Virtual Worlds and Metaverse Platforms:

New Communication and Identity Paradigms

Nelson Zagalo
Universidade do Minho, Portugal

Leonel Morgado
University of Trás-os-Montes e Alto Douro, Portugal

Ana Boa-Ventura
University of Texas at Austin, USA

Senior Editorial Director:	Kristin Klinger
Director of Book Publications:	Julia Mosemann
Editorial Director:	Lindsay Johnston
Acquisitions Editor:	Erika Carter
Development Editor:	Michael Killian
Production Editor:	Sean Woznicki
Typesetters:	Keith Glazewski, Natalie Pronio, Milan Vracarich, Jr.
Print Coordinator:	Jamie Snavely
Cover Design:	Nick Newcomer

Published in the United States of America by
Information Science Reference (an imprint of IGI Global)
701 E. Chocolate Avenue
Hershey PA 17033
Tel: 717-533-8845
Fax: 717-533-8661
E-mail: cust@igi-global.com
Web site: http://www.igi-global.com

Library of Congress Cataloging-in-Publication Data

Virtual worlds and metaverse platforms: new communication and identity paradigms / Nelson Zagalo, Leonel Morgado, and Ana Boa-Ventura, editors.
    p. cm.
  Includes bibliographical references and index.
    ISBN 978-1-60960-854-5 (hardcover) -- ISBN 978-1-60960-855-2 (ebook) -- ISBN 978-1-60960-856-9 (print & perpetual access) 1. Human-computer interaction. 2. Virtual reality. 3. Computer simulation. I. Zagalo, Nelson. II. Morgado, Leonel, 1970- III. Boa-Ventura, Ana, 1962-
  QA76.9.H85V587 2012
  006.8--dc23
                              2011018577

British Cataloguing in Publication Data
A Cataloguing in Publication record for this book is available from the British Library.

All work contributed to this book is new, previously-unpublished material. The views expressed in this book are those of the authors, but not necessarily of the publisher.

Table of Contents

Section 1
The World Arises: Creating Content

Chapter 1
User-Driven Content Creation in Second Life: A Source of Innovation?
> *Sisse Siggaard Jensen, Roskilde University, Denmark*

Chapter 2
> *Nuno Rodrigues, Polytechnic Institute of Leiria, Portugal*
> *Luís Magalhães, University of Trás-os-Montes e Alto Douro, Portugal*
> *João Paulo Moura, University of Trás-os-Montes e Alto Douro, Portugal*
> *Alan Chalmers, University of Warwick, UK*
> *Filipe Santos, Polytechnic Institute of Leiria, Portugal*
> *Leonel Morgado, University of Trás-os-Montes e Alto Douro, Portugal*

Chapter 3
Collective Building Projects in Second Life: User Motives and Strategies Explained From an
> *Bjarke Liboriussen, Copenhagen Business School, Denmark*

Chapter 4
> *Jacquelene Drinkall, University of New South Wales, Australia*

Section 2
Our Immersion: Entering the Metaverse

Section 3
Society Development: People, not Person

Section 4
Built for Fun: Playing in the Metaverse

Section 5
Sustenance: Virtual Health Care

Section 6
Life Happens: Religion, Morality, and Ethics

Detailed Table of Contents

Section 1
The World Arises: Creating Content

Chapter 1

> *Sisse Siggaard Jensen, Roskilde University, Denmark*

Second Life is conceived as an open space and symbolic world of affordances as to the user-driven co-creation of the content and agencies of the world. The questions asked are concerned with the ways in which the actors of three case studies design and mediate their Second Life agencies and how these choices contribute to user-driven content creation and possibly to innovative practises in a symbolic world.

Chapter 2

> *Nuno Rodrigues, Polytechnic Institute of Leiria, Portugal*
> *Luís Magalhães, University of Trás-os-Montes e Alto Douro, Portugal*
> *João Paulo Moura, University of Trás-os-Montes e Alto Douro, Portugal*
> *Alan Chalmers, University of Warwick, UK*
> *Filipe Santos, Polytechnic Institute of Leiria, Portugal*
> *Leonel Morgado, University of Trás-os-Montes e Alto Douro, Portugal*

With the increasing demand for more complex and larger models in different fields, such as the design of virtual worlds, video games, and computer animated movies, the need to generate them automatically has become more necessary than ever.

Users of "Second Life" invest considerable amounts of time, money, and creativity in collective building projects. Informed by a 14 month ethnography, this chapter explains why and how from an architectural perspective.

This chapter looks at Virtual Worlds in contemporary art practice, as well as the role of art and science in the creation of new technologically mediated telepathies.

Section 2
Our Immersion: Entering the Metaverse

This chapter explores the 3-D environment Second Life as a communication platform used by industry and science to create, design, develop, and distribute innovation. In order to achieve sustainable economic success in the context of global competition, companies need to optimize their communication activities within their innovation processes.

Chapter 6

This chapter argues that presence, the experience of "being- in-the-virtual-world," plays an underlying key role in most psychological processes connected with virtual worlds. Virtual worlds influence real life in a reciprocal loop, by shaping cognitive, psychological, and social processes of the real world.

Chapter 7

In the last few years much research regarding the advantages and potentialities of using Second Life in education came in to the spotlight. To identify which type of communication is most common among avatars and to understand if there is any similarity with communication in real life, we developed a case study that analyzed both verbal and nonverbal communication among Master degree students during six months.

Chapter 8

CarrieLynn D. Reinhard, Roskilde University, Denmark

This chapter argues for research studies focusing on how people make sense of virtual worlds when they engage with them, and to compare these situated sense-making processes amongst "virtual worlds technologies" as well as other types of media products. By mapping out and comparing such engagings, we may have a better understanding about what constitutes a virtual world.

Section 3
Society Development: People, not Person

Chapter 9

M. Toro-Troconis, Imperial College London, UK
N. J. Roberts, Imperial College London, UK
S. F. Smith, Imperial College London, UK
M. R. Partridge, Imperial College London, UK

This chapter describes the use of the nominal group technique to assess students' attitudes to game-based learning in the delivery of virtual patients in Second Life®. Two groups of undergraduate medical students (Yr 3, n=14) were invited to participate. The research question posed was: "In your opinion what are the advantages and disadvantages of learning in Second Life® compared with other methods?"

Chapter 10

Gaia Moretti, Libera Università Maria Ss. Assunta, Italy
Eliane Schlemmer, Universidade do Vale dos Rios dos Sinos, Brazil

Digital virtual spaces can contribute to change the traditional structure and definition of virtual communities, and can also contribute to their digital development, in the field of participation.

Chapter 11

Joao Mattar, Universidade Anhembi Morumbi, Brasil

This chapter addresses a resistance against the use of Second Life in education, which is based on the theory of technological minimalism. The main arguments of the resistance and the main concepts of the theory are discussed.

Section 4
Built for Fun: Playing in the Metaverse

Chapter 12

Michael Nitsche, Georgia Institute of Technology, USA

This chapter outlines three positions in the development of game spaces from the ideal of the perfect mindspace to the commercial reality of virtual worlds to the expansion of the game world into the physical environment into a hybrid space.

Chapter 13

Thiago Falcão, Federal University of Bahia, Brazil

In this chapter we inquire about the role the narrative acquires in the production of meaning resultant from the contact between players and environment, in the Massive Multiplayer Online Role-playing Game (MMORPG) World of Warcraft.

Chapter 14

Pascaline Lorentz, University of Strasbourg, France

The focus of this chapter is on the social impacts of virtual relationships on gamers in the gameplay. With the game The Sims®, we would like to analyze the process at stake in the relationship between the gamer and his Sim. The end justifies the means, so the gamer, here a teenager, has to figure out how to behave when he is an adult with responsibilities.

Chapter 15

Luís Carlos Petry, Pontifícia Universidade Católica de São, Brazil
Cristiano Natal Tonéis, Faculdades Metropolitanas Unidas de São Paulo, Brazil

Can we develop creative thinking? What is the role of games? Which characteristics of games can open up paths to creative thinking? The classical culture and the classical puzzles can give us an opportunity to answer these questions.

Section 5
Sustenance: Virtual Health Care

Chapter 16

Thomas D. Parsons, University of Southern California, USA

Actualization of the potential of virtual worlds for assessment will require the following: comparisons with well-validated neuropsychological measures, data storage, improved documentation of specific computer hardware and software used in experimental methods, and enhanced methods and result reporting by the researchers publishing studies on virtual worlds.

Chapter 17

With decades of experience in simulation, the health professions are comparatively well versed in virtual environments for training. More broadly, there is a growing body of experience and supporting evidence on the benefits of virtual worlds in professional information sharing, clinical simulation, healthcare delivery, and as a research tool.

Chapter 18

In this chapter we cover a range of areas where the metaverse, and notably Second Life, have been used to complement real life interventions in the field of public health. We particularly address those dealing with behavioral change and within these, we devote most of our work to addictive behaviors.

Section 6
Life Happens: Religion, Morality, & Ethics

Chapter 19

The Cardean ethnographic method was developed to study religious communities in the virtual world of Second Life. In our research, we faced a two-sided methodological problem. We had to theorize the virtual and its relation to the actual, while simultaneously creating practices for an effective ethnographic method. Our solution, named after the Roman Goddess of the hinge, Cardea, theorizes the "virtual" as desubstantialized and nondualistc; "residents," as fluid, multiple, and distributed cyborg-bodies; and "cloud communities," as temporary, outsourced groups of emotionally bonded residents.

Chapter 20

In this study, we examine in-world morality of frequent residents of Second Life (SL). Given the lack of systematic research on morality in non-gaming virtual worlds, we conducted an explorative small-scale, in-depth qualitative study with avid SL-residents.

This chapter focuses on the virtual world professionals being deployed within Second Life by companies and the appearance of their avatars. Virtual world professionals are considered to be persons who are deployed within a virtual world, such as Second Life, for the purpose of representing their company or organization within the virtual world.

This chapter provides a critical discourse analysis of French-Speaking players' personal and collective identity construction in World of Warcraft. Based on sixteen semi-structured interviews conducted online, we have analyzed how players introduce their avatars, the extent to which avatars correspond to or differ from players' real selves, and how players perceive and construct collective identity within their guilds.

Foreword

I can't say it was a religious experience, but Jesus was next to me. And he was dancing. On my other side, a dolphin floated a few feet above the ground on a surfboard. I think his date was the cute brunette who pirouetted non-stop, or maybe it was the pig that waddled around him in small circles. I can't be sure because I was really there for the music — Lambchop, a Nashville band playing live in Austin to this crowd of music lovers from around the world, and throughout the animal kingdom apparently.

As music lovers may know, Lambchop is very real, but Jesus and the rest of us weren't, at least that night. We were avatars drawn to the music or the inter-species socializing or the hope of seeing Michael Nesmith of Monkees' fame, the wizard behind the curtain of this virtual world concert called VideoRanch 3D. Every month or so Nesmith tapes a live band before a green screen and inserts it into VideoRanch. As a music nut, I love the opportunity to see bands with a colorful crowd. And as a developer, I'm thrilled to see the line between virtual and real worlds continue to blur.

While I make videogames for a living, I don't spend a lot of time in virtual worlds. My purview is handheld games — smartphones, DSs, mobile stuff like that. I'm often asked to help un-game-like organizations — workforce development non-profits, public radio stations, car dealerships (!) — bring games into their organizations. While they talk about game elements, such as avatars, rewards systems, and user-generated content, a game isn't really what they want. They want community. They want social stickiness. They want a digital forum that compels folks, regardless of geography, to convene and invest in a group, an idea, a movement.

That's what Nesmith is after with VideoRanch. Same for the petroleum engineering class I visited in which students were encouraged to make mistakes — big mistakes — on virtual oil wells where explosions and spills are corrected with a keystroke. And same for the simulator I tried that trains budding diplomats how to navigate the complex social norms of Afghanistan. They all are fostering community by creating safe worlds where we as users can create, communicate, and make a few mistakes.

I don't know if virtual worlds are encroaching on the real world, games are seeping into work, or everything we touch is becoming social and interconnected, and I don't think it really matters. What matters is we're inventing new ways to come together to share, create, and debate. It's thrilling. It's terrifying. And it continues to touch us in new ways.

Rodney Gibbs
Austin, Texas, November 28, 2010

Rodney Gibbs *is co-founder and CEO of Ricochet Labs, a developer of location-based smartphone apps. Esquire magazine calls QRANK, one of Ricochet's apps, one of the "80 people, places, and ideas that matter right now." Prior to Ricochet Labs, Rodney founded Fizz Factor, a developer of handheld and console games for EA, THQ, and Activision. Rodney serves on the boards of the International Game Developers Association, the Austin Film Society, and KUT, Austin's NPR affiliate.*

Preface

The metaverse is emerging, through the increasing use of virtual world technologies that act as platforms for end-users to create, develop, and interact, expanding the realm of human communication, interaction, and creativity. Not only researchers and scholars are experiencing the importance of this new field, but also industry is strongly investing in these domains, and – more important than that – society is responding with huge impacts and transformations.

This book presents texts whose focus is the scientific research on uses, effects, developments, and applications of various metaverse platforms, such as Second Life, Open Croquet, World of Warcraft, and others, providing a forum for the research community to present and discuss innovative approaches.

Whereas metaverse platforms are no longer a novel topic, they still pose challenges for the adaption of conventional research methodologies and communication practices with topics as: digital identity, collaboration, entertainment and playing, affective responses, educational objects, communication design, virtual space and digital representation, simulation and substitution, technology, and arts. The book's chapters present foundational research, models, case studies, and research results that researchers and scholars can port to their own environments to evolve their own research processes and studies. The chapters cover scenarios of intellectual disciplines and technological endeavors in which metaverse platforms are currently being used and will be used: computation, human-computer interaction, design, media and communication, anthropology, sociology, psychology, education, philosophy, theology, arts, and aesthetics.

The drive for creating this book originated from our practice of teaching and researching in this domain; reading material and in-depth research knowledge are still lacking, albeit growing in numbers and quality, but often locked into specific fields. We believe that novel platforms require researchers and practitioners to acquire broad perspectives of their use and potential across diverse fields of human knowledge, in order to support their own activities and inspiration.

For this purpose we initiated the SLACTIONS conference series, organizing SLACTIONS 2009 and supporting the organization of SLACTIONS 2010. We are also establishing a steering committee to support the worldwide organization of SLACTIONS 2011 and future events. These conferences have been extremely rewarding moments of cross-pollination of ideas between diverse fields of knowledge, with researchers from diverse fields presenting and discussing multiple perspectives, viewpoints, and approaches to the use, analysis, and development of metaverse platforms and their use.

The present book comes as a common base resulting from this multidisciplinary research effort. It aims to provide a reference guide for researchers and scholars, but also for practitioners, such as educators, artists, business professionals, communication professionals, and organizations looking for background on how to apply virtual worlds in their research, teaching, and business strategy: a set of pieces of knowledge with which one can open up new horizons to be creative.

The chapters, albeit diverse, form a structured encompassing view of the field. When reviewing and editing submissions, we took care to consider the overall structure of the book and how each chapter would contribute to the overall book. Hence, we follow a pathway style through the field, divided in to six sections:

1.　The World Arises: Creating Content
2.　Our Immersion: Entering the Metaverse
3.　Society Development: People, not Person
4.　Built for fun: Playing in the Metaverse
5.　Sustenance: Virtual Health Care
6.　Life happens: Religion, Morality, and Ethics

In section 1, about content creation, we present different views on how to create actual virtual content. Opening it, we present the most hard to manage perspective: user-created content and the richness of approaches and possibilities it brings – but also its challenges. Since this viewpoint is known to social and educational scientists, we complement it with a viewpoint well-known to computer scientists, but little known in other fields, and critical for massive spaces: automated, procedural generation of content. Then we expand both views by bringing in the matter of co-creation, a foremost issue in virtual worlds, where content can go beyond an individual's artifact into collecting creation. Finally, content creation in virtual platforms can support novel forms of artistic expression and reflection. We close this section with a provocative and inspiring view on how these platforms can be the heartland of different artistic approaches.

Content alone doesn't make a virtual world of course – at least not one warranting its consideration as a vibrant part of the metaverse. So chapter 2 deals with how people engage with these media, platform, or realms, and discover their new bearings. The section opens with a view on the communication affordances of virtual worlds and how they are being approached. Then we focus on the critical topic of avatars, and how they place a novel issue in terms of human-computer interaction: the identification of the avatar as an extension of one's persona and the role of this in the experience of using virtual worlds. We then conclude with two chapters that tackle a central detail whose impact is central to the experience: how verbal and non-verbal communication are used in worlds where three-dimensional space and embodiment are basic features, and how this affects the nature of person-to-person communication.

With the third section, about the development or emergence of societal relations in the metaverse, we take the reader a step further into these worlds. Now we delve into a concept more vast than a mere communication tool within a space, encompassing the notion that these worlds develop societies with their own rules, organization, and characteristics. We start from outside the metaverse, analyzing students' attitudes to the use of these platforms, to provide insights on how their deployment must indeed consider social dynamics; then we present a view from the inside, looking into the development of communities that leverage the new platform and its possibilities. Finally, we take a step back and consider how these two realities are aligned or confront current perspectives – in this case, for the field of education, an area where many practitioners and researchers have embraced the metaverse wholeheartedly.

The second half of the book stands on the perspectives and examples of the first half, and presents specific cases as food for thought.

The fourth section presents the entertainment perspective, with chapters that provide complementary perspectives: starting with the possibility of expanding both reality and virtuality into novel entertainment varieties, and concluding with a chapter on how virtual games may open up paths to creative thinking, a concept based on classical culture. Between them, two bridging chapters provide key perspectives on the role and development of narratives and their relation to user behavior in multi-user virtual world games, and on how aspects of social relationship may develop between the human and the virtual personas.

In the fifth section, the relationship between the virtual and the physical worlds are explored via a subject with a strong impact in everyday lives: health. We initiate this with a chapter on the potential of virtual worlds for neuropsychological assessment, which may drive the reader to consider how important a role metaverse platforms may play in the near future. Then we take a broader perspective on the potential for development of health professionals, and conclude with another example from the field, describing a virtual world's use to complement physical-world interventions in public health.

To conclude this pathway through which we (and the authors of all chapters) have been conducting the reader, we provide reflections on broader ideas: how does a virtual platform support a non-physical concept such as religion, whether morality and ethics are impacted or challenged by new means of social interaction, how professional users ponder their identity towards others via the embodiment of an avatar and its appearance, and – lastly, which is also the first dilemma – how our identities are constructed and perceived, through factual analysis of discourse and data.

So, we start from the basic building blocks of the metaverse, and conclude with issues which are present wherever humanity dwells. And this connection between the new virtuality and the ever-existing one is in itself also a concluding tenet from this book.

Nelson Zagalo
Universidade do Minho, Portugal

Leonel Morgado
University of Trás-os-Montes e Alto Douro, Portugal

Ana Boa-Ventura
University of Texas at Austin, USA

Acknowledgment

This book would not have been possible without the support of many colleagues and friends, but mainly without the happening that was the *SLACTIONS 2009 International Conference: Life, imagination, and work using metaverse platforms*. We're indebted to all people who took part in it, to all local organizers of physical chapters (Portugal, USA, Brazil, UK, China, Israel) and also to all paper presenters, who originated from all around the world. This conference was the debut work cooperation between the three editors of this book, and from it sprung connections with many keen researchers across the world. Together, the editors want to say thanks again to the institutions who supported and believed in this vision: NMC – New Media Consortium, SPCVideojogos – Sociedade Portuguesa de Ciências dos Videojogos, UTAD – Universidade de Trás-os-Montes e Alto Douro, UM – Universidade do Minho, and TACC – Texas Advanced Computing Center.

A big, hearty thanks goes especially to all our book contributors, who joined this endeavor and maintained their will till the end, to all reviewers whose insightful comments helped improve the overall content, and finally to all our editorial advisors who were responsible since the beginning for the great selection of texts we are now making available for the benefit of the public.

The editors want also to thank IGI Global for asking for this edited book and its staff for supporting it along the way: Mike Killian, Christine Bufton, Lindsay Johnston, Erika Carter, Kristin M. Klinger, and Jan Travers.

Nelson Zagalo
Universidade do Minho, Portugal

Leonel Morgado
University of Trás-os-Montes e Alto Douro, Portugal

Ana Boa-Ventura
University of Texas at Austin, USA

Section 1
The World Arises:
Creating Content

Chapter 1

User–Driven Content Creation in Second Life: A Source of Innovation?
Three Case Studies of Business and Public Service

Sisse Siggaard Jensen
Roskilde University, Denmark

ABSTRACT

In this chapter, Second Life is conceived as an open space and symbolic world of user-driven co-creation of content. The questions asked concern the ways in which the actors of three case studies design, mediate, and remediate their Second Life projects and how the choices they make contribute to user-driven content creation and possibly to innovative practices. To answer these questions, concepts of innovation, in particular closed and open innovation are introduced and motivations for engaging in co-creation are identified. It is suggested that we understand user-driven innovation in a world like Second Life in terms of symbolic reorganization of conceptual frameworks and meaning-making. Subsequently, the concept of remediation is suggested as a way to conceive of mediation in the cases studied. It is shown how difficult it is for actors to co-create, mediate, and remediate thus to generate user-driven innovative practices in two Danish business projects (Wonder DK and Times) and in one public service project (Literary). To conclude the analysis of the case studies, it is suggested that methods of creative co-creation and innovative practices can build on the concept of remediation borrowed from research on new media and redefined in virtual worlds.

DOI: 10.4018/978-1-60960-854-5.ch001

INTRODUCTION

Virtual worlds may be seen as built of symbolic bricks of signs and shapes; they are symbolic worlds of meaning-making and semioses (Matusitz, 2005). Questions and ideas are likely to emerge when we experience new meaning-making flows (Csikszentmihaily, 1996) in non-tangible virtual worlds that even question the very idea of what a world is. Questioning what is taken for granted often mobilizes creative energy, rethinking, and reinterpretation of agencies and engagements. In the case of Second Life, the Linden Lab firm's marketing of their product emphasizes that it is a tool for building a new world unbound by the tangible and physical (Au, 2008); a symbolic world which allows us to create shapes and signs "not possible in real life" in a compelling, surreal, and dream-like world to be experienced together with other residents accompanied by their avatars.

A virtual world like Second Life may thus be seen as a window of opportunity for mobilizing its residents' creativity of mediation and innovation as the content has to be provided and created by the users; creative qualities, which are often presented as a distinguishing feature of Second Life as compared to multi-user online role-playing games such as e.g., EverQuest and World of Warcraft. In Second Life there are no built-in storylines and no system of quests, experience points, classes, and roles as is the case in many role-playing games. In principle, everything in Second Life has to be provided by the residents who have chosen to settle, socialize, run business, attend cultural events, or just to have great in-world fun (Au, 2008; Boelstorff, 2008; Malaby, 2009). Let us therefore note that Second Life not only inspires but the general idea of the design actually requires the co-creation by the residents in order to make it a compelling and attractive experience. Therefore, to introduce Second Life to the market, a critical mass of residents is required to actually design and make the world. Yet obviously, for residents to run a project, a business, or a shop, it is also required

that *they* can attract the attention of other fellow residents to visit and partake in the activities of their projects, places and islands.

Thus, the user-driven content creation can be seen as a comprehensive experiment with user-driven innovation. Moving into Second Life, residents have to generate design ideas and realize these ideas whether they are running a business, conducting a series of talk-shows, arranging cultural events, producing machinimas or just travelling around the world to chat, socialize, go to ball-rooms to dance, or visit sex clubs. All of this may be seen as engagements, which entail communication and co-creation of new social agencies, norms, digital places, and environments. Only if the residents themselves can manage to design places, arrange events, and run a business can the world offer interesting and exciting in-world experiences.

QUESTIONS OF ANALYSIS

In this chapter, the practices of the user-driven content creation and user-driven innovation of the Second Life symbolic world is critically examined by analyzing three case studies of projects and actors who engage with or have been engaged with Second Life. The agencies of the Wonder DK, Times, and Literary projects are analyzed as seen from the perspective of mediation and innovation. Thus, in the analysis of the case studies, the ensuing questions that are dealt with are: In what ways do actors of the chosen case studies design and mediate their Second Life projects? And, how do their choices contribute to user-driven content creation and possibly to innovation in this symbolic world? To answer these questions, first, the concepts of innovation and remediation are introduced. Secondly, the three case studies are presented and then analysed, and finally some answers to the above stated questions are suggested.

CLOSED AND OPEN INNOVATION

Conceptions of innovation are many. Innovation may be seen as a research field (Krohn & van Daele 1998); a social constructivist inspired sociology (Latour & Woolgar 1979/86; Latour 2005); in the light of historical and/or economic understandings (Sundbo 2001, 2002); as collaborative network achievements (Gloor 2006); from a management and/or strategic perspective (Davis et al. 2005). The dynamics and processes may be conceived as individual and subjective qualities of creativity or as processes of cognitive problem solving (Simon 1977); as collective achievements when seen from a systemic view (Csikzentmihaily 1996) and/or social and knowledge intensive processes of learning when seen from a constructivist view (Darsøe 2009; Jensen 2008). In this analysis I will, however, focus on the distinction between closed and open innovation.

Generally speaking, this distinction is a dividing line and a recurring motif in each of the above mentioned approaches to innovation. The distinction is marked by the different relationships between the many parties involved in innovative practices. They may be subcontractors, other producers, universities or customers. In closed innovation, the R & D department of companies is seen as the main source of innovation. Knowledge, experiments, tests, etc., of innovative products and practices circulate in closed circuits kept secret until the products' introduction to the market. To illustrate this, I will refer to a definition of innovation, which is widely adopted in policy programs and statements (World Bank & OECD, 2009). From this point of view, innovation is seen as closely related to new *products* or *processes of commercial production*:

Innovation occurs when a new or changed product is introduced to the market, or when a new or changed process is used in commercial production (Baldwin & Hanel in Jensen, 2008, p. 31).

The closed innovation approach clearly demarcates the boundaries between the product and the consumer, the company and the market, the company and the suppliers, and the company and its competitors. If the end-users and consumers are consulted, it is primarily for quality and usability testing at the end of the innovation process and before the marketing.

However, examples of advantages gained from introducing ideas and knowledge from outside the company and of doing so early in the practices of innovation have also influenced the ideas of innovation and led to the open innovation concept. Open innovation denotes an assemblage of different ways to understand and produce innovation concerted by the fact that end-users are involved in early stages of the processes and practices. Among others, the inspiration for the conception of open innovation derives from software development and the open source movement. The digital technologies for communication, production, and design are among the mediators of this changing of ideas and practices of innovation. The personalization of the web, the building of online communities around a brand, the open source movements itself are some of the examples of this development. In his study about avatar-based Innovation, Thomas Kohler (2008) traces the development of ideas and practices which increasingly place the end-user(s), the consumer(s), as the initiator(s) of the innovation practices or even as part of the production and design itself. In this, he points to the notion of the "prosumer" to conceptualize this development.

In the case of Second Life, we find closed as well as open innovation depending on the optic of analysis. Seen from the Linden Lab perspective partly, the source code is public as the viewer is open source, which means that it is open to further development outside the control of the company. Also, the Linden Lab company keeps up a dialogue with in-world groups, bloggers, and online communities to gain the advantages of feedback and to appropriate the possible creativity of the users. Yet, the core business decisions of R&D are only made public or open to co-creation when it is a strategic advantage. Thus, the company seeks to balance the more traditional practices of the closed innovation approach and the open source tradition which urges them to make available their knowledge and sources for users to partake in the co-creation and design.

MOTIVATIONS FOR CO-CREATION

The question is however, what motivates the consumers and users to become active co-creators of the design and content? In his work, Kohler points out two main drivers. One is the recognition that results from being close to the brand, i.e. the Lindens; another is the experience itself. In order to engage the residents in a co-creation process, the experience itself should be compelling and fun, entertaining and appealing. It is important that the users see engagement as influential, with an impact that is visible and recognizable by other members of the community, even outside of it. Kohler (2008) refers to Bonsu & Darmody (2008) when he writes:

The authors convincingly outline the new mode of production, where the host Linden Lab facilitates unrestrained consumer freedom and empowerment. The creative capacities of each consumer of Second Life produce resources that are accessible to the community members and amenable to appropriation for corporate ends (Kohler, 2008, p. 67).

In concluding his study on avatar-based innovation, Kohler distinguishes the four different dimensions affecting the design of compelling and engaging experiences of co-creation. The dimensions are: desirability, usability, collaboration, and usefulness (Kohler, 2008, p. 194). To create a compelling and *desirable* setting for co-creation, the environment should be welcoming, comfortable, inspiring and stimulating and

provide a background for communication (DiPaola & Collins, 2002). In the case of Second Life, the place(s) has/ have to be distinguishable and memorable and generate a sense of place and a high degree of sensory immersion (Mullet, 2003). And importantly, the setting should emphasize collaboration, interaction, and modifiability of the content to inspire and serve as a starting point for further creation tasks (Randall et al., 2005). Referring to some of the classic studies of *usability* (Nielsen, 1999) this dimension first of all states that a compelling environment for co-creation should facilitate creativity and creation rather than generate obstacles to be overcome. The frequently stated needs are open architecture, ease of use, clear navigation, and structure, the latter in such a way as to balance structure and rules with "free-flowing, evolving processes" (Hornecker, 2008). To inspire collective consumer creativity, Kozinets et al. (2008) suggest an environment and content supported by help-seeking, help-giving, reflective reframing and reinforcing behavior. As for the third dimension, i.e. *collaboration*, ease of contact with the brand, e.g. Linden Lab, company interaction, and loosely knit communities of informal sociability, interpersonal interaction, and communication in "third places" are important drivers of engaging the co-creation (Steinkuhler & Williams 2006). Lessons learned from the many open source projects point to the important findings that modularity and granularity as well as integration mechanisms are needed. Finally, the fourth dimension of *usefulness* identifies the importance of a high degree of subjectivity and clear goals; and research also points out that learning and recognition have important parts to play in building and designing compelling co-creation experiences.

Let me summarize what has been said so far. Strategic decisions of the company and the introduction of the Second Life platform to the market follow a closed path of innovation (Au, 2008; Malaby, 2009) whereas the content creation of this symbolic world is conceived an open space of innovation, co-creation, and design made by the residents of the world. The business strategy of leaving open the space for residents' co-creation, the initiatives to motivate residents' creativity and innovation, and the traditional closedness of the platform's system development, all of this forms a complex network of innovative practices. Rather than understanding the open and closed innovation as mutually exclusive, in the Second Life case, they are networks of intertwined practices. Subsequently, Linden Lab faces a complexity of innovation due to, on the one hand, the rapid market developments of their field and, on the other hand, the unpredictability of co-creation of content. Their success depends on the residents' ability and creativity to design and create compelling and desirable content thus to attract traffic urging the residents to take yet another step of engaging their fellow residents in co-creating practices. In other words, there are several steps of innovative practices involved with an open space virtual world like Second Life. It depends on the users, the residents, and their motivation and ability to create compelling and desirable experiences targeting their fellow residents possibly even involving these in the co-creation. Hence, we may see Second Life as a major experiment with user-driven content creation in a complexity of networks of innovative practices.

FORMS OF REMEDIATION

The question of co-creation of content in the symbolic world of Second Life also implies an understanding of the mediations made out of symbolic bricks, codes, signs, and shapes. From the point of view of mediation, innovation can be understood in terms of symbolic reorganization of conceptual frameworks and meaning-making; a reorganization that allows actors to see and interpret things in new ways. One such example is the innovation that occurred when the understanding of human interaction with computers

changed from being seen as a military tool – with "commands" – to become the personal tool – with "clicks" - in a desktop metaphor (Nielsen et al., 2008). In both cases, metaphors have important parts to play. Thus, to conceive of innovation in terms of symbolic reorganization, the ambiguities of metaphors make possible a reframing of meaning-making. In this, symbolic innovations are different from the traditional understanding of innovation as a well-orchestrated, clearly defined set of actions that lead from the initial ideas to the introduction and marketing of new products and/ or commercial processes.

Bolter & Grusin (1999) suggest the notion of remediation to conceptualize their understanding of digital media and the reorganization of mediation and meaning-making that they bring. This concept of remediation is now briefly dealt with as it will assist us in the analysis of the case studies.

Remediation denotes a strategy of mediation. Basically, the concept of remediation refers to a process by which one medium is represented in another. If the photo of an ancient statuette from a historical museum is digitized and put on the web, then the digital version *borrows* from the original and aims at mirroring it without appropriation. If the same statuette is remediated to a digital encyclopedia with annotations and search functionalities added, it makes possible a *reshaping* of the ways in which to engage with the medium; the photo of the original statuette is reshaped and new options are added. *Redefining* and refashioning are remediation processes which almost aspire to alter and/ or absorb the old medium in the new. If the photo is remediated in a virtual world like Second Life and used as the texture of a virtual artifact that actors can use e.g., in processes of deconstruction and reconstruction, then the process of remediation profoundly redefines the old medium. The online games are obvious examples of games and movies being redefined in processes of remediation. The Star Wars Galaxies online game is an example of this. In conclusion, it may be said that the borrowing, reshaping and redefining of one medium in another are strategies progressively moving from continuity towards increased discontinuity of the remediation process. These processes of remediation and in particular the redefining of mediation hold potential for innovation as it is shown by the subsequent case studies.

CASE STUDIES: WONDER DK, TIMES, AND THE LITERARY PROJECT

The complexity and networks of open innovation practices of Second Life, the motivations identified that make users wish to partake in co-creation, and the conceptions of remediation, together these understandings form the conceptual framework for the analysis of the case studies. They include three Danish cases: the Wonder DK, Times, and Literary projects. These cases have been studied over time from the turn of the year 2006/ 2007 until 2010. Ethnographic in-world studies and participatory observations were conducted aimed to identify cases of relevance to the study of sense-making and user-driven innovation in virtual worlds (January 2007 to March 2008). Two of the cases have been followed until concluded: the Times and Literary projects, whereas the third case, the Wonder DK project, is still followed.

To follow up the ethnographic in-world studies, in situ iterative video interviews have been carried out covering five different foci of analyses: the choice of virtual world, the design of the projects' places and projects, the creation of personal mediators in the shape of avatars, the relationships with other residents and avatars of the world, the influence of this on the perception of self, and the weaving of the in-world agencies with those outside Second Life. Each case study is briefly introduced starting with the fully virtual business case Wonder DK leading on to the completely different business case of the Times project to end with the public service project Literary. In this chapter, the foci of analysis are motivations to co-create and steps taken by the actors to make their projects desirable, easy to use, collaborative, and useful. Thus, *designing* the places and projects, creating their *mediators* by the design of figures and avatars, and the framing of *social relationships* with other in-world residents and customers, these are three steps followed in the case analysis.

Wonder DK: A Virtual World Business Case

In the Wonder DK case, a start-up is run by a team of investors. Together they have invested in a Second Life island to run a fully virtual real estate business renting out land to outside businesses that wish to be present in Second Life. To develop this business concept and strategy, the manager is fulltime employed as he is to make a living of the Wonder DK start-up project. Renting out shops is the core content of the business. To frame this, the digital remediation of an image of a typical Danish provincial town is designed. It is a structured and well-planned design of an entire island as the manager finds that many design and places on the Linden Lab mainland are frightening examples of pointless and ill-designed projects and places. Therefore, the general framing of the Wonder DK is created by the manager with small shops all over the town surrounded by cozy streets, houses and squares together with agricultural and meadow-like areas, harbors and ships. The small shops are for rent preferable by outside businesses paying with the real money of outside economies and they are open to co-creation by the tenants. To ensure system performance only a limited amount of symbolic bricks and prims are available for the designing practices. Every Dane avatar who visits this place will immediately recognize the environment. They know how to navigate and find it amusing to see how the design is made. The first step taken by the manager of the business is to make sure that the design of the Wonder DK world is attractive, orderly and recognizable to convincingly convey the sense of a professional site.

Wonder DK is started in the wake of the Second Life hype in Denmark in early 2007 with extensive media coverage. To attract attention to the place, the team decided to remediate a famous fictional TV-series Matador about Danish society and history from the beginning of the 20th century until the Second World War. Buildings, cars, the famous wheelchair of the Mrs. Møge character, shops, etc., are remediated and the Second Life town Korsbæk is named after the provincial town that frames the story of Matador. These steps trigger attention. Many Danish residents entering Second Life visit the place to see and experience what Korsbæk looks like when remediated in a virtual world.

The mediator of the manager's in-world business – the avatar DC Aspen – is much in line with the design of the place and island. He is a remediation of the cultural image of a business man aimed to create a sense of professionalism and trust. The need to generate a sense of trust with his companion avatar DC Aspen is vital, according to the manager.

One of the frequently visited places of Korsbæk is the town square. It is an open space with a lot of information about activities in Wonder DK and other in-world events. Avatars hang out chatting and showing their animations at the town square. Town guides volunteer to show visiting avatars around the town thus getting a legitimate occasion to chat with the visitors. Importantly, the manager is almost always online often working 80 hours a week; he is easy to contact and soon also well-known for his knowledge about Second Life and his competence as to design.

The Wonder DK case is still running although the core business has changed. Increasingly, the content of the business includes Second Life design consultancies.

Times: A Virtual World Branch of a Company Outside Second Life

The Times business project paints a quite different picture. It is a virtual branch of an international company outside Second Life: a company with many affiliations all around Denmark. The core business of this company is to recruit temporary workers in order to match them with potential employers. One of the employees of a Danish branch of the company is supported by her immediate manager to start up a virtual branch in Second Life with the aim to explore if the virtual world holds potential for the endeavors of matching and recruiting. The top-managers of the company, however, do not see any sense in exploring this potential.

The approach taken by the project manager is to rent several places thus distributing the activities of the project. There is no centrally located place referring to the project and related activities. The distributed locations are designed with an approach quite different from Wonder DK. Instead of carefully remediated and well-known images as of Wonder DK, several distributed open spaces are designed. This is to adapt to the Second Life environment that requires freedom of movement, which is why it should be easy to fly in and out of the design. Any obstacle to this freedom of movement is seen as undesirable. The open spaces have no immediate reference or resemblance with the traditional images of a company or other environments. They are transparent and inspired by science fiction.

However, the urge and request to attract attention to the project is as strong as in the Wonder DK business whereas the strategy by which to meet these requests is different. Attention is drawn to the Times project by the design of the project manager's avatar, Helle, rather than by the design of the rented places. They only hold posters with information about the core business activities. The avatar is a funny-looking egg-or-balloon-like avatar wearing advertisements as clothing. To attract attention and make avatars aware of the project, Helle travels around the many islands of Second Life. Whenever there is an event, an arrangement, a network meeting, she attends it to start chatting with the avatars present about whatever comes up. The funny look of her advertising avatar easily shifts the chat to be about the Times business project. As part of this business strategy, an extensive in-world network is built. Networking with her companion avatar Helle is the most important part of doing business in a virtual world like Second Life, according to the project manager.

As mentioned, from the outset, the top-managers of the company did not support the project so by the end of 2007 the project was closed.

The Literary Project: A Public Service Institution

In the Literary project of a Danish public service institution, the very idea is to involve visitors of the place in activities of co-creation. Entering the virtual world in the wake of the intense media coverage in early 2007, this project is initiated and a project team is built with the aim of communicating to a wider audience how to enter this world. Public service, enlightenment, access to information, knowledge, and experience with media are some of the purposes and obligations of the institution. In line with this, the main idea is to spread and share with public audiences knowledge about virtual worlds, be they social worlds or gaming.

To realize the project aims a place is rented on the Linden Lab mainland just beside other early Danish Second Life projects. The design of the place is not planned in advance; rather, it is designed in spontaneous sessions of creation involving the project team as well as other visitors of the place. Thus, it is difficult to see what kind of place is designed, what the purpose of it is, and what to do at the place. It conveys a somewhat messy impression. On a wall it says: Literary,

which is the only mark that signifies what this place is about and who runs it. Thus, the design does not help visitors understand the aim and activity of the place. Also, it proves problematic that visitors are not able to create anything but messy and pointless design, according to the project team.

As for the mediating avatars, the project sets out with a shared workplace avatar expecting the colleagues of their institution to join their activities in Second Life. Within only a short while, the shared avatar is given up as it generates a lot of confusion. Avatars appear to be a personal matter and mediator. The many items in the avatar's inventory signify experiences and memory. Landmarks of the inventory tell the story of places visited by the avatar, items and clothes are bought and stored, looks and outfits, gestures and animations, all of these help generate an avatar's history and they are important for the personal mediation made possible by the avatar. Furthermore, it turns out that the colleagues do not use the avatar. Therefore, it is made a personal avatar and some new avatars are created. It proves too confusing to share an avatar not only for the project team but also for their in-world visitors never knowing who is accompanied by the avatar.

As mentioned, the general idea of the place is to help public audiences enter the place to learn how to design and create places, objects, etc., and to disseminate and create new kinds of Literary experiences. Over time, however, the strategy of co-design with public audiences is given up as it proves far too difficult to realize. Instead, the predominant activity of the place turns out to be meetings with a group of colleagues of the same profession. This group of colleagues meets on a weekly basis to discuss and debate the relevance of Second Life to wider audiences. To support these weekly meetings, the project buys an animated chair with an animation that creates a new chair each time an avatar joins the meeting; the chairs are scripted to form a circle to ask avatars in with this welcoming design and animation.

Due to a general reduction of staff, the project team member who is the driving force of the advancements of the project is not reappointed when his temporary employment expires. Therefore the project is closed over summer 2007.

CASE ANALYSIS

The analysis of the cases will now follow steps taken by each case with reference to the three foci: designing the places and projects, creating the mediators, and the framing of relationships with other residents and avatars. The concept of remediation and the motivations identified will guide the steps of the analysis.

Design of Place

In Wonder DK, the place is seen as immediately useful. It serves the business manager's purposes well and inspires co-creation. With a professional background in programming and a hobby of building environments for model railways, the manager is used to understanding scripting languages, planning places easy to navigate, and to build models of aesthetic quality. The steps taken help create a place useful for the owner and project manager, easy to navigate and use for other residents with their avatars, and the owner is in full control of the island's design. Most importantly, the idea of the remediation of the fictional TV-series Matador brings about a good start as it is conceived a compelling experience to visit the place. Thus the place and the business avatar DC Aspen is quickly widely known as Wonder DK attracts attention and traffic.

Compared to this, the Times project sets out with a disputed question of its usefulness. A divergence between the local and the international management means that the project is not fully supported and it starts with a very low budget. The project relies on the unpaid work of the project initiator. Her ideas of how best to design Second

Life places entail distributed places with open and transparent spaces. This adaptation to the virtual world however, complicates other residents and avatars' recognition of the places; they are difficult to remember, locate and understand. Most importantly, the places do not contribute a compelling experience only remediated information posters of job announcements. Renting the distributed places does not allow the project manager and designer to be in full control of the surrounding places and environments.

The Literary project is fully supported by the management of the institution. It is considered useful to explore and get to know about virtual worlds like Second Life. Yet, there are doubts as to the usefulness of this project among professionals from other similar institutions as they do not see engaging with virtual worlds as part of the public institutions' obligations. Still, the public service obligation is the aim of the Literary project targeted at public audiences. Renting islands on the Linden Lab mainland, the project team aims to educate and awaken the public awareness of the emergence of these new media. To realize this, the idea of the design is an open place for visitors to try out how to design and collaborate in Second Life. Thus, the explicit purpose of the project is co-creation of content. The place is, however, difficult to understand, the goal is not made clear, the design of places is difficult for the audiences targeted by the project, and the team has no control of the surrounding environments of the design. Therefore, the co-creation of content is given up. The experimental approach is followed up by the design of meditation bubbles to mediate surreal and funny experiences. These bubbles are also, it appears, difficult to understand and navigate for visitors who are not familiar with the Second Life environment.

Mediators

Avatars can be seen as personal mediators in virtual worlds. In the three Second Life cases, the avatars' design is vital for the projects to reach out and attract attention. The design of these avatars is approached differently.

Remediating the image of a business man, DC Aspen, is useful with regard to the purposes of the Wonder DK project. It is an avatar easy to understand and recognizable. Together with the design of the Wonder DK island this avatar inspires the trust of other residents and conveys an impression of responsibility important for doing business.

Compared to this, the design of the Times project's primary avatar, Helle, is meant to attract attention due to a very unusual outfit and appearance. This avatar design is vital to the nomadic business strategy of the project. The travelling avatar aims to spread the message about the project and to increase the awareness of its services. From an immediate point of view, it is difficult to understand and decode the avatar but that is part of the purpose, which is to convey a funny experience and with that, an invitation to chat. These adaptations to the Second Life world, however, are not obvious and useful when seen from the perspective of an international top management's point of view. The funny and unusual look, the nomadic approach, the distributed places inspired by sci-fi, does not appear convincing to a management full of doubts as to the relevance of this project. Even if meaningful when seen from the in-world perspective this approach collides with norms and expectations.

From the outset, a shared avatar is designed in the Literary project. Sharing the avatar proves very confusing. Never knowing what has happened to the avatar since the last logon, what objects and things have been bought, or how clothing and appearance have changed – all of this means that it is a very confusing experience to share the avatar. It generates large gaps in the memory of the owners. Further, the remediated intellectually-looking female avatar is a problem for one of the male members of the team. It is experienced as unpleasant to be a female avatar.

Social Relationships

The welcoming town square of Korsbæk creates an open square for avatars to meet, chat, pose, and dance showing their animations, creative media, and other in-world gadgets. In other words, it frames a compelling experience of social relationships with other residents and avatars of the group of Wonder DK as well as residents and avatars from outside the place. The framing of the social relationships is easy to use and as of social norms, it is acceptable to hang out at the town square together with other residents and avatars to also seek info about events and arrangements in Second Life.

The Times project's business strategy entails social relationships and chatting. It is a compelling experience to meet the unusual avatar of the project. The avatar's appearance is difficult to understand thus inviting to chat by awaking other residents' curiosity. Also it is easy to recognize and remember it. This design of the avatar is useful in the sense that it serves to realize the building of a network of business relations and knowledge sharing.

In the Literary project, the approach is experimental. The project team seeks to realize the "not possible in real life" approach while at the same time targeting wider public audiences. The experiments aimed to teach visitors how to design and co-create the project's place prove too difficult to understand, use, and learn. Subsequently, the actual content of the project is changed to frame weekly meetings of avatars and to host critical discussions and debates about the very idea of providing public services about virtual worlds like Second Life. Changing the aim, the project does not reach out to public audiences but to a circle of residents and professional colleagues.

Comparison

Comparing the different design of places it appears that the Wonder DK business meets many of the motivations identified that drive co-creation practices. It is conceived immediately useful for the business purposes, easy to use for other fellow residents, and the owner is well-reputed and in control of the place. It provides a compelling experience.

In the co-creation and design of projects and places different forms of remediation stand out. In the design of a typical Danish provincial town of Wonder DK the remediation borrows from an ideal typical and romanticized image. This cultural image is reshaped in the virtual world's environment. Using this well-known image, the new environment is made easily accessible. Also, the remediation of the fictional town of Korsbæk with many recognizable buildings, streets, vehicles, etc., it redefines the widely known TV-series. Thus, the Second Life residents can rent and design a shop to run a business in the remediated fictional town of Korsbæk. In the case of Wonder DK, remediation takes on forms of borrowing, reshaping as well as redefining. In particular, the redefining of the fictional town affords a compelling experience. The remediation of the Times project takes two main forms. The design of the project's distributed places inspires a science-fiction-like atmosphere borrowed from movies, fiction, and high-tech modes of expression. In contrast, the job advertisements remediate the content and lay-out by borrowing from well-known forms of announcement. In the Literary project, the design is experimental in the sense that it aims to spontaneously co-create the rented place together with casual visitors. No apparent remediation is part of the original design.

The remediation of the business man of the Wonder DK business as well as the intellectual-like female avatar from the Times project borrow from ideal typical cultural images to reshape these in the Second Life environment. In the Times project the choice and design of the avatar redefines the appearance of a project manager. The avatar does not make any reference to known images or conceptions except for the job advertisements worn by the funny-looking egg-and-balloon-like figure. Only the remediated advertisements give a hint of the purpose of the avatar.

In remediating the town square of Korsbæk, the design borrows from the ideal typical and romanticized picture of a cozy, friendly and welcoming Danish square to initiate social relationships; a pond with ducks, the typical green benches, paving stones, shops encircling the place, and Danish flags, they are cultural images that reshape and set the scene for chatting and socializing. As compared to this, in the Times project no places for social relationships are remediated whereas the nomadic avatar is vital for building the business and social networks. When the aim of the Literary project is changed, a meeting place is remediated in a minimalistic reshaping, whereas the animated chair that automatically includes a new avatar into the meeting circle redefines the meeting place. These weekly meetings serve to frame professional collaboration even if they also lead to arguments and disagreements.

In Table 1, the case analysis is condensed and held together with the motivations for co-creation as introduced earlier: compelling and desirable setting, usability, collaboration, and usefulness. By comparison, three examples are pointed out regarding openness and closedness of co-creation: the design of places in Wonder DK as compared with the Literary project, the avatar mediators of the Times as compared with the Literary projects, and the welcoming invitation of the Literary project's chair and the city guides of Wonder DK.

In Table 1, the case analysis of design of places, mediators, and social relationships is condensed and coded with reference to motivations for co-creation.

In Wonder DK, the design is a recognisable remediation which provides a compelling experience. However, to achieve an orderly and neat place, the owner is in tight control leaving only little room for co-creation. In this respect, the place is characterised by closedness. Compared to this, from the outset, the Literary project is

Table 1.

	1. Design of place	*2. Mediators*	*3. Social relations*
Wonder DK	• **[Useful]** Fully virtual business; real estate agent; renting out virtual shops. • **[Easy to use]** Remediation of cultural images of a Danish provincial town. • **[In control]** An island owned and controlled by the manager. • **[Compelling experience]** Remediation of a famous fiction TV-series. • **[Recognition]** Owner well-reputed and widely known in-world.	• **[Useful]** Avatar-based remediation of cultural images of a businessman. • **[Easy to understand]** Recognizable appearance and outfit. • **[Recognition]** Inspires trust in the business.	• **[Compelling experience]** Remediation of a Danish provincial town square: a central place for avatars to chat. Open space with info about events and in-world arrangements. • **[Easy to use]** Recognizable framing. • **[Collaboration]** Attractive meeting place. Owner's office at the corner of the square.
Times	• **[Doubts about usefulness]** A virtual branch of international recruitment company. • **[No control]** Renting places at different Danish places. • **[Difficult to understand]** Open and transparent remediation of science-fiction genre. • **[No compelling experience]** Remediation of posters announcing jobs. • **[Recognition]** Well-reputed and widely known in-world.	• **[Compelling experience]** Avatar-based remediation of a conspicuous advertisement pillar. • **[Difficult to understand]** Unusual outfit and looks. • **[Compelling experience]** Awaking attention.	• **[Compelling experience]** Travelling avatar. Awaking curiosity and initiating chat and contacts. • **[Easy to remember]** Recognizable due to unusual remediation • **[Collaboration]** Building networks.
Literary	• **[Doubts about usefulness]** Public service institution reaching out to public audiences. • **[No control]** Renting a place on the Linden Lab mainland. • **[No compelling experience]** Spontaneous, casual, and messy design. No obvious remediation. • **[Difficult to understand]** Not easy to recognize except for the name of the project on a wall. • **[Disputed]** Known in a circle of professionals	• **[Difficult to use and understand]** Avatar-based remediation of cultural images of an intellectual-looking avatar. A shared avatar changing appearance depending on who last used it. Confusing to owners and visitors.	• **[Difficult to use]** Experiments of co-design with public audiences • **[Collaboration]** Remediation of meeting place for colleagues within the same profession. • **[Compelling experience]** Chair with animation. Remediation of a welcoming gesture

completely open to co-creation even for casual by-passers. This approach leaves the project with a place difficult to understand. There is no apparent remediation; rather, the design appears to be messy. The places concerned, exemplify how difficult it is to balance the recognisable remediation of places with an open approach to co-creation. In both cases, the endeavour is to open the place for co-creation, yet, it proves difficult to realise.

In the Literary project, it is confusing to co-create a shared avatar. The changing appearance is difficult to understand for the project's visitors as well as for the members of the team. The open approach to the co-creation of the avatar is given up. In the Times project, it is also difficult to understand the avatar which is not a remediation of a known cultural image, but this confusion is part of the purpose. Awaking other avatars curiosity, the project manager incites them to co-create the network-building activities of the project.

The welcoming gesture of the animated chair invites other avatars to co-create the content of events at the Literary project's place. In Wonder DK, some of the regulars of the town-square-chat volunteer to show around visitors at the place; it provides in-world status to be part of the project. In both cases, the openness and the welcoming remediation encourage co-creation in terms of socialising and event-making.

CONCLUSION

Concluding the case analysis, I will point to two factors of importance: 1) the co-creation of compelling experiences and activities, and 2) the mastering of different forms of remediation. As mentioned earlier, in the case of Second Life there is a complexity of requirements regarding user-driven content creation and innovation. To make a symbolic world a compelling experience several steps have to be taken. First, the platform itself (i.e. Second Life) must be useful and easy to use but also inspire a compelling experience. Secondly, actors who contribute the content by co-creating and remediating shapes and signs must also be capable to design compelling experiences that are easy to understand, use, and remember if they aim to start projects targeting other residents, participants, or visitors. Thirdly, in itself, it is a difficult task to remediate cultural images of artifacts, clothes, places, buildings, environments, metaphors, and genres by means of symbolic shapes and signs. Thus, the open and user-generated content creation of Second Life invites the residents of the world to contribute new interpretations and experiences while at the same time it is a risky strategy for the providers of platforms (i.e. Linden Lab) as well as the in-world projects and businesses considering the complexity of the networks of innovative practices involved.

Remediation encompasses borrowing, reshaping, and redefining of mediated content. In Wonder DK, the cultural images of a cosy Danish provincial town and square is borrowed and reshaped along with the redefined TV-series Matador. The cultural image of the project manager of the Times project is a redefined conspicuous advertisement pillar travelling between places inspired by the remediated genre and images of science fiction. The meeting place of the Literary project with the animated chair is a redefined welcoming invitation to visitors of the place. The main problem is however that the competencies, creativity, and knowledge needed to create compelling experiences are scarce resources. To generate creative ideas and to remediate these ideas make high demands on knowledge, skills, imagination, and methods of seeing the familiar in new ways. To generate new understandings of known forms of mediation it takes rethinking, redefining, and remediation. Not only is creativity needed to borrow and reshape well-known mediations but so is the ability to add-on to these by creating new and hereto unknown experiences using the symbolic shapes and signs. The case studies show that to redefine shapes and signs in a virtual world it requires know-how about how to make useful, easy to use and navigate digital design as well as methods to reorganise conceptual frameworks and meaning-making. Remediation is an analytical concept that may help us develop such methods to advance innovative practices and design in virtual worlds.

ACKNOWLEDGMENT

This chapter is produced as part of the project "Sense-making strategies, and the user-driven innovations in Virtual Worlds" 2008-2011 (worlds. ruc.dk), which has received funding from The Danish Strategic Research Council, KINO committee, and the Nordic Virtual Worlds Network supported by the Nordic Innovation Centre (NICe).

REFERENCES

Au, W. J. (2008). *The making of Second Life*. New York, NY: Harper Collins Publishers.

Baldwin, M., & Hanel, P. (2003). *Innovation and knowledge creation in an open economy*. Cambridge, UK: Cambridge University Press. doi:10.1017/CBO9780511510847

Boelstorff, T. (2008). *Coming of age in Second Life - An anthropologist explores the virtual human*. Princeton, NJ & Oxford, UK: Princeton University Press.

Bolter, J. D., & Grusin, D. (2000). *Remediation – Understanding new media*. Cambridge, MA: MIT Press.

Bonsu, S. K., & Darmody, A. (2008). Co-creating Second Life. *Journal of Macromarketing, 28*(4), 355–368. doi:10.1177/0276146708325396

Chandra, V., Eröcal, D. P., Padoan, C., & Carlos, P. B. (2009). *Innovation and growth: Chasing a moving frontier*. World Bank & OECD Report. Retrieved from http://browse.oecdbookshop.org/oecd/pdfs/browseit/0309071E.PDF

Csikszentmihalyi, M. (1996). *Flow and the psychology of discovery and invention*. New York, NY: Harpercollins.

Darsøe, L., & Austin, R. (2009). Innovation processes and closure. *Journal of Management & Organization, 14*(5).

Davis, J., Sundbo, J., Gallina, A., & Serin, G. (Eds.). (2005). *Contemporary management of innovation*. London, UK: PalgraveMacmillan.

DiPaola, S., & Collins, D. (2002). A 3D virtual environment for social telepresence. *Proceedings of the Western Computer Graphics Symposium*.

Fuglsang, L., & Sundbo, J. (2002). *Innovation as strategic reflexivity*. London, UK: Routledge.

Gloor, P. (2006). *Swarm creativity. Competitive advantage through collaborative innovation network*. Oxford, UK: Oxford University Press.

Hatch, M. J., & Yanow, D. (2008). Methodology by metaphor: Ways of seeing in painting and research. *Organization Studies, 29*(1). doi:10.1177/0170840607086635

Hornecker, E. (2004). Analogies from didactics and moderation/ facilitation methods: Designing spaces for interaction and experience. *Digital Creativity, 15*(4), 239–244. doi:10.1080/1462626048520185

Jensen, H. S. (2008). *Research on innovation. Perspectives and views on processes of innovation*. Laboranova report.

Kohler, T. (2008). *Avatar-based innovation. Facilitating compelling co-creation experiences*. Unpublished dissertation, Innsbruck Universität.

Kozinets, R. V., Hemetsberger, A., & Schau, H. J. (2008). The wisdom of consumer crowds: Collective innovation in the age of networked marketing. *Journal of Macromarketing, 28*(4), 339–354. doi:10.1177/0276146708325382

Krohn, W., & van den Daele, W. (1998). Science as an agent of change: Finalization and experimental implementation. *Social Science Informatics, 37*(1), 191–122. doi:10.1177/053901898037001009

Latour, B. (2005). *Reassembling the social. An introduction to actor-network-theory* (1st ed.). Oxford, UK & New York, NY: Oxford University Press.

Latour, B., & Woolgar, S. (1979/86). *Laboratory life*. Princeton, NJ/ Chichester, West Sussex, UK: Princeton University Press.

Malaby, T. M. (2009). *Making virtual worlds: Linden Lab and Second Life*. New York, NY: Cornell University Press.

Matusitz, J. (2005). Deception in the virtual world: A semiotic analysis of identity. *Journal of New Media and Society*, *3*(1). Retrieved from http://www.ibiblio.org/nmediac/winter2004/matusitz.html.

Mullet, K. (2003). *The essence of effective rich Internet applications*. Macromedia White Paper.

Nielsen, K., Nielsen, H., & Jensen, H. S. (2008). *Skruen uden ende. Den vestlige teknologis historie* (3rd ed.). Odense, Denmark: Erhvervsskolernes Forlag.

Randall, T., Terwiesch, C., & Ulrich, K. T. (2005). Principles of user design of customized products. *California Management Review*, *47*(4), 68–85.

Simon, H. (1977). *Models of discovery*. Dortrecht, Holland: Reidel.

Steinkuhler, C., & Williams, D. (2006). Where everybody knows your (screen) name: Online games as third places. *Journal of Computer-Mediated Communication*, *11*(4), 885–909. doi:10.1111/j.1083-6101.2006.00300.x

Sundbo, J. (2001). *The strategic management of innovation: A sociological and economic theory*. Cheltenham, UK: Edward Elgar.

Sundbo, J. (2001). *The theory of innovation: Entrepreneurs, technology and strategy*. Cheltenham, UK: Edward Elgar.

KEY TERMS AND DEFINITIONS

Borrowing: A process whereby the content of some media is mirrored when remediated in new media.

Mediation: Signs and things that carry and transform meaning.

Open Innovation: Potential users or consumers of a product, service, event and/ or experience are involved in their development.

Prosumer: The boundaries between production and consumption are changed as consumption becomes a part of production and vice versa.

Redefining: A process whereby the content of some media is reinterpreted and transformed when remediated in new media.

Remediation: A process whereby the content of some media are made the subject of new media.

Reshaping: A process whereby the content of some media is adapted mainly as improvements and additions when remediated in new media.

Chapter 2
Procedural Virtual Worlds

Nuno Rodrigues
Polytechnic Institute of Leiria, Portugal

Alan Chalmers
University of Warwick, UK

Luís Magalhães
University of Trás-os-Montes e Alto Douro, Portugal

Filipe Santos
Polytechnic Institute of Leiria, Portugal

João Paulo Moura
University of Trás-os-Montes e Alto Douro, Portugal

Leonel Morgado
University of Trás-os-Montes e Alto Douro, Portugal

ABSTRACT

With the increasing demand for more complex and larger models in different fields, such as the design of virtual worlds, video games, and computer animated movies, the need to generate them automatically has become more necessary than ever. Manual tools are no longer sufficient to match this rising need, and the impact that automatic tools may have within these fields is essential and may lead to an adoption of virtual worlds in a growing number of applications. Indeed, it is possible to eliminate most of the effort associated with the creation of such environments, by providing tools that may generate "massive" 3D content automatically. In consequence these tools may lead to an exponential growth of virtual environments and represent an important turn into the design of realistic virtual cities, which may have a huge impact on virtual world users. This chapter discusses the very complex issue of where and when procedural modelling may be used and presents some solutions and methods that have been successfully used in the aforementioned fields of application.

INTRODUCTION

The continuous trend to use virtual worlds coming from several different domains, such as education and private sectors, leads to the need to efficiently create virtual environments. Indeed, in virtual worlds as well as in the competitive markets of film, video games and several other applications, there is a trend to rapidly produce digital content at low costs. Manually designing virtual environments, during long periods of time, is not a cost effective solution with limited valuable human resources in many situations.

DOI: 10.4018/978-1-60960-854-5.ch002

Within the present context, procedural modelling represents an effective solution to produce digital content which is, in numerous virtual worlds, often characterized by urban environments. In order to assure the realism of the final models there is the need to account for many architectural concerns. These are essential aspects when dealing with different applications, such as heritage worlds amongst others. The increasing number of virtual world users from diverse areas creates the need to provide tools, able to efficiently produce realistic urban environments featuring traversable structures (e.g. houses), which achieve architectural coherence.

Traditionally procedural modelling have been used mostly in film and games and is not, yet, a mainstream solution for the design of 3D content for virtual worlds, such as Second Life, Activeworlds or Croquet. It is a fact that some virtual worlds (e.g. Second Life) have well known native modelling tools, but these are not yet procedural. Some small procedural plug-ins do exist, often designed only to fulfil small specific requirements, such as the creation of textures. For these reasons, the next sections describe in which worlds may these procedural techniques and tools may be adopted and when and how it may be done. This chapter is mostly centred on the creation of urban environments, one of the targets of procedural modelling. Most virtual worlds, such as virtual worlds for socialization purposes, are often characterized by these type of models. The automatic content creation that can be achieved with such tools may deal with different features, such as the generation of clouds and textures, streets and roads, vegetation, houses and many other objects. These content generation have been used mainly in film and game industry but most of this features are often present in virtual worlds and may used in these in a similar way.

This chapter starts by presenting an overview of procedural modelling. Then the dilemma behind where, when and how should procedural modelling be used in virtual worlds is addressed. This is followed by a discussion of two possible targets of procedural modelling: reconstruction and generation. After that, some tools and techniques are described and finally some conclusions and future trends presented.

"GOING PROCEDURAL"

In the last few years, the use of algorithms to automatically generate virtual reality environments has become an effective solution for the production of digital content. In fact, the idea of automatically recreating environments with very little modelling effort is a fascinating idea that can lead to several benefits in different areas including virtual worlds (a few other examples include architecture, video games and movies). The goal is to place all, or most of the effort, of creating an environment in computer software. This means that the time spent by human resources, such as computer modellers or even a plain virtual world user who wants to create their own models, would be significantly reduced and their time may be used on more useful tasks.

The creation of virtual environments via an algorithm (instead of manually) is often identified as "generation" of virtual environments. Similarly, the set of techniques which rely on algorithms to generate these environments are often referred to as "procedural modelling" techniques. Although there are diverse techniques used in procedural modelling, such as grammar based techniques (e.g. L-systems[1]), fractals[2] and generative modelling[3], the general purpose of these is similar: apply parameterised algorithms to produce 3D virtual scenes. The result is to create 3D models or textures from user choices rather than manually modelling each of the environment features.

Procedural modelling techniques embody essential tools, in situations where it would be cumbersome to create 3D models manually, or where current software does not provide efficient means to produce those models. One particular situation, which reveals the huge advantages of such techniques, is their use in computer animations where one can easily imagine the amount of effort necessary to perform some manual tasks, such as perform characters movement including their hair and clothing. For these reasons recent animation movies use algorithmic simulations to perform characters animation. It is also easy to imagine several situations where procedural modelling may be useful such as the generation of "massive" 3D models to quickly populate a virtual world (e.g. traversable buildings for a whole city). As such there is an increase demand for tools that can produce 3D content, which in some situations requires automatic solutions as manual creation methods are no longer sufficient.

The generation of urban structures seems to be a very appealing target for the use of procedural techniques, since urban models embody most of the computer graphics environments in several areas. For this reason there has already been a number of papers produced concerning urban procedural modelling such as the work presented in "Procedural Modeling of Cities" (Parish & Müller, 2001), in "Real-time Procedural Generation of 'Pseudo Infinite' Cities" (Greuter, Parker, Stewart, & Leach, 2003), in "Instant Architecture" (Wonka, Wimmer, Sillion, & Ribarsky, 2003) and in "Procedural Modeling of Buildings" (Müller, Wonka, Haegler, Ulmer, & Gool, 2006).

One common characteristic amongst most of the existing methods within the field of urban procedural modelling, e.g. (Coelho, Bessa, Sousa, & Ferreira, 2007; Pascal Müller, et al., 2006; Parish & Müller, 2001; Wonka, et al., 2003), is the use of some kind of grammar (e.g. shape grammars: L-systems, split grammars[4], etc.), although the purpose may be very diverse (e.g. generate roads, determine building locations, generate building facades, etc.). Indeed, even within recent techniques ranging photogrammetry and/or LIDAR, grammars are also applied, e.g. (Aliaga, Rosen, & Bekins, 2007; Hohmann, Krispel, Havemann, & Fellner, 2009; Müller, Zeng, Wonka, & Gool,

2007). It is a fact that grammar approaches require many rules to generate the models but if, at first, this seems a clear disadvantage, compared to other approaches, the flexibility provided by grammars makes them a powerful tool for the generation of urban models. Furthermore, it is also possible to avoid the text-based complexity of grammars by designing efficient interactive visual editing systems for shape grammars, such as the one presented by Lipp et al. (Lipp, Wonka, & Wimmer, 2008).

Figure 1 presents a procedural generated virtual environment including algorithm generated objects (houses and roads) and manually designed objects (fences, trees and lightning poles). All of the houses in the picture are completely traversable and although some objects were manually designed they were algorithmically placed (via an L-system).

WHICH WORLDS?

The first question concerning the use of procedural modelling techniques in virtual worlds is where, i.e. in which virtual worlds may they be used? This raises another question, which types of virtual worlds exist?

The most popular virtual worlds are used for entertainment purposes. Most of them belong to the category of the so called Massively Multiplayer Online Role Playing Games (MMORPG) (Woodcock, 2008) and are games in their real sense as they have an inbuilt narrative or meta-narrative for the users which have in that game a specific purpose or goal to achieve. Some of the most played MMORPGs today are World of Warcraft (Warcraft, 2010), Lineage (Lineage, 2010) and RunEscape (RunEscape, 2008).

One other popular use of virtual worlds is for socialization purposes. The so called Massively Multiplayer Online Social Games (MMOSG) which, without necessarily imposing a narrative to the user, focuses on the social aspect of it as

Figure 1. Procedural generated environment

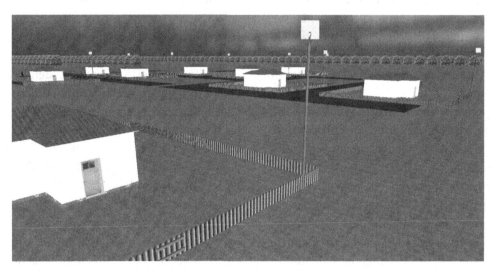

the main purpose, are expanding. Second Life (SecondLife, 2009) is currently the most well known virtual world of this kind, and the most open to content development by users, but many others have similar or greater popularity, e.g. IMVU (IMVU, 2010), particularly within the age groups of children and teenagers, e.g. Habbo Hotel (Hotel, 2010), Club Penguin (Penguin, 2010). The "Universe chart" in Kzero (KZero, 2010) shows the variety and popularity of virtual worlds universe.

One interesting aspect of some virtual worlds, MMOSGs in particular, is that as they don't have a goal to achieve or narrative to follow but rather they give the users the tools to make them. Second Life is well known by its 3D modelling tools (not procedural), which allow users the ability to program and control the behaviour of the world's objects. Other MMOSGs have lesser degrees of freedom in the level of control they give their users for creating content, but several provide tools that are adequate within the scope of this chapter (e.g. Activeworlds and Croquet). Virtual Worlds that have these two features give its users tremendous possibilities as worlds can be created and programmed for certain activities

as education, scientific research and collaborative work, amongst others.

These two perspectives see virtual worlds as pre-existing entities upon which one wishes to create content. A third perspective is that one may decide to create a virtual world from scratch, and provide the content from the start. This can be done using either a set of traditional programming tools or a special-purpose development library, such as Unity3D (Unity3D, 2010).

The potential of virtual worlds is very rich but has yet to be fully realised (Prentice, 2007). Still, there are already a great number of projects that take virtual worlds for education purposes (Ching-Song, Yan, & Jiann-Gwo, 2009; Dickey, 2005; Dreher, Reiners, Dreher, & Dreher, 2009; Natho & Pfeiffer, 2010) and training (Heinrichs, Youngblood, Harter, & Dev, 2008). These two uses of virtual worlds take advantage of, very often, virtual worlds as a simulating platform. Simulation may be seen as a technique "to replace or amplify real experiences with guided experiences, often immersive in nature, that evoke or replicate substantial aspects of the real world in a fully interactive fashion" (Gaba, 2004). Virtual worlds, as simulators, have some advantages over other types of simulators as high-fidelity simulators are expensive and students may be geographical far apart in virtual worlds (Heinrichs, et al., 2008), and in that virtual worlds can be more flexible in the range of educational activities, by leveraging the ability for students/trainees to create or modify content.

Other purposes for virtual worlds that are worth mentioning are the ones used for collaborative work (Back, et al., 2010; Bouras, Tegos, Triglianos, & Tsiatsos, 2007; Snowdon, Churchill, & Munro, 2001), scientific research (Bainbridge, 2007), virtual tourism (Bellotti, Berta, Gloria, Panizza, & Primavera, 2009) and military applications (3DSolve, 2010; Benford, Greenhalgh, Rodden, & Pycock, 2001). The commercial potential of virtual worlds is also subject of much research (Fang & Cai, 2009; Seidel & Berger, 2007).

Now, that a brief overview of has been presented the initial question persists. The fact is that independent of the type of virtual world there is a common feature amongst them, which is they all use 3D models, that represent nature, urban structures or even other human-made objects. Indeed it is easy to foresee a set of contexts where automatic 3D modelling mechanisms based on user parameters are useful. For example, a virtual city with hundreds or thousands of buildings can be implemented for real life simulations (e.g. earthquake damages scenarios) as virtual worlds may also have powerful physics engines integrated. These can also be useful for games and movies as new scenarios could easily be seen and tested since it would only be needed to change the pre-programmed rules for building creation.

These features makes procedural modelling a suitable tool for mostly all of the presented virtual worlds presented, since it ranges several different features ranging the simple generation of a texture, performing real objects animations (e.g. smoke, fire) to the complete generation of urban environments.

WHEN?

Once it is established the different types of virtual worlds which may benefit from procedural modelling it is also essential to determine when these techniques might be applied. This question does not have a straightforward answer since it is dependent of several aspects. For example, it depends of the availability of efficient methods/tools to produce the models. Most likely a common virtual world user who does not have any programming skills will not be willing to develop an algorithm to create virtual models.

Another example is the purpose for which the models are intended. It is not the same generating models for a pure imaginary world than for a world where the purpose is to represent real world structures. In fact, in procedural modelling techniques, the quality of the 3D models is closely related with the quality of the algorithm used to generate them, whereas in manual techniques the quality of the models is directly related to the skills of the human modeller.

Furthermore the choice of when to use a procedural technique is always dependent on the person who will design the world, either this is a computer graphics modeller or a common virtual world user. Most likely it is possible that, even when considering a procedural approach, the user would like to manually create some features or make some customizations thus producing a hybrid model. After all, as previously stated, the goal of procedural techniques is not to replace human resources or creativity but instead to provide efficient tools aiding the sometimes arduous and tedious task of producing complex 3D content.

These are just a few examples since there may be many other aspects constraining the use of procedural techniques. So, as may be understood there is not a unique answer of when to "go procedural". Though, one may say at the very least that procedural techniques are very likely the prime resort for the generation of virtual worlds, in present days, where it would be cumbersome to create 3D models manually or where current software does not provide efficient means to produce those models.

HOW?

The previous sections described where and when procedural modelling techniques may be used but did not described exactly the features of the different virtual worlds. This section presents how they may be used.

Most procedural modelling techniques address the generation of different features which may refer either to generation of static models or animated ones, allowing for the generation of models representing many of the physical objects present in our world. In (Watson, et al., 2008) the authors present a briefing of some of the vast quantity of procedural modelling "targets" and the corresponding techniques commonly used by several authors to generate or simulate each of them. L-systems are identified for the generation of plants (Prusinkiewicz, Lindenmayer, & Hanan, 1988), agent-based methods to model and animate different types of objects – e.g. particle systems to model fuzzy objects such as fire and smoke (Reeves, 1983) and Reynolds' boids to animate flocks, schools and herds (Reynolds, 1987), Perlin's noise to simulate clouds and natural textures (Perlin, 1985), and fractal techniques to synthesise natural landscapes (Fournier, Fussell, & Carpenter, 1982) or even simulate erosion effects on them (Musgrave, Kolb, & Mace, 1989).

All of these features make it possible to use procedural modelling in a large diversity of applications where different techniques may be used to couple with different aspects. For example, they may centre the attention on the generation of individual houses (Martin, 2005; Rodrigues, Dionísio, et al., 2008a, 2008b; Rodrigues, et al., 2009), on tall buildings and skyscrapers (Greuter, et al., 2003; Parish & Müller, 2001; Park, 2005), or on large urban environments (Bostrom, et al.,

2004; Willmott, Wright, Arnold, & Day, 2001), applying urban planning principles to the design of virtual environments (Ingram, Benford, Rd, & Bowers, 1996), modelling from architectural rules (Fuchs, 2006; Luca, Véron, & Florenzano, 2007; Rodrigues, Dionísio, et al., 2008a, 2008b; Rodrigues, Magalhães, Moura, & Chalmers, 2008), dealing with specific features as the generation of streets and roads (Chen, Esch, Wonka, Müller, & Zhang, 2008; Parish & Müller, 2001), or on house specific house features such as windows (Charbonneau, Boulerice, Booth, & Tidafi, 2006). Likewise, they may focus on modern architecture (Bessa, et al., 2005; Coelho, et al., 2007; Martin, 2005; Rodrigues, Dionísio, et al., 2008a, 2008b) or on heritage architecture, such as Roman (Müller, Vereenooghe, Ulmer, & Gool, 2005; Rodrigues, Magalhães, Moura, & Chalmers, 2007; Rodrigues, Magalhães, et al., 2008) or Mayan architecture (Müller, Vereenooghe, Wonka, Paap, & Gool, 2006). In another perspective, they may emphasise optimisation techniques, deal with real-time issues (M. Carrozzino, Tecchia, & Bergamasco, 2009; Döllner & Buchholz, 2005; Willmott, et al., 2001; Wonka, et al., 2006), or even address photo-realism (Müller, Vereenooghe, Vergauwen, Gool, & Waelkens, 2004) or high-fidelity (Sundstedt, Chalmers, & Martinez, 2004) concerns.

From all of the above it is clear that the requisites are not the same for each of the different applications where procedural techniques may be employed. The next section addresses the use of procedural techniques for two of their main purposes: reconstruction and generation.

RECONSTRUCTION/GENERATION?

At the beginning of this chapter some features of procedural modelling techniques were uncovered showing their undeniable advantages for the generation of new worlds. Indeed, often procedural modelling is the tool of choice when generation is in order. Additionally it may also prove to be useful to create virtual models representing structures lost in time, or even to create virtual models of existing structures. For these reasons it is important to first establish the significance of the terms reconstruction and generation within the present context, presented below:

- Reconstruction – creation of models using automatic techniques representing existing structures or creation of models representing structures no longer existing but for each there is enough evidences (i.e. ruins, floor plans, photographs, etc.) to faithfully reconstruct them.
- Generation – generation of new worlds, i.e. automatic creation of fictional structures not intended to represent any ever-existing structure.

Throughout the rest of this section the use of procedural techniques to perform the reconstruction and generation of structures is discussed, exemplified with heritage structures one of the main targets for "procedural reconstruction".

If the use of procedural techniques which produce fictional structures it is somewhat simple to realize in some areas (e.g. games), their use on areas such as archaeology where the general idea is to record historical fact it is not. Indeed, although these techniques should be carefully be thought out before they are employed in such area, since depending of the case study and purpose of the virtual models there may are more efficient methods (manual modelling), when realism is the main concern.

Some literature concerning procedural techniques has been used to create heritage models representing ancient structures. For example, in (Müller, et al., 2005) the authors wrote a set of rules to generate a virtual model of Pompei using CityEngine, a system introduced by Parish and Müller (Parish & Müller, 2001). Later, using the same system, the authors of "Procedural 3D Reconstruction of Puuc Buildings in Xkipche" (P.

Müller, et al., 2006), generated Puuc-style buildings similar to the ones that may be found in the ancient Mayan site of Xkipché, in Mexico. Without disregarding the efficiency of such techniques and tools the fact is that generation produces fictional structures, although in the present cases these are based upon known heritage construction rules or tries to reproduce features found in existing structures.

However, in structures showing more complex geometric harmony, the process used, i.e. the set of rules necessary to describe the physical geometry of the buildings may prove to be, in several cases, harder to achieve (or take more time) than when using traditional methods (manual modelling) or even impossible. Indeed, an experienced modeller may produce 3D models very efficiently when given adequate data (e.g. measurements, photographs, etc.) about a physical structure. Unfortunately, manual modelling does not allow the efficient reproduction of large virtual environments showing diversity (e.g. creation of different houses corresponding to a similar architectural style). For the above reasons and although the generation of models representing ancient structures may prove to have some interest or applications within archaeology and several other areas, when trying to faithfully reproduce an existing structure it does not always is a better solution. Therefore sometimes it is not desirable to use only algorithmically generated structures. The next section describes a way of using procedural modelling and yet maintaining realism in the models, by using a hybrid approach.

Realism

When addressing reconstruction or even considering a procedural technique for reconstruction it is important to think in which areas it may be applied. So, one may think at most obvious areas such as archaeology, architecture, etc. This raises some questions concerning the ability to represent or reconstruct structures using procedural methods since, for example, areas such as archaeology are highly driven by proof and realism.

Most known methods and tools for the automatic generation of models representing man-made structures usually rely on procedural techniques, which often produce models through the means of simple shape composition (or decomposition – depending on the technique). As previously mentioned these techniques sometimes do not allow the use of more complex objects. In areas such as archaeology, one main key point to recreate the past is the realism, which means that it is crucial do create features with a higher level of detail. Therefore, it is advisable to use manually modelled objects rather than to try to use some algorithm which would resemble the real structures that are pretended to be represented.

Producing these realistic models may be achieved either by designing them from known similar objects (e.g. artefacts, columns, windows, etc.) or even by replicating existing ones. This last option, however, does allow using faster reproductions, since there is the possibility of using automatic techniques such as laser scanning, to create the objects. Independently of how the models are created, the fact is that often there is evidence which indicate that most probably, within a certain architectural style, similar structures use identical features.

This is what led Rodrigues et al. in (Rodrigues, Magalhães, et al., 2008) to define a hybrid approach, i.e. an approach which joins both manual and procedural modelling, to meet the demanding concerns behind the reconstruction of heritage structures, but also providing most of the features brought by procedural techniques. Thus, the authors used an object database which may be used to represent some more specific house features. An example of this is the House of the Skeletons, a Roman heritage house of Conimbriga, Portugal. For the creation of the house several manual objects (e.g. triclinium window, impluvium, tuscan columns), modelled in an external application (3D Studio Max) were used, represented in Figure 2, and placed accordingly to grammar rules.

Integrating these objects into the final geometry is simply a matter of placing it in the desired place (e.g. impluvium, columns) or by subtracting the corresponding object geometry from the wall where they are to be placed (e.g. windows).

The grammar rules used in the approach were based on the knowledge left by Marcus Vitruvius Pollio – Roman architect and engineer who lived in the first century BC, author of "De architectura".

Moreover the same authors also provided a means to describe the whole geometry of a house through textual specifications (using a grammar) allowing both the generation of new houses but also the reconstruction of existing ones. This feature is particularly useful, because it allows a user with no knowledge or experience with modelling tools, to construct his/her own models through a set of textual specifications. These specifications were used to perform the reconstruction of the House

Figure 2. External objects; From left to right: triclinium window, impluvium, tuscan columns (Silva, Rodrigues, & Gonçalves, 2004)

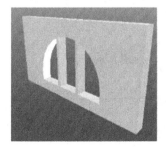
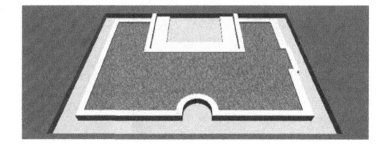

of the Skeletons which was then compared to a manual model showing very similar features. Figure 3 shows both of these models.

This approach may be considered a hybrid one, since it combines procedural techniques together with manually modelled objects. This allows a more realistic appearance of the final models and uses the best of both approaches: the efficiency of procedural techniques and the realism of manually modelling.

Automatic Reconstruction?

The previous section described how realism may be achieved using procedural modelling but one question still persists: how may procedural modelling techniques/tools be useful for areas such as archaeology?

The first answer to this question is to efficiently produce models of non-existing worlds for which there is some kind of knowledge (e.g. floor plans, photographs) to support the reconstruction of realistic environments.

Projects such as "Rome Reborn", "an international initiative whose goal is the creation of 3D digital models illustrating the urban development of ancient Rome from the first settlement in the late Bronze Age (ca. 1000 B.C.) to the depopulation of the city in the early Middle Ages (ca. A.D. 550)" (Rome, 2010), use both reconstruction, which currently is done manually, and generation. The buildings present in the digital model are divided into two kinds: "Class I" and "Class II" buildings. "Class I" buildings are manually modelled based on archaeological evidence (such as excavations, studies and ancient literary sources). "Class II" buildings are procedurally modelled from a digitization of the Plastico di Roma Antica, "a large plaster-of-Paris model of imperial Rome (16x17 meters) created in the last century" (Guidi, et al., 2005). The process consists of replacing the scan data from the digitization with geometrically simplified forms and the modelling of these simplified form faces with detailed architectural features (e.g. doors, windows, balconies). The process also included the correction of known errors present in the Plastico di Roma Antica. Another interesting feature about "Rome Reborn" is that CityEngine, an urban modelling software from Procedural Inc. described in section "Tools and Techniques", was used in "Class II" buildings. Rome Reborn is also published in the Internet as "Ancient Rome 3D" in Google Earth (A. Rome, 2010).

The second answer to the question presented is to support the generation of distinct possibilities to allow experts to draw some conclusions or conceive different hypotheses about lost worlds. For example in several Roman heritage sites (e.g. Conimbriga, Portugal) some parts of the city are yet uncovered or may even be lost. By taking as

Figure 3. House of the Skeletons; Left: manual model, Right: grammar model

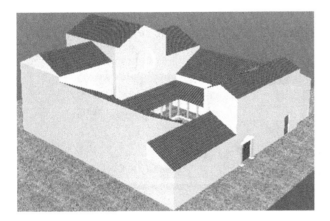

an example similar Roman cities it is possible to determine what may exist in most of the site. For this reason, Rodrigues et al. in (Rodrigues, Magalhães, et al., 2008) have designed an grammar approach which allows the specification of several features of a house, including incomplete specifications which allows the generation of several resembling models within an architectural style. The presented approach is demonstrated with the generation of several Conimbriga's Roman houses showing some dissimilarity amongst them.

The idea of generating structures similar to existing ones is not something new and not even confined to heritage. In fact, it is something that is pursued by several authors and may be referred as inverse procedural modelling. For example, (Aliaga, et al., 2007) describes an interactive system for the creation of new buildings in the style of others or for the modification of existing buildings. The idea is to create geometric models from photographs, divide the building into their basic external features (e.g. floors, windows, etc.) and create a grammar that captures the repetition patterns of these features. Then it allows the user to design building configurations from building blocks and finally to divide these building configurations into the several features, using the repetition patterns from the grammar. One of the most interesting aspects of this approach is the idea itself and its potential use in architecture. Nevertheless, there is still a great deal of interaction needed from the user, starting from the initial photograph mapping until the design of the final building blocks (nevertheless the interaction in this last step does make a lot of sense if the idea is for the user to provide new geometries). Another aspect to notice about this approach is that only facades are created.

TOOLS AND TECHNIQUES

Although recently procedural modelling is becoming mainstream in other applications, it has already been applied for a number of years in several applications such as games. The initial motivation for this relied in the fact that earliest computer games were limited by memory constraints of existing hardware and software. For example, "The Sentinel", a video game featuring 3D graphics allowed the generation of 10,000 different levels, which would be stored in about 64 KB of memory (another is "Elite", a space video game, which was initially planned to contain approximately 282 trillion galaxies with 256 solar systems each).

Nowadays the motivation is not exclusively related to hardware/software resources but also on the human resources necessary to produce large 3D environments. For this reason the trend to use procedural techniques to produce 3D models remains in modern games. Such is the example of ".kkrieger" and "Will Wright's Spore" which use procedural synthesis to generate the graphics (the first, ".kkrieger" has the particularity of packing video effects in less than 97 KB). Many more examples exist, such as the first-person shooter video games "Left 4 Dead" and "Left 4 Dead 2", released in 2008 and 2009 respectively.

Another example in a different area is the competitive movie industry where every year new movies rich in digital content, produced through procedural techniques, appear.

In the field of applications there is also some tools specific for the generation of different features, for example, to generate terrains there are tools available such as Terragen or Acropora; for trees, Speedtree; for urban structures, CityEngine (further described shortly) and Cityscape; for textures, Art of Illusion; to perform animations, Houdini, etc. Beside these applications there are also procedural plug-ins for existing applications, for example, Filter Forge is a plug-in for Adobe

Photoshop for designing procedural textures. These represent only a fraction of the available tools and most of these tools are not exclusively to one type of content. For example, some tools for the generation of urban environments may also allow the generation of terrains and trees. Furthermore, although some of these tools are available for free others are very expensive. So, it is really up to the user to choose the software which best fits their purpose.

(M. Carrozzino, et al., 2009), presented the City Modelling Procedural Engine (CMPE), a system for the automatic/semi-automatic reconstruction of virtual models of cities integrated in the XVR framework (Marcello Carrozzino, Tecchia, Bacinelli, Cappelletti, & Bergamasco, 2005), a framework for the development of Virtual Reality (VR) applications developed by some of the same authors. Indeed, mostly built with XVR, it uses 3D urban models and may include vehicle simulators, crowd behaviour simulators, according to the Pecchioli, Carrozzino et al. (Pecchioli, Carrozzino, & Mohamed, 2008), which also present a methodology to deal with the access to information related to Cultural Heritage.

In (CGV, 2010) several ongoing projects are also presented featuring High-Quality Urban Reconstructions by Fitting Shape Grammars to Images and derived Textured Point Clouds and also the generation of 3D city models, using existing data such as aerial photos and laser scans. Indeed such examples, e.g. (Hohmann, et al., 2009) proof that even procedural modelling approaches may also incorporate data and techniques used in photogrammetry and laser scanning.

One of the most remarkable tools, in the field of the procedural urban environments, is City Engine, a commercial software produced by Procedural Inc. (Procedural, 2009). City Engine is a 3D modelling software especially conceived for the generation of urban environments, using procedural techniques, which allows the generation of street networks which take into account the topography of the terrain. Furthermore, real city networks may be imported into this software, from several other programs such as OpenStreet-Map (OpenStreetMap, 2010). The software also includes a scripting language to develop architectural 3D content and an interface to parameterize specific building features (e.g. height, age). City-Engine also allows batch exports of 3D models for several file formats such as: Wavefront OBJ, Autodesk FBX, Autodesk 3DS, COLLADA DAE, MentalRay MI and Renderman RIB.

Some virtual worlds provide tools to develop 3D content (with scripts for behaviours if desired) but others rely on 3rd party tools for this task, as Blender or 3D Studio Max, giving the user "import content" tools. As this may be desirable, giving the users the liberty to use their favourite modelling tool, the lack of a common 3D modelling format, for the several virtual worlds, could also be a challenge as some problems of conversion between formats still exist. Presently, virtual world users may implement their own procedural techniques and tools for content generation, within the constraints of each platform (e.g., scripting languages, automated client software, etc.). Some 3rd party tools are available, with varying degrees of power and applicability, such as the ones described in this section, albeit its use is not widespread.

The dilemma behind using 3rd party tools is that these are not integrated in virtual worlds meaning the models have to be exported from 3rd party tools and imported to the virtual world. Beside conversion problems that may arise there is another aspect to take into consideration, which is the fact that 3rd party tools often produce dummy models, i.e. generic models which may not suit the virtual world. Indeed, although some virtual worlds allow the import of several formats, most of the time not all of the features of the format are supported due to constraints related with the virtual world. Furthermore, the models may be suitable for some applications but sometimes they are not appropriate for virtual worlds, which have to maintain some minimum performance. Additionally, the lack of a common format amongst virtual worlds sometimes constrains the use of certain application to produce the models.

The above reasons led Rodrigues et al., in (Rodrigues, et al., 2009) to present a framework prototype – ArchHouseGenerator – for the development of virtual models which integrates an "dedicated exporter", i.e. an exporter which takes into consideration the type of format being produced and the type of virtual world. Although this tool is not yet available to virtual world users some initial tests allow to produce models which were imported into a virtual world. The models were tested in a virtual world developed with virtual World SDK, OpenCroquet, a tool that "can be used by experienced software developers to create and deploy deeply collaborative multi-user online virtual world applications on and across multiple operating systems and devices" (OpenCroquet, 2009).

Figure 4 shows an OpenCroquet virtual world where a house produced with ArchHouseGenerator was imported and where its multi-user capabilities were also tested.

As it can be seen the world was rendered in two different machines synchronously – allowing the simultaneous presence of two users (here represented by rabbits – each one is seeing the other).

CONCLUSION AND FUTURE TRENDS

This chapter has presented the advantages, as well as disadvantages of using procedural modelling tools in the several types of virtual worlds. In addition, *where*, *when* and *which tools* are available to generate virtual models have been described. It is clear that, the purpose of procedural modelling in virtual worlds, is not to prevent virtual world users from designing their own worlds, but instead to provide an efficient tools to do so. Indeed, procedural modelling has been extensively used in several other areas and there is no reason to believe it will not be used the same way in virtual worlds.

The different types of existing virtual worlds determine where and when should procedural techniques be employed. When dealing with urban structures, the starting point for defining the way to create the physical models is to determine if the purpose of the models are the representation of existing structures or the generation of new ones. Procedural modelling is a very powerful tool but that does not mean that it is always the better solution. As described in this chapter many aspects determine the possible use of such techniques (e.g. type of virtual world, reconstruction/

Figure 4. Procedural generated traversable house (in an OpenCroquet multiuser world)

generation, number of models to create, etc.) and a conscientious choice has to be made in each case.

In this busy and competitive world the rush to generate digital 3D content may determine the overall adoption of procedural tools. This may also be a great opportunity to propel a virtual world to a new status as providing features not yet supported by all the others.

It is likely 3rd party generation tools would be integrated with virtual worlds' engines or, at the very least, would perform exports that are mode "virtual world friendly".

In addition, it is even more likely that future virtual worlds would have integrated their 3D modelling tools, as they currently have (e.g. Second Life), but also featuring procedural features, either natively supported or provided via plug-ins.

REFERENCES

Aliaga, D. G., Rosen, P. A., & Bekins, D. R. (2007). Style grammars for interactive visualization of architecture. *IEEE Transactions on Visualization and Computer Graphics*, *13*(4), 786–797. doi:10.1109/TVCG.2007.1024

Ancient Rome. (2010). *Ancient Rome*. Retrieved on June 13, 2010, from http://earth.google.com/rome/

Back, M., Childs, T., Dunnigan, A., Foote, J., Gattepally, S., Liew, B., et al. (2010). *The virtual factory: Exploring 3D worlds as industrial collaboration and control environments*. Paper presented at the Virtual Reality Conference (VR).

Bainbridge, W. S. (2007). The scientific research potential of virtual worlds. *Science*, *317*(5837), 472–476. doi:10.1126/science.1146930

Bellotti, F., Berta, R., Gloria, A. D., Panizza, G., & Primavera, L. (2009). *Designing cultural heritage contents for serious virtual worlds*. Paper presented at the Proceedings of the 2009 15th International Conference on Virtual Systems and Multimedia.

Benford, S., Greenhalgh, C., Rodden, T., & Pycock, J. (2001). Collaborative virtual environments. *Communications of the ACM*, *44*(7), 79–85. doi:10.1145/379300.379322

Bessa, M., Coelho, A. F. V. C. C., Moura, J. P., Ferreira, F. N., Cruz, J. B., & Sousa, A. A. d. (2005). *Modelação expedita de ambientes virtuais urbanos para utilização em dispositivos móveis*. Paper presented at the 13° Encontro Português de Computação Gráfica.

Bostrom, G., Fiocco, M., Puig, D., Rossini, A., Goncalves, J. G. M., & Sequeira, V. (2004). *Acquisition, modelling and rendering of very large urban environments*. Paper presented at the 3D Data Processing, Visualization, and Transmission (3DPVT), 2nd International Symposium.

Bouras, C., Tegos, C., Triglianos, V., & Tsiatsos, T. (2007). *X3D multi-user virtual environment Platform for collaborative spatial design*. Paper presented at the 27th International Conference on Distributed Computing Systems Workshops.

Carrozzino, M., Tecchia, F., Bacinelli, S., Cappelletti, C., & Bergamasco, M. (2005). *Lowering the development time of multimodal interactive application: The real-life experience of the XVR project*. Paper presented at the ACM SIGCHI International Conference on Advances in Computer Entertainment Technology, ACE 2005.

Carrozzino, M., Tecchia, F., & Bergamasco, M. (2009). *Urban procedural modeling for real-time rendering*. Paper presented at the 3rd ISPRS International Workshop 3D-ARCH 2009: 3D Virtual Reconstruction and Visualization of Complex Architectures.

CGV. (2010). *Computer graphics and knowledge visualization.* Retrieved on May 31, 2010, from http://www.cgv.tugraz.at/CGV/Research/Projects

Charbonneau, N., Boulerice, D., Booth, D. W., & Tidafi, T. (2006). *Understanding gothic rose windows with computer-aided technologies.* Paper presented at the 24th eCAADe Conference.

Chen, G., Esch, G., Wonka, P., Müller, P., & Zhang, E. (2008). Interactive procedural street modeling. *ACM Transactions on Graphics, 27*(3), 1–10. doi:10.1145/1360612.1360702

Ching-Song, W., Yan, C., & Jiann-Gwo, D. (2009). *A 3D virtual world teaching and learning platform for computer science courses in Second Life.* Paper presented at the Computational Intelligence and Software Engineering.

Club Penguin. (2010). *Club Penguin.* Retrieved on June 14, 2010, from http://www.clubpenguin.com/

Coelho, A., Bessa, M., Sousa, A. A. d., & Ferreira, F. N. (2007). Expeditious modelling of virtual urban environments with geospatial L-systems. *Computer Graphics Forum, 26*(4), 769–782.

Dickey, M. D. (2005). Three-dimensional virtual worlds and distance learning: Two case studies of Active Worlds as a medium for distance education. *British Journal of Educational Technology, 36*(3), 439–451. doi:10.1111/j.1467-8535.2005.00477.x

Döllner, J., & Buchholz, H. (2005). *Continuous level-of-detail modeling of buildings in 3D city models.* Paper presented at the 13th Annual ACM International Workshop on Geographic Information Systems.

Dreher, C., Reiners, T., Dreher, N., & Dreher, H. (2009). *3D virtual worlds as collaborative communities enriching human endeavours: Innovative applications in e-learning.* Paper presented at the Digital Ecosystems and Technologies.

3DSolve. (2010). *3DSolve.* Retrieved on January 5, 2010, from http://www.3dsolve.com/ov3d.html

Fang, Z.-C., & Cai, H. (2009). *Designing social commerce experience in 3D virtual world.* Paper presented at the 2009 IEEE Conference on Commerce and Enterprise Computing.

Fournier, A., Fussell, D., & Carpenter, L. (1982). Computer rendering of stochastic models. *Communications of the ACM, 25*(6), 371–384. doi:10.1145/358523.358553

Fuchs, A. (2006). *Outils numériques pour le relevé architectural et la restitution archéologique.* Nancy, France: Université Henri Poincaré.

Gaba, D. M. (2004). The future vision of simulation in health care. *Quality & Safety in Health Care, 13*(suppl 1), i2. doi:10.1136/qshc.2004.009878

Greuter, S., Parker, J., Stewart, N., & Leach, G. (2003). *Real-time procedural generation of 'pseudo infinite' cities.* Paper presented at the 1st International Conference on Computer Graphics and Interactive Techniques in Australasia and Southeast Asia.

Guidi, G., Micoli, L., Russo, M., Frischer, B., Simone, M. D., Spinetti, A., et al. (2005). *3D digitization of a large model of imperial Rome.* Paper presented at the Proceedings of the Fifth International Conference on 3-D Digital Imaging and Modeling.

Habbo Hotel. (2010). *Habbo Hotel.* Retrieved on June 14, 2010, from http://www.habbo.com/

Heinrichs, W. L. R., Youngblood, P., Harter, P. M., & Dev, P. (2008). Simulation for team training and assessment: case studies of online training with virtual worlds. *World Journal of Surgery, 32*(2), 161–170. doi:10.1007/s00268-007-9354-2

Hohmann, B., Krispel, U., Havemann, S., & Fellner, D. (2009). *CityFit: High-quality urban reconstructions by fitting shape grammars to images and derived textured point clouds*. Paper presented at the 3rd ISPRS International Workshop 3D-ARCH 2009: 3D Virtual Reconstruction and Visualization of Complex Architectures.

IMVU. (2010). *IMVU*. Retrieved on June 14, 2010, from http://www.imvu.com/

Ingram, R., Benford, S., & Bowers, J. (1996). *Building virtual cities: Applying urban planning principles to the design of virtual environments*. Paper presented at the ACM Symposium on Virtual Reality Software and Technology (VRST'96)

KZero. (2010). *KZero chart*. Retrieved on June 14, 2010, from http://www.kzero.co.uk/universe.php

Lineage. (2010). *Lineage*. Retrieved on May 1, 2010, from http://www.lineage.com

Lipp, M., Wonka, P., & Wimmer, M. (2008). *Interactive visual editing of grammars for procedural architecture*. Paper presented at the ACM SIGGRAPH.

Luca, L. D., Véron, P., & Florenzano, M. (2007). A generic formalism for the semantic modeling and representation of architectural elements. *The Visual Computer, 23*(3), 181–205. doi:10.1007/s00371-006-0092-5

Mandelbrot, B. B. (1982). *The fractal geometry of nature*. W. H. Freeman.

Martin, J. (2005). *The algorithmic beauty of buildings: Methods for procedural building generation*. Unpublished Honors Thesis, Trinity University.

Müller, P., Vereenooghe, T., Ulmer, A., & Gool, L. V. (2005). *Automatic reconstruction of Roman housing architecture*. Paper presented at the International Workshop on Recording, Modeling and Visualization of Cultural Heritage.

Müller, P., Vereenooghe, T., Vergauwen, M., Gool, L. V., & Waelkens, M. (2004). *Photo-realistic and detailed 3D modeling: The Antonine Nymphaeum at Sagalassos (Turkey)*. Paper presented at the Computer Applications and Quantitative Methods in Archaeology (CAA2004): Beyond the artifact - Digital interpretation of the past.

Müller, P., Vereenooghe, T., Wonka, P., Paap, I., & Gool, L. V. (2006). *Procedural 3D reconstruction of Puuc buildings in Xkipche*. Paper presented at the Symposium on Virtual Reality, Archaeology and Cultural Heritage (VAST).

Müller, P., Wonka, P., Haegler, S., Ulmer, A., & Gool, L. V. (2006). Procedural modeling of buildings. *ACM Transactions on Graphics, 25*(3), 614–623. doi:10.1145/1141911.1141931

Müller, P., Zeng, G., Wonka, P., & Gool, L. V. (2007). Image-based procedural modeling of facades. *ACM Transactions on Graphics, 26*(3). doi:10.1145/1276377.1276484

Musgrave, F. K., Kolb, C. E., & Mace, R. S. (1989). *The synthesis and rendering of eroded fractal terrains*. Paper presented at the 16th Annual Conference on Computer Graphics and Interactive Techniques.

Natho, N., & Pfeiffer, O. (2010). *A knowledge management system for educational scenarios in 3D virtual worlds*. Paper presented at the Second International Conference on Mobile, Hybrid, and On-Line Learning.

OpenStreetMap. (2010). *OpenStreetMap*. Retrieved on May 31, 2010, from http://www.openstreetmap.org/

Parish, Y. I. H., & Müller, P. (2001). *Procedural modeling of cities*. Paper presented at the 28th Annual Conference on Computer Graphics and Interactive Techniques.

Park, S. M. (2005). *Tall building form generation by parametric design process.* Chicago, IL, USA: Illinois Institute of Technology.

Pecchioli, L., Carrozzino, M., & Mohamed, F. (2008). *ISEE: Accessing relevant information by navigating 3D interactive virtual environments.* Paper presented at the 14th International Conference on Virtual Systems and Multimedia, IEEE VSMM.

Perlin, K. (1985). An image synthesizer. *SIGGRAPH Computer Graphics, 19*(3), 287–296. doi:10.1145/325165.325247

Prentice, S. (2007). *The five laws of virtual worlds.* Stamford, CT: Gartner Research, Gartner Inc. Publication ID: G00148019.

Procedural Inc. (2009). *Procedural Inc.* Retrieved on June 24, 2009, from http://www.procedural. com/

Prusinkiewicz, P., Lindenmayer, A., & Hanan, J. (1988). Development models of herbaceous plants for computer imagery purposes. *ACM SIGGRAPH Computer Graphics, 22*(4), 141–150. doi:10.1145/378456.378503

Reeves, W. T. (1983). Particle systems - A technique for modeling a class of fuzzy objects. *ACM Transactions on Graphics, 2*(2), 91–108. doi:10.1145/357318.357320

Reynolds, C. W. (1987). *Flocks, herds and schools: A distributed behavioral model.* Paper presented at the 14th Annual Conference on Computer Graphics and Interactive Techniques.

Rodrigues, N., Dionísio, M., Gonçalves, A., Magalhães, L., Moura, J. P., & Chalmers, A. (2008a). *Incorporating legal rules on procedural house generation.* Paper presented at the Spring Conference on Computer Graphics.

Rodrigues, N., Dionísio, M., Gonçalves, A., Magalhães, L., Moura, J. P., & Chalmers, A. (2008b). Rule-based generation of houses. *Computer Graphics & Geometry, 10*(2), 49–65.

Rodrigues, N., Magalhães, L., Moura, J. P., & Chalmers, A. (2007). *Geração automática de estruturas Romanas.* Paper presented at the CAA Portugal.

Rodrigues, N., Magalhães, L., Moura, J. P., & Chalmers, A. (2008). *Automatic reconstruction of virtual heritage sites.* Paper presented at the Symposium on Virtual Reality, Archaeology and Cultural Heritage (VAST 08).

Rodrigues, N., Magalhães, L., Moura, J. P., Chalmers, A., Santos, F., & Morgado, L. (2009, 24-25 September). *ArchHouseGenerator - A framework for house generation.* Paper presented at the Slactions 2009 International Conference: Life, imagination, and work using metaverse platforms, Babbage Amphiteatre, NMC Conference Center, Second Life.

Rome Reborn. (2010). *Rome Reborn.* Retrieved on June 13, 2010, from http://www.romereborn. virginia.edu/

RunEscape. (2008). *RunEscape.* Retrieved on May 1, 2008, from http://www.runescape.com

SecondLife. (2009). *Second Life.* Retrieved on July 29, 2009, from http://secondlife.com/

Seidel, I., & Berger, H. (2007). *Integrating electronic institutions with 3D virtual worlds.* Paper presented at the 2007 IEEE/WIC/ACM International Conference on Intelligent Agent Technology.

Silva, F., Rodrigues, D., & Gonçalves, A. (2004). *House of the skeletons - A virtual way.* Paper presented at the XXXII CAA - Computer Applications and Quantitative Methods to Archaeology Conference.

Snowdon, D., Churchill, E. F., & Munro, A. J. (2001). Collaborative virtual environments: Digital spaces and places for CSCW: An introduction. In Churchill, E. F., Snowdon, D. N., & Munro, A. J. (Eds.), *Collaborative virtual environments: Digital places and spaces for interaction* (pp. 3–17). London, UK: Springer-Verlag.

Sundstedt, V., Chalmers, A., & Martinez, P. (2004). *High fidelity reconstruction of the ancient Egyptian temple of Kalabsha*. Paper presented at the 3rd International Conference on Computer Graphics, Virtual Reality, Visualisation and Interaction in Africa.

Unity3D. (2010). *UNITY: Game development tool*. Retrieved on June 14, 2010, from http://unity3d.com/

Watson, B., Müller, P., Wonka, P., Sexton, C., Veryovka, O., & Fuller, A. (2008). Procedural urban modeling in practice. *IEEE Computer Graphics and Applications*, *28*(3), 18–26. doi:10.1109/MCG.2008.58

Willmott, J., Wright, L. I., Arnold, D. B., & Day, A. M. (2001). *Rendering of large and complex urban environments for real time heritage reconstructions*. Paper presented at the conference on Virtual reality, archaeology, and cultural heritage.

Wonka, P., Wimmer, M., Sillion, F., & Ribarsky, W. (2003). Instant architecture. *ACM Transactions on Graphics*, *22*(3), 669–677. doi:10.1145/882262.882324

Wonka, P., Wimmer, M., Zhou, K., Maierhofer, S., Hesina, G., & Reshetov, A. (2006). *Guided visibility sampling*. Paper presented at the ACM SIGGRAPH.

Woodcock, B. (2008). *MMOG chart*. Retrieved on April 21, 2008, from http://www.mmogchart.com/Chart8.html

World of Warcraft. (2010). *World of Warcraft*. Retrieved on May 1, 2010, from http://www.worldofwarcraft.com

ENDNOTES

[1] L-systems or Lindenmayer systems (named after their creator) consist of formal grammars and were introduced in 1968 by the Hungarian theoretical biologist and botanist from the University of Utrecht, Aristid Lindenmayer.

[2] A fractal is "a rough or fragmented geometric shape that can be split into parts, each of which is (at least approximately) a reduced-size copy of the whole" (Mandelbrot, 1982).

[3] Generative modelling, in computer graphics, is a procedural modelling technique where a shape is described by a sequence of processing steps.

[4] "Split grammars" were introduced by (Wonka, et al., 2003) and are three-dimensional design grammars based on the concept of a shape.

Chapter 3
Collective Building Projects in Second Life:
User Motives and Strategies Explained From an Architectural and Ethnographic Perspective

Bjarke Liboriussen
Copenhagen Business School, Denmark

ABSTRACT

Users of "Second Life" invest considerable amounts of time, money, and creativity in collective building projects. Informed by a 14-month ethnography, this chapter explains why and how from an architectural perspective. User motivation is explained with recourse to the concept of dwelling, and special attention is given to use of the architectural devices boundary and image. The user strategy employing such devices is summed up as a pop vernacular building strategy characterised by eclecticism but not by irony. Special attention is given to the way in which the avatar allows a sense of place to be bodily grounded in agency. Through its architectural focus on concepts such as place and dwelling, the chapter demonstrates the relevance of "old", i.e., pre-digital, experiences in virtual worlds.

INTRODUCTION

This chapter explores the phenomenon of virtual dwelling in "Second Life" (and, by extension, other virtual worlds). Both methodologically and theoretically it is informed by the idea that it is meaningful and productive to approach virtual dwellings as places. Methodologically, the notion of place points towards an ethnographic approach. Theoretically, it points towards architectural theory and related fields, especially the philosophy of space and place. These methodological

DOI: 10.4018/978-1-60960-854-5.ch003

and theoretical issues are addressed immediately below. I then turn towards my ethnography of a collective building project in "Second Life". The motivation for that collective building project will be explored through the concept of dwelling. User practices aimed at dwelling will be explained from an architectural perspective through the devices of *boundary* and *image*, and summed up as a building strategy of the *pop vernacular*. Throughout the chapter, special attention is paid to the ways in which the avatar functions as a device for giving the user a bodily grounded sense of agency and place.

PLACE, ETHNOGRAPHY, ARCHITECTURE

People in Virtual Places

In Tom Boellstorff's words (2008), virtual world ethnography presupposes that "virtual worlds are places", and thus "fieldsites [...] making an ethnographic approach conceivable" (p. 91). At heart, and bracketing its many variations and the discussions surrounding it, ethnography is about entering a place and staying in that place long enough to get a sense of its culture from the inside. The ethnographic approach is, however, not the only approach to studying virtual worlds, and this section gives a brief overview of how ethnography is situated in recent virtual worlds research.

Annette N. Markham (1998) offers three categories for the ways in which users can conceptualise an online community: as tool, as place, and as way of being. Based on Markham's work on (and in) text-based, online communities, the categories are meant to be a rough starting point for thinking about the myriad ways users approach such communities. The categories are also useful when surveying recent work on avatar-based, 3D virtual worlds such as "Second Life". Markham stresses that the three concepts are not used exclusively and that they form a continuum. On a day when

it seems to blend seamlessly into everyday life, a user might think of the virtual world as a way of being. Perhaps on the following day, the user thinks of it more as a place to be visited.

The tool approach is, e.g., employed by psychologist Nick Yee (2007) who have documented how the main tool for engagement with a virtual world, the avatar, influences not only how one is perceived by other users but also self-perception.

The notion of place is constantly present in Howard Rheingold's early book (1993) on "The WELL" (a text-based world preceding the World Wide Web with almost a decade). Place also makes itself present in Lisbeth Klastrup's work (2003) on "EverQuest" (SOE, 1999) in which she brings examples of how changes to virtual places radically alter social practices. A more recent article by Eric Hayot and Edward Wesp (2009) goes into detail with the social construction of place in "EverQuest".

The notion of the virtual world as a way of being underlies work focusing on the blurred boundary between online and offline. Examples are Mário J. L. Guimarães, Jr.'s ethnographic study of "The Palace" (2005), a 2D precursor to contemporary virtual worlds (Time Warner Interactive, 1995), and T. L. Taylor's ethnography (2006) of "EverQuest", tellingly titled "Play Between Worlds". In a sense, work focusing on blurred boundaries are a variant of the place approach, since there would not be a boundary, blurred or not, if the virtual world was not a place in its own right.

Based on the notion of place, ethnographic approaches have been used for text-based and two-dimensional virtual worlds. But the virtual world is, arguably, a place in a stronger sense when it is three-dimensional and engaged with through an avatar.

Avatars in Virtual Architecture

When users engage with virtual world places, they do so through and with an avatar. To understand the premise of virtual world ethnography, then, it is necessary to clarify the function of the avatar. Having an avatar opens up issues of identity and self-representation but what is important here is the avatar's fundamental function of affording users a sense of being in virtual place. That theme will be introduced here and then fleshed out later.

3D graphics and avatar allow correspondence between the movements of the user's actual body and movements in the space of the virtual world. This effect is known as *motor-isomorphism* (*motor* has to do with movement, *iso-* with things being the same). Even though a press of the W-key to move the avatar forward in "Second Life" is a very modest example of bodily movement, the user immediately perceives similarity between actual body movement and avatar movement. This similarity is suggestive of a space which is not the actual body's space. How could the body's movements be similar to other movements, if there was no space for these other movements to occur in? In 3D virtual worlds such as "Second Life", that most basic sense of space triggered by motor-isomorphism is enhanced by various *depth cues* such as *perspective* (in perspective, two parallel railway tracks famously converge in a single point), and *motion parallax* (e.g., a close tree seemingly moving faster than a far-away tree, when observed from a moving train), as described in perceptual psychology (see, e.g., Bruce & Green, 1990).

Crucial for the experience of avatar-based virtual worlds, movement through space is crucial for architectural experience as well. Architecture might be designed with a specific movement in mind, e.g., an imposing system of arches and staircases designed to impress the visitor on arrival, but architecture thrives on the relative freedom to take it in, literally on one's own pace. There are obvious differences between online and offline architectural experiences, but bracketing these differences allows us to tap into theoretical resources within architectural theory and related fields. When architectural theory is applied in order to improve game design, there is a tendency to

arrive at formalist understandings of architecture (e.g., the use of Christopher Alexander et al.'s tellingly titled "A Pattern Language" [1977] by Ljungström [2005] and Nitsche [2008]). As for this chapter, the issue is not game design but collective building projects aimed at dwelling. That issue calls for other parts of architectural theory to form the theoretical starting point, as I will discuss in the following.

Space and Place

When "Second Life" users, such as the ones of my ethnography, build virtual houses to feel at home, they are surely not engaged in an activity aimed at providing real-life housing. But they are, at least in some sense of that ambiguous word, doing architecture. Engaging in any discussion about "architecture" is to claim that the built environment is too important to be merely engineered in the most cost-effective way. Architects themselves often understand their craft in opposition to that of the engineers they work with on projects. The engineer might be able to construct buildings that fulfil required functions, but as the arguably most influential architect and architectural theorist of the 20th century, Le Corbusier, puts it (2008), the architect "[goes] beyond [...] the more or less utilitarian program" (p. 93). It is something of a mystery what exactly this "going beyond" the utilitarian means, and architectural theory often reflects on that mystery. One answer found in Le Corbusier (2000) is that although modernity is an "age of every conceivable ferocity: tumult, disorder, revolutionary inventions" (p. 304), the goal of modern architecture is to build "[homes]" that can "take [us] in" and "welcome [us]", despite the challenge posed by modernity (2008, p. 296).

This strand of Le Corbusier's thinking, that architecture should fulfil a basic, human need for a sense of home, has been emphasised by self-appointed heirs to the modernist legacy, such as Christian Norberg-Schulz (2000a). To highlight the theme of home, however, Norberg-Schulz and others had to clean up the theoretical toolbox of architecture, as it were. Modernist art forms had been defined by pointing out experiences and attributes unique to them, and modern architecture had defined itself as an art of "space" (Forty, 2000, p. 265), but there is something not quite homely about the concept of space. In fact, space has been used as one side of a conceptual dichotomy throughout all of the history of philosophy, "where 'space' connotes something undelimited and open-ended" (Casey, 1997, p. 77), and *place* its opposite. So to make the legitimate claim that Le Corbusier and his work focused on providing inhabitants with a sense of home, and by extension that "modern architecture [,] came into existence to help man feel at home in a new world" (Norberg-Schulz, 2000b, p. 6), Norberg-Schulz and others (including Juhani Pallasmaa and Aldo van Eyck [Forty, 2000, p. 271]) needed to switch from "space" to "place" as the core concept for understanding architecture. They did so from the late 1960s, calling on the philosophy of Martin Heidegger. I return to Heidegger's influential thoughts on architecture later.

Avatars in Places

Before turning to my own ethnography, this section offers further background information on the theoretical connections between sense of place and the phenomenology of having an avatar. Readers with no or little interest in the philosophy of place might want to skip ahead.

The space/place dichotomy just alluded to underlie a rich tradition in philosophy with high relevance for understanding virtual world experiences (see the list of further reading). Edward S. Casey (1997) has laid out the philosophical history of space and place as a multi-millennial conceptual oscillation between the two. Broadly speaking, Aristotle and Plato understood the connection between human and world in terms of place. Gradually, thinking about the world in terms of places gave way to a focus on space.

The peak of this complex transition is often said to be Newtonian *absolute space* or Cartesian *res extensa*. With Heidegger, the pendulum swings back towards place. After Heidegger came a number of "rediscoverers of place" (such as Foucault, Deleuze and Guatteri, and Tuan) who in Casey's account all had to react to Heidegger's work in some way, positively or negatively (p. 286).

Amongst all these eminent thinkers it is arguably Maurice Merleau-Ponty who is most relevant for understanding avatar-based engagement with virtual worlds (cf. the use of Merleau-Ponty in game studies, e.g., Klevjer, 2006; Nielsen, 2010). With Merleau-Ponty, the concept of place becomes contingent on a body, or rather, on a sense of bodily grounded agency. As Casey points out, Merleau-Ponty also gives place "a *virtual* dimension overlooked in previous accounts. A place I inhabit by my body [...] I come to a place as providing an indefinite horizon of my *possible* actions" (p. 230, emphases in the original).

For a user of "Second Life", this "virtual dimension" of "possible actions" means that even when a building is explored in *camera view* (i.e., with an avatar-disembodied, flying camera), the avatar still plays a role. Its presence is felt as a virtual avatar, meaning that the user's sense of proportion is informed by the out of sight avatar. The building is tall or low, big or small, as measured against the avatar. A slope is walk-constraining or walk-affording, depending on how the avatar is imagined to move up it.

An important nuance is, however, introduced with the concept of *inhabitation* (in the Casey quote above: "A place I inhabit"). Inhabitation highlights that relating to place through a sense of bodily founded agency goes beyond being able to perform a set of well-defined actions. Casey's summary of Merleau-Ponty's position can thus be read as a description of the avatar's role in virtual world experience (note the mention of "my virtual body"):

In noninstrumental settings as well, the body remains a constitutive force. A snowbound glade could not constitute a full-fledge place unless I could at least tacitly, by imputation, feel myself to be there bodily [...] Similarly, the lonely lighthouse is a place insofar as I can, by proxy, as it were, imagine someone's body (not necessarily my own) inhabiting it. In order to effect such imputations, I need to call on my virtual body, which is capable of inhabiting even the most remote and seemingly vacuous place. So long as something is a "possible habitat" for a possible body, it can count as a place. (Casey, 1997, p. 235, emphases in the original)

In a kind of projection, Merleau-Ponty calls upon his "virtual body" to "inhabit" the snowbound glade and the lonely lighthouse. In an essay on "The Place of Man", architect and architectural theorist Juhani Pallasmaa (2005b) expresses a sentiment close to Merleau-Ponty's: "In an environmental experience, there is an unconscious bodily identification with the object, a projection of the body pattern onto what is experienced, or a physical mimesis, an unconscious mimicry" (p. 75). Such projections are important not only in the experience of place in general but more specifically in the architectural profession, when architects work with models, drawings, and other representations of unrealised projects. With the avatar, projections gain a graphical focus and a more immediate bodily foundation. The avatar stands in for the otherwise purely imagined virtual body. The avatar is a device that aids in the inhabitation of virtual place by proxy. As it happens, *proxy* is a contraction of late Middle English *procuracy* which in turn stems from Latin *procurare* "take care of, manage", from *pro-* "on behalf of" and *curare*, "see to" (the OED). Proxy thus neatly sums up how the avatar acts on the user's behalf (pro-), yet is taken care of by the user (curare).

VIRTUAL DWELLING IN "SECOND LIFE"

Starting Point

Most would-be ethnographers of virtual worlds probably have experience with their virtual fieldsite before even considering doing ethnography. There have probably been unstructured excursions into the fieldsite giving rise to loosely formed research questions. Holding on to and reflecting on one's personal starting point for an ethnography might seem slightly narcissist but is also a way of grounding the ethnography.

My own, initial reaction to "Second Life" (in 2004) was one of recognition. This felt like my days (and nights) in "The Palace" almost ten years earlier (in 1996), back in the day when the line "we just got on the Internet!" commanded respect and envy. The sense of potential, if not promise, the odd encounters, the overwhelming generosity of strangers, the amazement at how human feelings were, so it felt, able to travel through a digital communications medium: It was all there, complete with the technological glitches which only served to underline the fact that we were all on a great, futuristic adventure. Informed by the philosophy of space and place I was reading at the time, initial reactions soon gave way to a sneaking suspicion that "Second Life" was not about limitless (cyber-) space but about places. Boundaries made themselves felt. I would glimpse an interesting, faraway building and fly towards it, only to hit a semi-invisible "glass wall" with a loud smack, left to peek into the forbidden land from a distance. If they did not secure their houses in this way, some users gained a degree of access control by building or renting houses floating high above ground level. What was going on?

To get a closer, micro-level look, I decided to do an ethnography centred on a group of "Second Life" builders. A *builder* is a commonly used term for a user with a certain expertise in wielding the design tools of "Second Life". Because of that expertise, the builder gains recognition amongst peers and is probably able to make money on his or her skills. The self-assigned "builder" label was used explicitly, and not without pride, by most of the users I followed.

Modelled on Christine Hine's examples in her book "Virtual Ethnography" (2000), and combining my initial curiosity about the use of boundaries with the conceptual dichotomy of place and space, I arrived on the following, very open questions to guide my attention:

Do "Second Life" users conceptualise their virtual world primarily in terms of space or place? Do they embrace a condition of placelessness? Or do they, on the contrary, develop attachments to virtual places? When it comes to "Second Life", is boundary no longer an organising principle? And how does one go about gathering material illuminating such questions?

Boundary

This section contains the main account of a collective building project I followed for 14 months (June 2007 to August 2008). During that time I regularly visited the group of builders, took scores of screenshots and logged all text chat. As soon as possible after the visits, I mixed screenshots and bits of text chat with my own reflections in field notes. Below follows a brief, chronological account of my time spent in the various places the group built. As that account draws to an end, Heidegger's philosophy of dwelling is reintroduced. This shift towards reflection illustrates anthropologist Tim Ingold's point (1994) that in ethnography, "a clear distinction between observation and interpretation, between the collection of data in the field and their placement within a theoretical framework, can not readily be sustained" (p. xvi). Ingold goes as far as to call ethnography "philosophy with people in it" (p. vii), a sentiment I share.

I met the leader of the group of builders, whom I will call Vlad, in early June, 2007. At that time I was quite literally trying to get through the glass walls of private places to get a better sense of what was going on inside them. Incidentally, my curious attitude has never offended anybody or raised any questions as to my identity. As it happens, there is a socially acceptable subject position standing ready for people indulging in flânerie. Sometimes users explicitly label such persons "explorers". I have had the explorer label attached to me on a number of occasions, for example when taking screenshots of private homes. To me, this makes it possible and acceptable for the researcher to stay in explorer character, so to speak, until initial contact and trust have been established with informants. None of the builders I approached took any offence when I came clean as a researcher, possibly several months after first contact. On the contrary, it might have seemed out of place to break the special "Second Life" atmosphere of playful fictiveness by prematurely providing "first life" information.

I chatted with Vlad in a "Second Life" gallery, and he told me he was "searchin [sic] for a home" for his "family" (June, 2007). The term "family" was recently agreed upon by him and a handful of other builders tied together by sexual orientation and an urge to establish a virtual "home". During the following months, several members of the group made frequent use of the terms "home" and "family" as their building project took shape as an intricate castle. The enterprise took continuous investments of time, money, and creativity. All of these investments were undertaken collectively. Costs were shared and the time-consuming creative work done by all family members (according to talent). In the early phase of the project, one of the builders earned the humorous honorific *lagooneer* as he was the one in charge of shaping a coastal area; an indication of how important building was to his "Second Life". In October, 2007, a neighbour was allowed to add a small structure in the same style as the main building, or as Vlad put it: "He linked it there because we both find it fitting", as if the places themselves had an inherent fit which both of the users happened to sense.

In late October, 2007, a rather well attended house warming party was held. According to the invitation's wording, oddly enough, the party's occasion was the "long time and hard but successfull [sic] work to build [the] Castle", rather than the castle itself. Conscious or not at the time, the wording proved appropriate in the following months as the family kept building and changing the castle. In April, 2008, the entire structure had to be taken down due to financial reasons out of the family's control, but the building continued at an even grander scale on newly bought and much larger grounds. A new ambition had crept in: to build something "fitting with the landscape" (Vlad's words), a landscape which was much more elaborate than the landscape surrounding the old place. The new landscape included mountains and forests. Having mastered the art of individual buildings, the builders now focused on the connection between house and landscape, something only tried out on a modest scale before.

In July 2008, Vlad told me something that I believe to be an apt summary of his building experience during the preceding 13 months: "a castle is never finished but it looks complete". The building might be "done" as *thing*, something standing in the landscape providing material for a nice screenshot. The building understood as *activity* is never over. Vlad thereby unknowingly hinted at the core of Martin Heidegger's philosophy of building.

Now, shifting towards reflection, Heidegger's thinking on architectural matters were done at a time when Germany was in the middle of rebuilding herself after being reduced to rubbles in the Second World War. Millions were rehoused in a fast and efficient way, using then modern building technologies. This provoked Heidegger to consider the difference between being housed and to truly dwell. It ultimately made him question

the basic assumption that building is an activity aimed at providing dwelling, i.e., an activity creating something entirely new. Building should, according to Heidegger (1971), be understood as a "construction" that is also a "cultivation"; cultivation of something that grows on its own, but needs someone to "to cherish and protect [it], to preserve and care for [it]" (p. 145). Cultivation-building is, however, only half of dwelling and must be complemented by construction-building:

Building in the sense of preserving and nurturing is not making anything. Shipbuilding and temple-building, on the other hand, do in a certain way make their own works. Here building, in contrast with cultivating, is a constructing. Both modes of building - building as cultivating, Latin colere, cultura, and building as the raising up of edifices, aedificare - are comprised within genuine building, that is, dwelling. (Heidegger, 1971, p. 145, emphases in the original)

Not only did the builders I followed explicitly build to dwell, to be "at home", but in Hedeggerian eyes they seemed to on the right, although endless, track to get there; "A castle is never finished but it looks complete". Protecting boundaries were crucial in securing building's "cultivation" aspect. On the few occasions on which I have entered private homes without permission (and been found out), I have been scolded with "doors are closed for a reason" or similar statements. I really did feel bad on these occasions, exactly like I would, had I been caught trespassing in the real world. Fortunately, it feels correspondingly good and immediately generates a sense of togetherness to be invited into someone's private place. Ceremonies of reception and rejection, inclusion and exclusion, constantly happen on the boundaries of "Second Life" places, and are important in generating dwelling.

Image

Taking the discussion of virtual world dwelling a step further, the home of Vlad's family featured several archaic symbols of domesticity, such as huts, fireplaces, and canopied beds. The same symbols showed up in other private places I visited. The "Second Life" practice of employing such symbols resonates with discussions of contemporary possibilities of dwelling within 1990s architectural discourse, and emphasises the crucial function of the avatar.

Juhani Pallasmaa (2005a) was among those concerned with dwelling in the 1990s. The architectural *images* necessary for establishing a sense of home, argues Pallasmaa, have been diluted. Inspired by phenomenological philosopher Gaston Bachelard's "The Poetics of Space" (1994), Pallasmaa understands an architectural image to resonate on a deeply personal and bodily level. Such an "image" is not perceived on exclusively visual terms. One of Pallasmaa's examples is the image of the *bed.* Surely beds are functional, i.e., they solve the problem of finding a comfortable place to sleep, but a bed used to be (and ought to be, it seems) "a miniature house within the house with physical and symbolic privacy". The contemporary bed, on the other hand, is often "a mere neutral horizontal plane, a stage of privacy" (p. 122).[1]

Pallasmaa takes the "flattened" bed to be part of the poor dwelling conditions of modern homes. The hearth, or stove, is also used as an example of a flattened home-image. Flattened from fireplace into a mere "[mantle] without the possibility of actual fire [...] The fireplace has turned from a device addressing the skin into a medium of visual pleasure" (p. 122). In order to provide true dwelling, homes have to combine images (authentic images, not the flat ones) with a basic, spatial sense of insideness.[2]

This is where the mass media come into Pallasmaa's criticism of the modern home. The television screen is assigned symptomatic status in the analysis. Pallasmaa acknowledges how the television has taken over the fireplace's role as focus for domestic sociality - and it can be added that the screens of gaming consoles and PCs function as such foci as well - but a screen and a fireplace allow for different kinds of domestic sociality. Pallasmaa generalises this to a distinction between "images [such as the fire-place, BL] that are deeply rooted in our common memory, that is, in the phenomenologically authentic ground of architecture" and "images [such as the "flat" screen images, BL] [that are] striking and fashionable perhaps [but do not] incorporate the personal identity, memories, and dreams of the inhabitants" (p. 124).

My starting point was that "Second Life" actually abounds with Pallasmaa's images of home. It is exceedingly and perhaps surprisingly easy to find groves, huts, fireplaces, and canopied beds in "Second Life". All of these small insides are flat, of course, as far as the screen goes, but less flat when the embodied and avatarial nature of user interaction is taken into account. A canopied bed, for example, is not just experienced on a screen but through and with an avatar, thus retaining some of its quality as "a miniature house within the house with physical and symbolic privacy". In a virtual world, a bed is inhabited by proxy when the avatar is there on the user's behalf, as the user's substitute and not merely as his or her representative. It is not entirely accurate, then, to make general statements such as "[i]n the virtual world the existence of a 'building' is purely symbolic" (Harry, Offenhuber, & Donath, 2008, p. 65). The purity of the symbolic is contaminated, as it were, by the user's sense of agency. This situation does allow for some sense of dwelling centred on architectural images, even though it is an interactive simulation of dwelling, not the authentic, offline thing.

The Pop Vernacular

The collective efforts of Vlad and his family were playful but there was also a sincerity to their projects that deserves a few words before the conclusion, as it sums up some of the themes covered so far. The family members showed a high level of commitment to common tasks and goals, and the mention of "home" never seemed ironic.

Paul Oliver (2003) has studied dwellings in all corners of the real world and notes a "widespread desire to create and build one's own dwelling" (p. 260). When this desire is realised, the self-made, architect-free, and often community-built dwelling is labelled a vernacular dwelling. Oliver is in accord with Heidegger's cultivation/construction dichotomy when he describes dwelling as "both process and artifact: it is the experience of living at a specific location and it is the physical expression of doing so" (p. 15).[3] Vernacular dwelling is in a sense what happens if Heidegger is read literately and dwelling and building understood synonymously. The most obvious and efficient way to obtain a feeling of being at home, then, would be for the dweller to dethrone the architect and build his or her own home, or at least have a substantial say in its building.

"Second Life" dwelling is often vernacular dwelling (existing alongside a big market for prefabs). When virtual dwelling is vernacular it could be labelled a "pop vernacular", a term I believe coined by Sam Jacob (2004). The term is intended to credit Pop Art for pioneering the utilisation of bits and pieces of popular culture and established art alike as a resource for creative work.[4] Vlad and family employed a similar strategy in their castle projects, mixing and matching elements belonging to diverse and sometimes contrasting styles and historical epochs. Pallasmaa's cosmic images of home (e.g., the fire-place) were thrown into the mix. This was not done at random by the users but with the explicit goal of attaining a sense of dwelling. Users do seem to have a sense of the power of architectural images of home. They in-clude deeply resonating images of home in their kitsch building, and they do so sincerely, i.e., without the irony characteristic of other modes of eclecticism, e.g., postmodernism.

FUTURE RESEARCH DIRECTIONS

As for the possibilities of obtaining as sense of dwelling by influencing the design of one's private home, preferably in co-operation with co-dwellers, virtual worlds are currently explored as a means of furthering that very possibility. Parts of the research project I have contributed to until recently, "Sense-making Strategies and Innovation in Virtual worlds" (funded by the Danish Strategic Research Council), is empirically based in architects' experiments with using virtual worlds to allow inhabitants (current or coming) into the architectural design process. At the time of writing, however, the innovative architects I have interviewed for the project are not so much fascinated by the virtual world's potential for letting clients wield design tools, as they are fascinated by two other aspects of virtual worlds. Firstly, the avatar, which can give the client a better sense of a proposed project through a bodily grounded sense of free movement through a 3D model. Secondly, the virtual world as a framework for social interaction letting those interested in investing in a building project, as well as those interested in architecture and design in a less committed way, exchange ideas and experiences. But the potential for letting the user into the design process is there, and that potential can be understood and nurtured by research based in a mix of ethnography of existing user practices, philosophy of space and place, architectural theory, and scholarship focusing on the crucial device of the avatar (scholarship which is mainly undertaken within computer game studies).

CONCLUSION

Some "Second Life" users invest considerable amounts of money, time, and creativity in buildings; "buildings" in the double sense of things and activities. They do so with the explicit goal of feeling at home. Because of their never-ending character, such projects resonate with Heidegger's thoughts on true dwelling being the result of both construction and cultivation. In virtual worlds, cultivation, or caring, is done through, with, and towards avatars. There is, in other words, a non-instrumental aspect to having an avatar which provides a sense of place. The avatar's original function is to be a graphical focus for navigation through space, but it also provides a sense of being in place, e.g., when small insides are encountered (canopied beds, small huts, the intimate circle around a fire-place, etc.).

The concepts of boundary, image, and the vernacular (as used in architectural discourse) illuminate virtual world user practices aimed at dwelling. Users rely very much on boundaries for generating a sense of dwelling; i.e., what Heidegger would call dwelling's cultivation aspect. They also rely on architectural devices constituted simultaneously by space and image, such as the fire-place and the sleeping-place. Their use of such devices is part of a pop vernacular building strategy, characterised by eclecticism but not by irony.

When young expert users of "Second Life" seek out new ways to obtain a sense of dwelling, it reminds us that virtual worlds call not only for fascination with what is new about them, but also for fascination with the old in the sense of the pre-digital. Virtual worlds offer renderings of very basic, human experiences in ways that are intriguingly new but based in something intriguingly old, namely, our relationship with places. Sense of place is a subject inviting lyricism and speculation. If approached stringently, however, and ethnography is a way of securing a certain amount of stringency, the subject of place adds to our understanding of virtual worlds and the ways we engage with them.

REFERENCES

Alexander, C., Ishikawa, S., & Silverstein, M. (1977). *A pattern language: Towns, buildings, construction*. Oxford, UK: Oxford UP.

Bachelard, G. (1994). *The poetics of space*. Boston, MA: Beacon Press.

Boellstorff, T. (2008). *Coming of age in Second Life: An anthropologist explores the virtually human*. Princeton, NJ: Princeton UP.

Bruce, V., & Green, P. (1990). *Visual perception: Physiology, psychology and ecology*. Hove, UK: Lawrence Erlbaum Associates.

Casey, E. S. (1997). *The fate of place: A philosophical history*. Berkeley, CA: University of California Press.

Forty, A. (2000). *Words and buildings: A vocabulary of modern architecture*. London, UK: Thames & Hudson.

Guimarães, M. J. L. Jr. (2005). Doing anthropology in cyberspace: Fieldwork boundaries and social environments. In Hine, C. (Ed.), *Virtual methods: Issues in social research on the Internet* (pp. 141–156). Oxford, UK: Berg.

Harry, D., Offenhuber, D., & Donath, J. (2008). Function follows form: The social role of virtual architecture. In Doesinger, S. (Ed.), *Space between people: How the virtual changes physical architecture* (pp. 64–70). Munich, Germany: Presetl.

Hayot, E., & Wesp, E. (2009). Towards a critical aesthetic of virtual-world geographies. *Game Studies, 9*(1).

Heidegger, M. (1971). Building dwelling thinking. In *Poetry, Language, Thought* (pp. 141-160). New York, NY: Harper Colophon.

Hine, C. (2000). *Virtual ethnography*. Los Angeles, CA: Sage.

Ingold, T. (1994). General introduction. In Ingold, T. (Ed.), *Companion encyclopedia of anthropology* (pp. xiii–xxii). London, UK: Routledge.

Jacob, S. (2004). *The pop vernacular*. Retrieved 6 October, 2010, from http://www.strangeharvest.com/mt/archive/read_mes/the_pop_vernacular.php

Klastrup, L. (2003). *Towards a poetics of virtual worlds: Multi-user textuality and the emergence of story*. Unpublished PhD thesis, IT University of Copenhagen, Denmark.

Klevjer, R. (2006). *What is the avatar? Fiction and embodiment in avatar-based single player computer games*. Unpublished PhD thesis, University of Bergen, Norway.

Krauss, R. (1972). Léger, Le Corbusier, and purism. *Artforum, 10*(8), 50–53.

Le Corbusier. (2000). *Modulor 2: Let the user speak*. Basel, Switzerland: Birkhäuser.

Le Corbusier. (2008). *Toward an architecture*. London, UK: Frances Lincoln Limited.

Ljungström, M. (2005). *The use of architectural patterns in MMORPGs*. Paper presented at the Aesthetics of Play Conference, Bergen.

Markham, A. N. (1998). *Life online: Researching real experience in virtual space*. Walnut Creek, CA: AltaMira.

Nielsen, H. S. (2010). The computer game as a somatic experience. *Eludamos, 4*(1), 25–40.

Nitsche, M. (2008). *Video game spaces: Image, play, and structure in 3D worlds*. Cambridge, MA: The MIT Press.

Norberg-Schulz, C. (2000a). *Architecture: Presence, language and place*. Milano, Italia: Skira.

Norberg-Schulz, C. (2000b). *Principles of modern architecture*. London, UK: Andreas Papadakis Publisher.

Oliver, P. (2003). *Dwellings: The vernacular house worldwide*. London, UK: Phaidon.

Ondrejka, C. (2007). Collapsing heography: Second Life, innovation, and the future of national power. *Innovations, 2*(3), 27–54. doi:10.1162/itgg.2007.2.3.27

Pallasmaa, J. (2005a). Identity, intimacy, and domicile: Notes on the phenomenology of home. In MacKeith, P. (Ed.), *Encounters: Architectural essays* (pp. 112–126). Helsinki, Finland: Rakennustieto Oy.

Pallasmaa, J. (2005b). The place of man: Time, memory, and place in architectural experience. In MacKeith, P. (Ed.), *Encounters: Architectural essays* (pp. 72–85). Helsinki, Finland: Rakennustieto Oy.

Pike, K. (1967). *Language in relation to a unified theory of the structure of human behavior*. The Hague, The Netherlands: Mouton.

Rheingold, H. (1993). *The virtual community: Homesteading on the electronic frontier*. Reading, MA: Addison-Wesley.

Rice, C. (2007). *The emergence of the interior: Architecture, modernity, domesticity*. London, UK: Routledge.

Sloterdijk, P. (2008). Excerpts from Spheres III: Foams. *Harvard Design Magazine, 29*, 38 52.

Taylor, T. L. (2006). *Play between worlds: Exploring online game culture*. Cambridge, MA: The MIT Press.

Venturi, R. (2002). *Complexity and contradiction in architecture*. New York, NY: The Museum of Modern Art.

Yee, N. (2007). *The Proteus Effect: Behavioral modification via transformations of digital self-representation*. Unpublished PhD thesis, Stanford University, USA.

ADDITIONAL READING

Architecture, Computer Games, Space

Aarseth, E. (2000). Allegories of Space. The Question of Spatiality in Computer Games. In Eskelinen, M., & Koskimaa, R. (Eds.), *Cybertext Yearbook 2000* (pp. 152–171). Finland: University of Jyväskylä.

Anders, P. (2001). Anthropic Cyberspace: Defining Electronic Space from First Principles. *Leonardo*, *34*(5), 409–416. doi:10.1162/002409401753521520

Babeux, S. (2005). *King of the Hill: Investigation and Re-appropriation of Space in the Video Game*. Paper presented at the Aesthetics of Play conference, Bergen, Norway.

Bartle, R. A. (2004). *Designing Virtual Worlds*. Berkeley, CA: New Riders.

Bartle, R. A. (2007). Making Places. In Borries, F. v., Walz, S. P., & Böttger, M. (Eds.), *Space Time Play: Computer Games, Architecture and Urbanism - The Next Level* (pp. 158–163). Basel: Birkhäuser.

Friedman, T. (1999). Civilization and Its Discontents: Simulation, Subjectivity, and Space. In Smith, G. (Ed.), *Discovering Discs: Transforming Space and Genre on CD-ROM*. New York: New York UP.

Gingold, C. (2003). Miniature Gardens and Magic Crayons: Games, Spaces, and Worlds. Unpublished MA thesis, Georgia Tech, Atlanta, USA.

Günzel, S. (2008). *The Space-Image: Interactivity and Spatiality of Computer Games*. Paper presented at the Philosophy of Computer Games, Potsdam, Germany.

Harry, D., Offenhuber, D., & Donath, J. (2008). Function Follows Form: The Social Role of Virtual Architecture. In Doesinger, S. (Ed.), *Space Between People: How the Virtual Changes Physical Architecture* (pp. 64–70). Munich: Presetl.

Jenkins, H. (2007). Narrative Spaces. In Borries, F. v., Walz, S. P., & Böttger, M. (Eds.), *Space Time Play: Computer Games, Architecture and Urbanism - The Next Level* (pp. 158–163). Basel: Birkhäuser.

Liboriussen, B. (2009). The Mechanics of Place: Landscape and Architecture in Virtual Worlds. Unpublished PhD thesis, University of Southern Denmark.

Stockburger, A. (2006). The Rendered Arena: Modalities of Space in Video and Computer Games. Unpublished PhD thesis, University of the Arts, London.

Wolf, M. J. P. (2001). Space in the Video Game. In Wolf, M. J. P. (Ed.), *The Medium of the Video Game* (pp. 51–75). Austin: University of Texas Press.

Avatar, Body, Digital Media, Architecture

Adams, E. (2002). *The Role of Architecture in Video Games*. Gamasutra.

Gregersen, A., & Grodal, T. (2008). Embodiment and Interface. In Wolf, M. J. P., & Perron, B. (Eds.), *The Video Game Theory Reader 2* (pp. 65–84). New York: Routledge.

Grodal, T. (2003). Stories for Eyes, Ears, and Muscles: Video Games, Media, and Embodied Experiences. In Wolf, M. J. P., & Perron, B. (Eds.), *The Video Game Theory Reader* (pp. 129–155). New York: Routledge.

Hansen, M. B. N. (2006). *Bodies in Code: Interfaces With Digital Media*. New York: Routledge.

Kalay, Y. E. (2004). *Architecture's New Media: Principles, Theories, and Methods of Computer-Aided Design*. Cambridge, MA: The MIT Press.

Kerckhove, D. d., & Tursi, A. (2009). The Life of Space. *Architectural Design, 79*(1), 48–53. doi:10.1002/ad.810

King, G., & Krzywinska, T. (2006). *Tomb Raiders and Space Invaders: Videogame Forms and Contexts*. London: I.B. Tauris.

Kolarevic, B. (2003). Digital Morphogenesis. In Kolarevic, B. (Ed.), *Architecture in the Digital Age: Design and Manufacturing* (pp. 12–28). New York: Taylor & Francis.

Leach, N. (2004). Virtual Dreamworlds. In O. C. Christine Calederón, Peter Dorsey (Ed.), *Beyond Form: Architecture in the Space of Media*. New York: Lusitania.

Wilhelmsson, U. (2006). What is a Game Ego (or How the Embodied Mind Plays a Role in Computer Game Environments). In Pivec, M. (Ed.), *Affective and Emotional Aspects of Human-Computer Interaction* (pp. 45–58). Amsterdam: IOS Press.

Philosophy of Space and Place

Augé, M. (1995). *Non-Places: Introduction to an Anthropology of Supermodernity*. London: Verso.

Casey, E. S. (1993). *Getting Back into Place: Towards a Renewed Understanding of the Place-World*. Bloomington: Indiana UP.

Casey, E. S. (1997). Smooth Spaces and Rough-Edged Places: The Hidden History of Place. *The Review of Metaphysics, 51*(2), 267–296.

Cresswell, T. (2004). *Place: A Short Introduction*. Malden: Blacwell.

de Certeau, M. (1984). *The Practice of Everyday Life. Berkely*. University of California Press.

Debord, G. (1995). *The Society of the Spectacle*. New York: Zone Books.

Grosz, E. (2001). *Architecture from the Outside: Essays on Virtual and Real Space*. Cambridge, MA: The MIT Press.

Lefebvre, H. (1991). *The Production of Space*. Oxford: Blacwell.

Relph, E. (1976). *Place and Placelessness*. London: Pion.

Tuan, Y.-F. (1974). *Topophilia: A Study of Environmental Perception, Attitudes, and Values*. New York: Comlumbia University Press.

Tuan, Y.-F. (1977). *Space and Place: The Perspective of Experience*. Minneapolis: University of Minnesota Press.

Virtual Ethnography

Escobar, A., Hess, D., Licha, I., Sibley, W., Strathern, M., & Sutz, J. (1994). Welcome to Cyberia: Notes on the Anthropology of Cyberculture [and Comments and Reply]. *Current Anthropology, 35*(3), 211–231. doi:10.1086/204266

Hine, C. (2005). Virtual Methods and the Sociology of Cyber-Social-Scientific Knowledge. In Hine, C. (Ed.), *Virtual Methods: Issues in Social Research on the Internet*. Oxford: Berg.

Williams, M. (2007). Avatar Watching: Participant Observation in Graphical Online Environments. *Qualitative Research, 7*(1), 5–24. doi:10.1177/1468794107071408

KEY TERMS AND DEFINITIONS

Architecture: Activity explicitly aimed at orienting a person in the world, and the results of such activity.

Boundary: Architectural device aimed at dwelling. Boundaries are often used for negotiating access to places.

Building: See dwelling.

Dwelling, or Building: An activity (typically undertaken collectively) that is also a place (providing shelter for a number of activities including education, entertainment, and rest).

Ethnography: Reflections on (aspects of) a culture based on the act of entering a place and then staying inside that place for a considerable amount of time.

Image: Architectural device aimed at dwelling and constituted both spatially and through iconic, two-dimensional representation. Examples: fireplace, sleeping-place.

Place and Space: Basic manifestations of the human urge to orient oneself inwards (place) and outwards (space) towards the world.

Pop Vernacular: Strategy for vernacular building characterised by eclecticism (but not by irony).

Vernacular Building: Activity unreflectingly aimed at orienting a person in the world, and the results of such activity. Cf. architecture.

ENDNOTES

[1] Also philosopher Peter Sloterdijk (2008), who has recently come to some attention amongst architects, notices the existential importance of small insides and of beds in particular: "The natural transcendence of night is articulated most closely in the built environment offering designed rest environments. Here the skin-I expands into a bed-I - surrounded by a room-I in a house-I. The purest sleep is one in an acosmic onion" (p. 51).

[2] The ambition of striking a balance between image and space is articulated in various ways within architectural theory, both as a statement about architecture in general (e.g., Frampton, 1975; Krauss, 1972) and as a statement about dwelling in particular (Rice, 2007). Although disgusted with postmodernism's relying overly on images, even Christian Norberg-Schulz (2000b) holds that "[l]ife in space [...] remains a mere physical fact if it is not endowed with meaning through images" (p. 50).

[3] Oliver (2003) would probably prefer *not* to be associated with Heidegger. He seems rather disdainful of the "Teutonic concept of *heim*/home, exploited in the imagery and media of northern Europe and America" (p. 261, emphasis in the original).

[4] Already Venturi (2002) stated that architecture owes a lot to Pop Art.

Chapter 4
The Art and Flux of Telepathy 2.0 in Second Life

Jacquelene Drinkall
University of New South Wales, Australia

ABSTRACT

This chapter looks at contemporary art practice in Virtual Worlds, and the effervescence of new techno-logically mediated telepathies. Avatar Performance Art by Jeremy Owen Turner and Second Front have explored a variety of Second Life telepathies, and have quickly earnt the title of Virtual Fluxus. Second Front's links to Western Front, Fluxus, Robert Filliou and the Eternal Network assist the continued internationalised new media and performance collaboration work with telepathy. As the body becomes obsolete, it develops new techlepathy[1].

INTRODUCTION

"Artistic activity is founded on high telepathy – a high contact – and everything which comes into its field becomes a sign, and is part of art. It is therefore evident that the primary problem of today's art has become the renovation and intensification of perception." (Lebel, 1968: 721)

Within Second Life (SL) there are a variety of emerging and established artists, art scenes, art galleries, residencies, sculpture parks, curators, artist-run spaces and an art market. Mario-Paul Martinez Fabre y Tatiana Sentamans detail key manifestations of art in SL (2007). There is the hyperformalism of Dancoyote Antonelli a.k.a. DC Spenseley that borrows from the graphic arts, mod-ernist abstraction and pixel algorithms (Martinez Fabre y Sentarmans, 2007: 55). There is avatar performance art, hybrid projects that are halfway between the real and the virtual such as the work of Eva and Franco Mattes a.k.a. 0100101110101101. ORG and video and animation is called Machinima (ibid: 55-62). Code Performance involves writing a script that can then be performed and changed by avatar performance artists when making the work. Code-scripts can also alter the behaviour

DOI: 10.4018/978-1-60960-854-5.ch004

of avatars as collaborators and audience as well as the environment (ibid: 66).

Second Front (SF) are the pioneering avatar performance artists in SL, co-founded by Jeremy Owen Turner, Tanya Skuce, Doug Jarvis, Patrick Lichty and others on November 23, 2006.[2] Gazira and Lichty also work as code-performance artists and they have brought code-performance to some SF artworks. Italian art-star avatar performer and 'code-wiz' Gazira was recruited quite early on by Turner. The SF website artist statement lists their influences as Dada, Fluxus, Futurist Synthesis, Situationism as well as performance artists such as Laurie Anderson and Guillermo Gomez-Pena. "Second Front creates score-based performances and interventions that challenge notions of traditional performance, virtual embodiment and the culture of immateriality." (Second Front, 2010) SF members often refer to the grandmother of performance art, Marina Abramović and Fluxus in artist statements, writings and remediations of her artwork. (Kildall, 2010; Lichty: 2009; Lichty, 2009a; Turner, 2010). References to Abramović in Lichty's writing are too many to be listed individually here, but many of his writings are easily accessible from his website (Lichty, 2010). Fluxus performance artist Robert Filliou was acknowldeged in an SF hybrid real-world gallery and virtual happening for Art's Birthday, a Fluxus tradition that Filliou invented, which involves local and global telepathic exchanges and performances (Fritz, 2007).

Artists Abramović (Abramović, 1993; 1996; 1998) and Filliou (Ruhrbeg, 2000, p. 589; Fritz, A., 2007) are also known for working with telepathy, as is Marcel Duchamp (Dalrymple Henderson, 1998: 101-111, 103; Drinkall, 2010; Lipsey, 1988: 98-101, 99). Duchamp and contemporary artist, psychoanalyst and art historian Bracha Lichtenberg-Ettinger recognise the importance of "psychic transgression ... [and] its irruption in the form of telepathy mysterious and mystical," (Lichtenberg-Ettinger, 2005: 211) to deliver "intersubjective transference relationships to the artistic

sphere, and to have them intersect with aesthetic experience." (ibid) Duchamp and Ettinger show how the "artist and the viewer transform the artwork and are transformed by it in different-yet-connected ways" where there is "a kind of aesthetic osmosis between the artist and the viewer via the artwork." (ibid) Telepathy is a hidden psychic force behind identity transformation. Telepathy cannot be separated from the Freudian concept of transference and the uncanny reality of shared language, feelings and empathy between the *I* and the *non-I*. Further, telepathy assists the generation of doppelgangers, puppet-selves, modified egos and alternate selves as Green discusses through looking at the artwork of Gilbert & George and Abramović/Ulay. (Green, 2000; Green 2001; Green, 2004) Duchampian telepathy aesthetics and Green's model of telepathetic and collaborative performance can occur in collaboration between avatars, between the 'real' self and the alternate avatar self, and between the creator and the viewer/participant end-user. Whilst nanotechnology and cyberspatial developments create new techlepathies in science (Finkelstein, 1999: 13), a number of collaborative SL avatar performance artists are remediating works by collaborative performance artists such as Abramović/Ulay and Fluxus and this is developing virtual and synthetic telepathies in art.

Dominico Quaranta, a prominent SL art critic, reports that the kitsch capitalist dystopia of SL is teeming with artists keen to develop their alter egos, meet other artists and collaborate, more so in SL than any other virtual world. (Quaranta, 2007) It is utopic for artists in terms of creating 'enormous' sculptures and installations works in SL, and the "lack of corporeality is compensated by the increase in specularity and cheap financial costs." (Martinez Fabre y Sentarmans, 2007: 64) "While real world venues frown upon dowsing an audience with napalm or crashing planes into it, not so is SL, where anything goes, and SF was quick to take advantage." (Wodell, 2008) SL artists are showing their work in experimental and established gallery spaces as well as major art biennales such as Venice and Shanghai.[3] Importantly for visual artists and performance artists, the avatar body modification options and Machinima platform in SL are widely considered the best of all the virtual worlds. (Martinez Fabre y Sentarmans, 2007; and Neustaedter and Fedorovokya, 2008).

The SL destination guide lists many new age, spiritual and religious destinations indexed under *Spirituality and Belief, Strange and Mysterious, Spirituality and Belief* (Second Life, 2010). However this paper focuses on SL technologically mediated telepathies (Porush, 1998) and techlepathies through the channel of contemporary conceptual performance art and its emerging presence in SL. Life as an avatar in SL is can be described as an Alice in Wonderland experience, where the Queen remembers the future as well as the past.

JEREMY OWEN TURNER'S AVATAR TELEPATHY

Turner has many avatars, some of which are performance artists, and Wirxli Flimflam is arguably his most infamous. In an interview Turner casually refers to instant messaging (IM) as telepathy.

"I cannot speak for all of my peers but I can say that any form of collaboration and rehearsal almost instantly takes some form of (virtually) tangible manifestation. We can literally beta-test any idea before taking it to an audience. In terms of performance, it helps to have the Instant Messaging (IM) system while performing and/or rehearsing because this form of telepathy allows the group to conduct themselves without leaking their improvised methods to the audience. Group performance in this regard becomes much easier to do." (Turner in Paech, 2007)

Turner says he was drawn to SL because of its godlike dimension. "I am into metaphysics and transcendental ideas…so cyberspace is really the most compatible medium for me." (ibid) SL "and

similar avatar worlds allow literally for a kind of magick to happen. Artists can truly become the shamans and sorcerers they have always wanted to be." (ibid)

The word telepathy is used to brand Professor Kevin Warwick's 'cyborg' emotion communication chips inserted in the human body (Drinkall, 2006 and 2009; Fleming, 2007) The invention of the term telepathy accompanied the invention of the telephone in the late 1800s and continues to have currency and shadow new technologies. Like other SL users, performance art avatars use dialogue 'channels' very similar to facebook chat windows to plan and undertake performances, collaborations, and gaming theatre. Gaming and avatar theatre offers further 'mind share' improvements on top of the social networking augmentation of the Internet. 'Channeling' reveals further techlepathy, resonating with both telecomunications and occult practice. Artist tricksters in SL learn to operate with sleight of hand, Linden currency and 'speculative intuition' (Martinez Fabre y Sentarmans, 2007: 52).

Facebook already facilitates games such as Farmville and credit cards have point reward systems, so it is a small leap from web 2.0 social networks to the next 2.0 expansion of the gaming layer. The suggestion of telepathy and promises of magic can seem like eccentric esotericism or alternatively like exaggerated public relations (PR) spin on the other. Artist intellectuals such as Turner enable 'high telepathy' to become increasingly contagious and effervescent within SL culture. Turner acknowledges he is simultaneously obsessed with both PR and the spiritual quest. This may have something to do with his SL medium. SL's two main assets are the promise that anything is possible including telepathy and teleportation, and of course its credit card operated Linden economy of companies, advertising strategies, landowners, artisans, service providers, artists and the homeless.

Turner has played and experimented with a wide range of virtual world game sites. In addition to being an avatar performance artist, he is also a social addict, art historian, musician and conceptual artist. Turner's work with virtual worlds and telepathy precedes SL. Turner practices astral travel and has his own private avatar in the real world.[4] The names for his SL avatars are derived from the secret name of his most personal and secret avatar that exists outside of SL (so far) and only in his mind and imagination. Onto Distro was his avatar in the Digitalspace Traveler Avatar Community. This avatar resembles a black TV screen with a face, and it suggests telepathic communication with the viewer from within the Yahoo time capsule:

I understand that there are entities that are trans terrestial and trans dimensional in scope, and in scale. Cyberspace and other occult worlds illustrate proof of that, as far as I'm concerned. Some of you have already spoken with me via telepathy using my limited mode of consciousness as a transmission medium."..."I think it is time this shallow 3D earthly society begins to embrace Alfred Lambremont Webre's exo-political approach to ET and ED, that is extra dimension entities such as yourselves." (Distro, 2006)

Turner's arguably most infamous avatar Wirxli Flimflam (2006-2010) recently left SL via suicide with great theatrical spectacularity (Turner, 2010a). A memorial plaque has replaced Wirxli's Warhol-like PR office. The suicide was a live gallery and SL avatar performance event. It involved artistic collaboration with SaveMe Oh[5] and machinima documentation. For Turner, it has presented an opportunity to explore life after death in Second Life, abstractions on the astral plane and delve deeper into SL as an afterlife. Although SL is gaining recognition as both a creative and capitalist economy in its own right (Schnapp and Shanks, 148) the death of an avatar artist has not had the same art market effects as the death of an actual artist. How do avatars die in SL - isn't it just life after life after life? SL can already resemble the afterworld with skull-headed and winged avatars.

On stage for Wirxli's final performance was a cube shaped 'prim' (an SL term to describe a primary shape or virtual object) with the text "If you are dead and you know it kill yourself." "The rights of an avatar are not the same as the rights of the associated person. (When people erase avatars of themselves is that suicide, homicide, or infocide?)" (Bainbridge, 2008) Was it just another event in avatar auto-bio-thanatography? How can you die when you are already dead? Where lies agency and culpability with avatacide?

Wirxli was also a member of the Avatar Orchestra Metaverse. In Figure 1 he is at centre front contributing to a telepathic sound-art performance within SL with peers from Avatar Orchestra Metaverse.[6] In the real world jazz musicians and band members in general often describe the experience of improvising on top of a score, collaborative fusion and charismatic shared intimacy as telepathy. Those developing artificial intelligence are studying improvisation cognition and *theories of mind* (Baumer, A. and Magerko B. 2009) - something all children develop when they learn to read the emotions and minds of others. Another avatar member of Avatar Orchestra Metaverse called Humming Pera explicitly identifies her contribution to SL as exploring sound, music, performance, telepathy and collaboration.[7] In the Wirxli FlimFlam memorial blog dated Monday May 14, 2007, Wirxli conjures improvised sound performance as a Duchampian readymade that is transmitted telepathically between avatars:

"...for this found-sound intro warm-up piece, we are literally just standing around, hanging out and telepathically transmitting our found sounds from our inventory directly into the public platz..."[8]

Wirxli committed suicide to earn the love and respect of SaveMe Oh on Valentines Day, 2010 at The Diablous Artspace. Appropriate to character, the wicked avatar performance and video artist SaveMe Oh takes all credit for Wirxli's suicide

Figure 1. Avatar Orchestra Metaverse (Jeremy O. Turner, 2007. Used with permission)

and final performance. SaveMe is the archetypal "soul-sucking" psychotic femme-fatal and "psychic vampire."[9] Wirxli wanted so much to be like her, to be with her and even to be her that he 'fell into her machinima', stalked her and in the end died for her. Such a strong identification borders on the telepathic. Stalkers often claim to communicate telepathically with their prey. In some cases the victim of stalking can begin to stalk the stalker and be caught within the psychic game playing of deranged love transference, psychic terror and dangerous telepathy. In the wider metaverse of Facebook and Twitter world the concept of 'friending' and 'following' someone is now synonymous with stalking, due to ease and addiction of life sharing with friends, acquaintances and strangers. In SL one 'befriends' someone in order to open IM telepathy/channeling and facilitate teleportation. In SaveMe Oh's blog (2010), Wirxli says: "SaveMe mesmerizes me." He follows her about, hangs out, squats in her studio and her UFO-Oh. He looses himself for this other. "I wish I was her or at least with her." (Turner, 2010a) SaveMe and Wirxli collaborate to create an SL fiction that performs telepathetic cyber love, death wish stalking, infatuation, as

well as mind control and thought insertion of the cruel femme-fatal cyborg.[10]

Qyxxql Merlin is a spiritual seeker who exists in order to meet all the major religious and spiritual leaders in SL (Turner, 2010d). *Qyxxql Merlin's LiveJournal* reports contact with various spiritual leaders in numerous blog entries such as *Gandhi's Salt Satyagraph Walk in Second Life, the Angel-Channeler Nina and the Mystic Twins, Nichiren Buddhism, Krishna Consciousness in Second Life* and *Islam in Second Life*. Qyxxql also reports on "his" experiences with a pagan ritual ground, Jewish candle lighting ceremony and Buddhist counseling. S/he blogs with interrogative detail about numerous Mormon Transhumanists SL seminars. Qyxxql has been documented in Turner's blog as having visited Wirxli's funerary plaque.

Qyxxql participates in MahatmaGandhi Chakrabarti's pilgrimage for the last three miles and reports "I am pleased that I was able to capture the energy between us as walkers. We did not speak that much during our walkabout. I really think we had an intuitive rapport that was bordering on the telepathic." (ibid) (See Figure 2) Qyxxql's blog documents a "transcendental yet intimate session that was held in Nina Lancaster's Healing Pool Centre for angelic transmissions and spirit-guided meditation." (ibid) Nina's friends, The Mystic Twins, counsel him further about his higher self and Qyzzql vows "I will expand my realm to include the "real" analog world alongside the "virtual" realms in order to achieve a quantum spiritual unity." (ibid)

Qyxxql is not an artist, but Turner certainly identifies as an artist and has shown in many galleries and Qyxxql is interested in telepathic/telepathetic SL artists and identities. Ghandi's great walk was projected into Eyebeam gallery in New York, 2008. Ghandi's real physical self Joseph DeLappe spent time on a treadmill in order to walk his avatar across islands in SL, and by the end of the pilgrimage he had walked 240 miles. Outside of SL, the collaborative performance artists Abramoviç/Ulay experienced pain, endurance, alchemical transformation, profound connection with earth minerals and energy lines of the planet, and even telepathy during their walk of China's Great Wall in 1988.

Qiezli Hixantapo is one of Turner's most recent avatars - a shimmering and jewel-like abstract non-humanoid. The audience, comprised mostly of other avatar performance artists and SF members, are both viewers and participants who ascend "the heavenly exit portal into the white void". "Qiezli Hixantapo greets them and giggles as their spirit guide" and "the reborn visitors play with Qiezli in the secondafterlife (or aftersecondlife)" (Turner, 2010) Qiezli shimmers because its skin carries the memory of SF performances as they are abstracted into four largely monochromatic modernist shapes. Qiezli wears a video texture that carries "a kind of abstracted 'life review' for the visitors". (Turner 2010) The remediated machinima of SF performances from the Ars Virtua archive are mapped onto the form to create a flickering distortion of the representational footage while the accompanying sound track continues to play (Turner, 2010). Qiezli is the reincarnation of Wirxli and Qyxxql, and its name is a derivation of both. Qiezli consists of four intersecting or clustered

Figure 2. Ghandi and Qyxxql at the end of Ghandi's 240 mile walk (Jeremy O. Turner, 2008. Used with permission)

geometeric shapes in the work *Last Exit,* 2010.[11] From amongst the other avatar artists viewing and participating in the performance SaveMe Oh delivers some further wallops to the newly reincarnated and sublime abstract avatar. In a 2010 collaboration called *Homology*[12] with another avatar performance artist Selavy Oh, Qiezli and Selavy exchange clothes and become the other. When Qiezli and Selavy practiced their exchange in the white void, Turner noted: "It was quite the gnostic and mystical experience - even for the artists!"[13] Wirixli escaped the deadly transference spell of SaveMe Oh into another 'second life' as a new and different being that can continues to exchange and collaborate with other SL artists. Qiezli is half 'human' avatar and half 'bot', which is a scripted automaton agent that Jeremy plans to use as a process of ongoing transformation and self-othering: "I was also thinking of giving it public access to certain trustworthy individuals as an open source identity."[14] Qiezli resembles some

early modernist abstractions in paint and sculpture. Kitsch pop-aesthetic attains a high-modernist conceptual affinity with Theosophical 'thought forms' and the 'movement of the triangle' central to Wassily Kandinsky's philosophy *Concerning the Spiritual in Art.* Turner recently left SF in order to undertake research into the anthropomorphism of non-humanoid avatars in SL in his Masters thesis titled *Neo-Modernist Visual Design of Avatars in Second Life* (See Figure 3, Figure 4).

SECOND FRONT

SF members are currently Gazira Babeli a.k.a. Gaz (Milan)[15], Fau Ferdinand a.k.a. Yael Gilks (London), Great Escape a.k.a. Scott Kildall (San Francisco), Bibbe Oh a.k.a. Bibbe Hansen (New York), Lizsolo Mathilde a.k.a. Liz Solo (St. Johns), Man Michinaga a.k.a. Patrick Lichty (Chicago), and Tran Spire a.k.a. Doug Jarvis (Victoria). Gazira

Figure 3. Qiezli resides in, and Qyqxxl peeks into, an arty secondafterlife (Jeremy O. Turner, 2010. Used with permission)

Figure 4. Selavy Oh and Qiezli's mystical exchange to become each other (Selavy Oh and Jeremy O. Turner, 2010. Used with permission)

is arguably the most famous in part due to the mysterious aura gained by not revealing her real life person. Doug Jarvis also co-curates an annual World Telekinesis Competition with Ted Heibert. This annual event involves real world game, play and competition as well as parapsychology, the occult and telekinetic aesthetics. This event receives submissions via internet from all over the world. Many members of SF exhibit their own art practice in galleries, for example Kildall exhibits SL digital prints as well as sculptural objects, video and installation. Kildall has explored technologically mediated telepathy in his work *After Though* 2010, which like Mariko Mori's *UFO Wave* translates EEG brainwave analysis of participants into an "emotional reflector" (Kildall, 2010).

Perhaps SF's most literal example of telepathy, collaboration and performance art is *Tower of Babelfish*, 2007:

Real world gallery visitors enjoyed a projected live online performance where Second Front enacted textual performances that communicated with spirits of four dead performers: Tristan Tzara, Ana Mendieta, Charlotte Moorman and Rudolf Schwarzkogler. The ghosts used AtlaVista's Babelfish engine as a means of trans-dimensional communication. (Second Front, 2010)

In *The Absolutely Last (and final) Supper*[16] performed by SF (See Figure 5) we see the artists

taking the position of Christ and his disciples, and with sly reference to Dan Brown they state it is Da Vinci code for the 21st century (Second Front, 2010). Communion engages a tele-presence with God by tasting his symbolically transubstantiated wine-blood. SF deliberately confronts the over-abundance of reproductions of masterpieces in SL, while at the same time create the work purely for live gallery exhibition. The seated avatars appear dressed for a rave and then briefly eat, drink and quietly commune collectively. However they soon start projecting red wine vomit-blood and jump up on the table to make full display of their pixilated tele-pathology for the distanced televisual audience. Telepathology is the diagnosis of blood and disease at a distance, mediated by computers and virtual reality technologies. SF offers the carnivalesque display of their 'semi-god' (Quaranta, 2008) symptom and the pathos of a bloodless kitsch performance. As a group engaged in both conceptual instruction and improvisation strategies, and performance for video/machinima, they engage what Krauss has identified as the telepathy of narcissistic performance for video aesthetics (Krauss, 1976). The appearance of partying and dying to be all at once more human, more cyborg and more god-like is both hilarious and haunting. The tableau vivant performance drifts away from the formality of its Christian references to resemble something like electro punk voodoo. A parallel can be drawn with their animal-cyborg behaviour and highly stylized animalistic and human figurative statuettes of traditional African Boh sculptures where sacrificial items such as blood and alcohol are combined with earth to coat the sculptures. This Boh ritual draws in positive spirits and wards off evil spirits. SF's remediation of Da Vinci shows that new or different technologies are accompanied by new or different mediations of spiritual communion.

Zombie Attack! 28 Avatars Later[17] uses the cult of zombie movies to critique SL, where all the bodies are far too perfect yet cyborg and zombie-like. Zombie culture is a horror genre parody of the contagion of crowd mentality that occurs in a street protest or large gathering where everyone starts behaving in the same way at the same time resulting in conformity at times, and a revolutionary eruption at others. Social theorists Gustave le Bon and more recently Mikkel Borch Jacobsen recognise that real world crowds are vulnerable to a telepathic contagion. Borch-Jacobsen describes the mysterious force within crowds as "indissolubly nonsubjectal and 'social,' [with nothing designated except] immediate communication with others…prior to any conscious-ness of self, and thus also prior to any consciousness of other. Taken to the extreme, it is thought transmission, telepathy." (Redfield, 1992) A sharing of identification, identity and telepathic contagion can also occur within the collaborative process. As telepathy theorist David Porush has shown, the viral nature of bodies, language and computers extends the telepathy metaphor (Porush, 1998).

With the help of Wirixli FlimFlam, Kildall produced a series of remediations of several iconic performance art pieces in SL in a series called *Paradise Ahead*, 2006-2007 (Kildall, 2010). The title of the work came from Kildall's concern with the demise of spiritual space in the modern age and his experience that he found "many in Second Life looking for transcendental experience." (Kildall in Quaranta, 2007) The concept for these works was entirely Kildall's and not a work of SF. Wirixli was only recruited as a helper, and only for part of the series. Wirixli's repeated presence could almost be suggestive of something more than just assisting, especially when work by collaborative artists Abramoviç/Ulay is repeated. However, other original artworks Kildall has remediated in

Figure 5. The Absolutely Last (and Final) Supper (Second Front, 2007. Used with permission)

this series such as those by Yoko Ono and Chris Burden required the relational assistance of other artists, helpers or viewing participants, without necessitating a more sustained partnership or formal artistic collaboration. Kildall's work deals more with the problematic issue of reproduction and remediation in performance art (Sant, 158) and his collaboration with Wirixli/Turner is confined within the group work of SF. Remediating performance into the virtual opens up "collective notions of emotional content in surreal space." (Kildall in Quaranta, 2007) It is in the work of the Mattes that collaboration of Gilbert & George and Abramoviç/Ulay is more closely mirrored by the artists' own intimate collaboration as artists who are partners. There is a difference between the telepathy of collaboration and the telepathy of a minor agent who helps, assists or participates. The telepathy of helpers requires less direct affective contagion to penetrate into and be recognised within the authorial identity, potentially creating more of a haunting shadow doppleganger. History reveals great telepathic assistants within Sandor Ferenczi, who assisted Sigmund Freud on his theory of telepathic transference, and Thomas Watson who attended séances and assisted Alexander Bell's invention of the telephone. Wirixli happily, generously and clownishly haunts Kildall's work.

The Wirixli FlimFlam memorial built by some of his other SF colleagues again clownishly haunts SL as he rides a SaveMe Oh horse backwards (see Figure 6, Figure 7).

WESTERN FRONT AND ETERNAL NETWORK

SF started as a SL extension of The Western Front artist run space.[18] Turner was born just after Western Front was established in 1973 with a focus on performance and new media. Turner credits friends of his parents, Michael Morris and Vincent Trasov, who co-founded[19] Western Front for getting him into art. Filliou's early and ongoing visits, performances, residencies and teachings are celebrated as the founding philosophy of Western Front. Filliou's work is very well represented in Western Front archives, including some of his Telepathic Music series. Filliou's *Telepathic Music Series* started with *Telepathic Music No. 2* made in 1973, and extended into the 70s. Filliou and George Brecht crystallised the Eternal Network, facilitating artists' work with telepathy via mail-art and performance. Together with George Brecht, Filliou founded the Eternal Network, which facilitated many of

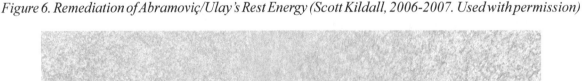

Figure 6. Remediation of Abramoviç/Ulay's Rest Energy (Scott Kildall, 2006-2007. Used with permission)

Figure 7. Wirixli helps Great Escape a.k.a. Scott Kildall in Paradise Ahead (Scott Kildall, 2006-2007. Used with permission)

his Telepathic Music works, mail art happenings and performances. Numerous other members of the Eternal Network spread throughout the world have also worked with telepathy (Drinkall, 2006). Filliou's invention of Arts Birthday continues as a global Eternal Network ritual and legacy that is most actively kept alive by Western Front and a sister new media arts community in Vienna. In terms of being an artist, Turner is a Western Front baby.[20] Eternal Network's mail-art network and artworks, happenings, performances and installation have evolved to include telematics, telepathy, email, and now SL and virtual worlds.

VIRTUAL FLUXUS

Quarenta declared SF to be 'virtual fluxus' very soon after it formed, and some may have thought this a bit premature and perhaps a burden for such an emerging artistic identity.[21] However, it is true that Turner and his SF friends and avatar performance friends share a deep connection to Fluxus, and that they remediate its spirit through original artworks as well as SL remediations of Fluxus artworks. Lichty sees Alan Kaprow's Happenings, Joseph Beuys social sculpture and

shamanism, and Nicholas Bourriard's Relational Aesthetics as the ideal influences for engagement with SL and virtual worlds. He points to Beuys as the artist with the best affinity to connect with the philosophy of Linden Lab. (Lichty, 2008)

A more recent addition to SF is the avatar Bibbe Oh a.k.a. Bibbe Hansen, daughter of important Fluxus artist Al Hansen (Second Front, 2010). Bibbe Hansen often performed in her father's theatrical avant guarde 'Happenings' as well as Andy Warhol films from the age of 13 when she starred opposite Edie Sedgwick in *Prison*. (Second Front, 2010) She continues to archive and exhibit her father's work. SF performed *Car Bibbe* in 2008 after a never performed Fluxus score that was created for her by her father (ibid). They also performed a new version of *Yoko Ono Piano Drop* created by Bibbe's father for Yoko Ono, and called it *Hansen-Ono Piano Drop* (ibid). The artwork *Virtual Fluxus* was performed October 27 2010 and involved collaboration with the important Fluxus artist Larry Miller. Miller is known for working with telepathy in his early Fluxus work, for example when he went under hypnosis to become and create artwork as his dead mother in the work Mom-me (Drinkall, 2007; Stiles, 2003: 75-88). In *Virtual Fluxus* Miller is dressed in tuxedo with a photo mask of his real and quite elder face of today. He introduces a series of short Fluxus artworks by himself, Bibbe and Man Machinaga a.k.a. Lichty. One of his own performances involves Bibbe and is called *See you in your dreams.* This artwork was written in 1977 with the instruction: appear in another's dreams (Virtual Fluxus, 2010). Lichty articulates some anxiety held by SF with this notion of being/becoming Virtual Fluxus, which is nevertheless outweighed with confident and critical ease. (Lichty in amyfreelunch, 2008). Lichty already had existing deep friendships with both Bibbe and Miller that preceded the founding of SF, and he is also familiar with some other Fluxus artists. Lichty describes the process of integrating Bibbe into the SF 'street gang' as very "organic" after Turner found out she was online (ibid).

ART, TELEPATHY AND REVOLUTION

In the otherworld of SL how do avatars identify with the Other and engage in issues of gender, conflict and representation? What is Other in this otherworld? How do avatars create changes in their own world, and perhaps the real world? One of the curators of Vancouver's Second Live Biennale of Performance Art 2007, called xox voyager, says, "Nothing can represent The Future better than a real-time, interactive 3-D space where fantastic people populate improbable architecture as they fly, teleport, and telepathically communicate their thoughts and dreams. Where do Native people fit into such a space?" (Fragnito, 2007) In James Cameron's blockbuster movie Avatar, the organic, cosmic 'gaia' telepathy of Na'vi comes up against the virtual world telepathy of humans - a form of military infiltration and surveillance. The human operated avatars use their military techlepathy in two ways – to love, learn from, collaborate and save the Na'vi or to stalk, manipulate and destroy the Na'vi. Lichty complains about alien fairies in SL as far too predictable vision of utopian

fantasmagoria as shallow othering of the young and beautiful avatars that dominate SL. Instead Lichty prefers the old and ugly ones as an affirmative attempt to represent alterity. Although there are plenty of homeless avatars, there is a virtual lack of representations of squallor, filth and dilapidation. Lichty does identify Virtual Darfur as a consciousness and social justice site. (Lichty, P. 2010)[22]

In terms of SL, it is artists who work between reality and virtuality with the greatest tension that are best placed to deal with issues of "gender, migration, micropolitics etc." (Martinez Fabre y Sentarmans, 2007: 69). Lichty creates animations for art activists The Yes Men, and there is a similar prankster and activist aspect within SF's work. SF have created activist interventions, for example *Breaking News*, 2008, was made in the abandoned SL buildings of Reuters. The 2007 work *Martyr Sauce* (See Figure 8) mobilized a peace demonstration within SL conflict zones. Some performance art avatars apparently lost their lives carrying peace placards whilst triggering animated psychedelic gerberas blooms and raining marijuana leaves. (ibid: 66). *Hazardous*, 2007, is a work made in response to the ill treatment of a fellow artist by the police. (Second Front, 2010)

It is claimed that a virtual happening occurred in SF's *Spawn of the Surreal* because of the involuntary audience 'participation' as the audience became part of the work. (ibid: 68) The avatar audience was given seats for the performance that were loaded with avatar-transforming code. At a specific time this code transformed their bodies into bizarre mutations. This work had a surreal and hallucinatory effect, causing some audience members to flee and log off, and others requesting a higher dose of the code. *28 Avatars Later* had a similar propagated disfiguring effect upon both performers and audience.

Fluxus artist and theorist Jean Jacque's Lebel's text 'On the Necessity of Violation,' was written in 1968 as an art treatise on telepathy, happenings and revolutionary aesthetics written just prior and

Figure 8. Martyr Sauce (Second Front, 2007. Used with permission)

after the May/June riots. Fluxus fused art, politics and telepathy, and the Eternal Network was also started in France in 1968. Filliou's *Permanent Creation Tool Shed*, 1969, promoted playful use of everyday tools - hammer, sickle, imagination and telepathy. A sign above Filliou's tool shed read something like: I am away on a trip at the moment, but leave your name with address and one day I will touch (contact) you via telepathy.[23] Lebel describes 'high-telepathy' of newly interdisciplinary art, radically connected to everyday life, politics and 'everything'. He questioned reliance on conventional theatres and galleries, and their status as sacred places. Happenings interpolate 'actual experience directly into mythic context', creating deep links between 'the actual and the hallucinatory', so we 'become one with our hallucinations.' (Lebel, 1996: 720) Lebel celebrated the *prophetic* role of art and 'mind-dancing hippies' (ibid: 722) to encourage people 'to be free of mental Stalinism' through 'guerilla theatre, street happenings and similar activities'. (ibid: 721) 'The Happening ... carries out transmissions' and 'imposes no restriction on affective ambivalence.'

(ibid: 720) Happenings involve extreme physicality and psychic activity. Lebel says:

Everything depends on the collective watchfulness, and on the occurrence of certain parapsychological phenomena. ... The Happening is not an invariable ceremony – rather, a state of mind, an act of clairvoyance. (Lebel, 1968: 720-71)

Some believe the revolution will not occur in social networking of Facebook and Twitter because it promotes weak ties, instead of strong cult-like ties between revolutionaries who keep each other's secrets and reinforce strong hierarchy (Gladwell, 2010). Daniel J Mounsey a.k.a. Pyewacket Kazyanenko reflects on the difference between SL compared to Facebook and Twitter and finds that there is a lot more scope for artist collaborations in SL (Bramwell, 2009). The Mattes' artwork *I know that it is all a state of mind* their avatars' action of repeatedly falling down triggered spontaneous and telepathetic avatar affect contagion. Eva and Franco kept falling over and over for hours. It was not meant to be a participatory artwork, but audience members also started falling down until the end of the performance. (Shindler, 2010) Lisa Blackman argues that theories of embodiment, affect and media need to acknowledge the workings of telepathy as a hidden force within contemporary forms of affective contagion (Blackman, 2010). What might be affective in real life is tele-affective in SL, with some ability to be touched at a distance. The Mattes report that performances in SL are much more interesting now than in 2007. "Now avatars are super fast at improvising with you; the result is, of course, unpredictable." (Mattes in Shindler, 2010) There is synthetic telepathy being developed within the Mattes' *Synthetic Performances*, reminds us that human telepathy has always been technologically mediated - as theorist of telepathy and technology David Porush has detailed. (Porush, 1998)

PERFORMANCE AND PAIN

Doctors constantly warn of damage to eyes, back, metabolism and mind through long periods of sitting at a computer. In Abramoviç/Ulay's most epic endurance work *Nightsea Crossing, 1981-1987,* the artists sat for days and weeks at a time in numerous galleries around the world at either end of a table without eating or speaking whilst maintaining each other's gaze. Instead of using a computer for mental travel they placed alchemical objects such as a boomerang covered in gold and a live python on the table at which they seated. Through extreme endurance of pain and exhaustion of sitting day after day an energy dialogue comprised of empathy, sympathy and telepathy was established with the audience and between the pair. The within and known to SF and the Mattes sometimes engage in endurance performance, where they continually move their mouse and click on keys to animate their avatar. Most are art university trained artists, art historians and/or critics and thus very knowledgeable of the history of conceptual, performance and time-based practices in art. Lichty writes and publishes prolifically,

and in one recent article on the subtleties of new media performance, he says that performance can be both the performer/creator and the viewer or end-user clicking computer mice (Lichty, 2010). Lichty acknowledges the tele-empathetic nature of comparative affect between live real performance and SL avatar performance: "empathy with Marina Abramoviç's bleeding belly in *Lips of Thomas* is questionably analogous to Man Michinaga's re-mediation of the piece." (Lichty, 2008) As yet, very few can profess to be working at the same level of physicality, danger and endurance as artists such as Abramoviç, but many involved with SF as well as the Mattes and Abramoviç herself are currently working through these problematics.

For Marina, a crucial element of performance art is endurance so we accepted [the directive] to perform for four days, for four hours a day. At the end, we were almost throwing up on the keyboards and for the first time, we felt pain that our avatars usually don't feel in our performances. (Mattes in Shindler, 2010)

SL artists such as Joseph DeLappe use a human-computer interface that uses the body in a more holistic way. The avatar performance artist Pyewacket Kazyanenko assists Stelarc's work in SL. It seems logical to suppose that Stelarc may also bridge his older-style, more 'real' endurance exercises with SL avatar performance. For DeLappe, physically demanding actions such as walking on a treadmill are used instead of being limited to a keyboard and computer mouse. Earlier artists such as Abramoviç are important muses and mentors for those seated at computers assisting the agency of avatar performance artists. Works by Great Escape and Wirxli have been made that show the pathos of eliminated risk and physical extremes, supplemented by superhuman fluorescent skin and cartoon levitation. Abramoviç herself is very interested in SL, and having seen the series *Synthetic Performances* of the Mattes she exclaimed that she wished she had thought of it. (Lichty, 2009d) In May 2010 Mattes reported *Synthetic Performances* continues as an ongoing project, and that they were creating two new works in collaboration with Plymouth Arts Centre and Abramović. (Schindler, 2010; and Plymouth Arts Centre, 2010). Abramović has expressed interest in working with scientists to make teleportation and time travel possible:

The are hundreds of parallel worlds. The fascinating thing about the idea of being in this space is that just by changing my wave-lengh, I could disappear in front of your eyes and reappear in the same room but in a different order, with another set-up. It could be incredible to work with both scientists and artists to make such things possible. You could really make time trips. (Abramović in Pijnappel and Abramović, 1990: 60)

In scientific experiments at Georgia Tech, real actors are combined with virtual ones within the same visual field, where a resident performance group called *Lets Try That* help test new technologies. "Avatars active on the virtual stage in Second Life are combined with the real-world actors in the physical performance space." (Farley K. et al, 2009) They observe that SL offers a dynamic performance platform that nevertheless has problems.

The animation control and render system is fixed, as well as the number of polygons used in a certain location. The use of dynamic lights and detailed avatar appearances is usually very limited, as both put heavy pressure on the render engine. (Farley K., Nitsche M., Bolter J. and MacIntyre B., 2009)

The experience of telepathy is not a confined to artists. Computer science researchers Dag Svanaes and William Verplank developed usebility tests of Tangible User Interfaces (TUIs). TUIs and wiimotes bring the whole body back into play for human-computer interface design. Their research reported that many who used TUIs described the experience in terms relating to the paranormal, such telepathy and voodoo. They believe that "magic and paranormal phenomena could be a fruitful place to look for new metaphors for TUIs." (Svanaes, D. and Verplank, W. 2000)

During our experimentation, we repeatedly found ourselves and others comparing our prototypes with paranormal phenomena: "This is like telepathy", "This is like Voodoo". This observation led us to explore our tacit expectations of the paranormal. Are there any common themes in our expectations of the magical? What is the structure of this world? (ibid)

Svanaes and Verplank refuse to reconcile their desire to know more about telepathy by limiting its usability/artistry as mere stage magic.

Tognazzini argues for the application of techniques from stage magic to interface design. We use "magic" to refer to belief systems different from that of Western rationality, that allow for phenomena that are "impossible" in the latter system. (ibid)

They seek a scientific belief system that will support this real experience of telepathy that people have through an appreciation of Quantum Mechanics and Bells Theorem, Relics and Magic and "The holistic universe and magic through resemblance" (ibid).

GHOSTS, SHELLS AND TELE-ACTORS

The artists Pierre Huyghe and Phillipe Parreno bought a readymade avatar called Annlee and invited contemporary artists to write scripts for her. (Warner, 2006: 331) The Annlee avatar commodity becomes animated with the potential emptiness of its virtual being as an endless medium for ventriloquising the thoughts of others. Annlee

"…changes the current between perceiver and perceived: she is haunted by us because without us she has no existence. Annlee never did have a soul – and her body possesses only appearance. She is "No Ghost Just a Shell." (ibid) In SL an avatar that remains after a person has logged off due to a glitch is called a "ghost." Pyewacket, whose first name was taken from a sixteenth century witches cat, has considered becoming a paranormal researcher into the glitches experienced in SL.[24] Pyewacket has been documented merging into the body of Wirixli, a common SL glitch that the Mattes anticipate will be fixed soon (Schindler, 2010).

Turner's metaphor of IM as telepathy doubles in computer associated weirdness with the twice-absent presence of communicating one's being as 'away from keyboard', typed in shorthand logo as 'afk'. The afk person haunts the virtual world as somewhere between online and offline as a ghostly absent presence (Boellstorff, 2008: 117). In a Derridean hauntological sense, Tom Boellstorff identifies the haunted afk as the essence of SL culture, where presence and emersion meet. For him as an anthropologist, afk is also where ethnography and the virtual meet - the participant observer is an "awkward presence" surveying the culture of the other. (ibid) Although Jacques Derrida himself did not have a computer he considered writing to be very performative, and the act of 'loosing' his *Telepathy* text for several years is an example of that. Derrida ventriloquises Sigmund Freud in *Telepathy*, speaking not as himself but as Freud. *Telepathy* is a lesser-known text than *The Spectres of Marx*, and both extend his interest in hypnotic and speculative phenomena.

The actions of avatars in machinima have an "orthopaedic touch" (Martinez y Sentamans, 2007: 60) involving what Lev Manovich refers to as 'tele-acting' and remote control in real time. The movement resembles zombie, robot and marionette-like qualities of some instructional conceptual performance, for example Gilbert & George's *Underneath the Arches* and *Bend It*

performances. Such real world performances are semi-autonomous, and can be puppet, automaton and mime-like where an elimination of personality is used to create an uncanny fusion between two selves while further distancing the viewers (Green, 2001: 139, 147, 152). In this example of early performance work "Each jerk is therefore a point at which an instance of virtuality occurs." (Green, 2001: 152) Alternatively, a line of concentrated smooth flight in SL is an instant of the otherworldly feeling more real.

CONCLUSION

Artists such as Turner and his avatar performance art friends and peers allow telepathy to be part of SL avatar performance art, unconsciously and through intellectual decisions to engage with transferential, technological and occult phenomena. Telepathic and transferential phenomena are active when creating an alternate or virtual self and/or selves, inside and outside of SL, and through sparks generated between the borders of real and virtual worlds. SL augments the creative schizoid nature of artistic personalities through the splitting and doubling of selves and ego modification. Avatar telepathy fictions can involve love, spiritual quests and high modernist aesthetics. The generation of secondafterlives in SL affirms that the avatar identity is extremely fluid, dynamic, exchangeable and telepathetic. Activist tendencies and Fluxus happenings are also accompanied by transferential and hypnotic phenomena, and this 'code' is present within SL. The performing body generates experiences of telepathy, as does the shared group and collaborative telepathy. Speaking through another, ventriloquising through soulless avatar shells and general computer and SL weirdness also allow telepathy to effervesce. SF and SL artists are remediating earlier technologically mediated telepathies and extending the cyborg flux of telepathetic art practice and historical lineage.

REFERENCES

Abramoviç, M. (1993). Art is about energy. *Art and Design, 8*(7-8), 32–37.

Abramoviç, M. (2010). *The pigs of today are the hams of tomorrow*. Plymouth Arts Centre. Retrieved October 17, 2010, from http://www. plymouthartscentre.org/ Press/ marinaAbramoviç. html

Abramoviç, M., & Abramoviç, V. *(1998). Time-space-energy or talking about asystemic thinking. In M.Abramoviç et al. (Eds.)*, Marina Abramoviç: Artist body-Performances 1969-1998 *(pp. 400-17). Milano, Italia: Edizioni Charta.*

Abramoviç, M., von Daniken, H. P., & Ruf, B. (1996). A conversation with Marina Abramoviç. In Landert, M. (Ed.), *Marina Abramoviç: Double edge* (pp. 11–47). Warth, Austria: Museum of Fine Art of the Canton of Thurgau, Kartause Ittengen.

Amyfreelunch. (2008). *New episode: Interview with Scott Kildall*. Retrieved November 14, 2010, from http://amyfreelunch.wordpress.com/ 2008/ 12/ 18/ new-episode-interview-with- scott-kildall/

Bainbridge, W. S. (2008). The rights of an avatar. *The Journal of Personal Cyberconsciousness, 3*(4). Retrieved November 4, 2010, from http:// www.terasemjournals.org/ pc0302/ wb3.html

Baker, C. (2003). Internal networks revisited: Telepathy meets technology. In *Digital Arts Conference 2003 Proceedings*. Retrieved September 23, 2009, http://hypertext.rmit.edu.au/ dac/ papers/ Baker.pdf

Baumer, A., & Magerko, B. (2009). Narrative development in improvisational theatre. In I. A. Iurgel, N. Zagalo, & P. Petta (Eds.) *Lecture Notes in Computer Science: International Conference on Interactive Digital Storytelling* (pp. 140-151) Berlin, Germany: Springer-Verlag.

Blackman, L. (2010). Embodying affect: Voice-hearing, telepathy, suggestion and modelling the non-conscious. *Body & Society, 16*, 163-190. Retrieved April 17, 2010, from http://bod.sagepub. com/ cgi/ content/ abstract/16/1/163

Boellstorff, T. (2010). *Coming of age in Second Life: An anthropologist explores the virtually human*. Princeton, NJ: Princeton University Press.

Bramwell, C. (2009). The second life of Pye. *Artlink, 29*(3), 68–70.

Brea, J. L. (2007). Collective telepathy 2.0 (the interconnected multitudes theory). In J. M. Prada (Ed.), *Inclusiva-net: New art dynamics in Web 2 mode* (pp. 36-50). Madrid, Espana: Área de las Artes. Retrieved October 22, 2010, from http:// www.medialab-prado.es/ mmedia/ 1098

Cohen, D. (2009). *Objet petit a(vatar): Psychoanalysis, posthumanism and the question of the self in Second Life*. Unpublished PhD thesis, University of Western Ontario, London Ontario Canada.

Dalrymple Henderson, L. (1998). *Duchamp in context-Science and technology in the large glass and related works*. Princeton, NY: Princeton University Press.

Drinkall, J. A. (2006). *Telepathy in contemporary, conceptual and performance art*. Unpublished thesis, University of New South Wales, Sydney. Retrieved from http://unsworks.unsw.edu.au/ vital/ access/ manager/ Repository/ unsworks:1561

Drinkall, J. A. (2007). *Social and political aesthetics of telepathy in Fluxus art and beyond*. Unpublished paper presented at Flux Conference, School of Art History, Cinema, Classics and Archeology, University of Melbourne.

Drinkall, J. A. (2009). Traumaculture and telepathetic cyber fiction. In I. A. Iurgel, N. Zagalo, & P. Petta (Eds.), *Lecture Notes in Computer Science: International Conference on Interactive Digital Storytelling* (pp. 163-173). Berlin, Germany: Springer-Verlag.

Drinkall, J. A. (2010). *Politics of telepathic collaborations: The 60s, the 80s and now*. Unpublished paper presented in Collaborations in Modern and Postmodern Visual Art Conference, Social and Aesthetics Research Unit, Monash University.

Farley, K., Nitsche, M., Bolter, J., & MacIntyre, B. (2009). Augmenting creative realities: The Second Life performance project. *Leonardo, 42*(1), 96–97. doi:10.1162/leon.2009.42.1.96

Finkelstein, A. B. A. (1999). Nanotechnology and cyberspace: Two roads to the same city. In *Proceedings for the Ninth General Assembly of the World Future Society*. Montreal, Canada: MacGill University.

Fleming, S. M. (2007). *The future of the brain*. In PhD 2, Neuroscience, Wellcome Trust Centre for Neuroimaging. Retrieved November 4, 2010, from www.ucl.ac.uk/ .../ RfP_EssayComp _LIFE_Fleming_ The_Brain_1_.pdf

Franganito, S. T. (2007). *xox Voyager's (Skawennati Tricia Fragnito's) curatorial statement*. In Vancouver's Second Live 2007. Retrieved October 17, 2010, from http://secondlive2007. blogspot.com/

Fritz, A. (2007). *Send us your art's birthday presence! Traces of art's birthday networks at the western front 1989-2007*. In Western Front Research Library. Retrieved November 4, 2010 from http://front.bc.ca/ research/ texts/ 3

Gladwell, M. (2010, October 4). Small change: Why the revolution will not be tweeted. *The New Yorker*. Retrieved November 4, 2010, from http:// www.newyorker.com/ reporting/ 2010/ 10/ 04/ 101004fa_fact_gladwell

Green, C. (2000). Doppleganger and the third force: The artistic collaborations of Gilbert & George and Abramoviç/Ulay. *Art Journal, 59*(2), 36–45. doi:10.2307/778099

Green, C. (2001). *The third hand: Collaboration in art from conceptualism to postmodernism*. Minneapolis, MN & London, UK: University of Minnesota Press.

Green, C. (2004). Group soul. Who own the artist fusion? *Third Text, 18*(6), 595–608. doi:10.1080/0952882042000285005

Kildall, S. (2010). *Scott Kildall*. Retrieved November 4, 2010, from http://www.kildall.com/

KoinUp blog, the immersive worlds guide. (2009). *SaveMe Oh*. Retrieved October 22, 2010, from http://blog.koinup.com/ 2009/ 12/ saveme-oh.html

Krauss, R. (1976). Video: The aesthetics of narcissism. In Battcock, G. (Ed.), *New artists video: A critical anthology* (pp. 43–64). New York, NY: E. P. Dutton. republished 1978

Lebel, J. (1968). On the necessity of violation. In Stiles, K., & Selz, P. (Eds.), *Theories and documents of contemporary art* (pp. 718–722). *Berkeley/Los Angeles, CA & London, UK*: University of California Press. republished 1996

Lichtenberg-Ettinger, B. *(2005). The art-and-healing-oeuvre: Metramorphic relinquishment of the soul-spirit to the spirit of the cosmos. In de Zegher & H. Teicher (Eds.),* 3 x abstraction: New methods of drawing by Hilma af Klint, Emma Kunz and Agnes Martin. *New York, NY & New Haven, CT: The Drawing Center, and Yale University Press.*

Lichty, P. (2000). The cybernetics of performance and new media art. *Leonardo, 33*(5), 351–354. doi:10.1162/002409400552810

Lichty, P. (2008). Why art in virtual worlds? E-happenings, relational milieu & second sculpture. *CIAC, 31*. Retrieved November 1, 2010, from http://www.ciac.ca/ magazine/ archives/ no_31/ dossier.htm

Lichty, P. (2009a). The translation of art in virtual worlds. *Leonardo Electronic Almanac, 16*, 4–5.

Lichty, P. (2009b). Wikipedia as art? In *Rhizome at the new museum*. Retrieved November 4, 2010, from http://rhizome.org/ discuss/ view/ 41713

Lichty, P. (2009c). *I know Gaz Babeli*. Retrieved November 1, 2010, from http://gazirababeli.com/ TEXTS.php? t=iknowgazbabeli

Lichty, P. (2009d). Lightening rod: Second front, reemergence of the happening and the integration of history. *CIAC, 33*. Retrieved October 29, 2010, from http://www.ciac.ca/ magazine/ perspective.htm

Lichty, P. *(2010)*. Patrick Lichty: Theorist – artist – curator. Asking question through art and media. *RetrievedNovember4, 2010, from*http://www.voyd.com/

Lipsey, R. (1988). Frantisek Kupka: The realm of rhythms and signs. In Lipsey, R. (Ed.), *An art of our own: The spiritual in twentieth century art* (pp. 98–106). Boston, MA: Shambhala.

MacDonald, G. L., & Boyce, J. S. (2008). Nanotechnology: Considering the complex ethical, legal, and societal issues with the parameters of human performance. *NanoEthics, 2*, 265–275. doi:10.1007/s11569-008-0047-6

Martinez Fabre, M. P., & Sentamans, T. (2007). The lapses of an avatar: Sleight of hand and artistic praxis in Second Life. In J. M. Prada (Ed.), *Inclusiva-net: New art dynamics in Web 2 mode* (pp. 51-76). Retrieved October 29, 2010, from http://www.medialab-prado.es/ mmedia/1099

Neustaedter, C., & Fedorovokya, E. (2008). *Presenting identity in a virtual world through avatar appearances*. In Kodak Research Labs and Graphics Interface Conference, (pp. 183-190). 25-27 May, Kelowna, British Columbia, Canada.

Paech, V. (2007). *Second front: Performance art in Second Life*. Artshub. Retrieved October 26, 2010, from http://www.artshub.com.au/ au/ newsPrint.asp? sid=159056

Pera, H. (n.d.). *Humming Pera biography*. Last.fm. Retrieved October 18, 2009, http://www.last.fm/ music/ Humming+Pera/+wiki/diff? &a=1&b=2

Pijnappel, J., & Abramoviç, A. (1990). Biography by Johan Pijnappel, interview Amsterdam. In Wijers, L., & Pijnappel, J. (Eds.), *Art meets science and spirituality* (pp. 54–63). London, UK: Academy Editions.

Porush, D. (1998). Telepathy: Alphabetic consciousness and the age of cyborg illiteracy. In Broadhurst Dixon, J., & Cassidy, E. J. (Eds.), *Virtual futures: Cyberotics, technology and post-human pragmatism, cyberculture singularities* (pp. 45–64). London, UK & New York, NY: Routledge.

Quaranta, D. (2007). *Remediations: Art in Second Life*. Retrieved November 6, 2010, from http://www.hz-journal.org/ n11/ quaranta.html

Quaranta, D. (2007, August 31). *Displaced familiarity: Interview with Scott Kildall*. In Spawn of the Surreal. Retrieved November 6, 2010, from http://spawnofthesurreal.blogspot.com/

Quaranta, D. (2008). *For God's sake!* The Spawn of the Surreal. Retrieved November 6, 2010, from http://spawnofthesurreal.blogspot.com/

Redfield, M. (1992). Book review Nicholas Royle- Telepathy and literature: The fictions of telepathy. *Surfaces, 2*, 27. Retrieved November 6, 2010, from http://www.pum.umontreal.ca/revues/ surfaces/vol2/redfield.html

Ruhrbeg, K., Schneckenberger, M., Fricke, C., Honnef, K., & Ingo, W. F. (2000). *Art of the 20th century*. London, UK/ Madrid, Spain/ New York, NY/ Paris, France/ Tokyo, Japan: Taschen.

Sant, T. (2009). Performance in Second Life: Some possibilities for learning and teaching. In Molka-Danielsen, J., & Deutschmann, M. (Eds.), *Learning and teaching in the virtual world of Second Life* (pp. 145–166). Norway: Tapir Academic Press.

Saveme Oh. (2010). *Death of an avatar*. Retrieved October 19, 2010, from http://savemeoh.yolasite.com/ death-of-an-avatar.php

Saveria Melissa Oh. (2010). *High heels but no soul*. Retrieved October 18, 2010, from http://www.vimeo.com/15462380

Schindler, K. (2010, May 28). Life after death: An interview with Eva and Franco Mattes. *Art 21*. Retrieved October 27, 2010, from http://blog.art21.org/ 2010/ 05/ 28/ life-after-death-an-interview- with-eva-and-franco-mattes/

Schnapp, J. T., & Shanks, M. (2009). Artereality (Rethinking craft in knowledge economy). In Maddoff, S. H. (Ed.), *Art school (Propositions for the 21st century)* (pp. 141–157). Cambridge, MA: MIT Press.

Second Front. (2010). *The pioneering performance art group in Second Life*. Retrieved November 4, 2010, from http://www.secondfront.org

Second Life. (2010). *Second Life destination guide*. Retrieved November 4, 2010, from http://secondlife.com/destinations

Stiles, K. (2003). Anomaly, sky, sex, and Psi in Fluxus. In Hendricks, G. (Ed.), *Critical mass: Happenings, Fluxus, performance, intermedia and Rutgers University 1958-1972* (pp. 60–88). Nebraska and New Jersey: Rutgers University Press.

Svanaes, D., & Verplank, W. (2000). In search of metaphors for tangible user interfaces. Designing augmented reality environments. In *Proceedings of DARE 2000 on Designing Augmented Reality Environment* (pp. 121-129). New York, NY: ACM.

Turner, J. O. (2006). *Onto Distro's official Yahoo time capsule speech*. Retrieved November 4, 2010, from http://video.google.com/ videoplay? docid=7699712386 719429816# Turner, J. O. (2010a). *In memory of Wirxli FlimFlam (2006-2010)*. May 2007. Retrieved October 17, 2010, from http://wirxliflimflam.blogspot.com/ 2007_05_01_ archive.html

Turner, J. O. (2010b). *Jeremy Owen Turner's classic blogs*. Retrieved October 29, 2010, from http://classicblogs.blogspot.com/

Turner, J. O. (2010c). *Last exit – Ars virtua*. Retrieved November 1, 2010, from http://www.youtube.com/ watch?v=q6Dmz PrmH3A

Turner, J. O. (2010d). *Qyxxql Merlin's LiveJournal*. Retrieved October 17, 2010, from http://qyxxql-merlin.livejournal.com/

Virtual Fluxus. (2010). *Virtual Fluxus*. Retrieved October 28, 2010, from http://www.mefeedia.com/ watch/ 33503241

Warner, M. (2006). *Phantasmagoria: Spirit vision, metaphors and media into the twenty-first century*. Oxford, UK: Oxford University Press.

(1939). Wodell. (2008). Performa 07 in Second Life: Brave new metaverse. *Art in America, 96*, 55.

ENDNOTES

[1] Professor Kevin Warwick often uses the term techlepathy. Warwick is developing brain-to-brain communication via cybernetics and robotics engineering to achieve technologically assisted telepathy (MacDonald Glenn and Boyce 2008: 269).

2   Canadians Jeremy Owen Turner, Tanya Skuce (then married and based in Vancouver) and Doug Jarvis sent out very spontaneous emails out to various other SL artists on November 23, 2006, and some others joined later that same day as co-founders. Numerous others have since been recruited and some, such as Turner and Skuce, have since left / taken a break. See also Lichty (2007). "The Apocraphal History of the Founding of Second Front". Retrieved October 29, 2009, from http://www.voyd.com/texts.html

3   The avatar China Tracy a.k.a. Cai Fei was included in the 2007 Venice Biennale curated by Robert Storr. *The Gate* is an installation that links the real Shanghai Biennale gallery space with the virtual world of Second Life's Odyssey Island, and was created by Belgian curators Yves Bernard and Yannick Antoin. Bernard and Antoin curated a number of avatar performance artworks such as *Falun Gong* and *Thriller*, 2010 – performed by Pyewacket Kazyanenko a.k.a Daniel Jay Mounsey and *Invisible Minority Report* - performed at by Cunzai Parx a.k.a. Ben Unterman, Keep Moving Mannonen a.k.a. Diego Silang Maranan, Jacquelene Utherwurldly a.k.a. Jacquelene Drinkall, Occlude Varthader a.k.a. and Mobileunit Loonie a.k.a. Sarah Coffin.

4   Facebook, email and skype conversations between the Turner and the author, late October, 2010.

5   SaveMe Oh, Retrieved November 4, 2010 from http://savemeoh.wordpress.com/

6   Avatar Orchestra. Retrieved November 4, 2010 from http://avatarorchestra.org/

7   Last.fm, Humming Pera Biography, 18.10.10 - http://www.last.fm/music/Humming+Pera/+wiki/diff?&a=1&b=2)

8   Monday, May 14, 2007; Avatar Orchestra Metaverse Concert at xxXtension... http://wirxliflimflam.blogspot.com/2007/05/avatar-orchestra-metaverse-concert-at.html. In Turner, J. (2010a)

9   Jeremy Owen Turner in Facebook conversation the author, October, 2010. Numerous Facebook, email and skype conversations took place during mid-late October and early November between Turner and the author, and Turner generously contributed numerous corrections and advice in the production of this text.

10   SaveMe Oh performed *High Heels But No Soul* in the SL Mormon Kingdom, with hair styled into two demonic black corkscrew styled hair-horns from her forehead, deadly weapon-style stiletto heals and cheeky dance routine filmed in the Mormon Kingdom and archived as machinima video.[1] Part of SaveMe Oh's performance art strategy incorporates confrontational and anti-social behaviours that result in her being banned from many SL regions, which are referred to as Sims in SL, by other SL avatar participants, for example when she made a racist comment about the Swiss provoked by Swiss religious intolerance. (Koinup, 2010) SaveMe Oh's hypnotic dance is a profane, provocative and militantly well-heeled display within the Mormon kingdom.

11   Turner, J.O. and Oh, S. (2010) Last Exit – Ars Virtua. Retrieved October 26, 2010, from http://www.youtube.com/watch?v=q6DmzPrmH3A

12   Turner, J.O. and Oh, S. (2010) Homology. Retrieved October 26, 2010, from http://www.youtube.com/watch?v=LdEcBhu8ygM

13   Selavy_Qiezli_ArsVirtua2010 Retrieved October 26, 2010, from Turner's personal facebook albumn

14   Turner, in conversation with the author, November 11, 2010.

15   (Lichty, 2008) Gazera Babeli's 'real' identity is a highly guarded secret. Selavy Oh, another avatar who guards her real life identity confided that she thought Babeli was used by several people including Lichty, although this was new speculation for Turner. Turner

and Selavy Oh in conversation with the author, November 11, 2010.

16   The Absolutely Last (and Final) Supper. Retrieved November 6, 2010, from http://www.youtube.com/watch?v=S4dRJW3SMe4

17   Second Front's "Zombie Attack! 28 Avatars Later..." Retrieved November 6, 2010, from http://www.youtube.com/watch?v=gByuAUcehrI

18   The Western Front http://front.bc.ca/mediaarts/events/1911 and curatorial statement http://front.bc.ca/exhibitions/events/816

19   Turner, in corrections he provided to the author for this paper, November 3, 2010

20   Turner's friendship with key Fluxus artist Douglas Davis lead him to contribute to an SL campaign to save a former Flux Co-op house in Wooster Street where Douglas resided.

21   Exibitart magazine. Milan. Italy, 2007

22   Lichty's text is an email sent to COFA Empyre Lists titled Alterity and Dystopia in SL – a response to dissidents in SL, written 2007.

23   Ruhrbeg, 2000, p. 589. The sign above Filliou's door said 'Le vagabond de l'art est toujours en voyage. Laissez nom et ('et' was then crossed out an replaced with 'sans') adresse, il vous touchera un jour sans doute. *(par telepathie)*.'

24   Facebook conversation between Daniel Jay Mounsey a.k.a. Pyewacket Kazyanenko and the author October 29, 2010.

Section 2
Our Immersion:
Entering the Metaverse

Chapter 5

The 3–D Innovation Sphere:
Exploring the Use of Second Life for Innovation Communication

Katrin Tobies
University of Leipzig, Germany

Bettina Maisch
University of St.Gallen, Switzerland

ABSTRACT

This chapter will explore the 3-D environment Second Life as a communication platform used by industry and science to create, design, develop, and distribute innovation. In order to achieve sustainable economic success in the context of global competition, companies need to optimize their communication activities within their innovation processes. In addition to identifying relevant trends at an early stage and generating marketable ideas, it is becoming increasingly important for companies to sufficiently communicate the usage and the meaning of innovations and to position themselves as consistent innovators. Virtual worlds like the high profile, realistically designed online environment Second Life offer far-reaching possibilities within the innovation management process – from ideating to market introduction. The objective of this chapter is to provide a systematic analysis of the communication paradigms in virtual environments. In particular, the main issues, challenges, opportunities, limits and trends of digital innovation communication will be discussed in the context of the 3-D world Second Life.

INTRODUCTION

In order to be economically successful, companies have to effectively communicate products and to position themselves as innovators. Three-dimensional virtual worlds provide a multitude of options for innovation management. While the number of reports about corporate activities in 3-D worlds has decreased significantly, three-dimensional virtual worlds are continually growing, both in terms of user numbers and the technological possibilities and the use scenarios these bring. In addition, studies on virtual worlds have gained new popularity in science and research. Research institutions and companies are continuing to explore the potential of these online environments for interaction with internal and external stakeholders in the course of innovation

DOI: 10.4018/978-1-60960-854-5.ch005

management (Kohler, Matzler, & Füller, 2009; Ondrejka, 2007). However, three-dimensional virtual worlds also appear to open up extensive possibilities for innovation communication, which have barely been examined to date.

This chapter contributes to the systematic analysis of the potential, limits and challenges of digital innovation communication. Basic information for the evaluation of current or future involvement in virtual worlds for the purposes of innovation communication will be presented using a systematic description of selected case studies from one of the first and most well-known virtual worlds – Second Life. This contribution describes the communication options provided by a 3-D online environment like Second Life, how companies can use such environments in their innovation processes and to what extent Second Life helps companies to position themselves as innovators.

VIRTUAL 3-D WORLDS

Virtual 3-D worlds are "immersive, three-dimensional, multi-media, multi-person simulation environments, where each participant adopts an alter ego and interacts with other participants in real time. World activity persists even if a player is off-line" (Wagner, 2008). In terms of their appearance, they can mimic the real world, but may also represent fantasy worlds. The common feature of all virtual worlds is that, because they are realized in digital form, they are not necessarily subject to any of the physical laws of reality. In the case of Internet-based virtual worlds, this is supplemented by the fact that they can be accessed online at any time, from anywhere in the world.

According to Frédéric Cavazza (2007) virtual worlds can be allocated to one of four forms of use:

- *Social:* worlds in which the main focus is on community building;
- *Game:* worlds that first and foremost serve online gaming;
- *Entertainment:* worlds consisting of music, videos and films;
- *Business:* worlds that specifically fulfill business purposes, including worlds used for the exchange and sale of goods or to simulate training.

These four categories (see Figure 1) can overlap in places, since a single world can serve more than one use aspect. The virtual 3-D world Second Life lies at the interface between all four areas, as it combines social interaction, gaming, entertainment, and business applications.

Second Life is an interactive 3-D online environment, which is not restricted to any specific subject matter and was created entirely by its users. It was set up in America in 1999 by Philip Rosedale, but did not go online until June 2003. Since then, it has undergone a continuous process of further development. In this world, users can create virtual landscapes and objects (buildings, apartments, items of clothing, etc.) and interact with one another in a broad variety of ways (chats, games, trading, organizing events, etc.). Anyone wishing to use Second Life has to register online, install a free software package and configure their own avatar. The avatar can be personalized in such detail using more than one hundred parameters that users can replicate their own individual personality and appearance in a way that is extremely true-to-life. Users can move through the virtual world and communicate with others via their avatar. Those who wish, in addition, to own land and create their own items have to purchase premium membership for 9.95 US Dollar per month (Linden Lab, 2010b).

Despite dwindling membership numbers since 2007, Second Life is considered to be the most

Figure 1. Categorization of virtual worlds. (Cavazza, 2007. Used with permission)

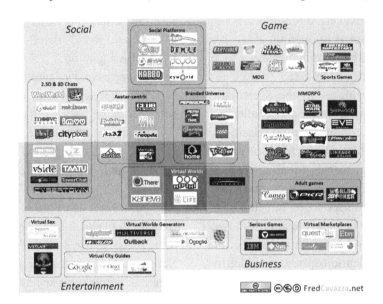

important 3-D world of its kind, both in terms of its profile and the number of users. More than 1.4 million residents logged-in worldwide within a 60-day period (as per May 2010, Linden Lab, 2010a). The majority of users are male, below the age of thirty and characterized by a high degree of affinity with computers (Fittkau & Maaß, 2007). In addition to individuals – and due largely to intense media interest in 2007 – companies, research institutes, private and government institutions can also be found in Second Life. In addition to companies like Adidas, BMW, IBM, Sony and Vodafone, Research Institutes of the German Fraunhofer-Society, the University of the Arts Berlin, Greenpeace, the German federal state of Baden-Württemberg, the Swedish consulate and many more all have or had a Second Life presence.

Second Life offers its users a wide range of development and activity options, enabling them to create their own content and interact with other users. The operators behind Second Life, Linden Lab, have not specified any differentiated gaming scenario, fixed rules, conditions or overarching purpose – indeed, quite the opposite: the inhabitants are free to design the platform according to their own ideas, interests and objectives, and can create their own games with no restrictions as to the size and genre within this world. Thus, not only a large number of role-playing communities, each with their own sets of rules, but also numerous fantasy, puzzle, problem-solving and strategy games have developed in which users can set out on adventures and search for treasure. There are also spheres in which weapons may be used to stage "Ego Shooter" games or murderous chases. On account of the fact that Second Life is deliberately used for relaxation and for actions with no specific purpose, the world has some of the characteristics of a game (Huizinga, 1939) in a Computer-generated three-dimensional setting. Overall, however, it embodies more an Internet-based infrastructure platform with user-generated content rather than a traditional game.

Furthermore, Second Life is open to targeted use for commercial ideas. It has a complete economic cycle, in which goods and services can be produced and traded with the Linden Dollar (L$) as its own currency. This virtual money can be purchased on stock markets and, in turn, exchanged for real currency. The exchange rate is approximately 260 Linden Dollars to 1 US Dollar (as per February 2010, Linden Research, 2010). In October 2008, turnover totaled more than 22 million US Dollars (Linden Research, 2008). The option of exchanging the virtual gaming money into real money has led to the creation of various forms of income in and around Second Life. The platform itself constitutes a distribution channel, as avatars can sell virtual and real products direct to other avatars. To this end, sales branches and flagship stores have been set up in-world, and on-line market places for Second Life products have even been created outside the platform, including ww.xstreetsl.com (English) and www.slmarket.de (German). Furthermore, the advertising communication opportunities mean that it is also possible to achieve indirect income in Second Life.

SECOND LIFE AS A COMMUNICATION PLATFORM

Not only private individuals, but also companies, associations, educational and research institutes utilize Second Life as a communication medium that can be used in a multitude of ways: for recruitment events, staff meetings, product presentations, counseling interview, to run courses and workshops, as an e-learning tool, for image and marketing purposes, as a sales area, or as a test area for experiments and scientific studies. In so doing, companies not only create virtual products, events and advertising to support internal and external communication, but also employee avatars and virtual company representative offices.

Employee Avatars

Employees can use avatars to complete tasks virtually. Avatars can interact in real time by simulating body language, in writing via a chat window and orally via Voice Chat. Thus, companies can use Second Life to carry out consultation and sales meetings, to exchange ideas with customers, run

internal training events or to bring together working groups that are scattered across the globe. The IT company IBM, for example, began its virtual involvement in October 2006 with a staff meeting, which was also attended by CEO Samuel Palmisano via his avatar. Since then, IBM has provided a significant proportion of customer services in Second Life, since some solutions are easier to explain using 3-D than per telephone or e-mail (Wilkens, 2006). German energy provider EnBW also uses Second Life for customer support purposes. Customers can log their electricity meter reading with a virtual member of service staff and obtain advice on tariffs and products. The advantages of this are manifold: it involves less time than real meetings and there are no travel expenses whatsoever. The feeling of actually being in the same place is greater than in telephone conferences, on account of the visual presence of the participants. The visual aspect furthermore makes it possible to use static, moving and, in particular, three-dimensional diagrams. Moreover, Second Life is independent of time or place, that is, it can be used anywhere in the world, 365 days a year at any time of the day or night. In addition, the potential anonymity – users are not required to state a real user name or authentic data when setting up their profile – means that participants may act more freely and thus provide the company with more open, critical feedback than they otherwise would.

Company Representations

A number of companies have set up not only virtual company headquarters, but also entire islands to bring their company, products and services closer to the interest public. Often, they serve image-building and marketing purposes to equal parts. Thus, these islands comprise a mixture of brand world, event platform, interactive showroom, sales point, service point and meeting place. The record company Sony BMG, for instance, invited fans from all over the world to virtual concerts on its "Media Island", advertising stars like Justin Timberlake and Christina Aguilera, as well as selling their music. Fashion label American Apparel, meanwhile, sells its clothing both in virtual stores on Lerappa Island and in the real world. Other well-known companies such as BMW, Amazon and TUI hoped to gain a greater media presence through their involvement in Second Life, resulting in an increase in popularity and a positive image transfer, since this proves that they are actively involved in a modern and innovative environment. Another reason for many was to gain experience in the professional use of a 3-D online world at an early stage, to equip them for the opportunities and challenges of three-dimensional Internet. As a result of the wane in media interest, however, many companies soon left Second Life.

In-World Advertising

A widespread form of communication in Second Life is the running of advertising campaigns: in-world advertising. Usually, standard forms of advertising are employed. Forms used in-world include posters, adverts, promotional films, sponsoring and mobile advertising media (head-up displays, signboards, rucksacks). German insurance company Gothaer used an advertising poster in its search for qualified employees for office and fieldwork, which linked users directly to the careers pages of its website.

Media agencies specialized in virtual worlds have already been set up, including The Otherland Group, the Inworld Advertising Network, YOUin3D.com and Second Promotion. They also offer behavior-based advertising campaigns. This is one of the huge advantages of Second Life, since here advertising can be integrated in a targeted fashion pursuant to specific criteria, and replaced as and when necessary. With the help of fixed user accounts, session cookies and IP-addresses, advertising can be personalized and systematically tailored to the interests of any given member. As logged-in users can also be geographically located,

the communication can furthermore be country-specific and run at certain times. Personalization like this facilitates greater attention and improved advertising impact. This is due not least to the fact that advertising messages may be experienced in a more emotional and positive light in a playful environment.

REQUIREMENTS FOR INNOVATION COMMUNICATION

The opportunities for communication and interaction in virtual 3-D worlds, such as Second Life, can also be used for the purposes of innovation communication. The concept of innovation communication addresses a relatively new field within the area of corporate communication. The term was coined and the concept developed and promoted by German researchers from the University of Hohenheim and University of Leipzig. In their understanding – which we adopt here – innovation communication is defined "as symbolic interactions between organizations and their internal and external stakeholders, dealing with new products, services, and technologies" (Mast, Huck, & Zerfaß, 2005; Mast & Zerfaß, 2005; Zerfaß, Sandhu, & Huck, 2004). It covers all systematic communication activities with the objective of fostering technological, economic and social novelties; this includes activities such as communicating the novelty itself, creating an understanding and trust in it, influencing its socially shared meaning pattern, and positioning the organization behind it as an innovator (Zerfaß, 2009).

Even though innovation communication is a field of activity in corporate communication, it requires its own methods and concepts to be tailored to the special features of novelties. As studies show (Mast, et al., 2005; Zerfaß, Swaran, & Huck, 2004), the challenge lies in the fact that new ideas and inventions are difficult to explain: for the most part they are complex and abstract, while their benefits and final target groups are initially unclear. Mainly because of their novelty, there is a lack of examples and experiences that could be used to explain their meaning and use. Thus, one task of innovation communication is to anchor a clear, positive image of the new product, service, process, or technology and its added value in the minds of relevant stakeholders. People must be given the opportunity to acquaint themselves with it and to trust the innovative power of the company behind it. Moreover, communicative interactions between the organization and its audiences need to establish social practices of the innovation. This is important as "innovation is more about creating meanings than it is about creating artifacts" (Toumi, 2002).

This means innovation communication is not simply transmitting information about a new product or service to relevant stakeholders, as the focus of prior studies in innovation management and marketing would suggest (e.g. Mohr, Sengupta, & Slater, 2009; Trommsdorff & Steinhoff, 2007). Rather, from a social science perspective, innovation communication is also about creating common patterns of meaning and establishing joint social practices (Zerfaß, 2005b, 2009). Accordingly, an innovation communication approach which emotionalizes and entertains and which visualizes and presents the specific uses, benefits, and meanings of the new product or service in a multi-sensual, experiential way is considered the most promising (Mast, Huck, & Zerfaß, 2006). Novelties demand simple, logical examples and an appealing, clear language (Mast, et al., 2006). Embedding in stories (storytelling), linking with current trends, gripping dramaturgy and sensationalism are also considered helpful (Mast & Zerfaß, 2005; Mast, Huck, & Zerfaß, 2006; Hoewner, Jansen, Jantke 2008; Fink 2009; Huck-Sandhu 2009).

Experience-based forms of communication in the real sphere and product samples for testing are particularly well-suited to fulfilling these requirements. For reasons of time and cost, however, these are often dispensed with. The virtual world

Second Life provides several opportunities to fill this gap. While it may not be possible to actually touch, taste, or smell new products, these can nevertheless be depicted true-to-life and simulated in virtual processes. As in the real world, interested parties can, through their avatars, actively try out new products and procedures and enter into dialogue with the companies or innovators behind them. This is considerably easier, faster, more cost-effective and entails less risk in a virtual environment. This is significant for the management of innovations, since time and budget are seen as the most crucial factors for success.

However, communication is key to making an innovation system work (Nordfors, 2004, 2006). An innovation system is built up by a complex set of interactions between those people, enterprises, institutions, research bodies, investors etc. that are essential to an innovation process (Lundvall, 1985). Therefore, it is vital that all internal and external stakeholder groups be incorporated. Close collaboration between employee communication, marketing and public relations (PR) is also very important (see Figure 2).

The objectives of innovation communication differ according to the stakeholder group (Zerfaß, 2005b, 2009). The purposes of internal innovation communication are primarily to support employees, but also to assist research and development (R&D) partners in the search for ideas and concepts, in initiating dialogue and enhancing product and process development. The task of innovation marketing is to optimize the introduction to the market and, thus, the diffusion and adoption of new products among customers, partners and competitors. The purpose of innovation PR, meanwhile, is to ensure an innovation-friendly environment throughout the entire innovation process in order to avoid potential opposition from decision-makers in politics, interest groups and the mass media.

Figure 2. Communication and stakeholders in the innovation process. (Adapted from Zerfaß, 2005a)

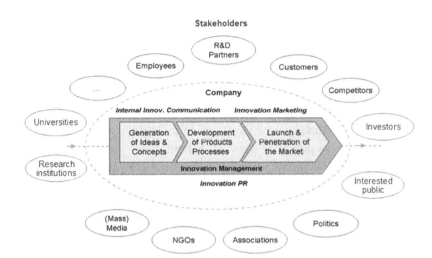

INNOVATION COMMUNICATION IN SECOND LIFE

To date, the metaverse has not been explored as a platform for innovation communication. Current investigations into innovation communication analyze conceptual frameworks (Nordfors, 2006; Zerfaß, 2005b; Zerfaß & Huck, 2007), the interlinking between corporate communication and journalism (Mast et al., 2005; Mast et al., 2006) as well as different communication instruments and formats (Zerfaß & Möslein, 2009). Furthermore, there are some studies which explore the use and potential of 3-D virtual worlds in innovation management. Several papers investigate the virtual product experience and customer participation in designing and manufacturing new products (Chase, 2008; Franz & Wolkinger, 2003; Füller & Matzler, 2007). Studies using the terms "Avatar based Innovation" or "Virtual Co-Creation", meanwhile, analyze the challenges and opportunities of Open Innovation approaches with respect to the online integration of customers (Kohler et al., 2009), amongst are also case studies which describe the use of internet platforms and Web 2.0 in corporate innovation practice (Erler et al. 2009; Helfrich 2009; Roschek 2009; Schläffer

2009). Other investigations focus on marketing aspects of 3-D worlds (Gierke & Müller, 2008; Hemp, 2006) including public relations, advertising (Barnes, 2007; Thomas & Stammermann, 2007) and branding (O'Guinn, Allen, & Semenik, 2008). However, to date, there has not yet been any investigation into which role virtual worlds can play for companies and their communication practices in innovation ecosystems.

Our research shows that several companies already use Second Life in their innovation communication. They use the virtual world during all phases of the innovation process, both for product communication and for corporate communication. The following examples illustrate how, with the help of Second Life, new ideas can be generated, new products developed, tested and marketed and the organizations behind these products portrayed as innovative. At the same time, we will evaluate the extent to which the virtual 3-D world is suitable for innovation communication.

Generation of Ideas and Development of Prototypes

Second Life serves as a development and testing laboratory for new ideas, products and services

(Kohler et al., 2009; Ondrejka, 2007). The reason behind this is obvious: with manageable expenditure in terms of staff and costs, companies can use Second Life to collect ideas, simulate products and present them to the target group. In this way, companies can find out whether the product innovation meets with approval among potential partners, co-producers and customers without any of the costs and risks entailed in a real physical introduction to the market (Bonsu & Darmody, 2008). Second Life also enables products to be developed further in a collaborative process, in line with the "Open Innovation" approach (Chesbrough, 2006). The lifelike, three-dimensional presentation of product developments and the option of being able to test these virtually, generally facilitates mutual understanding. Possible alterations can be taken into account at an early stage of development at a correspondingly low cost. The product designs can subsequently be implemented in real life and sent to selected target groups (lead users) to test their potential in the real world.

Reebok provides a good example of this. The sporting goods manufacturer allows its customers to individually design their shoes – purely virtually – for their avatar and, if they like them, as real one-off designs for themselves (Tedeschi, 2007). The Reebok shoe configurator allows individual components such as the sole, tongue, laces and upper to be designed in a variety of ways (mainly with respect to the color combinations). By making the customer a "Co-Producer" or "Prosumer" (Toffler, 1980), the manufacturer was able to identify trends and requirements at an early stage. The logistics and transport services provider Deutsche Post investigated new design and distribution ideas in Second Life by allowing visitors to create their own works of art on "Post Island", to take photographs and send them as a postcard to anywhere in the world (Jacob, 2008). The QUELLE Innovation Initiative also appeals to its customers' "inner inventor" and in March 2007 launched the first virtual laboratory in the world for inventors and creative individuals, sup-

porting them in the development of their ideas into market-ready products. This "ErfinderLand" provides information on patent procedures and marketing, a partner search facility for ideas and a sculpture garden in which users can evaluate current projects (Quelle InnovationsPartner, 2007b). In addition, inventor congresses and competitions are organized, e.g. expert chats on the subjects of inventing, designing and setting up a company (Quelle InnovationsPartner, 2007a).

The ideas and feedback in the Second Life community are also utilized by American hotel chain Starwood Hotels to develop and beta-test new products. The prototype of its new brand, the boutique hotel "Aloft", was first created by the company in the second world in the fall of 2006. Avatars were able to evaluate sample rooms, assess structural plans and have a say in the fittings, interior design and color palette used (Jana, 2006). Since then, the feedback collected has flowed into the real construction of these new design hotels, which are characterized by loft-style rooms, high ceilings, huge windows and public areas reminiscent of lounges. The first Aloft Hotel was opened in Montreal in June 2008, and the plan is to build a further 500 hotels by 2015 (Seipp, 2008).

Nevertheless, those wishing to generate and test ideas and new developments in Second Life must always be aware of the risk that competitors will quickly be able to copy them, since confidentiality of information is not sufficiently guaranteed in this environment. The highly sensitive nature of novelties and innovations at the pre-market stage means a protected development environment may well be the better choice in some cases.

Product Communication: Marketing New Products

Second Life can also serve to promote fully-developed product innovations on two levels: potential customers can view the products in a three-dimensional form (presentation level) and interact with the products or test them virtually (action level). Adidas, for instance, created a virtual store where the newest models from the current collection could be tested on a training course and purchased for avatars. The sporting goods supplier sold more than 20,000 virtual pairs of shoes, thereby boosting real sales (Hofer, 2007). In 2007, Sony Ericsson set up an interactive replica of its CeBIT trade fair stand on its own island in Second Life, where all product novelties could be examined in detail and avatars were able to request advice from specially-trained Sony Ericsson promoters (Sony Ericsson, 2007, see Figure 3).

Three-dimensional, multimedia realization of this kind allows for a realistic presentation and improved understanding of the form and dimensions of new products. This approach is particularly compatible with complex innovations that require some explanation. This is why energy company EnBW uses Second Life to outline its innovative energy generation systems, including a geothermal power plant. Second Life allows the boundaries of physical reality to be deliberately crossed. Thus, computer manufacturer Dell created a huge computer in Second Life, which was the size of a high-rise building in the virtual world and could be entered and interactively discovered by avatars. The altered dimensions made it pos-

sible to display elements that cannot ordinarily be seen with the naked eye, making them comprehensible and opening up an entirely new perspective (Second Opinion, 2006).

In addition to the true-to-life presentation, the advantage of Second Life is that innovations can be embedded in use scenarios and easily simulated. This not only highlights the product benefits and added value for the target group, but also means that immersion here is far greater than on many other Internet platforms. For example, the latest model launched by a car manufacturer can be experienced in Second Life in a much more direct fashion than in a vehicle configurator on a website. A Second Life visitor would be more likely to say that he/she had "test driven" the new car following a virtual test drive. Through this ostensibly direct handling of the object, the users are given a sense of having directly experienced it. Reservations regarding the product can be reduced or even eliminated entirely, as there is no risk involved in testing the products and they are not exposed to damage or wear and tear. However, despite the technical possibilities available, it is simply not possible to adequately replicate haptic and olfactory experience and real optical and acoustic experience on a 3-D platform. Matthias Schultze, Head of Customer Relationship

Figure 3. Customer advisor and CeBIT 2007 trade fair stand of Sony Ericsson in Second Life. (Sony Ericsson Mobile Communications International AB., 2007. Used with permission)

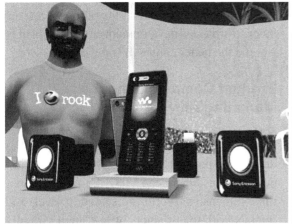 

Management and New Media at EnBW, sums it up as follows: "Second Life is only suitable for presenting new products to a limited degree, since, despite ongoing improvements, the platform is still far too complicated, too unstable and far too time-consuming to use for the majority of the population" (Schultze, 2008). This means there is even greater need to anchor product innovations in the real world. Close links between the virtual and the real world are thus a commonly used approach.

To market product novelties, Deutsche Post delivered packages of samples containing a changing selection of branded items, including products from Nestlé, Wilkinson, Zewa, skincare brand Dove, Burda publishing house, online video rental store Netleih and the mail service company DHL. Anyone who requested a TESTBOX on Post Island in Second Life received a free package of innovations relating to alternating topics such as wellbeing, entertainment or cosmetics with real products to try out at home. "The TESTBOX informs our customers about the latest trends in the various subject areas" says Claudia Schäfer, Head of the Innovative Products Division at Deutsche Post (Deutsche Post World Net, 2007). Well-known manufacturers used this method to publicize product novelties, to test their sales potential and obtain feedback. Users could leave comments on the products on an evaluation page.

Corporate Communication: Image Profiling as an Innovative Player

In addition to the communication of new ideas and products, companies use Second Life first and foremost in the course of their PR work. If a company is active in the area of new, innovative media, it is likely to be perceived by the public as an innovative player. Even the creation of a virtual representation in itself, or the implementation of special 3-D web measures, often garners free media coverage. For many companies, this was the original motivation behind their involvement

in Second Life. "Back then, at the beginning of 2007, the fact that we were here first enabled us to achieve really excellent and broad press communication", remembers Matthias Schultze, "and we were able to link the concepts of energy and innovative energy supply in Second Life with the EnBW brand" (Schultze, 2008).

Thus, with the help of a virtual world, the image of an innovative player can be strengthened twofold: first, by innovative communication via that medium (*how*); and second, by communicating innovations through that medium (*what*). In order to consistently present itself as an innovation leader using this modern form of Internet presence, the energy company regularly runs special promotions. It started with a football strip sponsoring campaign, then a discussion group involving Second Life participants; not long after, the permanent virtual branch office was established: Its purpose and main activities include interactive exhibits, film screenings, recruitment events, lecture series and quiz shows. The EnBW EnergyPark combines innovative communication measures with communication about company energy innovations, which can be explored interactively in the integrated Innovation Center (see Figure 4). The EnergyPark encompasses a) the "EnergyTower", a replica of Europe's largest lightning machine from the phæno Science Center in Wolfsburg, which explains the phenomenon of electrical surges in spectacular style, using a Tesla-Transformator with sparks flying off it; b) the "GeothermieCube", in which visitors can explore the varying heat levels within the earth and find out about the use of geothermal energy as a renewable energy source in the course of a virtual journey to the centre of the earth; and c) the "EnergyGlobe", a globe that simulates the changes occurring around the planet as a result of CO_2 emissions, population growth and climate change. Visitors can also gain an insight into how modern power plants work (CO_2 reduced coal power plant, wave power plant etc.), in "EnyCity" for an energy-efficient city of the future, as well as a large number of tips and trick to help save energy. Information is available in video format in the auditorium. In addition, every month EnBW runs a quiz with new questions on everything to do with energy, where players can win Linden Dollars and increasingly large volumes of traffic are being generated: more than 75,000 visitors have taken part in the quiz since autumn 2007 (EnBW Energie Baden-Württemberg AG, 2009b). The quantitative number of contacts in Second Life, however, remains relatively low. The EnergyPark has around 250 avatars visiting daily, while the EnBW company homepage had approximately 15,000 visitors daily in 2007 (Hildebrand, 2008). Seen in qualitative terms, however, it is assumed that customer contact in virtual worlds is considerably more intensive and, thus, has more long-lasting effects.

Deutsche Post also values Web 3-D as an ideal environment within which to build an innovative market presence. "What was to the fore in our involvement in Second Life was that we are able to communicate regarding our proven products, brands and services in a completely new way, providing new, creative perspectives for communication. We wanted to use this to emphasize our position as an innovative communications service provider", says Björn Jacob, project leader for Second Life in the Market Communica-

tion Division at the group (Jacob, 2008). In May 2007, the company opened its virtual presence – a true-to-life replica of its headquarters in Bonn – and tested new ideas by means of interactive promotions and competitions. At all times efforts were made to connect both worlds, in order to provide added value both online and offline, e.g. with the delivery of test boxes and postcards in the real world. Other promotions included the "Speed Academy Racing Cup", the virtual winter games, the adventure game "on the trail of the mysterious stamp" where players had to prove their skill, endurance and ability to multitask, and the sculpture competition "Summer, Sun, and the Travel Bug", where avatars could create works of art and postcard designs in the Post Tower's atelier. The best designers were rewarded with the prize of virtual land and Linden Dollars. Deutsche Post itself said that these promotions were in great demand among inhabitants of Second Life, yet actual use remained far lower than expected, despite the huge marketing efforts. Only a couple of hundred avatars visited Post Island weekly, with a total of slightly more than 10,000 guests over 9 months. The number of postcards sent was also only in the three-figure range per week. Despite the lack of response, Deutsche Post clearly demonstrated how companies can display

Figure 4. EnBW EnergyTower and EnBW EnergyGlobe in Second Life (EnBW Energie Baden-Württemberg AG, 2009a. Used with permission)

their innovative power and imbue their brand with emotion by becoming involved in Second Life. With the sending of postcards the company provided the first communication service of its kind between the virtual and the real world, delivering "as securely swiftly and dependably as always to anywhere in the world" (Jacob, 2008). By linking traditional, physical deliveries with an interface in a modern virtual 3-D world, Deutsche Post successfully positioned itself as an innovative logistics company company (see Figure 5).

Many other companies use the continually growing offers of Second Life, which are also improving in terms of quality, to present themselves to the interested public as innovative and modern. A number of educational institutes and seminar organizers relocated their teaching events, workshops and courses in the artificial world (Billig, 2009). EnBW is also investigating how Second Life can be used for additional fields of action, e.g. for e-learning, conferences, internal seminars, and team meetings in internal communication as well as for e-recruiting in personnel procurement. The positive public perception and the successful positioning of the energy company as a Second Life expert made a significant contribution to generating the necessary interest in the company, even cross-sector. "If one experiences certain success with a topic, people are more likely to go along with it. Internally, we see this in the fact that areas that do not have any direct links with virtual worlds now are prepared to look into additional forms of use together with us", says Matthias Schultze (Schultze, 2008).

However, new web technologies are not given a fixed place in the communications mix of all players. Following Adidas (summer 2007), Mercedes (spring 2008) and Reuters (winter 2008), Deutsche Post also withdrew from the parallel world in spring 2008: "It became clear to us that we had largely exhausted the possibilities within Second Life", says Björn Jacob justifying this decision (Jacob, 2008). A group representative furthermore explained their withdrawal on the basis of the fact that the company's own offers were not being used frequently enough, the design possibilities of the platform too limited, operation too complicated and the technical requirements in terms of computer systems too high (Hildebrand, 2008). Many organizations entered Second Life with high expectations which were raised by a lot of enthusiastic praises in the media around 2007, but they also withdrew fast when they realized that Second Life needs to be used properly and that this platform is only one interesting channel for digital communication amongst others.

Figure 5. The Post Tower and opening event for the adventure game "on the trail of the mysterious stamp" of Deutsche Post in Second Life. (Deutsche Post AG, 2007. Used with permission)

RECOMMENDATIONS FOR SUCCESSFUL INNOVATION COMMUNICATION IN VIRTUAL WORLDS

Companies use Second Life primarily as an innovative research laboratory: to test out new ideas, to experiment with modern communication methods, to try a new form of marketing presence and thereby position themselves as an innovative company. Some companies, bolstered by the media hype and the fear of missing out on a development, were able only to gain a brief and temporary insight into the opportunities and limits in virtual worlds. Others are still involved today in new projects, testing the innovative and sustainable options within the online world to actively promote their own development. Below, we summarize a number of recommendations as to how a company's own actions and representations in the course of innovation communication can be successfully used to gain new visitors. Strategic planning, implementation and control of such activities is even more important since Second Life, while it is one of the most popular 3-D online platforms, still has not been able to reach a mass audience.

A virtual representation should be every bit as "alive" as real life. A successful presence thus demands a dialog-oriented, personal support, continual maintenance, ongoing further developments and above all an apparent added value – both for the individual visitor and for the virtual world per se. This requires that a company not only knows its target group, but also the field in which that target group is active (Mediaedge:cia, 2005).

Added value can be created e.g. through a personal contact person in the virtual company presence, through permanently available attractions and up-to-date additional services. What is important is that companies not only represent themselves with virtual buildings, but also that they are present with avatars. They should reveal themselves personally to their visitors, enter into active dialog with them and be constantly present.

Virtual advisors provide important persuasive work through their direct customer contact. The virtual service offerings must correspond to that available in the real world. This, however, demands constant support in real life. To facilitate close communication between the company and the visitors, EnBW installed feedback boxes on its island, set up an EnBW-Group, whose members can be informed via Internet mailing lists, and operates an avatar that actively approaches guests, answering questions and providing suggestions. The effort involved in this is much greater than for normal Internet, also to ensure that the presence in Web 3-D is always up to date.

It is also important that visitors are provided with an entertaining, action-based program. Interactive, varied and new promotions all the time are very important to the success of a representation. Being up to date is a vital element. According to EnBW's experiences, comparably short update cycles of approximately 2-3 months are required. However, these promotions do not always have to be groundbreaking. "Recently I came to the conclusion that it is the really simple things that work here", advises Matthias Schultze, "many simple mechanisms will also work on a platform like this" (Schultze, 2008). Providing new highlights regularly appears to be more important. The energy company held a series of talks in 2007 for example: every three weeks there was a presentation on a specific main topic followed by an opportunity for discussion. Figures recorded by Deutsche Post furthermore demonstrate that numbers of visitors can be boosted significantly through interactive promotions (Jacob, 2008). What must be kept in mind in this context is that the offers are tailored to the technical features of the platform. Projects requiring elaborate graphics and staging larger in-world events are possible only to a limited extent with the technology currently available.

CONCLUSION AND FUTURE RESEARCH

The suggestions put forward here present, by means of an example, the potential and the limits to innovation communication in virtual worlds like Second Life. The study does not, however, claim to be comprehensive.

It can be assumed that 3-D online worlds and the opportunities that can be realized therein will develop further. They are still at the beginning of a huge process of development, but they have the potential to develop into the Internet of the future in the course of the next few years. Those who already test and learn to understand these worlds today are at any advantage. Björn Jacob also confirms that, despite its withdrawal from Second Life, Deutsche Post intends "to continue to intensively explore the development of 3-D worlds and, when the time is right, to become involved again" (Jacob, 2008). With increasing bandwidth, growth in Internet usage, improved technology, more straightforward operation, inter-operability between worlds, growing media interest and an entertainment and games industry that is beginning to become established, companies are set to invest more in virtual worlds. There is already huge potential for greater use: by 2011, around 90 percent of German households will have an Internet connection, around 80 percent will have broadband by 2015 (Medienboard Berlin-Brandenburg, 2008).

Despite the fact that the number of traditional media users and gamers is likely to remain considerably larger, it can be assumed that virtual 3-D worlds will establish themselves in future as an important communication and information platform, thereby providing additional opportunities for innovation communication. New visualization technologies will initially result in improved graphics with almost photo-real images. Further developments will show which communications platforms are able to establish themselves on the market and whether interfaces between the various platforms will develop, allowing users to switch with ease from one world to the next. However, virtual worlds are able to meet specific communication demands and to reach specific stakeholders, but their potential should be estimated realistically to avoid possible new disappointments.

It follows that companies will have to continue to familiarize themselves with the forms of communication, presentation and interaction in Web 3-D in good time, in order to be in a position to fully exploit the opportunities that arise in a profitable manner. In doing so, the use of new Web technologies in innovation communication must always be carefully weighed up. Thus, there is a need for ongoing systematic exploration of virtual worlds in media, communications and economic sciences.

REFERENCES

Barnes, S. (2007). Virtual worlds as a medium for advertising. *ACM SIGMIS Database*, *38*(4), 55. doi:10.1145/1314234.1314244

Billig, M. (2009). Das surfende Klassenzimmer. An deutschen Hochschulen finden immer mehr Seminare in virtuellen Welten statt. *Berliner Zeitung*. Retrieved February 2, 2009, from www.berlinonline.de/berliner-zeitung/archiv/.bin/dump.fcgi/2009/0211/wissenschaft/0006/ index.html

Bonsu, S., & Darmody, A. (2008). Co-creating Second Life: Market – consumer cooperation in contemporary economy. *Journal of Macromarketing*, *28*(4), 355. doi:10.1177/0276146708325396

Cavazza, F. (2007). *Virtual universes landscape*. Retrieved December 1, 2009, from http://www.fredcavazza.net/2007/10/04/virtual-universes-landscape/

Chase, S. C. (2008). *Virtual worlds as collaborative environments for design and manufacturing: From idea to product*. Paper presented at the International Workshop on Virtual Manufacturing, Turin, Italy.

Chesbrough, H. W. (2006). *Open innovation. The new imperative for creating and profiting from technology*. Boston, MA: Harvard Business School Press.

Deutsche Post World Net. (2007). *In Second Life bestellen, in First Life ausprobieren. TESTBOX der Deutschen Post liefert aktuelle Markenprodukte frei Haus*. Retrieved November 10, 2009, from www.testbox.de/secondlife

EnBW Energie Baden-Württemberg. (2009a). *Second-Life-Bildmotive zum Herunterladen*. Retrieved December 01, 2009, from http://www. enbw.com/content/de/impulse/enbw_webwelt/ second_life/ download-bilder/index.jsp

EnBW Energie Baden-Württemberg. (2009b). *Verquizt noch mal – das erste Second-Life-Quiz zum Thema 'Energie'*. Retrieved January 10, 2009, from www.enbw.com/content/de/impulse/ enbw_webwelt/second_life/energyquiz

Erler, H., Rieger, M., & Füller, J. (2009). Ideenmanagement und Innovation mit Social Networks – Die Swarovski i-flash Community. In Zerfaß, A., & Möslein, K. M. (Eds.), *Kommunikation als Erfolgsfaktor im Innovationsmanagement* (pp. 391–401). Wiesbaden: Gabler. doi:10.1007/978-3-8349-8242-1_24

Fink, S. (2009). Strategische Kommunikation für Technologie und Innovation – Konzeption und Umsetzung. In Zerfaß, A., & Möslein, K. M. (Eds.), *Kommunikation als Erfolgsfaktor im Innovationsmanagement* (pp. 209–225). Wiesbaden: Gabler. doi:10.1007/978-3-8349-8242-1_11

Fittkau & Maaß. (2007). *Ergebnisse der 24. W3B-Umfrage*. Retrieved August 1, 2008, from http:// www.w3b.org/ergebnisse/w3b24/

Franz, R., & Wolkinger, T. (2003). *Customer integration with virtual communities*. Paper presented at the 36th Hawaii International Conference on System Sciences.

Füller, J., & Matzler, K. (2007). Virtual product experience and customer participation – A chance for customer-centred, really new products. *Technovation, 27*(6-7), 378–387. doi:10.1016/j. technovation.2006.09.005

Gierke, C., & Müller, R. (2008). *Unternehmen in Second Life: Wie Sie virtuelle Welten für Ihr reales Geschäft nutzen können*. Offenbach: GABAL Verlag GmbH.

Helfrich, M. (2009). Community Generated Innovation – Vernetzung von Verbrauchern und Kreativen auf der Ideen-Community Tchibo ideas. In Zerfaß, A., & Möslein, K. M. (Eds.), *Kommunikation als Erfolgsfaktor im Innovationsmanagement* (pp. 367–378). Wiesbaden: Gabler. doi:10.1007/978-3-8349-8242-1_22

Hemp, P. (2006). Avatar-based marketing. *Harvard Business Review, 84*(6), 48–56.

Hildebrand, J. (2008). *Anhaltende Flucht aus der virtuellen Scheinwelt*. Retrieved March 02, 2009, from www.welt.de/wams_print/article1655456/ Anhaltende_Flucht_aus_der_virtuellen_Scheinwelt.html

Hoewner, J., Jansen, M., & Jantke, K. (2008). *Von der Spinnovation zur Sinnovation*. Düsseldorf.

Hofer, M. (2007). *Der geplatzte Traum vom zweiten Leben*. Retrieved March 2, 2009, from http://www. sueddeutsche.de/computer/939/320809/text/

Huck-Sandhu, S. (2009). Innovationskommunikation in den Arenen der Medien – Campaining, Framing, Storytelling. In Zerfaß, A., & Möslein, K. M. (Eds.), *Kommunikation als Erfolgsfaktor im Innovationsmanagement* (pp. 195–208). Wiesbaden: Gabler. doi:10.1007/978-3-8349-8242-1_10

Huizinga, J. (1939). *Homo Ludens. Vom Ursprung der Kultur im Spiel* (*Vol. 19*). Reinbek: Rowohlt.

Jacob, B. (2008). *Deutsche post world net, department market communication, project leader Second Life*. Written Interview, April 2, 2008.

Jana, R. (2006). *Starwood Hotels explore Second Life first*. Retrieved March 2, 2009, from www.businessweek.com/innovate/content/aug2006/id20060823_925270.htm

Kohler, T., Matzler, K., & Füller, J. (2009). Avatar-based innovation: Using virtual worlds for real-world innovation. *Technovation, 29*(6-7), 395–407. doi:10.1016/j.technovation.2008.11.004

Linden Lab. (2010a). *Economic statistics (Raw data files), logged_in_users.xls*. Retrieved February 6, 2010, from http://secondlife.com/statistics/economy-data.php

Linden Lab. (2010b). *Linden Lab Offiziell: Zusatz-Benutzerkonto FAQ*. Retrieved May 1, 2010, from http://wiki.secondlife.com/wiki/Zusatz-Benutzerkonto_FAQ_%28KB%29

Linden Research. (2008). *Second Life pricing list*. Retrieved December 8, 2008, from http://static-secondlife-com.s3.amazonaws.com/corporate/Second_Life_Pricing_List_20081208.pdf

Linden Research. (2010). *LindeX™ market data*. Retrieved May 5, 2010, from http://secondlife.com/statistics/economy-market.php

Lundvall, B.-A. (1985). *Product innovation and user-producer interaction*. Aalborg, Denmark: Aalborg University Press.

Mast, C., Huck, S., & Zerfaß, A. (2005). Innovation communication outline of the concept and empirical findings from Germany innovation. *Innovation Journalism, 2*(7). Retrieved May 20, 2009, http://www.innovationjournalism.org/archive/INJO-2-7.pdf

Mast, C., Huck, S., & Zerfaß, A. (2006). *Innovationskommunikation in dynamischen Märkten. Empirische Ergebnisse und Fallstudien*. Berlin, Münster: LIT.

Mast, C., & Zerfaß, A. (2005). *Neue Ideen erfolgreich durchsetzen. Das Handbuch der Innovationskommunikation. Frankfurt a. M.* FAZ Frankfurter Allgemeine Buch.

Mediaedge:CIA. (2005). *Playing with brands*. Retrieved February 18, 2008, from http://www.mecglobal.com/output/Page1463.asp

Medienboard Berlin-Brandenburg. (2008). *Games – Informationen zum Medienstandort Berlin-Brandenburg*. Retrieved August 18, 2008, from http://www.deutsche-gamestage.de/WebObjects/Medienboard.woa/media/9064

Mohr, J., Sengupta, S., & Slater, S. (2009). *Marketing of high-technology products and innovations* (3rd ed.). Upper Saddle River, NJ: Prentice Hall.

Nordfors, D. (2004). The role of journalism in innovation systems. *Innovation Journalism, 1*(7). Retrieved August 18, 2008, from www.innovationjournalism.org/archive/INJO-1-7.pdf

Nordfors, D. (2006). PR and the innovation communication system. *Innovation Journalism, 3*(5), Retrieved August 18, 2008, from www.innovationjournalism.org/archive/INJO-3-5.pdf

O'Guinn, T., Allen, C., & Semenik, R. (2008). *Advertising and integrated brand promotion*. Cincinnati, OH: South Western College Pub.

Ondrejka, C. (2007). Collapsing geography (Second Life, innovation, and the future of national power). *Innovations: Technology, Governance, Globalization, 2*(3), 27–54. doi:10.1162/itgg.2007.2.3.27

Quelle InnovationsPartner. (2007a). *Experten-Chat im Quelle ErfinderLand*. Retrieved March 1, 2009, from http://www.quelle-innovationsinitiative.de/aktuell_detail.php?id=18&count=6&image=18/image18.jpg&nav1=aktuell

Quelle InnovationsPartner. (2007b). *Quelle InnovationsInitiative öffnet ErfinderLand in Second Life*. Retrieved March 1, 2009, from http://www.quelle-innovationsinitiative.de/aktuell_detail.php? id=15&count=6&image=15/ image15.jpg&nav1=aktuell

Roschek, J. (2009). Web 2.0 als Innovationsplattform – Wie multimediale Kollaboration bei Cisco interne und externe Innovationspotenziale mobilisiert. In Zerfaß, A., & Möslein, K. M. (Eds.), *Kommunikation als Erfolgsfaktor im Innovationsmanagement* (pp. 379–389). Wiesbaden: Gabler. doi:10.1007/978-3-8349-8242-1_23

Schläffer, C. (2009). Interne Innovations-Communities mit Bewegtbild-Formaten – Generierung von Innovationsideen bei der Deutschen Telekom und T-Mobile. In Zerfaß, A., & Möslein, K. M. (Eds.), *Kommunikation als Erfolgsfaktor im Innovationsmanagement* (pp. 403–413). Wiesbaden: Gabler.

Schultze, M. (2008). *EnBW, Director CRM und New Media*. Telephone Interview, April 25, 2008.

Second Opinion. (2006). *Infinite vision media. Expressing brands in 3D*. Retrieved March 2, 2009, from http://secondlife.com/newsletter/2006_12/html/developer.html

Seipp, B. (2008). *Den neuen Hotelmarken in die Betten geguckt*. Retrieved March 1, 2009, from www.welt.de/reise/article2573514/Den-neuen-Hotelmarken-in-die-Betten-geguckt.html

Sony Ericsson. (2007). *Sony Ericsson builds at Second Life*. Retrieved March 13, 2007, from http://www.sonyericsson-secondlife.com/downloads/Pressemitteilung_Second%20Life_CeBIT_English.pdf, press release

Tedeschi, B. (2007, June 11). Awaiting real sales from virtual shoppers, e-commerce report. *The New York Times*. Retrieved February 28, 2009, from www.nytimes.com/2007/06/11/business/11ecom.html

Thomas, W., & Stammermann, L. (2007). Der Markt für In-Game Advertising. In W. Thomas & L. Stammermann (Eds.), *In-Game Advertising – Werbung in Computerspielen* (pp. 11-25). Wiesbaden: Gabler.

Toffler, A. (1980). *The third wave (Vol. 1)*. New York, NY: Morrow.

Toumi, I. (2002). *Networks of innovation*. Oxford, UK: University Press.

Trommsdorff, V., & Steinhoff, F. (2007). *Innovationsmarketing*. München: Vahlen.

Wagner, C. (2008). Learning experience with virtual worlds. *Journal of Information Systems Education, 19*(3), 4.

Wilkens, A. (2006). *IBM weitet Aktivitäten auf „Second Life" aus*. heise.de. Retrieved January 3, 2009, from http://www.heise.de/newsticker/IBM-weitet-Aktivitaeten-auf-Second-Life-aus--/meldung/82490

Zerfaß, A. (2005a). Innovation readiness. A framework for enhancing corporations and regions by innovation communication. *Innovation Journalism, 2*(8), 1–27.

Zerfaß, A. (2005b). Innovationsmanagement und Innovationskommunikation. Erfolgsfaktor für Unternehmen und Region. In C. Mast & A. Zerfaß (Eds.), *Neue Ideen erfolgreich durchsetzen. Das Handbuch der Innovationskommunikation* (pp. 16-42). Frankfurt a. M.: Frankfurter Allgemeine Buch.

Zerfaß, A. (2009). Kommunikation als konstitutives Element im Innovationsmanagement – Soziologische und kommunikationswissenschaftliche Grundlagen der Open Innovation. In Zerfaß, A., & Möslein, K. M. (Eds.), *Kommunikation als Erfolgsfaktor im Innovationsmanagement. Strategien im Zeitalter der Open Innovation* (pp. 23–56). Wiesbaden: Gabler. doi:10.1007/978-3-8349-8242-1

Zerfaß, A., & Huck, S. (2007). Innovationskommunikation: Neue Produkte, Technologien und Ideen erfolgreich positionieren. In Piwinger, M., & Zerfaß, A. (Eds.), *Handbuch Unternehmenskommunikation* (pp. 847–858). Wiesbaden: Gabler.

Zerfaß, A., & Möslein, K. (2009). *Kommunikation als Erfolgsfaktor im Innovationsmanagement: Strategien im Zeitalter der Open Innovation*. Wiesbaden: Gabler. doi:10.1007/978-3-8349-8242-1

Zerfaß, A., Sandhu, S., & Huck, S. (2004). Innovationskommunikation. Strategisches Handlungsfeld für Corporate Communications. In Bentele, G., Piwinger, M., & Schönborg, G. (Eds.), *Kommunikationsmanagement*. Loseblattwerk.

Zerfaß, A., Swaran, S., & Huck, S. (2004). Kommunikation von Innovationen. Neue Ideen und Produkte erfolgreich positionieren. *Kommunikationsmanager*, *1*(2), 56–58.

KEY TERMS AND DEFINITIONS

Communication Platform: Describes a sphere of communication that is relatively freely accessible to all individuals and organizations and in which the participating players can communicate, interact and exchange ideas with one another about various topics and opinions. These spheres may be constituted by different communication mediums and interaction forms including physical and virtual means, e.g. by face-to-face talks, events, online-mediated forms (blogs, virtual worlds, online-communities), mass-medial forms (radio, television, newspapers) and others.

Innovation: Describes all technical, economic and social novelties that successfully establish themselves on the market or within an organization, are acknowledged as being new and encompass a change in social practices. This can apply to new products, services, technologies, processes, structures, business models etc. The word "innovation" literally means "novelty" or "renewal" and is derived from the Latin "novus" meaning "new" and "innovatio" meaning "a new creation".

Innovation Communication: Describes all systematic communication activities – carried out by organizations with their internal and external stakeholders – which have the objective of fostering new products, services, technologies, processes, ideas, and concepts. This includes strategic activities in all stages of an innovation process, such as communicating the novelty itself, supporting its further development, influencing its socially shared meaning pattern, creating an understanding and trust in it, and positioning the organization behind it as an innovator. Innovation communication is a field of activity in corporate communication.

Innovation Management: Describes the systematic planning, steering and controlling of innovations in organizations. The process includes several steps, amongst them (1) the search for and generation of new ideas and concepts and the evaluation thereof, (2) the development of new ideas and concepts into new products and services, and (3) the implementation and diffusion of these new products and services into the market.

New Product Communication / Market Entry Communication of Innovation: Describes the communicative introduction of the innovation to the market. The objective is to have a positive effect on the diffusion and adaption of the novelty among the target groups, thereby helping it to become successful.

Virtual Innovation Communication: Related to all innovation communication activities, which take place in computer-generated environments respectively the Internet. This can take place in all interactive mediums, such as e.g. in virtual 3-D worlds (Second Life, World of Warcraft etc.), blogs, forums and social networks.

Chapter 6
What's Real?
Presence, Personality and Identity in the Real and Online Virtual World

Benjamin Gregor Aas
University of Amsterdam, The Netherlands

ABSTRACT

To understand virtual realities and the effect on its users, empirical research into a variety of social and psychological domains has to be conducted in online virtual environments. It is argued that presence, the experience of being-in-the-virtual-world, plays a key role in most psychological processes connected with virtual worlds. A short overview of studies addressing personality, identity, emotions, and stereotypes in virtual reality is given, to subsequently offer improved approaches, by using a setup that compares participants on an individual level. Furthermore, potential cohort-differences are discussed; there is reason to believe that people who have grown up with computers, Internet, and virtual worlds experience and use virtual worlds differently than those who haven't. Finally, it is hypothesized that virtual worlds influence real life in a reciprocal loop, by shaping cognitive, psychological, and social processes of the real world and – seemingly paradoxical – might even trigger experiencing the real as real.

INTRODUCTION

A lot has been written about (online) virtual realities: their economic potential, their communicative potential, their social potential, their therapeutic potential and their psychological and cognitive potential (and risk). On one hand, so called 'immersionists' believe that virtual realities function as an entirely new world with their own features of social, economic and psychological aspects that are to some extend different from the real material world, potentially following their own specific processes - I will denote the real material world as 'real world' and online virtual worlds as 'virtual worlds' throughout this chapter (Wadley, 2008; Turkle, 1995; Boellstorff, 2008). On the

DOI: 10.4018/978-1-60960-854-5.ch006

other hand, there are the 'augmentationists'. They understand virtual worlds as an extension of the real life, to which the aspect of virtuality is merely added and argue that processes of social, economic and psychological nature in virtual worlds function the same way as in real life. They "expect people to behave in the same way in the virtual environment as they would in an equivalent real-world situation" (Friedman, Steed & Slater, 2007b, p. 252). To put it short, both sides agree that there are some commonalities and some differences between the real and the virtual world, starting off from the two extremes of a continuum.

This differentiation appears somewhat blurry, for it does not add clarification, nor does it make specific predictions about what is going on when people enter the virtual world. A basic demand one must have towards a concept or theory is not fulfilled, namely that no strong conclusions can be drawn from such a distinction. When it comes to very basic aspects of personality, identity or mood, substantial knowledge about potentially existing differences between real life and virtual life, is missing.

Central to a proper understanding of virtual realities is the proper understanding of the real world. One method that is widely used to achieve this understanding is the empirical scientific method, which can be applied to virtual worlds as well as to real life questions. This book chapter will therefore try to give a short compilation of theories that are most basic to the understanding of human behavior in the virtual world. In a first step, the very basic concept of presence, which underlies all other experiences within virtual lifes, will be discussed (How real is the virtual? Do people experience presence in virtual environments?). The focus will then be shifted on the psychology of virtual worlds, especially personality, identity and emotion aspects of virtual worlds (second step). Thirdly, an attempt will be made to predict how virtuality influences real life in a reciprocal loop, performing the step back from the virtual life into the real life. This, it is analyzed, might be essential to understand how the virtual and the real merge into one. Where possible, short sketches for improvements of research in virtual worlds will be given.

BACKGROUND

At the University of Amsterdam and many other places, there is ongoing research concerning the possibility to use virtual platforms for psychological therapeutic interventions (Meyerbröker & Emmelkamp, 2010). To give such research and practical implementation a sound basis, it is inevitable to understand underlying processes and yield a sound conceptualization of what is going on, when humans go virtual.

PRESENCE, PERSONALITY AND IDENTITY IN THE REAL AND ONLINE VIRTUAL WORLD

Presence in Virtual Reality

The concept of presence can mainly be traced back to 20th century philosophy. 'Being-in-the-world' (in-der-Welt-sein) and 'being' (Dasein) add a basic structure of emotional authenticity to the more interpretation- and thought-focused philosophical approaches and trends of that time (Heidegger, 1927; 2006). "The 'production of presence' points to all kinds of events and processes in which the impact that 'present' objects have on human bodies is being initiated or intensified" (Gumbrecht, 2004, p. xiii). This is a more modern version of how everything surrounding us not only conveys meaning, but also always contains an emotional (read 'presence-like') component. In virtual worlds, 'being-in-the-world' receives a new notion, raising the question to what extent a mere digital and data-driven environment can create such a feeling of presence.

Riva, Waterworth and Waterworth (2004) follow Damasio's approach of subdividing the self into a proto-, core- and extended-self. They apply this distinction to the concept of presence, resulting, firstly, in a proto presence, which can be described as the experience of 'being' an embodied person (self vs. non self). Secondly, a core presence can be discriminated, which is the coherent, perceptual 'being-in-the-world', the stream of outside reality we experience (self vs. present external world). Thirdly, these entities interact in an extended presence, the reflective, significance creating 'being-a-person' (self relative to present external world). It is hypothesized that the overall "experienced presence is mediated by the integration of these three layers of presence […] and the extent to which conscious attention is focused on one layer" (Waterworth, Waterworth, Mantovani & Riva, 2010, p. 8). From these authors' point of view, the sketched approach can be applied to real world experiences as well as to virtual world experiences. An experienced gamer might describe a situation in a 3-D game, where he is totally sucked into the world and in 'the flow' of the virtual reality. As a result, even though the eliciting stimuli are merely virtual, he might experience coherent real life bodily sensations. When playing a couple of hours and accidentally falling from a virtual skyscraper – even in a non-immersive 3-D game – it can occur that the gamer senses his intestines cramp together. This person, one might argue, has exported the three layers of presence into the virtual world (the embodied proto presence might be influencing his 'guts') and his attention is focused on virtual stimuli (the experience of 'flow'). In other words, in the same way the integration of the three presence layers in real life can be distinguished and informs about the experienced presence, the virtual presence can be subdivided into the same three levels and follow the same processes. From this conceptualization one can predict how real a virtual world will appear to a user. The sense of presence can be described as the function of how well the online world user identifies with his avatar (proto-level), how well the virtual world yields coherent and convincing stimuli (core-level) and how smooth, immediate, continuous and detailed interaction between avatar and 3D-world is (extended-level).

An attempt to translate such conceptual considerations into the practical realm of a questionnaire is undertaken by the *Igroup Presence Questionnaire* (IPQ; Schubert, Friedmann & Regenbrecht, 1999; 2001). Using linear equation modeling, these authors find that a certain sense of being in the virtual environment or presence is best reflected by three distinct factors, namely 'spatial presence' (feeling present in the virtual world), 'realness' (consistency between virtual and real world) and 'involvement' (being concentrated on the virtual world). As described by Riva et al. (2004), 'spatial presence' and 'realness' are found back in the above mentioned integration of presence layers, and 'involvement' is related to focused conscious attention.

Empirical research on presence focuses mostly on how presence mediates virtual world experiences (Do participants feel present in the virtual?) and very rarely on presence in the real world. As described before, even in everyday life, people supposedly experience different grades of presence. Some studies use presence questionnaires as a control mechanism when running experiments in virtual worlds or hypothesize about the mediating influence of presence on behavioral outcome measures (e.g. Jin, 2009). Surprisingly, no empirical research has been conducted yet, whereby similar situations in real and virtual life are tested and compared in terms of presence. Such a simple comparison could clarify whether, and if so, in what respect, presence differs in the real and the virtual.

To have knowledge about the role of presence is not only important per se, but also to draw the right conclusions when comparing the real and virtual worlds in terms of personality, identity and emotion - the psychology of the virtual.

Psychology of Virtual Reality

Whereas presence is a relatively young concept, emotion, identity and especially personality have infiltrated scientific and everyday life very deeply. A first conceptualization of personality and personality differences draws back to ancient Greek ideas of body fluids, introduced by Hippocrates, that were supposed to influence temperament. Today, there are numerous theories and studies circling around the very broad topic of personality; psychotherapists even use a whole cluster of personality disorders to understand peoples' misbehavior and inability to adapt to their social environment. The historic idea of body fluids does not attract too much attention anymore; it is, nevertheless, still one of the big debates in psychology, whether the personality of a person is mostly 'hard-wired' in its genetic code or a consequence of its social environment throughout life and learned. Most researchers and therapists would probably subscribe to the idea that personality is a product of both, but would still find themselves troubled when asked about the flexibility and alterability of personality over time. In the field of psychotherapy, a clear answer to this question is necessary, to know how to treat patients with a personality pathology; when it comes to virtual worlds, the consequences are less dramatic, but it remains astonishing that some online virtual world users keep reporting to experience their avatars as distinct from themselves and even ascribe them an own, virtual personality. Most definitions see personality as a stable and unchangeable concept of the sum of the attributes of a person (Mischel, 1999); so it seems tautological to expect an incoherent personality between the real and the virtual world.

In a recently published study, 34 participants filled in a personality questionnaire twice, once in a pen and paper version and once with their personalized avatar in the online virtual reality of Second Life on a virtual testing screen (Aas, Meyerbröker & Emmelkamp, 2010). Strikingly,

as can be seen in Figure 1, no significant differences between the real life version and the virtual version for any personality trait are found, even though there was a half year delay between the two tests. From this result, the authors conclude that when it comes to extraversion, friendliness, conscientiousness, neuroticism and development, the virtual personality does not differ from the real personality or, in other words, that there is no such thing as a distinct virtual personality.

Even though this study yields interesting results, it still has some drawbacks. There should be, as a first point, larger samples; virtual realities offer a great opportunity to easily gather data from a highly diverse sample. Therefore, this study is currently being conducted on a bigger scale via internet and Second Life, but it is too early to make statements about results.

Second, one could argue that the setup of the study is only of correlational nature. In a true experiment, participants are supposed to be manipulated in a certain way to make statements about their expected behavior and test clear hypotheses. Using the experimental approach, one could manipulate e.g. specific emotions using computer- and text based paradigms which have subsequent effect on negotiation behavior (Kleef, De Dreu, & Manstead, 2004). Eventual differences in outcome behavior between the real life and virtual life situations might then be ascribed to a lack of presence or differences between the virtual and real personality. If there was something like a virtual personality that differs from the real world, the manipulation of specific emotions might process in different ways or remain domain specific.

Third, one might possibly use the concept of identity. Theories surrounding this concept allow persons to carry a whole variety of identities, as e.g. experiencing different identities in certain social situations. It seems plausible that one acts differently at work, at home or on the basketball court. Different social situations demand different sets of behavior. There might be something like a core identity, but identity theory inhers a greater

Figure 1. Means of the real life and virtual Second Life version of 5 personality traits (with standard error bars; adapted from Aas et al. 2010)

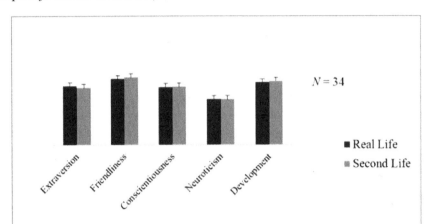

flexibility as a concept within persons (Tajfel & Turner, 1984). It is, however, difficult to find good measures of identity in real life, let alone for virtual environments. One possibility could be to look at stereotypes of people and their influence on identity perception. It is known that activation of certain ethnic and social identities results in a simultaneous activation of stereotypes, or in other words, stereotypical thinking often is a significant part of an identity, that can directly influence behavior (Bargh, Chen & Barrows, 1996). Can this process be found in virtual life as well? Which cues do users of virtual worlds – implicitly – take into account when drawing conclusions about the person behind an avatar? One hypothesis could be that within the virtual, people rely less on variables that can be manipulated, e.g. skin color, gender or age. The virtual world simply yields less and – by nature – more mediated information than real life. This might be the reason why the step from text-based chat to voice-based chat in virtual worlds is experienced as a big one. In real life, it is the body appearance that gives first and deep cues. In virtual worlds, one can choose which 'channels' to open and it is mostly voice that is the first real life channel that is used in virtual surroundings. Since those first cues potentially

trigger stereotypical thinking, there are simply fewer cues available to draw conclusions from in virtual worlds; this might in turn be experienced by the user as being more open towards anyone around. Own openness and expectation of others' openness might set communication into a positive direction from the very beginning. Such reasoning can be cast into an experimental setup. It has been found that, within an immersive virtual reality, stereotypical behavior existed in a similar way as it is found in real life situations (Dotsch & Wigboldus, 2008). In this study, participants approach a Dutch or Moroccan avatar waiting at a virtual bus stop. Results show that, when asked to read numbers on the chest and back of an avatar, people tend to have less eye-contact, keep a bigger distance from the northern African type than the Caucasian avatar and show a higher skin conductance rate in this situation, pointing towards higher stress levels. Similarly, it has been found that characters of the same gender maintain a bigger distance from each other in virtual worlds (Yee, Bailenson, Urbanek, Chang, & Merget, 2007), sales techniques like the foot-in-the-door and door-in-the-face approach also function in virtual worlds (Eastwick & Gardner, 2009) and the conformity in individual attitudes on sex is mediated by the cohesion of the virtual group one is in (Friedman et al., 2007b).

Unfortunately, in this respect exemplary for most studies, these studies only test participants within the virtual world and do not compare them (individually) with real life data. Rightly, the authors conclude that stereotypes do exist in virtual life as they do in real life, but it would be even more insightful, if for the same participant the same cues were found to function in different worlds in a similar procedural way. It might be that differences exist, for the subset of virtual online world users who perceive their avatars as distinct from themselves.

In a next step, it is important that studies conducted in immersive online virtual worlds are repeated for non-immersive virtual environments, and in frequently used online platforms. Furthermore, presence, gender and questions evolving around identity could be taken into account. With such an approach, it would be possible to draw firm conclusions on identity (-shifts) in virtual and real life.

Cohort-Effect of Experiencing Virtual Worlds

A dad tells his daughter about the good old times, when everything was fine, the people friendly, the summers hot and the world just more relaxed without computers and all that. The girl responds: 'But if you had no computers, how did you access internet?'

Another related topic that lacks profound research is the question whether and how people that grow up with modern technical devices, computer usage and virtual worlds differ from people who did not, in terms of the above raised questions of presence, personality, identity et cetera. There is a good chance that people of 30 years and older – in fact those who are in good research positions – have a different perception of virtual worlds. Just as I was watching my parents struggle to deal

with emails, the generation of children growing up now will look at their parents the same way when these try to communicate and navigate in online virtual worlds of twenty years from now. When it comes e.g. to presence in virtual reality, the mere fact of not being used to handle those worlds, might be an obstacle that 'pushes' one out of the immersive experience. For someone used to it with peers doing the same, there might be no hesitation at all. Again, this possibility could be researched in a straightforward manner by applying the setup of almost any of the above introduced studies and running the experiments twice in real life and virtual worlds to compare data afterwards. Such research might also inform about, how to enhance the accessibility of online worlds for anyone how is new to virtual worlds.

From evolutionary psychology it is known that learning a second language is best and easiest achieved between the ages of two to five, the critical period (Snow & Hoefnagel-Höhle, 1978). In fact, it makes it easier to learn a third language later in life as well. Accordingly, there might be a process underlying the usage of virtual worlds that is best learned early in life as well, so that intuitive handling of virtual worlds could have a critical period as well. On the other hand, it might be just a matter of time spent in the virtual world and learning. It is certainly not impossible for older people to acquire good capabilities to lead a 'second life'; however, having contact with computers and virtual realities early in life might enhance how to navigate and communicate digitally and therefore let emerge subsequent experiences of (naturalistic) immersion. In contrast, common usage of virtual worlds might also lead to a less naturalistic and more realistic – read 'virtualistic' – usage of the virtual worlds. One could raise the question, why we still feel the urge to let our avatar sit down on virtual chairs to feel comfortable (Yee, Ellis & Ducheneaut, 2009). Even though we know that it is just an avatar, people behind the screen still respond by moving towards somebody, when the other avatar does so as well, but at the same time, they experience their personal space intruded if an avatar stands too close (Friedman et al., 2007b). These kind of real-world-virtual-world coherencies might disappear in people that grew up with the virtual world. For them, using the PC and virtual environments as a mere tool might be more pronounced than in older people.

Reciprocal Influence From the Virtual Onto the Real World

Reasoning up to this point was performed in the direction of the real life to the virtual life. Concepts and processes from real life are for some part found in the virtual worlds, but apparently differences exist as well. The question remains, how the real life is influenced by the virtual. By that, I do not only mean how our lives are changed in terms of communication possibilities and large scale networking, but also the question whether distinctive virtual features have influence on how we perceive and behave in real life. This reverse process has reached wide acceptance in art, where content or graphics take more and more online forms in real life as well; this is true for language as well, where computers and internet yield fertile (metaphorical) concepts for non-technical entities (thinking e.g. of the brain as a computer with working memory, hard ware and software).

The internet makes communication and gathering information easy and very accessible. Educational institutions react on this evolution by placing the focus of their didactic curricula not only on knowledge, but also the act of acquiring and selecting knowledge. The reasoning is that if the pool of almost all knowledge is just a mouse click – or screen touch – away, it is more useful to be able to know where to look and to decide quickly which sources to trust and which not, than to merely accumulate factual knowledge. This factual 'what' is then outsourced into the online internet cloud. Selection of information and remembering already acquired knowledge however demand different cognitive resources.

People who grow up in a modern information- and communication society might automatically adapt to these cognitive demands and, as a consequence, perceive not only computer based environments like the internet in a new way, but also the real world around them. In fact, the two environments of the real world and the technical might grow closer together and indivisibly merge into one – in terms of devices to access online worlds and the necessary cognitive resources.

This process is likely to occur not only for internet, but also for virtual worlds. As already picked up briefly above, virtual worlds not only add a new experience to everyday life, but the way these worlds are built, the way they function and the benefits they bring, will influence human cognitions and psyche in a reciprocal turn (Sanchez-Vives & Slater, 2005). It is found that participants given a taller avatar in Second Life have more aggressive negotiation behavior in real life afterwards, as compared to smaller avatars (Yee & Bailenson, 2007). This short-term effect might foster itself in people that go online on an everyday basis. In fact, this is the basic rationale behind (research on) virtual therapy: Virtual realities trigger a certain fear response of e.g. height, spiders or social situations, to subsequently allow the patients to apply therapeutic psychological interventions like gradual desensitization, recognition of the irrationality of the fear response, application of relaxation techniques and social skills training. Somebody who is for example afraid of meeting people in public or speaking to strangers, might experience communication via virtual platforms as less intriguing and harmful, always having the possibility to leave an undesired situation with a single mouse click. Step by step, the virtually experienced positive situations and practiced skills might translate into real life.

Besides such therapeutic and desired effects, there might also be some more subtle ones. In a virtual reality, one has control over the appearance and communication channels at use. The virtual mask of the avatar might enhance the openness in conversations. Even though there is less direct contact, behind an avatar, people prone to show themselves in too positive light in real life, might be capable of showing more of their true self in a virtual environment and lose the fear of committing failures. The controllability of communicative situations might however, in an unfavorable process, impair peoples' capability to make contact in real life. Somebody neurotic in real life might even get more neurotic when only communicating in virtual rooms. To put it short, the 'nerd' might become even more nerdy; people with good social capacities might even increase their skills and benefit from virtual realities.

To wrap the main part of this chapter up, it is interesting to finally look at the reciprocal effect of virtual realities on the concept of presence, as introduced in the first part. As stated there, the intensity of feeling present in a virtual world is thought to be a key factor in understanding the relation between virtual and real world. Furthermore, authors like Gumbrecht (2004) try to implement the concept of presence in the humanities, interestingly without touching the topic of virtuality. The growing use of internet and virtual worlds, the technization and digitalization of communication and information creates a 'second world' in which the actor is no longer embodied and an absence of certain senses is the consequence, especially olfaction, gustation, touch and to some extent audition. In other words, a primacy of vision is the consequence of the digital revolution. The fact that people spend more and more time in such un-embodied virtual worlds, makes it almost inevitable that they experience the virtual world – at least unconsciously – as real. Simultaneously, the virtualization of everyday life and the experience of sensual absence will also rebound in stating questions about presence in real life. In short: Setting a virtual world next to the real world makes it easier and more prominent to ask questions about the realness of the real world. This 'experiencing the real as the real' is closely connected to Heidegger's 'being-in-the-world',

which in reaction might conceptualize itself in the idea/concept of presence automatically. Doing so, virtual worlds not only add a dimension to everyday life as a new place to go, but might also give rise to a stronger need to reflect on one's existence and – paradoxically – experience the real as real.

CONCLUSION AND FUTURE RESEARCH DIRECTIONS

This chapter presents ideas and research on how people behave in and experience virtual realities. A key feature of virtual worlds appears to be how present someone feels when entering such a world. It is argued that people experience the virtual as part of their real life (augmentation) or as an own separate world (immersion), but that the intensity of presence is a key factor for understanding whether social, cognitive and psychological processes function the same way in both environments.

In a second step, the psychology of virtual worlds is then introduced, presenting research which shows that real life personality, real life emotions and real life identity/stereotypes do exist in virtual worlds in a similar way. It is pointed out that there is, however, a lack of empirical research that experimentally compares these processes between the worlds. Despite evidence that some psychological processes cohere between the virtual and the real world on a global level, it remains unclear, whether this argumentation holds true for individuals as well. It is possible that people who experience strong presence in virtual worlds and perceive their avatar as distinct from themselves, display a non-corresponding virtual personality, identity or stereotypes.

In a next step, it is argued that there might not only be differences in virtual experiences in terms of presence, but also related to age. It is plausible that there exists a cohort effect in a way that adolescents who grow up with computers and virtual worlds from an early age onwards, have a more direct and natural usage of digital environments.

Finally, it is being discussed, in what respect virtual worlds influence the real world in a reciprocal loop. Distinctive features of digital environments as e.g. dis-embodiment of communication, control over appearance and general settings or absence of sensual stimuli leading to a primacy of vision will shape the perception, experience and communication in real life as well.

It is not only important and interesting to understand virtual worlds and effects between the real and the virtual per se, but it is also inevitable to have this profound knowledge to use virtual worlds as online research and sales platforms. To mention just some benefits of online research, more information can be accumulated from a worldwide sample, only restricted by computer- and internet-access. Seen that most psychological research is conducted by first year undergraduate students, the (virtual) internet sample is not only bigger and easier to access, but also has a higher degree of diversity. Some cross-cultural aspects are for example automatically ruled out, when an experiment is conducted 24/7 in an internet based online 'worldwide' world. Furthermore, the costs can be dramatically reduced; not only because no more laboratories are needed, but also because a high degree of automatization can be achieved. Virtual robot avatars could undertake assignments to execute experiments (Friedman et al., 2007a). This is not only cheap, but also makes experimenter effects completely controllable, traceable and manipulable. In fact, this manipulability is one of the most interesting features of virtual worlds from an experimental psychologist's point of view. One can not only change – and track – real life coherent variables in virtual life, but also a whole variety of variables that are fixed or not existing in real life. Think of having two bodies/avatars to control at the same time; what happens to heartbeat when an avatar is falling from a skyscraper or dying; what is the consequence of an avatar that suddenly starts to move by himself and the user loses control? These questions can be addressed in virtual settings very easily and set the stage for a new entry into research on the mind. Replicating the idea of the rubber hand illusion, it is possible to experience a virtual arm as part of one's own body (Slater, Perez-Marcos, Ehrsson & Sanchez-Vives, 2008). In this experiment, participants have their real arm tapped, but have synchronous visual input of a virtual arm, projected towards their body, being tapped, too. After some minutes, they report experiencing the visual arm as real. This experience can even be taken further to encompass whole out-of-body experiences; when participants see themselves depicted as avatars from behind as they are stroked in a virtual world and have the coherent real body sensations, they begin to locate their true body position in the avatar rather than in their real body (Lenggenhager, Tadi, Metzinger & Blanke, 2007). Such an out-of-body experience can hardly be induced in a real life setting, so if one wants to continue in this line of research, it is necessary to accumulate knowledge on the effects and processes of virtual worlds thoroughly. This is also necessary, because new technologies will contribute to closing the gap between the real and the virtual world. On the one hand, as the success of the Nintendo-Wii game console shows, the virtual will be more and more embodied, closing the gap from the virtual side. The game, and by that the virtual world, is brought deeper into real life. On the other hand, the gap will be closed more and more from the real life side as well. It has been shown that brainwaves can be recorded by an EEG in a way that it is possible to control mouse cursors and by that navigate avatars in virtual worlds. Such a tool allows a person to let his avatar do what he wants by thinking alone and this will most certainly have beneficial influence on the experienced presence in virtual worlds.

This point appears even more crucial, when following modern neuroscientists and anthropologists that take even a step further, stating that all self-consciousness and culture is in the end just a virtual projection of reality in us humans (Metzinger, 2003; Boellstorff, 2008).

REFERENCES

Aas, B. G., Meyerbröker, K., & Emmelkamp, P. M. G. (2010). Who am I - and if so, where? A study on personality in virtual realities. *Journal of Virtual Worlds Research, 2*, 5.

Boellstorff, T. (2008). *Coming of age in Second Life: An anthropologist explores the virtually human.* Princeton, NJ: Princeton University Press.

Dotsch, R., & Wigboldus, D. H. J. (2008). Virtual prejudice. *Journal of Experimental Social Psychology, 44*, 1194–1198. doi:10.1016/j.jesp.2008.03.003

Eastwick, P. W., & Gardner, W. L. (2009). Is it a game? Evidence for social influence in the virtual world. *Social Influence, 4*, 18–32. doi:10.1080/15534510802254087

Friedman, D., Steed, A., & Slater, M. (2007a). *Research bots in Second Life.* Retrieved October 10th 2010 from: http://portal.idc.ac.il/en/schools/ Communications/ research/Virtuality/Pages/ SLbots.aspx

Friedman, D., Steed, A., & Slater, M. (2007b). Spatial social behavior in Second Life. *Lecture Notes in Computer Science, 4722*, (p. 252).

Göritz, A. S., & Moser, K. (2006). Web-based mood induction. *Cognition and Emotion, 20*, 887–896.

Gumbrecht, H. U. (2004). *Production of presence: What meaning cannot convey.* Stanford University Press.

Heidegger, M. (1927, 2006). *Sein und Zeit.* Tübingen: Niemeyer.

Jin, S.-A. A. (2009). Modality effects in Second Life: The mediating role of social presence and the moderating role of product involvement. *Cyberpsychology & Behavior, 12*(6), 717–721. doi:10.1089/cpb.2008.0273

Lenggenhager, B., Tadi, T., Metzinger, T., & Blanke, O. (2007). Video ergo sum: Manipulating bodily self-consciousness. *Science, 317*(5841), 1096–1099. doi:10.1126/science.1143439

Metzinger, T. (2003). *Being no one: The self-model theory of subjectivity.* Cambridge, MA: MIT Press.

Meyerbröker, K., & Emmelkamp, P. M. G. (2010). Virtual reality exposure therapy in anxiety disorders: A systematic review of process- and outcome studies. *Depression and Anxiety, 27*(10). doi:10.1002/da.20734

Mischel, W. (1999). *Introduction to personality* (6th ed.). Fort Worth, TX: Harcourt Brace.

Riva, G., Waterworth, J. A., & Waterworth, E. L. (2004). The layers of presence: A bio-cultural approach to understanding presence in natural and mediated environments. *Cyberpsychology & Behavior, 7*(4), 402–416. doi:10.1089/ cpb.2004.7.402

Sanchez-Vives, M. V., & Slater, M. (2005). From presence to consciousness through virtual reality. *Nature Reviews. Neuroscience, 6*, 332–339. doi:10.1038/nrn1651

Schubert, T., Friedmann, F., & Regenbrecht, H. (1999). Embodied presence in virtual environments. In Paton, R., & Neilson, I. (Eds.), *Visual representations and interpretations* (pp. 268–278). London, UK: Springer-Verlag.

Schubert, T., Friedmann, F., & Regenbrecht, H. (2001). The experience of presence: Factor analytic insights. *Presence (Cambridge, Mass.), 10*, 266–281. doi:10.1162/105474601300343603

Slater, M., Perez-Marcos, D., Ehrsson, H. H., & Sanchez-Vives, M. (2008). Towards a digital body: The virtual arm illusion. *Frontiers in Human Neuroscience, 2,* 6. doi:10.3389/neuro.09.006.2008

Snow, C. E., & Hoefnagel-Höhle, M. (1978). The critical period for language acquisition: Evidence from second language learning. *Child Development, 49*(4), 1114–1128. doi:10.2307/1128751

Tajfel, H., & Turner, J. C. (1986). The social identity theory of intergroup behavior. In Worchel, S., & Austin, W. (Eds.), *Psychology of intergroup relations* (pp. 7–24). Chicago, IL: Nelson-Hall.

Turkle, S. (1995). *Life on the screen: Identity in the age of the Internet.* New York, NY: Simon & Schuster.

Van Kleef, G. A., De Dreu, C. K. W., & Manstead, A. S. R. (2004). The interpersonal effects of anger and happiness in negotiations. *Journal of Personality and Social Psychology, 86,* 57–76. doi:10.1037/0022-3514.86.1.57

Wadley, G. (2008). Talking and building: Two studies of collaboration in Second Life. *Workshop on virtual worlds, collaboration, and workplace productivity, at CSCW, San Diego.*

Waterworth, J. A., Waterworth, E. L., Mantovani, F., & Riva, G. (2010). On feeling (the) present. *Journal of Consciousness Studies, 17*(1–2).

Yee, N., & Bailenson, J. (2007). The Proteus effect: The effect of transformed self representation on behavior. *Human Communication Research, 33,* 271–290. doi:10.1111/j.1468-2958.2007.00299.x

Yee, N., Bailenson, J. N., Urbanek, M., Chang, F., & Merget, D. (2007). The unbearable likeness of being digital: The persistence of nonverbal social norms in online virtual environments. *Cyberpsychology & Behavior, 10,* 115–121. doi:10.1089/cpb.2006.9984

Yee, N., Ellis, J., & Ducheneaut, N. (2009). The tyranny of embodiment. *Artifact, 2,* 1–6.

ADDITIONAL READING

Baecker, D. (2007). *Studien zur naechsten Gesellschaft.* Frankfurt am Main: Suhrkamp.

Bainbridge, W. (2007). The scientific research potential of virtual worlds. *Science, 317,* 472–476. doi:10.1126/science.1146930

Bargh, J. A., Chen, M., & Burrows, L. (1996). Automaticity of social behavior: Direct effects of trait construct and stereotype activation on action. *Journal of Personality and Social Psychology, 71*(2), 230–244. doi:10.1037/0022-3514.71.2.230

Bargh, J. A., McKenna, K. Y. A., & Fitzsimons, G. M. (2002). Can you see the real me? Activation and expression of the "true self" on the internet. *The Journal of Social Issues, 1,* 33–48. doi:10.1111/1540-4560.00247

Bessiére, K., Seay, A. F., & Kiesler, S. (2007). The ideal elf: Identity exploration in world of warcraft. *Cyberpsychology & Behavior, 10,* 530–535. doi:10.1089/cpb.2007.9994

Botgirl Questi. (2008). You can help investigate human and avatar personality by taking brief test. Retrieved 12 November 2008, from: http://botgirl.blogspot.com/2008/05/you-can-helpinvestigate-human-and.html.

De Nood, D., & Attema, J. (2006). Second Life. Het tweede leven van virtual reality. *EPN rapport.* Retrieved June 5, 2008, from http://www.epn.net

Emmelkamp, P. M. G. (2005). Technological innovations in clinical assessment and psychotherapy. *Psychotherapy and Psychosomatics, 74,* 336–343. doi:10.1159/000087780

Gallego, M. J., Botella, C., Garcia-Palacios, A., Banos, R. M., & Guillen, V. (2008). A self-help treatment via the internet for fear of public speaking: A single case study. *Psicología Conductual, 16*(2), 323–340.

Gonzalesa, A. L., & Hancocka, J. T. (2008). Identity shift in computer-mediated environments. *Media Psychology, 11*(2), 167–185. doi:10.1080/15213260802023433

McKenna, K. Y. A., & Bargh, J. (2000). Plan 9 from cyberspace: The implications of the internet for personality and social psychology. *Personality and Social Psychology Review, 4,* 57–75. doi:10.1207/S15327957PSPR0401_6

Precht, R. D. (2007). *Wer bin ich – und wenn ja, wie viele? Eine philosophische Reise*. München: Goldmann.

Schubert, T., Friedmann, F., & Regenbrecht, H. (1999). Embodied presence in virtual environments. In Paton, R., & Neilson, I. (Eds.), *Visual representations and interpretations* (pp. 268–278). London: Springer-Verlag.

Tellegen, A., & Atkinson, G. (1974). Openness to absorbing and self-altering experiences ("absorption"), a trait related to hypnotic susceptibility. *Journal of Abnormal Psychology, 83,* 268–277. doi:10.1037/h0036681

Turkle, S. (1997). Multiple subjectivity and virtual community at the end of the Freudian century. *Sociological Inquiry, 67,* 72–84. doi:10.1111/j.1475-682X.1997.tb00430.x

Wagner, B., & Lange, A. (2008). Internet-basierte Psychotherapie 'Interapy. In Bauer, S., & Kordy, H. (Eds.), *E-Mental Health. Neue Medien in der psychosozialen Versorgung, 9, 105- 120*. Heidelberg: Springer Medizin Verlag.

Westerhoff, N. (2007). Therapie 2.0. *Gehirn und Geist, 3,* 92–97.

Wigboldus, D. H. J. (2006). Virtuele stereotypen. *Psycholoog, 41,* 442–448.

KEY TERMS AND DEFINITIONS

'Being-in-the-World': A basic structure of (emotional) authenticity as opposed to the more interpretation- and thought-focused philosophical approaches.

Core Presence: A coherent, perceptual 'being-in-the-(virtual?!) world'.

Extended Presence: A reflective, significance creating 'being-a-person'.

Identity: A person's conception and expression of their individuality or group affiliations.

Mood Induction: Experimental technique to influence mood in a specific direction for a short time.

Personality: The stable and unchangeable concept of the sum of the attributes of a person.

Presence: Points to all kinds of events and processes in which the impact that 'present' objects have on human bodies is being initiated or intensified.

Proto Presence: The experience of an embodied 'being'

Stereotype: A commonly held public belief about specific social groups or types of individuals.

Chapter 7
Verbal and Non–Verbal Communication in Second Life

Sara Pita
Universidade de Aveiro, Portugal

Luís Pedro
Universidade de Aveiro, Portugal

ABSTRACT

In the last few years, several studies concerning the advantages and potentialities of using Second Life in education came to spotlight. To identify which type of communication is most common among avatars and to understand if there is any similarity with communication in real life, a case study was developed in order to analyze both verbal and non-verbal communication among Master degree students.

This chapter will explain how this study was conducted, as well as the results and the conclusions drawn from it. After the data analysis we concluded that avatars rarely use kinesic communication - although there is, in Second Life, an inventory full of gestures - using instead verbal communication. In fact, it was very clear that individuals use written code to express their emotions, thus increasing the number of participations. Non-verbal communication had a small role in interaction, proxemics was influenced by space, and finally, appearance didn't reveal the true personality of the user.

INTRODUCTION

Second Life (SL) is known by its potential to enhance social communication, interaction and information sharing. This virtual environment is also interactive and dynamic, allowing users to experience situations beyond one's physical and financial constraints (Appel, 2006, p.4). In fact, several teachers, doctors, architects, businessmen and many others use SL to develop their daily activities, because it is a realistic and persistent environment, and because it expresses a sense of presence and a sense of immersion. SL also has several advantages for educational professionals, especially regarding content creation, role-playing and socialization.

However, in order to use virtual worlds in classrooms, it is fundamental to understand how individuals relate with each other and what pedagogical strategies are more efficient in those

DOI: 10.4018/978-1-60960-854-5.ch007

environments. To fulfill these goals, the present research was out forward, over the period of a year, aiming to understand the verbal and non-verbal behavior of several Portuguese master students in Second Life.

Words have an enormous importance in our lives because they can express feelings, enlighten, excite. Therefore language can be a great instrument or a hazardous weapon. (Toomey, 2000).

But communication doesn't necessarily mean speaking: pre-historical men used gestures, postures and movements to get in touch with other individuals. Davis (1979) however acknowledges the value of words, adding that words are beautiful, exciting, and important, although also expressing a belief that words have been overestimated since they represent neither the full nor the partial communicated message. Indeed, verbal communication cannot be analyzed without non-verbal communication, because doing so might jeopardize the effectiveness of the whole purpose of interaction. To fully understand the meaning of verbal messages, individuals have to take into account intonation, intention, environment, interaction, interlocutor and non-verbal communication (Streeck, 1993, *in*Leathers, 1997). As Kendon (1972) stated *"the flow of movement in the listener may be rhythmically coordinated with the speech and movements of the speaker."* (*in*Weitz, 1979, p. 89)

Non-verbal communication is responsible, in real life, for 65 to 70 percent of human interaction (Birdwhistell, 1970, *in*Leathers, 1997). The way we look, the way we place ourselves and the gestures we make are very expressive and say a lot about/of our emotions. These items are studied by several disciplines, namely proxemics and kinesics. Obviously, non-verbal communication is quite different in SL and in real life, but there are some points in common.

Since we have described the two major concepts that underlie our study it is now important to present its main aims which were to identify how individuals relate with each other in SL and

to identify whether there is any similarity with real life interaction, so as to adjust SL classroom strategies to both the teachers' and the students' needs. Furthermore, we also wanted to:

1. Understand the interaction typologies – verbal and non-verbal communication – among students in Second Life and their relevance to education;
2. Understand the impact of interaction between individuals concerning the increase of sense of community;
3. Identify the advantages of interacting in virtual worlds when compared with the advantages of traditional communication means.

COMMUNICATION TYPOLOGIES

Verbal Communication

Language is a tool to accomplish one's goals and success (Ng e Bradac, *in*Szuchewycz, 1995), because it can develop, modify or overthrow the power someone has. Although it is very important, language is not the only constituent of the communicative process, since the non-verbal acts, such as movements, postures and facial expressions, also express feelings and emotions.

Although it might look simple, the analysis of verbal communication requires the consideration of multiple variables. Since language is full of ambiguities it is necessary to use complementary signs to get the message through (Toomey, 2000). Verbal messages can be used to fulfill four main functions:

1. Give information on people's attitude;
2. Provide personal information about the speaker and his state of mind;
3. Report the intensity of speaker's emotions;
4. Present relational information.

Hymes (1984) and Jakobson (*in*Hébert, 2006) have considered six functions:

1. Referential – it analyzes context and content;
2. Metalinguistic – it analyzes the code and language itself;
3. Expressive – it focus attention on the speaker's emotions;
4. Connotative – it emphasizes the speaker's intention to influence the attitudes and behavior of the receiver;
5. Poetic – it focus on the shape and structure of the message;
6. Phatic – it establishes and maintains interpersonal contact.

Verbal communication is about sharing information, not only regarding the speaker's character, but also his/her emotions, believes and attitudes. Therefore, verbal communication is an incredible network whereby messages, means and the communication process itself work together.

To sum up, verbal messages give us information on the participants, space, time and intrinsic meaning. However, each and every message should be analyzed to avoid mistakes and misunderstandings. Speech acts can have different intents and it is, therefore, extremely important to analyze them not only taking into account the reaction they will produce in the receiver but also their communicational expressivity and context.

During the analysis of speech acts we have considered several parameters which helped us to classify each message. These parameters are related to the expression of emotions, the qualitative participation in a debate and the proximity between the intervenients. Some of these parameters will imply gathering specific words and will be detailed in the next chapters.

Non-Verbal Communication

Hickson & Stacks (*in*Leathers, 1997) describe non-verbal communication as a process to manipulate actions and expectations and to show feelings and believes whether they are intentional or not. Leathers (1997) defines non verbal communication as *"the use of interacting sets of visual, vocal and invisible communication systems and subsystems by communicators with the systematic encoding and decoding of nonverbal symbols and signs for the purpose of exchanging consensual meaning in specific communicative contexts"* (p.11). Therefore, non-verbal communication can be an effective way to explain ambiguous oral messages and to indicate how accurate and cohesive they are.

Non-verbal acts have many functions, namely the reinforcement or replacement of verbal messages and the clarification of some indistinct concepts. They also emphasize emotions and express feelings in a genuine and discreet way. More, these acts control social situations since they can guide one's behaviors and impressions. Finally, non-verbal communication is often quicker than verbal messages:

"The reaction must be quick and reflexive, with no time to ponder or talk. And whenever such situation occurs, the slower and exhaustive verbal codifications are out of the question for practical reasons and are clearly more time-consuming and inefficient than nonverbal reactions" (Reusch & Kees, 1956, inLeathers, 1997, p.8).

Given that non-verbal communication has so many functions, it encompasses several disciplines, namely kinesics, proxemics and appearance. Although appearance has a huge impact in everyday communication, in SL is hard to analyze its importance since users can freely edit their avatars. Despite this fact, we will explain, in the following section, each one of these three areas.

Kinesics

Kinesics studies observable, isolate and meaningful movements, such as gestures, facial expressions and postures that occur during interpersonal communication (Leathers, 1997). According to Birdwhistell, "*kinesics is concerned with abstracting from the continuous muscular shifts which are characteristic of living physiological systems those groupings of movements which are of significance to the communication process and thus to the interactional systems of particular groups*" (*in*Leathers, 1997, p. 67).

Kinesics analyzes movements taking into account their intentionality, awareness and cohesion within verbal discourse. Through this analysis, the researcher can justify some attitudes, feelings and even the self-esteem of the subject (Leathers, 1997).

Postures are also an important element of kinesics, whether in real life or in Second Life. Scheflen (1964, *in*Leathers, 1997) classifies postures in three different types:

1. Postural movements keep other people away or bring them closer together;
2. Individuals stay near their interlocutors, showing interest in communicating with all participants;
3. Posture indicates haughtiness or modesty.

In fact, postures can influence the way other people perceive us and how they react to our speech, facilitating or hindering the continuity of communication (Weitz, 1979).

Proxemics

Proxemics is the study of movements in a space, of the positioning of objects and of the distance between people (Hall, 1968). To clearly understand this concept, we have to understand the meaning of both space and distance; the first one refers to the location or environment where interaction occurs and the use that people make of it. According to Hall, the organization of space can prevent spontaneous interactions (*in*Leath-

ers, 1997). Unfortunately, educational spaces are organized in such a way that they intimidate students and support distance when they should promote closeness, involvement and interaction.

Distance depends on the affiliation or privacy needs (Leathers, 1997). Collier (1975, *in*Davis, 1979) and Leathers (1997) argue that people come closer to people whom they like and care for, standing face-to-face or side-by-side. The positioning also determines status and hierarchical role; leaders tend to adopt a central position - though this might be a spontaneous attitude.

Davis (1979) also holds that it is possible to foresee some psychological characteristics from the place people take in a conversation; for instance, shy people tend to keep away from other participants. This author adds that a circular disposition is taken whenever there is no clear leadership (Davis, 1979).

In order to analyze proxemics it is important to observe people's movements in spontaneous environments, because spatial configurations can determine human behavior (Davis, 1979). Furthermore, it is essential to observe people's attitudes, since they might express feelings and emotions that would not be told orally.

Appearance

Appearance is also an essential element of non-verbal communication. According to Birdwhistell (*in*Davis, 1979) individuals are influenced by society to look in a certain way. Mass media, culture or religion exerts pressure over individuals, making their desire to fit in more important than their own individuality.

Physical appearance, namely the type of body, weight and height, clothes and accessories also influences others perspective towards us. So, appearance may define social identity: a gothic man, for instance, is easily identified with his group (Leathers, 1997).

WORK PLAN AND COLLECTED DATA

When SL became a famous platform, a group of students and teachers of the University of Aveiro (Portugal) decided to explore this new environment. Because they were studying the use of different technologies in education, especially Web 2.0 tools, SL seemed to be an interesting new platform where they could meet, talk and share information. These meetings, which were always held after working hours, soon drew the attention of other people, which also wanted to learn and speak about the way technology enhanced learning.

In order to analyze both components of communication in the aforementioned meetings we created two main observation grids. The verbal communication grid was actually based on studies by Philips (2000) and Rourke et al. (2001). These authors studied the way people interact in virtual environments like LMS (learning management system). The non-verbal communication grid, on the other hand, was more complex to build since there are many different components, some of which are not considered in a 3D virtual environment, namely facial expressions. Despite this restriction, we have studied and included kinesics, proxemics, intentionality and appearance components in this data collection instrument (Davis, 1979; Leathers, 1997; Weitz, 1979).

Table 1 shows the several parameters and descriptors of the verbal communication grid.

Affective Parameter

This parameter refers to all the sentences in which users express feelings, emotions, beliefs, values or their state of mind. Greetings, verbal reinforcement, expressive icons (☺, ☹, …) and onomatopoeic words are some of the most common examples of affective elements.

Real Life Parameter

Virtual worlds as well as web 2.0 tools are growing because of their social capacity, since they have the ability to spread knowledge regardless distance. In this parameter we consider all sentences relating to events that occur in real life.

Interactive Parameter

To define the descriptors of the interactive parameter we have used a Philips' study (2000) as reference, because it analyzes the quality of interaction between students in virtual environments like LMS. Although LMS and 3D virtual worlds are very different, participations are quite similar because both use written code, making sharing easier and potentially empowering argumentation skills.

Sentences representing appreciation for the other's point of view or showing reference to a specific subject were classified as interactive. These speech acts not only showed tolerance and respect but also contributed to enhance the communicative process.

This parameter also included questions that present one's point of view.

Table 1. Verbal communication parameters

PARAMETER	DESCRIPTOR
Affective	Expression of emotions Demonstration of users' state of mind Greetings
Social	Presentation of events which take place outside SL
Interactive	Resumption of previous discussion Clear allusion to someone else's topic Questioning others directly Showing one's appreciation for others' opinion
Cohesive	Sense of community Using vocative
Participative	Number of sentences collected Number of sentences on a specific topic Diversity of topics in discussion

Cohesive Parameter

These sentences are intrinsically related with the affective content, since they express the sense of community. Expressions like "our group" or "our point of view", the use of the personal pronoun "we" and others are just a tiny example of this sense of belonging which is increased by familiarity. Once again, greetings, resumption of previous topics, sharing social information and indicating a specific topic were considered cohesive elements. Using the first name to speak to someone was also an expression of cohesion, regardless its common use in SL.

Participative Parameter

This parameter counts the sentences that were written down along the meetings.

We decided to consider the sentence as the unity of analysis, like Henri (1992) did in his study. Participative and interactive parameters, for instance, showed us how important these meetings were and how involved users in this community of practice and learning were. On the other hand, the affective parameter gave us tools to understand the emotions and the relationship between individuals, some of which were conveyed to real life.

Since we had to analyze non verbal communication in real time, verbal communication was studied *a posteriori*, always taking into account the avatar's behavior and his/her non verbal acts.

In fact, one of our parameters was intentionality, which was used to compare verbal messages with non-verbal attitudes (gestures, movements or simply appearance), because they might disclose the true meaning of verbal messages (Davis, 1979).

Although there were obvious differences between non-verbal communication in a real environment and in SL, we have discovered some similarities, namely kinesics and proxemics. Physical features, however, were hard to evaluate because avatars can freely choose their appearance.

The non-verbal grid was divided into four main parameters regarding avatars' behaviors and attitudes (Davis, 1979, Knapp, 1992) (See Table 2).

Kinesics

Gestures are the most ancient way of communication and therefore their relevance cannot be devalued. In real life interaction, non-verbal acts can replace speech. However, in SL, these gestures are especially used to reinforce certain oral messages. This parameter includes both the gestures available in the inventory and the gestures created by SL users.

Physical Features

In real life, appearance has an important role in social relationships, because it shows people's expectations, believes, desires, needs... Physical features can influence the personality of an individual and can determine the group to which he/she will belong. Although we might make some assumptions regarding the impact of the avatar's appearance in his/her personality, there is not a clear proof showing this relationship.

Table 2. Non-verbal communication parameters

PARAMETER	DESCRIPTOR
Kinesics	Gestures in SL inventory Gestures created by users
Physical features	Avatars' appearance Sense of belonging to a social group Influence of the avatar's appearance in his/her behavior Identification through appearance Setting one's status
Proxemics	Understanding space and position Organization of a group in a specific space Immediacy or distance between avatars
Intentionality	Expression of emotions Verbal communication reinforcement Identifying if verbal and non-verbal acts are totally out of step

Nevertheless, appearance is the easiest way to recognize someone in a crowd or to define his/her importance in a certain group.

Proxemics

The position people assume in the presence of other people or towards space can have different meanings. In fact, some positions and postures clearly show some degree of intimacy among avatars. Positioning can also reveal someone's status and role in the community, especially when they take a central place.

The last descriptor of this parameter refers to the group's behavior as a collective entity.

Intentionality

This last parameter intends to analyze the relation and cohesion between verbal and non-verbal acts. In some cases, non-verbal acts can show emotions, even though they are not linked to a specific oral message. Concerning intentionality we also evaluated if non-verbal acts were used as a reinforcement of speech.

As we mentioned before, the majority of participants in this study attended a master degree in Multimedia in Education lectured in the University of Aveiro. Despite this fact, the openness of the meetings soon attracted other researchers, students and scholars, which came from different cities and countries. Since the avatars came from different places, these meetings happened in different locations, for example the Island of the University of Aveiro, Portucalis, and the Island of PT Inovação. The topics of discussion were mainly related with education in virtual worlds.

DATA ANALYSIS AND RESULTS

Next, we will present and discuss the information gathered in the six meetings we have observed. In these meetings the number of participants, mostly Portuguese students, never exceeded forty. Although we have analyzed the information according to a qualitative perspective all data will be showed using graphics. The written messages and the non-verbal acts were all treated with the help of software of qualitative analysis (QSR Nvivo), respecting the parameters put forward in the observational grids.

Verbal Communication Results

There was an average of 27 users from different educational institutes in the meetings we have attended. In fact, the less crowded meeting was on the 8th January 2008, when users discussed the topic of interaction design. The presence of so many people in these meetings showed the importance of SL and its sense of community. This huge participation can be shown through the number of messages collected, in a total of 6423 sentences (See Figure 1).

The number of messages collected on the 24th January meeting showed that users talk intensely about that specific topic. The two first meetings were about topics related with education or with SL benefits or disadvantages and gathered mainly Master students, as this discussion began in real life classroom. Most meetings were related with a conference on Communication, Education and Training in SL held in the University of Aveiro, which probably influenced this amount of participation.

After collecting avatars' messages we have analyzed them according to the parameters previously presented. Next, we will represent the global analysis, which will respect the order of parameters, because this is the best way to understand and frame some of the conclusions drawn. Since descriptors are a little extensive, we adopted an alphabetic system, in order to represent each one of them:

A.   Expression of emotions;
B.   Demonstration of users' state of mind;

Figure 1. Number of sentences per meeting

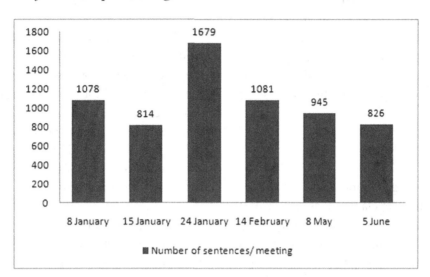

C. Greetings;
D. Presentation of events which take place outside SL;
E. Resumption of previous discussion;
F. Clear allusion to someone else's topic;
G. Questioning others directly;
H. Showing one's appreciation for others;
I. Sense of community;
J. Using vocative.

These descriptors belong to different parameters, respectively affective (A, B, C), social (E, F, G, H), cohesive (I, J) and interactive. Figure 2 represents the amount of messages in each parameter, being obvious the supremacy of the interactive parameter over others. However, this parameter has more descriptors than the others, which might have influenced this result.

Once more, we want to stress that written messages were analyzed in context to understand the true meaning of that specific speech act. The same sentence can be classified in a multiplicity of parameters, according to its meaning and intention.

Messages are often labeled as interactive or affective. In meetings like these, in which people are supposed to express their opinion, it is normal to argue, to expose ideas, to reveal a state of mind or to greet.

Figure 3 allows us to confirm that descriptor E has a significant difference when compared with the remaining descriptors. The use of vocative – descriptor J – is also often used, since avatars need to identify who they are talking to.

Furthermore, it is important to notice that the sense of community was visible regardless the

Figure 2. Percentage of messages per verbal communication parameter

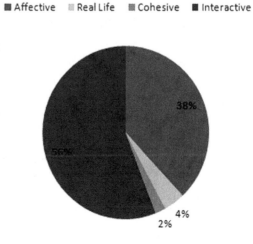

number of messages. Avatars use words like "community", "all", "people", "group", "folks", as well as personal pronouns ("we" and "ours").

In order to clear up this analysis and given the fact that we have only showed the global results we will specify each parameter by giving some examples.

Affective Parameter

Messages expressing emotions, beliefs, states of mind and intimacy are classified as affective. It is important for us, as researchers, to analyze not only the explicit meaning of sentences, but also the subjective one, because people are not always objective. Despite this fact, there were some speech acts hard to classify due to its multiple meanings.

To descriptor A – "expression of emotions" – correspond all sentences expressing feelings such as:

- [13:23] **Avatar1:** *This space makes me feel safe...*
- [14:05] **Avatar2:** *yet??*
- [14:29] **Avatar3:** *(what a shame...)*
- [15:10] **Avatar4:** *Hallelujah!!!!*

- [15:33] **Avatar5:** *I love it!*

Descriptor B, corresponding to the "demonstration of users' state of mind", gathered messages that use humor, emoticons and expressive punctuation. In order to recognize humoristic sentences, researchers consider the context and punctuation, since there is no intonation available, as it happens in a real life situation.

In order to show this descriptor, we have collected the following messages:

- [13:22] **Avatar1:** *lol*
- [14:10] **Avatar2:** *:)*
- [14:20] **Avatar3:** *:D*
- [14:15] **Avatar4:** *heheheheheheh*

The last affective descriptor (C) includes not only greetings, but also messages showing personal incentives and support.

- [13:22] **Avatar1:** *good night everybody, sorry i'm late*
- [15:24] **Avatar2:** *C U:)*
- [15:02] **Avatar3:** *good news:D*
- [14:16] **Avatar4:** *go on!!*

Figure 3. Number of sentences per descriptor

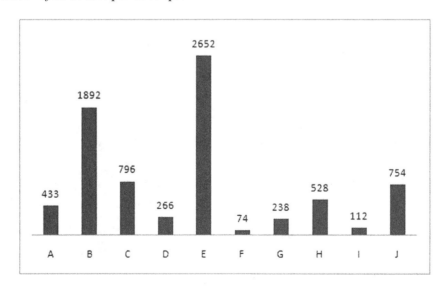

As we can see, these messages do not have a direct relationship with the argument. Nevertheless they allow us to deduce the existent relationship between avatars.

Real Life Parameter

This parameter is characterized by messages relating to events that took place in real life and do not influence directly avatars' behavior and experience in the virtual world. We also classify as social all the messages relating to the users' opinion on the importance of topics in their daily life.

Even though there were not many messages of this kind, there are some examples:

- [14:12] **Avatar1:** *I was in DSI until last year...*
- [14:35] **Avatar3:** *I just arrive from BCN.*
- [14:37] **Avatar4:** *Prima is a journal promoted by CETAC.MEDIA (UA and UP)*
- [14:07] **Avatar6:** *I know one's made and sold in a typical fair at Setubal*

Interactive Parameter

This parameter has a large amount of messages, because it refers to argumentative sentences that carry on an argument (E) or bring in a new discussion (H).

The next messages are just an example of descriptor E:

- [14:22] **Avatar1:** *well, at the beginning what attracted me the most on* SL, *was the possibility of communicate and meet people from other cities and countries*
- [13:22] **Avatar2:** *Metaphor is a challenge to communication...*
- [14:21] **Avatar3:** *In this second stage we want to reinforce the development of areas to support students and to enhance socialization*

- [14:44] **Avatar4:** *I want to show you an experience...*

When avatars use a message to make comments about a certain topic or to mention directly the work or the opinion of someone else, there is a specific reference (F). The sentences below show how interested the avatars are in the discussion and in the resumption of argument.

- [14:42] **Avatar1:** *and there isn't, on SL, the means to fulfill our dreams as Avatar7 says?*
- [13:29] **Avatar2:** *I'll add, Avatar8: The arousing of new era...the dawn of the ancient ways to communicate*
- [15:41] **Avatar3:** *with the goal, as Avatar10 said, of involving more Brazilian people*
- [15:26] **Avatar4:** *in one of the meaning, I believe it was in the first one, Avatar10 raise a relevant question, which I'm about to explain*

Descriptor G includes messages in which avatars show their respect and appreciation for somebody's opinion, indicating intimacy and proximity between the users. The next sentences exemplify this fact:

- [14:52] **Avatar1:** *I agree*
- [13:22] **Avatar2:** *oh Avatar7...great ideia*
- [15:08] **Avatar3:** *exactly, Avatar8*
- [15:24] **Avatar4:** *that's great:D*

The last interactive descriptor does not relate exclusively to interrogative questions, since there are also many declarative sentences employed to stimulate argument and to raise new topics. Here are some examples:

- [14:36] **Avatar1:** *aren't we encouraging controversy by defending the idea that SL is a game?*

- [14:26] **Avatar3:** *when you spoke about Portuguese-speaking community, did you mean academic and scientific one?*
- [14:42] **Avatar4:** *Avatar7, do you want to speak a bit about Avatar8 professional and personal path?*
- [14:14] **Avatar5:** *Can you explain me once again the context, since I didn't understand it quite well?*

Cohesive Parameter

Group cohesion is a very important issue in any social situation. At SL the sense of community (I) is really important and avatars show how deep the relationship that unites them is by using some specific words, such as "group", "our", "community" or "we".

- [14:13] **Avatar1:** *hello everybody*
- [13:24] **Avatar2:** *He!!! I have my family from SL community calling me every where*
- [14:13] **Avatar3:** *Hi, folks!*
- [15:32] **Avatar4:** *I like to see u all together…*

The other descriptor in this parameter is the use of vocative. In SL it is necessary to use the first name so that people know who they are talking to, unlike it happens in real life communication.

- [13:26] **Avatar1**: *Avatar8, this is good or bad, if we're talking about socialization on second life?*
- [14:18] **Avatar2:** *Avatar10, make the introductions*
- [14:20] **Avatar3:** *Avatar11, please turn that voice down*
- [14:33] **Avatar4:** *Avatar8… lead the argue*

In conclusion, verbal communication is the most important mean to socialize and interact in SL. Results showed that 43% of the messages were interactive, while 37% were affective. These results mean that individuals are participative, interested and active in the debate, choosing to express their opinion rather than just listen to others' ideas. The affective parameter also reveals the intimacy between individuals, which led them to express their emotions and feelings.

Non-Verbal Communication Results

The analysis of non-verbal acts was made in real time with the support of an observational grid. After recording each act, we crossed this reference with the verbal speech in order to analyze its cohesion and veracity. Although this section of communication is qualitative, the results will be presented through graphics.

Physical features are difficult to analyze just through the observation of meetings. As we have mentioned earlier, individuals are totally free to edit their avatars, independently of their real personality. This makes it really difficult to set people's personality or to identify the group to which they belong just by their appearance.

Even though we can't make any assumptions regarding the user's personality or behavior, we can notice that some of them choose an eccentric appearance. Even if there isn't any connection between appearance and behavior, eccentricity can promote their recognition while in a huge group. To corroborate this fact, we have chosen several messages in which avatars talk about some particular features:

- [14:31] **Avatar1:** *I've blue hair, almost green… bad premonition*
- [15:08] **Avatar2:** *and blue eyes…*
- [13:41] **Avatar3:** *I love your cloak*
- [13:42] **Avatar4:** *remembers me Cruela*
- [13:42] **Avatar5:** *phantom of the opera…*

In conclusion, the first parameter of non-verbal communication only allows us to identify people in a group; however, it is impossible to indicate their status or any trace of personality. In order to get this information we suggest the application of questionnaires.

Kinesics

Users have a huge amount of avatars gestures in the SL inventory at their disposal. Additionally, they can create their own gestures. There are 35 gestures, some of which are different according to gender to simulate several of the non-verbal acts used in common interaction. The creation of gestures was indicative of the knowledge of avatars regarding the use of scripting tools. Besides, it also illustrated their interest in this virtual environment. Although many gestures were used, we've noticed users prefer to express themselves in written code, using emoticons, interjections and idiomatic expressions. From the inventory, it became quite clear that users use "Laugh" the most; however, many of them choose to write it down in the following way: [14:15] **Avatar1:** *hehehe-heheheh*" or "[14:20] **Avatar2:** *HiHiHiHiHiHi*".

Since avatars choose to replace gestures for speech acts, the percentage of non-application is bigger than its use (See Figure 4).

We can point out some reasons to justify this behavior. First, its timing, since there is a time frame between the application of gesture and the speech act that can lead to incoherency and incomprehension of the true message. Second, the lack of knowledge of gestures use; and third, the habit of using emoticons or written sentences to express feelings, emotions, humor…

These three reasons can probably be the cause for the devaluation of gestures, which, in some meetings, were not even used at all. Figure 5 shows a comparison of the six meetings.

It is important to clarify that although percentage reveals a high application of gestures; numbers are quite lower, corresponding to only one dozen of gestures per meeting.

Throughout meetings we have realized that several avatars, especially those with a better knowledge of this particular virtual world, create

Figure 4. Global results for application of gestures

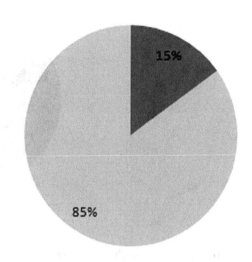

some gestures, namely "All right", "Aahhh!" or "Miauu". However, this fact did not emphasize the avatars' interest on the application gestures. From the 35 gestures at avatars disposal, "Clap", "Chuckle", "Laugh", "Wow" and "Yes" are the most frequently used.

After the comparison between verbal and non-verbal communication, we've noticed that all gestures used by avatars intended to emphasize other people speaking act. In order to corroborate the cohesion between these two components of interaction, we will present the written message and the respective gesture.

At 14:58, 24th January, an avatar used the gesture "*Nod*" to express his/her agreement to Avatar3's opinion: [14:58] **Avatar3:** *credibility, presence…*

In the same day, at 14:31, an avatar used the gesture *"Aahh"* to show his/her support to the information given by the slides and wrote simultaneously [14:31] **Avatar4:** *well done.*

In February, an avatar joke about cats, writing [15:05] **Avatar1:** *unless you're a cat.* In response Avatar2 used the sound *"Miauu".*

Figure 5. Global percentage of gestures per meeting

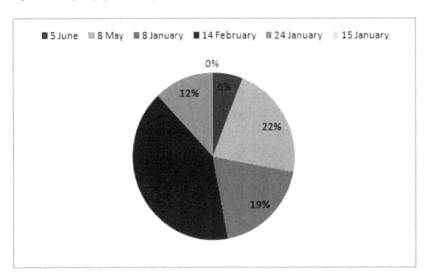

The final example happened on the 05th June, at 14:20, when an avatar used the gesture "Boo" to emphasize his divergence regarding another avatar's opinion. At the same time another avatar used "All right" to simulate his/her agreement. These gestures were used in response to the following message [14:20] **Avatar5:** *that's a rap… would you want to go to coffee, sit down a bit?*

The application of these gestures throughout all the meetings shows the cohesion and coherence between verbal and non-verbal communication. Curiously, we have noticed that even when the gesture could entirely replace the written code, avatars used rather both of them.

Proxemics

Throughout the meetings we have noticed that avatars adopt a certain position in order to see all participants, even if it means having to change place regularly. Indeed, although real users have a clear perspective of other avatars, they try to take the better place.

Avatars like circular disposition better, adopting a different disposition only when the space is preconceived. This fact happened in two of the meetings, in which the leader used slides to

expose his/her ideas (See Figure 6). Curiously, avatars said that they rather like to be seated in circular way, like they do in real life:

- [13:47] **Avatar1:** *don't you think we can talk better in orange seats?*
- [13:47] **Avatar2:** *we're in a circle*
- [13:48] **Avatar3:** *I like it better*

The position avatars took in the meetings reveal their sense of community and the intimacy between them. So, if they adopt a circular positioning they will engage in argue actively, unlike what it happens when they sit side by side. Comparing a meeting in which the space wasn't restricted

Figure 6. Snapshot retrieved 08 January 2008

to another one in which it was necessary to look at slides, we have noticed that avatars were less participative in the second case, because their focus was on the slides being presented and not on the discussion itself. Circular positioning also helps to understand the closeness between users and their sense of belonging to a group, as non-verbal theories advocate.

Although the previous items are quite similar in real life communication, we cannot identify how close individuals are by their positioning or their personality. In fact, even when they were apart, avatars participated actively in discussion. However, in some cases avatars took a leadership position, when the meeting was of their responsibility.

In conclusion, proxemics gave us enough material to understand the relationship between avatars and to identify a sense of community and of belonging to a group. Even though there were some similarities with real behavior, namely the circular position when in group contexts, it was difficult to establish a connection between their positioning and the avatars' personality or importance in the meeting. However, in some meetings we have noticed that avatars take a leadership position, acting as moderators.

CONCLUSION

The main goal of this research was to identify which type of communication avatars liked better, so that teachers and other scholar agents could have a deeper understanding of communication patterns that emerge in this particular virtual world. After analyzing the information, we have realized that users communicate mostly through written code.

Despite the success of verbal communication, we have realized that the absence of non-verbal acts, such as postures and gestures, devalue the power of interaction, when compared with everyday life, because a lot of interpersonal communication happens through non-verbal communication.

Throughout this research we have collected 6423 sentences, proving that individuals are really interested in debates and want to share their knowledge and opinions. Even when avatars' intention is to express their emotions, they prefer to use emoticons or written expressions.

Although the affective parameter was relevant to the overall superiority of verbal communication, the interactive parameter gathered much more messages. All the descriptors in the interactive parameter refer to debate, not only with messages regarding its resumption, but also boosting.

Results have showed individuals are active, engage in debates and want to contribute to ongoing discussions. Curiously, users didn'tmention many events happening in real life, probably because they see SL as an opportunity to live another life. Results also reveal that users regularly use vocative, because they need to specify the person they are talking to. This discloses a flaw in SL interaction which might be overcome through a more powerful database of gestures and movements.

The cohesive parameter did not give us much information, but we could foresee the sense of community and the union between avatars, when they used specific words or expressions.

In relation to non-verbal results, we have concluded that it is difficult to establish a connection between the avatar's appearance and the user's behavior or status. In order to obtain this information it is essential to apply questionnaires and interviews. Although the majority of the descriptors in the appearance parameter could not be analyzed, observation showed that physical features are an excellent way to identify a person.

The proxemics parameter revealed that when avatars adopt a circular disposition in the group, they wish to share experiences and to point out their equal status. Even when there was a leader or a moderator, avatars chose to use an informal speech.

After the analysis of each type of communication, we have compared results and concluded that there is cohesion between both of them and that, in addition, non-verbal acts were used especially to emphasize the meaning of the messages.

This research has given us some clues on the impact of these virtual worlds in education, namely on the use of informal spaces to create a friendly environment and to enhance spontaneous interactions. The absence of an authority figure and the use of open and creative spaces also help individuals to talk to one another, exposing their ideas and opinions freely. Despite this fact, we can't firmly say that SL is a useful tool to improve learning and a powerful instrument to use in classroom. If a teacher wants to use this kind of virtual environment, we suggest the implementation of discussion activities.

In conclusion, we can say that verbal communication is the most used type of interaction in SL, in spite of weakening the content of the messages. So, it might be useful to improve nonverbal communication, not only by increasing the gestures available in the inventory, but also by developing new postures and movements.

FUTURE RESEARCH DIRECTIONS

Throughout this chapter we have indicated some future research directions that might give educators and researchers a new background on this particular virtual world.

One of the studies we consider important is concerned with the relationship between avatars' life in SL and users' real life. This could tell us more about behavior, learning and teaching habits, allowing educators to adopt the most useful strategies to achieve their learning goals.

Another important research direction is related with the analysis of these two components of communication in multicultural groups in order to realize the impact that this interaction has in real and in second life.

Finally it could be helpful to develop a system to improve non-verbal communication, so that avatars can understand the full meaning of messages by intonation and postural movements.

FURTHER READINGS

Exodus to the virtual world: how online fun is changing reality, by Edward Castronova

Castronova discuss the growing popularity of virtual worlds, such as Second Life and World of Warcraft, and why these virtual environments can shift social, political, educational and economic paradigms.

Interpersonal communication and human relationships, by Mark Knapp

This book explains, through the use of common experiences, several principles and theories of interpersonal communication. Its main aim is to motivate readers to understand and critically think about their own relational communication and those of others.

Successful nonverbal communication: principles and applications, by Dale Leathers

In this book Leathers demonstrates the importance of nonverbal messages to the success of interpersonal communication. The author presents nonverbal cues and their functions, as well several tests for measuring and developing nonverbal communication skills.

REFERENCES

Appel, J. (2006). Second Life develops education following: Virtual worlds being used by some educators and youth groups for teaching, socialization. *eSchoolNews: Tecnology News for Today's K-20 Educator.* Retrieved April 11, 2010, from http://www.eschoolnews.com/news/topnews/index.cfm?i=42030&CFID=3971087&CFTOKEN=31042212

Davis, F. (1979). *A comunicação Não-verbal.* São Paulo, Brazil: Summus.

Hall, E. (1968). A system for the notation of proxemic behavior. *American Anthropologist, 65*(5), 1003-1026. Retrieved May 23, 2008, from http://www.jstor.org/stable/668580

Hébert, L. (2006). The functions of language. In L. Hébert (Dir.), *Signo: Theoretical semiotics on the Web.* Retrieved May 23, 2008, from http://www.signosemio.com/jakobson/a_fonctions.asp

Henri, F. (1992). Computer conferencing and content analysis. In A. Kaye (Ed.), *Collaborative learning through computer conferencing* (pp. 117-135). NATO ASI Series, 90, The Najaden Papers. Heidelberg, Germany: Springer-Verlag.

Knapp, M. (1992). *Interpersonal communication and human relationships.* Boston, MA: Allyn & Bacon.

Leathers, D. (1997). *Successful nonverbal communication: Principles and applications.* Boston, MA: Allyn & Bacon.

Phillips, R. A. (2000). *Facilitating online discussion for interactive multimedia project management.* Heriot-Watt University and Robert Gordon University. Retrieved 20 June, 2008, from http://otis.scotcit.ac.uk/eworkshop.htm

Rourke, L., Anderson, T., Garrison, D. R., & Archer, W. (2001). Assessing social presence in asynchronous text based computer conferencing. *Journal of Distance Education, 14*(2). Retrieved June 6, 2006, from http://cade.athabascau.ca/vol14.2/rourke_et_al.html

Szuchewycz, B. (1995). Power in language: Verbal communication and social influence. *Canadian Journal of Communication, 20*(2). Retrieved May 29, 2008, from http://www.cjc-online.ca/index.php/journal/article/view/874/780

Toomey, M. (2000). The power of language. In M. Toomey (Ed.), *Liberation psychology: The choice of intimacy not conquest.* Retrieved May 29, 2008 from http://www.mtoomey.com/book_language.html

Weitz, S. (1979). *Nonverbal communication: Readings with commentary.* New York, NY: Oxford University Press.

KEY TERMS AND DEFINITIONS

Convention: What people say to respect society rules.

Community: Group of individuals gathered to discuss subjects of common interest, to share experiences and knowledge, and to enjoy each other's presence. This community can be a practice or a learning one and it stimulates the interaction and relationship between individuals, regardless of their geographical location.

Immersion: User's ability to control information and objects as he/she does in real life situations. The deeper the users are engaged in this virtual world, the higher their sense of realism is, and so the more they believe they experiencing real situations.

Intentionality: Cohesion between written or verbal message and kinesics and proxemics movements.

Kinesics: Study of observable and meaningful movements happening throughout interpersonal communication like gestures, facial expressions or postures.

Non-Verbal Communication: Communication based on visual, vocal and invisible systems, with the main goal of emphasizing, clearing up or replacing speech acts.

Proxemics: Study of people's positioning and behavior in space. It also studies the distance between individuals during a conversation and the relative position of objects.

Sense of Presence: User's belief that the virtual world is real, because it has some similarities with real life such as gravity or topography. This concept can be linked to immersion, since the user believes that he/she is in a real environment and that he is able to interact with people and objects.

Verbal Communication: Oral language, it is the most common type of communication in an interactional setting, although not the most important one. This type of communication should be analyzed according to the meaning and intention of the verbal acts.

Chapter 8
Virtual Worlds and Reception Studies:
Comparing Engagings

CarrieLynn D. Reinhard
Roskilde University, Denmark

ABSTRACT

Across the various fields, discourse communities, and paradigms studying virtual worlds, there are disagreements about the object of their studies. The nature of what virtual worlds are, and how to study them, are in flux. For some, this flux has benefits. However, the flux is potentially a problem for the study of virtual worlds from the audience and reception studies paradigm. Without knowing what can be labelled as a "virtual world," it is hard to study how people engage with a virtual world and to discuss what is found as ecologically valid. This chapter argues for research studies focusing on how people make sense of virtual worlds when they engage with them, and to compare these situated sense-making processes amongst "virtual worlds technologies" as well as other types of media products. By mapping out and comparing such engagings, we may have a better understanding about what constitutes a virtual world.

INTRODUCTION

As a new computer-based technology, a new communication medium, a new entertaining pastime, a new instructional tool, and a new venue for self-expression, virtual worlds have become the "object of interest" for a variety of academic fields and public discussion. The introduction of any new media technology, content, or genre often causes the same pattern of questions, problems and approaches from academics and the public (Golub, 2010; Manovich, 2003; Marvin, 1988). The introduction tends to be met with questions over what is the new technology, how does it

DOI: 10.4018/978-1-60960-854-5.ch008

impact people, how are people using it, and how can it be beneficially integrated into society and culture.

By positioning virtual worlds as a new media technology, I am consciously highlighting how virtual worlds have been undergoing a similar period of answering these questions. As with media innovations before it, this is a period of flux for virtual worlds technologies. This period is seen in the disagreements that exist regarding the conceptualization of the technologies, contents, and users of these media products.

Being in a period of flux has both advantages and disadvantages. On the advantages side, those who are innovating virtual worlds have latitude in what they should do to have their final media product be considered as aligned with the terrain of products known as virtual worlds technologies. On the disadvantages side, those who are studying how and why people engage with virtual worlds, and the impact doing so can have, find themselves perhaps troubling over how to study such objects. This chapter approaches the study of virtual worlds from the audience and reception studies paradigm, which would consider the flux a disadvantage with the potential to be advantageous.

My proposal for handling this flux is the propagation of methods that centralize the comparison of media engagings through situated sense-making processes. My assumption is that comparisons will provide fuller understandings of what is unique about engaging with virtual worlds, thereby helping us to better conceptualize virtual worlds. Empirical work on mapping the similarities and differences amongst virtual worlds, and between virtual worlds and other media products, may help handle the flux by providing bottom-up, empirically based definitions and typologies. We often know what something is by knowing what it is not. If we want to know what a virtual world is, especially to those who engage with them, then we should know what they consider a virtual world is and is not.

We should study virtual worlds as one medium among others in people's media landscapes by comparing these engagings with other media products (Dovey & Lister, 2009; Hermes, 2009). By mapping out people's engagings with a variety of media products, we can understand the convergences and divergences amongst various virtual world technologies and between virtual worlds and other media technologies. In order to map out this terrain of reception, we should utilize an interpretivist perspective to understand how people make sense of their engagings with media products (Dervin & Foreman-Wernet, 2003).

First, I review the flux and disagreements of conceptualizing this new media technology. Second, I review the types of comparison studies that have already been done and discuss where they lack a) comparisons to other media products and b) an interpretive perspective on engaging with media products. Third, I propose the need for methods for studying comparisons that understand situations of media engagings as complex, situated sense-making processes. Fourth, I discuss different types of methods that could be useful in this endeavor, with examples of work my colleagues and I have done to this end at the Virtual Worlds Research Project at Roskilde University (http://worlds.ruc.dk).

THE PROBLEM OF FLUX

In a top-down approach to audience and reception studies, how we study engaging with a virtual world depends on how we define what a virtual world is (Boellstorff, 2010; Schroeder, 2008). In these media reception situations, the entry point usually depends on the media product chosen: do we want to study violent television, emotional films, multiplayer games, and so forth. To say we want to study how, why, when, and where people engage with a "virtual world", for XYZ reasons, we would first have to define what is a virtual world and why the one we have chosen to study qualifies as such. Without knowing what is and is not a "virtual world", it is difficult to make claims about what happens when a person engages with a virtual world, or to apply what is learned from one such engaging to other virtual worlds. This not knowing is the flux that I discuss in this section.

Defining Virtual Worlds

To study a virtual world, and a person's engaging with it, we begin with the problem "what is a virtual world?" From an exploration of the literature produced from research into virtual worlds technologies across numerous discourse communities, I have found a multiplicity of answers to this question (Reinhard, 2010a). So as not to impose my own definition into this confusion, I refer to these material/digital objects as "virtual worlds technologies", creating an umbrella term for the assortment of technologies being grouped together for or associated with this field of research. The multiplicity indicates that a certain amount of disagreement surrounds these material/digital objects and the phenomena associated with them. Throughout this research, it appears that academics differ on three important considerations: the classification of virtual worlds as a medium, the definition of boundaries of separation and inclusion, and the jargon or terms used to label these technologies.

The first consideration focuses on whether or not virtual worlds technologies can be classified as communication medium. Academics differ on classifying these technologies as a "communication medium" or as a "metamedium" with a variety of communication modalities or channels. Wadley, Gibbs and Ducheneaut (2009) argue that virtual worlds are not themselves "communication media", but simulations of three-dimensional space within which different channels of "virtual communication media" are implemented. Others argue they are more than what a modern day conceptualization of a medium allows for: to Boellstorff (2008), virtual worlds offer more to

people than any other medium before them by providing places for human cultures to evolve. This initial classification is important if we want to understand how virtual worlds technologies relate to the array of media products people engage with on a daily basis.

The second consideration focuses on what are the features a virtual world technology needs to have to be defined as a virtual world. That is to say, academics differ on what is the definition of a virtual world. According to Bell and Robbins-Bell's (2008) joint analysis of the etymology of the term, the term "virtual worlds" goes back to 1965 and Ivan E. Sutherland's idea that through computer screens we can see a virtual world. This usage was repeated by Richard Bolt in 1980. This idea of the computer as window into a new world grew in 1980s as computers became powerful enough to construct/maintain/model "complex natural environments", so that before the rise of the internet, anything "beyond the screen" was a virtual world.

With the rise of internet and networked computers in the 1990s, virtual worlds became conceived as multiple and interacting. In what was apparently the first contemporary definition, Bruce Damer in 1997 mentioned "navigable visual digital environments...inhabited by users represented as avatars" (as quoted in Bell & Robbins-Bell, 2008). Following Damer, other formal definitions include:

- **Richard Bartle (2003):** environment that its inhabitants regard as being self-contained.
- **Raph Koster (2004):** spatially based depiction of a persistent virtual environment, which can be experienced by numerous participants at once, who are represented within the space by avatars.
- **Edward Castronova (2004):** crafted places inside computers that are designed to accommodate large numbers of people.

- **Mark Bell (2008):** A synchronous, persistent network of people, represented as avatars, facilitated by networked computers.
- **Sarah Robbins-Bell (2008):** persistence; multiuser; avatars; wide area network.
- **Ralph Schroeder (2008):** persistent virtual environments in which people experience others as being there with them - and where they can interact with them.
- **Tom Boellstorff (2010):** places of human culture realized by computer programs through the Internet, a definition that includes online games but excludes things like email and websites, and thus even social networking sites like Facebook.

Across these definitions we see the following similarities in what are defining characteristics: people, computers, and space/place. Differences include: persistence, presence, avatars. None of these definitions specifically address the representation of the world, via computer graphics (2D or 3D) or text -- although Boellstorff (2010) stated a virtual world does not need "visuality" -- and the necessity of the interaction to be synchronous versus asynchronous.

It appears academics agree that the label "virtual worlds" applies to a specific array of digital technologies that require certain actions of the user to engage with them. Specifically, the material object(s) of a computer-network produces a digital space within which people can gather. Beyond that, agreements breakdown, especially given the continual emergence of objects that could be virtual worlds, such as Facebook games like Zynga's *Farmville*, or networked console videogames like Sony's *Little Big Planet*. Without agreed upon boundaries for what constitutes a "virtual world", what results is a vast array of related virtual worlds technologies that may not all be the same when it comes to how a person engages with them.

The third consideration focuses on the labels being used when academics discuss what it was

they have studied. The use of different terms becomes the jargon through which academics communicate. The focus here is on the multitude of terms being employed across discourse communities. Additionally, they appear to be interchangeable, and are sometimes stated without reflection or explanation for why that term was used. By going through research publications, I have generated the following list of terms, grouped by their conceptual similarities:

- virtual community, online game, digital game, social game, casual game
- MOOD (Multi-User Object Oriented Domain/Dungeon), MUD (Multi-User Dungeon/Domain), MMO (Massive(ly) Multiplayer Online), MMOG (Massive(ly) Multiplayer Online Game), MMOSG (Massive(ly) Multiplayer Online Social Game), MMORPG (Massive(ly) Multiplayer Online Role-Playing Game)
- (3D) MUVE (Multi-User Virtual/Visual Environment), SVWE (Social Virtual World Environment), MUSE (Multi-User Simulated Environment)
- networked world, virtual world, synthetic world, digital world, mirror world, sim, simulation, social virtual world, gaming virtual world, metaverse
- 3D platform, virtual environments, synthetic environments, 3D environments, CVE (Collaborative Virtual Environment), IVE (Immersive/Intelligent Virtual Environment), DVE (Distributed Virtual Environment), 3D web, 3D internet
- virtual reality, networked virtual reality

The array of terms is vast, and oftentimes they conceptually overlap, creating confusion about what is being said when one term could, or could not, stand in for another. Saponaro (2007), in trying to explain in a school assignment paper what is *Second Life*, shows the slipperiness of the labels as well as their interrelatedness: "Second Life is defined trough different acronyms: MUVE (Multiplayer Virtual Environment) is the most used, but it's even ascribed at the MMOGs' family (Massively Multiplayer Online Game), wherein it's defined as a MMOSG (Massively Multiplayer Online Social Game) to distinguish it among other role play games (MMORPG)." Without agreed upon terms, communication can become complicated and unsuccessful.

Virtual Worlds as New Media

While we may disagree as to what constitutes a virtual world, or even what to call such objects, there is no denying that virtual worlds technologies are positioned as new media. They are a new media technology because they are, or at least rely on, digital media. They require computer code for programming the multimedia content of text, audio and visual that produces the digital environments within which individuals interact with each other and the environment (Bell, 2008; Schroeder, 2008).

However, being a new medium indicates that these technologies are undergoing a period of flux as societies and cultures determine how to "manage" them. Gitelman and Pingree (2003) argued that when any new media technology is introduced into society and the marketplace, if it is able to maintain and grow in presence, then it will enter a period of flux in which its presence challenges the "ritualized conventions of existing media".

...when new media emerge in a society, their place is at first ill defined, and their ultimate meanings or functions are shaped over time by society's existing habits of media use (which, of course, derive from experience with other, established media), by shared desires for new uses, and by the slow process of adaptation between the two. The 'crisis' of a new medium will be resolved when the perceptions of the medium, as well as its practical uses, are somehow adapted to existing categories

of public understanding about what the medium does for whom and why. (p. xii)

Lievrouw and Livingstone (2002) argued there exists a process of innovation in new media development, where existing devices, practices, and arrangements are continually being innovated by designers, users, and regulators. The more innovative and iterative turns taken amongst these actors, the more normalized the new media becomes, reducing the ideological tension and conceptual flux that originally surrounded it.

With each new media technology introduced, we can see the same recurring ideological tensions (Manovich, 2003). In the 1800s, new communication technologies were met with the same tension of "fascination and fear" (Marvin, 1988) as today's virtual worlds technologies (Golub, 2010). These tensions fuel public and academic interest in studying the new media technology. The particular interest is in how the different behaviors implicated by the new technology support either side of the tension. As virtual worlds technologies become more integrated into people's everyday lives, then this period of flux and tension typically dissipates. What the technology is will crystallize, and how societies and cultures can manage them will become normalized. We will know we have reached that point when this period of flux has diminished.

Of course, one method to make this period diminish may be through judicious study and mapping of the various definitions and terms being used by academics, and even other actors like practitioners, designers and the public. Such a solution would ultimately entail having "the" definition and "the" jargon agreed upon through negotiation of all the actors' epistemological and ontological stances. I am suggesting a solution that entails gathering further evidence as to how people make sense of virtual worlds technologies as part of their everyday lives and the mediascape within which it is entangled. Understanding how people make sense of these technologies, in relation to each other and to other media technologies, could provide empirical evidence to help academics and others have a basis for the negotiation of answers to the question of "what is a virtual world".

COMPARING ENGAGINGS

It is my contention that virtual worlds technologies should be studied as just another medium people engage with during their daily lives. I make this assertion based on three reasons. First, differentiations between "new" and "old" are unnecessary. According to media historian Carolyn Marvin, other generations have remarked about the shifts in technology and society: "If our own experience is unique in detail, its structure is characteristically modern." (1988, p. 3). Each new medium does not emerge from a vacuum to become a unique object: the new develops out of the potentials and pitfalls of the old. Instead of seeing engaging with virtual worlds technologies as being unique due to the characteristics of the technologies, we need to recognize that all media technologies are unique due to their specific characteristics.

Second, virtual world technologies appear to be three types of communication media simultaneously. They are the result of computer networked technologies, where computers communicate with each other. They are a visual and auditory manifestation of a digital environment that communicates the representation of the environment to the user. They are a framework of communication channels, which allows for users to communicate with each other. What results is a communication technology that is simultaneously a mass medium and an interpersonal medium.

Third, differentiations between what happens inworld versus offline unnecessarily separate engaging with virtual worlds technologies from engaging with other media products. This tension appears in the extent to which academics will define the virtual world as being separate from the "actual" world due to "membrane" of

technology or "magic circle" conceptualizations (Golub, 2010). Any "membrane" must be seen as permeable due to the user bringing into the world his or her own lived experiences (Malaby, 2009). By placing virtual worlds technologies within these "magic circles", we further the conceptualization of them as unique and worthy of special consideration, reinforcing the flux that surrounds them. Instead, these technologies need to be understood for how they are as interwoven into people's lives as other media technologies.

There have been studies that have compared engaging with virtual worlds to engaging with "real world", or the physical world, or comparing engagings with different virtual worlds technologies. I discuss these two trends in the following sections, followed by how such studies fail to address the types of comparisons needed to be useful to handling the flux.

Comparing the Physical and the Virtual

Studies have compared experiences in a virtual world to experiences in the physical world. The typical approach is to ascertain if some psychological, sociological or cultural aspect of living in the "real world" will manifest similarly or differently in a "virtual world". Even studies that do not explicitly compare the physical world to a virtual world appear implicitly interested in understanding how similar or different "being" in the latter is compared to the former (examples: Fox & Bailenson, 2009; Lo, 2008; Pena, Hancock & Merola, 2009). Currently, one line of inquiry on this topic informs the argument on the viability of virtual worlds as places for experimenting to understand and/or modify human behaviour (see Gillath, McCall, Shaver & Blascovich, 2008; Moore, Wiederhold, Wiederhold & Riva, 2002). Overall, underlying questions in these comparison studies focus on how close virtual worlds can replicate, represent, and remediate the physical world and human behaviours from it.

The majority of these studies appear to focus on the performance of specific cognitive or physical tasks. Flannery and Walles (2003) experimentally tested whether or not knowledge about what constitutes an office in the physical world would be accessed when evaluating a virtual office. Mania and Chalmers (2001) experimentally compared learning in virtual reality set-ups and a more traditional physical world classroom for memory retention. Jackson, Zhao and Witt (2009) conducted a survey to understand the relationship of morality between the physical world and virtual worlds. Bideau, Kulpa, Ménardais et al (2003) experimentally compared a handball goalkeeper's actions in the physical world and a virtual reconstruction of a stadium. In an experiment, Arnold, Farrell, Pettifer and West (2002) had participants complete a skilled motor task of passing a metal hoop across a series of joined metal pipes: either first in the real world, or first in a virtual world accessed via a head mounted display.

Studies that compare internal and external behaviors tend to be focused more on narrow aspects of engaging with the virtual world: motor tasks, memory retention, and so forth. There is less focus on aspects of engaging that are more complicated, such as enjoyment or communication practices (Golub, 2010), or on considering a number of these factors concurrently. An example of a study comparing more complex practices comes from Castronova, Williams, Shen et al's (2009) experimental and survey examination of economic systems and behaviors in MMORPGs. While less complex than economics, Friedman, Karniel and Dinur (2009) employed the virtual world *Second Life* in an experiment to compare group discussions inworld and outworld.

Comparing Different Media Technologies

More similar to the argument being made in this chapter are those studies that have compared different media technologies to various virtual worlds technologies. In a longitudinal study, Smyth (2007) randomly assigned people to play one of four types of games for a month: arcade, console, sole computer, or MMORPG. In an experiment, Persky and Blascovich (2007) tested for the impact of violent content on aggressive tendencies between people playing a desktop computer game or an immersive version accessed via head mounted display. Chen and Raney (2009) experimentally compared playing a Nintendo Wii game or a Flash game about boxing, or watching a DVD clip, for impacts on mood. Bailenson, Patel, Nielsen et al (2008) analyzed an experiment on learning Tai Chi moves from video versus virtual reality.

Sometimes this type of comparison study will overlap with studies comparing physical world to virtual world performance when one of the media technologies studied is a physical, tangible object. In an experiment about sense-making, Antoniettei and Cantoia (2000) compared a static image of art to an immersive virtual environment. For their experiment, Mania and Chalmers (2001) compared task performance when information was communicated via a physical lecture, a desktop virtual environment, a head mounted virtual reality, or audio only. In another experiment, Antoniettei and Mellone (2003) had people play either the physical or virtual version of a game and compared performance with each.

Where Lacking Comparisons Persist

The studies discussed above are examples of trends in research that compare engaging with a virtual world technology to something else. Looking across these studies, they tend to lack the two aspects that I aruge are necessary for making deep understandings out of such comparisons: the type of deep understandings that could help us address the question of "what is a virtual world". First, they lack a focus on comparing the complex, situated sense-making processes involved with engaging with these virtual worlds technologies. Second, there has been more work done comparing virtual worlds technologies to each other and the physical world than comparing them to other media products.

First, the majority of these studies are experimental, quantitative, and focused on specific aspects of engaging without consideration of the complexity involved in these media reception situations. They appear to study the media reception situation from the perspective of the technology, and how the features of the technology impact the engaging with it. Sometimes the research brings in sociodemographic and/or psychographic features of the person to test for interactions with the technological features, such as Persky and Blascovich (2007) comparing gender, violent and nonviolent content, and desktop versus head mounted display. However, overall, there is less consideration for the mediating, moderating, and interacting influences of the sense-making processes that occur within the situations of engaging. Without accounting for these influences, the actual operations of a person engaging with a technology, and how a person understands what is a virtual world, especially in comparison to other media products, cannot be fully understood (Reinhard & Dervin, 2010; Potter & Tomasello, 2003).

Second, most previous works have focused on virtual worlds technologies, specifically digital games and virtual reality interfaces. Less work appears to have been done on what researchers would more generally consider to be virtual worlds, given the most agreed upon definition discussed previously. Digital games found in arcades, on console systems, and standalones on computers are not persistent, networked digital environments that continue progression without the involvement of the player. Virtual reality interfaces may provide access to a virtual world, but the presence of a head mounted display, haptic gloves, and other related interface devices is not sufficient to say there is a virtual world being studied. In most studies that utilize VR interfaces, what is called a "virtual world" is just a digital environment. Thus, there appears to have been more work done to compare

virtual worlds technologies than virtual worlds to other media technologies and the physical world, with some exceptions (examples: Castronova et al, 2009; Friedman et al, 2009; Smyth, 2007).

Additionally, there has been less focus on comparing virtual worlds technologies to media products that are further removed from them taxonomically. That is, most of the comparisons to other media technologies have been similar in terms of being a game (ex. Antoniettei & Mellone, 2003; Persky & Blascovich, 2007; Smyth, 2007) or something else that requires visual cues (ex. Antoniettei & Cantoia, 2000; Bailenson, Patel, Nielsen et al, 2008; Chen & Raney, 2009; Mania & Chalmers, 2001). Such comparisons make theoretical and conceptual sense, given the similarities in engaging with such technologies, and thus more should be done to understand such overlaps. However, we may also learn new similarities, and differences, when we compare virtual worlds technologies to media products that appear to be less similar to them, such as music and books.

STUDYING COMPARISONS

In this section I explain my suggestion for how to compare engagings with different media products. It is my argument that to truly compare, we need to understand all the ways engagings can overlap, and to make comparisons in those overlaps for similarities and differences. In order to understand these overlaps, we need to map out engagings. I am suggesting a focus on complex, situated sense-making processes for comparing engagings with the variety of media products that constitutes the everyday lifeworlds of users (Reinhard & Dervin, 2010). What I discuss in this section are a) what are situated sense-making processes, and b) what are methods to measure these processes for comparing media reception situations.

Situated Sense-Making Processes

When studying a media reception situation, the focus should be neither on the person nor the virtual worlds technology, but on those times and spaces when the person and the technology interact within the situation and how the person makes sense of such interactions (Giddings, 2009; Reinhard & Dervin, 2010). The main analytical interest should be the mapping of differences and similarities as not just due to technological or content features and/or sociodemographic or psychographic features, but on complex, situated sense-making processes. There needs to be a focus on the complex, interconnected internal and external cognitive, affective, and behavioural processes that constitute sense-making as it occurs during the engaging. This call for focusing on situated sense-making processes comes from other researchers as well.

Some researchers have argued on the intertwinement of online and offline sense-making. Golub (2010) argued for the need to study not just the users when inworld, but also how those worlds they engage with are part of the larger fabric of their lifeworlds. Marvin (1988) argued that since we always use our bodies to engage with any media, engaging with a new medium draws upon the body's experience with older media: we make sense of the new based on what we know from the old. Malpas (2009) argued that virtual worlds are not autonomous from the non-virtual world of people's everyday lives: the systems that constitute virtual worlds are dependent for their structure and meaning on the pre-established systems that constitute the non-virtual world. Thus, how we make sense of a virtual world is similar to how we make sense of other engagings with other, older media products, which is also related to how we make sense of the non-mediated experiences we have in our everyday lives. There is no online life and offline life: there is just "life".

Some researchers have argued for the need to study the situation within which the engaging oc-

curs as the main unit of analysis. Dervin made it her primary conceptual focus in her Sense-Making Methodology (Dervin & Foreman-Wernet, 2003) that can be applied to compare different media products with one another (see Dervin & Song, 2005; Reinhard, 2008). Hoelig and Hasebrink (2008) argued to shift analytical focus from the media technology to the user-within-situation to understand what is being done with any media product. Combining these arguments with those made above, there is the foundation for an argument that supports studying situated sense-making processes. That is, to understand this intertwinement between the online and offline – to understand the cognitive and affective processes of making sense of just "life" – we need to take a situationality approach to our studies of media reception. With a microscopic focus on the situation we can see the operations that occur as people make sense of their lives, whether online or offline.

What I and others are advocating is for audience and reception studies that focus on mapping these complex, situated sense-making processes during media reception situations. To do so requires a methodological and methodical focus on a) understanding sense-making processes and b) comparing media reception situations that involve differing media products. By positioning virtual worlds technologies as media products, I extend this theoretical, methodological, and methodical suggestion to the creation of studies to understand people's engagings with virtual worlds. What follows are my suggestions for how methodological approaches and research methods could be applied to this pursuit, with examples given from work my colleagues and I have already done.

Three Approaches to Methods

I do not consider there to be just one methodological approach or method that can be usefully applied in this endeavor. Instead, a variety of methods could be applied, as they currently exist or with some alteration. Such methods could be employed from a quantitative or qualitative approach, as long as the method is anchored in the dual requirements to measure situated sense-making processes for the purposes of comparing media reception situations.

Instead of bifurcating into quantitative and qualitative, a better distinction would be to consider how researchers locate the media reception situations. There are at least three ways to do this. In this final section, I discuss what I see as these three locations, with examples that illustrate the type of studies being done to compare engagings from them. These locations are: a) "recollection", locating the media reception situation in the past experiences of everyday life; b) "everyday", locating the media reception situation in the everyday experience as it occurs; c) "artificial", locating the media reception situation in the laboratory experience as it occurs.

Recollection

On approach would be to compare engagings by locating the media reception situations that have already occurred in the course of the person's everyday life. The methods for this approach would focus on people's recollection of the engaging and the situated sense-making processes from it. Interviews, questionnaires and focus groups have a long history of being used for this purpose, replete with advantages (e.g. cost effectiveness) and disadvantages (e.g. problems of recall). With the proper anchoring on situated sense-making processes and comparing engagings, these methods could be applied from either a quantitative or qualitative approach.

Indeed, so fundamental are these methods that they would likewise be useful in measuring situated sense-making processes for the other two locations. What separates them into their own approach is the focus on recollection. While recollection may play a role in the everyday and the artificial, it is central to this approach: through these methods, the past can be recalled from the person's memory. Additionally, while there are problems associated with recall -- in that people may not be able to faithfully recite the engagings moment-by-moment -- there are means by which to adjust the method to account for this lacking. One approach would be to utilize an interview, questionnaire or focus group informed by Dervin's Sense-Making Methodology (Dervin, 2008).

Other approaches can be seen in the studies that, to some extent, appear to be accounting for this dual focus on situated sense-making processes and comparing engagings. There have been studies focused on understanding in more depth the sense-making processes of engaging with one virtual world. Shin (2009) conducted a quantitatively intensive survey analysis of *Second Life* users to understand motivations to engaging with the world. Oliver and Carr (2009) interviewed couples who played *World of Warcraft* together to understand how they make sense of playing as it related to other aspects of their lives.

Other studies have sought to compare experiences with a more than one virtual world. Kieger (2010) surveyed self-identified entrepreneurs of two virtual worlds, *Second Life* and *Entropia*, for how used the worlds and made sense of them for business purposes. Still others have looked at virtual worlds compared to other media products. Sivunen and Siitonen (2010) interviewed international organizational teams and their use of media technologies for communicating and compared them to MMO gaming clans' communication techniques.

With all these examples, the recollections tend not to be situationally anchored; although, it is not unheard of. With Sivunen and Siitonen (2010), the MMO gaming clan members were asked to answer the interview questions with the recollection of specific situations. Anchoring the interview, questionnaire or focus group to specific situations would yield even more information about the sense-makings people had when engaging with these virtual world technologies.

Everyday

A second approach would be to locate and understand people's sense-making in these engagings in the context of their everyday lives. Unlike recollection, the focus would be to understand the sense-makings as they occurred within the context of the person's daily life. Traditionally, such a focus has been the purview of ethnographies. While there are other methodological approaches, given the history of ethnographies in social sciences, I will focus my discussion on how ethnographic approaches can be useful for studying situated sense-making processes to compare engagings.

Ethnographies have helped us understand how various media products are integrated into the everyday lives of people, and the sense they make of these media products as part of their lifeworlds (Moores, 1993; Bird, 2003). Ethnographic approaches use a variety of methods, such as participant-observation, text analysis, focus group and interview. At a meso-level analysis, a media ecology approach focuses on the specific situational contexts in which sense is made before, during and after engagings with virtual worlds and other media products. This approach could provide an in-depth analysis of "what people *really* do with media, rather than what we imagine they *might* do, or what close readings of texts *assume* they might do" (Bird, 2003, p.191, italics in original). At a micro-level analysis, Giddings (2009) has called for a moment-by-moment ethnographic analysis of gameplay as it occurs ("microethology"): his argument is based on the need to understand the moment(s) of intersection between technology, content and user.

There have been examples of ethnographic methods used to study people's engaging with virtual world technologies from the vantage of within the physical world and/or in a virtual world (i.e. virtual ethnography). One approach is to have an in-depth investigation of one virtual world. Boellstorff (2008) conducted a two year ethnographic study of the cultures and inhabitants of *Second Life*. Others have done less intensive ethnographic studies by going inworld with specific questions in mind. Ostrander (2008) studied situated sense-making processes when she examined information seeking behaviors in *Second Life*.

Another approach is to compare more than one virtual world. Researchers observed behaviors at specific types of locations across a variety of worlds (*Star Wars Galaxy, City of Heroes, Second Life, EverQuest II, World of Warcraft, EverQuest Online Adventures,* and *There*) to understand how they were being constructed as public spaces or "third places" (Moore, Gathman & Ducheneaut, 2009). Voulgari and Komis (2010) combined their participant observations with interviews of players to understand collaborative problem-solving processes in *Lineage II* and *Tribal Wars*.

Other ethnographies have approached the subject from the position of seeing the engaging with the virtual world in a larger framework of engagings and lived experiences. Golub (2010) discussed his experience with a guild in *World of Warcraft* for how they utilized a variety of media technologies across their lives to conduct guild business. Albrechtslund (2010) followed gamers' storytelling on different websites to understand their processes of meaning making as it related to their identity constructions. In studying *Whyville. net*, the researchers focused analytically on "an insider gaming practice" which allowed them to follow the users' activities across gaming spaces, both online and offline (Feldon & Kafai, 2008; Fields & Kafai, 2008).

However, none of the examples given were studies that compared situations of engaging with different media products. Those studies that looked at use of media technologies outside of the virtual world were primarily interested in how such technologies were integrated into the person's engaging with the virtual world. A media ecology ethnography, combined with a "microethology", would be intensive and expensive, but also expansive for our knowledge, and thus worthy of the investment.

Research Example

The following is an example of an ethnographic study that compared media reception situations involving two different types of virtual worlds. The particular research focus was on how people made sense of their avatars in specific situations and in general. My colleague on the Virtual Worlds Research Project, Sisse Siggård Jensen (2009; 2010) conducted participant observations and in-situ video interviews at the homes or offices of users of Second Life and players of EverQuest. During these sessions, the interviewees led her through their own experiences with the respective virtual world, discussing and interpreting their actions for her during these research journeys.

Jensen analyzed these "sense-makings in practice" for how the people discussed the role of their avatars. She found similarities in how people discussed their avatars across the different types of engagings people had with the virtual worlds, and thus across the two very different virtual worlds. She argued that analyzing these engagings with virtual worlds through the interpretive perspective of the users helped her to find similarities between the gaming-based world and the user-driven world.

What Jensen's work shows is the utility of studying sense-makings to compare different virtual worlds. Because her topic was focused on understanding avatars, there was no feasible way to compare these engagings to the variety of media products that do not contain avatars. However, her focus on comparing through sense-making processes is the reason this study is included as an example for how an ethnographic method could be applied to this line of study being proposed.

Artificial

The third approach would locate media reception situations within artificial conditions. Essentially, this would entail examining engagings as they occurred outside of the context of a person's everyday life. Commonly, this approach utilizes the artificiality of the laboratory to create media

reception situations under controlled conditions. While, typically, experiments approach data collection from a quantitative approach, they could be restructured for a more qualitative approach to measure situated sense-making processes (Reinhard, 2010b). As experiments traditionally have structures for making comparisons among conditions, the addition of a qualitative data collection would help to compare situated sense-making processes.

Indeed, the artificiality of the experimental framework could illuminate the sense-making processes by allowing for a moment-by-moment analysis of them. Dervin (2008) discussed how what appears to be, to the observer, a cohesive, solitary situation can be broken down into "micro-moments" of time-space: in essence, mini-situations embedded in the larger situation. German reception theorists such as Iser (Holub, 1984) have discussed how there exists "gaps" structured into a text that influence the process, over time, of reading the text. Thus, each moment of engaging with a media product could require sense-making.

To understand situated sense-making processes in-depth, a moment-by-moment accounting of them would be useful to understand how they relate to the media product and the context of the situation. The ability to control the conditions of the engaging in an experiment could facilitate such a mapping. Josephs (2000) discussed the utility of the artificial lab environment "to slow down the meaning-making process in order to gain access to it." (p. 124). Talk aloud protocols could be combined with recollection and observation methods to surround the situated sense-making processes as they occurred and afterwards.

Such an experimental design requires more measurement of sense-making than the application of pre- and post-test questionnaires typically allow. One example of a more involved measurement comes from Hindmarsh, Heath and Fraser (2006), who analyzed people's conversations while they engaged with a desktop virtual reality interface.

However, they did not study a virtual world, and they did not compare the sense-making of the VR interface to other media technologies.

Research Example

The following is an example of a study I conducted where I examined how novice users made sense of the two types of virtual worlds, gaming and social, in comparison to two older media products, film and video games. The two virtual worlds I studied were City of Heroes and Second Life. I controlled for different types of media technologies to produce media reception situations with different requirements on their actions and, possibly, their sense-makings. To do so, I utilized the framework of the experiment to structure the comparisons, while I used various qualitative methods to measure the situated sense-making processes (Reinhard, 2010b).

The study was a within-subjects experimental design with in-depth qualitative interviews employed alongside talk aloud, surveys and observations as the data collection methods. Data collection occurred while participants were engaging with the media products, via talk aloud protocols, and afterwards when they were asked to recall and compare these situations in open-ended questionnaires and interviews structured using Dervin's Sense-Making Methodology (Reinhard & Dervin, 2010).

I analyzed how the participants discussed their engagings with the four media products. In this analysis, I focused on areas of potential overlap to compare sense-makings that occurred when engaging with the virtual worlds to console videogames and movies. By using Sense-Making Methodology, I was able to illustrate how situated sense-making processes can provide locations of potential overlaps within which to compare engagings with different media technologies (Reinhard & Dervin, 2010). Using these overlaps, similarities could be found across these engagings in how people had questions about the engaging, what they found helped or hindered them as they

engaged, and the roles their past experiences and expectations played in how they made sense of the engaging.

As with Jensen's study, I collected data on the participants' engagings as they occurred. I also sought their recollection of what happened using Sense-Making Methodology to probe the experience and have them discuss how it connected to their everyday lives. As with both studies, the focus on situated sense-making processes allowed us to find similarities alongside differences in how these engagings compare. The analysis of these comparisons has just begun. Thus far, the foundation has indicated the utility of combining the artificial construct of the experiment with the interviewing for situated sense-making processes.

CONCLUSION

Virtual worlds are no more special than any media technology that existed before them. All media technologies have affordances and constraints due to their technological structures, which may align or differ with other media technologies, and which may be more or less useful for some purpose than another. But each new media remediates upon the older (Bolter & Grusin, 1999), reconfiguring the old to offer something new until the trajectory of media technologies is a long history of innovation (Marvin, 1988). Thus, virtual worlds are unique and worthy of study, just as each media product has unique characteristics that make it worthy of study. Virtual worlds are both different and no different than every other media product that constitutes the fabric of a person's lifeworld. As such, they should be studied in conjunction with studying those other media products in how a person makes sense of each as it relates to her life.

Because we are in a period of flux, where our understanding of and the potential for virtual worlds are being forged, there are great opportunities to explore how we study people's engagings with them. Indeed, doing so may better help us handle this flux. The approach advocated here is not top-down theorizing but bottom-up empiricizing: to understand how the people who engage with these technologies make sense of them in comparison to other media technologies for what sets these technologies apart into something categorizable as "virtual worlds". Supporting research that seeks to map the similarities and differences of engaging with virtual worlds to engaging with other, more established media products could foster the growth of virtual worlds to reach their full potential.

The methodological and methodical approaches discussed in this chapter are but one potential means for handling the issue of what is a virtual world. I am arguing that any of those approaches could be useful in handling the problem if they are structured a) to understand situated sense-making processes during the engaging with b) different media products. The approaches suggested are not to say we should ignore differences that arise in these comparative studies. However, we will not know about similarities that exist until we look for them. These proposed approaches are my suggestions for where and how to start looking. The examples given are from studies that have only begun to go looking. I hope others will be inspired to go looking after reading this chapter.

In order for virtual worlds to become more normalized, to emerge from the flux and become more fully integrated into societies and cultures, we have to stop focusing on them, and start focusing on the people who engage with them. Only when we can show how virtual world users, and non-users, make sense of these virtual worlds can we show the potential they offer as a new computer technology, a new communication medium, a new entertaining pastime, a new instructional tool, and a new venue for self-expression.

REFERENCES

Albrechtslund, A. M. (2010). Gamers telling stories: Understanding narrative practices in an online community. *Convergence: The International Journal of Research into New Media Technologies, 16*, 112–124. doi:10.1177/1354856509348773

Antonietti, A., & Cantoia, M. (2000). To see a painting versus to walk in a painting: An experiment on sense-making through virtual reality. *Computers & Education, 34*, 213–223. doi:10.1016/S0360-1315(99)00046-9

Antonietti, A., & Mellone, R. (2003). The difference between playing games with and without the computer: A preliminary view. *The Journal of Psychology, 137*(2), 133–144. doi:10.1080/00223980309600604

Arnold, P., Farrell, M. J., Pettifer, S., & West, A. J. (2002). Performance of a skilled motor task in virtual and real. *Ergonomics, 45*(5), 348–361. doi:10.1080/00140130110120510

Bailenson, J. N., Patel, K., Nielsen, A., Bajscy, R., Jung, S.-H., & Kurillo, G. (2008). The effect of interactivity on learning physical actions in virtual reality. *Media Psychology, 11*(3), 354–376. doi:10.1080/15213260802285214

Bartle, R. A. (2003). *Designing virtual worlds*. Berkeley, CA: Peachpit Press.

Bausinger, H. (1984). Media, technology and daily life. *Media Culture & Society, 6*, 343–351. doi:10.1177/016344378400600403

Bell, M. W. (2008). Toward a definition of "virtual worlds.". *Journal of Virtual Worlds Research, 1*(1). Retrieved from http://jvwresearch.org/ index.php ?_cms=1248915995.

Bell, M. W., & Robbins-Bell, S. (2008). Towards an expanded definition of "virtual worlds.". In Villares, F. (Ed.), *New digital media: Audiovisual, games and music* (pp. 125–134). Rio de Janeiro, Brazil: E-Papers.

Benoit, B., Kulpa, R., Ménardais, S., Fradet, L., Multon, F., & Delamarche, P. (2003). Real handball goalkeeper vs. virtual handball thrower. *Presence (Cambridge, Mass.)*, *12*(4), 411–422. doi:10.1162/105474603322391631

Bird, S. E. (2003). *The audience in everyday life: Living in a media world*. New York, NY: Routledge.

Boellstorff, T. (2008). *Coming of age in Second Life: An anthropologist explores the virtually human*. Princeton, NJ: Princeton University Press.

Boellstorff, T. (2010). A typology of ethnographic scales for virtual worlds. In Bainbridge, W. S. (Ed.), *Online worlds: Convergence of the real and the virtual*. London, UK: Springer-Verlag. doi:10.1007/978-1-84882-825-4_10

Bolter, J., & Grusin, R. (1999). *Remediation: Understanding new media*. Cambridge, MA: The MIT Press.

Castronova, E. (2004). *Synthetic worlds: The business and culture of online games*. Chicago, IL: University of Chicago Press.

Castronova, E., Williams, D., Shen, C., & Ratan, R., Xiong, Li., Huang, Y., & Keegan, B. (2009). As real as real? Macroeconomic behavior in a large-scale virtual world. *New Media & Society*, *11*, 685–707. doi:10.1177/1461444809105346

Chaffee, S. H., & Metzger, M. J. (2001). The end of mass communication? *Mass Communication & Society*, *4*(4), 365–379. doi:10.1207/S15327825MCS0404_3

Chen, Y. S., & Raney, A. A. (2009). *Mood management and highly interactive video games: An experimental examination of Wii playing on mood change and enjoyment*. Paper presented at the International Communication Association Conference May 2009, Chicago.

Dervin, B., & Foreman-Wernet, L. (Eds.). (2003). *Sense-Making Methodology reader: Selected writings of Brenda Dervin*. Cresskill, NJ: Hampton Press.

Dervin, B., & Song, M. (2005). *Reaching for phenomenological depths in uses and gratifications research: A quantitative empirical investigation*. Paper presented at the annual meeting of the International Communication Association, New York City, May. Retrieved from http://communication.sbs.ohio-state.edu/ sense-making/ art/ artabsdervinsong05 icaUG.html

Dovey, J., & Lister, M. (2009). Straw men or cyborgs? *Interactions: Studies in Communication and Culture*, *1*(1), 129–145. doi:10.1386/iscc.1.1.129_1

Feldon, D. F., & Kafai, Y. B. (2008). Mixed methods for mixed reality: Understanding users' avatar activities in virtual worlds. *Educational Technology Research and Development*, *56*, 575–593. doi:10.1007/s11423-007-9081-2

Fields, D. A., & Kafai, Y. B. (2008). A connective ethnography of peer knowledge sharing and diffusion in a tween virtual world. *International Journal of Computer-Supported Collaborative Learning*, *4*(1), 47–68. doi:10.1007/s11412-008-9057-1

Flannery, K., & Walles, R. (2003). How does schema theory apply to real versus virtual memories? *Cyberpsychology & Behavior*, *6*(2), 151–159. doi:10.1089/109493103321640347

Fox, J., & Bailenson, J. N. (2009). Virtual virgins and vamps: The effects of exposure to female characters' sexualized appearance and gaze in an immersive virtual environment. *Sex Roles*, *61*(3-4), 147–157. doi:10.1007/s11199-009-9599-3

Friedman, D., Karniel, Y., & Dinur, A. L. (2009). Comparing group discussion in virtual and physical environments. *Presence (Cambridge, Mass.)*, *18*(4), 286–293. doi:10.1162/pres.18.4.286

Gauntlet, D. (2009). Media studies 2.0: A response. *Interactions: Studies in Communication and Culture, 1*(1), 147–157. doi:10.1386/iscc.1.1.147_1

Giddings, S. (2009). Events and collusions: A glossary for the microethnography of video game play. *Games and Culture, 4*(2), 144–157. doi:10.1177/1555412008325485

Gillath, O., McCall, C., Shaver, P. R., & Blascovich, J. (2008). What can virtual reality teach us about prosocial tendencies in real and virtual environments? *Media Psychology, 11*(2), 259–282. doi:10.1080/15213260801906489

Gitelman, L., & Pingree, G. B. (2003). *New media, 1740-1915*. Cambridge, MA: The MIT Press.

Golub, A. (2010). Being in the World (of Warcraft): Raiding, realism, and knowledge production in a massively multiplayer online game. *Anthropological Quarterly, 83*(1), 17–45. doi:10.1353/anq.0.0110

Hermes, J. (2009). Audience studies 2.0: On the theory, politics and method of qualitative audience research. *Interactions: Studies in Communication and Culture, 1*(1), 111–127. doi:10.1386/iscc.1.1.111_1

Hindmarsh, J., Heath, C., & Fraser, M. (2006). (Im)materiality, virtual reality and interaction: Grounding the "virtual" in studies of technology in action. *The Sociological Review, 54*(4), 795–817. doi:10.1111/j.1467-954X.2006.00672.x

Hoelig, S., & Hasebrink, U. (2008). *What do people do when they use the internet? Communication modes as an integrated concept for the analysis of media use in converging media environments.* Paper presented at the 2nd European Communication Conference, ECREA, Barcelona, Spain, November 26-29.

Holub, R. C. (1984). *Reception theory: A critical introduction*. New York, NY: Methuen.

Jackson, L. A., Zhao, Y., Witt, E. A., Fitzgerald, H. E., & von Eye, A. (2009). Gender, race and morality in the virtual world and its relationship to morality in the real world. *Sex Roles, 60*(11-12), 859–869. doi:10.1007/s11199-009-9589-5

Jensen, S. S. (2009). Avatars and their use of avatars: An empirical study of avatar-based sense-makings and communication practices in the virtual worlds of EverQuest and Second Life. *MedieKultur, 47*, 29–44.

Jensen, S. S. (2010). *Transformative interrelations of actors and their companion avatars: Sources of social innovation? Case studies of actors playing the game of EverQuest and inhabiting the social world of Second Life.* Paper presented at the 3rd ECREA Pre-Conference "Avatars and Humans: Representing Users in Digital Games", Hamburg, Germany, October 12th.

Josephs, I. E. (2000). A psychological analysis of a psychological phenomenon: The dialogical construction of meaning. *Social Sciences Information. Information Sur les Sciences Sociales, 39*, 115–129. doi:10.1177/053901800039001007

Koster, R. (2004). A virtual world by any other name? *Terra Nova* blog. Retrieved from http://terranova.blogs.com/terra_nova/2004/06/a_virtual_world.html

Lievrouw, L. A., & Livingstone, S. (2002). The social shaping and consequences of ICTs. In L. A. Lievrouw & S. Livingstone (Eds.). *Handbook of new media* (1-16). Thousand Oaks, CA: Sage Publications.

Lo, S. (2008). The impact of online game characters outward attractiveness and social status on interpersonal attraction. *Computers in Human Behavior, 24*(5), 1947–1958. doi:10.1016/j.chb.2007.08.001

Malpas, J. (2009). On the non-autonomy of the virtual. *Convergence: The International Journal of Research into New Media Technologies, 15,* 135–139. doi:10.1177/1354856508101579

Mania, K., & Chalmers, A. (2001). The effects of levels of immersion on memory and presence in virtual environments: A reality centered approach. *Cyberpsychology & Behavior, 4*(2), 247–264. doi:10.1089/109493101300117938

Manovich, L. (2003). New media from Borges to HTML. In Wardrip-Fruim, N., & Montfort, N. (Eds.), *The new media reader* (pp. 13–25). Cambridge, MA: The MIT Press.

Marvin, C. (1988). *When old technologies were new: Thinking about electronic communication in the late nineteenth century.* New York, NY: Oxford University Press.

Moore, K., Wiederhold, B. K., Wiederhold, M. D., & Riva, G. (2002). Panic and agoraphobia in a virtual world. *Cyberpsychology & Behavior, 5*(3), 197–202. doi:10.1089/109493102760147178

Moore, R. J., Gathman, E. C. H., & Ducheneaut, N. (2009). From 3D space to third place: The social life of small virtual spaces. *Human Organization, 68*(2), 230–240.

Moores, S. (1993). *Interpreting audiences: The ethnography of media consumption.* Thousand Oaks, CA: Sage Publications.

Oliver, M., & Carr, D. (2009). Learning in virtual worlds: Using communities of practice to explain how people learn from play. *British Journal of Educational Technology, 40*(3), 444–457. doi:10.1111/j.1467-8535.2009.00948.x

Ostrander, M. (2008). Talking, looking, flying, searching: Information seeking behaviour in Second Life. *Library Hi Tech, 26*(4), 512–524. doi:10.1108/07378830810920860

Pena, J., Hancock, J. T., & Merola, N. A. (2009). The priming effects of avatars in virtual settings. *Communication Research, 36*(6), 838–856. doi:10.1177/0093650209346802

Persky, S., & Blascovich, J. (2007). Immersive virtual environments versus traditional platforms: Effects of violent and nonviolent video game play. *Media Psychology, 10*(1), 135–156.

Potter, W. J., & Tomasello, T. K. (2003). Building upon the experimental design in media violence research: The importance of including receiver interpretations. *The Journal of Communication, 53*(2), 315–329. doi:10.1111/j.1460-2466.2003.tb02593.x

Reinhard, C. D. (2008). *Gendered media engagings as user agency mediations with sociocultural and media structures: A Sense-Making Methodology study of the situationality if gender divergences and convergences.* Doctoral dissertation, Ohio State University.

Reinhard, C. D. (2010a). *Our definitions and metaphors: Discussion of how researchers and designers as users make sense of virtual world technologies.* Paper presented at Virtual Worlds Research Group International Research Workshop, June 7-9, Copenhagen.

Reinhard, C. D. (2010b). Interviews within experimental frameworks: How to make sense of sense-making in virtual worlds. *Journal of Virtual Worlds Research, 3*(1). Retrieved from http://jvwresearch.org.

Reinhard, C. D., & Dervin, B. (2010). *Situations of media engagings: Comparing the new and the old through sense-making.* Paper presented at the Association of Internet Researchers Conference 11.0, October 21-23, Gothenburg, Sweden.

Robbins-Bell, S. (2008). *Using a faceted classification scheme to predict the future of virtual worlds.* Presented at the Association of Internet Research Conference, 9.0, Copenhagen, Denmark.

Saponaro, A. (2007). *Assignment 3: Second Life as didactic environment.* Retrieved online from http://www.ielmers.com/ saponaro/ portfolio/ ITDE8012/ Assignment_3 _SecondLifeInEducation.pdf

Schroeder, R. (2008). Virtual worlds research: Past, present & future. *Journal of Virtual Worlds Research, 1*(1).

Shin, D. (2009). The evaluation of user experience of the virtual world in relation to extrinsic and intrinsic motivation. *International Journal of Human-Computer Interaction, 25*(6), 530–553. doi:10.1080/10447310902963951

Sivunen, A., & Siitonen, M. (2010). *Comparing experiences on leadership in virtual teams and online multiplayer gaming clans.* Paper presented at the International Communication Association Conference, June 2010, Singapore.

Smyth, J. M. (2007). Beyond self-selection in video game play: An experimental examination of the consequences of massively multiplayer online role-playing game play. *Cyberpsychology & Behavior, 10*(5), 717–721. doi:10.1089/cpb.2007.9963

Suh, K. S., & Chang, S. (2006). User interfaces and consumer perceptions of online stores: The role of telepresence. *Behaviour & Information Technology, 25*(2), 99–113. doi:10.1080/01449290500330398

Voulgari, I., & Komis, V. (2010). "Elven Elder LVL59 LFP/RB. Please PM me": Immersion, collaborative tasks and problem-solving in massively multiplayer online games. *Learning, Media and Technology, 35*(2), 171–202. doi:10.1080/17439884.2010.494429

Wadley, G., Gibbs, M. R., & Ducheneaut, N. (2009). *You can be too rich: Mediated communication in a virtual world.* Paper presented at OZCHI 2009, November 23-27, 2009, Melbourne, Australia.

ADDITIONAL READING

Blumer, H. (1969). *Symbolic interactionism: Perspective and method.* Englewood Cliffs, NJ: Prentice-Hall, Inc.

Bordwell, D. (1989). *Making Meaning: Inference and rhetoric in the interpretation of cinema.* Cambridge, MA: Harvard University Press.

Dervin, B. (2008). *Interviewing as dialectical practice: Sense-Making Methodology as exemplar.* Paper presented at International Association for Media and Communication Research (IAMCR) 2008 Annual Meeting, July 20-25, Stockholm, Sweden. [available from: dervin.1@osu.edu]

Gauntlet, D. (2005). *Moving Experiences: Media effects and beyond* (2nd ed.). Bloomington, IN: Indiana University Press.

Hall, S. (1973/1993). Encoding, decoding. In During, S. (Ed.), *The Cultural Studies Reader* (pp. 90–103). New York: Routledge.

Hine, C. (2000). *Virtual Ethnography.* Thousand Oaks, CA: Sage Publications.

Höijer, B. (1992). Socio-cognitive structures and television reception. *Media Culture & Society, 14,* 583–603. doi:10.1177/016344392014004006

Iser, W. (1978). *The Act of Reading: A theory of aesthetic response.* Baltimore, MA: John Hopkins University Press.

Jensen, K. B. (2010). New media, old methods: Internet methodologies and the online/offline divide. In Consalvo, M., & Ess, C. (Eds.), *The Handbook of Internet Studies* (pp. 43–58). London: Wiley-Blackwell.

Jensen, K. B., & Rosengren, K. E. (1990). Five traditions in search of the audience. *European Journal of Communication, 5,* 207–238. doi:10.1177/0267323190005002005

Katz, E., Blumler, J. G., & Gurevitch, M. (1974). Utilization of mass communication by the individual. In Blumler, J. G., & Katz, E. (Eds.), *The Uses of Mass Communications: Current perspectives on gratifications research* (pp. 19–34). Beverly Hills, CA: Sage Publications.

Lindlof, T. R., & Shatzer, M. J. (1998). Media ethnography in virtual space: Strategies, limits, and possibilities. *Journal of Broadcasting & Electronic Media, 42*(2), 170–189.

Livingstone, S. (1990). *Making Sense of Television: The psychology of audience interpretation.* New York: Pergamon Press.

Livingstone, S. (1999). New media, new audiences? *New Media & Society, 1*(1), 59–66. doi:10.1177/1461444899001001010

Lull, J. (1990). *Inside Family Viewing: Ethnographic research on television's audiences.* New York: Routledge.

Moores, S. (1994). Texts, readers and contexts of reading: Development in the study of media audiences. In Graddol, D., & Boyd-Barrett, O. (Eds.), *Media texts: Authors and Readers* (pp. 256–272). Philadelphia, PA: Multilingual Matters Ltd.

Morley, D. (1992). *Television, Audiences and Cultural Studies.* New York: Routledge.

Reinhard, C. D., & Dervin, B. (2009). Media uses and gratifications. In W. F. Eadie (Ed.). *21st Century Communication.* Thousand Oaks, CA: Sage Publications.

Rogers, E. M. (1962). *Diffusion of Innovations.* New York: Free Press.

Salen, K., & Zimmerman, E. (2004). *Rules of Play: Game Design Fundamentals.* Cambridge, MA; London, England: MIT Press.

Schrøder, K., Drotner, K., Kline, S., & Murray, C. (2003). *Researching Audiences.* New York: Oxford University Press.

Schrøder, K. C. (1994). Audience semiotics, interpretive communities and the 'ethnographic turn' in media research. *Media Culture & Society, 16,* 337–347.

Staiger, J. (2005). *Media Reception Studies.* New York, NY: New York University Press.

Taylor, T. L. (2006). *Play between Worlds: Exploring Online Game Culture.* Boston, MA: MIT Press.

Turkle, S. (1995). *Life on the Screen: Identity in the Age of the Internet.* New York: Simon & Schuster.

Van Dijk, J. (2004). Digital media. In Downing, J. D. H. (Ed.), *The Sage Handbook of Media Studies.* Thousand Oaks, CA: Sage Publications.

Vorderer, P., & Bryant, J. (2006). *Playing Video Games: Motives, responses, and consequences.* Mahwah, NJ: Lawrence Erlbaum Associates.

Webb, S. (2001). Avatar culture: Narrative, power and identity in virtual world environments. *Information Communication and Society, 4*(4), 560–594. doi:10.1080/13691180110097012

KEY TERMS AND DEFINITIONS

Engaging: The series of physical and interpretive actions and reactions that occur when in contact with a media product.

Media Product: Any combination of media technology and mediated content that is produced to be consumed, i.e. to be engaged with by individual(s) that may, or may not, include the original producer(s).

Sense-Making: The internal behaviors, both affective and cognitive, and external, observable behaviors involved in working to understand one's self, life, and the world.

Situated Sense-Making Processes: The affective and cognitive activities that include judgments, interpretations, decisions, emotions, learnings, inspirations, and so forth that over the course of a particular media reception situation.

Virtual Worlds: The use of computer-aided, networked technology to produce a representation of a space (graphical or textual) that becomes an ongoing and persistent place for people to engage with each other, synchronously or asynchronously, and the space, to the extent that the producers of the space permit such interaction.

Virtual Worlds Technology: Those technological artifacts that connect to or contain content and, via our engaging with them, produce experiences that in some way result in and involve the sense of being in a geometrically defined space to interact with others online.

Section 3
Society Development:
People, not Person

Chapter 9
Students' Perceptions About Delivery of Game–Based Learning for Virtual Patients in Second Life

M. Toro-Troconis
Imperial College London, UK

N. J. Roberts
Imperial College London, UK

S. F. Smith
Imperial College London, UK

M. R. Partridge
Imperial College London, UK

ABSTRACT

This chapter describes the use of the nominal group technique to assess students' attitudes to game-based learning in the delivery of virtual patients in Second Life.

Two groups of undergraduate medical students (Yr 3, n=14) were invited to participate. The research question posed was: "In your opinion what are the advantages and disadvantages of learning in Second Life compared with other methods?" Thirty items were generated in each group, then reduced to 10 items. These were classified into 3 themes 1) learning experience, 2) clinical exposure, and 3) technical experience. Results from the first group focused on the learning experience highlighting its importance for clinical diagnosis and a structure for learning. The second group focused on the clinical exposure although they were ambivalent about the advantages of this type of delivery mode. Results show interesting findings highlighting the virtual patients developed follow a very linear approach which is not challenging enough for medical students at that level.

DOI: 10.4018/978-1-60960-854-5.ch009

INTRODUCTION

Anecdotal evidence from teachers suggests that the impact of gaming on millions of learners, who grew up playing best-selling games such as SimCity is starting to be felt (Squire 2002). According to Prensky (2001), these learners or *'digital natives'* are native speakers of the digital language of computers, video games, mobile phones and any other digital technology that easily become available. Some authors recognise the fact that these learners have a cognitive style characterised by multi-tasking while learning, with short attention span during learning and an exploratory and discovery approach to learning (Asakawa & Gilbert, 2003; Bain & Newton, 2003; Prensky, 2005). However, the term *'digital native'* has been recently expanded by Prensky (2009) to fit a wider audience that has grown up in the era of digital technology. Prensky defines a new term *'digital wisdom'* emphasizing that the use of digital technology in our everyday lives makes us wiser.

Digital tools already extend and enhance our cognitive capabilities in a number of ways. Digital technology enhances our memory, for example, via data input/output tools and electronic storage. Digital data-gathering and decision-making tools enhance judgment by allowing us to gather more data than we could on our own. (Prensky, 2009)

Video and computer games are in many ways a 'perfect' learning mechanism for this group (Prensky 2006). Learning by games results in the acquisition of new knowledge, the transfer of learning, the development of intellectual skills (abstraction, anticipation, strategy-building, problem-solving, spatial representation, function-movement relationship), and the development of behavior and attitudes (Whelan, 2005; Sauve et al, 2007).

The term game-based learning has emerged as a generic name for the use of games for learning or educational purposes. It has also been termed 'serious games', and includes fully immersive virtual worlds, in which learners can take on virtual presence within these worlds (Joint Information Systems Committee 2007). Gee (2003) also observed how successful game play and experiential learning opportunities have been shown to share common aspects.

The game-based learning activities for the delivery of virtual patients were designed based on the four-dimensional framework developed by De Freitas and Oliver (2006) and discussed by the authors in other publications (Toro-Troconis et al, 2008), which provides a close relationship with the systems of Activity Theory (Kuutti, 1996). The learning types described by Helmer (2007): Demonstration, Experiential Learning, Diagnostic activities, Role-Play and Constructive Learning were also taken into account for the design. And finally, it is worth highlighting the last three influential factors taken into account in the design which were described by Begg (2005): Emergent Narrative, originally described by Murray's (1997), The Responsive Environment and the Psycho-social Moratorium originally described by Gee (2003).

The framework focuses on four main dimensions in advance of using games and simulations (De Freitas & Oliver, 2006):

- particular context where learning takes place, including macro-level contextual factors.
- attributes of the particular learner or learner group.
- internal representational world of the game or simulation and
- pedagogic considerations, learning models used, approaches, etc.

The Faculty of Medicine at Imperial College London developed a Respiratory Ward in Second Life with a series of virtual patients' activities following the framework and modes of representation mentioned above. A range of game-based elements were introduced and delivered to the learner via a Heads Up Display (HUD), which aims to keep the learner informed of his/her progress, showing the patients treated by the learner, how far the learner is in the diagnostic process, his/her scores and the top scores for each patient (Figure 1). A demo on YouTube can be accessed at: http://tinyurl.com/mwpm2r

The game-based learning activities aim to drive experiential, diagnostic and role-play learning activities within the 3-D world, aiming to support students as they select investigations and make diagnoses. The Respiratory Ward was developed with five virtual patients, each with a different respiratory condition, and each includes elements of medical history, differential diagnosis, inves-

tigations, working diagnosis and production of a management plan.

The delivery of virtual patients in Second Life benefit from target user input during development. Focus groups composed of undergraduate medical students have been organised to gather feedback about attitudes and barriers when accessing virtual patients in Second Life. As an alternative to the focus group, the Nominal Group Technique (NGT), originally developed by Delbecq, Van de Ven, and Gustafson for organizational decision making and problem solving was used. The NGT is a highly structured group process that is used to generate prioritised list of responses to a question or problem (Delbecq et at, 1975; IoM, 1985). A primary purpose of the NGT is to ensure

Figure 1. Virtual Patient at the Respiratory Ward – Imperial College London region in Second Life

that opinions of all participants receive equal representation (Hall, 1983).

One of the criticisms of nonstructured focus groups is that there is often a tendency for discussions to become dominated by the opinions of the most self-assured personalities in any group. The NGT aims to limit this potential by offering and forcing equal opportunities for each participant to express their opinion (Carney, O. et al, 1996).

EXPERIMENTAL METHODOLOGY

Participants

This investigation focused on two groups of Year 3 undergraduate medical students. On average, par-

ticipants were 21 years old (+/- 1.26). The gender distribution of the respondents was 7% female (n = 1) and 93% male (n = 13). Two sessions were held with 6 in one group, and 8 in the other.

Process

An introduction to the virtual hospital and the Virtual Respiratory Ward was given to each group of students. The students spent 30 minutes assessing five virtual patients at the Respiratory Ward in groups of two (Figure 2).

The moderation of the NGT was not researcher-led which avoided domination of the leader's concerns rather than those of the participants. Three members of staff led the process and students were asked to consider the following question:

Figure 2. Students assessing a virtual patient at the virtual Respiratory Ward

"In your opinion what are the advantages and what are the disadvantages of learning in Second Life compared with other methods?".

The NGT process consisted of 6 stages (Figure 3).

Results

The NGT was held at Imperial College, Sir Alexander Fleming building, London in April 2009. The results of the NGT include the items generated and the voting that gave the consensus opinion on important items for inclusion. Initially, 30 possible items that could be important in assessing the advantages and disadvantages of learning in Second Life, following a game-based learning model for virtual patients were generated by the two groups. The 30 items generated by participants during the silent phase and subsequently ranked during the voting phase can be seen in Table 3 & 4. Table 1 & Table 2 only show the top 10 items selected in each group.

Following the first round of voting, participants had an opportunity to view the voting results and express their opinions or discuss queries if it was considered some items had been emphasized incorrectly in their opinion. The discussions that preceded the first round of voting clearly influenced how individuals ultimately voted. Ten items had received final votes in both groups resulting in greater consensus (Table 5).

The established items have been grouped into three main areas in Table 5:

1. Learning experience (L)
2. Clinical exposure (C)
3. Technical experience (T)

DISCUSSION

The results of this NGT process established ten items generated in each group to be taken into account for the design of game-based learning for

Figure 3. The NGT process

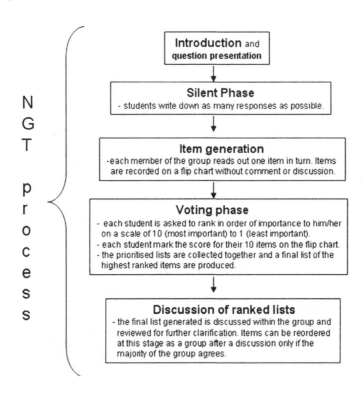

Table 1. Top ten items generated by nominal group technique that are important when learning in Second Life (Group 1).

Suggested item (n=30)	Number of votes	Number of participants scoring item
Predictability – removes thought process becoming mechanical process.	19	4
Gives opportunity to discuss issues in a safe environment.	8	2
Useful as reinforcement of other teaching.	27	4
Easier to validate learning by supervisor.	4	1
Easy to organise structure for self learning.	0	0
Restrictive choice of tests/no option to add new investigations (limited capacity to make mistakes).	16	3
Repeatable, go back to virtual patients.	0	0
Focusing on passing exams not seeing the unusual "real life exposure" on the wards.	12	2
Difficult to cover all material needed to become a doctor – reinforcement aid.	0	0
Extended Matching Questions (EMQs) where you can walk around/given differential diagnosis.	6	1
Items generated by the nominal group technique with the question: "In your opinion what are the advantages and disadvantages of learning in Second Life compared with other methods?"		

Table 2. Top ten items generated by nominal group technique that are important when learning in Second Life (Group 2).

Suggested item (n=30)	Number of votes	Number of participants scoring item
Second Life can be vandalized.	2	1
Negative view about Second Life.	4	1
Potential to become over dependant on e-learning methods.	12	3
Students may use Second Life too much stopping them from interacting in real world.	0	0
Can't ask specific questions during history taking.	24	4
Can't see advantage over other forms of e-learning.	22	3
Bridges gaps between lecture and hospital – framework for years prior to clinical practice.	23	6
Too simple to teach diagnostic skills, more complicated scenarios needed, should allow you to make mistakes.	56	7
No control over spending money in Second Life.	1	1
Potential to learn blood results.	6	1
Items generated by the nominal group technique with the question: "In your opinion what are the advantages and disadvantages of learning in Second Life compared with other methods?"		

virtual patients in Second Life. This process has determined content validity by assuring students agreement on the items to be evaluated further.

The final items generated by Group 1 were mainly focused on the Learning Experience with

a total of 107 points. The second most popular item among Group 1 was focused on the Clinical experience with a total of 62 points leaving only 21 points to the Technical experience item.

Table 3. Items generated by nominal group technique that are important when learning in Second Life (Group 1).

Suggested item (n=30)	Number of votes	Number of participants scoring item
Predictability – removes thought process becoming mechanical process.	19	4
Gives opportunity to discuss issues in a safe environment.	8	2
Useful as reinforcement of other teaching.	27	4
Easier to validate learning by supervisor.	4	1
Easy to organise structure for self learning.	0	0
Restrictive choice of tests/no option to add new investigations (limited capacity to make mistakes).	16	3
Repeatable, go back to virtual patients.	0	0
Focusing on passing exams not seeing the unusual "real life exposure" on the wards.	12	2
Difficult to cover all material needed to become a doctor – reinforcement aid.	0	0
Extended Matching Questions (EMQs) where you can walk around/given differential diagnosis.	6	1
Would be better for clinical beginners – helps structure thinking.	17	2
Distracted by emails in Second Life.	8	1
Miss out on practical stuff – only theory.	4	1
Time taken away from learning - technical issues.	4	1
Not designed for teamwork, no expert to ask unless they happened to be there.	3	1
Too spoon fed for Seniors.	0	0
Motivating for junior levels.	4	2
Very easy to use in own time, anywhere.	21	4
Students can work at their own speed.	7	1
Break from other formats of learning.	20	3
	0	0
Mimics game, conditioned to enjoy games, making learning memorable.	0	0
More applicable to learning on the wards ties in with wards.	9	1
Integrates learning that is not covered in other ways, e.g. breath sounds and other things not always taught together as a package.	22	3
Not good learning tool. Couldn't ask questions/insufficient information.	9	1
Structured way to learn – framework for learning.	19	4
Unrealistic presentation of symptoms.	5	3
Reduces the doctor/patient relationship and associated skills – antisocial.	15	2
Does not compare for experiences on the ward.	14	3
Tedious – may skip after the first patient.	0	0
Items generated by the nominal group technique with the question: "In your opinion what are the advantages and disadvantages of learning in Second Life compared with other methods?"		

There was great discussion about the advantages of learning the process of clinical diagnosis using this type of delivery mode. However, the fact that this way of learning may become mechanical was pointed out. Some discussion was based on the clinical disadvantages focused on the restrictions of tests available and the simplicity of the clinical cases. Similar approaches were found

Table 4. Items generated by nominal group technique that are important when learning in Second Life (Group 2).

Suggested item (n=30)	Number of votes	Number of participants scoring item
Second Life can be vandalized.	2	1
Negative view about Second Life.	4	1
Potential to become over dependant on e-learning methods.	12	3
Students may use Second Life too much stopping them from interacting in real world.	0	0
Can't ask specific questions during history taking.	24	4
Can't see advantage over other forms of e-learning.	22	3
Bridges gaps between lecture and hospital – framework for years prior to clinical practice.	23	6
Too simple to teach diagnostic skills, more complicated scenarios needed, should allow you to make mistakes.	56	7
No control over spending money in Second Life.	1	1
Potential to learn blood results.	6	1
Bugs in system, slow running of programme.	13	2
Useful for EMQs.	15	3
Useful for platform for older students to help.	9	2
Wider variety of cases – bank of cases abnormal presentation.	35	6
Easy to monitor what people do.	0	0
Motivation when Imperial is exploring new methods of learning.	1	1
Aliases can be confusing to find friends.	0	0
Chance to encounter scenarios you wouldn't encounter in the hospital.	47	7
Seems more fun and interactive like playing a game.	16	5
Makes you think about the tests you order.	43	7
Takes a lot to get used to the controls.	16	2
Only the person buying the tests sees the results. Results can't be shared.	0	0
Not realistic, don't practice communication skills.	45	7
Don't have to travel to hospital should make you more productive.	17	3
Scenarios make you remember / learn better.	25	3
Combines all the elements of diagnosis in one programme, history, exams, etc.	14	4
Sound bleed in different patients.	0	0
Explanations about results are good.	32	5
Procrastination in team/group work.	0	0
Can work in groups.	11	3
Items generated by the nominal group technique with the question: "In your opinion what are the advantages and disadvantages of learning in Second Life compared with other methods?"		

Table 5. Final votes during NGT - Group 1 and Group 2.

Suggested item (n=10) Group 1	Number of votes		Suggested item (n=10) Group 2	Number of votes	
Useful as reinforcement of other teaching.	27	L	Too simple to teach diagnostic skills, more complicated scenarios needed, should allow you to make mistakes.	56	C
Integrates learning that is not covered in other way, e.g. breath sounds and other things not always taught together.	22	L	Chance to encounter scenarios you wouldn't encounter in the hospital.	47	C
Very easy to use in own time, anywhere.	21	T	Not realistic, don't practice communication skills.	45	C
Break from other formats of learning.	20	L	Makes you think about the tests you order.	43	C
Predictable – removes thought process, becomes mechanical process.	19	L	Wider variety of cases – bank of cases, abnormal presentation.	35	C
Structured way to learn – framework for learning.	19	L	Explanations about results – good.	32	C
Would be better for clinical beginners – helps structure thinking.	17	C	Scenarios – make you remember / learn better.	25	L
Restrictive choice of tests/no option to add new investigations (limited capacity to make mistakes).	16	C	Can't ask specific questions during history taking.	24	L
Reduces the doctor/patient relationship and associated skills – antisocial.	15	C	Bridges gaps between lecture and hospital – framework for years prior to clinical practice.	23	L
Does not prepare for experiences on the ward.	14	C	Can't see advantage over other forms of e-learning.	22	L
Items groups according to the following areas: Learning Experience: **L** Clinical Exposure: **C** Technical Experience: **T**					

in both groups where they identified this type of delivery more suited for clinical years, highlighting the fact that this way of learning might help medical students structure clinical thinking. The group also pointed out how the delivery of virtual patients in this way would reduce doctor/patient contact and would not prepare them for experiences on the ward. The only item discussed around the technical experience area was the advantage of accessing virtual patients in their own time, anywhere.

The final items generated by Group 2 concentrated mainly on the Clinical exposure with a total of 282 points. This group highlighted the fact that this delivery method was too simple to teach diagnostic skills and more challenging scenarios were required. Few items related to the Learning

experience were discussed mainly focused on the advantage of making students remember better bridging the gap between lectures and clinical work. A small amount of students did not see the advantage of learning in the virtual hospital over other forms of e-learning. This may be due to the fact students are used to a wide variety of interactive e-learning materials which are already embedded in the curriculum and they are already used to accessing and learning from.

The gender distribution of the respondents was not even with a high representation of males (93% n=13) in comparison to females (7% n=1). However, recent studies carried out at undergraduate medicine level at Imperial College London shows interest findings which do not highlight significant gender differences in attitude when learning following a game-based learning approach in Second Life (Toro-Troconis & Mellström, U., 2010).

CONCLUSION

Consensus of these student groups has established 20 items to be considered for the delivery of virtual patients following a game-based learning model in Second Life. With increased educational research investigating interventions to evaluate the educational advantages of virtual worlds, such an instrument will be critical for the non-biased qualitative analysis of these learning environments.

It is clear from the group items generated that there are mixed opinions about how useful they find learning in this way and no major technical issues were found. On the other hand, the clinical experience was found to be too simple for the delivery of virtual patients at Year 3 undergraduate medicine level, suggesting the delivery of this type of virtual patients should be aimed at earlier years in the undergraduate medical curriculum. More challenging scenarios following a branching model and a '*responsive environment*' that does not necessarily follow one right path (Murrary, 1997; Begg 2007), should be constructed to target higher level cognitive skills at more advanced clinical years. Further thought needs to be given to the type of clinical scenarios and skills acquisition best suited to this form of learning. This may involve scenarios where students can select investigations or interventions which could cause harm in real life such that experience can be obtained without risk. Role-play - multi-user game-based learning activities may also be developed in which students could work together, with their responses affecting the overall learning experience of the group. This approach would challenge more advanced medical students in their diagnosis processes emphasizing communication and Inter professional skills. This model would also exploit the multi-user capacity presented in virtual worlds.

REFERENCES

Asakawa, T., & Gilbert, N. (2003). Synthesizing experiences: Lessons to be learned from Internet-mediated simulation games. *Simulation & Gaming*, *34*(1), 10–22. doi:10.1177/1046878102250455

Bain, C., & Newton, C. (2003). Art games: Pre-service art educators construct learning experiences for the elementary art classroom. *Art Education*, *56*(5), 33–40.

Begg, M., D. Dewhurst, and H. MacLeod. (2005). Game informed learning: Applying computer game processes to higher education. Innovate 1 (6).

Begg, M., Ellaway, R., Dewhurst, D., & Macleod, H. (2007). Transforming professional healthcare narratives into structured game-informed-learning activities. *Innovate* 3 (6). Retrieved on July, 13, 2009, from http://www.innovateonline.info/ index.php?view=article &id=419

Carney, O., McIntosh, J., & Worth, A. (1996). The use of the nominal group technique in research with community nurses. *Journal of Advanced Nursing*, *23*, 1024–1029. doi:10.1046/j.1365-2648.1996.09623.x

De Freitas, S., & Oliver, M. (2006). How can exploratory learning with games and simulations within the curriculum be most effectively evaluated? *Computers & Education*, *46*(Special Issue), 249–264. doi:10.1016/j.compedu.2005.11.007

Delbecq, A. L., Van de Ven, A. H., & Gustafson, D. H. (1975). *Group techniques for programme planning: A guide to nominal group and Delphi process*. Glenview, IL: Scott Foresman and Company.

Gee, J. P. (2003). *What video games have to teach us about learning and literacy*. New York, NY: Palgrave MacMillan.

Hall, R. S. (1983). The nominal group technique for planning and problem solving. *The Journal of Biocommunication*, *10*, 24–27.

Helmer, J. (2007). *Second Life and virtual worlds.* Learning Light Limited. Retrieved July 13, 2009, from http://www.epic.co.uk/content/ news/ nov_07/Second_Life_ and_Virtual_Worlds_ JH.pdf

Institute of Medicine (IoM), Division of Health Sciences Policy. (1985). *Assessing medical technologies.* Washington, DC: National Academies Press; Methods of Technology Assessment.

Joint Information Systems Committee. (2007). *Game-based learning. E-learning innovation programme.* Briefing papers. Retrieved on July 13, 2009, from http://www.jisc.ac.uk/publications /publications/pub_ gamebasedlearningBP.aspx

Kuutti, K. (1996). Activity theory as a potential framework for human computer interaction research . In Nardi, B. A. (Ed.), *Content and consciousness: activity theory and human-computer interaction* (pp. 17–44). Cambridge, MA: MIT Press.

Murray, J. (1997). *Hamlet on the holodeck: the future of narrative in cyberspace.* Cambridge, MA: MIT Press.

Prensky, M. (2005). *Adopt and adapt. 21st-century schools need 21st-century technology.* Edutopia. Retrieved on July 13, 2009, from http://www.digitaldivide.net/ articles/view.php?ArticleID=786

Prensky, M. (2006). *Don't bother me mom – I'm learning.* St Paul, MN: Paragon House.

Prensky, M. (2009). H. sapiens digital: From digital immigrants and digital natives to digital wisdom. *Innovate, 5*(3), 1. Retrieved on August 11, 2010, from http://www.uh.cu/static/ documents/ TD/H.%20Sapiens %20Digital.pdf

Sauvé, L., Renaud, L., Kaufman, D., & Marquis, J. S. (2007). Distinguishing between games and simulations: A systematic review. *Educational Technology & Society, 10*(3), 247-256. Retrieved on July 13, 2009, from http://www.ifets.info/ journals /10_3/17.pdf

Squire, K. (2002). Cultural framing of computer/ video games. *The International Journal of Computer Game Research, 2*(1). Retrieved on July 13, 2009, from http://www.gamestudies.org/ 0102/squire/

Toro-Troconis, M. and Mellström, U. (2010), Game-based learning in Second Life®. Do gender and age make a difference?, *Journal of Gaming and Virtual Worlds* 2:1, pp. 53-76, doi: 10.1386/ jgvw.2.1.53_1

Toro-Troconis, M., Mellström, U., Partridge, M., Meeran, K., Barrett, M., & Higham, J. (2008). Designing game-based learning activities for virtual patients in Second Life. *Journal of Cyber Therapy and Rehabilitation* 1(3):227–239. Retrieved on July 13, 2009, from http://www1.imperial. ac.uk/ resources/62DCE340-6816- 4254-B4C0- 03A16B54EF0A/

Whelan, D. L. (2005). Let the games begin! *School Library Journal, 51*(4), 40–43.

Chapter 10
Virtual Learning Communities of Practice in Metaverse

Gaia Moretti
Libera Università Maria Ss. Assunta, Italy

Eliane Schlemmer
Universidade do Vale dos Rios dos Sinos, Brazil

ABSTRACT

Characteristic of the contemporaneous age, and taking advantage of the diffusion of digital technologies, virtual communities are diffusing in the organization's culture such as places where members can learn, work, or simply meet. The evolution of the same digital technologies, and the development of Digital Virtual Worlds in 3D (such as Second Life), permits now to think of new tools for the organizational communities and for communities in general that could build new knowledge, share common practices, and work together in immersive and collaborative spaces. Digital virtual spaces can contribute to change the traditional structure and definition of virtual communities, and can also contribute to their digital development, in the field of participation.

INTRODUCTION

This paper aims to present the possibilities offered by some new technologies and cultural paradigms to the organizational world, particularly investigating the concept of Virtual Learning Community of Practice in the context of 3D technologies. Therefore the concept of Metaverse and the characters of Metaverse technology will be useful to define the possibilities that could be realized in the field of the Virtual Community.

Starting from the importance and the characters of the so-called " contemporaneous Age", and from the centrality of the digitalization process, we are going to describe Virtual Learning Communities of Practice as communities that produce knowledge, make subjects express their emotions, create spaces of collaboration and cooperation. The success cases of UNISINOS (ECODI Ricesu c ECODI PPGs) will show the role of Metaverse technology in the creation of several Virtual Learning Communities of Practice.

DOI: 10.4018/978-1-60960-854-5.ch010

BACKGROUND

According to Castells (1999), the contemporaneous age can be called 'Information Age': main processes and functions are growing organized in Nets. These Nets put in order a new social morphology, and the diffusion of Net logic modifies productive, cultural and social processes, and also experience processes. Therefore, Net is a system of interconnected elements that can also connect to other elements, creating other Nets and creating "new orders in the world and in heads" (Eco, 2004, p. 162).

The new paradigm of Information Age consist in the capacity of information and communication technology in diffusing the Net into the social structure. The power of information and communication flows is more important and stronger than political power: to be or not to be present in the Net and in relation with other nets is a crucial element to dominate and transform society. In this framework, virtual communities play an important role, because communities live in Nets and constitute Nets: the same constitution of the Net passes trough people that are in it, building relations with other people, building infinite Nets.

Moreover, according to Veen e Vrakking (2006), a new generation is emerging in the contemporaneous age: the Digital Natives. This generation lives absorbed by digital/virtual tools and environments, using them daily to connect with people, especially building communities.

According to Levy (1999) and Palloff and Pratt (1999), virtual communities are defined as electronic Nets of interactive communication, constituted by sharing interests, knowledge, common projects and tools to realize it, established in a cooperation process. Communities can also be characterized by identity processes (Turkle, 1999; Wenger, 2006): members of communities experiment 'sense of membership' because of sharing common contents. Members are involved, moreover, by social relations and interactions: because of this, Levy (1999) and Castells (1999) state that the importance of Digital Technologies is in offering the possibility of creating and implementing communities. In developing communities, emotions play an important role: members of communities express themselves online trough different tools, not only writing; voice, 'smiles' and graphic/video expressions contribute to communicate different feelings. Therefore, different digital technologies offer the possibility of members sharing emotional ties; in the case of Metaverse technology, this possibility is developed by textual language, voice, graphics and sign language. It means that the members' personality can be expressed by his way of writing, his opinions in a discussions, the customization of his own avatar and so on; Virtual Learning Communities of Practice are surely involved in this process, and are based on maintaining relations and developing new interactions.

Neal Stephenson coined the term Metaverse in his postmodern novel Snow Cash (1992), where it represents a fictional virtual world. For the author, Metaverse is a lifelike private and public utility, an extension of the physical world's real space within an Internet virtual space. Therefore, Metaverse is constituted in cyberspace, and according to Lemos (2002) it is the technological incarnation of the old daydream of creating a parallel world, a collective memory, with the imagery, myths and symbols, pursuing man since ancestral times, and is materialised with the creation of DVW3Ds, where subjects represented by avatars experience immersion in a digital virtual environment, by interacting and creating several 3D spaces for living and living together, thus allowing parallel worlds to emerge. DVW3Ds are multimedia environments (Boccia Artieri, 2004), permitting communication through supporting technologies, 3D representation, computer-graphics modelling. DVW3D are materialised through 3D graphic representations and require human actions to come into being. Without the acting of e-citizens through their avatars, DVW3D would not come about at all. Any action by the avatars has real-time results; that is, at the very instant the avatar acts, the DVW3D is modified and updated. The Digital Virtual World offers multiple ways to interact, which may be developed using different languages: textual, oral, gestural and graphic.

According to Klastrup (2003), a virtual world is a persistent online representation, which contains the possibility of synchronous interaction between users and between the user and the world that exists within the framework of a space designed as a navigable universe. Virtual worlds are worlds you can move in, by means of a persistent representation of the user, in contrast to the worlds represented by traditional fiction, which are presented as inhabited by real people, but not actually inhabitable (Klastrup, 2003: 2).

According to Schlemmer (2004), a DVW3D may be a relatively faithful facsimile of the physical world, or it may be an unique creation based on entirely imaginary representations, modelling itself on non-physical space for digital-virtual living together. These worlds may have rules of their own, and its inhabitants can make use of their creative powers, since they are not limited to any existent physical rule. One of the key characteristics of DVW3D is that they are dynamic systems that change in real time as subjects interact with it.

VIRTUAL COMMUNITIES

Online learning developed by the constitution of Virtual Learning Communities of Practice–VLCP represents, nowadays, not only a world tendency but, moreover, a reality that develops both in formal education (Institutions, Universities and Research Centers), and informal education (organization and firms).

The term "virtual communities" (VCs) gained strength in 1993, with Rheingold's book "The Virtual Community". According to Rheingold (2004) virtual communities are "... social aggregations that emerge on the network when a group of people carries on public discussions long enough

and with enough human emotion, to form networks of relationships in cyberspace." However other researchers, over time, have also dealt with this definition, such as Lévy (1999) and Palloff and Pratt (1999) that define "virtual communities" such as interactive electronic communication networks, formed from affinities of interests, ideas, projects and mutual exchange values are established in a cooperation process.

According to Castells (2003), there are two main aspects on which the VCs work: free and horizontal communication (linked to global practice of free expression that arise with the creation of the Internet), and shared values (that he calls "formation of autonomous networks," which means that any subject can form a group and disseminate its own information). Thus, the development of a VC is based on *interconnection*, through contacts and interactions of all kinds, involving and incorporating different forms of expression as well as the diversity of interests, values and imaginations, including the expression of conflicts.

According to Turkle (1999), a community is linked to identity; therefore a community cannot exist in the interim. Turkle (1999) is interested in the effects of "identity" in the experiential online, which involves the feeling of permanence experienced when one assumes a role, becoming part of the life of another one, which is typical of the community. "It will come, however, to call the places not transient Internet community, because I believe that the issue remains open. In any case, I turn to them in that effects of identity. To them, to weave personal stories." (Turkle, 1999, p. 2).

A VC is constituted by people who share the same interests and goals, and that interact using different languages (textual, oral, gestural and graphic), over various digital technologies which have the Internet as a platform. Thus, a collective VC is semi-permanent, depending on the maintenance and on the interest of the participants, because it feeds the flow of interactions and concerns and human relations that are deterritorialized in the digital virtual space.

Looking for the production of knowledge related to VCs, we find derivations such as virtual learning communities - VLCs, virtual relationship communities - VRCs, virtual community of practice - VCPs, among others, both expressions of a culture of real virtuality. In this chapter we will discuss VLCs and VCPs in particular.

In our perspective, a "virtual learning community" (VLC) can be understood as a group of people that act and interact through *telepresence*, and *through digital virtual presence* (Schlemmer et alii, 2008 - 2009), sharing common interests and learning together, defining learning objectives, strategies and actions, in order to achieve them in a timeless time and in a communication stream of digital virtual nature. The main purpose is *learning*.

In our perspective, a "virtual community of practice" (VCP) has as its main objective to exchange information- generate and share knowledge - mainly linked to professional practice and it can be linked to formal organizations or informal. According to Moretti (2009)

"Produce knowledge for an organization not only means to acquire information and data, but rather create a dynamic system in which data, information and experiences are connected to produce a greater overall knowledge than the simple sum of the initial knowledge. To do this, an organization needs to develop the production of knowledge in each element that is part of it. The basic elements that constitute an organization are, according to the theory of Argyris and Schon (1998), Porter (2003), Nonaka (1998), Wenger (2000, 2006), Davenport and Prusak (2005), men who work in the organization. This means that the main producers of knowledge are workers, and on the other hand, the technological artifacts with which they work. (...) The men who work are actually the only ones able to produce new knowledge. However, the process of creating

new knowledge is not automatic, nor for men. The knowledge produced by an individual is the result of experiments, theoretical knowledge, skills he possesses. (Moretti, 2009 p. 5:06)

For VLCP we intend here a Virtual Learning Community of Practice that daily learn, work and act in and for the organization whom concern. In our perspective (Moretti, 2009) a Virtual Community of Practice is rarely not also a Virtual Learning Community; practices developed by the community become knowledge available for all the members (and, at least, for the organization), and a continue process of learning is developed into the community's activities.

Nonaka and Takeuchi (1998) build a model describing the organizational knowledge flows; in their model, organizational knowledge passes through several processes of sharing tacit and explicit knowledge, sharing tacit knowledge through sharing experiences and processes of creation knowledge. Creation of knowledge, in particular, can be developed in spaces called BA (Nonaka, Konno, 1999); a BA is a common context where knowledge is created, shared and used through interaction processes. A BA, in our opinion, can be considered as a community-space where members can share and create knowledge, also through the sharing of tacit knowledge (experiences and implicit knowledge). Surely, a BA is a formalized and structured space; but one of its most important characteristics is represented by the interaction among the members, the *frequenters* of the common space. The BA is a "shared space for emerging relationships", and it could be virtual, physical, mental, or a combination of different "spaces"

Organizations have to think of nonconformist ways and practices in online learning and in the constitution/implementation of virtual communities; this means, finding new tools to improve people's competencies in communities, learning processes and development of good practices (Wenger, 2006). In our opinion, the Metaverse technology, which enables the creation of DVW3D (Digital Virtual worlds in 3D), offers this possibility both to formal training Institutions and to productive organizations. We suggest that constitution of VLCPs in DVW3Ds can be an important opportunity for those organizations (i.e. international organizations) that desire improving their Learning Communities of Practice offering to them Digital Virtual Environments where they can share experience, practices, emotions, and producing new knowledge, in order to their own organization turn more productive and competitive.

VIRTUAL LEARNING COMMUNITIES

In this part, we suggest a brief analysis of the nature of Virtual Learning Communities, and an identification of their role in productive organizational processes; we also suggest some tools to improve their activity and production, using Digital Technological Tools.

The members of a VLC – that lives in its members' actions and interactions - can share knowledge, experiences, ideas and information, and they can, therefore, produce knowledge cooperating. Virtual Learning Communities build themselves in practices of interaction in the Net, an interactive process that involves the community's objectives, rules and tools to achieve them; depending by the type of technology utilized to implement the community, interaction can be realized through different languages (oral, textual, graphic, sign). Some underlying functions of Virtual Learning Communities are identified by De Marchi & Costa (2006) as to produce knowledge, to collaborate and to manage all the process. These elements represent the basis of development for this kind of communities, but their full potential is not possible without an environment where develop them. The cooperation and collaboration between community members forms the environment. This can take place only in an environment that offers the possibility of virtual meetings, interactions between participants and so on. Finally, a Learning Community cannot exist without the development of 'participation culture'; each member knows the importance of relating with others, and they all know the importance of the common projects they are working on together.

A Virtual Learning Community is mainly a formal community, but even informal communities of learning can be developed. This depends on the nature of learning, a participative and shared process, but also a process in which the knowledge transfer is in act. Members of Learning Communities can acquire knowledge through lessons and formal ways of learning, but can also develop processes of learning by doing, developing learning through their experience and pratical/tacit knowledge.

VIRTUAL COMMUNITIES OF PRACTICE

According to Wenger (2006), communities of practice (CoPs) are groups of people that share a common interest for something that they achieve to do better together than alone; CoPs are group of people working together and sharing practices, experiences and working methodologies . CoPs are groups of people, defined by three characteristics: the domain (of a certain common and shared interest), the community (members participating in activities together) and the practice (sharing resources and methodologies to work).

CoPs can be organized in informal or formal groups. According to the first definition of Wenger (2006), CoPs should be mainly informal groups, in order to enhance the sense of membership built by the own members. In the second version of Wenger's CoPs theory (2007), CoPs are groups that can be quite formalized, as the organization can build spaces and tools (bulletin board, mailing lists, video conferences, newsletters, forum, wiki, blogs) to improve the CoPs' activity. In our opinion, one version doesn't exclude the other one: informality is one of the elements of a CoP because of the interaction among members, a process that develops in different ways depending on the structure of formal or an informal groups. Formal process of creation and implementation of a CoP permits to insert the same structure of the community into the organizational frame, as a substantial part of the entire organizational frame. In our opinion, also according with Daniel, Schwier and McCalla (2003), CoPs are characterized by informal learning goals and distribution of responsibilities. This is valid mainly for distributed communities of practice, for their definition, communities of members are geographically distributed on different countries.

In our perspective, Communities of Practice can be developed in an informal way through Virtual Technologies. According to Schlemmer (2008, 2009), virtual tools can be used to develop characters of communities such as emotionality, sense of membership, collaboration and cooperation. We define a Virtual Community of Practice such as a CoP developed in Digital Virtual Environments (like DVW3Ds or Web 2.0 environments); this kind of community can be fundamental for the developing of productive organizations, because the underlying elements of organizations are people (Porter, 2003; Nonaka, 1998; Davenport and Prusak, 2006; Moretti, 2009).

The community's "level of virtuality" can be different, if we are using Digital Virtual environments or Web 2.0 tools for its development; in the second case, we call it "secondary virtuality" (Moretti, 2010). This type of virtuality is characterized by sharing and interacting mainly through text and voice; the user is represented by what he writes or says, and often groups work without having an interaction between their virtual representation. In this "secondary virtuality", it is possible to write, read, discuss, work or learn together, but it is not possible, in most cases, to sense the presence of the users and to perceive and build the digital space around their own.

Digital Virtual Worlds in 3D, that we call a type of "primary virtualty", permit

the creation of three-dimensional online graphic environments, where the subject can be telepresent through an avatar (avatar-driven telepresent), a 3D graphical representation through which s/he can interact making a kind of 'digital-virtual life' emerge. This 'digital-virtual life' has shaped and being shaped by a human being represented by a 'digital-virtual self' in its relations with other digital-virtual 'selves' represented by 'technologised bodies' organising in communities in the cyberspace, creating digital-virtual social nets, shaping and being shaped by this culture. (Schlemmer, Trein, Oliveira, 2009)

VIRTUAL LEARNING COMMUNITIES OF PRACTICE IN METAVERSE

According to Moretti (2010), the concept of Community of Practice cannot be separate from the one of Learning Community. A Community of practice, in fact, always learns from the experience of its members, situations and projects; and members always learn together, one from the other: learning is possible in sharing practices.

We can define "virtual learning community of practice" (VLCP) a community constituted by the sharing practice, the study and discussion of topics of common interest within the members of the community, and rules and performance standards that are set through negotiation within the group. The contents of a VLCP is produced during the interactions that arise from discussions, reflections and readings that can be suggested by any member of the community. The knowledge is built as the subject learns the process of self-organization of conceptual thought, as it needs to coordinate its views with other views, arguments, evidence provided by community members. Thus, through VLCPs it is possible to produce knowledge in a dialogic relationship, founded on collaboration and cooperation, where all members can develop their capacity of expression and listening, in a process of autonomy (in terms of identifying their own needs learning, as well as ways to develop it) and authorship (with regard to responsibility for the content of their action / interaction, the relationships that produce knowledge or establishing). Monitoring and evaluation is undertaken by all members continuously.

Individuals who act and interact in VLCPs become more committed and responsible for their own learning, they feel more engaged in contributing to the learning advancements of their colleagues, which enables individuals to establish and strengthen emotional ties, besides providing the development of processes of collaboration and cooperation. The success of a VLCPs depends on the active contribution of each of its members over time, so that through collaboration and cooperation it can achieve the common goals set by the community.

VLCPs are born fundamentally in relation with the need of innovation, competencies development and in the belief that the needs of the learner cannot always be satisfied by the formal education and classic training courses. Online Learning doesn't need a classic and hierarchic structure like traditional courses: learning passes trough social processes, experiences and knowledge share. This new 'format' of social organization modifies the way in which people are in relation with information, learning and production of knowledge: according to Castells (1999), one of the ways to develop communities and, therefore, produce and share knowledge (Nonaka, Takeuchi, 1998) is the informal way.

Digital Virtual Technologies can implement this kind of community: according to Moretti (2010), VLCPs can be developed in Digital Virtual Environments because of the presence of different kinds of expressing cooperation and collaboration. In DVW3Ds, above all, members of communities can collaborate not only in writing documents together (that happens, for instance, in tools such as Google Docs or Wikis), but also in building objects together, in realizing simulations or participating them in order to experiment digital training. The immersion, fundamental character of DVW3Ds, permits the development of interactions between members; they can build knowledge objects, they can build a digital representation of abstract concepts, they can share experiences and practices in an environment that permits a lot of (virtual) actions.

We suggest that use of DVW3Ds permits the realization of the so-called (Castells, 1999) 'real virtuality', a 'virtuality' experimented from members trough their avatar, digital virtual representations that members use in order to live and work in virtual worlds.

In our perspective, the use of Metaverse Technology for the development of communities can be shown in the definition of ECODI (Schlemmer, 2008, 2009).

An ECODI is a digital space, namely a physical space but created through the contribution of ICTs; it is a 3D space where people and objects are characterized by three-dimensionality, that provides the sense of "presence" more than in a chat or an environment of Web 2.0. The digital space is populated by virtual objects and users, and they interact with each other, that is, an environment, understood as a space of relations.

An ECODI could not exist without people who populate it, i.e., in the case of DVW3Ds, the Avatars, bearers of users' personality that is expressed through them: an empty ECODI doesn't exist, since the reports that are interwoven among avatars are the foundation of the own existence of the digital space.

An ECODI is a "room" for coexistence, which means that avatars interact with each other in the digital space creating the own space, that is characterized as the sum of their relations, not as a private space, but as a shared space, that can be one of the privileged places for the creation and implementation of virtual communities.

The use of Metaverse Technology (Second Life) to create and support VLCPs was developed in several UNISINOS research projects, such as UNISINOS Island, ECODI RICESU and ECODI UNISINOS VIRTUAL. All these projects aimed, on the first side, to offer to the University Community spaces of digital connivance and interaction between users, and to develop learning processes and creation of good practices in the field of Education and Professors Training; on the other side, the Research Group GP e-du UNISINOS CNP/q, that has planned and developed these projects, has also developed its research in the field of Technology Learning through the observation of its members and their activities.

CASE STUDIES

The research design was "explorative" (Di Franco 2001). The goals of the study are to find out new relationships among learning and community's phenomena, to define post-hypotheses and suggest drivers for further research (Guala 2000). The field research followed two steps:

a. Field research, based on qualitative methodologies;
b. Data analysis and interpretation.

According to Yin (1984), the research design adopts different methodologies, in order to make possible the triangulation of data. In accordance with the research design, each step of the study was aimed at building new categories and defining emerging variables for the next phases of the research. According to Richards and Moore (2009), the Group has followed the hermeneutic approach where the researcher has to pay attention in dialogue processes of share and interaction that happen in the research setting, because they represent the ground for building meanings.

The field research followed the following steps:

a. Analysis of the context and preliminary research;
b. Field research, based on qualitative methods;
c. Data analysis and interpretation, aimed to the formulation of ex - post research hypothesis for further investigations.

Communities were investigated starting from the perceptions of the communities' own members, and from their technologic and intellectual products. The phases of the field study:

1. open-ended interview with the Community manager (s);
2. documents collection and analysis;
3. analysis of communities' distance communication tools (blog, forum, chat, meetings in Second Life);
4. semi-structured interviews with the core group and the coordinator of the community.

UNISINOS Island. The project was developed in 2006, aiming to create the representation of the University, in the Second Life Metaverse. Then some icons of UNISINOS were simulated, such as: Communitary Center and Library (these space are simulations of physic spaces); Research Group - Digital Education – GP e-du UNISINOS/CNPq, Convivence Center, sandbox, and others; these spaces are imaginary spaces, created with the propriety of MDV3D).

This project represents the "main box" for the development of all the other investigations and projects realized through the Metaverse technology. The aim of the project was to create a general ECODI where events and specific researches should be realized.

The main reason for the creation of the island in SL was UNISINOS Research in Education, where we seek to better understand how to place the processes of teaching and learning using this technology. One goal was to create a virtual space of digital information, communication and interaction for the academic community UNISINOS, so that teachers, researchers and students can explore, experiment and experience this new space within the Education Online while potentiating the processes of teaching and learning, so are the objects of research for GP e-du.

This project is open to the entire academic community of UNISINOS, and currently the main activity developed in the context of the island UNISINOS refers to research on Digital Education. Such research involves the creation of space and exploration, experimentation and

experience of these spaces for students and teachers. On the UNISINOS Island are also available general information about the University, spaces of interaction for digital virtual coexistence are presented dissertations, Meetings digital virtual research groups, exhibitions, events, among others.

ECODI-RICESU (Digital Virtual Living Space of the Network of Catholic Institutions of Higher Education). The project was developed in 2007/2008, and consisted specifically in creating a virtual space of digital information, communication and interaction for the development of a virtual learning community of practice within the Network of Catholic Institutions of Higher Education – RICESU, and development of training

Figure 1. UNISINOS Island

UNISINOS in physic space

UNISINOS in DVW3D (Second Life)

Living Area

Research Group - Digital Education – GP e-du
UNISINOS/CNPq

processes for building 3D spaces in the Metaverse Second Life, offered for Catholic Institutions of Higher Education - IESCs that integrate RICESU in the context of GT-EDUDI. The ECODI was built and realized into the UNISINOS Island.

This project incorporated two stages, as follows:

- The first milestone was the acquisition of an island in the Metaverse-SL to create the Island RICESU (modeled using the specific characteristics and properties of the technology of Digital Virtual Worlds in 3D), which took shape after the creation of different spaces Digital Virtual 3D - EDV3D for common use of RICESU such as the "host" virtual digital RICESU, the joint projects of the Network, as well as areas for collaborative / cooperative work, spaces for meetings, discussions, lectures, among others, created with the objective of bringing about the formation of ECODI to enable the development of VLCs and VCPs in the context of Digital Education, and more specifically for Education Online in Metaverse. Therefore, the core of coexistence Network (common area of RICESU) was constituted by spaces for each IESCs that integrate RICESU, so that they can develop their specific projects.

- The second step consisted in offering two training processes (of 80 hours) for IESCs teachers / researchers / practitioners that integrate RICESU. Each of IESCs indicated a teacher from the areas of pedagogy, technology - 3D design and programming and architecture; these three professionals were the beginning of what could become a subgroup of research and development in Metaverse technology. Thus, each component of the IESC RICESU indicated three participants to represent them in both the formative process, aiming to create "nodes" of institutional development

and educational proposals in Metaverse, contributing to the development of both local and network actions, constituting a micro-grid (micro-community) to allow the creation of a new GT, the GT-ECODI RICESU. Therefore, 13 teams of different IESCs were built, totalling 39 physically distant participants, who have worked together in a digital virtual presence, in the context of the island in RICESU MDV3D-SL. Besides the teachers, counselors and responsible for training processes, three teams were formed with the members of GP e-du. Each team consisted of a guiding master and a scholar in basic scientific research, responsible for monitoring four IESCs 4; one team was responsible for five IESCs. These teams had the primary function of monitoring the learning process of participants. Methodology and materials (texts, tutorials, videos, challenges, etc.) used in the two training processes were built by GP e-du, which caused the need to create specific objects in space for the training process, as panel integrator (help, mural, schedule meetings, guidelines for large screen projection, virtualteca, diary, forum, central teleports, etc). Participants also used it as a space for the development of training processes, the "trunk" of their own IESC, where they deposited the challenges made to their IESC, which developed the project-based learning problems. These spaces can be viewed in the following figures. During the training process, besides the SL Metaverse, different technologies were used, such as: blog, discussion forums, Youtube, etc.

Currently, the main activities developed in the context of ECODI-RICESU refer to meetings of the Steering Committee, meetings of the WG - Working Groups and organization/development of virtual events, developed in SL. In the context of different spaces that integrate the IESCs ECODI-RICESU it is possible to perceive different levels of development and activity patterns and distinct objectives. For example, in the PUCSP space it is possible to observe an audience that is used for presentations, events, meetings, etc.. In the PUCRS space, we found an area where general information is available on the University, exhibition spaces for works and researches in the context of SL and also a digital virtual space for meetings, meetings, lectures, presentations, etc. There is also an area where simulations are created. Therefore, by walking around the island you'll find that each IESC develops some kind of activity in those spaces created.

It is interesting to note the rise of a suvra-community of practice, constituted by several members of the 13 Universities. Members of 13

Institutions developed a form of virtual interaction that was finalized to the creation of several common projects between the suvra-community and the local organizations on Brazilian ground, i.e. international projects and collaborations between institutions and local productive systems. They realized several joint projects in the South of Brazil, developing them mainly in Second Life and partly using e-mails, forum and blog. One example of a common developed project is the constitutions of GE (Grupo de Estudo), in which members are from different institutions, and work on common themes: Business and Administration, Digital Library, Quality, Collaborative Technologies, and others.

ECODI UNISINOS VIRTUAL - 2009/2010. The project deals specifically with the development of a Digital Virtual Living space for the

Figure 2. RICESU Island

RICESU Project – space for collaborative projects

Integrator Panel - training space

CEUCLAR
(Centro Universitario Claretiano)

PUCSP (Pontificia Universidade
Católica de São Paulo)

provision of Online Education in the context of UNISINOS VIRTUAL - Graduation. The digital virtual space reflects a methodology that promotes processes of teaching and learning grounded in an epistemological interactionist / constructivist / systemic approach, that currently arises as an area of coexistence of provocative learning.

In this context two pilot projects are being developed: the subject "Physics of the Earth System", linked to the graduate course in Physics, and the discipline "Teaching and Learning in the Digital World", linked to the Pedagogy graduate course.

Results of this projects are still in development, because the period of research observation is still not ended; nowadays, students' communities in the ECODI are developing capacities and competences of:

- Creation of new objects in collaboration with other members;
- Collaborative work around a creative idea;
- Collaborative production of learning, quantifiable in the exchange of lessons' materials, production of tests, reports and learning documents;
- Creation of various digital virtual communities, that rise in the Second Life Metaverse, in UNISINOS spaces, and then continue to grow up both in Second Life and in the Real World and other technology tools (Web 2.0: forum, blog, chat, wiki etc.)

ECODI PPGs (Programas de Pós-Graduação) UNISINOS - 2008-2010 - "Virtual Space in Digital Living Programs Graduate (stricto sensu) - ECODI-PPGS UNISINOS: a proposal for the researchers' training". The project is focused on creating a space for information, interaction and research development of educational practices and processes of teacher-researchers, in the context of the Graduate (stricto sensu - SS) - UNISINOS, in order to constitute a Living Space in Digital Virtual - ECODI (Schlemmer et al.

2006, Schlemmer 2008). In this context the Program Graduate Education and Graduate in Business Administration is also involved.

Several activities are currently developed in ECODI PPGs: Research in Digital Education (teaching and learning processes with Metaverse Second Life technology); Classes at the undergraduate and postgraduate level (Masters and PhD); Extension courses – continuous training; Workshops; Work Guidelines for graduation, Master and PhD thesis; Meetings of the Research Group; Display / exhibition of works; scientific and academic events (participation and organization) - International Congress on Education; Presentation of papers; Lectures; Defense of dissertation and PhD thesis.

This last projects, still in the development phase, aims to use the potentialities of DVW3Ds not only for under-graduated and graduated students but also for PhD students and high-level education people. Nowadays, the number of Master and PhD thesis discussed (and sometimes realized) in the ECODI is growing up (we have 5 discussion only in 2010, into the PPG in Education); the participation of professors is growing up too, after the first period of "learning to learn" about the platform and technology's use. The so-called "Digital Divide" plays here an important role, not only because of the problem of the use of technology, but mostly because of the problem of "faith" in the technology possibilities. It is interesting to note here that the development of this specific project was possible only after the presentation of the results of the others projects to the Academic Community. The Academic Community needed not only "quantitative" results, but after all, a motivation to participate in a project different by the others and that previewed a direct involvement of Professors and Researchers.

MAIN FINDINGS AND DISCUSSION

It is important to realize that in the universe of human relationships, communities represent a trend significantly growing up in recent times, both for the more formal characteristics, which constitute different types of organization, as for informal ones, that constitute different contexts linked mainly to Web environments. Thus, all kinds of communities live together, from the most traditional, territorial based community, to those constituted by different social movements and built in digital virtual spaces, such as VLCPs; VLCPs permit the emergence of spaces rich in subjects' action and interaction, in the context of sharing practices and building knowledge collaboratively and cooperatively.

In this framework, perspectives and trends are to identify communities of online gamers, particularly those linked to form MMORPG (Massive Multiplayer Online Role Playing Games), focused on meeting game challenges. These communities develop collaborative and cooperative competition, where each player competes against the others to be the best player, and to get the most relevant items. However, many times, the competitors come in groups and the player needs to join a group and to establish a relationship of collaboration and cooperation in order to achieve certain common goals. Therefore, players that provide a higher level of cooperation and greater numbers of bonds

Figure 3. ECODI UNISINOS VIRTUAL

Avatars in interactions in ECODI UNISINOS VIRTUAL

Physics of the Earth System Class

Teaching and Learning in the Digital World Class

Construction space of the Teaching and Learning in the Digital World Class

Figure 4. PPGs working

of this type become more evolved. This concept can be applied to different organizations, which can benefit from it. Another perspective and a tendency for VLCPs, consists precisely in VLCPs nomads-hybrid, ie VLCPs using different Web 2.0 technologies combined with 3D web technologies such as Digital Metaverse and Virtual Worlds in 3D, including games and simulations. What does "nomads hybrid" mean? Hybrids subjects have a physical and digital identity, such as a physical existence (physical body) and digital virtual existence (body technologized-avatar); they live simultaneously in the physical world and in the digital virtual world. Both "spaces" are exploitable, and these "spaces" don't refer to a "pure space" as an a priori condition of experience of the world as we find in Kant (1983) apud Schlemmer (1998), but constitutes the main object of experience, where the *avatar* and the *subject* (an individual not separable in his multiple identity) lives, creating and re - creating his identity; he lives, creating digital virtual living spaces, where a world happens.

Does the "digital native", the "zapping generation" (Veen, Vrakking, 2006), is building his objectivity and subjectivity from this hybrid dimension? They are nomads because of their constant roaming, ignoring boundaries, to search for new spaces that can satisfy their desires and interests.

"While experts are still talking about the real and virtual, people are building a life in which borders are increasingly permeable .(...) In the future, the porous borders will be most interesting to study and understand (Turkle, 1999, p. 118)

According to Turkle (1999), the defense of the borders between virtual and real efforts to locate certain types of experience in one or other dimension; currently is prevalent among specialists than among users, citizens of virtual communities, to refuse the idea of the existence of defined borders, and to clearly express the human desire to have access to several things simultaneously.

"Real relationships are those in which people feel connected enough to give them importance. It is these relationships that determine the way each is perceived (...) or the way they see their own ability to relate to others. " (...) In life online, people find themselves in a position to play different roles, adopting different personalities in different parts of the network. See and experience many aspects of themselves. Living intensely this multiplicity (...) In this sense, life online resumes an aspect of everyday life to take him to a higher grade. (...) For many people, the virtual community allows a freer expression of many aspects of themselves. But it is also something that you live in the "rest of life." (...) To the extent that things are closed and the space is reduced, cyberspace offers something on the order of space-game: a chance to trial absent from the rest of his life in the RV (...) I want to stress that the best possibilities for the development of the communities are in places where they cross the virtual experiences and the rest of life. " (Turkle, 1999, p. 119, 120, 121)

Members of this generation live together, co-inhabit new spaces, being through and in the communities created, leaving the concept that exists only one space to live, one community, one world, one universe.

REFERENCES

Castells, M. (1999). *A sociedade em rede*. São Paulo, Brazil: Paz e Terra.

Castells, M. (2003). *A Galáxia da Internet: Reflexões Sobre a Internet, os Negócios e a Sociedade*. Rio de Janeiro: Zahar.

Daniel, B., Schwier, R. A., & Mccalla, G. (2003). Social capital in virtual learning communities and distributed communities of practice. *Canadian Journal of Learning and Technology, 29*(3).

Di Franco, G. (2001). *EDS: Esplorare, descrivere e sintetizzare i dati. Guida pratica all'analisi dei dati nella ricerca sociale*. Milano, Italia: Franco Angeli.

Eco, U. (2004). *Il nome della rosa*. Milano, Italia: Bompiani.

Guala, A. (2000). *Metodi della ricerca sociale*. Roma, Italia: Carocci.

Kant, I. (1983). Crítica da Razão Pura . In *Os Pensadores*. São Paulo, Brazil: Abril Cultural.

Lemos, A. (2002). *Cibercultura. Tecnologia e Vida Social na Cultura Contemporânea*. Porto Alegre: Sulina.

Lévy, P. (1999). *Cibercultura*. Rio de Janeiro: Editora 34.

Moretti, G. (2009). *Mundos digitais virtuais em 3D e aprendizagem organizacional: uma relação possível e produtiva*. In IV Congreso de la Ciber-Sociedad 2009: Crisis Analógica, Futuro Digital. Disponível em: http://www.cibersociedad.net/congres2009/es/coms/ mundos-digitais-virtuais-em-3d-e-aprendizagem-organizacional-uma-relasao-possivel-e-produtiva/644/

Moretti, G. (2010). *La simulazione come strumento di produzione di conoscenza: ComunitÃ di apprendimento e di pratica nei mondi virtuali*. PhD thesis in Communication Sciences and Complex Organizations, LUMSA University, Rome, Italy, National Library of Rome.

Nonaka, I., & Konno, N. (1999). *The concept of "Ba": Building a foundation for knowledge creation*. USA: Butterworth – Heinemann.

Nonaka, I., & Takeuchi, H. (1998). *The knowledge creating company*. Milano, Italy: Guerini e Associati.

Palloff, R. M., & Pratt, K. (1999). *Building learning communities in cyberspace - Effective strategies for the online classroom*. São Francisco, CA: Jossey-Bass Publishers.

Piaget, J. (1973). *Estudos sociológicos*. Rio de Janeiro, Brazil: Companhia Editora Forense.

Rheingold. H. (2004). The virtual community: Homesteading at the electronic frontier. Retrieved from http://www.rheingold.com/vc/book

Richards, L., & Moore, J. M. (2009). *Fare ricerca qualitativa*. Milano, Italy: FrancoAngeli.

Schlemmer, E. (1998). *A representação do espaço cibernético pela criança, na utilização de um ambiente virtual. Programa de Pós Graduação em Psicologia, Universidade Federal do Rio Grande do Sul. Dissertação*. Porto Alegre: Mestrado em Psicologia do Desenvolvimento.

Schlemmer, E. (2002). AVA: Um ambiente de convivência interacionista sistêmico para comunidades virtuais na cultura da aprendizagem. Porto Alegre: URFGS. *Tese (Doutorado em Informática na Educação) Programa de Pós Graduação em Informática na Educação, Universidade Federal do Rio Grande do Sul.*

Schlemmer, E. (2005). Ambiente virtual de aprendizagem (AVA): Uma proposta para a sociedade em rede na cultura da aprendizagem. *In: Carla Beatris Valentini; Eliana Maria do Sacramento Soares. (Org.). Aprendizagem em Ambientes Virtuais: compartilhando idéias e construindo cenários*, (pp. 135-160). Caxias do Sul.

Schlemmer, E. (2005). Metodologias para Educação a Distância no Contexto da Formação de Comunidades Virtuais de Aprendizagem . In Barbosa, R. M. (Ed.), *Ambientes Virtuais de Aprendizagem* (pp. 29–49). Porto Alegre.

Schlemmer, E, (2008). ECODI – A criação de espaços de convivência digital virtual no contexto dos processos de ensino e aprendizagem em Metaverso. IHU Ideias, São Leopoldo, ano 6. n. 103 (caderno).

Schlemmer, E. (2009). *Telepresença*. Curitiba: IESDE Brasil S.A.

Schlemmer, E., Trein, D., & Oliveira, C. (2009). Metaverse: Telepresence in 3D avatar-driven digital-virtual worlds. *TIC Revista D'Innovación Educativa, 2*, 26–32.

Scotti, E., & Sica, R. (2007). *Community management. Processi informali, social networking e tecnologie Web 2.0 per la gestione della conoscenza nelle organizzazioni*. Roma: Apogeo.

Turkle, S. (1999). Fronteiras do real e do virtual. Entrevista concedida a Federico Casalegno. In *Revista FAMECOS, 11*, dezembro.

Veen, W., & Vrakking, B. (2006). *Homo zappiens. Growing up in a digital age*. London, UK: Network Continuum Education.

Wenger, E. (2006). *Comunità di pratica. Apprendimento, significato, identità*. Milano, Italy: Raffaello Cortina.

Wenger, E. (2010). *Communities of practice: A brief introduction*. Retrieved from http://www.ewenger.com/ theory/index.htm

Wenger, E., Mcdermott, R., & Snyder, W. (2007). *Coltivare comunità di pratica*. Milano, Italy: Guerini e Associati.

KEY TERMS AND DEFINITIONS

Avatar: Digital and graphic user's representation in digital virtual worlds in 3D.

Digital Virtual Worlds in 3D (DVW3Ds): Immersive worlds graphically built and represented in the Internet, such as Second Life.

ECODI: Space of digital virtual cohabitation in digital virtual worlds in 3D, where avatars can meet, work together and built objects.

Virtual Communities (VCs): Communities living mostly in the Web, interacting through text messages and collaborative tools of Web 2.0.

Virtual Communities of Practice (VCPs): Virtual communities whose main objective is working together, sharing and creating knowledge and practices.

Virtual Learning Communities (VLCs): Virtual communities whose main purpose is learning together.

Virtual Learning Communities of Practice (VLCPs): Virtual communities whose members work together, and learn trough the sharing knowledge and using common practices.

Chapter 11
Technological Minimalism vs. Second Life:
Time for Content Minimalism

Joao Mattar
Universidade Anhembi Morumbi, Brasil

ABSTRACT

This chapter addresses a certain resistance against the use of Second Life in education, which is based on the theory of technological minimalism. The main arguments behind this resistance and the theory's basic concepts are discussed. Then a critique of an example of the application of technological minimalism to the use of Second Life in education follows. Technological minimalism advocates the minimum use of technology needed to transmit content. The text argues that in the current stage of education technology potential educational tools should not be chosen based on that criterion. Technology and education cannot be easily separated anymore. As a conclusion, this chapter suggests a new form of minimalism: a minimalism of content.

INTRODUCTION

There is a personal and existential motivation behind this chapter. When I started to use Second Life (SL) in education in 2007, Brazilian distance education researcher Wilson Azevedo was the main critic of my experiences. He based his criticism on Mauri Collins' and Zane Berge's concept of technological minimalism (TM). While we

debated in a mailing list, I enrolled in the course 'Teaching and Learning in Second Life' at Boise State University (Spring 2008), and guess who the professor was? Mauri Collins! The mother, if you will, of the argument used by Azevedo to criticize the use of SL in education was my instructor about (and in) SL. But that was not the whole puzzle: the "father" of the argument, Zane Berge, also followed the course in SL, as an

DOI: 10.4018/978-1-60960-854-5.ch011

observer. In my debate with Azevedo, I could use the authority of my teachers in SL and he could use the authority of the proponents of TM – but they were the same educators! This chapter tries to make sense of that surreal experience.

The chapter is based on bibliographic reviews as well as my own experiences with SL. Furthermore, my thoughts were also shaped by my debate with Azevedo and some discussions I had with both Collins and Berge during the course.

I initially address the main arguments by Azevedo against the use of SL in education. Subsequently I criticize the principles of TM and an article by Berge where these principles are applied to SL. I then conclude with a discussion about education technology and a proposition of a new type of minimalism.

The objectives of this theoretical chapter are, though, to present and discuss a common resistance against the use of SL (and, therefore, virtual worlds) in education, and propose a new focus for education technology. A focus that is not based on the criterium of minimum technology, but on minimum content.

BACKGROUND

Second Life is an online 3D virtual world developed by Linden Lab and launched in 2003. Users can interact with each other through avatars, their 3D virtual representation, using voice and text chat, in addition to other tools. Objects can be easily built, to which scripts, textures, animations, and gestures can be added.

SL is being used as a tool by many institutions around the world, as the following selected examples illustrate. Mattar (2008) discusses the use of SL as a learning environment. Molka-Danielson & Deutschmann (2009) present a Scandinavian educational project in SL, with guidance on building simulations and integrating virtual worlds into education. Clark (2009) presents the use of SL for teaching genetics. Wankel & Kingsley (2009)

explore the theory and case studies on the use of virtual worlds in education. Other references will be indicated during this chapter.

Other authors, however, criticize the use of SL in education. Young (2010) argues that there was a hype much more related to marketing than to education, and now colleges and universities are retreating.

One of these critiques is based on the theory of TM, defined by Collins & Berge (1994) as the minimum use of technology in support of instructional objectives. There are many simpler technological alternatives to virtual worlds available, according to the principle of TM, therefore there would be no sense in using SL in education. (Berge, 2008)

Although TM is not a pervasive principle, its arguments can be taken as typical examples of general positions against the use of virtual worlds in education. Azevedo's arguments, in turn, can then be taken as a didactical application of the principle of TM for evaluating the use of virtual worlds in education. These ideas will be discussed in this chapter.

AZEVEDO'S CRITIQUE OF SECOND LIFE

In several discussions in a distance education mailing list in Portuguese (Lista EaD-L), Wilson Azevedo argues against the use of SL in education. His arguments can be divided into four main points: funnel, smoke, withdrawal, and 3Ducation. A brief discussion of each of them follows.

Funnel

There is a technological funnel to use SL, through which only a few can pass, what turns it into an elitist and exclusionary tool.

This is actually a real funnel, which should however open up as hardware develops and bandwidth increases. In UK universities, for instance, already fewer academics are complaining about technical issues when using SL, such as inadequate equipment (Kirriemuir, 2009). In addition, the virtual world's applications may be considered cheaper than video conferencing. (Badger, 2008)

Smoke

Too much smoke, little fire: SL was a bubble. Too much artificial noise in the beginning, with many potential uses foreseen in education, but no real benefits. What will remain, two years from now (that was 2007), when the fascination has passed? No practical applications and no impact in distance education.

Even if correct, Azevedo's prophecy covers only half of the hype cycle. An innovation graph usually shows that, after a technology trigger and a peak of expectation takes place there might be a period of disillusionment, and that, in turn, might be followed by a slope of enlightenment and a plateau of productivity. And what piques the interest of an educator is not exactly a SL graph, but a graph that shows the use of virtual worlds in education.

Less than one year after Wilson's prophecy, Kelton (2008) stated:

Many people believed that virtual worlds would end up like the eight-track audiotape: a fond memory of something no longer used (or useful) [Azevedo used PointCast as an example]. Yet today there are hundreds of higher education institutions represented in three-dimensional (3D) virtual worlds such as Active Worlds and SL. Indeed, the movement toward the virtual realm as a viable teaching and learning environment seems unstoppable.

Where are we now, years after Wilson's prophecy? Harrison (2009) discusses how education followed an inverse path as an exception to the hype and subsequent disappointment with SL by corporations:

Education is thriving in Second Life. This enthusiastic subculture is abuzz within the Second Life realm, constantly interacting inside and outside Second Life. Educators are exploring every possible tool the 3D virtual world offers and establishing best practices along the way.

It is also worth registering the growing use of SL as an environment for academic events. While only 1,200 or so different avatars participated in Second Life Best Practices in Education in 2007, in 2009 3,647 participated in Virtual Worlds Best Practices in Education and more than 6,000 in the 2010 version. These numbers demonstrate that SL is still a valuable tool for educators.

Withdrawal

A very high percentage of users (much higher than in other Internet services) creates accounts in SL but never comes back. SL is not attractive for the majority of its registered users who never become active. We should listen to them to better evaluate SL's applicability to distance education.

Elizabeth Knittle explains the feeling of an educator getting "inworld" (inside Second Life) for the first time:

I looked around and I thought, this is crazy. I just couldn't see the value of it, so I left. But then people starting blogging about it – a lot of people – so I had to reconsider. I decided that if I was going to understand this thing and be able to answer questions about it intelligently, I really just had to suck it up and get in there and participate. Once I connected with people inworld, it made all the difference. (Waters, 2009)

The movement of education in virtual worlds continues and to evaluate the pedagogical use of environments such as SL there is a need for immersion in them. Azevedo admits he has entered one or two times, walked around, felt it, and did what the majority of users do: never went back.

This is not the description of a user withdrawal, but of an educator refusing to test a tool.

3Ducation

What difference does the use of 3D simulations make to learning? There is no more than dazzle in the answers available. Those who use SL in education were not able to show that a significant difference exists, that is to say, they were not able to prove positive results on the use of virtual worlds in education.

Educators who are inworld provide lots of answers, among them: 3D graphical setting, game-like environment, multimedia presentation tools, experiential learning, experimentation, immersion, simulation, cross-reality, role-play, social network knowledge construction, collaboration, co-creation, retention, participation, engagement, the use of avatars, sense of social presence, understanding the learning process, price, etc. (Batson, 2009; Calongne, 2008; Dawley, 2009; Harrison, 2009; Lifton, 2007; Lifton, Laibowitz, Harry, Gong, Mittal, & Paradiso, 2009; Lifton & Paradiso, 2009; Trein, 2010; Walker & Rockinson-Szapkiw, 2009; Wallace & Maryott, 2009; Weusijana, Svihla, Gawel, & Bransford, 2009)

According to Clark (2009), online education created a need for online laboratory experiences, and SL offers a new dimension to scientific education:

Virtual experiments performed in Second Life laboratories offer students activities that are both hands-on and minds-on, making it possible for students to replicate classic experiments or perform laboratory activities that might be too dangerous, too expensive, or too time-consuming in the real world.

Historically the discussion of interaction in distance education did not give much importance to the learner/interface or learner/technology component of the learning environment. To the three categories of interaction initially proposed by Moore (1989) – learner/content, learner/instructor, and learner/learner, Hillman, Willis, and Gunawardena (1994) add a fourth one: the interaction between the learner and the interface, justified by the development of technologies used in distance education. In addition, Burnham and Walden (1997) talk about a learner-environment interaction, an interplay or mutual influence between the learner and his or her environment, which helps or hinders learning.

Mattar (2008) argues that SL provides an interesting type of interaction for students, professors, and content with the environment. 3D virtual worlds have brought back to the learning experience at least part of the sense of a physical space that was taken from us by traditional learning 'environments'. When an avatar gets too close to you, it bothers you. When you bump into an avatar, you apologize. Educators who master virtual worlds' pedagogy have the opportunity to design new, creative and unpredictable types of learning.

Kapp & O'Driscoll (2010) present a long discussion on how three-dimensional environments force us to review our pedagogical principles, supporting learning and collaboration. Content-centered instructional design models are inappropriate both for the scenario we live in and for today's students. The authors argue that design is the key element in 3D environments.

TECHNOLOGICAL MINIMALISM

Follows a discussion of what is explicitly the basis for all of Azevedo's arguments: the theory of TM.

This is the famous definition of TM (Collins & Berge, 1994):

We are defining technological minimalism as the unapologetic use of minimum levels of technology, carefully chosen with precise attention to their advantages and limitations, in support of well defined instructional objectives.

completed by:

There is wisdom in technological minimalism – the more bells and whistles a delivery technology has, the more expensive and complex the equipment needed, the greater the limitations on student access, the greater the claims on time and travel (e.g. to live videoconference sites), the more extensive the technical support needed and the greater the chance of inopportune equipment failure.

First of all, as this article was written more than fifteen years ago, there is naturally a need to revise some concepts. As one example, the authors state that "content can not interact, hold a dialogue, nor answer back" referring to Moore (1989). This discussion was actually later extended by Anderson (2003), who introduced the concept of content/content interaction. It is possible today, with web 2.0 tools, to produce learning objects in which content, from a certain moment on, starts to renew and update by itself, through interaction with other objects and content. You can, for instance, build a RSS page about a topic, so during a course this page will be automatically updated, without need for interaction with human beings.

The main concept of the article that needs to be revised, however, is the one of TM itself. In 1994 students were different from today so minimal technology today is different from minimal technology fifteen years ago. Besides that, what is minimal for an educator who does not regularly use digital tools might also be significantly different from what is minimal for an educator who has already adequately integrated technology into his teaching practices.

Why, then, not think about different levels of technology in a course, so that a student could choose the optimal level according to his or her preferences? Why limit the level of technology in a course to the minimum, if some (or many?)

students might prefer, and feel motivated by, more technology? Why leave the technological level decision only in the hands of the instructor?

Six years later, Collins and Berge (2000) state: "'Technological minimalism' is a valid methodological stance that can guide choices among technologies that are already proven to be robust, available, and relatively inexpensive."

As technologies change rapidly those choices are not so simple. But we can also be afraid that TM, read literally, would prevent us from testing the pedagogical potential of new technologies that are still not robust, available and inexpensive. This is one of the motivations behind the resistance to test SL in education, as it is clear on Berge's text (2008), commented in the next section.

One interesting example of the application of TM is the analysis of the use of video in education. Collins and Berge (2000) discuss the negative impact of streaming video technologies, which had added cost, but not gains to learning. However, we know today that video and animations, when appropriately used, open pedagogical possibilities we cannot reach simply using text or minimal technology. Snelson (2008), for example, researches these results. It is not, though, just a simple question of adding a little bit of technology to one side, and measuring the results on the other, to check if it is worth it: everything changes. Even if using video, audio, and animations really does not guarantee an automatic gain in teaching and learning, this does not mean that we should not use these technologies. This is a basic fallacy: if the growth of *A* does not guarantee the improvement of *B*, so no (or minimum) *A*. Learning is not simply the measurable results of an equation, but a journey of exploration.

Technology is not the cure for education, but this does not mean we need to be afraid of it. Instead of cutting it down to a minimum we need to develop faculties' abilities to explore and effectively use technology in education, through quality professional development programs. (Mattar, 2009)

BERGE'S CRITIQUE OF SECOND LIFE

A typical example of the application of TM to education is Berge's critical review of SL (2008). The reasoning is the same: if an easier alternative is available, why use something more complicated? "Generally, teachers and students in *SL* cannot accomplish anything that they could not accomplish in regular Websites" (p. 30). Almost everything done in SL (with many more barriers) can be performed online. According to Berge, there is no justification to use SL in education unless educators figure out what to do in 3D virtual worlds that can't be more easily done in other environments. Neither is it worth the steep learning curve to master its effective use.

A typical technological minimalist should then sit down and wait until a specific technology matures and becomes useful in education, as if testing and adapting technologies for educational purposes should not also be the responsibility of an educator. Either technology would become educational by itself or other educators should test these tools, while the technological minimalist comfortably watches, encapsulated and protected from any mistakes by not experimenting.

SOLUTIONS AND RECOMMENDATIONS: EDUCATION TECHNOLOGY AND CONTENT MINIMALISM

Education Technology is the research and practice field of the use of technological tools in education. It involves exploring the pedagogical potential of these tools and integrating them into education.

The obsession with a minimum level of technology cannot imprison us and block our tests. As the medium is, in many cases, at least part of the message, technology is not simply a support for the transmission of content – actually, no software is pedagogically neutral. In this sense,

TM can be seen as a 'conceptual' minimalism, an excessive theoretical simplification, which might limit (instead of improving) learning.

The choice for TM should be the minimum level of technology needed to reach an objective. This presupposes that it is simple to compare levels of technology and outcomes; that the level of technology does not affect the results; and that the objectives of a course should be pre-determined before it starts. An opposite perspective, however, claims that the curriculum – and learning objectives – should be open and indeterminate, collaboratively built during the course upon the world of the real students. Peters (2004, p. 62), for example, states that in the post-industrialized distance education, the objectives are usually unknown in the beginning of the learning process, which is not systematic, but random and intuitive. Curricula should be open to discovery, investigation, improvisation, indetermination, creativity, and innovation, conceived as something in course, unstable and dynamic. From this perspective, there is simply no way of pre-determining the minimum of technology needed to reach well-defined instructional objectives. And the reason for that is that there are no well-defined objectives, nor content, before the learning experience starts.

So much concern about the use of technologies above the minimum may not make sense anymore, and some educators might be using the TM argument to justify their resistance to learn new technologies, needed to teach the new generation of students, or at least adequately communicate with them. After all, why learn or teach our students how to use technology instead of doing pure teaching? Why should we confuse the delivery platform with what is being delivered?

Clark (1983) claims that media are "mere vehicles that deliver instruction but do not influence student achievement any more than the truck that delivers our groceries causes changes in our nutrition" (p. 445). But nutrition does not include interaction with the truck, while education implies interaction with and within technology.

The truck is not an environment for nutrition, while technology is an environment for education. In a layer even previous to the metaphor, delivery of instruction is exactly what Freire (1982) criticized as the "banking concept" of education.

Collins and Berge (2000) argue that, leaving technology aside, students and teachers could concentrate on what matters most – teaching and learning. This presupposes a clear separation between technology (or form, on one side) and education (or content, on the other). There seems to be a certain level of naivety in this belief: here is the content we want to transmit, predetermined, and for that transmission we should find the minimum level of technology. If we use more technology than needed, we risk spending resources and taking the focus from content. As if technology did not alter, radically, many times, the content itself. As if learning to use new tools would not be, in its own right, a precious type of learning. As if siding with minimum technology would mean a great victory, or a great choice. As if it would be wiser to stop in time because of the constant progress of technology.

The TPCK – Technological Pedagogical Content Knowledge model, on the contrary, proposes the integration of content, technology, and pedagogy (Angeli & Valanides, 2009; Mishara & Koehler, 2006). Technology cannot be clearly separated from education anymore, it is not possible to conceive both unbound. Depending on the technology you choose the *learning outcomes* will be different. Technology is not neutral in relation to education; it is not possible to project educational objectives, slice them, and at the end simply choose the minimum technology to deliver that content. The tools affect not only content, but the whole process of teaching and learning. The equation became much more complex.

According to Batson (2008), for more than twenty years we stated that it was not about technology, but about education. This rhetoric, however, does not make sense anymore, if it ever did, because it does a disservice to us. We should

not be ashamed to say: it is about technology in the same sense that it is about education, not an education carriage pulling the subaltern technology.

Focusing on education does not preclude focusing on technology, just as not focusing on technology does not guarantee better focus on education. The level of technology used changes the educational process and its outcome.

According to constructivism, the focus of education is not on content, but on the process (Kanuka & Anderson, 1999). Quinn (2005) claims that we should not think about the design of content, but on constructing experiences and environments for learners to make decisions and reflect about the decisions made. Our starting point should not be to organize content, but how the learner will act. Digital game-based learning theory (Prensky, 2007) teaches us to start from engagement and interaction, not from content and instructional design. Richardson (2006) points as a great change in education the collaborative construction of social content. As virtual worlds like SL involve a predisposition to collaborate, there is no need to create and recreate courses and content all the time: "At its core, Second Life is a rich ecosystem of learning experiences that are open to the public. Teachers don't have to create everything from scratch." (John Lester as cited in Waters, 2009)

The use of web 2.0 tools, games, and 3D virtual worlds, without fear of venturing above a minimum technological level, allow us to think of a 'minimalism of content'. That is to say, to include a minimum level of ready content in the design of courses, while motivating the learning and use of tools by students to search, collect, organize, and produce content during the course. Different tools and different levels of technology should be adopted according to the interests of different students. This can be accomplished without an intense focus on content (there is free content available to be used for almost any course) and without fear of technology. Instead of instructional designers trained to polish content, we need designers capable of developing technology, environment, interaction and learning:

We often see the roles associated with design as content or institutionally centred – instructional designers, project managers, graphic artists, network specialists. However where are the designers for learning or the interactive architects? Where are the collaborative environment specialists? We operate in a learner-centred collaborative context and yet our design models are too often predicated on face-to-face and teacher-centred paradigms. If we are to achieve the full potential and benefits that an online environment affords then we must rethink the philosophies and practices that we bring to the design environment. (Sims, 2006)

FUTURE RESEARCH DIRECTIONS

Many more studies are certainly needed on the use of virtual worlds in education. Augmented reality and mobile devices have brought new dimensions for the use of virtual worlds in education, such as dual or cross-reality (Lifton 2007, Lifton et al 2009, Lifton & Paradiso 2009) and mobile simulations and games (Klopfer, 2008).

The importance of the environment in experiences in virtual worlds is also a very interesting area of research. As online education used, since its beginning, primarily text interfaces, the interaction of teachers and students with the virtual environment can be analyzed as a new variable in the educational process, and its results measured.

The character of the representation of our identity in avatars, and how it affects online learning, is also a growing and interesting area of research. Schlemmer, Trein, & Oliveira (2009) and Trein (2010) are exploring this direction. Trein's research concludes that with the creation of virtual digital identities in SL the user feels engaged in a rich, immersive and interactive experience due to the sense of being the avatar and an integral part of the environment. As a consequence, the

synchronicity of being together and the possibility of expressing our corporality in virtual worlds increase the feeling of presence and belonging, contributing to the overcoming of the paradigm of distance and the lack of physical presence in online education.

3D Virtual Worlds push us to explore new pedagogies, questioning the excessive importance given to content in online education, and new technologies allow us to exercise unimaginable ways of socializing, interacting, and learning. Peer 2 Peer University (http://p2pu.org/), for example, is an online community of open study groups organized around open content available online, and peer to peer assessment.

CONCLUSION

This chapter has criticized several reservations against the use of Second Life in education based on the principles of technological minimalism. What is being proposed is that 3D virtual worlds, such as Second Life, bypass the need to establish a minimum use of technology in education, in addition to calling for a minimum of content. Data and content do not give us meaning; interaction does:

Content has always been the center of the human-computer interface. We have lived now for decades with the 'desktop' and the 'filing cabinet' being the primary metaphor for the human-computer interaction. In learning, we spent years implementing learning management systems that are essentially prisons for learning content. We had a focus on content that reflected the hierarchy of our organizations and of our learning models that were available at that time. Now with the emergence of live avatar-based virtual environments, we have the opportunity to move beyond content, beyond rigid hierarchies, beyond the desktop, to a learning environment focused on the context of learning. (Burns, 2010, p. xi).

We should not be afraid of using more technology. Instead, we should be wary of poor quality professional development programs for teachers to integrate technology into education. While our students master several tools such as virtual worlds, many teachers are still far behind in using these tools in education. As Chris Dede states:

I believe the greatest challenge facing educators is empowering students to master such 21st century skills as understanding and resolving complex, novel situations; collaborating with a diverse team both face-to-face and across distance; and producing knowledge by filtering and synthesizing information. This requires fluency in information technology for collaboration, information synthesis, and decision making. Schools of education should make these types of learning experiences central to teachers' preparation. (Thatcher, 2005)

Technological minimalism will not help us with that challenge. It is interesting that this perspective finds an echo in Berge's new work. One year after his mentioned article, he completely changes the tone when referring to Second Life (Smith and Berge, 2009):

The possibilities for educational success are virtually endless.

Second Life is distance education 2.0. Development of MUVEs will take distance education to new heights over the next decade. In-world educational events will be the primary source for distance education.

Trips to museums, theaters, conferences, school, and many other places can be accommodated in-world because of the technology of digital imitation and design. Because of that, another benefit to in-world learning is that it can be a more cost effective alternative to distance education.

This is the same person but a new discourse, which somehow ends the puzzle: time has come for the death of technological minimalism, and maybe the birth of content minimalism.

Second Life is today a free and open tool with which educators and students are intensively experimenting, and the importance of these experiments is not the level of technology used, but the courage of these educators and students to explore new dimensions in teaching and learning. Furthermore, the inspiration for these experiments is not technological minimalism. This technological minimalism, in its original approach, would not allow us to engage in these tests, for which the importance of content is lower than interaction. Second Life will die someday, but this reflection may form the foundation not only for the exploration of other virtual worlds, but also of new technologies that might potentially be used in education.

REFERENCES

Anderson, T. (2003). Modes of interaction in distance education: Recent developments and research questions. In Moore, M. G., & Anderson, W. G. (Eds.), *Handbook of distance education* (pp. 129–144). Mahwah, NJ: Lawrence Erlbaum.

Angeli, C., & Valanides, N. (2009, January). Epistemological and methodological issues for the conceptualization, development, and assessment of ICT–TPCK: Advances in technological pedagogical content knowledge (TPCK). *Computers & Education, 52*(1), 154–168. doi:10.1016/j.compedu.2008.07.006

Badger, C. (2008, December). *Recipe for success with enterprise virtual worlds.* Fortrera. Retrieved from http://www.forterrainc.com/ images/ stories/ pdf/ recipe_for_success_10509.pdf

Batson, T. (2008, June 8). It IS about technology: Integrating higher ed into knowledge culture. *Campus Technology*. Retrieved from http:// campustechnology.com/ articles/ 2008/ 08/ it-is-about-technology -integrating-higher-ed -into-knowledge-culture.aspx

Batson, T. (2009, March 18). Is simulation as good as real life? *Campus Technology*. Retrieved from http://campustechnology.com/ Articles/ 2009/ 03/ 18/ Is-Simulation-as-Good- as-Real-Life. aspx? Page=1

Berge, Z. L. (2008, May-June). Multi-user virtual environments for education and training? A critical review of Second Life. *Educational Technology*, *48*(3), 27–31. Retrieved from http://it.coe.uga. edu/ itforum/ ETSecLife.pdf.

Burnham, B. R., & Walden, B. (1997). *Interactions in distance education: A report from the other side*. Paper presented at the 1997 Adult Education Research Conference, Stillwater, Oklahoma.

Burns, R. (2010). Preface. In Kapp, K. M., & O'Driscoll, T. (Eds.), *Learning in 3D: Adding a new dimension to enterprise learning and collaboration* (pp. xi–xiv). San Francisco, CA: Pfiffer.

Calongne, C. M. (2008, September/October). Educational frontiers: Learning in a virtual world. *EDUCAUSE Review, 43*(5). Retrieved from http:// www.educause.edu/ EDUCAUSE% 2BReview/ EDUCAUSEReviewMagazineVolume43/ EducationalFrontiersLearningin/ 163163.

Clark, M. A. (2009, August/September). Genome Island: A virtual science environment in Second Life. *Innovate, 5*(6). Retrieved from http://www. innovateonline.info/ index.php? view=article& id=562

Clark, R. E. (1983). Reconsidering research on learning from media. *Review of Educational Research, 43*(4), 445–459.

Collins, M., & Berge, Z. L. (1994, September/ October). *Guiding design principles for interactive teleconferencing*. Paper presented at the Pathways to Change: New Directions for Distance Education and Training Conference, University of Maine at Augusta. Retrieved from http://www.emoderators. com/ papers/ augusta.html

Collins, M., & Berge, Z. L. (2000, November/ December). Technological minimalism in distance education. *The Technology Source*. Retrieved from http://technologysource.org/ article/ technological_minimalism_ in_distance_education/

Dawley, L. (2009). Social network knowledge construction: Emerging virtual world pedagogy. *Horizon, 17*(2), 109–121. doi:10.1108/10748120910965494

Freire, P. (1982). *Pedagogia do oprimido* (11th ed.). Rio de'Janeiro, Brazil: Paz e Terra.

Harrison, D. (2009, February 02). Real-life teaching in a virtual world. *Campus Tecnnology*. Retrieved from http://campustechnology.com/ Articles/ 2009/ 02/ 18/ Real-Life-Teaching-in-a-Virtual-World.aspx

Hillman, D. C. A., Willis, D. J., & Gunawardena, C. N. (1994). Learner- interface interaction in distance education: An extension of contemporary models and strategies for practitioners. *American Journal of Distance Education, 8*(2), 30–42. doi:10.1080/08923649409526853

Kanuka, H., & Anderson, T. (1999). Using constructivism in technology-mediated learning: Constructing order out of the chaos in the literature. *Radical Pedagogy, 1*(2).

Kapp, K. M., & O'Driscoll, T. (2010). *Learning in 3D: Adding a new dimension to enterprise learning and collaboration*. San Francisco, CA: Pfiffer.

Kelton, A. J. (2008, September/October). Virtual worlds? Outlook good. *EDUCAUSE Review*, *43*(5). Retrieved from http://www.educause. edu/ EDUCAUSE+Review/ EDUCAUSEReviewMagazineVolume43/ VirtualWorldsOutlookGood/ 163161.

Kirriemuir, J. (2009, June). *Early summer 2009 Virtual World Watch snapshot of virtual world activity in UK HE and FE*. Virtual World Watch. Retrieved from http://virtualworldwatch.net/ wordpress/ wp-content/ uploads/ 2009/ 06/ snapshot-six.pdf

Lifton, J. H. (2007). *Dual reality: An emerging medium*. PhD thesis, Massachusetts Institute of Technology. Retrieved from http://www.media. mit.edu/ resenv/ pubs/ theses/ lifton_phd.pdf

Lifton, J. H., & Paradiso, J. A. (2009, July 27-29). Dual reality: Merging the real and virtual. *Proceedings of the First International ICST Conference on Facets of Virtual Environments* (FaVE), Berlin, Germany. Retrieved from http://web.media.mit. edu/ ~lifton/ publications/ lifton_2009_07_fave. pdf

Lifton, J. H. H. H. H., Laibowitz, M., Harry, D., Gong, N. W., Mittal, M., & Paradiso, J. A. (2009, July-September). Metaphor and manifestation - Cross-reality with ubiquitous sensor/actuator networks. *IEEE Pervasive Computing. Mobile and Ubiquitous Systems*, *8*(3), 24–33.

Lista EaD-L. (n.d.). *Distance education mailing list* (in Portuguese). Retrieved from http:// www.ggte.unicamp.br/ gecon/ sites/ GGTE/ index_html?foco=HTML/ 753

Mattar, J. (2008, February 20). Second Life is not a learning environment... but why not? *De Mattar* (blog). Retrieved from http://blog.joaomattar. com/ 2008/ 02/ 20/ second-life-is-not-a-learning-environment-but-why-not/

Mattar, J. (2009, October 21). Professional development models for educators. *De Mattar* (blog). Retrieved from http://blog.joaomattar.com/ 2009/ 10/ 21/ professional-development- models-for-educators/

Mishra, P., & Koehler, M. J. (2006). Technological pedagogical content knowledge: A new framework for teacher knowledge. *Teachers College Record*, *108*(6), 1017–1054. doi:10.1111/j.1467-9620.2006.00684.x

Molka-Danielson, J., & Deutschmann, M. (2009). *Learning and teaching in the virtual world of Second Life*. Trondheim, Norway: Tapir Academic Press.

Moore, M. G. (1989). Three types of interaction. *American Journal of Distance Education*, *3*(2), 1–6. doi:10.1080/08923648909526659

Peters, O. (2004). *A educação a distância em transição: tendências e desafios* (p. 62). Trad. Leila Ferreira de Souza Mendes. São Leopoldo, RS: Ed. Unisinos.

Prensky, M. (2007). *Digital game-based learning: Practical ideas for the application of digital game-based learning*. St. Paul, MN: Paragon House.

Quinn, C. N. (2005). *Engaging learning: Designing e-learning simulation games*. San Francisco, CA: Pfeiffer.

Richardson, W. (2006). *Blogs, wikis, podcasts, and other powerful web tools for classrooms*. Thousand Oaks, CA: Corwin Press.

Schlemmer, E., Trein, D., & Oliveira, C. J. (2009). The metaverse: Telepresence in 3D avatar-driven digital-virtual worlds. *Revista d'Innovació Educativa, 2*, 26-32. Retrieved from http://gpedunisinos. files.wordpress.com/ 2009/ 03/ 02.pdf.

Sims, R. (2006). Beyond instructional design: Making learning design a reality. *Journal of Learning Design, 1*(2), 1–7. Retrieved from http://www.jld.qut.edu.au/ publications/ vol1no2/ documents/ beyond% 20instructional% 20design.pdf.

Smith, M., & Berge, Z. L. (2009, June). Social learning theory in Second Life. *MERLOT Journal of Online Learning and Teaching, 5*(2), 439-445. Retrieved from http://jolt.merlot.org/ vol5no2/ berge_0609.pdf

Snelson, C. (2008). Web-based video in education: Possibilities and pitfalls. *Proceedings of the Technology, Colleges & Community Worldwide Online Conference*, (pp. 214-221). Retrieved from http://etec.hawaii.edu/ proceedings/ 2008/ Snelson2008.pdf

Thatcher, M. (2005, March 15). The back page (vol. 16). Q&A with Chris Dede. *Tech&Learning*. Retrieved from http://www.techlearning.com/ article/ 3704

Trein, D. (2010). *Educação online em metaverso: a mediação pedagógica por meio da telepresença via avatar em MDV3D*. Master Thesis, Universidade do Vale do Rio dos Sinos - Unisinos, São Leopoldo-RS, Brasil.

Walker, V., & Rockinson-Szapkiw, A. (2009). Educational opportunities for clinical counseling simulations in Second Life. *Innovate, 5*(5). Retrieved from http://www.innovateonline.info/ index.php? view=article& id=711

Wallace, P., & Maryott, J. (2009). The impact of avatar self-representation on collaboration in virtual worlds. *Innovate, 5*(5). Retrieved from http://www.innovateonline.info/ index.php? view=article& id=689

Wankel, C., & Kingsley, J. (2009). *Higher education in virtual worlds: Teaching and learning in Second Life*. Bingley, UK: Emerald Group Publishing Limited.

Waters, J. K. (2009, January 1). A Second Life for educators. *THE Journal*. Retrieved from http://thejournal.com/ Articles/ 2009/ 01/ 01/ A-Second-Life-For-Educators.aspx? Page=1

Weusijana, B. V., Svihla, D. G., & Bransford, J. (2009). MUVEs and experiential learning: Some examples. *Innovate, 5*(5). Retrieved from http://www.innovateonline.info/ index.php? view=article& id=702

Young, J. R. (2010, February 14). After frustrations in Second Life, colleges look to new virtual worlds. *The Chronicle of Higher Education*. Retrieved from http://chronicle.com/ article/ After-Frustrations-in-Second/ 64137/

ADDITIONAL READING

Aldrich, C. (2005). *Learning by Doing: A Comprehensive Guide to Simulations, Computer Games, and Pedagogy in E-Learning and Other Educational Experiences*. San Francisco, CA: Pfeiffer.

Au, W. J., Platel, R., Rymaszewski, M., Ondrejka, C., & Gorden, S. V. Cé,... Rossig. (2008). *Second Life: The Official Guide*. 2nd ed. Indianapolis: Wiley.

BBC. (2009, February 4). *Children Taught in Second Life*. Available from http://news.bbc.co.uk/ newsbeat/ hi/ technology/ newsid_7869000/ 7869303.stm

Beja, M. (2009, March 27). Online Students at Bryant & Stratton College Will Graduate via Second Life. *The Wired Campus*. Retrieved from http://chronicle.com/ blogPost/ Online-Students-at-Bryant/ 7180

Coleman, B. (2009, July-September). Using Sensor Inputs to Affect Virtual and Real Environments. *PERVASIVE computing*, IEEE CS, 2-9. Available from http://cms.mit.edu/ people/ bcoleman/ publications/ coleman-x-reality-proof.pdf

Collins, C. M., & Millard, R. W. (2008, September/October). Galapagos Islands in Second Life. *EDUCAUSE Review, 43*(5). Retrieved from http://www.educause.edu/EDUCAUSE+Review/EDUCAUSEReviewMagazineVolume43/GalapagosIslandsinSecondLife/163177.

Corrêa, B. C. (2009). *A Construção do conhecimento nos metaversos: educação no Second Life* (Master Thesis, Universidade Braz Cubas, Mogi das Cruzes-SP, Brasil). Retrieved from http://www.joaomattar.com/Bruno_Correa_UBC-Dissertacao-2009.pdf

Fernandes, D. A. A. (2010). *Os ambientes virtuais tridimensionais e a educação para a biologia: possibilidades e interações acerca do ensino de ciências e biologia no metaverso do Second Life* (Unpublished Master Thesis, Pontifícia Universidade Católica de Minas Gerais, Belo Horizonte-MG, Brasil).

Gecelka, R. (2009). *Vivências, benefícios e limitações: registro sobre o uso do Second Life em uma experiência educacional* (Graduate Course Final Paper, Universidade Católica de Brasília, Florianópolis-SC, Brasil). Retrieved from http://www.iea.com.br/sites/default/files/TCC_Rodrigo_Gecelka_da_Silva.pdf

Gibson, D., Aldrich, C., & Prensky, M. (2007). *Games and Simulations in Online Learning: Research and Development Frameworks*. Hershey, PA: Information Science Publishing.

Gomes, E. T. (2008). *Ciência, tecnologia e educação em rede: as significações da ciência nos ambientes virtuais de aprendizagem – AVAs* (Master Thesis, Universidade do Sul de Santa Catarina, Palhoça-SC, Brasil). Retrieved from http://www3.unisul.br/paginas/ensino/pos/linguagem/disserta/189.htm

Harrisson, D. (2009, March 18). Second Life's Role in a Curriculum. *Campus Technology*. Retrieved from http://campustechnology.com/Articles/2009/03/18/Teaching-in-the-Trenches-Second-Lifes-Role-in-a-Curriculum.aspx

Harrisson, D. (2009, March 22). Engaging Students in Virtual Learning. *Campus Technology*. Retrieved from http://campustechnology.com/articles/2009/04/22/engaging-students-in-virtual-learning.aspx

Harrisson, D. (2009, March 4). Second Life: Engaging Virtual Campuses. *Campus Technology*. Retrieved from http://campustechnology.com/Articles/2009/03/04/Second-Life-Engaging-Virtual-Campuses.aspx

Innovate Journal of Online Learning (2009, June/July), *5*(5). Available from http://innovateonline.info/

Journal of Virtual Worlds Research. Available from http://jvwresearch.org/

Kirriemuir, J. (2009, June). *Early summer 2009 Virtual World Watch snapshot of virtual world activity in UK, HE, and FE*. Available from http://virtualworldwatch.net/wordpress/wp-content/uploads/2009/06/snapshot-six.pdf

Klopfer, E. (2008). *Augmented Learning: Research and Design of Mobile Educational Games*. Cambridge, MA: MIT Press.

Klopfer, E., Osterweil, S., Groff, J., & Haas, J. (2009). *Using the Technology of Today in the Classroom of Today: The Instructional Power of Digital Games, Social Networking and Simulations, and How Teachers Can Leverage Them*. Education Arcade; MIT. Retrieved from http://education.mit.edu/papers/GamesSimsSocNets_EdArcade.pdf

Layne, C. (2008, February 21). Ball State wins inaugural of Blackboard Greenhouse Grant for Virtual Worlds. Available from http://www.bsu.edu/ update/ article/ 0,1384,38104-5107-57275,00.html

Lorenzo, G. (2001, April 1). Technological Minimalism: A Cost-Effective Alternative for Course Design and Development. *Distance Education Report, 5*(7), 8.

MacManus, R. (2009, July 14). Cross reality: When sensors meet virtual reality. *ReadWriteWeb.* Retrieved from http://www.readwriteweb.com/ archives/ cross_reality_when _sensors_meet_ virtual_reality.php

Metaworld2. (Livestream). Available from http:// www.livestream.com/ metaworld2

Oblinger, D. G. (2006, May). *Simulations, games, and learning.* EDUCAUSE Learning Initiative white paper. Boulder, CO: EDUCAUSE. Retrieved from http://www.educause.edu/ ir/ library/ pdf/ ELI3004.pdf

Review Magazine, E. (2008, September/October). *43*(5). Available from http://www.educause.edu/ EDUCAUSE+ Review/ ERVolume432008/ EDU-CAUSEReview MagazineVolume43/ 163160

Schlemmer, E. (2010). *Ecodi-Ricesu – formação/ capacitação/ação pedagógica em rede utilizando a tecnologia de metaverso.* Paper presented at XV Endipe – Encontro Nacional de Didática e Prática de Ensino. Belo Horizonte, Brasil. CD-ROM.

SocialPresence3D. (Wiki). Available from http:// socialpresence3d.wikispaces.com/

Valente, C., & Mattar, J. (2007). *Second Life e Web 2.0 na Educação: o potencial revolucionário das novas tecnologias.* São Paulo: Novatec.

Weusijana, B. F., Svihla, V., Gawel, D., & Bransford, J. (2009). MUVES and and Experiential Learning: Some Examples. *Innovate Journal of Online Learning 5*(5). Retrieved from http:// www.innovateonline.info/ pdf/ vol5_issue5/ MUVEs_and_ Experiential_Learning-__ Some_ Examples.pdf

KEY TERMS AND DEFINITIONS

Avatar: Three-dimensional computer representation of a user in virtual worlds and games.

Content Minimalism: Theory, proposed in this chapter, which takes the focus away from content in education.

Digital Game-Based Learning: The process of integrating video games into the educational process.

Educational Technology: The research and practice field of the use of technological tools in education.

Second Life: Online 3D social virtual world developed by Linden Lab.

Technological Minimalism: Theory that proposes the minimum use of technology in support of instructional objectives.

Virtual Worlds: Computer-based simulations in which users can interact with one another and, in many cases, create objects.

Section 4
Built for Fun:
Playing in the Metaverse

Chapter 12

The Players' Dimension:
From Virtual to Physical

Michael Nitsche
Georgia Institute of Technology, USA

ABSTRACT

This chapter outlines three positions in the development of game spaces from the ideal of the perfect mindspace to the commercial reality of virtual worlds to the expansion of the game world into the physical environment into a hybrid space. The third position will be investigated further as the argument looks into peculiarities of the evolving hybrid space that result from the combination of changes to the physical through the fictional space. This continues the ongoing dissolution of the magic circle's boundaries and illustrates how fictional worlds expand into even non-game locations. Building on Popper's system of the 3 worlds, it is suggested that today's fictional game worlds have already changed our physical environments. In that, it partially closes the argument back to the earliest dreams of cyberspace but arrives not at a new mindspace to "log in" but instead at a new physical space in need of re-evaluation.

INTRODUCTION

Early on, spatiality has been noted as a defining element of digital media. However, the *kind* of space involved changed over time. Starting from a perspective mainly informed by Human Computer Interaction (HCI) and Game Studies, this paper looks at the development of space in video

games as it reaches out of the digital virtuality into the physical domain. This is a necessarily limited view at the complexities of the debate about space and our engagement with it. It focuses at the increasing role of the physical domain in digital game worlds and will sketch out three steps in the development of video game spaces: from an idealistic mindspace to the contested virtual game worlds of commercial video games to the more current interconnections between physical

DOI: 10.4018/978-1-60960-854-5.ch012

and virtual game spaces. Although this paper will suggest three – rather roughly defined – positions in this development, it should be noted that these positions do not necessarily contradict each other in practice. As our involvement with game worlds grows from an ongoing media history and widening literacy, these three categories should be seen as interwoven and parts of an ongoing evolution. To clarify their differences, though, they will be treated as separate entities.

The three entities outlined here represent three different yet interconnected answers to the question posed by the spatial representation and practices in digital media. Thus, instead of an excluding view that would replace one stage with a new one, it is suggested to understand the argument for stages as a cumulative one. Game worlds can be understood as mindspaces as well as virtual worlds as well as hybrid spaces. The differentiation, as will be argued in the closing section, happens in our actual engagement with them, which can shift rapidly.

CYBERSPACE

Ever since the early days of digital media, visionaries saw them as a new accessible space and a world to explore. Howard Rheingold hoped that cyberspace may be "a new laboratory of the spirit" (Rheingold, 1991). Supporting the idea of the "spirit world" Barlow claimed "[o]urs is a world that is both everywhere and nowhere, but it is not where bodies live. We are creating a world that all may enter without privilege or prejudice accorded by race, economic power, military force, or station of birth" (Barlow, 1996). Reflected in these positions we see the visions of Gibson and other visionaries as they popularized that mix of Science Fiction and technological origins that came together to seed "cyberspace." But it had to be a mainly futuristic forward-looking perspective.

Gibson's work, and the Cyberpunk genre in general, have principally served to excite interest in newly developing interactive computer systems. In a social order whose economic and technological rationale still seems centered on a Marinettian notion of progress - where 'progress is right, even when it's wrong' - the lack of address to the cautionary aspects of the genre is perhaps understandable. It is not surprising that a society preoccupied with technology and consumerism can more readily grasp the potential pleasures of new media rather than predictions of the social decay they might cause. Whatever Gibson's (best) intentions, his work has created a desire for cyberspace technologies in advance of their production. Their current unavailability thereby renders them objects of desire par excellence for a high-tech consumer culture untroubled by vague speculations as to their dystopian potential. (Hayward, 1993)

Inspired by the promise of the new digital technology and its usage, the prophets of cyberspace called for a new kind of space, defined by a new society, somehow stepping beyond the problems of the flesh, at times stepping beyond the biological altogether (Moravec, 1988). These were places to "log in" to a higher level of cyber-enhanced consciousness and "drop out" of reality with its social, economic, and political flaws.

Visionaries such as Douglas Engelbart, whose perspective originated not from the cyberspace fiction of Gibson but from a more practical and technological basis, promised "augmenting man's intellect" (Engelbart, 1988) with the help of this new technology. In Engelbart's case, this famously included the mouse as control device that offered new interaction options to the user. Others expanded this perspective to a conquest of new knowledge spaces through digital technology. Cyberspace as such a deterritorialized knowledge space was seen as the "civilization's new horizon" (Levy, 1997). As a techno-social construct offering "a form of *universally distributed intelligence*" its aim was to provide "the mutual recognition and enrichment of individuals rather than the cult of fetishized or hypostatized communities" (Levy, 1997).

As references to existing communities in many of these works show, these perspectives were certainly not devoid of social context. Many scholars noted that these new spaces had to be discussed in the context of existent cultural studies that offered valuable debates from the conquest of the "new world" as digital colonialism (Gunkel & Gunkel, 1997) to questions of body, gender, and identity (Stone, 1998). The space itself, though, remained a kind of new and yet-to-be-defined location with new opportunities focused on the improvement of the individual as well as the "collective intelligence" of the community at large.

VIRTUAL WORLDS

When the first wave of game worlds became available on household computer systems it looked very different from the promised cyberspace systems. Instead of embarking on the quest for a new freedom offered by the technology, these commercially available worlds remediated existing forms from architectural structures to interactive functionality and audio-visual presentation (Bolter & Grusin, 1999). With remediation comes a re-implementation of existing media politics. The result were not the digital promised lands but familiarized virtual worlds that could be discussed with the help of disciplines such as anthropology or cognitive sciences. For example, instead of logging in like Neo in *The Matrix* and downloading knowledge modules to ones brain, these worlds were seen as bases for perceptual learning (Greenfield, 1984). Perceptual qualities, cognitive processes during play, and psychological states such as flow or immersion offered criteria adapted from neighboring disciplines to analyze these worlds. It is telling that an extended discussion in academia worried about which discipline

should be responsible for the critical analysis of these worlds – now that they had become artifacts available and worthy of study. The more the game environments consolidated as media, the more the players' relationship to them became relevant. One did not seamlessly log in to a new world but the limitations of our perception influenced our orientation in the virtual space (Henry, 1992), spatial understanding was realized as dependent on navigation in physical spaces (Anders, 1998; Darken & Sibert, 1993), gender was not eliminated in these worlds but found new forms of representation (Jenkins, 1998), navigation was identified as crucial (Guenzel, 2008), as was the interplay between spatial construct and visual presentation (Nitsche, 2009).

Revisiting their hopeful positive outlooks visionaries like Rheingold adjusted their projections. Rheingold had to admit that the "unalloyed positive social benefit" (Rheingold, 2000) that was attributed to cyberspace in earlier writings (in this case: in Rheingold's original 1985 edition of the same book) had not materialized. The predicted new enlightenment had not happened here – at least not yet. Instead, these worlds turned into virtual piazzas, arenas, and labyrinths. The designed spaces of all those ever-evolving game worlds lay the grounds for the emergence of game worlds as fictional environments in countless video game settings. They used existing fictions, physical and cognitive conditions, and media techniques to form their own entities. The Sony Playstation 2 slogan "Live in Your World. Play in Ours" illustrates that eventually these game spaces were seen and marketed as self-sufficient environments next to the "real" world. Players visited these worlds from time to time, and engaged with their particular rules and regulations.

Instead of a holistic virtual mindspace, these spaces were legion and defined by clear demarcation lines – each one defined by a unique configuration incompatible to the others'. Each game set up a world for its own. As Dodge and Hitchins realized, when they worked on maps for cyberspace structures: "cyberspace does not consist of one homogenous space; it is a myriad of rapidly expanding cyberspaces, each providing a different form of digital interaction and communication" (Dodge & Kitchin, 2001). These spaces offered access and opportunity for personal growth as outlined by many scholars before but in a highly specific way. Their effects were suddenly measured, contextualized and compared to other media, and their inner workings were gradually disseminated in relation to their individual rule systems in the discipline that emerged as its new academic home, Game Studies. The resulting game worlds might not answer the call for a consciousness-enhancing unified virtual future but they proved to be immensely successful as virtual playgrounds. Their new spatial structures offered solutions to many problems of game design from the aforementioned remediation to narrative, cinematic and dramatic influences. Maybe most importantly, these worlds were realized as dynamic social spaces where emergent play could evolve. One social construct that seemed to work exceptionally well in this context was the idea of the "magic circle."

The arena, the card-table, the magic circle, the temple, the stage, the screen, the tennis court, the court of justice, etc., are all in form and function play-grounds, i.e. forbidden spots, isolated, hedged round, hallowed, within which special rules obtain. All are temporary worlds within the ordinary world, dedicated to the performance of an act apart. ((Huizinga, 1950) here cf (Salen & Zimmerman, 2006))

The conditions of engagement with these worlds was seen as something outside our daily routine, as a special state that transforms players according to the circumstances of the virtual arenas they enter. Within these circles, societies formed based on the conditions of the given worlds and the interactions with them. Depending on the provided virtual environment, different groups evolved:

clans, tribes, guilds, countless chat communities, and virtual citizens of branded individual online worlds. Often these communities were described as equipped with new technological features around which a specific community could evolve as it allowed users to express and explore their own (and others') social realities. The technical prowess of the underlying virtual world co-shaped the forming of the community. The new evolving communities where investigated by countless scholars from very different perspectives including the social activities within these worlds (Ducheneaut, Yee, Nickell, & Moore, 2006). Based on these shared social realities, players formed connections that expanded beyond the virtual and into the physical world (Taylor, 2006). Even though these effects were noticed by many, a certain surprise prevailed when they materialized. Seemingly shocked, some authors realized that real social life grew on the Petri dish provided by the virtual (Dibbell, 1999). The virtual world had become an accepted own fictional location that attracted a lot of research to the degree that the reference back to the social realities of the players had to be re-discovered.

HYBRID SPACES

To repeat the initial caveat: the three positions marked out here are presented as historical, that means that there are continuous overlaps and gradual transformations. It also allows for breaks, rejections, and full-blown refutations to develop over time. These, too, are part of virtual space history. Some of the most acclaimed visionaries of the cyberspace era, like Lanier, have turned into sharp critics (Lanier, 2009). Consequently, the positions outlined so far should be read as debated and dynamic points on a trajectory. Along this trajectory one finds the third position suggested here. It is based on the aforementioned growing interdependencies between the virtual and the real and might be best introduced with the commercial campaign at the launch of Nintendo's

Wii console in its difference to the Playstation 2 slogan used to identify the second stage of game space development above. Instead of praising the qualities of the new hardware, showing off the graphical wonders of the new generation, or at least advertising the titles available at launch date, Nintendo's TV commercials looked from the virtual world into the living room. A camera seemingly set inside the TV set observed players in their living rooms using the new Wii controller as they were obviously interacting with something off-screen behind the camera. The virtual world they played with remained left open to the imagination of the audience, supported by sound, movement of the controller, and occasional light or visual effects. Instead of looking into the virtual to introduce a polygon-constructed playground, the Wii looked outwards into the living room to emphasize the physical as part of their concept of the game world. The result illustrates the shift of perspective that led to a new invasion from the virtual game world into the physical realms of daily life.

Effects of the digital revolution have been identified from transformations of urban landscapes (Mitchell, 1995), to public spaces, and individual model homes such as Georgia Tech's "Aware Home." On the one hand, we find the emergence of "smart spaces" equipped with new technology that adds new functionality to the location, like technologies for assisted living or more efficient work places. On the other hand, we sense the expansion of fictional worlds that infuse the existent space with new meaning instead of actual functionality. This effect depends on technology such as new interfaces, new sensors, new hard- and software, but it uses them as stepping-stones to develop a fiction and not as an end of means. The result of these worlds is not the visible and functional presence of new technologies to provide new forms of usability through digital technology but a change of the existent perception of the everyday surroundings through expanding game universes. While both are interconnected,

the goal is not an expansion of the technology but the development of the fiction.

Augmented Reality applications display information on my favorite restaurant, hovering as virtual bubbles right next to it. Google Map's street view positions "me" next to "my house" which looks most likely different than it does in the present physical world. The Build-A-Bear Workshop expanded from physical shops to create your own stuffed animals to an online service where animals are designed virtually and then shipped to their future owners – or remain completely digital in their video games. This is not only a technical expansion but also a fictionalization of my physical surroundings. As a result, we have to re-think our existing spaces as the new dimension of the digital has been added to them.

SERIOUS PLAY

Facilitating this kind of rethinking, the role of the game systems had to change. A key word of the evolution of game systems is the notion of convergence. Here, convergence is applied as a step into a new quality of space. The formerly distinct game console became a networked media center, able to replace traditional TV formats by streaming downloadable content and offering increasingly hybrid services like Netflix or facebook next to their original gaming domain. Media usage – including game usage – evolved into an open field of experimentation. Because these media had become partially responsible as contributors to the socialization process of their audiences, the blurring of media boundaries also blurred the confinements of the virtual playground. The effect can be traced in the reactions of the visitors to these playgrounds. The perception of some players to take a game world as "real" or "serious" is not new. Already in 1990, at the dawn of online worlds, Richard Bartle, one of their pioneers interrogated the blurring between offline and online life, between playing it and "living it":

Surely, though, things which wield this kind of emotional power over people can't be mere games? The passions roused in (traditional) MUAs [= Multi-User Adventures] have the kind of fire to them normally reserved for religious or political evangelism. People aren't so much playing the MUA as living it. (Bartle, 1990)

Bartle's virtual environments were predominantly text-based but that did not stop players from including them in their version of "reality." Even given the technical limitations, these worlds were immensely attractive for players. Not unlike cyberspace's conscious-altering qualities, excessive play experience was described as "addictive:"

MUDs [= Multi-User Dungeons] are addictive, as we who play them are well aware. Gibson and the rest were right about the addictive possibilities of cyberspace. They were just wrong about the magnitude. (Bryant Durrell, founder of the online world Islandia cf (Bartle, 1990))

Where to find a balance between the two poles was and still is debated but the infusion of the physical world with digital space – as exemplified with the Wii launch – does not necessarily follow the dualism of virtual versus real, online versus offline, play versus life. It combines them.

A second example to illustrate this emergence of a hybrid space are Alternate Reality Games (ARG) and their battle cry of "This is Not a Game." The Wii still embraced the living room of the player from a fixed perspective, namely that of the stationary console. In contrast, ARGs, posterchilds of convergence, cannot be located in a single media form or location. In fact, "[p]art of what characterizes an ARG is that the game universe is not explicitly limited to a particular piece of software or set of digital content" (Kim, Allen, & Lee, 2008). If the playground is not defined anymore, then the perception of an ongoing play state and play space can take over. As the play state becomes part of the everyday-life,

the formerly clearly located game world leaps into the physical everyday-world to change our perception of and engagement with this former non-game world. McGonigal traces these effects in an ARG community's response to the attacks on the World Trade Center: after the 9/11 attacks, discussions flared up in the Cloudmaker community – key ARG players – whether the network of many collaborating players in a game world could be used to solve the mystery of the attacks. As ARGs mainly depend on the cooperation of players in solving very complex puzzles that are seemingly situated in the "real" world, this appeared to some players as a viable option. It had become a way of life.

For many, working closely with the Cloudmakers group had profoundly affected their sense of identity and purpose, to the point that a game mentality was a natural response to real-world events. (McGonigal, 2003)

Not only did the play activity change the players' abilities and performances, but the missing boundaries of the play space also changed their engagement with the physical world and the historical problem at hand. The game space's functionality, part of its virtuality, had been integrated into the non-game space via the extension of the fictional universe. Explaining this effect, McGonigal refers back to Levy's principle of "collective intelligence." For her, an ARG such as *I Love Bees* has the power to facilitate "a visceral, first-person, hands-on experience of collaborative cognition, networked cooperation, and real-time coordination. Players develop a familiarity with CI [= Collective Intelligence] techniques through direct experience" (McGonigal, 2008). For game spaces, this means that the spatial practices of the player change. The player rapidly moves between physical and digital, fictional and factual, and these movements, physical as well as imagined, are the new frontier to be investigated.

The way these players make sense of their surrounding spaces shift and alters the quality of physical space as well as that of the fictional digital game world. In this case, digital media project a new quality onto already existing environments even if there is no factual change in their physical conditions but only a perceptual shift. The Cloud-makers did not have a pre-designed puzzle at their hand for 9/11, there were no definite clues in the media landscape pre-implanted, but players looked at the situation as a game state. The physical world had been changed by the "virtual realities" of the digital game construct.

SHAPING SPACES

Game worlds today use both techniques. They invade the physical spaces with the help of new technology just like "smart spaces" and they expand the fictional world through a shift of perception. Both are interconnected. An ARG like *I Love Bees* that uses GPS-based treasure hunts as well as complex networks of web sites and code snippets, expands beyond a given horizon because these technologies are accepted to be ubiquitous in our every day life.

We had a few basic design principles: Come into the players' lives in every way possible. We hosted Web sites for you to browse, sent emails to your inbox, and arranged for faxes to be sent to your office 'by mistake.' We got a gravel-voice Microsoft employee to record a menacing message from a robot revolutionary and then called players on their phones, which was electrifying, particularly at the home where a player's grandmother answered the call. (Then we had a polite conversation with the police, but that's another story.)" (Sean Steward, author for The Beast cf (Montola, Stenros, & Waern, 2009))

Because the game includes usage of formerly non-game devices (like the telephone) its effects reach beyond the agreed-upon-demarcation line that was the magic circle. A teddy from Build-A-Bear might be born in digital space but will sit on a real world toy chest. Because these technologies travel with us, blend into their surroundings, and increasingly are found everywhere, the interconnected game space can be everywhere. Convergence and ubiquitous computing have driven the development of game worlds into a phase where they are not bound anymore to be experienced through a window that carries the player away through immersion into the virtual, but instead they diffuse into any location they want. Because we do not have to log in anymore, no place is left untouched and the logging out becomes the real challenge.

Game spaces as virtual stages have developed an expressive vocabulary that does not merely reject the limitations of the magic circle "inside" a computer system. Video game worlds have outgrown the magic circle as they settle in today's media space. A wave of new interfaces such as guitars (*Guitar Hero*), bongos (*Donkey Konga*), complete band set ups (*Rock Band*), dance mats (*Dance Dance Revolution*), motion controllers (Nintendo's Wii), steering wheels, cameras (Microsoft's Kinect), microphones, cell phones and tablet computer as game platforms as well as many other technologies have digitized our households. Not only do they change existing architecture, as the coffee table has to give way for the *Rock Band* drum set, but they are also signs of the acceptance of the hybrid space as a fictional space. As more technologies become commonplace in our environments, this projection grows more likely – even if these technologies are not actively used by the audience. The media landscape often successfully closes this loop for us, often via commerce. A Green Day video for their song "Last of the American Girls" might be delivered by the avatars of their video game

Green Day: Rock Band performing the piece on a virtual game stage for a broadcast on the television network MTV, which acquired the game company Harmonix, designers of *Rock Band*, in 2006. The video creates an association with the game even for those who do not play or do not own that specific version of the *Rock Band* franchise and it spreads the game's visuals as equal to other MTV videos to everybody watching the video broadcast. The connection is much more effective for the viewers familiar with the game and its functionality, though. For those players/ viewers the game world and non-game world have morphed into a hybrid navigated by the player, not unlike it did in *I Love Bees*.

Its first shift was their playful participation in the music through the game that stages the player as part of the band; the second is the re-shaping of the "reality" of Green Day itself. In a media-driven world that has already seen fictional pop stars like the cartoon pop band Gorillaz, a virtual Green Day line up remains credible enough. That this change is indeed very "real" surfaced in the debates on Kurt Cobain's representation as a playable avatar in *Guitar Hero 5* that were seen as threatening to his legacy. His widow, Love, called them "lethal" (Michaels, 2009), as they depicted Cobain as a singer of songs that were not seen appropriate to his musical status. The possible misrepresentation of the artist as a virtual being and the public's reaction show that the borderlines have blurred between the musician's performance space, the virtual game space, the media space, and the actual singer and band members, who are simulated in the avatars' movements and lip synched animations. As the representation comes full circle through countless commercial media outlets, the effects of the converging hybrid game space become at times painfully tangible.

The shift questions the distinction between fiction and non-fiction and presents an epistemological challenge. As this change into hybrid game spaces is an ongoing phenomenon that is still gaining momentum, the challenge remains open but to describe this shift and its effects on our knowledge of the world, the essay concludes with a reference back to the philosophy of Karl Popper. Popper argues for three different, yet equally "real" worlds:

- World 1 consists of the physical facts such as plants, humans, magnetic and physical forces.
- World 2 is the mental/ psychological world consisting of experiences, individual thoughts, beliefs, and emotions.
- World 3 is the world of "products of the human mind" (Popper, 1980) that are not individual experiences but interchangeable objects such as language, fiction, and scientific theories.

Especially Popper's defense of an absolute knowledge in World 3 has been debated but this debate is not at the heart of how his distinction will be applied here. Following Popper's model, WiFi coverage as a question of signal strength and transmitter positioning is an element of World 1; the data of a specific web page, such as the text of a digitized Shakespeare writing would be part of World 3; a web user reading this text and developing an unique understanding of it would be part of World 2. However, a simple transition of this model on more dynamic and interactive texts is not unproblematic (Tavinor, 2005). In interactive digital media a data set would not rely on a single version of the Shakespeare play but instead provide a "possible world" realized in a dynamic manifestation of the text that could be a blog, a game session, a chat room, or an event organized by the Second Life Shakespeare company. We might speak of rules and systems as underlying and shared elements of the "human mind." In other words, a pre-designed quest in *World of Warcraft* is a World 3 object, conducting the quest and the player's experiences are a World 2 object, the computers involved are World 1 objects.

In comparison, Benedikt argues: "cyberspace, we might now see, is nothing more, or less, than the latest stage in the evolution of *World 3*, with the ballast of materiality cast away—cast away again, and perhaps finally" (Benedikt, 1991). It was the goal of this essay to point out that this "casting away" of the materiality is in fact *not* the defining action and that, instead of disappearing, the "ballast of materiality" is returning to a center stage, changed and reinvigorated by the digital.

Bolter and Grusin are closer to this argument as they argue against Benedikt that "cyberspace refashions and extends earlier media, which are themselves embedded in material and social environments" (Bolter & Grusin, 1999). But while remediation sees an evermore-complex family tree of media rooted in social and physical conditions, Popper separates into different interconnected worlds of different distinct "realities." Without disagreeing with Bolter/ Grusin, this essay used the media aspect as a means of transition between those "realities." It is through the experience of information through various media that the "reality" of the game world affects the "reality" of every other world and that the game space can spill over into the world of our everyday life.

Where do these trends lead us? A change of reality has been discussed particularly in pervasive gaming communities (Montola, et al., 2009) with a specific emphasis on the game design mechanisms that facilitate such a change. Spinning it further, the concept of a "gamification" of life has been recently popularized (Priebatsch, 2010; Schell, 2010), which is based on an even more aggressive inclusion of game mechanics in everyday world behavior. This can include reward points for appropriate social behavior or personal performance – from points collected for using public transportation to motivational rewards to support a more sustainable personal lifestyle. Gamification implies that game rules take over real world conditions. To the extent that this is based on an extension of the fictional world created by a virtual system, this claim mirrors the argument made in this chapter. But unlike the emphasis on the means in which the game design can re-shape the real world in an almost law-like force, the emphasis here is on the fictional. Our everyday environments tend to become play grounds not because of the law of a game highscore, enforced by implanted sensors, tracked by huge data mining endeavors, and tied to some grand reward scheme of necessarily gigantic proportions. The change this paper suggests grows from a different understanding of our surroundings based on the connections of game worlds across the boundary of real and virtual. It does not depend on additional hardware but on the realization that the digital world has become part of the physical one. Existent game consoles have already changed our surroundings. As this reality sinks into our consciousness these consoles' game worlds re-shape our idea of the world we live in. Gamification is not taking over life but game worlds simple fall into place in the framework that Popper presented and future discussions need to realize this new unity of space to truly make sense of the digital worlds we create.

REFERENCES

Anders, P. (1998). *Envisioning cyberspace: Designing 3D electronic spaces*. New York, NY: McGraw-Hill Professional.

Barlow, J. P. (1996). *A declaration of the independence of cyberspace*.

Bartle, R. A. (1990). *Interactive multi-user computer games*. MUSE Ltd. British Telecom.

Benedikt, M. (1991). *Cyberspace: First steps*. Cambridge, MA: MIT Press.

Bolter, J. D., & Grusin, R. (1999). *Remediation: Understanding new media*. Cambridge, MA & London, UK: MIT Press.

Darken, R. P., & Sibert, J. L. (1993). *A toolset for navigation in virtual environments*. New York, NY: ACM Press.

Dibbell, J. (1999). *My tiny life. Crime and passion in a virtual world*. London, UK: Fourth Estate Ltd.

Dodge, M., & Kitchin, R. (2001). *Mapping cyberspace*. New York, NY/ London, UK: Routledge.

Ducheneaut, N., Yee, N., Nickell, E., & Moore, R. J. (2006). *"Alone together?": Exploring the social dynamics of massively multiplayer online games*. Paper presented at the SIGCHI conference on Human Factors in computing systems.

Engelbart, D. C. (1988). A conceptual framework for the augmentation of man's intellect. In Greif, I. (Ed.), *Computer-supported cooperative work: A book of readings* (pp. 35–65). Morgan Kaufmann Publishers Inc.

Greenfield, P. M. (1984). *Mind and media: The effects of television, video games, and computers*. Cambridge, MA: Harvard University Press.

Guenzel, S. (2008). The space-image. Interactivity and spatiality of computer games. In S. Guenzel, M. Liebe & D. Mersch (Eds.), *Conference Proceedings of the Philosophy of Computer Games 2008* (pp. 170-188). Potsdam, Germany: Potsdam University Press.

Gunkel, D. J., & Gunkel, A. H. (1997). Virtual geographies. The new worlds of cyberspace. *Critical Studies in Mass Communication, 14*, 123–137. doi:10.1080/15295039709367003

Hayward, P. (1993). Situating cyberspace. The popularisation of virtual reality. In Hayward, P., & Wollen, T. (Eds.), *Future visions. New technologies of the screen* (pp. 180–204). London, UK: British Film Institute.

Henry, D. (1992). *Spatial perception in virtual environments: Evaluating an architectural application. Unpublished MScie.* University of Washington.

Huizinga, J. (1950). *Homo ludens. A study of the play-element in culture*. Boston, MA: The Beacon Press.

Jenkins, H. (1998). Complete freedom of movement: Video games as gendered play spaces. In Cassell, J., & Jenkins, H. (Eds.), *From Barbie to Mortal Kombat: Gender and computer games*. Cambridge, MA: MIT Press.

Kim, J. Y., Allen, J. P., & Lee, E. (2008). Alternate reality gaming. *Communications of the ACM, 51*(2), 36–42. doi:10.1145/1314215.1340912

Lanier, J. (2009). Future tense. Confusions of the hive mind. *Communications of the ACM, 52*(9), 112–113. doi:10.1145/1562164.1562192

Levy, P. (1997). *Collective intelligence. Mankind's emerging world in cyberspace* (Bononno, R., Trans.). Cambridge, MA: Perseus Books.

McGonigal, J. (2003). *This is not a game: Immersive aesthetics and collective play*. Paper presented at the 5th International Digital Arts and Culture Conference.

McGonigal, J. (2008). Why I love bees: A case study in collective intelligence gaming. In Salen, K. (Ed.), *The ecology of games: Connecting youth, games, and learning* (pp. 199–208). Cambridge, MA: The MIT Press.

Michaels, S. (2009, September 10). Courtney Love to sue over Kurt Cobain Guitar Hero appearance. *The Guardian*. Retrieved 13 July 2010, from http://www.guardian.co.uk/ music/ 2009/ sep/ 10/ courtney-love-kurt-cobain

Mitchell, W. J. (1995). *City of bits*. Boston, MA: MIT Press.

Montola, M., Stenros, J., & Waern, A. (Eds.). (2009). *Pervasive games: Theory and design. Experiences on the boundary between life and play.* Amsterdam, The Netherlands: Morgan Kaufmann.

Moravec, H. (1988). *Mind children: The future of robot and human intelligence.* Cambridge, MA & London, UK: Harvard University Press.

Nitsche, M. (2009). *Video game spaces. Image, play, and structure in 3D worlds.* Cambridge, MA: MIT Press.

Popper, K. (1980). Three worlds (lecture given April 7, 1978). In Ashby, E., Popper, K., & Hare, R. M. (Eds.), *Tanner lectures on human values* (pp. 143–167). Salt Lake City, UT: University of Utah Press.

Priebatsch, S. (2010). *The game layer on top of the world.* Paper presented at the TED Boston. from http://www.ted.com/ talks/ seth_priebatsch_the _game_layer_on_ top_of_the_world.html

Rheingold, H. (1991). *Virtual reality.* London, UK: Secker & Warburg.

Rheingold, H. (2000). *Tools for thought. The history and future of mind-expanding technology* (new edition (first edition 1985) ed.). Cambridge, MA: The MIT Press.

Salen, K., & Zimmerman, E. (Eds.). (2006). *The game design reader. A rules of play anthology.* Cambridge, MA/ London, UK: The MIT Press.

Schell, J. (2010). *When games invade real life.* Paper presented at the DICE 2010.

Stone, A. R. (1998). *The war of desire and technology at the close of the mechanical age.* Cambridge, MA: MIT Press.

Tavinor, G. (2005). Video games, fiction, and emotion. In Y. Pisan (Ed.), *The Second Australasian Conference on Interactive Entertainment* (pp. 201-206). Sidney, Australia: University of Technology, Sydney.

Taylor, T. L. (2006). *Play between worlds. Exploring online game culture.* Cambridge, MA & London, UK: MIT Press.

Chapter 13

Structures of Agency in Virtual Worlds:
Fictional Worlds and the Shaping of an In-Game Social Conduct

Thiago Falcão
Federal University of Bahia, Brazil

ABSTRACT

In this chapter we inquire about the role that the narrative acquires in the production of meaning resulting from the contact between players and environment, in the Massive Multiplayer Online Role-playing Game (MMORPG) World of Warcraft[1]. We posit that through the process of agency, the authorial narrative, structurally positioned at the conceptual core of the virtual world, may contribute to the diversity of variables involved in the creation of a framing (Goffman, 1974) in which the users will engage in interaction among themselves. According to Dramaturgical Sociology, the resulting meaning from an interaction strongly depends on the context in which it is situated; such notion is precisely the reason why, by observing an environment so intensely imbued by symbols from popular culture, European folklore and medieval fantasy, we may also examine how such signs may assist in the creation of behavioral scripts – and how these are played by the players interacting in the virtual world.

"In the theatre the audience wants to be surprised - but by things that they expect."
Tristan Bernard, French Dramatist

DOI: 10.4018/978-1-60960-854-5.ch013

Despite the usual media framing referring to MMORPGs as mere video games – or, in an oversimplification, *games* – it is necessary to point out that such terminology does not convey a proper treatment of the complexity caught up in the social and psychological facets of these environments. Such phenomena lacks two distinct characteristics of these virtual worlds: (1) firstly, it summarily ignores the aspects of world that are projected by the environments, with their own rules, acting up both inherently, concerning the rules of the world, or related to the practices of appropriation, evoking the social rules created by the players on their own; (2) secondly, if we take a closer look in the functions such environments are prone to assume, we may approach a ruling that may address virtual worlds not as merely game systems, but will focus on the features concerned with the communication processes or spatial appropriations. Previous research in this field has pointed out several of these practices, ranging from behavioral modifications based on contact with virtual worlds (Yee, 2007) to the possibility of experimenting an environment like *World of Warcraft* (Blizzard Entertainment, 2004) as an arena for mere *flânerie* through a digital theme park (Aarseth, 2009).

This latter proposition sustains the core of the argument of this paper. Aarseth (2009) brings forth, by discussing spatial practices in *World of Warcraft*, the thoughts of Angela Ndalianis (2005) about the various aspects of contemporary entertainment and how the diegetic space, leaves the safe haven of cinema and television screens and transports itself to theme parks in which we are able to wander through the fictional world and watch wonders that previously could only be experienced through special effects. However, there is another of Ndalianis' (2005) arguments that is directly connected to Aarseth's (2009) thoughts:

Entertainment forms such as computer games, comic books, theme parks, and television shows have become complexly interwoven, reflecting the interests of multinational conglomerates that have investments in numerous media companies. One media form serially extends its own narrative spaces and spectacles and those of other media as well. Narrative spaces weave and extend into and from one another, so much so that, at times, it

is difficult to discuss one form of popular culture without referring to another (Ndalianis, 2005, p. 157).

Aarseth (2009) is especially concerned how Ndalianis (2005) deals with theme parks as environments in which we are able to enter the diegesis. The Norwegian scholar establishes a comparison in order to address the spatial practices developed by *World of Warcraft* (*WoW*) players. If Ndalianis (2005) is particularly interested in aspects of the Jurassic Park franchise – the movie, the video game and the theme park at Orlando (FL, EUA) – Aarseth (2009) approaches the problem from another angle: he believes the way visitors behave at theme parks is very alike to the way *WoW* players build up their gameplay practices.

According to him (Aarseth, 2009), such comparison is legitimate because *WoW* players are not able to effectively modify the world under their avatars – and even if they try to do it, by engaging mobs and slaying monsters, these quickly re-spawn, and the *locus* returns to its initial state.

While some MMOGs allow their players to create buildings and govern towns or districts, in Azeroth the player is a ghost-like guest on an uncaring, slick surface, a stranger in a strange land. The nature of the game dynamics can be compared to a theme park ride, the Fordist paradigm of assembly-line mass entertainment as pioneered by Disney: "Move along, please, more enjoyable monsters and sights await around the next corner." The flying transporter beasts on their fixed trajectories resemble most of all a scenic conveyor belt or a monorail train taking tourists or workers to the next attraction or work site (Aarseth, 2009, p. 114, emphasis added).

Although the deliberation about entertainment venues seems to depart from the argument of this paper, it is necessary to point out that the emphasis added to the citation presents an interesting thought: even though MMORPGs are usually considered an immediate reference on how open-ended a video game can actually be, such possibilities are certainly subordinated to the Worlds of Code (Pargman, 2003) created by the programmers and designers responsible for the construction of the virtual world as a symbolic product subject to consumption – and as ergodic text (Aarseth, 1997).

It is important, at this point, to realize that video games are devices that enclose a particular feature, commonly referred as the simple presence of interactivity. They require a particular kind of action so they are able to produce any meaning. Even though we may say that traditional representational media demands activity from readers, Galloway (2006) clarifies that there are several differences separating video games from books and movies – and this is the reason why he dismiss the idea of interactivity and embrace the notion that video games are actually an "action-based medium" (Galloway, 2006, p. 3). Given that we are heading towards this argumentation, we should introduce, in order to add a measure of complexity, the notion of *agency*, which basically is how a player may exert his will into the game world. Even though we shall properly address this concept further in the paper, it is worthy to note that although the range of actions that a character in *WoW* can perform is absolutely conditioned by the player's will, it is also conditioned by the actions the system allows him to execute.

If we consider video games as devices structured by a close relationship between rules and fiction – composition previously defended by Juul (2005) – and specially considering our recent work regarding the immersive process related to video games (Ferreira and Falcão, 2009), this paper aims at (1) discussing the fact that if we consider a specific facet of the notion of *agency* concerned with MMORPGs, (Krzywinska, 2009; Murray, 1997), we may be able to achieve a particular understanding of the completeness of such

process. We actually would rather refer to such process as merely illusory – vision supported by the work of additional researchers (MacCallum-Stewart and Parsler, 2007; Krzywinska, 2009) – and finally posit that such illusion actually is structured between the diegetic and systematic aspects of a MMORPG, or, in a simpler way, that the illusory agency process may be split into two branches, one related to the rules, the other related to the narrative supporting the environment. Our efforts questioning the agency process intend to, finally, (2) express that the fictional agency may incur in the formation of behavioral scripts, suggesting actions and attitudes that should be performed by the players – both concerning the aspects of the gameplay, the social aspects of the situational context.

ON THE COMPOSITION OF MMORPGS

According to the work of Jesper Juul (2005), the pivotal understanding of video games as composed by rules and fiction is the offspring of a debate that defines the field since the 1990s, when Espen Aarseth (1997) published his treatise on the systematic and interactive aspect of certain types of text – *cybertexts* – and Janet Murray (1997) published her essay on the dramatic nature of the new aspects of media. Even though both books are not the only ones defending their respective alignments – Espen Aarseth's *Cybertext: Perspectives on Ergodic Literature* and Janet Murray's *Hamlet on the Holodeck: The Future of Narrative in Cyberspace* – they certainly are the more emblematic, therefore, more often cited when addressing the dichotomy ludology-narratology.

Historically, narratology has been more universally discussed which caused the first video game studies to concern the fictional aspects of such media (Murray, 1997; Ryan, 2001; Laurel, 1993). The issue on addressing this medium solely through this specific theoretical lens, obviously is due to the lack of a simple component, the key to this research: the fact that video games are, after all, games.

In video games, the performance of the actor is actually demanded by the system, and without it there is no possible event. Meanwhile, if we observe the so-called 'passive' narratives, the spectator/reader solely allows the diegetic events to follow their course, and the action performed by him is restricted to the psychological and cognitive processes involved in the act of fruition (Machado, 2007).

This discrepancy between video games and traditional representational media, however, must be carefully handled: scholars like Janet Murray (1997) consider this dichotomist notion rather dangerous, believing, instead, that the game is but a particular form of drama, where a great amount of the classic strategies of narrative analysis will still work.

Although every game has its rules, we often come across games that besides rules, also project a fictional world that helps to frame the context and position the characters in a particular given universe. According to Juul (2005, p. 121), rules and fiction compete for the players' attention– even they showing up traces of asymmetry. This is related to the fact that we can talk about rules without necessarily referring to fiction, although it is impossible to deal with fiction in video games without considering the rules portrayed in the universe. Juul (2005, p. 123) discuss this issue when addressing what he calls *incoherent worlds* – worlds where the narrative cannot necessarily explains what happens in the game world, and the only thing that can actually do that is the rules.

It is interesting to remark that when discussing fiction, and considering the fact that the video games can actually project worlds, Juul (2005) makes use of the concept of possible worlds, borrowed from analytical philosophy. According to the author, "In its most basic form, possible worlds can be understood as abstract collections of states of affairs, distinct from the statements describing those states" (Juul, 2005, p. 122). What he is trying to convey is the fact that in any work that makes use of a fictional world – a book, for instance – the portrayed scene is far much smaller than the world around it. Take British writer J. K. Rowling's *Harry Potter and the Philosopher's Stone*, for instance: the action takes place in a British countryside castle. However, we expect – we even know – that the world outside Hogwarts is as big and detailed as the world we experience in a daily basis.

Although we may be imbued by the conscience that the fictional world projected by a specific work on a specific medium is larger than what we actually contemplate, we may affirm that such gaps also depend strongly of the readers/ players in contact with any given world. This is why we consider these worlds as *incomplete* (Juul, 2005, p. 122) taking us to the *principle of minimal departure* (Ryan, 1991, 48-60), created by Marie-Laure Ryan to deal with the problem of incompleteness in fictional worlds: she believes that when a piece of information about a particular world is not specified by its author, we usually fill in the blanks, using our understanding of reality. Such explanation prevents authors of describing minimal and transparent rules when portraying their worlds, like the law of gravity, for example. This issue is deeply related to how these fictional worlds may be represented in video games in general. According to Parlett (1999, p. 6), "How representational a game is depends on the level at which it is being played and the extent of the player's imagination."

The idea of discussing rules and fiction is to address properly the elements of game presented in a MMORPG. It's valid to highlight the fact that if such environments tend to display aspects of a game, they are also projected in order to be used as virtual environments dedicated for the phenomena of mediated communication. It is not uncommon at all to observe players engaged in strictly social activities, such as chatting on public channels, interacting with one another, role-playing. Taking *World of Warcraft* as an example, this feeling becomes even more present: although there may be meaning on experiencing the world in a lonely way – thus interacting with the authorial cybertext only – the world is designed according to a specific logic where the effective evolution will only be achievable by participating on a larger – quasi-omnipresent – network of people controlling other characters and building up both a social-economic, as well as psychological fabric. Concerning this social prerogative present in *WoW*, Aarseth (2009, p. 115) states that the proper understanding to such phenomena is accepting that it consists of a "automatic social cruelty" – a craving for frequently interaction with a personal network of contacts and with the 'generalized other', to reference Mead's notion (1934), for generally it is not enough to deal only with the limited group of known people from offline contexts, if the objectives are related to effective progression in the MMORPG.

Those who fail the group fail themselves in the quest for leveling up, and soon find themselves looking for another group. The automatic social cruelty of this mechanism is as elegant as it is unethical. Casual players must fend for themselves; disloyalty to the group and to the game is its own punishment. On a higher institutional level, the guilds function as player-policed assembly lines in an attempt to ensure that the most dedicated players receive all the rewards and benefits the game has to offer (AARSETH, 2009, p. 115).

We should make clear, at this point, that MMORPGs are a particular component of a larger category: the virtual worlds. This conceptual separation is due to the fact that virtual worlds are generally projected to be interaction environments, supposedly disregarding the game structure here represented through the dialogue between rules and fiction. And even when they do it, they place the responsibility of creation of rules

and fictional spaces in the component of social appropriation. This may be seen, for example, in *Second Life* (Linden Lab, 2003), where complex rules of etiquette were created by users, as well as islands which are dedicated to a specific fictional aspect: replicating places from *WoW* or the Victorian England.

ON (ILLUSORY) AGENCY

We have mentioned before that what characterizes video games as a medium that is different from traditional representational media is the necessity of interaction – the need for the player to act, pressing buttons and controlling levers so there is a narrative progression, thus making the story being told develop further. The main difference, therefore, is the fact that we are finally able to control the actions of the main character of a tale, deciding what will be done and which ways will it take.

According to Brazilian scholar Arlindo Machado (2007), one of the particular components of the immersive process in video games is the notion of *agency*, where the actor experiences the feeling that his decisions actually matter to the decisions placed in particular determining points of a narrative. The point here is: when interacting with a text, are we able to experience this so-called sense of influence?

Strictu sensu, the answer is yes – as mentioned by Machado (2007), an electronic narrative needs interaction to work properly. Even in the most simple cases – a two way flux, for example – one of the options need to be chosen, so the reader would be able to access specific points in the story.

If we observe through a wider lens, though, we may realize that no matter how open ended and full of possibilities is the narrative, it will always answer to a matrix of results that was predicted by the game designers. When this does not happen, if an appropriation or an accident of gameplay reveals a detail that was not projected, the game will likely experience a glitch, or a bug.

This line of thinking leads us to question the true application of the agency process, due to the fact that what happens is actually programmed, projected. Further: consider, for example, games where the agency only gives the player the possibility of changing a few features of the character, never experiencing power over the story being told (MacCallum-Stewart and Parsler, 2007). It is worth mentioning that such issue is not restricted to single player video games, where the reader experiments production of meaning in a relationship that may be generally reduced to a human-machine interaction; meanwhile, we may identify this same subject in the relationship established between readers and *WoW*, where it is actually enhanced by the way the quest system links players and the world.

In *World of Warcraft*, there are thousands of choices at hand to be made: the player may work in secondary professions, simply chat, and pursue more mounts or vanity pets. Everything is subscribed to decisions of the game design. It is possible, then, to question the idea of agency, to address it, according to Krzywinska, as illusory:

Undertaking quests lends the player a sense that they are playing a role in the history of the game world. While this is important in stitching the player into the game's overarching narrative, it is however a form of 'illusory" agency because it is patently obvious to any player that they undertake the very same tasks already completed by others (Krzywinska, 2009, p. 127).

We are not saying there is no appropriation on the side of the players. According to Janet Murray (1997), one of the features that help defining the MUD culture is precisely the capacity of dealing with transforming environments, even if it is not a material transformation. The author (1997, p. 145) relates a story where a student, tired of slaying dragons, simply began to host parties. The

additional players would bring food and drinks, and role-play their characters, conferring them a personality. In *World of Warcraft*, such appropriations do exist: servers are separated by categories, and there are those in which role-playing not only is possible, but also endorsed.

This behavior apparently provides an extension to the sense of agency, since interaction between players may create a variable amount of narratives. However, following the same logic portrayed previously, non-projected system actions are impossible to perform. Combat between members of the same faction, for instance, may only be performed in special circumstances, what limits the possibility of story creation.

However, we may realize the illusory agency works on distinct ways – and that, as explained by Murray (1997), such appropriations actually give the players the possibility of experiencing new situations, enhancing the agential forms, setting them free, until they find out another attempt of suppression by the system. We should acknowledge that unlike the sense of consequence that keeps us from doing whatever we want in the *offline* world; in a MMORPG the internal laws of the system limit behaviors severely. On a daily basis, theoretically, at least, nothing keeps us from doing whatever we want to, but to each action, there are consequences that must be dealt with. Although the idea that every action leads to a consequence is also true in a MMORPG, some actions simply cannot be performed by the way the internal rules work. Once more, the decisions of game design frame the way the players may act.

We may, then, refer to agency as a relative process that could be split into two different branches, both of them answering to the structure chosen to represent the above-mentioned aspects of games in MMORPGs. Our intention is to particularly posit this division into two micro-processes, subscribed to the notion of agency, where the (1) first will take action concerning specifically rules, and the (2) second will be interested in the action concerning the narrative factor of the MMORPG. From this point forth, applying this division, we will address these micro-processes as (1) *operational agency* and (2) *diegetic agency*, respectively.

In the first of the micro-processes, we deal with (1) operational agency, that concerns specifically the issues related to the rules of a game. Using this concept, it is expected that we analyze purely the gameplay. Operational agency consists of the feeling of accomplishment the player experiences when interacting through interfaces, with the game, returning a direct answer on the digital environment. Regarding *WoW* and the structure of progression (Juul, 2005) through which the game design frames human behavior, this sense of operational agency would evolve in a progressive way, according to the levels a character acquires – a level 70 character has way more possibilities of action concerning its interface than a level 7 character, for instance. In order to illustrate with a game subscribed to the structure of emergence (Juul, 2005), in which the rules are completely stated the moment the player engages the activity, consider *Tetris* (Alexei Pajitnov, 1984): the pressing of a button just to make the falling pieces rotates is a case of operational agency.

In the second case, regarding (2) *diegetic agency*, we will consider specifically the actions a player may perform concerning the advancement of the narrative aspects involved in the game. We may realize that it is impossible to discuss diegetic agency without mentioning interface operation mechanism – which takes us to Juul's (2005) questioning about the phenomenological superiority of the technical-systematic aspects of the rules.

Concerning *World of Warcraft*, diegetic agency may work on two different ways: the first (a) regards the way the player levels, making choices and completing quests – which, we may argue, although deeply connected to the rules system, also have a strong narrative background that explains to the player the idea of travelling to another city to deliver a letter, or slaying a thousand mobs so you can find one single object; this quality of agency

focuses on the progression of a series of stories that takes the player, according to his level, to the end of the game – it tells the story in a slightly chronological way, since the player may ignore one or entire sequences of quests.

Such stories may involve chores a player would provide to a community, like the quest "*Are we there, Yeti?*", in which the player should use a toy to scare non-player characters (NPCs) at the town of *Everlook*, in the zone known as *Winterspring*; or may be part of complex sequences known as *chains*, that usually represent significant events to the fictional world of *Azeroth*. As a fine example, we have the *chain* "*Veteran of the Wrathgate*" that portrays an important point on the recent story of the MMORPG.

The second way *diegetic agency* may be found in *World of Warcraft* regards (b) strategies of role-playing: ways players, after creating their characters, may confer personalities and live their own stories which may or may not be connected to authorial narrative as built up by the producer of the MMORPG. It should be pointed out that role-playing is considered more a strategy of appropriation than properly a practice inherent to the environment. According to MacCallum-Stewart and Parsler (2009), a player that consciously role-plays in *WoW* seeks to create a character that transcends the game mechanics, and therefore, produces a plausible, self-defined reality.

This is not to say that the player lives their character's life (though some do), but rather that they direct that character's actions, not as a player controlling a game avatar, but rather like an author, scripting their protagonist (MacCallum-Stewart and Parsler, 2009, p. 226).

This precise sub-category of the micro-process of fictional agency is of great concern for this paper: does the actual idea of dealing with the limitation of actions influenced by the narrative aspect of the world and supported by the discussion on illusory agency limit the behavioral possibilities in an environment like an MMORPG by creating scripts? We seek to argue about this possibility by establishing an articulation between Dramaturgical Sociology and the theoretical body previously discussed in this piece.

ON HOW THE WORLD (OF *WARCRAFT*) MAY BE A THEATRE

The effort to compare the aspects of social reality as experienced and the dramatic theater construction, presents itself as a fruitful area for scientific research. Erving Goffman, Canadian sociologist who lived in the United States in the 1950s, by publishing the book *The Presentation of Self in Everyday Life*, coined the term and defined boundaries for what is now referred to as the Dramaturgical Theory (or Dramaturgical Sociology) - having been inspired, by the work of literary theorist Kenneth Burke, who in 1945 proposed a theoretical apparatus referred to as 'Dramatism': a method for understanding the social uses of language.

The sociological apparatus proposed by Goffman (1959) had the intention to understand the way in which the micro-social relations occur, which, for the sociologist, can be understood as performances on a big stage - hence the importance of that famous Shakespearean quote that illustrates the Globe Theater in London: "*Totus Mundus Agit Histrionem*" (All the World is a Stage), which turned into a premise of dramatic sociology: "All the world is not, of course, a stage, but the crucial ways in which it isn't are not easy to specify" (GOFFMAN, 1959, p. 72).

The central idea of the most important work of Goffman, *The Presentation of Self in Everyday Life*, that gives a basis to the dramaturgical sociology is that social reality, formed from the interaction process, can be explained if directly confronted with the specific relativity concerning the way the representations of tragedies occur "In a play, actors try to convey to an audience a particular impression of the world around them. Through the use of scripted dialogue, gestures, props, costumes, and so on, actors create a new reality for the audience to consider" (Kivisto and Pittman, 2007, p. 272).

However, even if we consider the contribution of Goffman (1959) for the field of sociology and communication studies, it is important to emphasize that the Canadian was not the only one to make a direct comparison between human behavior and dramatic structures. Brenda Laurel (1993), in her book *Computers as Theatre*, takes a step forward, not speaking about relationships face to face that Goffman speaks, but trying to encapsulate the full range of computer mediated interaction.

Published in 1993, and under the need of a theoretical update*, given the transformation of social contexts–and especially the use of computer and telecommunication technologies as vectors of mediated interaction – the author offers an important contribution to this work by doing this structural analysis of mediated interaction and by using the Aristotelian dramatic categories. The category of *Enactment* offers us a wide viewing angle, especially for the differentiation made by the author (Laurel, 1993, p. 50) in the drama, spectacle is all that is seen - but in activity between man and computer, it becomes simply the sensory dimensions of the action being represented: visual, auditory and kinesthetic. The definition of the category, to the author, goes perfectly with the argument assumed in this work: "Aristotle defined the enactment in terms of audience rather than the actors" (1993, p. 51).

It is important to realize that, for the Canadian sociologist, the reality and the very notion of self are also defined in terms of audience: Goffman (1959) believes that a subject and his situational context could not be defined individually, or in a unitary way, but instead, according to everything –all of the intertexts and symbolic representations – inherent to his surroundings.

This self itself does not derive from its possessor, but from the whole scene of his action . . . this self is a product of a scene that comes off, and not a cause of it. The self, then, as a performed character, is not an organic thing that has specific location . . . [the individual and his body] merely provide the peg on which something of collaborative manufacture will be hung for a time. And the means for producing and maintaining selves do not reside inside the peg (GOFFMAN, 1959, p. 252).

Then given the importance of interaction and social environment in training both the behavior and the very essence of the subject - and with reservation we can speak of such things - the environment in which the interaction occurs, then, and where the social context is build, it is always an extremely important variable in this study. It is necessary to mention that although Goffman's most representative work is The Presentation of Self in Everyday Life, the key concept used to investigate virtual worlds - the script one - was coined in his *Frame Analysis* (1974).

To finally demonstrate, with a quite fruitful example, how the fictional agency occur in the interaction between players, we should focus on the concept of script, to see how this happens and how it interacts with the elements of rhetorical fantasy and, therefore, suggests behaviors. Schechner (1988) believes that the scripts actually not necessarily imply exact actions - better than that, they suggest only codes of conduct - types of actions that should be used. Scripts are nothing more than "basic code of an event" - they consist of statements of actions: to act, when to act, how to act, to perform rituals in a certain event; a wedding, for instance.

Besides the concept of scripts - pre-determined sequences of actions that define a situation well known to the speaker, and can be grouped in a schemata - Frame Analysis (Goffman, 1974) offers the very concept of frame; previously used by Bateson (1972) to explain the ways of negotiation that the subjects can arrange the level of abstrac-

tion which a message should be understood, the concept is reworked by Goffman (1974) in a way that a frame provides not only as a message to be understood - but what kind of messages can be expected in an interaction: structures of expectations are formed, for the Canadian sociologist (Goffman, 1974), on whatever face to face interaction by introducing frames that organize the speech and guide the interaction situation.

In an implementation in the field of game studies, Goffman's sociology was used by Klastrup (2003) to explain how the frames of representation in virtual worlds occur. For the Danish scholar, whenever we enter a virtual world, we take the role of actors, ready to work in a representation of ourselves that may be more or less according to our personality offline. This proposition is similar to what Goffman (1959) believes: we can consider, making the seemingly simple relationship between the Canadian sociologist and Danish researcher, that to enter into a virtual world can be considered simply entering a new social context - where we can be caught up by living with new audiences, we have the ability to develop new characters and build new representations.

The elements of rhetoric associated with the medieval fantasy genre, however, act as symbolic delimiters of the social context when a player enters in the MMORPG World of Warcraft. Thus, when entering the world, the player, through the social framing structure as suggested by Bateson (1972), regarding the reception of messages and metacommunication; and by Goffman (1974), in the creation of expectation cascades, both purely communicative (which may flow from the game or the players, the object or activity) and social - adjusts to the social reality experienced, knowing that such representations may be - or not - engendered. "We perform differently, also in a virtual world, depending on the specific cultural and social setting that we find ourselves situated in" (Klastrup, 2003, p 196).

We, therefore, believe that such fictional elements of *WoW's* structure - which, according to

Krzywinska (2009, p. 124) combine elements of a classical mythology plot, fruits of recent hybridization between the classical forms of myth and the rhetorical structures of fantasy and derivative forms of popular culture and video games – work to strongly influence the social context, thus limiting the number of actions that can be developed by a character when interpreting the role chosen for this.

We should realize, however, that the information encapsulated by the game's fictional discourse are not few - they permeate various cultural moments and dialogue with various subcultures: the race of gnomes, for example, is given to experimenting with technology, approaching the ideals of *steampunk* fiction; while the race of the *draenei*, given its origin and arrival in the world of *Azeroth* (in case of the fall of its space cruiser - *Exodar*) interacts very strongly with aspects of science fiction. That many elements gives vent to numerous forms of ownership and fictional agency, when the players dialogue.

ON PERFORMING AND SATISFYING EXPECTATIONS

Practices of role-play like those referenced above happen when the players choose to concentrate in the creation of a personality to a chosen character – and when they perform the actions of the character as if they were their own. However, *World of Warcraft's* game design restricts a great number of possibilities of creation of a personality by the time of the character's choice. As pointed out by MacCallum-Stewart and Parsler (2009), the limitations of the avatar's customization frustrate several role-play expectations. That also happens because each one of the selectable races is portrayed in a sexy way, with large muscles, hips and breasts, among other features.

The main argument concerning the issue of role-playing in online environments concerns the fact that the agonistic aspects of the game are way

too evident to be ignored – and the traditional pen-and-paper RPG is experienced in a different manner. Most of the players, according to MacCallum e Parsler (2009, p. 227), are interested in leveling their characters, and to role-play does not help this aspect, instead, it slows progression down.

The only facet of core gameplay in World of Warcraft likely to be affected by role-play is the building of interpersonal relationships, which can in turn lead to more productive gameplay. However, these relationships can be built up equally well without the need to role-play (MacCallum and Parsler, 2009, p. 227).

Our aim here is not, however, 'what motivates the act of role-playing', but to focus on an *a posteriori* effect: once such nature of performance is set in motion, what kind of behavior will the player develop? The example brought into light to illustrate such argument happened at the *Lothar* server, in the Chinese version of *WoW*. *Ironforge*, home of the dwarves was being invaded by a massive group of members of the opposite faction, the Horde, and both players and NPCs from the Alliance were already defeated, exposing the lone sovereign Magni Bronzebeard. Standing by the side of the king, Plapla (Figure 1), a paladin character, confronted alone the whole raid group approaching the king. We need to step back a moment and pay attention to the player's intentions, here: he or she could simply run from the city or exit the game for a moment, for as soon as the king died, *Ironforge* would be left alone. Instead, Plapla drew her sword and shield and used the chat system to threat the enemy arm. She, then, yelled "*thou shall not be passed*" and the battle took place.

Despite the obvious syntax error, Plapla's utterance (which should have been *Thou shall not pass*) may have been based on pure chance – a simple coincidence – but it could have been interpreted as referencing one of the more important works concerning the relationship between mass

Figure 1. Plapla and Magni Bronzebeard against the Horde

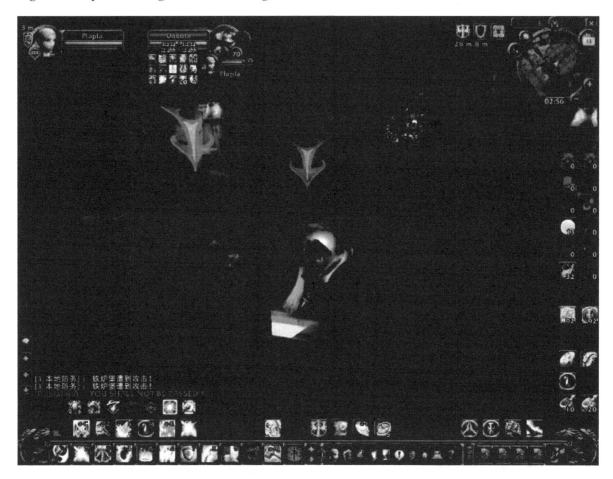

media and medieval fantasy, genre which *WoW* draw its essence from. *Thou shall not pass*† is a famous phrase used by Gandalf in his struggle against the balrog of Morgoth, at the bridge of Khazad Dûn – in the first of the movie adaptations of Tolkien's *Lord of the Rings* trilogy, entitled *The Fellowship of the Ring* (2001), for the cinema.

We should state that the behavior portrayed by the player controlling the character is part of an archetype that echoes through the rhetoric of fantasy, and alludes to outnumbered and decadent heroes – the Rohirrim in their struggle at Helm's Deep, or Gondor's decadence at the Pelennor Fields – who sacrificed for a greater cause, on a further reference to Tolkien's work (1954).

We should realize that according to the theoretical background previously discussed in this paper, Plapla's behavior is originated in the narrative features of the MMORPG. A quick evaluation of the situation would show that on a matter of gameplay, there was not much to be done, since no personal gameplay technique would change the outcome of the circumstances – summarizing, there was no way Plapla could appeal to the rules to help, the situation was set. Such narrative characteristics are not exclusive to the MMORPG: as we previously highlighted, its fictional structure strongle dialogues with a number of other works framed the same genre – medieval fantasy, in this case – and with a whole lot of other symbolic structures of contemporary culture.

Conforming to what is expected from a player who engages the practice of role-playing, the actions of a character are led through the same direction the rhetoric of fantasy seems to guide: the one that says it is better to die honorably in the battle fields than run and become a coward. Yee (2007) has discussed behavioral confirmation – the theory suggesting that the expectations of a perceiver may be enough to make a target behave in a particular way. "In line with self-perception theory, they conform to the behavior that they believe others would expect them to have" (Yee, 2007, p.27). Two factor, then, would act as limiters – and upholders, at the same time – of the sense of agency: (i) the symbols shared with the rhetoric of fantasy – that work as scripts drawn through the history and through a dialogue within the culture – that would teach us, eventually, certain guidelines on how to behave in particular situations; and (ii) the expectations – if we address *role-players*, of course – of the players, of the generalized other, in a given situational context.

FINAL THOUGHTS

Through this paper, we have discussed the notion that the narrative may offer modes of appropriation and fruition, concerning the MMORPG *WoW*, that are not necessarily linked to the way the rules of the game act on the player. More: we have argued that such narrative draws borders and ensues a particular behavior – or at least, behavioral expectations – that may influence, according to the modes of gameplay (MacCallum-Stewart and Parsler, 2009) how the player will approach the MMOG.

We sought to emphasize through the argument that some notions of Canadian sociologist Erving Goffman, as well as a number of other theoretical devices that are concerned with the matter of behavioral dramaturgy may be applied to analyze the behavior of characters and players in virtual worlds – the narrative steps up to be an important

part of the technical and social variables involved in this process, clearly appearing in the definition of the situational context.

Finally, the major contribution aimed by this paper to the field of game studies is the execution of a critical thought related to the notion of agency (Murray, 1997; Machado, 2007; Krzywinska, 2009; MacCallum-Stewart and Parsler, 2007); we have posited the division of the agency process into two micro-processes, according to the structure of understanding of video games as cybertexts, aiming to shed some light over the associations between the facets of games and fictional spaces.

REFERENCES

Aarseth, E. (1997). *Cybertext: Perspectives on ergodic literature*. Baltimore, MD: The John Hopkins University Press.

Aarseth, E. (2009). A hollow world. World of Warcraft as spatial practice . In Corneliussen, H. G., & Rettberg, J. W. (Eds.), *Digital culture, play, and identity. A World of Warcraft reader*. Cambridge: MIT Press.

Bateson, G. (1972). *Steps to an ecology of mind*. New York, NY: Ballantine Books.

Ferreira, E., & Falcão, T. (2009). *Through the looking glass: Weavings between the magic circle and immersive processes in video games*. Digital Games Research Association 2009 Conference: Breaking New Ground: Innovation in Games, Play, Practice and Theory. London, UK.

Galloway, A. (2006). *Gaming: Essays on algorithmic culture*. Minneapolis, MN: University of Minnesota Press.

Goffman, E. (1959). *The presentation of self in everyday life*. Garden City, NY: Doubleday.

Goffman, E. (1974). *Frame analysis*. New York, NY: Harper & Row.

Juul, J. (2005). *Half-real. Video games between real rules and fictional worlds*. Cambridge, MA: MIT Press.

Kivisto, P., & Pittman, D. (2007). *Goffman's* dramaturgical sociology: Personal sales and service in a commodified world. In Kivisto, P. (Ed.), *Illuminating social life: Classical and contemporary theory revisited*. London, UK: Pine Forge Press.

Klastrup, L. (2003). *Towards a poetics of virtual worlds*. Doctoral Thesis presented to the IT University of Copenhagen.

Krzywinska, T. (2009). World creation and lore: World of Warcraft as rich text . In Corneliussen, H. G., & Rettberg, J. W. (Eds.), *Digital culture, play, and identity. A World of Warcraft reader*. Cambridge, MA: MIT Press.

Laurel, B. (1993). *Computers as theatre*. Londres, UK: Addison Wesley.

Lemert, C., & Branaman, A. (Eds.). (1997). *The Goffman reader. Massachussets*. Blackwell Publishers.

MacCallum-Stewart, E., & Parsler, J. (2007). *Illusory agency in vampire: The masquerade – Bloodlines*. Retrieved from http://bit.ly/ 9PJPjX

MacCallum-Stewart, E., & Parsler, J. (2009). Role-play vs. gameplay: The difficulties of playing a role in World of Warcraft . In Corneliussen, H. G., & Rettberg, J. W. (Eds.), *Digital culture, play, and identity. A World of Warcraft reader*. Cambridge, MA: MIT Press.

Machado, A. (2007). *O Sujeito na Tela. Modos de Enunciação no Cinema e no Ciberespaço*. São Paulo, Brazil: Paulus.

Murray, J. (1997). *Hamlet no Holodeck. O Futuro da Narrativa no Ciberespaço*. São Paulo, Brazil: UNESP.

Ndalianis, A. (2005). *Neo-Baroque aesthetics and contemporary entertainment*. Cambridge, MA: MIT Press.

Parlett, D. (1999). *The Oxford history of board games*. Oxford, UK: Oxford University Press.

Ryan, M. L. (2001). *Narrative as virtual reality. Immersion and interactivity in literature and electronic media*. Baltimore, MD: The John Hopkins University Press.

Schechner, R. (1988). Drama, script, theater and performance . In Schechner, R. (Ed.), *Performance theory*. New York, NY: Routledge.

Yee, N. (2007). *The Proteus effect. Behavioral modification via transformations of the digital-self representation*. Unpublished Doctoral Thesis presented to the Department of Communication and the Committee of Graduate Studies of Stanford University.

KEY TERMS AND DEFINITIONS

Agency: In her book named *Hamlet on the Holodeck: The Future of Narrative in Cyberspace*, Janet Murray (1997) posited interactivity as the combination of the procedural and the participatory properties of a system, which together would namely afford the pleasure of agency. Similar, in a way, to its socio-philosophical counterpart, agency refers to the capacity of individuals to act independently and to make their own free choices.

Dramaturgical Sociology: Dramaturgy is a sociological perspective stemming from symbolic interactionism. The term was first adapted into sociology from the theatre by Erving Goffman, who developed most of the related terminology and ideas in his 1959 book, The Presentation of Self in Everyday Life.

Virtual Worlds: A virtual world is a genre of online community that often takes the form of a computer-based simulated environment, through which users can interact with one another and use and create objects. Virtual worlds are intended for its users to inhabit and interact, and the term today has become largely synonymous with interactive 3D virtual environments, where the users take the form of avatars visible to others graphically.

MMORPGs: Massively multiplayer online role-playing game (MMORPG) is a genre of computer role-playing games in which a very large number of players interact with one another within a virtual game world.

Quests: Quests are tasks performed by a player so he/she receives, as a reward, experience points, money or important items, which will help him/her evolve. For details about the World of Warcraft quest system, refer to Corneliussen and Rettberg (2009).

Role-Playing Games: Role-playing games (RPG) are a broad family of games in which players assume the roles of characters in a fictional setting.

World of Warcraft: World of Warcraft, often referred to as WoW, is a massively multiplayer online role-playing game (MMORPG) by Blizzard Entertainment, a subsidiary of Activision Blizzard. It is the fourth released game set in the fantasy Warcraft universe, which was first introduced by Warcraft: Orcs & Humans in 1994.

ENDNOTES

* Although such update does represent an interesting path to be taken, it is not the purpose of this article to provide it, due to our current specific goals concerning the agency process.

† Originally "You cannot pass", in the first tome of the trilogy (1954).

1 ©2004 Blizzard Entertainment, Inc. All rights reserved. World of Warcraft, Warcraft and Blizzard Entertainment are trademarks or registered trademarks of Blizzard Entertainment, Inc. in the U.S. and/or other countries.

Chapter 14

Is There a Virtual Socialization by Acting Virtual Identities?
Case Study: The Sims®

Pascaline Lorentz
University of Strasbourg, France

ABSTRACT

This chapter will present sociological analysis of the offline video game The Sims®, from the first version to the third one. The focus is on the social impacts of virtual relationships on gamers at stake in the gameplay. With the game The Sims®, we would like to analyze the process of socialization involved in the relationship between the gamer and his Sim. The gamer, here a teenager, has to figure out how to behave when he is an adult with responsibilities. The primary socialization is his family, and the secondary one is the avatar in the game; we will demonstrate that gamer will learn all the classical steps of socialization that lead to become a social being and are included in the gameplay. The study of these two times of the socialization process is relevant because they take part of the construction of the Self. Nowadays, teenagers also become a social being and an adult through gaming at video games.

This chapter relies on a sociological doctoral research led in France, in Russia, and in United Arab Emirates. Results of the survey tell us how most gamers of the poll use characters to experiment social life and build identities by confronting their virtual behaviours.

INTRODUCTION

The difference between gaming and learning could be very narrow and for a few years, serious games have been developed and studied by researchers because they have noticed that a video game can teach the gamer something (Greenfield, 1994 ; Gee, 2003) and *vice versa*. Simulators and simulation games used to be classified among what we now call serious games. Incidentally, when Will Wright proposed his video game, *The virtual dollhouse*, which is a simulation of life, nobody supported his idea (Ichbiah, 1998). The point of the game is to manage the life of a Sim, an avatar,

DOI: 10.4018/978-1-60960-854-5.ch014

and to deal with his wishes and aspirations. The difficulty is the independence of the Sim. This virtual character is able to do actions on his own. Managers thought that a video game simulating life would not be able to entertain gamers, which is what it was supposed to be aimed at.

However simulating life has always been the goal of video games creators and a few years after the first try, the American engineer, Will Wright, achieved to convince a new manager to develop his game. Now, *The Sims®* has become famous world wide.

Howbeit, few sociologists focused on this video game as a work field. Hence, the wish of working on it for a doctoral research in Sociology appeared. This chapter will present a sociological point of view on virtual worlds about communication between the gamer and his avatars. Past research focused on interactions between gamer – computer – gamer it consists in a real relationship with its codes and norms up to what is going on when there is no other gamer at the end of the network. In his book, Dubey (2001) argued that the utopia of virtual society would rely on the technical substitute of social link and would be built by virtual knots. Where lonely people, connected to each other by a virtual network, live the main idea would be the need of rethinking social life (Bouvier, 2005). Besides, Schmoll (2000) explained that virtual worlds existed through the reality of the commune imaginary universe created and shared by gamers. This argument can be pursued in more details with the example of online communities. As a matter of fact, these communities are real thanks to the relationships their members have created and maintained. Thus, we could consider that there is no interest for studying social relationships in a game with a gamer – computer system interaction. Leaving the topic of online communities on one side, we shall give a different approach to another aspect of virtual communication. If it is said that communication has to be between two different people, can we also say that there is communication between one real person and

a virtual one? Gamers spend a huge amount of time playing their favourite game. Is it conceivable that there is nothing happening during this gaming time? All the social process involved in this relationship takes a part in the construction of gamers' identity (Süss, 2006). We may foresee the opportunity of studying various social aspects of virtual life. This text relies on a sociological doctoral research led with 180 teenagers living in Strasbourg in France ("S"), in Moscow in Russia ("M") and in Abu Dhabi in United Arab Emirates ("AD"). The sample is small because the point is to study the correlation between different variables in a homogenous population (Javeau, 1990). There is 55% of girls and 45% of boys in this sample. They have filled a survey composed of 67 questions and some of the results appear in the text below.

The point is about focusing on what the social impacts of these virtual relationships and all the effects of communication between the gamer and his avatars are. We will give the same meaning to virtual characters, avatars and Sims with no distinction. Can we claim that these relationships are pointless, they have no social impacts, and are useless – and have no effects on gamers – just because they take place between a real gamer and its virtual identity? This is precisely why we shall analyze the gameplay of the video game *The Sims®*, then explain the process of socialization which takes place in this gameplay and we will finally develop the way gamers use avatars to fulfil social experiences.

THE SIMS® PRESENT A REAL VIRTUAL LIFE

In this first part, the purpose will be to expose and underline all the social aspects and possibilities of communication in the game *The Sims®*. The player has to deal with many status bars related to Sim's needs such as Hunger, Energy, Social, Comfort, Social, Hygiene, Bladder and Room for the first version. If the status bar is green, the Sim is satisfied. On the contrary, if it turns red, the Sim will become more and more independent and it will be harder to manage him.

Possibilities of Interaction with the Gameplay: A Very Rich Virtual Communication

The desire for gaining constitutes one of the main motivations of video game players. However, *The Sims*® is a no-end game rewarded by no victory at all; the only purpose is to stay alive. But this is not so simple, because the creation and/or the maintenance of relationships will - through meetings, exchanges, and discussions - constitute the principal activity of the latter, intra and inter-family.

This section is about all the different kinds of relationships (family, friendly, professional) the avatar can maintain during the game. First of all, the gamer has to create his own character then he has to imagine his own life that is to say to buy a house, to find a job, to meet new people and make friends with them, improve his knowledge, practice sport or music or paint. The avatar will have three different centres of relationships: his house, his office and community places. This aspect is one of the most important changes in different versions of the game. In the first one, all the action is focused on the household. Then, in the second, there are more possibilities to go out and to meet new people. In the last one, relationships are the main point and the gamer can, thanks to his Sim, go wherever he wants to, except to the office. It should be noted that the place granted to the relational aspect in the three versions evolves somewhat, while remaining essential. But the level of difficulty can be raised up by increasing the number of Sims living in the same house. If the gamer chooses to get a roommate for his avatar, he will have to handle their relationship too. After a while, someone could move in and there would be a household to orchestrate.

Practically, the rules of the game remain the same for all versions but the easiest way to make the Sim differs. Thus, in the first version, it is the number of friends which determines the social position of the Sim! Compelled to invite someone every day to maintain these bonds, the latter hardly has any entertainments. As the Sim does not get older, we consider the situation wealthy when the avatar has almost twenty friends and is at the top of his career. In the second version, on the other hand, prospects of promotion require fewer friends, the wages depending first of all on professional skills. As time is taken into account, a delirious time trial has settled up and the gamer has to do everything to get his avatar wealthy before his retirement. In addition, the Sim does not have more leisure time, because an increased attention must be carried to the children, who also grow up. In the last opus, the relational aspect is essential. Less easy than in the other versions, striking up a friendship is more difficult and above all takes a lot of time to be solid.

The principal difference existing between the first and second and third versions resides in the integration of the concept of time and, consequently, of the cycle of life: the character is born, grows, becomes an adult, ages and dies. During their virtual existence, Sims become parents and are in charge of the education of their children, whose physical and intellectual development is taken into account by the interfaces of the game. For example, the characters will have to teach the baby to walk, thus contributing to his good motor development. Although the father has the opportunity of playing a big role in the education of his children, the question of parental leave arises exclusively for the mother, who remains at home to take care of the baby. It is then possible to call upon a nurse - which is systematically a woman, so that the mother can rest, enjoy other occupations or go back to work.

We can notice that a lot of different ideas, values and norms are presented in the game. The interest of this type of game is the fact that the player expresses himself but also the training and the incorporation of behaviour relative to a character. As Goffman (1959) said, *"life is a theatre"* where the subject plays a part. In these video games, the people are offered a multitude of roles which they may incarnate or not whenever they have dangerous actions to perform (soldier, spy…). Games consisting in simulations of life have an enthralling interest for the young people. The rules and the codes which reign there must be integrated by the players to continue the game (Padilla-Walker, 2006). When the rules approach the rules which are applicable in the real world, the use of these games has a considerable stake.

Values and Norms Set in the Game

Games form integral part of the culture and:

"culture arises in the form of play that it is played from the very beginning" (Huizinga, 1955).

This game was created by an American engineer so the point is to simulate American life and values. Analyzing these values is relevant to understand what the ideology of the game is. The main idea of the game is relationships and their maintenance and the point is about which actions the gamer has to give priority to reinforce these bounds. The game consists of standards and rules and the interactions are framed. For example, a Sim who meets a new Sim cannot fly into his arms and the direct consequence of such an inappropriate act, or sanction, is the rejection of the Sim he has met, along with a red status bar. This attempt at transgression of the standard implies its assimilation by the gamer. In fact, the interactions are coded and the gamer must understand that to make friends, there are different stages which have to be respected there. In general, he must start talking to the Sim he has met, then after a certain time, depending on his feelings; he can be

allowed to joke or to raise less general questions and so on. In this example, we note that the game follows rules which are flexible but present. At this point, we can apply Durkheim's analyses (1893) about societies and social sanctions. As he has argued, a behaviour which is not appropriate will be sanctioned in a social way.

Indeed, this game is controlled by standards which will produce values. What is interesting is precisely the fact that these modes of interaction, as Trompenaars (1995) showed it, depend on the cultures to which the subjects belong and consequently, the players will integrate the standards of the game, which in fact was created by American developers, who have been socialized according to American values. To illustrate this matter, let us take the example of the meeting between two people of countries from southern Europe and between two people from northern Europe. The perception of distance is completely different because inhabitants of southern Europe definitely have closer contacts than those living in northern Europe as the American anthropologist Hall (1973) explained. Consequently, the players coming from different cultures will assimilate values they are not traditionally accustomed to.

Concerning close relationships, the game appears rather *avant-garde*, insofar as the avatar is free to maintain heterosexual, homosexual and/or bisexual relationships. More largely, couples can be formed in a completely free way, without any social, ethnic or sexual discrimination. Devoted to the topic of sexuality in the first version of the game, Consalvo's study observes that:

"it allows players the chance to create worlds of their own choosing—worlds that can include "Sim" people of varying genders, races and sexual orientations who coexist without homophobia, racism or sexism" (Consalvo, 2003).

Moreover, the game allows polygamies or bisexual characters and single-parent families. Furthermore, a large scale investigation on the public of *The Sims*® needs to be carried out to determine whether for teenagers who play this game, this sexual tolerance constitutes an additional factor of interest or not.

In fact, this liberal aspect of the game is a seducing point for teenagers because they are more open-minded (Percheron, 1980) to new ideas and social schemes. However the poll shows that teenagers have a very conservative way of thinking gender choices. For instance 78% of them give a priority to cooking knowledge for women and 66.5% to mechanical knowledge for men. Likewise, only 24.6% of them choose to adopt children and among them 3.3% say that they choose adoption because the couple is composed of people from the same sex. By the way, 62.3% are composed of families. Further, 59% of them answer "no" to the question: "Do you make different generations of your Sim live together?", although it could be a very helpful strategy. Albeit young people are quite liberal for political ideas and the gameplay is really rather open-minded as far as their way of gaming is concerned, they are very conservative for their way of gaming.

The main idea of the game is that money helps you to get a better life. The consumerist ideology of the game has often been criticized (Flanagan, 2003; Pearce, 2006) but the point is to simulate life. Of course, a kind of parody of life can be perceived (Frasca, 2001) but teenagers do not feel it. They say:

"it is like real life" (Girl, 13, M), "it is everyday life but virtual" (Boy, 14, M), "it is better than real life because I can do everything I want to" (Girl, 13, AD); "the game helps us for our future life" (Boy, 13, AD).

For teenagers, the game is simply a simulation of real life and they consider it that way.

Meritocracy is completely part of the game and is an underlying ideology. If the Sim does everything he can, like working hard, being friendly, buying good quality items, cooking well and resting enough, he will become wealthy as well as happy. Teenagers are not so credulous because they realize important matters:

"I can notice the difficulty of being an adult and the simplicity of being a kid" (Boy, 14, AD).

Gamers can use cheating codes that 9.5% of them employ, to get money with any efforts. They understand that codes change the gaming activity:

"Life is difficult without cheating codes" (Boy, 15, AD).

So, as a whole, the game promotes capitalistic and meritocratic values.

After analyzing values and norms set in the game, we shall wonder if there can be socialization through gaming at *The Sims*® or how a gamer can be socialized through gaming.

A REAL SOCIALIZATION THROUGH A VIRTUAL WORLD

We are now going to use theoretical paradigms about socialization. The goal is to demonstrate that there could be a virtual socialization through video gaming.

When Caillois studied games in 1958, he was far from suspecting that one of its concepts was perfectly adapted to the gamers of *The Sims*®. Indeed, the mimicry category of games suits well to this video game and he explained:

"any game supposes temporary acceptance, if not of an illusion (even though this word means enter in the game: in-lusio), at least of a closed, conventional universe and, with certain regards, fiction." (Caillois, 1958).

The goal of this type of game is to interpret a character and to take pleasure in doing it. The main point for us is the observation it makes on the actor-player. He says:

"as it is about a play, it is not primarily question of misleading the spectator. The child who plays train can refuse to be kissed by his father by saying to him that the engines are not kissed, it does not mean that he really believe he is a true engine." (Caillois, 1958).

Thereby, we shall focus on the process happening during the game.

Implication of the Gamer in Playing Practice

The virtual body resulting from the virtual reality has singular characteristics and a main aim which is to answer the greatest possible realism. In fact, the virtuality of this body does not spare the gamer its realistic constraints. As Milon specified:

"it [the virtual body] is different from the artificial body to the direction where the artificial body is a body entirely manufactured and factitious. The virtual body is consequently (...) a not yet updated body which potentially contains all the evolutions of the real body" (Milon, 2006).

Since Greenfield wrote:

"I claim that these games (video games) exert a cognitive influence with large scales, they allow a social diffusion of processes of perception and knowledge, which without being unknown in our civilization, were never popularized at this point" (Greenfield, 1994).

Scientists agree to admit that video gaming can generate gamers' knowledge (Gee, 2003; Shaffer, 2007). Then, the question is more about the gamer's attitude, is he passive or active? If he is only passive, he is subjected to choices he has to do for his avatar. As well, it would be only a reaction to a stimulus sent by the system. The relationship between the player and his Sim would be reactivity or interactivity? By studying the relationship between the gamer and his characters more deeply, we shall try to understand if this relationship can be defined as interactive. Using Weissberg's definition (2000), a double determination of the interactive posture which is both an auto-communication and a meta-communication appears, he separates these two aspects because for him auto-communication is made up of accounts and the meta-communication places the communicating person in the centre of the communication process production. Thus on the one hand, the player will be rocked by the gameplay and on the other he will act on it to modify it and adapt it to its will. Weissberg even says that:

"the program works like a simulator of role composing" (Weissberg, 2000).

So, we can note that the player does not confine himself to reacting, answering the stimulus of the gaming software. In the meta-communication, he is the creator of the dialogue and he intervenes. The player of video games is not passive; he does not undergo his activity. On the contrary, he is an actor who will direct his practice according to his choices. As Sid Meier said:

"the play is a succession of interesting decisions" (Meier, 2004).

He has a margin of freedom and uses it to be able to act on the game. In research on video games, the modding studies the way the gamers create new forms of games inside the gameplay. With regard to the game *The Sims®*, Tanja Sihvonen (2009), a Finnish doctor in media sciences, has led her work about modding, which analyzes all the games the gamers have created inside the game. This attitude shows that the player's reactivity dominates his activity. According to it, reactivity and activity are different considering the origin of the action, i.e. in the case of reactivity it is not the player who is the cause of it, and he only answers to it. The gamers of *The Sims®* are able to create games in their play and they intervene by meta-communication to influence the play activity. Moreover, the game studied here is a simulation of life and the protagonists' actions have consequences the gamers take into account when they make their choices. In fact, in the study, we noted that the children will tend to test behaviours in the game to see what occurs before adopting them in real life:

"to see what really occurs" (Boy, 13, S) and "to make them do silly things in The Sims to avoid them in true life" (Boy, 14, M).

Thus, we can see that the children who play are aware of the consequences of their actions because they test them in the game before doing them for real. This is closely akin to the idea that they need to give meaning to their practice (Tisseron, 2006). So, we can maintain that the relationship between the gamer and his Sim is interactive and we suppose that social mechanisms can happen through it.

Socialization is the social process which makes a subject become a social being. Indeed, as of childhood, the new born evolves in a particular social context. He learns how to behave and answer people's expectations. This process will last throughout life and comprises various stages: primary socialization in the family, secondary socialization at work. We are particularly interested in the question of knowing if a process of socialization between a subject and an avatar, that is to say a virtual character, exists. The gamers of *The Sims®* must orchestrate the life of a virtual character. Many constraints frame the playing practice and the player must respect them. Whereas

the studied players are involved into a construction of an identity, why makes them incarnate such or such role in the play?

The socialization can be virtual because of all the choices the gamers have to make during their game. Actually, in *The Sims®*, gamers build lives for their avatars and embodiment is really intense due to these responsibilities.

Elements Learned through Gaming

Recently, the study about avatars by the Norwegian researcher Rune Klevjer (2006) explained why it is not because the events are imaginary or unreal that the objective facts, generated by standards and rules, do not have a certain reality. Before him, Kendall Walton's work (1990) took up the idea that representations are fictions but it does not mean that they are not true. This leads us to think that this virtual interaction has real consequences, which can generate socialization.

The game enables gamers to integrate a lot of different social competencies and the appropriate way to behave. As the gamer orchestrates a Sim's life from birth to death, a girl claims she learned:

"how to take care of a family, to manage money, to live alone" (Girl, 12, AD).

When the Sim is a baby, the gamer has to take care of him continuously, namely to feed him, to change him, to wash him, to entertain him, to have him rest and so on. All these activities, though very basic, are understood and assimilated by the gamers. As a boy says:

"I learn how to take care of the baby, it's difficult" (Boy, 12, AD).

At primary school, the Sim has homework to do every day, which takes a lot of time. At the same time, the Sim will try to strike up relationships with his schoolmates. His parents will scold them for acting foolishly. The interesting point is the evolution of the baby Sim, because every action he has done, viz. every choice the gamer has done for him, are taken into consideration and all these choices influence the future temper and knowledge of the baby Sim. Hence gamers realize that they should take care of Sims babies because of the future.

Then the teenager Sim enters secondary school and can work part-time to earn some pocket money. From this moment on, the Sim will discover love relationships, family constraints, difficulties of adult life. If the gamer chooses a job for his teenager Sim, he quickly realizes that there is not so much free time left. As we have said, relationships are at the heart of the game and opus after opus it is more and more difficult to manage them while being over-booked by various activities. Our gamers are teenagers, they look for learning how sociability works (Danic, 2006), how relationships can be maintained, how seduction has an impact on someone else. They say:

"I learn how friendship is stricken up" (Boy, 14, AD), "I learn to organize my schedule" (Boy, 13, M), "I learn to build relationships and to maintain them" (Girl, 13, AD).

After all this education time, the Sim grows up and becomes an adult. The game will provide him with a professional life and does not let the gamer watch what happens at work but in the last opus, the gamer can choose between "Hardwork", "Meeting colleagues", "Helping the boss", "Nothing unusual", "Try something new", *etc.* for his Sim's attitude. Choosing a state of mind is not neutral, because professional life is part of secondary socialization and identity is developed at work (Dubar, 1992). Power, ambition, hierarchical relationships, team spirit, strategy are all at stake in professional life. The teenagers reproach the game for not letting them orchestrate their Sims at school and at work. They want to manage their Sims' actions everywhere and continuously. This reproach shows the intellectual embodiment of the gamers.

All these aspects seem very basic but there are not because they are at the root of rules in modern societies. To this end, we have to learn how to behave, what we can say, what we can do and especially the limits of our freedom. Through gaming *The Sims*®, teenagers really become aware of all these phenomenons. They finally consider that they take part in an entire world which is ruled, even better that they should consider their actions plus their consequences before deciding and acting. This point matters to understand the construction of a social being because the effects on teenagers' behaviours are the first aspect. Afterwards, teenagers will think about themselves and try to consider who they want to be and how they can become who they want to be.

CHOOSE YOUR VIRTUAL IDENTITY AND ACTION!

Then the gamer has to choose between two different approaches of his avatar identity before embodying his Sim. Video games captivate the young people and they are devoted to it without limits, they represent a kind of *"numerical modelling clay"* (Tisseron, 2006) and the difference with the plays of yesteryear is not so big:

"the offline player does nothing else but engage in a high-tech version of the traditional plays of childhood" (Tisseron, 2006).

Just as a child used to do with his toys, the players will learn how to behave through the playing practice. We will study these two different cases and explain the reasons why the gamer chooses one or another.

From Classical Virtual Identity...

The first stage of socialization by interpretation of roles proposed by the American sociologist, George Herbert Mead (1934), is the imitation of *"The significant other"*, i.e. the mother, the father, the teacher. In fact, according to Mead, the children, while adopting a role they know well, will socialize and integrate the various behaviours that the society, in which they grow up, expects. Thus, the young child will learn how to behave in society because he seeks to be defined in it by interpreting the roles of the others. As we say, the player has an interactive relationship with his Sim and we postulate that while interpreting various roles via his characters, socialization is in process. So do we allow us to take up Mead's expression *"The significant other"* to say that this virtual other is much closer to the identity of the player. What we want to show here is that when the gamer and the Sim he creates are alike, the realism of the game supports the process of identification. In the group where players and the characters they have created are alike, we mainly find the youngest teenagers of the sample, that is to say 39.5% are 12 years old and less. They are mainly boys - 65% of them- and they regularly play as soon as they do not have school. This group of players will create a character which resembles them so as to be able to test social behaviours but also so as to learn, in a virtual way, how to react in society. As a matter of fact, adolescents want to know what can happen if they adopt such a behaviour or not.

Thus it is like if the child "imitated", according to the meaning of Tarde (1890), of the social behaviours but there in a virtual way. Due to the very simple idea of the gameplay, everyone can play at *The Sims®* even if they have never played video game before (Griebel, 2006). The reason is that a gamer's first reflex is to create a Sim who resembles him and to orchestrate his life according to his own wishes.

Notwithstanding, this is a game and players understand easily and quickly which action is allowed and which is not. For instance, if the goal is to make the biggest number of friends, the gamer had better not try to insult another Sim or hit him. The consequences of his actions are easily understandable and the gamer, here a teenager, will integrate these social rules implicitly.

Nevertheless, after practising with a virtual self who resembles him for a while, the gamer will choose to create an avatar, which is very different from him, the dreamed self.

…to Non-Common One!

After experiencing a virtual self who is very like him, the gamer, getting older, will try a virtual identity which is very different from his own. On account of the fact that:

"a game is a universe in which a player must unroll a particular story in a whole of possible" *(Natkin, 2004).*

The gamer of *The Sims®* can overstep the limit of his imagination and to this end play with a very original Sim. Indeed, the game is so full of possibilities that teenagers will be able to enjoy themselves to the full. Thus, by getting older, children move to another stage of socialization by interpretation of *"The generalized other"* (Mead, 1934) to characterize fictional figures created by the child who will invent a role. Sometimes the gamer gives up fictional characters, and sometimes he invents a role. However, Mead insisted on the normalized and regulated aspect of this phase of the game. Indeed, the child becomes aware of the fact that he takes part in a ruled society. The child goes further to search for his own identity by confronting it with the others. In this group, girls are in the majority (56%), the average age is 13 years old and the players use version number 2 as much as version number 3. This element translates the gamers' will to use the most possibilities the game offers, point of the last version (namely the third). With this stage, we notice that the teenager seeks to transgress these rules, by creating an atypical character, in order to have fun:

"it is funny, they are different from others" (Boy, 13, AD), "to have fun especially what I cannot do with myself" (Boy, 14, AD), "because you don't often see original people in real life so it is funny to see what an original Sim can do" (Girl, 14, M).

The players, here adolescents, continue their training of life in society and thus socialize gradually themselves by incarnating various roles. Initially they seek to define their identity with respect to themselves then they will seek their identity by confrontation with the glance of the others. The virtual Sim enables them to carry out experiments which they could not try in real life. They are perfectly aware of the limits of their actions in life and clearly state it:

"to test things which we can't in real life" (Boy, 12, S), "we can do what we want like killing parents so that the teenagers are quiet" (Girl, 14, AD), "to make silly things without being scolded" (Girl, 13, S).

As Pierre Bruno explains:

"the playing element in the game of simulation is the knowledge to acquire" (Bruno, 1992),

and it is this very particular aspect of the game *The Sims®* which appeals to so many teenagers. This process of acquisition of social competences shows that the player, while being embodied in his practice, approaches the game in a cognitive way and integrates norms and rules explicitly and implicitly. Thus, as the gamer builds his identity socially via the playing practice, we observe that the interactivity, which characterizes the relationship between the player and the characters, could take the shape of an interaction, although virtual. All these identity paradigms have a very significant role in the gamer's real life.

CONCLUSION

According to all of these facts and theories, we have to admit that the virtual relationship between the gamer and his avatars has a real role, social effects and behavioural consequences. Even if this social process seems to be virtual for the most refractory people, we can say that there is at least a "Sim socialization". First results of the survey tell us that most polled gamers agreed to confess that they learn something when they play. Some of them even say they feel *"more prepared for real life"* (Boy, 12, S) after all. In fact, all these identity paradigms have a very important role in the gamer's real life.

In addition, I wish to underline that this game is very appreciated by girl gamers, which distinguishes it from the video game field. In an article in a French journal (Lorentz, 2011), I analyze this process and the reason why this game is the first one that girls have massively adopted. At the end of this analysis, it is possible to affirm that the video game The Sims®, which was not specifically created for girls, has certain particular characteristics: not only does it hold the public's attention, but it also appeals to it, because of the presence of gendered stereotypes integrated as of childhood, singularly by the means of toys. This point is also relevant because the construction of gender is a part of an identity paradigm and youth is the decisive time of life for it.

REFERENCES

Bouvier, P. (2005). *Le lien social*. Paris, France: Gallimard.

Bruno, P. (1992). Le jeu de simulation dans. In B. Gilles (dir.), *Le jouet: valeurs et paradoxes d'un petit objet secret*, (p. 69). Paris, France: Autrement, collection Mutations

Caillois, R. (1958). *Les jeux et les hommes*. Paris, France: Folio Gallimard.

Consalvo, M. (2003). *It's a queer world after all: Studying The Sims and sexuality*. Retrieved from http://www.glaad.org/ publications

Danic, I. (2006). La culture des 12-15 ans: Les lascars pour modèle. In Sirota (dir.), *Eléments pour une sociologie de l'enfance*. Rennes, France: Presses universitaires de Rennes, collection Le sens social.

Dubar, C. (1992). *Socialisations et identités professionnelles*. Paris, France: Armand Colin.

Dubey, G. (2001). *Le lien social à l'ère du virtuel*. Paris, France: PUF.

Durkheim, E. (1984). *The division of labour in society*. New-York, NY: Macmillan.

Flanagan, M. (2003). Une maison de poupée virtuelle capitaliste? The Sims: domesticité, consommation et féminité. In M. Roustan (Ed.), *La pratique du jeu vidéo: Réalité ou virtualité?* Paris, France: L'Harmattan.

Frasca, G. (2001). The Sims: Grandmothers are cooler than trolls. *The International Journal of Computer Game Research, 1*(1).

Goffman, E. (1959). *The presentation of self in everyday life* (pp. 106–140). Anchor Books.

Greenfield, P. (1994). Les jeux video comme instrument de socialisation cognitive. *Reseaux*, 67.

Griebel, T. (2006). Self portrayal in a simulated life: Projecting personality and values in The Sims 2. *Games Studies, 6*. Retrieved from http://www.gamestudies.org

Hall, E. T. (1973). *The silent language*. New York, NY: Anchor.

Huizinga, J. (1955). *Homo Ludens, a study of the play element in culture* (p. 46). Boston, MA: Beacon Press.

Ichbiah, D. (1998). *La saga des jeux video*. Paris, France: Pocket.

Javeau, C. (1990). *L'enquête par questionnaire: Manuel à l'usage du praticien*. Bruxelles, Belgium: Editions d'organisation.

Klevjer, R. (2006). *What is the avatar? Fiction and embodiment in avatar-based single player computer games*. Doctoral dissertation, University of Bergen in Norway.

Lorentz, P. (2011). La construction des représentations sexuées à travers la pratique ludique: L'exemple des Sims. In Le Breton & Schmoll (Ed.), *Jeux et enjeux*. Strasbourg, France: Revue des Sciences sociales.

Mead, G. H. (1934). *Mind, self, and society* (Morris, C. W., Ed.). Chicago, IL: University of Chicago Press.

Meier, S. (2004). *Jeux vidéo et médias du XXIème siècle. Quels modèles pour les nouveaux loisirs numériques?* (p. 6). Paris, France: Vuibert.

Milon, A. (2006). *La réalité virtuelle avec ou sans le corps?* Paris, France: Autrement, collection Le corps plus que jamais.

Natkin, S. (2004). *Jeux vidéo et médias du XXIème siècle: Quels modèles pour les nouveaux loisirs numériques?* Paris, France: Vuibert.

Padilla-Walker, L. (2006). Adolescents, developmental needs of, and media. In J. Jensen Arnett (Ed.), *Encyclopedia of children, adolescents, and the media*. SAGE Publications. Retrieved from http://www.sage-ereference.com/ childmedia/ Article_n419.html

Pearce, C. (2006). *Toward a game theory of game. First Person: New Media as Story*. Performance, and Game.

Percheron, A. (1980). Se faire entendre. In Mendras, H. (Ed.), *La sagesse et le désordre*. Paris, France: Gallimard.

Schmoll, P. (2000). Les mondes virtuels, entre imagerie et imaginaire. *Sociétés, 70*(4), 33–46.

Shaffer, D. W. (2007). *How computer games help children learn*. Palgrave Macmillan.

Sihvonen, T. (2009). *Players unleashed! Modding The Sims and the culture of gaming*. Doctoral dissertation, University of Turku, Finland.

Süss, D. (2006). Socialization and media. In J. Jensen Arnett (Ed.), *Encyclopedia of children, adolescents, and the media*. SAGE Publications. Retrieved from http://www.sage-ereference.com/childmedia/ Article_n419.html

Tarde de, G. (2003). *Les lois de l'imitation, étude sociologique*. Book Surge Publishing.

Tisseron, S. (dir.). (2006). *L'enfant au risque du virtuel*. Paris, France: Dunod.

Trompenaars, F. (1995). *The seven cultures of capitalism*. Piatkus Books.

Walton, K. (1993). *Mimesis as make-believe*. London, UK: Harvard University Press.

Weissberg, J.-L. (2000). *Présences à distance. Déplacement virtuel et réseaux numériques: Pourquoi nous ne croyons plus la télévision?* Paris, France: L'Harmattan, collection Communication et civilisation.

ADDITIONAL READING

Aarsand, P. A. (2007, May). Computer and Video Games in Family Life: The digital divide as a resource in intergenerational interactions. *Childhood*, *14*, 235–256. doi:10.1177/0907568207078330

Anderson, C. A., Gentile, D. A., & Buckley, K. E. (2007). *Violent Video Game Effects on Children and Adolescents: Theory, Research, and Public Policy*. USA: Oxford University Press Inc. doi:10.1093/acprof:oso/9780195309836.001.0001

Atkins, B. (2006, Apr). What Are We Really Looking at?: The Future-Orientation of Video Game Play. *Games and Culture*, *1*, 127–140. doi:10.1177/1555412006286687

Calleja, G. (2007, Jul). Digital Game Involvement: A Conceptual Model. *Games and Culture*, *2*, 236–260. doi:10.1177/1555412007306206

Consalvo, M. (2006, Feb). Console video games and global corporations: Creating a hybrid culture. *New Media & Society*, *8*, 117–137. doi:10.1177/1461444806059921

Edery, D., & Mollick, E. (2008). *Changing the Game: How Video Games Are Transforming the Future of Business*. Financial Times Prentice Hall.

Gee, J. P. (2003). *What video games have to teach us about learning and literacy*. Palgrave Macmillan.

Gee, J. P. (2008, Jul). Video Games and Embodiment. *Games and Culture*, *3*, 253–263. doi:10.1177/1555412008317309

Hayes, E. (2007, Jan). Gendered Identities at Play: Case Studies of Two Women Playing Morrowind. *Games and Culture*, *2*, 23–48. doi:10.1177/1555412006294768

Herman, L. (1999). *The Fall and rise of video-games. Rolenta Press*. Phoenix: Union.

Iacovoni, A. (2004). *Game Zone: playgrounds between virtual scenarios and reality*. Basel: Birkhäuser.

Kent, S. L. (2002). *The Ultimate History of Video Games: From Pong to Pokemon and Beyond-The Story Behind the Craze That Touched Our Lives and Changed the World*. Prima Life.

Lauwaert, M. (2007, Jul). Challenge Everything?: Construction Play in Will Wright's SIMCITY. *Games and Culture*, *2*, 194–212. doi:10.1177/1555412007306205

Martey, R. M., & Stromer-Galley, J. (2007, Oct). The Digital Dollhouse: Context and Social Norms in The Sims Online. *Games and Culture, 2*, 314–334. doi:10.1177/1555412007309583

Metzinger, T. (2003). *Being No One*. Cambridge: MIT Press.

Molesworth, M., & Denegri-Knott, J. (2007, Apr). Digital Play and the Actualization of the Consumer Imagination. *Games and Culture, 2*, 114–133. doi:10.1177/1555412006298209

Murphy, S. C. (2004, Aug). Live in Your World, Play in Ours': The Spaces of Video Game Identity. *Journal of Visual Culture, 3*, 223–238. doi:10.1177/1470412904044801

Myers, D. (2006, Jan). Signs, Symbols, Games, and Play. *Games and Culture, 1*, 47–51. doi:10.1177/1555412005281778

Nesson, R. and C. (2008, Aug). The Case for Education in Virtual Worlds. *Space and Culture, 11*, 273–284. doi:10.1177/1206331208319149

Salen, K., & Zimmerman, E. (2004). *Rules of Play. Game Design Fundamentals*. Cambridge, MA: MIT Press.

Schwartz, L. (2006, Aug). Fantasy, Realism, and the Other in Recent Video Games. *Space and Culture, 9*, 313–325. doi:10.1177/1206331206289019

VanDeventer, S. S., & White, J. A. (2002, Mar). Expert Behavior in Children's Video Game Play. *Simulation & Gaming, 33*, 28–48. doi:10.1177/1046878102033001002

Wolf, M. J. P., & Perron, B. (Eds.). (2003). *The video game theory reader*. New York: Routledge.

Yee, N. (2006, Jan). The Labor of Fun: How Video Games Blur the Boundaries of Work and Play. *Games and Culture, 1*, 68–71. doi:10.1177/1555412005281819

Chapter 15
The Epistemological Character of Puzzles in the Metaverse

Luís Carlos Petry
Pontifícia Universidade Católica de São, Brazil

Cristiano Natal Tonéis
Faculdades Metropolitanas Unidas de São Paulo, Brazil

ABSTRACT

This chapter discusses cognitive abilities that can be developed by means of the metaverse. We are concerned with developing virtual environments capable of providing, in a world full of challenges, more than adventures and excitement meant to push the narrative forward. In the search for recovering classical concepts and integrating them into the metaverse we also seek their episteme so that experience construction can be contemplated by means of lateral thinking, that is "thinking about thinking" in a way similar to the Greek concept of mathema. Can we develop creative thinking? What is the role of games? Which characteristics of games can open up paths to creative thinking? The classical culture and the classical puzzles can give us an opportunity to answer these questions.

INTRODUCTION

Since ancient times, puzzles have been used by people to reconstruct knowledge for new generations. In other words, the knowledge developed and accumulated throughout generations has been transmitted to new generations by means of thought-provoking puzzles, which have been making possible the reconstruction of past knowledge. Creative thinking and some abilities such as imagination and abstraction have been associated to the process of reconstructing the knowledge developed by our ancestors.

The "living world" – *lebenswelt* – also encompasses what is known as metaverse and therefore this dimension of our experience is in constant metamorphosis. We can try a ride in a new world or we can even take advantage of this experience in the metaverses to create relevant cognitive structures, venturing ourselves beyond the mere

DOI: 10.4018/978-1-60960-854-5.ch015

"being together" to accomplish the "being with" (*mitsein*) in the metaverses world, and in this way, develop abilities as logical-mathematical reasoning, imagination, and abstraction in a creative manner.

In the following parts of this article, we are going to resort to two examples of games to consider the world of metaverses. One of them - Myst *Uru-live* - opens up ways for the collective construction of knowledge and the other, the academic game *Ilha Cabu*, poses a paradigm of transposition of puzzles into metaverses. These two examples will help us grasp the epistemological possibilities displayed by puzzles as a means for broadening horizons and enabling several forms of thinking (lateral thinking) in metaverses.

An Ontological Issue: The Creative Thinking and Puzzles as a Discovery Game

Considered as the basis of the Western World, Greek culture is the birth place of the *promethean* perspective centered in the production and the transformation of knowledge, which in our times can be interpreted as a continuous game of cognitive transformations undergone by our culture and science. We've reached this state of affairs along with Freud (1915), Lacan (1953), Fink (1960) and Gadamer (1960), due to the amplification of the idea of the epistemophilical pulsion (*Wissentrieb*), which concerns the essential structure of the game of desire of the subject who expresses himself in the game of language and knowledge. It will be in the continuum of the gorge opened by this game structure that we find the world of games displaying genuine movements of psycho-cognitive transformations and reconstructions. It is precisely at the interface between knowledge and games that the open dimension of the metaverses is found. Although the issue under discussion allows for multiple approaches, we will follow the analysis of the game Myst (1993-2010), which is modeling and paradigmatic at the same time,

as has been pointed out by Murray (2003) and Manovich (2001). Based on the analysis of Myst we intend to show the recovery of classical values and, at the same time, point out the process and the objective of the construction of knowledge.

It is important to point out that thinking about games and metaverses comprises the consideration of the creativity involved in playing a game; that is, in the game we are faced with the incessant playing and endless possibilities which are associated with our own actions in the living world.

On considering the philosophical ideas about games, Gadamer's works are worth considering. Gadamer (1999) states that the correlations between the movements in games and the actions accomplished by men in the living world make men and games become involved in a relationship based on mutual complicity. It is inside the game that man fulfils his purposes. The game is supposed to be taken seriously. It is then that game and man turn out to share the same nature in a co-constitution process that is realized in the game itself. This state of affairs concerns movements of "back and forth" which correspond to cultural expressions such as "to play a game". This everyday expression reveals the gender and the ontological structure of the game activity: the verb "play" followed by the noun "game" takes into account the movement which persists in the incessant action of playing, comprising its act and its strength, extending its semantic scope in such a way that meaning can only be expressed in the following way: "we play and the game plays with us". It is precisely then, at the moment of action between man and game that the games' ontological character emerges.

It is possible to say: "enter a game" or "play a game". What happens here is a relation, which implies both the game and the player: a "back-and-forth" in a continuous movement. It is inside this movement structure that the player has the possibility to create and recreate his experiences regarding the game. Those who play know very well what the game is and that which is being done is 'just a game' but they do not know what they 'knows' in this activity, as Gadamer (1999:175) shows us. This perspective prompt us to assert that it will be in the game, in fact in any kind of game, that reside the essential experiences which will lead us to new discoveries.

This has to do with the fact that in the movement of the game we, as subjects of the game, are capable of "living other lives", in the same way one who can live a life expressing himself in fantasy, in reading, in watching a movie or in any other kind of expression stemming from self-transformation. It will be in the act of playing, in the fantasies as aesthetics forms of the game, that humanity expresses its desires, fears, fantasies and dreams. It is in the game that the experience of past, present and future traditions meet. As Gadamer (1999) warns us "it is the game that is played or that unravels itself as game (*sich abspielt[1]*). In fact, no fixed subject is playing there. The game is the consummation of the movement as it is.

It is in this perspective that our ontological reflection enables us to state that *we are one with the game.* Upon entering it, the player and the game blend together inside the game itself. It will be inside the game that both creativity and imagination may grow, making it possible for the player to access his creative and reality-transforming potential. On maintaining himself *in* the game, the player gets hold of a space for the exploration of experience. Thus, creativity and imagination constitute themselves in dispositions which are enhanced and fulfilled at the very happening of the phenomena, culminating in the sense to be achieved *inside* and *by* the own game. In his work *Homo Ludens,* Huizinga (1938) argued that games belong to an absolutely primary category of human life, as essential as reason (*Homo sapiens*) and utensil making (*Homo faber*). The *Homo ludens,* being at the same time contiguous and at the basis of *Homo sapiens* and *Homo Faber* categories, stands for the basis and development of culture, and is one of its ontological columns.

Agreeing with Huizinga (1990) who states the game is prior to culture, we observe that the game is constituted in one of its ontic basis or, according to Heidegger (1927) in *Sein un Zeit*, the game would constitute itself in one of *Dasein's* existential ways. Supporting the same point of view, Huizinga show us that the concept of game presents itself as a distinguishing and fundamental factor, being present in everything which occurs in the human world. Huizinga (1990) states that *it is in the game and through the game that civilization is born and develops.* Being part of the culture, the game is constituted in the striking engine of its transformation. There is a mysterious potency, something which defines the game and at the same time makes it enigmatic, enchanted, encompassing everyone who engages in such an activity. Huizinga also identifies it as a practical activity: playing a game, which, when free and consciously taken as "not serious" and exterior to daily life, possesses the capacity to absorb game and player in a process, which we have more recently referred to as *immersion,* following Murray (2003). It is an activity free of all appeal, material and exterior to the game and which has no interest apart from the game itself. It is accomplished inside its own space-time limitations and further limited by rules, which are specific to the game itself.

Since the definition established by Huizinga, the word "game" has been assigned to a multitude of human manifestations as, for example, to any type of competition, production of knowledge (from enigmas to puzzles), poetry (as a "game of words" or simply wordplay), art, craftsmanship, philosophy and ultimately to culture as a whole. It is based on this perspective that many scholars after him begin to think of the man's world as a continuous and ever-changing game (see for example Fink, 1960; Gadamer, 1960).

However, to understand the meaning of the phrase "not serious" as assigned to games by Huizinga, we need to regard the expression from its phenomenological point of view. It is not about bringing out something trivial or not important. To the contrary, the phrase "*not serious*" puts the game into a dimension other than bureaucratic: "*not serious*" indicates that the game has a character of immanent freedom. Huizinga states that games in their "*non-serious*" character seduce and cast us into it, making us absorbed by it both in space and time, and freeing us from everything else. We adhere to games spontaneously, "get inside it" and, by means of this movement, we proceed to a state of suspension of reality outside games. It is in this sense that we open up possibilities to several forms of freedom manifestations, such as fantasy and imagination, expressed inside the space for playing. It is certain that when we play it is pleasure we aim at. But, unlike many daily activities, we do not have ways to predict or even anticipate their appearance inside games. For us to be able to face the effects of games, we have to let ourselves be led inside it by the game's own movement, every time we re-enter it. We frequently say: new game, new surprises. Recalling here Heraclitean thought, in the same way as we never bathe in the same waters and everything flows as well as changes, in games, everything changes and flows. Such a thing concerns the "back-and-forth" movement proposed by Gadamer.

When the philosopher points out this "back-and-forth" movement he wants to draw attention to the fact that "playing is being played" (Gadamer, 1999, p.181). With that expression he means that it is in the very act of being played that the game reflects its playful behavior, and then the game and the player become one. The player can not be thought of as a mere participant, but as a compound unity, being the game-player inside the creative and particular universe of the game's space, in which the rules point the way to be taken and by which it is possible to stay in the game and make it go on. On the other hand, this game conception shows us that the game does not sub exists in pure dependency of the player. To the contrary, the game will always be there, being the responsible for provoking and instigating the player to persist in it. That aspect has more recently been pointed

out in relation to digital games (Cf. Turkle, 1997 and Murray, 2003). The approach presented here shows us that *we play the game and by it we are played*: "the real subject of the game [...] isn't the player, but the game itself. It is the game which keeps the player in the path, which draws him in the game, and which keeps him there" (Gadamer, 1999:181).

If we agree to a concept of game based on an ontological condition and intend it to be completely identified on digital games, it is imperative to choose an exemplar model able to illustrate our conceptual perspective. In order to do it, we have chosen among the array of existing games, a paradigmatic game (as Murray, Manovich and others have pointed out) which was created in the 90's, as a first-person game and got, in 2010, a new version including first and third person modalities. It is the series of games *Myst* (1993; 1998; 2001; 2003; 2004; 2005; 2006; 2008; 2010). Currently it has been transformed in a genuine metaverse. According to many researchers, such as Trukle, Murray, Manovich, Miles among others, *Myst* can be considered, along with *Doom,* created in 1993 and *Zork,* created in 1980, as a *paradigm-game,* given that they not only constitute a landmark in the history of technology and games, as well as they introduce the fundamental models of computer narrative, interface and playability that are still largely used in the communities of both producers and users. Notwithstanding the numerous attributes of *Myst,* there is one which is worth calling attention to: *puzzles* inserted in a narrative between two worlds (the virtual nature of the game and the real nature of the book).

By presenting puzzles as components of the story, as portals to new worlds or yet challenges and allegories that shed some light on the elements of the narrative or on the story of a character, *Myst* presents a crucial component, introducing the practical idea of game (*puzzle)* inside the play (*game).* There are many kinds of *puzzles* in *Myst,* from those involving the concatenation of behavior patterns to produce a given result to jigsaws of varying complexity. In this sense, a jigsaw – *puzzle* – consists in a game in which the player must solve a given problem and, to solve it he has to make use of reasoning (in many different modalities). The *puzzles* define a way of playing, in which the primacy of reasoning overcomes any other type of psycho-social-cognitive competence.

David Miles (1996) defends the point of view that *Myst* represents a new and compact art form, since it gathers characteristics of different classical origins. In *Myst* there is a combination of forms and representations considered by some digital media critics as outdated. The form of narrative in *Myst* pay classical RPG games such as *Zork²* and *Dungeons & Dragons³* the reverence they deserve Furthermore, the narrative structure associated in an innovative and tridimensional way of navigation in *Myst* makes the player remember a syncretic epic adventure that combines elements of Homer's Odyssey and Julio Verne's science-fiction genre. Another striking feature of *Myst* concerns its style. It can be thought as a "movie" varying between *surrealism* and *art-nouveau* whose creation was motivated by the will of improving *puzzle* resolution. In 1996, as Heim made prophecies about the metaverse, Miles envisioned all the potential that a narrative associated to a game could offer to players and to culture.

Discussing the relations between *ludology* and *narratology*, Frasca (1999) states that a *puzzle* in the ludological concept would be equivalent to a *ludus,* that is to say, it would be equivalent to a problem which needs to be overcome so that the player can move forward in the game. Walking around the spaces of *Myst*, the player is faced with innumerable possibilities of exploration. Each player, at his own game pace, has the possibility of reconstructing *Myst's* story in different ways and through different paths. As a system and a game, *Myst* introduces a culture and an architecture that stems from its narrative structure. This culture is based on one of the elements of the game nature, which resides in its surprise element, thus building the base of its mysteries. It is the *puzzle* that

provides the elements of connection between the narrative, the local culture and its structure of mystery. It is by facing, uncovering and deciphering the *puzzles* in *Myst* that the player assimilates more and more elements of the *Myst* culture and, thus, is able to understand its story better. In his analysis of Myst, Carroll (1997) presents us a surprising description of what we are capable of developing in this mysterious world of *Myst*, in which as he points out the player must turn into a talented amateur archeologist. In order to accomplish that the player must view every artifact and ask, "What is that for? What does it do? Which physical principles are being followed? What biological urge is being served?" Speculation is not just encouraged; it is necessary".

If we are convinced by the arguments given in the preceding brief discussion of the game *Myst*, we will certainly reach the conclusion that such speculations (hypothesis) are at the basis of the logical-mathematical thinking we inherited from the West. It is based on the question dialectics that explanation can be built as an answer or yet, it is from new evidences that we are able to reconstruct the question, given a process of reversibility and transposition. On linking facts that are apparently distinct we are, in other words, inferring global hypothesis from local conclusions and these global hypothesis are to be verified *a posteriore*. In here, a movement can be detected in the game and the space-time element in which it occurs is the *puzzle*. It is in this sense that the puzzles of *Myst* and the logical-mathematical thought structures are associated. For a *puzzle* is an open and organized logical structure which foster a reflexive process culminating in the comprehension of a given problem which constitutes the *puzzle* itself. In a way, at the same time direct and derivate, the way of investigation and experiencing of a *puzzle* culminates in a broadening of horizons, that is to say, it comprises a magnification of the aesthetical experience taken in its phenomenological sense. The continued *puzzle* resolution process will indicate, as an effect on the subject of the experiment, a magnification of his potential to formulate and, consequently, solve problems. Here resides the central nucleus of the transposition and reversibility issues regarding problem solution and they require more complex cognitive constructions. Both mathematics and logic history teach us that sometimes we must "think in a different way" and look for a new prism to solve a given problem. Puzzles certainly offer a wide array of possibilities for this kind of thinking experience.

We note that the broadening of horizons, which is made possible by the experience with puzzles, stimulates acquiring an open way of thinking about the activity of dealing with problems of any kind. It is then a continued process we wish to stimulate and this process can be described as "the game of reorganizing ideas" such as the idea of building hypothesis or "promoting different ways of thinking. This is what De Bono (1970) called "lateral thinking"[4]. The *lateral thinking* approach is promising since in real life, when we are faced with problems, we are involved in an activity frequently more alike to that of solving a *puzzle* than solving a traditional mathematical question.

The ability of solving problems encompasses a series of implicit competences in the process. We certainly are not prone to solving a problem we happen to understand. The challenge and the stimulus are to solve problems, which are unknown to us. For Goldstein & Levin (1987), problem solving is one of the ways of thinking and it can be considered the most complex of all intellectual functions. Solving problems is one of the highest level cognitive processes and requires the modulation and control of a lot of fundamental routines or abilities (Goldstein & Levin, 1987). The mankind evolutionary history has to do with looking for challenges. The development of cultures and consequently civilizations point out to the strength and the commitment of human thought on problem solving. The development of abilities of observation, generalization, simulation and abstraction are intrinsically related to problem resolution. All of these abilities and challenges are faced by the game player and among the games, *Myst,* for its narrative features organized around puzzles is exemplar.

If it is true that the structure of *Myst's* design is organized as an navigable space (Manovich, 2001), open to the production of a more and more mutable narrative (Murray, 2003), it is also true that the more we chronologically advance through the versions of *Myst* (from 1993 to 2010), the more we tend to find both the organization and manifestation of a logic of discovery (Tonéis & Petry, 2008), which assumes innumerable though hard to be parameterized proportions. Once immersed in the *game* the player will be able, within his navigation and investigation, to go deeper and get to know it better. Consequently, he will be able to learn how to solve problems or to learn from the game the method to solving problems. Provided that this is the emerging form of communication which is experienced, our biggest challenge is overcoming our limitations regarding the abilities to observe and correlate pieces of information. However, this situation implicates in the meeting of the player and the game with its puzzles, a situation which must be defined as an experience with the puzzle being part of the game.

.It is an experience that can be understood as an encounter, a happenstance that moves us and invites us to new discoveries. It underlies all personal experience and derives from a reflexive process. When something happens and moves us, it causes a transformation, because the reflexive act has a high transformative value and consequently influences the actions following it. This experience in a given situation is designated by us here as an *aesthetic experience*, and it constitutes itself in an important piece of conceptual work on phenomenology (Gadamer, 1999; Petry, 2003; Tonéis & Petry, 2008). In this case, the secret passion between aesthetic experience and interactive puzzle's organization structured on principles of mathematical logic, is one of the key elements to problem solving.

Based on the previous statements, we argue that a cognitive discovery or the solution to a problem which has drawn all our attention tend to generalize its impact to other spheres of our lives. Such a discovery certainly derives from a reflexive experience, for in situations where we develop a method "to get out of the problem" or "to overcome an obstacle" as is the case in one of the game's puzzles being analyzed in this article. This act turns out to be a way of acting positively towards the construction of personalized knowledge, even when it is developed in a cooperative environment. We truly believe *puzzles* in games are powerful engines driving the continuity of the narrative since the building of the narrative relies on the player's actions. In order to get to know more about the *Myst's* story, for example, we need to overcome the obstacles put in our way. In fact, "these "puzzles" are similar in nature to the tasks mythological heroes faced when pursuing their goals and the various difficulties heroes in fairytales face when are sent on some mission" (Berger, 2009, p.77). When we accept the invitation to travel to *Myst Riven*, for example, no much detail about how to complete the mission is given to us. We find ourselves in a situation similar to that of explorers/players, with all the implications that playing and exploring have. It is in this sense that we interpret what Shigeru Miyamoto, Nintendo's main designer, said in an interview about games. He thought of games as a trigger for adults to go back to being primitive, primary ways of thinking and remembering. An adult is a child who has more ethics and morals, and that is it. As a child, I am not creating a game. I am in the game. The game is not for children it is for me. It is for an adult who still has the character of a child[5].

In the interview given by Miyamoto, he refers to one of the characteristics of the game, that of "being for me", which Merleau-Ponty would refer as "be with him". This characteristic designates the point of encounter between the player and the game, both of them becoming "one" and it is, as such,

fundamental to the problem solving process. Inside the game environment it is the player who attributes meaning to the problem, that is to say, we signify what is real from abstractions and reflections and it is in this movement of discovery, surprise and encountering that we develop our mathematical-logical thinking, based on which the construction of inferences and correlations between objects that are apparently unrelated is built. We enter the game and risk ourselves in an activity by our own choice and wish to join it. This characteristic of the game is clarified in the following declaration "the attraction that the game exerts over the player resides exactly in that risk". The game allows the player to enjoy a freedom of choice which is, at the same time, considered risky and hopelessly restricted" Gadamer, (1999:181). The "play" and the "be played", the double invariant determined by the game reveals the oldest characteristic of humankind, the production of knowledge, the possibility of learning by exploring and many times making mistakes and looking for new ways to improve oneself. This was probably what has happened in the history of mankind and in the intense exchange of information and knowledge applications. The question isn't "what we do" or yet "what should we do", but what, beyond our wanting and doing comes upon us or happens to us as Hegel expresses himself: when you give shape to what is conceived and reproduced in thought, you give shape to yourself. That statement of his refers to the fact that when men acquires some kind of "power' (*können*), he gains, by means of this power, a self-conscience. In other words, the human beings have a working conscience because they are able to understand what is correct to say and know that work gives shape to what is con conceived and reproduced in thought

Giving shape to one's "own self" is being aware of one's own self. It is also sharing experience and accomplishing it because in that way experience is accomplished too. In this sense the aesthetic experience gets really close to the conception of digital universe, as we have mentioned before in this article. The production of knowledge converges with the idea of shaping oneself. We understand knowledge as result of a process, a work, or an intellectual effort, prior to the praxis and the technicality. This kind of knowledge, which is at the same time specialized and 'spatialized', falls between common sense and reflexive knowledge and in spite of not being scientific, tends towards it, because as it moves away from common sense it starts correcting itself or even rejecting common sense. In this way, we enrich common sense with the results from science. The construction of personal knowledge that permeates this scientific-historical knowledge, even departing from today's common sense is, most of the times, the result of some past scientific investigation.

"To be a conscience, or prior, to be an experience, is to communicate with the inner world, with the body and with others, to be with them rather than being beside them" (Merleau-Ponty, 2006:142). *With others*, in other words, consciously knowing them, overcoming the frontiers of what is already known, means conquering the unknown in search of new experiences. In this sense, conscience is an experience undergoing a reflexive process, which endows us with re-learning traits.

A reevaluation of the knowledge assisted by our senses and based on the association between this and other worlds, which in former times used to be considered prior to modeling of new concepts is necessary either in the context of facing a puzzle in games or facing everyday problems. In a process of assimilation and accommodation, such experiences turn into conscious knowledge for the possibility of resolution of new challenges that may come[6]. When "we are", we are open to things, we are prone to things which might happen to us and affect us. We, then, reach some enlightening into the concept of aesthetic experience. This experience takes place in a world, be it virtual or real, in the solitude of a contemplative observer, in some enthusiastic participation in a big party and, in this way, memory, learning and conscience

become linked. It affects us and moves us pointing out to the privileged moments in which the being is open to opportunities. It indicates us that the resulting comprehension will be operative, though not *machinic* (Stein, 2003, p.45).

In fact, we do not know the actual possibilities for being the learning experience creative, for learning to experience creativity, or yet for learning how to develop a creative and innovative thought. In spite of that, we can offer opportunities for thoughtful experiences to manifest themselves in all their potentiality in situations such as games, for example. But we know that human creativity reveals and manifests itself into innovative associations and combinations of plans, models, feelings, experiences and facts. We believe that it is highly relevant to present opportunities and encourage individuals to search for new experiences, to test hypothesis and, mainly, to establish new forms of dialogue. We consider a *puzzle* to be a way of broadening horizons and creating possibilities and, in this way, we are able to build up dreams which are translated in this willingness to imagine new worlds, to construct inner worlds even before any kind of sensitive impression is obtained. For the one who is open to creative thought, the dream becomes reality at the very moment one dreams, for it starts to be built, incorporated into one's activities in many different ways.

Among the games containing puzzles that function as engines of a complex narrative, *Myst* stands out, among other things, because it acquires real-time multi-user characteristics on the Web, allowing the members of the community of game players to meet and exchange ideas, to come up with plans together, etc. Myst is a special kind of metaverse whose potential not only enlarges the narrative's horizons, but also claims for a new approach to its puzzles from a psycho-social-cognitive perspective. It is in this way that the *Myst* series, and more recently the *Myst Uru Live – online* series – evolved as a form of metaverse which contributes to the development of the community of its players and to cyberspace explorers. By means of the avatars, each player can take part in the adventure in *Uru live*, solving the mysteries of the *D'ni* civilization and playing the role of a cyber-archaeologist. In a collaborative way, we are guided to the interior of the metaverse and as we face its puzzles new ways of thinking emerge, corroborating to the spontaneous development of each subject and in doing so we equally contemplate all the components of its psycho-social universe. Whenever we withdraw from the structure of a puzzle its logic we are moving towards successive discoveries which will culminate in the learning of new ways of thinking.

Davidson (2008) in his research work about the Myst series analyzed the structure of the game narrative in three different media: the CD-Rom, the comic book and the book. His research, focusing on the involvement of its players in these apparently divergent medias, revealed the immersive power of the game. He also demonstrated that the structure of the work transcended the digital universe, highlighting another important aspect: it is the hypertextual construction of *Myst's* story, which compelled its narrative to be communicated through different medias. This can be the most remarkable change in our times: our digital culture doesn't follow a single media or a linear form since it is released in multiple forms, medias and aesthetics. We are inter-connected; we build hyperlinks with the intent of amplifying our knowledge, our relations and our actions. The *Uru live* metaverse offers the player the opportunity for taking part in a story in which his presence in the community of players is essential, not only to getting a solution for the puzzles but also to the building of the narrative, which, by different medias, transforms players into more than readers and navigators-explorers. In fact, it transforms us into co-authors and co-actors of an open story. The open story and the puzzles form the modeling structure of the discovery logic developing process in the heart of the community of players. In it, creativity has fertile soil to thrive on.

The Ontologic Puzzles in the Process of Knowledge Construction

We are aware that creativity can undergo great changes as we engage into puzzle solving in this immersive narrative media known as the metaverse. The metaverse can be enriched by making use of classic puzzles because they provide an adequate environment to presenting logical problems taken from the history of problems which have troubled human thought. Such a procedure based on Murray (2003) and Manovich (2001) involves the transformation of a problem from mathematical-logic history into a puzzle inside a metaverse is called transposition. Transposition can be seen as an historical and cultural factor and a way of providing "new links" to the development of creative processes. In the process of building a puzzle, taking *Myst* as a paradigm, transposition deals with mathematical logic problems in the metaverse environment. In the process of solving a *puzzle* the concern is with the technical mathematical logic language used to formulate concepts and to create the immersive environments, such as metaverses and games, which exhibit relevant cognitive abilities which can be acted upon by game players. The formulation of puzzles by our research team and their incorporation into the metaverses and games takes into account the process of transposition. This was the case of the game and metaverse project entitled *Cabu Island*[7] which comprises a great number of puzzle transpositions.

As in *Myst*, *Cabu Island* uses puzzles to entice the player to develop creative ways in order to search for solutions to the problems. Upon arrival on *Cabu Island* the player sees a huge Hanoi Tower, built in stone and placed at the top of a mountain. The Hanoi Tower alludes to the myth of creation and its presence gives the player the clue that the game is about to start.

Recalling Miles (1996:4), who argued that *Myst* is in accordance to the fourth law of medias proposed by Marshall Mcluhan: "the initial development of a new media will recover characteristics of the previous medias.", we might say that the design project developed in Myst works out the recovery of conventions and forms of literature, cinema and graphical design, combining them in the *multimedia-hypertext-CD-ROM*[8] media. The same happens in *Cabu Island, a* kind of academic game, which recovers previous forms of cognitive constructions with the objective of giving rise to new interpretations. *Cabu Island* introduces logical-mathematical transpositions in the form of puzzles. One such an example of transposition consists of the formulation of a problem based on a story taken from the *Treatise of the Art of Arithmetics,* by Bento Fernandes[9]. The story is about an apple orchard.

A gentleman has fallen for a lady and can't have from her his wish. The lady wants him to bring her 9 apples from the King's garden. Fulfilled that condition, she shall accept him joyfully. Then the gentleman goes to the King's garden and there he comes upon 3 doors, and in front of each door there is a doorman; the first doorman tells him he can go on, but that he has to give him half the apples he had brought plus 2. The second doorman tells him he can go on, but that he has to give him half the apples that he had brought plus 3. The third doorman also tells him he can go on but that he has to give him half the apples he brought minus 4. I ask you: how many apples does this gentleman needs to pick up so that, at the end, he has exactly 9 apples, no more no less than that after giving each doorman the number of apples which has been asked for? (Lagarto, 2009)

In order to derive a formula for calculating the required number of apples we can rely on the conceptual understanding of an abstract and functional numerical model. A function is defined by an equation. Then, *"x"* can stand for the number of apples. The most important thing is getting out through door 1 ("gate" in the case of *Cabu Island*)

holding 9 apples, so that the gentleman can give them to the lady.

Being "x" the total number of apples,

Door (gate) 1: $x - 0,5x - 2 = 9 \rightarrow 0,5x = 11 \rightarrow x = 22$

{The gentleman should be carrying 22 apples when he passes through the second door}

Door (gate) 2: $x - 0,5x - 3 = 22 \rightarrow 0,5x = 25 \rightarrow x = 50$

{The gentleman should be carrying 50 apples when he passes through the third door}

Door (gate) 3: $x - 0,5 x + 4 = 50 \rightarrow 0,5x = 46 \rightarrow x = 92$

{Therefore, the gentleman will have to get 92 apples if he wants to held 9 at the end}

In search of the heuristics for solving the puzzle, we came to find different ways of thinking, one of them being the recursive algorithm, i.e. by means of a deductive reasoning we can choose the opposite direction from that proposed by the puzzle. Given that at the end nine apples must be hold, it is by the end that we must begin. How many apples have we got to collect? The arrival at a port is the output of the previous one and that characterizes what is called a recursive algorithm, since the last gate in the entry will be, for the sake of the exit, the first one.

The main idea in this game development is to observe the construction of knowledge as a natural process. The result of this process is to show the building up of knowledge as a product of a mental dynamics. A mythological Ent's creature and three guardians were used to show the transformation of a logic problem into a game experience. The Ent claims an apple to the player. Apples can be found in a tree in the center of the maze. But on the way to the apple tree, there are three guardians who also demand a certain number of apples to the player. The player is the one who performs the actions regarding knowledge transformation because he needs to create a strategy to calculate the number of apples necessary to give to each guardian and leave one apple for the Ent. A

Analyzing the total number of apples necessary to solve this puzzle, we can build up a relation between the number of apples to the Ent denoted "x" and the total number of apples to be picked up in the Tree denoted "y", based on the following *ratio*:

$$y = 8x + 20$$

If x = 1, then y = (8 * 1) + 20 = 8 + 20 = 28. Therefore, to deliver one apple for Ent, we would have to pick up 28 apples. The same applies to the original problem if we want to deliver the final nine apples to the lady, then we have to pick "y = (8 * 9) + 20 = 92" apples.

We have considered the potential of games for knowledge construction processes. At the same time, we argued that logical mathematics is a powerful instrument for man's cognitive development and the learning processes of making decisions, given the fact the it provides us ways to exercise our creativity. D'Ambrosio (2002:4) states: "mathematics provides the necessary instruments for an evaluation of the consequences of the chosen decisions". The essence of ethical behavior is a result of the knowledge of the consequences of the decisions we make. So we can build up knowledge that structures itself through reevaluations. Such an opportunity must be present at every moment of our formation. It is not the amount of information, nor the sophistication in Mathematics that can, alone, provide useful knowledge, but the ability to put that knowledge into context. With that in mind, we wish to enjoy the potential of metaverses on the widest array of human life.

CONCLUDING REMARKS

Thinking in a creative and innovative way, as well as exercising the potential of solving problems in the world we live in is an ability, which can also be developed by using games. Traditional elements can be incorporated into games and be associated to enriching experiences of high playability. Everything that moves us, takes our time and changes us is capable of turning us into epistemologists, detectives, researchers, etc. Thinking about new ways of thinking immersed in the digital universe and being part of an exciting story, we are much more than characters, we are the main actors of our own development. Lateral thinking and mental agility are essential in a changing world.

Looking for new ways to create metaverses which encompass a bigger number of applications aiming at building up cognitive structures in any kind of field, for example in education and in business, requires a deep analysis of the theoretical pre-assumptions which support them and a thorough research of the classical-scientific literature. The human being is not defined solely by work, but by game as well. Not only children, but also adults like and need to play. That is why we watch soccer matches, for example. We are much more *Homo ludens* than *Homo economicus*. We do not live solely for economic interests. In the *Homo ludens*, the *homo mitologicus* lives on, that is, we live in the light of myths and faith, being conscious or not about it. Men are at the same time prosaic and poetical. As Hölderling stated, men inhabit the earth poetically, but also prosaically, and if prose did not exist, then men could not enjoy poetry. Even truer today, when science discreetly abandons certain mechanical elements to assimilate the game between the certainty and the uncertainty, puzzles can be used to encourage the constant spirit of discoveries starting from the groundings of all primordial uncertainty.

On valuing self-correction, something, which can be done in metaverse environments, each individual becomes capable of regulating his abilities. Enlarging his observation and analysis capacity, the individual can improve his current cognitive abilities. The self-esteem, resulting from overcoming obstacles in a *game*, becomes an ally in his search for possible methods to solve problems, since his aims are not restricted to simply "getting the right answers". By offering an opportunity to the creation of their heuristics, adolescents and young adults will feel more free to explore, to assume their errors and to self-regulate, each of them operating on a certain level, but always doing it in a significant way. Even if logic and mathematics can look mysterious to them, they will not be seen as their adversaries anymore. The main contribution of this chapter is not discussing the concepts and methods related to games but something much more fundamental which has to do with the belief that games and metaverses, by means of the aesthetical experience they provide, can be thought of as sophisticated forms of human intellect which hold the legacy of the tradition accumulated by our ancestors and which can be projected into the digital existence unveiled to the *Dasein*.

REFERENCES

Berger, A. A. (2009). *Video games: A popular culture phenomenon* (3rd ed., pp. 73–83). Piscataway, NJ: Transaction Publishers.

Bondía, J. L. (2002). Notas sobre a experiência e o saber de experiência. *Revista Brasileira de Educação*, *19*, 20–28. doi:10.1590/S1413-24782002000100003

Carroll, J. (1994, August). Guerrillas in the Myst: From garage start-up to the first CD-ROM superstars. *Wired*, 70-73.

Carroll, J. (September, 1997). (D)riven. *Wired Digital*. Retrieved June 15, 2009, from http://wwww.wired.com/ wired/ 5.09/ riven.html

D'Ambrosio, U. (July, 2002). *Que matemática deve ser aprendida nas escolas hoje?* Teleconferência no Programa PEC – Formação Universitária, patrocinado pela Secretaria de Educação do Estado de São Paulo. Retrieved from http://vello.sites.uol.com.br/ aprendida.htm

Davidson, D. (1999). *The journey of narrative: The story of Myst across two mediums*. National Communication Association Convention, Chicago, IL. Retrieved from http://waxebb.com/ writings/ journey.html

Davidson, D. (2008). *Stories in between: Narratives and mediums @ play*. ETC Press.

De Bono, E. (1968). *New think: The use of lateral thinking in the generation of new ideas*. New York, NY: Basic Books.

De Bono, E. (1970). *Lateral thinking: Creativity step by step*. New York, NY: Harper & Row.

De Bono, E. (n.d.). *Edward de Bono's authorised website*. Retrieved May 12, 2010, from http://www.edwdebono.com/ index.html

Dudeney, H. E. (2008). *Os Enigmas de Canterbury. Espanha: RBA editora*. Desafios Matemáticos.

Edmunds, L., & Dundes, A. (1981). The sphinx in the Oedipus legend. In Edmunds, L. (Ed.), *Oedipus, a folklore casebook*. Madison, WI: The University of Wisconsin Press.

Fauvell, J., & Gray, J. (1992). *The history of mathematics - A reader*. London, UK: The Macmillan Press ltd.

Fink, E. (1966). *Le Jeu comme symbole du monde (1969)*. Paris, France: Minuit.

Frasca, G. (1999). *Ludology meets narratology: Similitude and differences between (video) games and narrative*. Retrieved January 12, 2010, from http://www.ludology.org/ articles/ ludology.htm

Freud, S. (1999). *Triebe und Triebschicksale* (pp. 209–232). Frankfurt am Main, Germany: Fischer.

Gadamer, H. G. (1999). *Verdade e método: Traços fundamentais de uma hermenêutica filosófica.* Petrópolis. Vozes, 3. ed.

Goldstein, F. C., & Levin, H. S. (1987). Disorders of reasoning and problem-solving ability. In Meier, M., Benton, A., & Diller, L. (Eds.), *Neuropsychological rehabilitation.* London, UK: Taylor & Francis Group.

Heidegger, M. (2006). *Sein und Zeit.* Tübingen: Niemeyer.

Huizinga, J. (1990). *Homo Ludens: O jogo como elemento da cultura.* São Paulo, Brazil: Perspectiva.

Katz, V. J. (2007). *The mathematics of Egypt, Mesopotamia, China, India, and Islam: A sourcebook.* Princeton, NJ: Princeton University Press.

Kearsley, G. (1994-2003). *Lateral thinking: DeBono.* Retrieved January 18, 2004, from http://tip.psychology.org/debono.html

Lacan, J. (1996). *O seminário, livro 01: Os escritos técnicos de Freud.* Rio de Janeiro, Brazil: Jorge Zahar Editor.

Lagarto, M. J. (2009). *História da matemática medieval* (History of Medieval Mathematics). Retrieved on March 10, 2009, from http://www.malhatlantica.pt/ mathis/ Problemas/ macas/ macas.htm

Manovich, L. (2001). *The language of new media.* Cambridge, MA: The MIT Press.

Mayer, P. (1996). Representation and action in the reception of Myst: A social semiotic approach to computer media. *Nordicon Review of Nordic Popular Culture, 1,* 237–254.

McLuhan, M. (1964). *Understanding media: The extensions of man.* Cambridge, MA: The MIT Press.

Merleau-Ponty, M. (2006). *Fenomenologia da percepção.* São Paulo, Brazil: Livraria Martins Fontes Editora.

Miles, D. (1999). The CD-ROM novel Myst and McLuhan's fourth law of media: Myst and its retrievals. In Mayer, P. (Ed.), *Computer media and communication: A reader* (pp. 307–319). Oxford, UK: Oxford University Press.

Murray, J. (2003). *Hamlet no holodeck: O futuro da narrativa no ciberespaço.* São Paulo, Brazil: UNESP.

Petry, L. C. (2003). *Topofilosofia: O pensamento tridimensional na hipermídia.* Tese de Doutorado, São Paulo: PUC-SP.

Piaget, J. (1970). *A Gênese das Estruturas Lógicas Elementares. Trad. Álvaro Cabral.* Rio de Janeiro: Zahar.

Piaget, J. (1977). *A tomada de consciência.* São Paulo, Brazil: Melhoramentos/Editora da Universidade de São Paulo.

Stein, E. (2003). *Nas proximidades da antropologia: Ensaios e conferências filosóficas.* Ijuí. Editora UNIJUÍ.

Tonéis, C. N., & Petry, L. C. (2008). Experiências matemáticas no contexto de jogos eletrônicos. *Ciências & Cognição, 13*(3), 300-317. Retrieved from http://www.cienciasecognicao.org/ pdf/ v13_3/ m318317.pdf

ENDNOTES

[1] *Sich – own* and *abspielt* – game, thus, sich abspielt points to the fact that game and player are the game itself, in a single movement.

[2] Zork was one of the first interactive fiction games written for computers. Zork's first version was made in 1977-1979 in a DEC PDP-10 computer by Tim Anderson, Marc Blank, Bruce Daniels and Dave Lebling and implemented in the MDL programming language. All four of them were members of the dynamic modeling group. Zork was

the name given originally to an unfinished program by a MIT hacker. It was also adapted into a book series.

[3] Dungeons & Dragons (abbreviated D&D or DnD) is a mediaval fantasy RPG originally developed by Gary Gygax and Dave Ameson, and published the first time in 1974 in the USA by TSR, company of Gary Gygax. The game is published by Wizards of the Coast. Its origins are the miniature wargames (mainly Chainmail). D&D's publication is considered as the origin of modern RPGs and was published in Brazil by Grow. D&D players create characters who embark on imaginary adventures in which they face monsters, gather treasures, interact between themselves and earn experience points to become incredibly powerful as the game moves forward.

[4] According to the Oxford English dictionary, Lateral Thinking is "…a way of thinking which seeks the solution to intractable problems through unorthodox methods, or elements which would normally be ignored by logical thinking." Edward De Bono differentiates this from vertical thinking, which can be described as traditional, logical thought; vertical thinking looks at a reasonable view of a problem or situation and works through it, generally in a path of least resistance. On the other hand, Lateral Thinking suggests that the student or problem solver should explore different ways of examining a challenging task, instead of accepting what appears to be the solution with seemingly the most potential and going forward. De Bono is not opposed to vertical thinking; he sees Lateral Thinking as complementary (each make the other more effective). De Bono has indicated that the difference between Lateral Thinking and vertical thinking can be expressed in several ways: alternatives (think of many ways beyond the obvious approach), nonsequentiality (jump out of

the frame of reference or work from several points and link them together), undoing selection processes (think outside of logical progression into pathways that might seem wrong), and attention (a shift in the direct focus of concern).

[5] Next Generation Magazine. Available in <http://pt.wikiquote.org/wiki/Videogame>. Accessed on 26 Oct. 2008).

[6] Here, as the terms assimilation and accommodation suggest, we reference constructivism.

[7] The game and metaverse project Ilha Cabu is part of a Doctorate's research at Pontifical Catholic University of São Paulo developed by Arlete dos Santos Petry in the Post-Graduate Program in Communication and Semiotics. The title of the thesis is "O jogo como condição da autoria e produção do conhecimento" (The play as a condition of authorship and knowledge production). The computational implementation was made by Mario Madureira Fontes. The project's site is: http://www.ilhacabu.net

[8] At the historical occasion of Myst's launch it was the CD-ROM, which evolved to the DVD-ROM and we still currently have other Media forms and even cyberspace as a topos digital offering many online games. If we analyze from the point of view of communications theory, specifically from MacLuhan, we can say that online games are an evolution as a form of media and programming.

[9] Bento Fernandes published his Treatise of the Art of Arithmetic in 1555. It presents rules to execute numerical operations and to solve problems which were useful to merchants and Frei Lucas de Burgo's doctrines for the resolution of equations of first and second degrees". Available in: <http://www.mat.uc.pt/~jaimecs/livrogt/2parte1.html>. Accessed on 15 fev. 2010).

Section 5
Sustenance:
Virtual Health Care

Chapter 16

Virtual Simulations and the Second Life Metaverse:
Paradigm Shift in Neuropsychological Assessment

Thomas D. Parsons
University of Southern California, USA

ABSTRACT

In neuropsychology's received paradigm, the "normal science" of assessment and treatment planning appears to be approaching a paradigm shift: first, there are the general developments in other neurosciences that inform the practice of neuropsychological assessment. Second, there is the shift in the purpose of neuropsychological assessment from differential diagnosis of brain pathology to predictions about activities of everyday functioning and treatment planning. Third, there is growing need that neuropsychologists update their outdated technology for ecologically valid assessments. The impending paradigm shift may be well served to include the utility of virtual worlds for ecologically valid neuropsychological assessments. Actualization of the potential of virtual worlds for assessment will require the following: comparisons with well-validated neuropsychological measures, data storage, improved documentation of specific computer hardware and software used in experimental methods, and enhanced methods and result reporting by the researchers publishing studies on virtual worlds.

INTRODUCTION

Neuropsychological assessment represents an integration of a systematized neurological assessment of functional cortical and subcortical systems and a precise scaling of psychometric measurement.

A typical neuropsychological assessment evaluates several aspects of psychological functioning. In addition to measures of intelligence (e.g., IQ) and achievement, the neuropsychological assessment is made up of a battery of tests to examines multiple areas of functioning that also have an

DOI: 10.4018/978-1-60960-854-5.ch016

impact on performance of activities of daily living. The following represents a set of cognitive functions that is likely to be assessed: learning/memory, intelligence, language, visuoperception, and executive-functioning. The historical development of neuropsychology has resulted in a "normal science" that is informed by developments in psychology, neuroscience, neurology, psychiatry, and computer science. Each of these "informing disciplines" has gone through changes that challenge theory and praxes of neuropsychological assessment. These changes are what Kuhn (1962/1996) describes as paradigm shifts, in which new assumptions (paradigms/theories) require the reconstruction of prior assumptions and the reevaluation of prior facts. For psychology, the paradigmatic shifts are found in the move from mentalism (i.e., study of consciousness with introspection) to behaviorism (Watson, 1912), and then cognition (Miller, 2003) as now understood through connectionist frameworks (Bechtel & Abrahamsen, 1990). Neurorehabilitation has undergone a paradigm shift as a result of influences from basic and clinical research (Nadeau, 2002). For psychiatry (e.g., neuropsychopharmacology) the "paradigm shift" has been found in an understanding of psychiatric disorders and molecular biology models that account for gene/environment/development interaction (Meyer, 1996). Likewise, neuroscience has seen a shift related to the understanding of communication between nerve cells in the brain—shift from predominant emphasis upon electrical impulses to an enhanced model of chemical transmission (Carlsson, 2001). For neurology (and a number of related branches of neuroscience) a shift is found in new ways to visualize the details of brain function (Raichle, 2009). Finally, we are seeing shifts in computer science in the areas of social computing (Wang, 2007), information systems (Merali and McKelvey, 2006), and even the video game industry (Zackariasson and Wilson, 2010).

Developments in the area of neuropsychological assessment parallel several of Kuhn's observa-tions concerning the nonlinear trend of progress in the history of science (Kuhn, 1962/1996). For example, the naive assumption that traditional neuropsychological assessment procedures would continue to maintain prominence following the advent of neuroimaging characterized an earlier status quo, a period Kuhn referred to as normal science. The untenable presumption that traditional paper-and-pencil batteries (or automated computerized versions) were generally capable of forming accurate judgments about the everyday functioning (i.e., ecological validity) of persons tested on the basis of observation was another received belief that characterized this soon to be archaic era of practice. According to Kuhn, "paradigms" are initially recognized scientific achievements that for a period provide model problems and solutions to a community of practitioners. For the most part neuropsychologists are interested in "normal science" research based upon previous neuroscientific realizations that provide the foundations for neuropsychology's further practice. From a Kuhnian perspective, the unprecedented achievements of notable neuropsychologists, for example Wernicke or Luria, have provided the context for the neuropsychological research of the next generations and their theories are adequately open ended to allow for a variety of problems to be explored. For example, the localization and connectionist theories begun by Wernicke culminated in Luria's (1973) theory of three interacting functional systems. From a Kuhnian perspective, the attainment of a paradigm is found in its potential for achievement in still unfinished examples and normal science consists in the actualization of this potential. Further, normal science is interested in answering questions and a revolution occurs in response to a "crisis" when theory and praxis cannot be integrated and neuropsychological research problems can no longer be adequately resolved. In neuropsychology, such a paradigm shift would result in a community of neuropsychologists coming to view their theory and practice quite differently.

The advent of neuroimaging caused a crisis state in the normal science of neuropsychological assessment. During a pre-neuroimaging paradigm focusing on localization, neuropsychologists received referrals from neurosurgeons to psychometrically localize brain damage. However, over the past few decades a number of developments in neuroimaging have made virtually obsolete the normal science of localization by neuropsychologists. Unfortunately, technological progress in clinical neuropsychology has not been made at the rate that is found in the other clinical neurosciences (Dodrill, 1997). As a result, the normal science of neuropsychology is increasingly being questioned as it uses outdated methods (e.g., paper-and-pencil tests). What is needed is a shift to technologically advanced and ecologically valid neuropsychological assessment that made predictions of the patient's real world functioning. A response to this need may be found in the virtual worlds that are being created for clinical neuropsychology applications. Potential virtual world use in assessment and treatment of human cognitive and affective processes is becoming recognized as technology advances. Such simulation technology appears to be distinctively suited for the development of ecologically valid virtual worlds, in which stimuli are presented in a consistent and precise manner. As a result, subjects are able to manipulate objects in a virtual world that proffers a range of potential task demands.

A further development of this emerging paradigm for clinical neuropsychologists may be found in the expanding metaverse of virtual worlds such as Second Life (SL; Linden Lab, San Francisco, Calif.) that proffer tools (i.e. scripting and graphics) and environments that facilitate the creation of virtual environments that can be made available to potentially thousands of research subjects in an economical manner (Bainbridge, 2007). The population of users in Second Life has reached more than six million virtual citizens (Boulous, 2007). Within virtual worlds, it is possible to systematically present cognitive tasks targeting

neuropsychological performance beyond what are currently available using traditional methods. Reliability of neuropsychological assessment and treatment of affective and cognitive disorders can be enhanced in virtual worlds by better control of the perceptual environment, more consistent stimulus presentation, and more precise and accurate scoring. Virtual worlds may also improve the validity of neurocognitive measurements via the increased quantification of discrete behavioral responses, allowing for the identification of more specific cognitive domains. Virtual worlds could allow for cognition and affect to be assessed and treated in situations that are more ecologically valid. Participants can be evaluated in a virtual world that simulates the real world, not a contrived testing environment.

Virtual worlds offer the option to produce and distribute identical "standard" simulation environments in which performance can be measured and treated. Within such digital scenarios, normative data can be accumulated for performance comparisons needed for assessment/diagnosis and for treatment/rehabilitation purposes. In this manner, reusable archetypical virtual worlds constructed for one purpose can also be applied for applications addressing other clinical targets. This chapter will provide a review of such a retooling approach using virtual environments that were originally developed as a controlled stimulus environment in which cognitive processes could be systematically assessed in persons with various neurocognitive and affective deficits.

The organization of this chapter is as follows. In section one a brief overview will be given of the historical development of clinical neuropsychology's normal science and the crisis state that is leading to a paradigm shift. In section two, a brief discussion of current applications of computer-based neuropsychological assessment are described. In section three, there will be a discussion of the utility of virtual worlds for ecologically valid neuropsychological assessments that make use of current technological advances.

Obstacles and limitations are discussed in section four. A discussion of future directions is given in section five.

NEUROPSYCHOLOGICAL ASSESSMENT: FROM LOCALIZATION TO ACTIVITIES OF DAILY LIVING

The neuropsychological assessment has historically been characterized as both a refinement and an extension of the neurological examination (Benton, 1985). Much of what is now considered part of neuropsychological assessment originated from localizationist attempts of late nineteenth and early twentieth century physicians to improve evaluation of the cognitive capacities of persons with brain disease (e.g., Broca and Wernicke aphasics). Part of this has to do with the fact that many widely used neuropsychological tests were constructed before the advent of neuroimaging and emergence of much of the currently available information relating altered behavior to brain dysfunction. During this pre-neuroimaging era localization required clinical neuropsychology to establish standardized assessment measures for a normal science capable of identifying the neurocognitive effects of brain dysfunction. Standardized assessment in neuropsychology is largely due to its historic development from Alfred Binet's tests of intelligence and the United States's entry into the World War I in 1917 (see Anastasi and Urbina, 1997 for a review). During this time Robert Yerkes, Arthur Otis, and the American Psychological Association developed a group administered version of the Stanford-Binet (i.e., Army Alpha), and a novel group administered assessment composed of nonverbal tasks (i.e., Army Beta). A shift occurred with Yerkes (1917) move Binet's age-scale approach (i.e., tasks fluctuate with age and developmental level) to a point-scale methodology (i.e., tests selected based upon specified functions) over. Ultimately,

the Army group administered measures reflecting an amalgamation of Yerkes's point-scale approach and Binet's task-specific approach to measuring cognitive performance. Further, a performance scale developed by David Wechsler was included in an Army battery, (1920) that was made up of subtests developed primarily by Binet and World War I psychologists. A major shift in testing occurred when Wechsler applied testing procedures (i.e., group and individual) developed for normal functioning persons to the construction of a clinical test battery. Following World War I, Wechsler assembled the Wechsler-Bellevue battery, which included both Verbal and Performance Scales. By the 1940s a number of specialized neurocognitive tests were available to clinicians for assessing the mental capacities of persons with brain disease. The additive effects of these tests provided the foundation for the normal science found in today's neuropsychological assessment procedures (see Lezak et al., 2004).

As mentioned above, during a period focusing on localization, the normal science of neuropsychologists involved the development and administration of measures based upon a localization paradigm that focused upon double dissociation—two neocortical areas are functionally dissociated by two behavioral measures, each measure is affected by a lesion in one neocortical area and not the other (Pribram, 1971). It is important to note, however, that with the advent of neuroimaging, the need for neuropsychologists to localize brain damage has been greatly reduced. Unfortunately, many neuropsychologists continue to rely on "localization" as the chief basis for validating neuropsychological tests. As Ronald Ruff has contended, although neuroimaging caused the role of neuropsychology to shift from localization to documentation of neuropsychological deficits for prediction of real world functioning, clinical neuropsychologists many times fail to develop ecologically oriented assessments and continue to use localizationist-developed test batteries (Ruff, 2003).

Clinical neuropsychologists are increasingly being asked to make prescriptive statements about every-day functioning (Long, 1996). This new role for neuropsychologists has resulted in increased emphasis upon the ecological validity of neuropsychological instruments. To establish ecological validity of neuropsychological measures, neuropsychologists focus on demonstrations of either (or both) verisimilitude and veridicality (Franzen and Wilhelm, 1996). By verisimilitude, ecological validity researchers are emphasizing the need for the data collection method to be similar to real life tasks in an open environment. For the neuropsychological measure to demonstrate veridicality, the test results should reflect and predict real world phenomena (Chaytor and Schmitter-Edgecombe, 2003).

In addition to the controversy related to whether or not current indices found on commonly used paper-and-pencil neuropsychological tests give us sufficient detail for prediction of the potential everyday difficulties likely to be faced by patients (Wilson, 1993), a dearth of research has addressed the degree to which neuropsychological testing is ecologically valid (Nussbaum et al., 1995). Review of the ecological validity of neuropsychological tests has provided support for the superiority of verisimilitude tests as the results from these measures tended to be more consistently related to the outcome measures than the traditional paper-and-pencil tests. However, a problem for the verisimilitude approach is that these instruments do not appear to be migrating from research laboratories into the applied settings of clinical neuropsychologists (Rabin et al., 2007). An additional problem for this approach is that although these neuropsychologists have developed instruments that more closely approximate skills required for everyday functioning, have not made use of advances in computer technology. As a result, they are in danger of continuing the negative trend that deemphasizes psychology's role as a science.

COMPUTER AUTOMATION OF PAPER-AND-PENCIL TESTS

In the 1980s there was some initial interest in computerization of various assessment measures and neuropsychologists transferred a number of paper-and-pencil measures to the personal computer platform. Initial attempts at assessing the equivalence of these measures to traditional tests were made. A few examples of computerized versions of traditional paper-and-pencil neuropsychological tests include: the Raven's Colored Progressive Matrices; the Peabody Picture Vocabulary Test; Category Test subtest of the Halstead Reitan Battery; and the Wisconsin Card Sorting Test. Further, in the past decade, a number of computerized tests of neurocognitive function have been developed: CogSport, ImPACT, ANAM, and Headminder. Computer-based neuropsychological assessments offer a number of advantages over traditional paper-and-pencil testing: increased standardization of administration; increased accuracy of timing presentation and response latencies; ease of administration and data collection; and reliable and randomized presentation of stimuli for repeat administrations (Schatz & Browndyke, 2002).

Despite these computerized versions of traditional paper-and-pencil neuropsychological tests, the vast majority of current neuropsychological assessment procedures represent a technology that has not changed since the first scales developed in the early 1900s (e.g., Binet and Simon's first scale in 1905 and Wechsler's in 1939). For the past few decades, the Wechsler scales (in various manifestations; e.g., WAIS-R, WAIS III) have been the most widely used neuropsychological tests. While automated versions were developed of the original WAIS in 1969 and again in 1980, these automations provided only rudimentary stimulus presentation and limited data recording. Since the 1980s, the automated versions are all but abandoned and now the focus is upon slight revisions of the paper-and-pencil versions with computerized scoring. In fact, the latest revisions of the Wechsler scales (e.g., Wechsler Adult Intelligence Scale—Third Edition; Wechsler Intelligence Scale for Children—Fourth Edition) offer little more than cosmetic change and improved standardization. This lack of technological advancement of the Wechsler scales is important because according to a 2005 study surveying assessment practices and test usage patterns among 747 North American, doctorate-level clinical neuropsychologists, the Wechsler Scales were the most frequently used tests in their neuropsychological assessments (Rabin, Barr, and Burton, 2005).

Robert Sternberg (1997) pointed out over a decade ago the discrepancy between progress in cognitive assessment measures like the Wechsler scales and progress in other areas of technology. Sternberg used the example of the now obsolete black and white televisions, vinyl records, rotary-dial telephones, and the first commercial computer made in the United States, UNIVAC I to illustrate the lack of technological progress in the standardized testing industry. According to Sternberg, currently used standardized tests differ little from tests that have been used throughout this century. For example, while the first edition of the Wechsler Adult Intelligence Scale appeared some years before UNIVAC, the Wechsler scales (and similar tests) have hardly changed at all (aside from primarily cosmetic changes) compared to computers. Although one may argue that innovation in the computer industry is different from innovation in the standardized testing industry, there are still appropriate comparisons. For example, whereas millions of dollars spent on technology in the computer industry typically reflects increased processing speed and power; millions of dollars spent on innovation in the testing industry tends to reflect the move from multiple-choice items to fill-in-the-blank items. Sternberg's statements are as true now as they were over a decade ago. While neuropsychology emphasizes its role as a science, its technology is not progressing in pace with other clinical neurosciences. Sternberg also

points out neurocognitive testing needs progress in ideas, not just new measures, for delivering old technologies.

The recent shifts in computer science in the areas of social computing (Wang, 2007), information systems (Merali and McKelvey, 2006), and even the video game industry (Zackariasson and Wilson, 2010) reflect a growth in telecommunication and internet-based technologies. Given these advances, it is becoming increasingly possible to conduct social and behavioral science research via the internet. Researchers have reported the development and use of a handful of internet-based neurocognitive assessment measures. An internet-based neurocognitive screening for adult head injuries has been developed (Erlanger et al., 2003); the Cognitive Stability Index (CSI). The CSI assess neurocognitive functioning in persons with known or suspected primary central nervous system illness (Erlanger et al., 2002). The CSI is made up of ten subtests that comprise four domains: attention, processing speed, response time, and memory. In addition to use with adult head injury, it has been applied as a measure of cognitive function in patients with mild to moderate traumatic brain injury (Erlanger et al., 2003; Erlanger et al., 2002), Alzheimer's disease (Lichtenberg et al., 2006), and multiple sclerosis (Younes et al., 2007). Other internet-based cognitive assessments include IntegNeuro and WebNeuro. These assessments are being used in healthy controls and clinical populations. Reliability, validity, and norms for comparison with clinical groups are being established for both the IntegNeuro (Paul et al., 2005) and the WebNeuro (Silverstein et al., 2007).

While standard neuropsychological measures have been found to have adequate predictive value, their ecological validity may diminish predictions about real-world functioning (Chaytor and Schmitter-Edgecombe, 2003). Regardless of the medium (e.g., paper-and-pencil; computer automations; or internet delivered), traditional neurocognitive measures may not replicate the diverse environment in which persons live. Additionally, standard neurocognitive batteries tend to examine isolated components of neuropsychological ability, which may not accurately reflect distinct cognitive domains (Parsons et al., 2004a, 2005). Only a handful of neuropsychological measures have been developed with the specific intention of tapping into everyday behaviors like navigating one's community, grocery shopping, and other activities of daily living. Of those that have been developed, even fewer make use of advances in computer technology. It is important to note that the ones that have been applied to computer technology also run this risk of not offering the ecological validity needed for assessment of real world functioning.

VIRTUAL WORLDS OFFER ADVANCED ECOLOGICAL VALIDITY

Virtual worlds offer an advanced computer interface that allows humans to become immersed within a computer-generated simulation. Potential virtual world use in assessment and rehabilitation of human cognitive processes is becoming recognized as technology advances. Since virtual worlds allow for precise presentation and control of dynamic perceptual stimuli, they can provide ecologically valid assessments that combine the veridical control and rigor of laboratory measures with a verisimilitude that reflects real life situations. Additionally, the enhanced computation power allows for a range of the accurate recording of neurobehavioral responses in a perceptual environmental that systematically presents complex stimuli. Such simulation technology appears to be distinctively suited for the development of ecologically valid environments, in which stimuli are presented in a consistent and precise manner. As a result, subjects are able to manipulate three dimensional objects in a virtual world that proffers a range of potential task demands.

Virtual world applications that focus on treatment of cognitive (see Rose et al., 2005; Parsons 2009a) and affective disorders (see Powers & Emmelkamp, 2008; Parsons et al., 2008a), as well as assessment of component cognitive processes are now being developed and tested: attention (Law et al., 2006; Parsons, et al., 2007) spatial abilities (Beck et al., 2010; Parsons et al., 2004b), retrospective memory (Parsons & Rizzo, 2008b), prospective memory (Knight & Titov, 2009), spatial memory (Astur et al., 2004; Goodrich-Hunsaker and Hopkins, 2010); and executive functions (Elkind et al., 2001; Pugnetti et al., 1998; McGeorge et al., 2001). The increased ecological validity of neurocognitive batteries that include assessment using virtual scenarios may aid differential diagnosis and treatment planning. Within a virtual world, it is possible to systematically present cognitive tasks targeting neuropsychological performance beyond what are currently available using traditional methods (Rizzo et al., 2004). Reliability of neuropsychological assessment can be enhanced in virtual worlds by better control of the perceptual environment, more consistent stimulus presentation, and more precise and accurate scoring. Virtual worlds may also improve the validity of neurocognitive measurements via the increased quantification of discrete behavioral responses, allowing for the identification of more specific cognitive domains (see Gaggioli et al., 2009). Virtual environments could allow for neurocognition to be tested in situations that are more ecologically valid. Participants can be evaluated in an environment that simulates the real world, not a contrived testing environment (see Gorini et al., 2008). Further, it offers the potential to have ecologically valid computer-based neuropsychological assessments that will move beyond traditional clinic or laboratory borders.

Technological advances in computing and the World Wide Web in the last couple decades (Abbate, 1999) have allowed for internet-based virtual worlds testing with potentially more diverse samples in respect to socioeconomic status, sex, and age than traditional samples that are often drawn from undergraduate university students (Gosling et al., 2004). Virtual worlds are made up of online communities in which persons inter-relate in simulated environments. The continued progress in the development of robust technologies such as more rapid and secure internet connections has led to the ever increasing interest in social networks (Boulos & Wheeler, 2007). Virtual worlds provide users to experience social interaction as they participate in individual and group activities. The virtual world Second Life proffers multiple medical and health educational projects (Boulos, Hetherington, & Wheeler, 2007). Although these programs focus primarily on the dissemination of medical information and the training of clinicians, a handful of private islands in Second Life (e.g., Brigadoon for Asperger's syndrome; Live2give for cerebral palsy) have been created for therapeutic purposes. In a recent article by Gorini et al (2008), the authors describe such sites and the development and implementation of a form of tailored immersive e-therapy in which current technologies (e.g., virtual worlds; bio and activity sensors; and personal digital assistants) facilitate the interaction between real and 3-D virtual worlds and may increase treatment efficacy.

In a recent article in *Science*, Bainbridge (2007) discussed the robust potential of virtual worlds for research in the social and behavioral sciences. For social and behavioral science researchers, virtual worlds reflect developing cultures, each with an emerging ethos and supervenient social institutions (for a discussion of supervenience see Hare, 1984). In addition to the general social phenomena emerging from virtual world communities, virtual worlds provide novel opportunities for studying them. According to Bainbridge (2007), virtual worlds proffer environments that facilitate the creation of online laboratories that can recruit potentially thousands of research subjects in an automated and economically feasible fashion. Virtual worlds like Second Life offer scripting and graphics tools that allow even a novice computer user the means necessary for building a virtual laboratory. Perhaps even more important is the fact that social interactions in online virtual worlds (e.g., Second Life) appear to reflect social norms and interactions found in the physical world (Yee et al., 2007). Finally, there is the potential of virtual worlds to improve access to medical rehabilitation. Klinger and Weiss (2009) describe the evolution of virtual worlds along to two dimensions: 1) the number of users; and 2) the distance between the users. According to Klinger and Weiss, single user and locally used virtual worlds have developed into three additional venues: 1) multiple users located in the same setting, 2) single users remotely located, and 3) multiple users remotely located. According to Klinger and Weiss, single user, locally operated virtual worlds will continue to be important for rehabilitation within a clinical or educational setting. However, the literature, to date, has been limited to descriptions of system development and reports of small pilot studies (Brennan, Mawson, & Brownsell, 2009). It is anticipated that this trend is changing and future years will see evidence of the effectiveness of such virtual worlds for therapy.

OBSTACLES AND LIMITATIONS

For social and behavioral scientists to make good use of internet-based virtual worlds, there is need for empirical, procedural, ethical, and professional practice guidelines. A general literature review reveals that most internet-based virtual worlds' development efforts have been conducted in relative isolation with varying standards for data transmission, platform dependence, normative comparison, and clinical application. Although guidelines are emerging for internet and data storage issues among collaborative researchers who are scattered geographically (Marshall & Haley, 2000), many virtual world studies fail to provide sufficient quantitative information to allow readers to evaluate the appropriateness of the analysis and to draw their own interpretations. For example, a Meta-analysis by Parsons and Rizzo (2008a) found that the inadequate characterization of results and design across studies made it impossible to carry out an analysis to determine the influence of moderator variables upon treatment effects. Hence, for clinical variables, such as presence, immersion, anxiety and/or phobia duration, demographics (e.g. age, gender, and ethnicity), it was not possible to calculate correlation coefficients because numerous studies did not report exact values, and, for some parameters, the number of studies was too small to meaningfully interpret the r value. While the application of virtual worlds to social and behavioral science can increase the ecological validity of these studies allowing for results to generalize beyond the controlled laboratory context (Rizzo et al., 2004), the ecological approach to such research runs the risk of being inconsequential because scientific progress necessitates greater emphasis on experimental control (Banaji and Crowder, 1989). As a result, there is a consistent tradeoff between enhanced fidelity and experimental control.

There are some relatively obvious practical and technical limitations of virtual world-based assessment that will cause clinical neuropsychology to be slow in adopting computerization on a large scale. For example, synchronization between the user's computer processor and the user's internet connection occurs with varying amounts of delay, or error, in timing. As a result, it will be difficult to standardize or control this delay with a degree of consistency. At one time this was an issue for any computerized testing. However, researchers have since developed software solutions that provide near-millisecond accuracy (Westall et al., 1989). Hence, there is a need for both the development of internet-based measures and "measure development" software. Further, there is the issue of crucial sources of error in computerized neuropsychological assessment (Cernich et al., 2007). For example, various configurations and operating systems are in use. A further example may be found

in real-time versus store-and-forward Internet-based assessment. These issues emphasize the need for technology standardization in which internet-based information may be exchanged. At minimum, researchers should use the American Psychological Association's (APA) established guidelines for the development, administration, and interpretation of computerized assessments (APA, 1986, 1987). Given the many changes that have occurred in the years since these guidelines were developed, there is need for a documented standard beyond those recommendations offered by the APA. There is a need for neuropsychology to update such guidelines and maintain a professional and guiding presence. Clinical practice is increasingly being impacted by the internet's ability to disseminate rapidly vast amounts of information and facilitate the instantaneous exchange of ideas.

Another issue is that the automated nature of virtual world measures does not allow an examiner to interrupt or stop the assessment and "test the limits" or be more flexible with their evaluation. Further, virtual world assessments may not provide as much qualitative information as standard evaluations in which a clinician examines the type of errors a patient makes and the strategies a patient might use to arrive at his or her answers (Woo, 2008). Hence, any computerized assessment should not remove a clinician from the equation. Instead, virtual worlds, like automated neuropsychological assessments, should be viewed as a tool to be used by a clinician, and not a replacement of the clinician.

FUTURE RESEARCH DIRECTIONS

The "normal science" that makes up clinical neuropsycholoy's cognitive and affective assessment is informed by developments in psychology, neuroscience, neurology, psychiatry, and computer science. The paradigm shifts that have occurred in each of these "informing disciplines" may reflect an impending paradigm shift in neuropsychology.

This impending shift is also reflected in the ways in which traditional paper-and-pencil assessments of cognition and affective presentations have been replicated with general equivalence to their paper-and-pencil predecessors. Likewise, virtual world applications that focus on treatment of cognitive (see Rose et al., 2005; Parsons 2009a) and affective disorders (see Powers & Emmelkamp, 2008; Parsons et al., 2008a), as well as assessment of component cognitive processes are now being developed and tested. One example of such developments can be found in a set of projects at the University of Southern California's Institute for Creative Technologies (USC/ICT). At USC/ICT, a number of projects have been designed, developed and implemented using a Virtual Iraqi/Afghani theme. The Virtual Iraq/Afghanistan world uses virtual environments to assess and treat combat related trauma, such as posttraumatic stress disorder (PTSD) and traumatic brain injury (TBI). This example is used because it represents the evolution from 1) paper-and-pencil and automated computer assessments to a virtual world environment (Virtual Reality Cognitive Performance Assessment Test); 2) extension of VRCPAT to a virtual reality exposure therapy; and 3) finally an instantiation of in Second Life.

First, in one set of these environments at USC/ICT, Thomas Parsons (Parsons et al., 2008a, 2008b, 2008c, 2009b) and colleagues have recycled the virtual graphic assets built for the combat tactical simulation training game, Full Spectrum Warrior, to develop a Virtual Reality Cognitive Performance Assessment Test (VRCPAT). The VRCPAT project is embedding the metrics and 2D stimulus presentations from a well established computerized assessment battery of cognitive function known as the Automated Neuropsychological Assessment Metrics (ANAM) and validating the results on standard paper-and-pencil measures. Preliminary results suggest that the VRCPAT measures a capacity that is a valid test that provides a unique opportunity to reliably and efficiently study cognitive function within an ecologically valid environment.

Second, in related work at USC/ICT, Albert Rizzo, Parsons, and colleagues, are using the same Virtual Iraqi/Afghani environment for virtual reality exposure therapy (VRET) with soldiers who have experienced trauma resulting in disrupted affect. The Virtual Iraq/Afghanistan system built from a user-centered design process has been tested in an open clinical trial with PTSD-diagnosed active duty service members. The participants were service members who recently redeployed from Iraq and who had engaged in previous PTSD treatments (e.g., group counseling, SSRIs, etc.) without benefit. The VRET exposure exercises followed the principles of graded prolonged behavioral exposure and the pace was individualized and patient-driven. Initial analyses of results from the first 20 Virtual Iraq treatment completers have indicated positive clinical outcomes. Of the first twenty patients to complete treatment 16 no longer meet diagnostic criteria for PTSD at post treatment. It is important to note that the VRCPAT and the VRET for combat-related PTSD projects developed at USC/ICT are not online virtual worlds. Instead, the Virtual Iraqi/Afghani world uses an offline immersive virtual environment.

Third, virtual world environments that mimic USC/ICT's VRET approach have been developed at USC/ICT in Second Life by Jackie Morie. The Second Life instantiation is called the Transitional Online Post-deployment Soldier Support in Virtual Worlds (TOPSS-VW). The TOPSS-VW project uses the facility of online virtual worlds to create a place of camaraderie and healing for returning United States military veterans—virtual space that can help them deal with problems related to their time of service and also assist in their reintegration into society (Morie et al., 2009). Finally, Parsons and Morie at USC/ICT are currently planning to implement VRCPAT in a Second Life Virtual Iraq/Afghanistan. The goal will be to development and validate a handful of internet-based neurocognitive assessment measures using Second Life.

CONCLUSION

The historical development of neuropsychology has resulted in a "normal science" that is informed by developments in psychology, neuroscience, neurology, psychiatry, and computer science. Each of these "informing disciplines" has gone through changes that challenge theory and praxes of neuropsychological assessment. Developments in the area of neuropsychological assessment parallel several of Kuhn's observations concerning the nonlinear trend of progress in the history of science. For example, the naive assumption that traditional neuropsychological assessment procedures would continue to maintain prominence following the advent of neuroimaging characterized an earlier status quo, a period Kuhn referred to as normal science. The untenable presumption that traditional paper-and-pencil batteries (or automated computerized versions) were generally capable of forming accurate judgments about the everyday functioning (i.e., ecological validity) of persons tested on the basis of observation was another received belief that characterized this soon to be archaic era of practice.

A further development of this emerging paradigm for clinical neuropsychologists may be found in the expanding metaverse of virtual worlds such as Second Life. Within virtual worlds, it is possible to systematically present cognitive tasks targeting neuropsychological performance beyond what are currently available using traditional methods. Reliability of neuropsychological assessment and treatment of affective and cognitive disorders can be enhanced in virtual worlds by better control of the perceptual environment, more consistent stimulus presentation, and more precise and accurate scoring. Virtual worlds may also improve the validity of neurocognitive measurements via the increased quantification of discrete behavioral responses, allowing for the identification of more specific cognitive domains. Virtual worlds could allow for cognition and affect to be assessed and treated in situations that are more ecologically

valid. Participants can be evaluated in a virtual world that simulates the real world, not a contrived testing environment. Virtual worlds offer the option to produce and distribute identical "standard" simulation environments in which performance can be measured and treated. Within such digital scenarios, normative data can be accumulated for performance comparisons needed for assessment/diagnosis and for treatment/rehabilitation purposes. In this manner, reusable archetypical virtual worlds constructed for one purpose can also be applied for applications addressing other clinical targets.

REFERENCES

Abbate, J. (1999). *Inventing the Internet*. Cambridge, MA: MIT Press.

American Psychological Association. (1986). *Guidelines for computer-based tests and interpretations*. Washington, DC: American Psychological Association.

American Psychological Association Committee on Professional Standards & Committee on Psychological Tests and Assessment. Division 40. (1987). Task force report in computer-assisted neuropsychological evaluation. *Clinical Neuropsychologist, 2*, 161–184.

Anastasi, A., & Urbina, S. (1997). *Psychological testing* (7th ed.). New York, NY: McMillian.

Astur, R. S., Tropp, J., Sava, S., Constable, R. T., & Markus, E. J. (2004). Sex differences and correlations in a virtual Morris water task, a virtual radial arm maze, and mental rotation. *Behavioural Brain Research, 151*, 103–115. doi:10.1016/j.bbr.2003.08.024

Bainbridge, W. S. (2007). The scientific research potential of virtual worlds. *Science, 317*, 472–476. doi:10.1126/science.1146930

Bechtel, W., & Abrahamsen, A. (1990). *Connectionism and the mind.* Cambridge, MA: Blackwell.

Beck, L., Wolter, M., Mungard, N. F., Vohn, R., Staedtgen, M., Kuhlen, T., & Sturm, W. (2010). Evaluation of spatial processing in virtual reality using functional magnetic resonance imaging (FMRI). *Cyberpsychology, Behavior, and Social Networwing, 13,* 211–215. doi:10.1089/cyber.2008.0343

Benton, A. L. (1985). Some problems associated with neuropsychological assessment. *Bulletin of Clinical Neurosciences, 50,* 11–15.

Boulos, M. N., & Wheeler, S. (2007). The emerging Web 2.0 social software: An enabling suite of sociable technologies in health and healthcare education. *Health Information and Libraries Journal, 24,* 2–23. doi:10.1111/j.1471-1842.2007.00701.x

Boulous, M. N., Hetherington, L., & Wheeler, S. (2007). Second Life: An overview of the potential of 3-D virtual worlds in medical and health education. *Health Information and Libraries Journal, 24,* 233–245. doi:10.1111/j.1471-1842.2007.00733.x

Brennan, D. M., Mawson, S., & Brownsell, S. (2009). Telerehabilitation: Enabling the remote delivery of healthcare, rehabilitation, and self management. *Studies in Health Technology and Informatics, 145,* 231–248.

Carlsson, A. (2001). A paradigm shift in brain research. *Science, 294,* 1021–1024. doi:10.1126/science.1066969

Cernich, A., Brennana, D., Barker, L., & Bleiberg, J. (2007). Sources of error in computerized neuropsychological assessment. *Archives of Clinical Neuropsychology, 22,* 39–48. doi:10.1016/j.acn.2006.10.004

Chaytor, N., & Schmitter-Edgecombe, M. (2003). The ecological validity of neuropsychological tests: A review of the literature on everyday cognitive skills. *Neuropsychology Review, 13,* 181–197. doi:10.1023/B:NERV.0000009483.91468.fb

Dodrill, C. B. (1997). Myths of neuropsychology. *The Clinical Neuropsychologist, 11,* 1–17. doi:10.1080/13854049708407025

Elkind, J. S., Rubin, E., Rosenthal, S., Skoff, B., & Prather, P. (2001). A simulated reality scenario compared with the computerized Wisconsin card sorting test: An analysis of preliminary results. *Cyberpsychology & Behavior, 4,* 489–496. doi:10.1089/109493101750527042

Erlanger, D., Kaushik, T., Cantu, R., Barth, J. T., Broshek, D. K., Freeman, J. R., & Webbe, F. M. (2003). Symptom-based assessment of the severity of a concussion. *Journal of Neurosurgery, 98,* 477–484. doi:10.3171/jns.2003.98.3.0477

Erlanger, D. M., Kaushik, T., Broshek, D., Freeman, J., Feldman, D., & Festa, J. (2002). Development and validation of a Web-based screening tool for monitoring cognitive status. *The Journal of Head Trauma Rehabilitation, 17,* 458–476. doi:10.1097/00001199-200210000-00007

Franzen, M. D., & Wilhelm, K. L. (1996). Conceptual foundations of ecological validity in neuropsychological assessment. In Sbordone, R. J., & Long, C. J. (Eds.), *Ecological validity of neuropsychological testing* (pp. 91–112). Boca Raton, FL: St Lucie Press.

Gaggioli, A., Keshner, E. A., Weiss, P. L., & Riva, G. (Eds.), *Advanced technologies in rehabilitation - Empowering cognitive, physical, social and communicative skills through virtual reality, robots, wearable systems and brain-computer interfaces.* Amsterdam, The Netherlands: IOS Press.

Goodrich-Hunsaker, N. J., & Hopkins, R. O. (2010). Spatial memory deficits in a virtual radial arm maze in amnesic participants with hippocampal damage. *Behavioral Neuroscience, 124*, 405–413. doi:10.1037/a0019193

Gorini, A., Gaggioli, A., Vigna, C., & Riva, G. (2008). A Second Life for e-health: Prospects for the use of 3-D virtual worlds in clinical psychology. *Journal of Medical Internet Research, 10*, e21. doi:10.2196/jmir.1029

Gosling, S. D., Vazire, S., Srivastava, S., & John, O. P. (2004). Should we trust Web-based studies? A comparative analysis of six preconceptions about Internet questionnaires. *The American Psychologist, 59*, 93–104. doi:10.1037/0003-066X.59.2.93

Hare, R. M. (1984). Supervenience. *Aristotelian Society, 58*, 1–16.

Klinger, E., & Weiss, P. L. (2009). Shifting towards remote located virtual environments for rehabilitation. *Proceedings of the Chais Conference on Instructional Technologies Research*. Haifa, Israel.

Knight, R. G., & Titov, N. (2009). Use of virtual reality tasks to assess prospective memory: Applicability and evidence. *Brain Impairment, 10*, 3–13. doi:10.1375/brim.10.1.3

Kuhn, T. S. (1996). *The structure of scientific revolutions* (3rd ed.). Chicago, IL: University of Chicago Press.

Law, A. S., Logie, R. H., & Pearson, D. G. (2006). The impact of secondary tasks on multitasking in a virtual environment. *Acta Psychologica, 122*, 27–44. doi:10.1016/j.actpsy.2005.09.002

Lezak, M. D., Howieson, D. B., Loring, D. W., Hannay, H. J., & Fischer, J. S. (2004). *Neuropsychological assessment* (4th ed.). New York, NY: Oxford University Press.

Lichtenberg, P. A., Johnson, A. S., Erlanger, D. M., Kaushik, T., Maddens, M. E., & Imam, K. (2006). Enhancing cognitive screening in geriatric care: Use of an Internet-based system. *International Journal of Healthcare Information Systems and Informatics, 1*, 47–57. doi:10.4018/jhisi.2006070103

Long, C. J. (1996). Neuropsychological tests: A look at our past and the impact that ecological issues may have on our future. In Sbordone, R. J., & Long, C. J. (Eds.), *Ecological validity of neuropsychological testing* (pp. 1–14). Delray Beach, FL: GR Press/St. Lucie Press.

Luria, A. R. (1973). *The working brain: An introduction to neuropsychology*. New York, NY: Basic Books.

Marshall, W. W., & Haley, R. W. (2000). Use of a secure Internet website for collaborative medical research. *Journal of the American Medical Association, 284*, 1843–1849. doi:10.1001/jama.284.14.1843

McGeorge, P., Phillips, L., Crawford, J. R., Garden, S. E., Della Sala, S., & Milne, A. B. (2001). Using virtual environments in the assessment of executive dysfunction. *Presence (Cambridge, Mass.), 10*, 375–383. doi:10.1162/1054746011470235

Merali, Y., & McKelvey, B. (2006). Using complexity science to effect a paradigm shift in Information Systems for the 21st century. *Journal of Information Technology, 21*, 211–215. doi:10.1057/palgrave.jit.2000082

Meyer, R. E. (1996). Neuropsychopharmacology: Are we ready for a paradigm shift? *Neuropsychopharmacology, 14*, 169–179. doi:10.1016/0893-133X(95)00074-N

Miller, G. A. (2003). The cognitive revolution: A historical perspective. *Trends in Cognitive Sciences, 7*, 141–144. doi:10.1016/S1364-6613(03)00029-9

Morie, J. F., Antonisse, J., Bouchard, S., & Chance, E. (2009). Virtual worlds as a healing modality for returning soldiers and veterans. *Studies in Health Technology and Informatics, 144,* 273–276.

Nadeau, S. E. (2002). A paradigm shift in neurorehabilitation. *The Lancet Neurology, 1,* 126–130. doi:10.1016/S1474-4422(02)00044-3

Nussbaum, P. D., Goreczny, A., & Haddad, L. (1995). Cognitive correlates of functional capacity in elderly depressed versus patients with probable Alzheimer's disease. *Neuropsychological Rehabilitation, 5,* 333–340. doi:10.1080/09602019508401476

Parsons, T. D., Bowerly, T., Buckwalter, J. G., & Rizzo, A. A. (2007). A controlled clinical comparison of attention performance in children with ADHD in a virtual reality classroom compared to standard neuropsychological methods. *Child Neuropsychology, 13,* 363–381. doi:10.1080/13825580600943473

Parsons, T. D., Cosand, L., Courtney, C., Iyer, A., & Rizzo, A. A. (2009b). Neurocognitive workload assessment using the virtual reality cognitive performance assessment test. *Lecture Notes in Artificial Intelligence, 5639,* 243–252.

Parsons, T. D., Larson, P., Kratz, K., Thiebaux, M., Bluestein, B., & Buckwalter, J. G. (2004b). Sex differences in mental rotation and spatial rotation in a virtual environment. *Neuropsychologia, 42,* 555–562. doi:10.1016/j.neuropsychologia.2003.08.014

Parsons, T. D., & Rizzo, A. A. (2008a). Affective outcomes of virtual reality exposure therapy for anxiety and specific phobias: A meta-analysis. *Journal of Behavior Therapy and Experimental Psychiatry, 39,* 250–261. doi:10.1016/j.jbtep.2007.07.007

Parsons, T. D., & Rizzo, A. A. (2008b). Neuropsychological assessment of attentional processing using virtual reality. *Annual Review of Cybertherapy and Telemedicine, 6,* 23–28.

Parsons, T. D., & Rizzo, A. A. (2008c). Initial validation of a virtual environment for assessment of memory functioning: Virtual reality cognitive performance assessment test. *Cyberpsychology & Behavior, 11,* 17–25. doi:10.1089/cpb.2007.9934

Parsons, T. D., Rizzo, A. A., & Buckwalter, J. G. (2004a). Backpropagation and regression: Comparative utility for neuropsychologists. *Journal of Clinical and Experimental Neuropsychology, 26,* 95–104. doi:10.1076/jcen.26.1.95.23932

Parsons, T. D., Rizzo, A. A., Rogers, S. A., & York, P. (2009a). Virtual reality in pediatric rehabilitation: A review. *Developmental Neurorehabilitation, 12,* 224–238. doi:10.1080/17518420902991719

Parsons, T. D., Rizzo, A. A., van der Zaag, C., McGee, J. S., & Buckwalter, J. G. (2005). Gender and cognitive performance: A test of the common cause hypothesis. *Aging, Neuropsychology, & Cognition, 12,* 78–88.

Paul, R., Lawrence, J., Williams, L., Richard, C., Cooper, N., & Gordon, E. (2006). Preliminary validity of "integneuro": A new computerized battery of neurocognitive tests. *The International Journal of Neuroscience, 115,* 1549–1567. doi:10.1080/00207450590957890

Powers, M. B., & Emmelkamp, P. M. (2008). Virtual reality exposure therapy for anxiety disorders: A meta-analysis. *Journal of Anxiety Disorders, 22,* 561–569. doi:10.1016/j.janxdis.2007.04.006

Pribram, K. H. (1971). *Languages of the brain.* Englewood Cliffs, NJ: Prentice-Hall.

Pugnetti, L., Mendozzi, L., Attree, E. A., Barbieri, E., Brooks, B. M., & Cazzullo, C. L. (1998). Probing memory and executive functions with virtual reality: Past and present studies. *Cyberpsychology & Behavior, 1*, 151–162. doi:10.1089/cpb.1998.1.151

Rabin, L., Barr, W., & Burton, L. (2005). Assessment practices of clinical neuropsychologists in the United States and Canada: A survey of INS, NAN, and APA Division 40 members. *Archives of Clinical Neuropsychology, 20*, 33–65. doi:10.1016/j.acn.2004.02.005

Rabin, L. A., Burton, L. A., & Barr, W. B. (2007). Utilization rates of ecologically oriented instruments among clinical neuropsychologists. *The Clinical Neuropsychologist, 5*, 727–743. doi:10.1080/13854040600888776

Raichle, M. E. (2009). A paradigm shift in functional brain imaging. *The Journal of Neuroscience, 29*, 12729–12734. doi:10.1523/JNEUROSCI.4366-09.2009

Rizzo, A. A., Pair, J., Graap, K., Treskunov, A., & Parsons, T. D. (2006). User-centered design driven development of a VR therapy application for Iraq war combat-related post traumatic stress disorder. *Proceedings of the 2006 International Conference on Disability, Virtual Reality and Associated Technology,* (pp. 113-122).

Rizzo, A. A., Schultheis, M. T., Kerns, K., & Mateer, C. (2004). Analysis of assets for virtual reality applications in neuropsychology. *Neuropsychological Rehabilitation, 14*, 207–239. doi:10.1080/09602010343000183

Rose, F. D., Brooks, B. M., & Rizzo, A. A. (2005). Virtual reality in brain damage rehabilitation [Review]. *Cyberpsychology & Behavior, 8*, 241–262. doi:10.1089/cpb.2005.8.241

Ruff, R. M. (2003). A friendly critique of neuropsychology: Facing the challenges of our future. *Archives of Clinical Neuropsychology, 18*, 847–864. doi:10.1016/j.acn.2003.07.002

Schatz, P., & Browndyke, J. (2002). Applications of computer-based neuropsychological assessment. *The Journal of Head Trauma Rehabilitation, 17*, 395–410. doi:10.1097/00001199-200210000-00003

Silverstein, S. M., Berten, S., & Olson, P. (2007). Development and validation of a World Wide Web-based neurocognitive assessment battery: WebNeuro. *Behavior Research Methods, 39*, 940–949. doi:10.3758/BF03192989

Sternberg, R. J. (1997). Intelligence and lifelong learning: What's new and how can we use it? *The American Psychologist, 52*, 1134–1139. doi:10.1037/0003-066X.52.10.1134

Wang, F. Y. (2007). Toward a paradigm shift in social computing: The ACP approach. *IEEE Intelligent Systems, 22*, 65–67. doi:10.1109/MIS.2007.4338496

Watson, J. B. (1912). Psychology as the behaviorist views it. *Psychological Review, 20*, 158–177. doi:10.1037/h0074428

Westall, R., Perkey, M. N., & Chute, D. L. (1989). Millisecond timing on Apple's Macintosh revisited. *Behavior Research Methods, Instruments, & Computers, 21*, 540–547. doi:10.3758/BF03202886

Wilson, B. A. (1993). Ecological validity of neuropsychological assessment: Do neuropsychological indexes predict performance in everyday activities? *Applied & Preventive Psychology, 2*, 209–215. doi:10.1016/S0962-1849(05)80091-5

Woo, E. (2008). Computerized neuropsychological assessments. *CNS Spectrums, 13*, 14–17.

Yee, N., Bailenson, J. N., Urbanek, M., Chang, F., & Merget, D. (2007). The unbearable likeness of being digital: The persistence of nonverbal social norms in online virtual environments. *The Journal of CyberPsychology and Behavior*, *10*, 115–121. doi:10.1089/cpb.2006.9984

Yerkes, R. M. (1917). Behaviorism and genetic psychology. *Journal of Philosophy, Psychology, and Scientific Methods*, *14*, 154–160. doi:10.2307/2940700

Yoakum, C. S., & Yerkes, R. M. (1920). *Army mental tests*. New York, NY: Holt. doi:10.1037/11054-000

Younes, M., Hill, J., Quinless, J., Kilduff, M., Peng, B., & Cook, S. (2007). Internet-based cognitive testing in multiple sclerosis. *Multiple Sclerosis*, *13*, 1011–1019. doi:10.1177/1352458507077626

Zackariasson, P., & Wilson, T. L. (2010). Paradigm shifts in the video game industry. *Competitiveness Review*, *20*, 139–151.

ADDITIONAL READING

Gorini, A., Gaggioli, A., & Riva, G. (2007). Virtual Worlds, Real Healing. *Science*, *7*, 1549. doi:10.1126/science.318.5856.1549b

Kuhn, T. S. (1957). *The Copernican Revolution: Planetary Astronomy in the Development of Western Thought*. Cambridge, Mass: Harvard University Press.

Kuhn, T. S. (1974) Logic of discovery or psychology of research, in: Schilpp, P.A. (Ed.) *The Philosophy of Karl Popper, Vols. I and II The Library of Living Philosophers* (Open Court Press).

Kuhn, T. S. (1977). *The Essential Tension. Selected Studies in Scientific Tradition and Change*. Chicago: University of Chicago Press.

Kuhn, T. S. (2000). *The Road Since Structure* (Conant, J., & Haugeland, J., Eds.). Chicago: University of Chicago Press.

Moore, K., Wiederhold, B., Wiederhold, M., & Riva, G. (2002). Panic and Agoraphobia in a Virtual World. *Cyberpsychology & Behavior*, *5*, 197–202. doi:10.1089/109493102760147178

Ready, R. E., Stierman, L., & Paulsen, J. S. (2001). Ecological Validity of Neuropsycho-logical and Personality Measures of Executive Functions. *The Clinical Neuropsychologist*, *15*, 314–323. doi:10.1076/clin.15.3.314.10269

Riva, G. (2009). Virtual reality: an experiential tool for clinical psychology. *British Journal of Guidance & Counselling*, *37*, 335–343. doi:10.1080/03069880902957056

Riva, G., Mantovani, F., & Gaggioli, A. (2004). Presence and rehabilitation: toward second-generation virtual reality applications in neuropsychology. *Journal of Neuroengineering and Rehabilitation*, *1*, 9. doi:10.1186/1743-0003-1-9

Riva, G., Raspelli, S., Algeri, D., Pallavicini, F., Gorini, A., Wiederhold, B. K., & Gaggioli, A. (2010). Interreality in Practice: Bridging Virtual and Real Worlds in the treatment of Posttraumatic Stress Disorders Cyberpsychology. *Behavior & Social Networking*, *13*(1), 55–65. doi:10.1089/cyber.2009.0320

Rizzo, A. A., & Kim, G. (2005). A SWOT analysis of the field of Virtual Rehabilitation and Therapy. *Presence (Cambridge, Mass.)*, *14*, 1–28. doi:10.1162/1054746053967094

Rizzo, A. A., Schultheis, M. T., Kerns, K., & Mateer, C. (2004). Analysis of Assets for Virtual Reality Applications in Neuropsychology. *Neuropsychological Rehabilitation*, *14*, 207–239. doi:10.1080/09602010343000183

Rizzo, A. A., Strickland, D., & Bouchard, S. (2004). Issues and Challenges for Using Virtual Environments in Telerehabilitation. *Telemedicine Journal and e-Health, 10,* 184–195. doi:10.1089/tmj.2004.10.184

Silver, C. H. (2000). Ecological validity of neuropsychological assessment in childhood traumatic brain injury. *The Journal of Head Trauma Rehabilitation, 15,* 973–988. doi:10.1097/00001199-200008000-00002

Wiederhold, B., & Wiederhold, M. (2000). Lessons learned from 600 virtual reality sessions. *Cyberpsychology & Behavior, 3,* 393–400. doi:10.1089/10949310050078841

Wood, D., Wiederhold, B., & Spira, J. (2010). Lessons Learned from 350 Virtual-Reality Sessions with Warriors Diagnosed with Combat-Related Posttraumatic Stress Disorder. *Cyberpsychology, Behavior, and Social Networking, 13,* 3–11. doi:10.1089/cyber.2009.0396

KEY TERMS AND DEFINITIONS

Crisis State: According to Kuhn, this occurs where a new paradigm has emerged and draws allegiances because of problems with the current paradigm.

Ecological Validity: To establish ecological validity of neuropsychological measures, neuropsychologists focus on demonstrations of either (or both) verisimilitude and veridicality. By verisimilitude, ecological validity researchers are emphasizing the need for the data collection method to be similar to real life tasks in an open environment. For the neuropsychological measure to demonstrate veridicality, the test results should reflect and predict real world phenomena.

Neuropsychological Assessment: A neuropsychological assessment typically evaluates multiple areas of cognitive and affective functioning. In addition to measures of intelligence and achievement, it examines a number of areas of functioning that also have an impact on performance in activities of daily living.

Normal Science: Kuhn's idea that the theory and praxes of a scientific community (e.g., neuropsychologists) are firmly based upon one or more past scientific achievements that the scientific community acknowledges for a time as supplying the foundation for its further practice.

Paradigm: Kuhn defines a scientific paradigm as having the following: 1) that which the researchers in the scientific community choose to observe and scrutinize; 2) the kind of questions that are supposed to be asked by researchers in the scientific community; 3) the structure of these questions; and 4) the ways in which the results of scientific investigations should be interpreted.

Paradigm Shift: From a Kuhnian perspective, this represents a shift in professional commitments to shared assumptions that occurs when an anomaly subverts the existing tradition of scientific practice.

Scientific Community: Kuhn's idea of a scientific community entails that neuropsychologists as a community cannot practice its trade without some set of received beliefs.

Virtual Reality: An advanced form of human–computer interaction, in which users are immersed in an interactive and ecologically valid virtual environment.

Chapter 17
Virtual Worlds and Health:
Healthcare Delivery and Simulation Opportunities

David Holloway
Metaverse Journal, Australia

ABSTRACT

With decades of experience in simulation, the health professions are comparatively well versed in virtual environments for training. More broadly, there is a growing body of experience and supporting evidence on the benefits of virtual worlds for professional information sharing, clinical simulation, healthcare delivery, and as a research tool. Virtual worlds have empirically demonstrated outcomes as a simulation tool that increases knowledge and of health professionals, and initial explorations in regard to healthcare delivery show promise. Key challenges for wider adoption of virtual worlds within the health professions include a lack of established standards around privacy, a fragmented approach to collaboration and marked skepticism toward virtual worlds as a platform for health care delivery. Recommendations for formalised collaboration mechanisms, agreement on standards, and future research avenues are put forward, with a focus on virtual worlds as a tool that increasingly will be central to professional learning and practice.

INTRODUCTION

A majority of the focus on virtual worlds to date has been on their applicability to education more broadly as opposed to health care specifically. For health professionals, health researchers and academics, a range of unique opportunities and challenges present themselves in relation to virtual

DOI: 10.4018/978-1-60960-854-5.ch017

worlds, which have evolved to be a cost-effective, clinically appropriate learning tool, health intervention environment and research platform.

This chapter will therefore look at three broad areas on virtual worlds and health. First, the use of virtual worlds for general training purposes and professional information sharing will be discussed. Second, the context for the use of virtual worlds for clinical simulation will be established, including a case study showing its utility in the field of surgery. The related area of clinical modeling for more effective health care delivery will also be explored, with examples of work underway on hospital workflow logistics and the use of smart objects. Finally, the use of virtual worlds as a health research tool will be illustrated, with a particular emphasis on the link between virtual world and physical world health behaviours.

The three areas for discussion provide a snapshot of the work underway within the health field, but do not encapsulate its full breadth. The issue of addiction has been purposely avoided as the research base is markedly disparate to the other areas discussed in this chapter, so doing it justice within the space constraints is difficult. For a small proportion of the population, use of virtual worlds can indeed become problematic. This is no way detracts from the larger population that currently and potentially will benefit from virtual worlds, but the negative aspects should not go unacknowledged.

BACKGROUND

Clinical Simulation: The Link to Virtual Worlds

The utilisation of virtual worlds within the health domain has arguably been a longer term one than in other fields. This is predominantly due to the regular use of simulation in the medical, nursing and allied health fields over many decades. The use of three-dimensional (3D) simulations for specific surgical procedures is particularly well established, with the earliest references to its use occurring in 1987 for fibre-endoscopy (Cooper and Taqueti, 2008).

For nursing and most allied health professionals, clinical simulation is also a standard component of undergraduate training and remains a tool for workplace-based learning. The rationales for their use in the health professions are obvious in a lot of respects: a semi-realistic learning envi-

ronment, the ability to make mistakes without causing harm and the ability to reflectively discuss both adverse and desired outcomes. Simulation has traditionally been of a procedural nature i.e. insertion of a urinary catheter, but this has been expanded to the psychosocial aspects of healthcare delivery such as health assessment and counseling, to the point that procedural training may be more considered a clinical laboratory process than true simulation.

There is a large body of research work confirming the efficacy of clinical simulation – with some caveats. A study by Bambini et al (2009) confirmed the utility of traditional simulation mechanisms in improving clinical judgement, communication and general confidence. Gordon and Buckley (2009) in an assessment of graduate nurses' ability to respond to patient clinical emergencies, not only found an improvement in technical confidence but also an increase in non-technical aspects such as information sharing, voicing concerns and using external resources. A systematic review of the 2003-2007 literature on the efficacy of high-fidelity simulation in health sciences training, found an overall increase in assessment and clinical skills performance – whilst also recommending a more rigorous and uniform approach to evaluation of simulation outcomes (Harder, 2010).

A framework proposed by Jeffries (2005) is a useful basis for any discussion on nursing and simulation. The framework identifies the pivotal role simulation can play in generating learning outcomes, whilst increasing satisfaction and self-confidence of those who have participated. It emphasises the role simulation plays in developing critical thinking skills, which are crucial for any nurse to demonstrate competence in an increasingly complex working environment. A discussion paper from Clancy et al (2008) emphasises the utility of virtual environments in simulating complex systems that nurses work within on a daily basis. Specifically, the authors assert that such simulations deliver superior outcomes for both patient and nurse due to their ability to encapsulate the whole system as opposed to traditional reductionist approaches that attempt to investigate one small aspect in isolation. A 2011 multisite evaluation study of an end-of-life simulation for nursing education demonstrated enhanced student knowledge in caring for someone at the end of their life, as well as increased levels of self confidence, communication skills and satisfaction with the approach overall (Fluharty et al, 2011).

Virtual Worlds and Health: The Broader Picture

The body of research and practice on health and virtual worlds is at formative stages, with an emphasis to date on describing the current and future virtual worlds landscape and recommending broad areas for further research. One key exception to this, as will be discussed below, is psychosocial research in areas such as the link between avatar and physical world health behaviours, viewpoint. The relative familiarity of the health professions with simulation has meant that the step to 3D immersive platforms is a smaller one than for a lot of disciplines. For the sake of this discussion, a virtual world is defined as any platform that provides an immersive, avatar-based three-dimensional space. As will be illustrated in detail below, virtual worlds that offer end-user content creation (such as Second Life, Unity3D and OpenSim) tend to provide the most substantive options for the health professions, but other platforms do provide adjunct benefits for health-based research or interventions, and these will be discussed as well.

The supporting research literature on health-related use of virtual worlds has grown significantly over the past decade in particular. The following table provides a gauge of the explosion in virtual worlds research since 1991. For the sake of this illustration, the use of the search term 'virtual reality and health' was used, with the search completed in January 2011 and limited to peer-

Table 1. Health-related virtual worlds research 1991-2010

Database name	1991-2000 results*	2001-2010 results*
Ovid MEDLINE	48	163
PsycINFO	14	160
CINAHL	199	1729
Google Scholar	56400	115000

reviewed research or authored books (excluding the Google Scholar component).

This growth in research and discussion on virtual worlds and health is most evident in the psychosocial domain, which is unsurprising given the cognitive basis of most current virtual reality experiences. Additionally, the psychology of immersion, addiction and interaction in 3D environments involves complexities that sit intrinsically within the psychosocial domain and tend to be researched from that perspective. The growth in research within the medical and nursing fraternities has remained substantial but of a comparatively smaller quantum. The establishment of journals devoted to the topic area has also fostered the level of research undertaken – The *Journal of Virtual Worlds Research* is one notable example, although *The Journal of Medical Internet Research* and *Presence* also regularly publish peer-reviewed virtual worlds research, amongst others. This is providing the critical mass of publications to ensure less explored aspects of virtual worlds and health are investigated and disseminated.

Some significant challenges remain in regard to the more widespread use of virtual worlds in healthcare training and delivery. First, ensuring a uniform clinical simulation environment for users can be problematic. The higher-end PC requirements for use of a large number of the platforms can provide a roadblock in education environments where numerous learning activities are priorities for the same infrastructure. Second, there continues to be some instinctive resistance to avatar-based platforms from both those receiving the training and those responsible for delivering it. A qualitative review of six papers on that issue showed that educators unfamiliar with the area tended to assume virtual worlds weren't of real educational value and that they were similar to lower level arcade games (Rice, 2007). Third, for true adoption of these environments for healthcare interventions, significant work around privacy and medical record storage needs to occur. Like their 2D counterparts, virtual worlds have a long way to go before safe and effective medical record storage becomes the status quo.

There are medium-term solutions on the horizon for all of these issues however. The increasing maturity of web-based virtual worlds will assist in driving adoption as the combination of perceived usefulness for communication and ease of use evolves. For the so-called 'digital natives' - those who have grown up knowing nothing other than internet access - there is a natural affinity to using online mechanisms for health information, due to their attitude to technology being informed by their constant exposure (Fetscherin et al, 2008). This exposure is quickly expanding to the use of immersive environments for purposes other than entertainment and socialisation. The success of the American Cancer Society's Relay for Life in Second Life is one such example of non-profit volunteer work being undertaken virtually (ACS, 2008). Overall, there is real momentum toward innovative and cost-effective clinical simulation and virtual worlds are central to this. In relation to privacy and medical records storage, work is well underway to confirm international standards, which could then be implemented within virtual environments.

Augmented Reality: On the Close Horizon

Although Augmented Reality (AR) isn't the focus of this discussion, its combination with virtual environments for health-related purposes is evolving, with such mechanisms having been touted for more than fifteen years (Kancherla et al, 1995). The ability to overlay information from the virtual environment onto a physical patient or device is the next obvious step in utilisation of virtual worlds in the health professions. One hypothetical example would be the use of avatars for initial training of midwives in antenatal assessment and then using an Augmented Reality mechanism to overlay the key components of the assessment onto a physical patient to bridge the gap between simulation and reality. Inversely, a busy antenatal clinic may collect assessment data from a cohort of women and then use that data to inform the behaviours of the avatars used in clinical simulations. This essentially occurs now in informing the projects developed to date, but AR mechanisms will allow for better synchronisation between learning environments.

An Issue of Promise

Virtual worlds provide both opportunities and challenges in regards to health. The only certainty is that awareness of these environments is critical for all health professionals, in order to gauge their effectiveness for both those within the professions and for the populations they serve. The research base for virtual worlds and health is burgeoning, with much more work yet to be done to establish a concrete foundation for their day-to-day utilisation across the board. To ensure widespread adoption, a rigourous evidence base needs to be confirmed, with the examples cited in this discussion part of the initial cohort achieving that objective.

HEALTH PROFESSIONAL TRAINING AND EDUCATION

Arguably the most obvious use of virtual worlds in the health context comes with the initial or ongoing training of health professionals. Specific clinical simulation will be covered later in this chapter, however there is a wide range of general health education and training initiatives already implemented within virtual worlds. The availability of more general health science education and training is particularly relevant to disciplines where aspects of health sciences such as biochemistry, genetics and physiology are required as theoretical background rather than being intrinsic to practice. Being able to use immersive options for learning can provide cost effective learning and increase retention of knowledge via increased engagement with the subject matter and a fuller understanding of its context (Cannon-Bowers and Bowers, 2009; Wankel and Kingsley, 2009).

Broadly, the areas where virtual worlds are utilised include health-related science (anatomy, physiology, epidemiology), core health information (diseases, health risk factors) and professional information sharing (forums of mutual clinical interest, conferences). Each will be discussed below, including points on future evolution likely in each area.

Health-Related Science

The use of 3D environments to illustrate health-related science concepts is very well established, particularly within the anatomy and physiology fields. There are numerous non-immersive 3D anatomical modeling options available to students, however those are not the focus here. Using Second Life as an immersive example, over the past five years a range of anatomical models have been developed that provide a particularly unique opportunity: the ability for an avatar to walk through key anatomical structures. A well-established example of this is the Ohio State University's model of the human testis (Danforth, 2008), which has been established in Second Life for well over three years. It provides a large scale, multi-stage anatomical exhibit covering both the structures themselves in addition to detailed, real-time physiological illustrations - in this case the various stages of sperm development.

Biology concepts are pivotal to most disciplines in the health professions, and a range of work has been conducted in that field in virtual worlds. Evolution, genetics and genetic mutations have been a popular focus from a range of institutions in both Second Life and OpenSim. This popularity is partly due to the scripting language in both environments providing the ability to simulate issues such as mutation in an effective way. One example of this is the work being done in Open-Sim by Dr Paul Decelles, whereby evolutionary processes are being explored through replication of virtual organisms (Decelles, 2010). Projects like this provide a useful learning opportunity for health professionals learning the human sciences as it provides an illustrative point that consolidates knowledge in that area.

Epidemiology is another area of interest and from a mainstream media viewpoint, the Massively Multiplayer Online Role-playing Game (MMORPG) World of Warcraft was cited as a test-bed for disease transmission. After a glitch in a 2005 software patch released by Blizzard Software, players who engaged in battle with a dungeon boss called 'Hakkar', were infected with 'Corrupted Blood' which depleted their health. This is a normal gameplay mechanic, but in this specific case the disease was able to be transferred out of the dungeon in question to the wider World of Warcraft population. This led to widespread 'deaths' amongst lower-level players, with the associated inconvenience of needing to walk back to one's corpse in-game. A discussion paper by Logfren and Fefferman (2007) citing this particular event, identified the opportunities for reproducing epidemic scenarios using large virtual environments like World of Warcraft.

There were key weaknesses in the 2005 event however, including the fact that the transmissibility was 100% and the level of applicability to physical world human movements was limited - there has been a degree of criticism of the level

Figure 1. Dalaran – a city in World of Warcraft

of enthusiasm about what is argued as a flawed model (Williams, 2010). That said, the use of virtual worlds for epidemiological research remains a fertile area for exploration. In a discussion paper on modeling epidemics, Gordon et al (2009b) make the argument that the link between avatar and human is potentially strong enough in freer environments like Second Life to allow for substantive modeling of epidemics such as HIV/AIDS transmission due to the ability for all the relevant behaviours to be simulated. Although outcomes to date have been sparse in this specific area, there is certainly agreement that virtual worlds can be a useful adjunct to physical world modeling. With the ongoing growth of virtual worlds usage and as these worlds become more nuanced, the potential for epidemiological research grows even more evident.

Consumer Health Information Provision and Support

As a collaborative, social platform, virtual worlds provide a strong option as a health information

and health support tool. This is an area where less complex worlds such as IMVU and Habbo also boast communities with a health-specific focus, but this discussion will focus on the more complex communities and presences that have evolved.

The University of Plymouth has a presence in Second Life dating back to July 2007, devoted to sexual health education. It combines video tutorials, live seminars and interactive quizzes and initial evaluations has shown it to be popular although determining outcomes is problematic, given the limitations in measuring traffic to particular areas in Second Life. One of the cited successes came with a seminar on sex and disability, with the presenting speaker stating that the attendance was much higher in Second Life than it would have been face-to-face due to the sensitivity of the topic (Kamel Boulos and Toth-Cohen, 2009; Kamel Boulos, 2010). In the absence of metrics gleaned from the virtual world platform, more traditional session evaluation tools continue to be pivotal, and even as in-world measurement improves, those tools will continue to be important.

During 2010 a research project was undertaken by Murdoch University's Kirsty Best, on the utility of Second Life for supporting those experiencing Myalgic Encephalitis / Chronic Fatigue Syndrome. The qualitative research focused on the role of Second Life as a means to reduce social isolation for those experiencing the illness. At time of writing the feedback from participants was showing outcomes in regard to lessened social isolation and increased knowledge around managing life with Myalgic Encephalitis / Chronic Fatigue Syndrome. Cited negatives included the complexity of the technology and issues for some participants in installing and using Second Life effectively (Holloway, 2010).

A project led by the Texas Obesity Research Center at the University of Houston is also worth noting in this section because of its focus on providing evidence-based information around obesity. For the research, active recruitment was undertaken within Second Life, with 162 participants taking part in a range of interventions including extensive information provision on diet and physical activity. Activities were centred on three areas: a 'Café Pavilion', 'Physical Activity Pavilion' and 'Information Pavilion'. Specific activities included choosing foodstuffs from a virtual refrigerator with associated recipes and dietary guidelines, avatar engagement in physical activities such as walking and jumping for 30 minutes maximum per day, and completion of questionnaires on diet and physical activity. The results of the project showed mixed results - on the positive side, the authors state that "obesity prevention interventions can be effectively designed and implemented within virtual worlds" (Siddiqi et al 2010). Less desirable outcomes revolved around retention of participants and user-experience issues with Second Life – a regular finding of virtual worlds research to date.

The three examples cited here illustrate the ability for health professionals to disseminate relevant information to populations that may be otherwise difficult to access, or where the sensitivity of the topic makes face-to-face interventions more challenging. Additionally, health professionals can learn a great deal from the communities of mutual interest that have developed around health issues – such groups provide an ideal base on which to build collaborative projects with health consumers.

Professional Information Sharing

The use of virtual worlds for information sharing between health professionals is well-established. Second Life has been the focus of the majority of work, although more recently OpenSim has gained significant traction, as has Unity3D. One of the key challenges in this area is actually defining the scale of information sharing occurring.

This author has encountered a range of professional groups within Second Life since 2006, including nursing, medicine, counseling and mental health. Some come under the auspice of professional bodies; others are driven by university academics, with the remainder being formed by communities of interest within professions. One of the latter is the Online Therapy Institute, which focuses on Second Life and its usefulness in counseling / therapy. Founders DeeAnna Merz Nagel and Kate Anthony see virtual worlds offering an improved level of sensory experience over other 'remote' counseling modalities such as web-chat and discussion forums, with a related improvement in therapeutic outcomes (Holloway, 2009). Their initial work in Second Life has been in the information-sharing domain, providing familiarity instruction and a virtual space for collegiate interaction. There is an acceptance that virtual worlds like Second Life do continue to have limitations in regard to establishing identity and ensuring privacy (Gorini et al, 2008), and that until such issues are resolved it is difficult to offer substantive counselling interventions outside of finite research study boundaries. The concepts of privacy and identity in virtual worlds are fraught with challenges, including the likelihood that an individual seeking counselling within a virtual world is predicated on a desire for absolute anonymity, and the professional challenges that brings.

Another noteworthy example of professional information sharing is the International Virtual Association of Surgeons (IVAS), which had its first conference in 2008. Initiated as a demonstration of the cost-effectiveness of virtual conferences, the central purpose of the meetings are sharing of information, including discussion of medical imaging, research studies and related professional issues. IVAS' continued growth is not assured however, with concerns acknowledged around verifying identity and the inability to conduct true hands-on workshops that would be possible in a face-to-face context (Leong et al, 2008). However, the fact that IVAS has had some success to date within one of the most highly-technical, 'hands-on' professions, bodes well for the use of virtual worlds more widely as an information sharing tool.

Looking at the issue of information sharing in virtual worlds more broadly, the use of open-source virtual worlds like OpenSim will arguably lead to more effective information sharing, for three reasons. First, there is an established body of evidence that the success of virtual communities is related to the degree of system quality, service quality and information quality (Lin and Lee, 2006). Therefore, OpenSim's lower price point, ability for greater end-user customisation and the boutique customer service approach by some grid administrators meet those criteria for success. Second, the ability to create an OpenSim-based world behind a firewall at minimal cost provides a superior option for professional information sharing where security of information is a priority or where the scale of content creation makes worlds like Second Life cost-prohibitive. Finally, collaboration in the health professions is most successful where common structures are in place, and OpenSim provides interoperability with Second Life and the gamut of OpenSim-related grids.

In the longer term, the drive toward secure, interoperable virtual environments that provide nuanced content creation options will be critical for the adoption of virtual worlds as a central information-sharing tool for the health professions. At present, those involved are early-adopters and innovators providing proof-of-concept modeling that will form the basis of that longer-term view.

CLINICAL SIMULATION

Virtual Worlds as Simulation

As discussed in the Background section above, clinical simulation is a well entrenched learning tool with a significant body of evidence supporting it. The large majority of this evidence revolves around the use of simulation laboratory settings rather than virtual environments; however, the body of literature on simulation and virtual worlds is growing as well. It is also arguable that the bulk of the evidence supporting laboratory simulation can be applied to virtual worlds to some extent, in that virtual worlds are essentially another tool in the simulation arsenal. There are certainly issues specific to these environments that do not apply to more traditional simulations, but there are as many similarities as differences. Cooper and Taqueti (2004) illustrate the lack of clarity around the clinical simulation field generally, citing the fact that in procedural simulation, there has been no review of the field and that there remains confusion over definitions and outcomes of simulation beyond a particular device or approach. A review of surgical simulation by Sturm et al (2008) found that although clinical simulation did transfer successfully to the live clinical environment, the ten randomized trials and one comparative study were "of variable quality and did not use comparable simulation-based training methodologies".

The lack of definitional clarity to date with clinical simulation provides a unique opportunity for the nascent area of virtual worlds-based simulation. Because of the relative infancy of 3D virtual worlds, the reality is that there are only a handful of platforms complex enough to accommodate effective simulation. If work is continued on standardisation and interoperability between platforms, then some of the pitfalls of the simulation field more widely (lack of replication of research areas, fragmentation of approaches) may be avoided. There has been some significant work on this to date, through the open-source OpenSim and its high degree of interoperability with Second Life protocols. Additionally, OpenSim allows for use of other virtual worlds protocols, which has been demonstrated successfully with the Unity3d platform over the past couple of years (Hughes, 2009). If the level of cooperative evolution and innovation continues, then more rigorous research outcomes are likely to be generated as the foundation on which research methodologies are applied becomes more solid and widely accepted.

Clinical Simulation: Limitations and Successes

In addition to the Imperial College case study given below, a number of virtual world clinical simulations have been developed that have demonstrated positive outcomes. All have a commonality in that they address specific clinical pathways, require accurate replication of clinical decision-making and provide a comprehensive simulation experience transferable to actual clinical practice. Additionally, each has cited similar limitations that require further investigation. To illustrate the specifics of the successful and not-so-successful aspects of clinical simulation, it is pertinent to cite two examples: the Second Life in Education in New Zealand (SLENZ) project and a research initiative by the University of Alberta.

The SLENZ project contained a midwifery clinical simulation at the core of its activities, with the aim to build (in Second Life) a best-practice birthing unit, within which midwifery students could then be trained in a range of aspects of the birthing process from the initial phone call from the expectant mother through to delivery of post-

natal care. According to a qualitative evaluation undertaken on the project (Winter, 2010), the combination of the best-practice birthing facility and the ability for students to role-play both the midwife and birthing woman provided useful outcomes from the perspective of both the students and the educators. More specifically, a number of the students participating had their skepticism toward the virtual world simulation (and to some extent Second Life) turned around to the point of agreement that the simulation was a very useful tool. On the negative side, both the students and the educators involved found the learning curve for Second Life quiet steep, experienced technical difficulties including bandwidth issues due to the remote locations of some students, and found that the need to employ an experienced Second Life content creator provided a set of challenges (Winter, 2010).

The University of Alberta initiative also contained two aspects. The first was the development of scenario-based training simulations for Emergency Medical Technicians (EMT) that involved procedural and communication domains. The second was a communications skills education program utilising 'Standardized Patients' – in this case Second Life avatars. In both cases, similar outcomes to the SLENZ experience were demonstrated, with yet again an emphasis on the inherent limitations of consumer virtual worlds like Second Life and a desire for exploration of even more flexible and comprehensive environments for simulation development (Chodos et al, 2010).

The SLENZ and University of Alberta experiences to a large extent encapsulate the challenges for simulation in non-specialist virtual environments. There is a growing awareness of their usefulness, mixed with concerns over their complexity and the need to overcome resistance to their use. This resistance is exacerbated by negative coverage by some of the mainstream media revolving around sex, gambling, addiction and relationship breakdowns. Once relevant exposure to virtual worlds occurs, resistance tends to break down and in its place awareness develops of the scope of learning opportunities that these environments provide.

Simulation: The Future

Although simulation is one of the most well entrenched aspects of virtual environments and health, the drive to improve the quality of simulation is greater than ever. The cost-effectiveness of virtual worlds like OpenSim and Second Life, whilst providing opportunities for more widespread simulation use, have a great deal of evolution to undertake before providing the level of immersion that some of the more specialist virtual reality devices can provide. That evolution is likely to occur at an increasingly accelerated pace, is likely to have mirroring of physical world data at its core, and will heavily involve augmented reality mechanisms where appropriate. The increasing interest by government in the use of virtual worlds may also provide a catalyst for more substantive funding of non-commercial virtual worlds development. The United States Government in particular has an active virtual worlds strategy and the conjunction of the Defense Forces' interest in virtual worlds support for returned servicemen (as discussed below) is likely to be one of the key drivers for quality improvement in the space worldwide.

Case Study: Imperial College London

Surgical simulation is well entrenched in medical training, but widening its use has been dependent on cost and availability. The Department of Biosurgery and Surgical Technology at the Imperial College London, formed the Medical Media and Design Laboratory (MMDL) in 2007, focused specifically on "innovative and efficient means for communicating complex health messages, the visualisation of future health care delivery models, medical device development, professional networking and educational tools for patients and

staff." (Imperial College London, 2010). Over the time of its operation, the MMDL has instigated a number of projects:

Medical Device Education
A simulation was created within Second Life designed to increase familiarity with specific medical devices such as insulin infusion pumps. Eleven surgical nurses, of which ten were novice users of the specific insulin pump, completed a clinical scenario with a scripted patient avatar and an in-world instructor. The feedback from the nurses involved showed that all felt it was a useful training tool, there was increased confidence in using the physical world equivalent of the device, and 82% were willing to recommend the training to colleagues (Kinross et al, 2009). The applicability of medical device familiarity training for both emerging and experienced clinicians is absolute: just as virtual worlds continue to evolve at a rapid pace, so do the iterations of medical devices available. For universities and health delivery services, the ability to script virtual world objects that replicate new medical devices is both cost-effective and clinically effective in that most educators are unable to supply real working versions of each new medical device being used.

Clinical Scenarios
A number of clinical scenarios have been developed for both doctors and nurses, to develop clinical decision-making skills. In this instance, an avatar patient was scripted to exhibit a range of symptoms, with the health professional required to undertake an appropriate assessment, make a relevant diagnosis and provide the appropriate care with the equipment provided in the simulation (Imperial College London, 2010). The degree of intricacy of the simulation allows for a near-direct mirroring of actual clinical practice and work environment, which informed the development of the hospital wards and treatment areas. At time of writing, substantive outcomes of the clinical scenarios were still being written

up, with the MMDL team confident of replicating the medical device study results cited above in regard to learning outcomes. Another related project underway involves a scenario designed to train health professionals in gaining informed consent from individuals with a learning disability. The 'Pathways for Consent' project, although quite different to assessing medical needs, uses the same delivery medium and is essentially identical in that the highly configurable nature of objects in Second Life means that a unique simulation experience is generated.

CLINICAL WORKFLOW MODELING

Unlike clinical simulation, which tends to be focused on individual outcomes, clinical modeling primarily involves processes and workflow. The ability to create content in virtual worlds that replicates the physical world provides a number of opportunities for those looking at improving how medical facilities work, whether they be hospitals, ambulances or community health centres. Thompson and Hagstrom (2008) provide a useful summary of the link between smart objects, health care and virtual worlds. The key benefit is the ability to test the interaction of smart objects such as Radio Frequency Identification (RFID) tagged devices with the wider facility environment to determine both the benefits and challenges of that interaction. Using a hospital as an example, smart objects may be the medical devices that adjust their behaviour based on biometric data, the lighting system that ranges from low light to operating theatre quality depending on the number of staff present in the room, or an orthopaedic chair that communicates with each patient's RFID tag and adjusts its position based on clinical need. The modeling of these devices within the virtual world allows for the identification of issues and prioritisation of improvements. As Eguchi and Thompson (2010) state: "the smart object interface protocols we develop can be platform-agnostic, so they can operate either in the real or virtual world". This is the critical point for clinical modeling in virtual worlds: direct interoperability with the physical one. Once that has been achieved, a major barrier to widespread acceptance amongst the health professions is potentially overcome – the concern over applicability to everyday practice.

Stroulia et al (2009) illustrate the close interaction between the virtual and physical worlds with their Smart Condo project. It provides for assisted living at home through the extensive use of sensors to support a range of medical and daily living needs, with the data gathered visualised within Second Life. Once again there is an opportunity to use physical world trends, in this case home-based care as a cost-effective alternative to traditional care options, to promote the effectiveness of virtual worlds in healthcare delivery – in this case to visualise clinical data. To state the case even more emphatically: there is finally the potential to build a useful clinical picture of an individual's management of their health and related activities of daily living, in their own home, with its implications for improved management including the crucial psychosocial aspects of health.

Although the work on clinical modeling in virtual worlds is at a formative stage, it does provide an opportunity to increase awareness of its usefulness amongst populations of people who may not otherwise have realised its application. The work on smart objects and assisted living gives virtual worlds a direct influence on activities of daily living for elderly people, or others with multiple co-morbidities including chronic disease. This not only involves their use as test-beds for physical world implementation, but includes their use as data visualisation tools for health professionals involved in case coordination of numerous individuals with varied health issues. The data visualization aspect also potentially provides the opportunity for a health professional to replicate a complex in-home model for a different individual with similar needs, saving time and money com-

Figure 2. An avatar patient for assessment

pared to starting over for each person. Once this level of adoption has occurred, virtual worlds will be no stranger a concept than personal medical alarms are currently.

VIRTUAL WORLDS RESEARCH AND HEALTH OUTCOMES

Intrinsic to the progression of any field is the ability to bridge the divide between research and practice. The driving force for the health professions is improving the health of individuals and the communities they reside in, so given the relatively short existence of 3D virtual worlds, the real health outcomes being demonstrated are encouraging. Two broad categories encapsulate the work completed to date: studies comparing virtual worlds to other modalities, and virtual worlds specific research, with the latter the focus of this discussion. The unique attributes of the virtual world environment provides both opportunities and challenges for the researcher, particularly around issues of consent, confirming identity and scheduling follow-up where required. The focus of a lot of research undertaken within virtual worlds

has fallen into two areas: ethnographic studies of behaviour, or measurement of impact on actual health (mental or physical).

Ethnographic Studies

Virtual worlds by their nature offer a different level of interaction between individuals and groups compared to either physical world interactions or non-3D online interactions. Ethnographic studies of virtual worlds populations have occurred for well over a decade, a notable example being the detailed study of a multi-user dimension (MUD) written by Cherny (1999). A striking recent example is a study by Portnoy et al (2010), which investigated the degree to which virtual environments could indicate propensity to engage in risky interpersonal behaviours, even though the ramifications of virtually exhibiting those behaviours is essentially non-existent. As has been demonstrated in a range of contexts across virtual worlds research, the results showed that the sense of presence generated for the participants was significant enough to perceive interpersonal risk in the absence of actual negative consequences.

Sexuality and sexual health have been one of the more dominant aspects of ethnographic research undertaken to date, and this is an area that has obvious connotations for the health sector. Boellstorf (2008), in his extensive anthropological investigation of Second Life, devotes a significant amount of time to the issues of intimacy, friendship and sexuality. Not surprisingly there were a range of views expressed to the author during his fieldwork, but the common and somewhat unsurprising theme is that to a large degree, the behaviours exhibited in virtual worlds either are a reflection of, or a reaction to, their physical world iterations. To a large extent this is the central value of health research in virtual worlds: the ability to engage with people who are using virtual worlds to express themselves more openly than they otherwise would have. This can lead to the identification of strategies to improve health outcomes, delivered within virtual worlds, in more traditional health contexts, or in both environments. The real power of ethnographic research for the health professions is reinforcing the fact that virtual worlds are not a technological aspect to be factored in – they are just another extension of human expression that needs to be considered in a holistic approach to health.

Health Impacts

One of the larger bodies of evidence that demonstrates the impact of virtuality on health, is research into the use of virtual reality to ameliorate the effects of Post Traumatic Stress Disorder (PTSD). One of the more recent studies by Wood et al (2010) involved the use of virtual reality tools in treating 30 military personnel over 350 sessions, with the results confirming the use of Virtual Reality Exposure Therapy as an effective and safe intervention. Rizzo et al (2009) investigated the use of the 'Virtual Iraq / Afghanistan' PTSD Therapy Application on 20 personnel and found that 16 no longer met the diagnostic criteria for PTSD after treatment. During 2010, the United States' Defense

Advanced Research Projects Agency (DARPA) announced a funding opportunity to develop its 'Healing Heroes' program, which is to provide comprehensive telehealth support to its active and veteran military personnel who have experienced PTSD, traumatic brain injury or major depressive episodes. The first layer of the support requested for development is "avatar-based simulation, virtual environments, serious games, web comics, and other forms of 'new media'" (DARPA, 2010).

The research to date on PTSD and virtual environments illustrates to a large extent the roadmap for virtual worlds development in coming years. The military-level work in this area involves more than just visual and auditory immersion – the use of smells, sensations and temperature are also utilised, as are a range of mechanisms such as meditation, visualisation techniques and physiological monitoring. Translated to the broader community, these more intensive immersive techniques are already being utilized. Gaming consoles like the Nintendo Wii have provided a lot of momentum in regard to promulgating the concept of haptic interfaces, with research supporting the use of virtual reality as an adjunct to other treatments. With the technology now at a consumer level, it is allowing more widespread analysis of its efficacy. Using virtual reality for individuals who have had a stroke has led to more effective rehabilitation (Merians et al, 2002; Kim et al 2008). A subsequent study using the Nintendo Wii has also demonstrated positive rehabilitation outcomes (Saposnik et al, 2010). Other platforms such as the Sony Playstation and Microsoft Xbox have recently followed suit with location aware controllers or motion detection, further cementing the approach in the wider community.

A final area of significant momentum in virtual worlds health research, is on the link between an individual's physical world health behaviours and those of the avatar they control. The link between the size, shape and physical activity behaviours is a focus of interest for its potential application to preventative health measures in a society where gaming and sedentary pursuits have continued to grow. A study by Dean et el (2009) utilized 'heavy' and 'thin' avatars in Second Life to interview respondents on their physical activity and weight. The published findings involve only 29 respondents and the authors emphasise the findings as preliminary, but they warrant discussion for the trends they flag. The first outcome was support for the hypothesis that those engaging in physical activities in Second Life were more likely to engage in physical world exercise. Second, those who had thin avatars reported a lower average Body Mass Index than those with larger avatar sizes. Finally, those who were interviewed by a researcher with a thin avatar were nearly twice as likely (64.3% versus 33.3%) to report that they believed their avatar to be also thin. The respondents interviewed by the heavy avatar were nearly twice as likely to report that they didn't believe their physical world weight and size to be 'about right' compared to those interviewed by the thin avatar (66.7% versus 35.7%). These findings, when expanded upon with further research, are likely to be pivotal in regard to the design of health interventions within virtual environments.

SOLUTIONS AND RECOMMENDATIONS

The claim is repeatedly made in this chapter that virtual worlds provide a useful option for the health professions, albeit at an early stage of development. For the adoption of these environments to become widespread and intrinsic to both education and clinical practice, it is proposed that the following steps need to occur:

Interoperability

The current state of play with interoperability between virtual worlds is mixed. Although OpenSim and Second Life have commonalities, and the hypergrid protocol allows for movement between OpenSim worlds, there remains a raft of difficulties. A more formalised dialogue needs to be established, with the aim of maximising interoperability between all virtual environments. There is some significant momentum toward web-based virtual worlds and this may be the foundation of interoperability efforts, but the ideal outcome would be an outcome-driven interoperability framework rather than one driven by technology considerations only. Any such developments should include input by educators and health professionals.

Agreement on Standards for Simulation in Virtual Worlds

The research literature on the use of simulation in the health professions points to the need for agreement on simulation standards to ensure maximum quality of simulation but also to provide the basis on which more significant, replicable research can be undertaken. Development of standards would require an inter-disciplinary body, which would seek input from each profession on needs idiosyncratic to that profession. The scale of such an undertaking would best be integrated into current professional peak body structures – although the current level of awareness of virtual worlds issues makes this a longer-term proposition. In the meantime, key innovators in the field collaborating on standardisation would provide the impetus for the work required.

Central Directory of Places for Professional Information Sharing

The current body of health information existing within virtual worlds is highly fragmented, and due to the well-developed virtual worlds being 3D, data is difficult to search for in the traditional sense. The vacuum has been filled to date by informal efforts around Wikis and other knowledge-bases. There remains a need for a peer-refereed repository of information on virtual worlds and health. The ability to achieve this will hinge on the broader issue of acceptance of virtual worlds as a key tool for the health professions, as only then will there be a 'specialty' that resources can be devoted to.

E-Health Standards Compliance

Critical to the evolution of virtual worlds as a health intervention will be their articulation with emerging e-health standards. The Health Level Seven (HL7) protocols have been under development for many years, and user interfaces are a core component (Health Level Seven International, 2010). Ensuring that future virtual worlds development is cognisant of HL7 standards is the key part of the equation – the standards themselves are broad enough to easily accommodate the needs of new virtual worlds applications.

Further Development of Expertise in Data Visualisation Within the Health Professions

With few exceptions, a disconnect exists between those developing virtual worlds and interpreting their data, and the health professions. With the burgeoning growth in online health initiatives, there needs to be a greater emphasis on capability development in data visualisation within the health field. This has obviously already occurred with the growth in health informatics as a specialty, but the sub-specialty of analysing the data gleaned from virtual worlds interventions and its relationship to real world outcomes, is at best in its infancy.

An Agreed Research Agenda for the Health Professions

As has been demonstrated in this discussion, there remains an enormous amount of work to be done to establish the empirical framework for the use of virtual worlds in health. Like any research endeavour, it needs to be driven by the key decision-makers within each respective field. In most cases these are the educators and senior clinicians who determine both research and education priorities. Without a collaborative dialogue, the risk of unwanted replication of research in some areas, lack of replication in others and no research activity in key areas remains a high risk. The growing interest in translational research provides some promise here, as the professions look to take advantage of the linking opportunities such an approach engenders.

FUTURE RESEARCH DIRECTIONS

The scope for future research in regard to virtual worlds and health is enormous. The nature of virtual worlds has provided some challenges for researchers attempting to apply traditional research techniques, but adaptation has certainly occurred and will continue to evolve. A key component of future research will be the establishment of agreed approaches to data collection in virtual worlds where establishing identity can be challenging and where protecting privacy rightly remains a key concern.

More specifically, it is proposed that the following research areas warrant particular attention:

Avatars as Vehicles for Health Behaviour Change

The research to date on the link between avatars and physical world lifestyle change is promising. Further in-depth quantitative studies looking at the outcomes of virtual world health interventions around lifestyle risk factors need to be undertaken. This may revolve around an interactive module offered within a virtual environment, with group support also provided in the same context. To ensure that any evidence of success is emphatic, the measurement of outcomes should include objective biometric measurements rather than reliance on self-reported data as has largely occurred to date.

Therapeutic Interventions for Distorted Body Image

As discussed above, perception of self appears to translate to an individual's avatar, and vice-versa. Further research on the psychology and sociology of body image and therapeutic interventions delivered in virtual worlds could provide another tool to engage individuals who otherwise may not seek out assistance. The efficacy of computer-brain interfaces to directly control avatar appearance with thoughts or emotions is a related area deserving of further attention.

Decision-Making

Research on simulation supporting clinical decision-making is well established, but decision-making more broadly needs further exploration. Whether it is sexuality, substance use, peer interaction or informed consent, virtual worlds provide a unique option that needs rigourous definition. Creating scenarios in virtual environments that inculcate decision-making skills is a relatively simple task that could deliver substantial outcomes in a range of health-related areas, particularly in enhancing confidence and competence in clinical practice.

Integration

The acceptance of virtual worlds within the health professions will require a solid evidence base that places them within an overall framework rather than as a standalone tool. This is already the case to some extent, but further research that demonstrates the successful integration of face-to-face, 2D online and 3D online aspects in required, whether as a health intervention or clinical education tool.

CONCLUSION

Health professionals have never faced bigger challenges in managing the health of individuals or populations. The pace of technological change, combined with the shrinking health workforce comparative to a growing population, means that cost-effective options for training, collaboration and intervention has never been more imperative. There is a respected history within the health professions for clinical simulation, and this is likely to provide the basis on which acceptance of virtual worlds will become widespread within the university sector. Like any initiatives adopted academically, the ability to bridge the gap between theory and clinical practice will be critical in the coming decade to ensure this emerging field gains the attention it deserves. There is no certainty that virtual worlds will become central to clinical practice. What is certain is that virtual worlds hold enough promise to test their claims in a detailed and rigorous way, to support the research to date that points to their ability to gain health outcomes not able to be achieved elsewhere. It is the uniqueness of virtual environments, combined with the emotional power that individuals place in their avatars, that makes a powerful case for collaborative translational research to confirm the role virtual worlds will play in the health professions.

REFERENCES

American Cancer Society. (2010). *Relay for Life® in Second Life®*. Retrieved 3rd July 2010, from http://www.relayforlife.org/ relay/secondlife

Bambini, D., Washburn, J., & Perkins, R. (2009). Outcomes of clinical simulation for novice nursing students: Communication, confidence, clinical judgment. *Nursing Education Perspectives*, *30*(2), 79–82.

Boellstorff, T. (2008). *Coming of age in Second Life*. Princeton, NJ: Princeton University Press.

Boulos, M. N. K. (2010). *Social Web (Web 2.0) and the 3D Web (Virtual worlds and Second Life®)* Retrieved from http://www.healthcybermap.org/ sl.htm

Boulos, M. N. K., & Toth-Cohen, S. (2009). The University of Plymouth sexual health SIM experience in Second Life®: Evaluation and reflections after 1 year. *Health Information and Libraries Journal, 26*(4), 279–288. doi:10.1111/j.1471-1842.2008.00831.x

Cannon-Bowers, J. (2009). Synthetic learning environments: On developing a science of simulation, games, and virtual worlds for training. In Kozlowski, S. W. J. (Ed.), *Learning, training and development in organizations*. New York, NY: Routledge Academic.

Cherny, L. (1999). *Conversation and community: Chat in a virtual world*. Stanford, CA: CSLI Publications.

Chodos, D., Stroulia, E., Boechler, P., King, S., Kuras, P., Carbonaro, M., & de Jong, E. (2010). *Healthcare education with virtual-world simulations*. Cape Town, South Africa: ACM.

Clancy, T. R., Effken, J. A., & Pesut, D. (2008). Applications of complex systems theory in nursing education, research, and practice. *Nursing Outlook, 56*(5), 248–256. doi:10.1016/j.outlook.2008.06.010

Cooper, J. B., & Taqueti, V. R. (2004). A brief history of the development of mannequin simulators for clinical education and training. *Quality & Safety in Health Care, 13*(supplement 1), i11–i18. doi:10.1136/qshc.2004.009886

Danforth, D. R. (2008). Development of an interactive virtual 3-D model of the human testis using the Second Life platform. *Biology of Reproduction, 78*(129), 319.

Dean, E., Cook, S., Keating, M., & Murphy, J. (2009). Does this avatar make me look fat? Obesity and interviewing in Second Life. *Journal of Virtual Worlds Research, 2*(2), 3–11.

Decelles, P. (2010). *OpenSim evolution simulation I* [Web page]. Retrieved July 1, 2010, from http://slbiology.blogspot.com/2010/02/opensim-evolution-simulation-i.html

Defense Advanced Research Projects Agency. (2010). *DARPA-BAA-10-62 healing heroes (HH) broad agency announcement (BAA) for information processing techniques office (IPTO)*. Retrieved July 1, 2010, from http://www.darpa.mil/ipto/ solicit/baa/BAA-1062_PIP.pdf

Eguchi, A., & Thompson, C. (2010). *Smart objects in a virtual world*. Presented at the Acxiom Laboratory for Applied Research, Conway Arkansas, April 9, 2010.

Fetscherin, M., & Lattemann, C. (2008). User acceptance of virtual worlds. *Journal of Electronic Commerce Research, 9*(3), 231–242.

Fluharty, L., Hayes, A. S., Milgrom, L., Malarney, K., Smith, D., Reklau, M. A., et al. (2011). A multisite, multi-academic track evaluation of end-of-life simulation for nursing education. *Clinical Simulation in Nursing*. In press. Retrieved May 2, 2011 from http://www.nursingsimulation.org/article/S1876-1399(10)00164 -7/abstract

Gordon, C. J., & Buckley, T. (2009). The effect of high-fidelity simulation training on medical-surgical graduate nurses' perceived ability to respond to patient clinical emergencies. *Journal of Continuing Education in Nursing, 40*(11), 491–498. doi:10.3928/00220124-20091023-06

Gordon, R., Bjorklund, N. K., Smith, R. J., & Blyden, E. R. (2009b). Halting HIV/AIDS with avatars and havatars: A virtual world approach to modelling epidemics. *BMC Public Health, 9*(Suppl 1), 1–6.

Gorini, A., Gaggioli, A., Vigna, C., & Riva, G. (2008). A second life for e-health: Prospects for the use of 3-D virtual worlds in clinical psychology. *Journal of Medical Internet Research, 10*(3), e21. doi:10.2196/jmir.1029

Harder, B. N. (2010). Use of simulation in teaching and learning in health sciences: A systematic review. *The Journal of Nursing Education*, *49*(1), 23. doi:10.3928/01484834-20090828-08

Health Level Seven International. (2010). *Health Level Seven International* [Web page]. Retrieved on 1st July 2010, from http://www.hl7.org

Holloway, D. (2009). Interview – DeeAnna Nagel and Kate Anthony. Online Therapy Institute. *The Metaverse Journal*. Retrieved July 1st 2010, from http://www.metaversejournal.com /2009/03/30/ interview-deeanna-nagel-and-kate-anthony-online-therapy-institute/.

Holloway, D. (2010). ME/CFS Support in Second Life. *Metaverse Health*. Retrieved July 1st 2010, from http://www.metaversehealth.com /2010/03/ me-cfs-support-in-second-life/

Hughes, I. (2009). We have all the pieces - Unity3d, OpenSim, Evolver, Smartfox. *Life At The Feeding Edge*. Retrieved July 4th 2010 from http://www. feedingedge.co.uk /blog/2009/12/15/ we-have-all-the-pieces-unity3d-opensim-evolver-smartfox/

Imperial College London. (2010). *Medical media and design laboratory (MMDL)*. Retrieved 15th June 2010, from http://www1.imperial.ac.uk/ medicine/research/researchthemes /healthtechnologies/ simulation/mmdl/

Jeffries, P. R. (2005). A framework for designing, implementing, and evaluating simulations used as teaching strategies in nursing. *Nursing Education Perspectives*, *26*(2), 96–103.

Kancherla, A., Rolland, J., Wright, D., & Burdea, G. (1995). A novel virtual reality tool for teaching dynamic 3D anatomy. In *Proceedings of Computer Vision, Virtual Reality, and Robotics in Medicine '95* (CVRMed '95).

Kinross, J. M., Lee, H., Patel, V., Chan, M., Das, A., & Miles, K. … Darzi, A (2009). *Virtual worlds are a novel interdisciplinary platform for medical device training*. In Society of American Gastrointestinal and Endoscopic Surgeons Annual Meeting. Phoenix, Arizona, USA.

Leong, J. J., Kinross, J., Taylor, D., & Purkayastha, S. (2008). Surgeons have held conferences in Second Life. *British Medical Journal*, *337*(2), 683. doi:10.1136/bmj.a683

Lin, H. F., & Lee, G. G. (2006). Determinants of success for online communities: An empirical study. *Behaviour & Information Technology*, *25*(6), 479–488. doi:10.1080/01449290500330422

Lofgren, E. T., & Fefferman, N. H. (2007). The untapped potential of virtual game worlds to shed light on real world epidemics. *The Lancet Infectious Diseases*, *7*(9), 625–629. doi:10.1016/ S1473-3099(07)70212-8

Merians, A. S., Jack, D., Boian, R., Tremaine, M., Burdea, G. C., & Adamovich, S. V. (2002). Virtual reality-augmented rehabilitation for patients following stroke. *Physical Therapy*, *82*(9), 898–915.

Portnoy, D., Smoak, N., & Marsh, K. (2010). Perceiving interpersonally-mediated risk in virtual environments. *Virtual Reality (Waltham Cross)*, *14*(1), 67–76. doi:10.1007/s10055-009-0120-7

Rice, J. W. (2007). New media resistance: Barriers to implementation of computer video games in the classroom. *Journal of Educational Multimedia and Hypermedia*, *16*(3), 249–261.

Saposnik, G., Teasell, R., Mamdani, M., Hall, J., McIlroy, W., & Cheung, D. (2010). Effectiveness of virtual reality using Wii gaming technology in stroke rehabilitation: A pilot randomized clinical trial and proof of principle. *Stroke*, *41*(7), 1477–1484. doi:10.1161/STROKEAHA.110.584979

Siddiqi, S., Mama, S., & Lee, R. E. (in press). Developing an obesity prevention intervention in networked virtual environments: The international health challenge in Second Life. *Journal of Virtual Worlds Research*.

Stroulia, E., Chodos, D., Boers, N. M., Huang, J., Gburzynski, P., & Nikolaidis, I. (2009). Software engineering for health education and care delivery systems: The smart condo project. *Proceedings of the 2009 ICSE Workshop on Software Engineering in Health Care*, (pp. 20-28).

Sturm, L. P., Windsor, J. A., Cosman, P. H., Cregan, P., Hewett, P. J., & Maddern, G. J. (2008). A systematic review of skills transfer after surgical simulation training. *Annals of Surgery, 248*(2), 166–179. doi:10.1097/SLA.0b013e318176bf24

Thompson, C. W., & Hagstrom, F. (2008). Modeling healthcare logistics in a virtual world. *IEEE Internet Computing, 12*(5), 100–104. doi:10.1109/MIC.2008.106

Wankel, C., & Kingsley, J. (2009). *Higher education in virtual worlds: Teaching and learning in Second Life*. United Kingdom: Emerald Group Publishing Limited.

Williams, D. (in press). The mapping principle, and a research framework for virtual worlds. *Communication Theory*.

Winter, M. (2010). *Second Life education in New Zealand: Evaluation research final report*. New Zealand: CORE Education. Retrieved 5th July 2010, from http://slenz.files.wordpress.com/2010/03/slenz-final-report-2_-080310cca.pdf

Wood, D. P., Wiederhold, B. K., & Spira, J. (2010). Lessons learned from 350 virtual reality sessions with warriors diagnosed with combat-related posttraumatic stress disorder. *Cyberpsychology, Behavior, and Social Networking, 13*(1), 3–11. doi:10.1089/cyber.2009.0396

ADDITIONAL READING

Banakou, D., & Chorianopoulos, K. (2010). The Effects of Avatars' Gender and Appearance on Social Behavior in Online 3D Virtual Worlds. *Journal of Virtual Worlds Research, 2*(5).

Beard, L., Wilson, K., Morra, D., & Keelan, J. (2009). A Survey of Health-Related Activities on Second Life. *Journal of Medical Internet Research, 11*(2), e17. doi:10.2196/jmir.1192

Bessière, K., Pressman, S., Kiesler, S., & Kraut, R. (2010). Effects of Internet Use on Health and Depression: A Longitudinal Study. *Journal of Medical Internet Research, 12*(1), e6. doi:10.2196/jmir.1149

Blascovich, J., Loomis, J., Beall, A. C., Swinth, K. R., Hoyt, C. L., & Bailenson, J. N. (2002). Immersive virtual environment technology as a methodological tool for social psychology. *Psychological Inquiry, 13*(2), 103–124. doi:10.1207/S15327965PLI1302_01

Boulos, M.N.K. (2010). *Networked social media in learning, teaching and research*.

Boulos, M. N. K., & Maramba, I. (2009). Pitfalls in 3-D Virtual Worlds Health Project Evaluations: The Trap of Drug-Trial-Style Media Comparative Studies. *Journal of Virtual Worlds Research, 2*(2).

Bush, H. (2009). Practice makes perfect. *Hospitals & Health Networks, 83*(3), 28.

Gonzalez, V. G. (2009). Towards a Virtual Doctor-Patient Relationship: Understanding Virtual Patients. *Journal of Virtual Worlds Research, 2*(2).

Haidar, E. (2009). Clinical Simulation: A Better Way of Learning? *Nursing Management, 16*(5), 22.

Kardong-Edgren, S. E., Starkweather, A. R., & Ward, L. D. (2008). The Integration of Simulation Into a Clinical Foundations of Nursing Course: Student and Faculty Perspectives. *International Journal of Nursing Education Scholarship, 5*(1), 1–16. doi:10.2202/1548-923X.1603

Parker, B. C., & Myrick, F. (2009). A Critical Examination of High-Fidelity Human Patient Simulation Within the Context of Nursing Pedagogy. *Nurse Education Today, 29*(3), 322. doi:10.1016/j.nedt.2008.10.012

Prentice, R. (2005). The Anatomy of a Surgical Simulation: The Mutual Articulation of Bodies In and Through the Machine. *Social Studies of Science, 35*(6), 837–866. doi:10.1177/0306312705053351

Riva, G., Raspelli, S., Algeri, D., Pallavicini, F., Gorini, A., Wiederhold, B. K., & Gaggioli, A. (2010). Interreality in Practice: Bridging Virtual and Real Worlds in the Treatment of Posttraumatic Stress Disorders. *Cyberpsychology, Behavior, and Social Networking, 13*(1), 55–65. doi:10.1089/cyber.2009.0320

Rizzo, A. A., Difede, J., Rothbaum, B. O., Johnston, S., McLay, R. N., & Reger, G. (2009). VR PTSD Exposure Therapy Results with Active Duty OIF/OEF Combatants. *Medicine Meets Virtual Reality 17. Studies in Health Technology and Informatics*, 277–282.

Stevens, J. E. (1995). The Growing Reality of Virtual Reality. *Bioscience, 45*(7), 435–439. doi:10.2307/1312785

University of Plymouth. Presentation, accessed 2nd July 2010 at http://www.slideshare.net/ sl.medic/networked-social-media-in-learning-teaching-and-research

Waxman, K. T. (2010). The Development of Evidence-Based Clinical Simulation Scenarios: Guidelines for Nurse Educators. *The Journal of Nursing Education, 49*(1), 29. doi:10.3928/01484834-20090916-07

Wiecha, J., Heyden, R., Sternthal, E., & Merialdi, M. (2010). Learning in a Virtual World: Experience with Using Second Life for Medical Education. *Journal of Medical Internet Research, 12*(1), e1. doi:10.2196/jmir.1337

Windsor, J. A. (2009). Role of Simulation in Surgical Education and Training. *ANZ Journal of Surgery, 79*(3), 127–132. doi:10.1111/j.1445-2197.2008.04829.x

Woodruff, S. I., Edwards, C. C., Conway, T. L., & Elliott, S. P. (2001). Pilot Test of an Internet Virtual World Chat Room for Rural Teen Smokers. *The Journal of Adolescent Health, 29*(4), 239–243. doi:10.1016/S1054-139X(01)00262-2

KEY TERMS AND DEFINITIONS

OpenSim: an open-source virtual world platform loosely based on the Second Life architecture.

Second Life: a virtual world in existence since 2002 which allows creation of unique content that remains the intellectual property of the creator.

Simulation: the utilisation of methods to replicate real clinical situations without causing harm.

Unity3D: A multi-platform game development tool with relatively simple content creations options and the ability to create web-based virtual worlds.

Virtual World: a computer-based simulated environment, within which users can interact and create objects.

Chapter 18

Virtual Worlds and Behavioral Change:
Overcoming Time/ Space Constraints and Exploring Anonymity to Overcome Social Stigma in the Case of Substance Abuse

Ana Boa-Ventura
University of Texas at Austin, USA

ABSTRACT

This chapter discusses how virtual worlds (VWs) have been and are being used for the prevention and treatment of addictive behaviors related to substance abuse. The substances covered are tobacco, alcohol, and illegal drugs. By definition, physical health concerns the body but there is an indisputable physiological component to mental health (for example, vitamin D is related to depression). I suggest that embodiment – as a distinctive characteristic of VWs when compared to other virtual spaces (e.g.: chatrooms) - should present great potential for health professionals when considering VWs for the design of prevention or treatment health programs. VWs free users of time and space constraints. This further justifies the use of VWs as alternative or complementing spaces of intervention. The anonymity of these environments reinforces this idea, as addictions that were socially acceptable just a few years ago have become socially stigmatizing (e.g.: smoking). In the case of virtual worlds such as Second Life, anonymity is combined with embodiment, and this compounded effect, which is anything but simple, is particularly important for health professionals and health promotion advocates interested in exploring the use of virtual worlds in the treatment of substance abuse.

DOI: 10.4018/978-1-60960-854-5.ch018

CHAPTER'S ORGANIZATION AND SCOPE

Given the centrality of the 'body' in VWs, section 1 focuses on embodiment by approaching the topic under five different spotlights offered by five different disciplines that have 'embodiment' as a key topic: Feminist and Gender Studies, Ethics and Moral Philosophy, Psychology, Film studies and Health.

Sections 2 offers some background information on addictive behavior and provides a framework for the study of addictive behavior related to substance abuse in the field of Health. Prevention and treatment in this field make use of practices that are evidence based. Some of these practices include social support – such as face-to-face meetings - and access to information of medical authority. These will be summarized in that section.

Section 3 discusses VW-assisted health interventions for the treatment of substance abuse. For this chapter, I am considering alcohol, tobacco and illegal drugs. This overview, based on type of substance abuse, underlines not only the commonalities but also the specificities across types of substance abuse. It does so by presenting them as both challenges and opportunities for VW- based health interventions, whether they are geared to prevention or treatment.

Section 4 presents a proof-of-concept that I have developed and designed: the 'biographic space'. It is a storytelling-based space in Second Life (SL) that explores the media richness of VWs to represent the state of change of the user of that space in her struggle against addiction.

These are the sections covered by this chapter.

When discussing vast topics such as this one and presenting it to a community that is not necessarily in the field of Health, it is equally important to say what a chapter does not cover. Hence, in the next paragraph, I justify why some areas are not within the scope of the discussion.

An important part of publications in the area of Health and virtual worlds has been devoted to Education and the use of virtual worlds for higher education in Health. Although the importance of this topic is irrefutable, this chapter is not devoted to the use of VWs for the education and training of professionals and students in the field of Health in general or of addictive behavior in particular.

Although computers can cause addiction, this chapter is not about the so called 'electronically-induced addictions' such as compulsive Internet use (including time spent in virtual worlds), computer game playing, or online gambling. In fact, it should be noted than in clinical settings, health professionals are skeptical about using the term 'addiction' to these cases, and prefer 'process addiction' to designate dependencies to processes - as opposed to dependencies to substances (Brenner, 1998).

TERMINOLOGY USED

Central to this chapter are notions of two very different disciplines: virtual worlds on one hand and substance abuse, on the other. So, I must clarify the terminology pertaining to both, very distinct, fields, before proceeding any further.

The term 'substance abuse' is used in this chapter as a synonym of a pattern of harmful use of any substance, whether natural or chemically prepared, for the purpose of altering one's mood. Drugs are the main type of substance that drive abuse for purposes of mood alteration (Roberts & Koob, 1997). For purposes of this chapter, I will consider patterns of harmful use, for mood alteration, of alcohol, nicotine and illegal drugs.

For the term ' virtual world', this chapter adopts Richard Bartle's definition (2003) in his "Designing Virtual Worlds", which is an excellent reference book on virtual worlds. Bartle makes a clear distinction between real, imaginary and virtual by noting that virtual is all that is not while having the effect or form of that which is. Bartle goes on to stress that since virtual worlds simulate environments, when different individuals can simultaneously affect the environment, the world is known as being a 'multiuser environment'; and that the environment, however, continues to exist independently of being visited / occupied by individuals and so, and in most cases, it develops internally regardless of visitors and occupants. Bartle calls this property the 'persistence' of virtual worlds.

Bartle points out other features that most virtual worlds share: (1) a physics that is particular to the world (automated rules that allow users to impact the world); (2) interaction of individuals with the environment and other users of the environment is channeled through a character or representation of the self; (3) feedback to actions in the world takes place almost instantaneously. Furthermore the word is shared and (at least to some extent) persistent.

According to this definition, a strategic war game, for example, would not classify as virtual world since the user is not mapped onto a single avatar.

I would add, for further clarification, a few more lines on self-representation in VWs, multiusage and 'game quality' of a VW:

Self-representation - Although the term 'virtual world' is used today to designate 3D virtual environments, not all virtual worlds have anthropomorphic (or even graphic) depictions of users as avatars. The avatar is the proxy of a user operating in a virtual 3D world. However, this proxy may be an abstract depiction, or for instance, a sound.

Multiusage - When VWs allow for multiple users and the content and engagement is similar to those of a game, these worlds may be called MMORPGs (massively multiplayer online role playing games).

'Game quality' of a VW - There has been a lot of discussion on whether popular VWs such as Second Life can be called a game, let alone a MMORPG. Whether to consider a VW a game is largely a function of the specific context of use and the persuasive strategies used by its creators to keep users engaged and interacting. For purposes of this chapter I will not delve into those fine distinctions. In line with Bartle's definition, and in this chapter, a VW will not be considered a game unless there is a clear underlying script or at least an objective laid out as a sequence of actions the user must take when interacting with the environment.

I will use 'avatars', 'residents, 'members' or 'citizens' to designate users of a VW. These terms are not innocuous in terms of branding strategies on behalf of the VW developers. The Linden Labs, for example, label their Second Life members of 'residents' arguably to promote loyalty among their pool of users with a paid membership.

Finally, and in section 4, I use the term 'self-organized communities' to designate spontaneously formed groups of individuals whose reason for organization and whose agenda are 'born' in the virtual environment and not in real life. As opposed to federal agencies, NGOs and corporate organizations that exist in real life and have a presence in one or more VWs, then, self-organized communities do not have a preexisting formal organization in real life. However, it is not uncommon that the regularity and / or intensity of work in the VW leads to the organization expanding to real life as well.

1. THE IMPORTANCE OF EMBODIMENT IN VIRTUAL WORLDS

As mentioned in the Terminology section, though virtual worlds are often used as a synonym of 3D virtual worlds, not all virtual environments include a user representation in the form of an avatar. The embodiment may be achieved in other more subtle and abstract ways, such as a proxy: a visual (or aural) minimal / abstract representation that simply signals tele-presence. Often, that representation is, however, a full avatar (a visual representation of the self), built according to the sophistication and customization allowed by specific virtual world considered. I believe this is important to clarify as 'embodiment' is, as I defend elsewhere (Boa-Ventura & Saboga-Nunes, 2010), an important quality of digital environments used in Health in general, and in the treatment of addictive behaviors related to substance abuse in particular.

Having an avatar representation in a world such as Second Life means that I can coincide in space and time with other people who are also embodied through their avatars in the same space and time that I am visiting. This opens up interesting discussion on the feeling of community, as it relates to the treatment of substance abuse and I will discuss it after summarizing next a number of methodological approaches to the body.

Feminist and Gender Studies

Feminist and gender studies have played a key role in emphasizing the role of embodiment in cyberspace (Haraway, 1994). Indeed, feminist theory is particularly well suited to discuss and understand embodiment (Meynell, 2009). I think this credit is due because, like Sherry Turkle and Char Davies, I believe that the body occupies a central position in VWs... a position that, I add, must be taken seriously in any VW-mediated health intervention. The reputed invisibility online as well as what Hansen called the "decoupling identity from any analogical relation to the visible body" (Hansen, 2006: 145) deserves some justified skepticism today, especially when taken as one step towards an idealized race and gender neutral 'environment'. Increasingly graphic, with high audio and video quality, today's virtual worlds put embodiment back in

the center of the real-virtual diode. Although this is central to VWs- assisted health interventions, this introduces a series of considerations, not the least of which being the continuation of gender and race discrimination in the virtual world. Furthermore, the proxy representation is synonym with over-simplification and reduction, which promotes traditional stereotypes.

Ethics and Moral Philosophy

Philosophers including those in the field of Ethics and Moral discuss embodiment in cyberspace - or cyborgisation - as the undermining of the power of the body by the Internet. However, more recently. prominent scholars in this field argue for the importance of reclaiming this body agency, which they see as an anchor for values. Steve Matthews (2008) notes that "if IT affects the way others see me, especially in virtue of the ways it alerts various modes of social communication, then it will come to affect the way I see myself". (144) The use of prosthetic enhancement along the lines of Stelarc's work has been the subject of heated discussion in the realm of Ethics. One school of thought is the transhumanist school, which defends prosthetics on the basis of its power to surpass human limitations (from Newtonian limits like speed to more human limitations such as health deterioration and age). Opponents to transhumanism describe what they believe to be biases propelling the development and acceptance of such technologies. Namely, non- transhumanists see a bias towards functionality and efficiency that, they claim, may compel assent to a view of human people de-emphasizing what they consider to be humanity's and personhood's defining characteristics, in favor of a different sort of 'values': upgrades, versions, and utility.

Psychology

A number of scholars have been looking at to what extent can findings of social interaction in the read world propagate to virtual worlds, given the virtual representation of the self (through an avatar). Gaze, attractiveness and interpersonal distance are some of the attributes that have been studied in virtual worlds with the aim of comparing how they play out in virtual settings, when compared to real world.

Yee and Bailenson (2007) used de-individualization and self- perception theory (Bem, 1972), to conduct a study where they concluded that virtual reality users may adjust their identity to that of their avatars rather than the more expected opposite phenomenon. This is known as the Proteus effect. The same authors note that " in line with self-perception theory, [users in online environments] conform to the behavior that they believe others would expect them to have" (p. 274). In their study avatar's height and attractiveness were the two physical features of the avatar (features of the virtual embodiment) relevant in the study. Overall, more attractive avatars, as well as (on a separate study) taller avatars positively affected other avatars' trust and willingness to become intimate. This is line with studies in classical psychology on attractiveness (see, for instance Dion, Berscheid, & Walster, 1972). In Proteus Effect research, avatars' interactions with other avatars are influenced by their own and other avatars' physical characteristics (Dean, Cook, Keating & Murphy, 2009).

Fox and Bailenson (2009) found that humans' real world behavior is influenced by their own self-representing avatars' behavior. In their experiment, participants who watched their self-representing avatars (which were designed to mimic to an extent their real physical characteristics) being physically active (such as running on a treadmill) were more prone to engage in exercise in the next 24 hours than those participants who watched an avatar doing nothing or a non self-representing avatar doing exercise.

In particular, Bailenson et al (2003) concluded that in their experiment on behavioral and emotional reactions to an avatar's personal space invasion and body space "participants exhibited patterns of interpersonal distance behavior with respect to virtual humans similar to that which decades of research using actual humans have demonstrated" (831)

In a way, these studies in Psychology – notably those conducted by Yee and Bailenson (2007) and Bailenson et al (2003) - are at the basis of any validation of health interventions in Second Life as they report conclusions of experiments that suggest that healthy behaviors evidenced by avatars in virtual worlds may affect healthy behaviors in real life.

Film Studies

Several film theorists have discussed Dziga Vertov's kino-eye in light of current virtual worlds. Landay, for example contextualizes this new virtual kino-eye within well grounded film theories of gaze and spectatorship such as Christian Metz, Anne Friedberg and Vivian Sobchack (Landay, 2009). Among the insights brought by these theorists, one is particularly relevant to a discussion of VWs and embodiment: Francesco Casetti's idea that cinema at the cutting edge (like IMAX or 2001 Space Odyssey) relates not to 'more than movies' (as IMAX theaters advertise themselves) but rather to the return to the real drive of 'going to the movies', whereby the apparatus acts like a "snare ready to capture whoever enters its radius of activity" (Casetti, 1998:8-9). Different VWs allow for different default camera positions. VWs may offer different gazes, depending on the number of camera views allowed in world. For example, in SL the default camera view is positioned from behind the avatar's head while in other VWs, the default view maybe a bird's eye view of the avatar or its front view.

Health

In the field of Health, 'embodiment' in online environments is arguably a problem of trust/

reputation. If one cannot meet the medical care or health information provider face-to-face or, worse, if these specialists are embodied in what seem to be little more than on-screen animated cartoons, can one trust the medical authority of the information received? In the specific case of mental health embodiment as in a having agency over a representation of my real body may be an empowering process. Many have reported on the liberating effect of the use of Second Life by physically impaired individuals. Many scholars in the field see empowerment as a goal for therapy (Tomm, 1987; Anderson & Goolishian, 1988; Gergen, 1994).

However, the idea of accessing an environment that allows for the embodiment of both patients and care provider / health professional / health information provider is complicated by regulations such as HIPA (Health Information Privacy Protection Act) in the US. These regulations need to be in place to ensure that personal medical information is not accessed by others (or, in the case where there is an unintentional public disclosure, that release of information is not sanctioned by universities or federal agencies).

The article 'Does this avatar make me look fat?' (Dean et al, 2009) was a groundbreaking study conducted by a team of the NGO 'RTI International' (based at the Triangle Research Park, North Carolina) on the impact that the virtual representation of the self - the avatar – has on the real self. These findings - along with those of earlier studies in Psychology mentioned above (Bailenson et al, 2005; 2007; Fox & Bailenson, 2009) may have a tremendous impact in the analysis of VWs potential in behavioral change, as they suggest that by reaching virtual patients (avatars), health interventions can actually lead to behavioral change in the real life patients / individuals.

2. FUNDAMENTALS OF SUBSTANCE ABUSE AND ADDICTIVE BEHAVIOR

The Brain's Reward Circuit and Substance Use and Abuse

The use of certain substances – such as nicotine, alcohol and illegal drugs such as marijuana – often leads to addiction and psychological dependency. This is, in fact, what justifies the change from substance use to substance abuse. The use becomes abuse because drugs increase the concentration of dopamine in the brain's reward circuit. This reward circuit ultimately aims at survival. Dopamine is the chemical involved with sex drive and satisfying hunger (Kelley, 2002).

When one craves for a specific food and one finally consumes it, there is a feeling of pleasure, which is channeled via a surge of dopamine. Substances like nicotine and heroin entail an abnormal surge of dopamine and because the brain remembers that surge, it wants to experience it again, and again (and yet again).

In his or her attempts to quit tobacco, there is, in the smokers' brain, a battle between the limbic system (primitive brain) and the part of the brain that controls rational thought.

To increase the problem, abnormal surges of dopamine change the way in which dopamine receptors normally work. By becoming less receptive to the effects of the body's natural dopamine, the ability to experience pleasure decreases. Use therefore may become abuse. This is the nature of the cycle of addiction – a body that is de-sensitized to normal levels of dopamine and needs ever-increasing exposure to drugs (whether smoking, drinking or shooting intravenous drugs) to experience the same amount of pleasure that in the beginning of the process, a single cigarette, glass of alcohol or injection would impart (Volkow, 2009).

Factors with Positive Impact in Traditional (not Computer-Supported) Interventions for the Treatment of Addictive Behavior on the Basis of Substance Abuse

A number of randomized clinical trials (RCTs) have shown that Internet-based treatment is as effective as face-to-face treatment (and more effective than no-treatment). However, research has focused more on anxiety and mood disorders, (burn-out, panic, depression, headache, insomnia) than substance abuse (where obesity seems to be the most common type of behavioral disorder studied). In this section I will cover those factors that health professionals have been integrating in the design of interventions for the treatment of substance abuse, in traditional settings (in other words: in non-computing settings). In fact, a number of factors may positively impact treatment by hindering the development of substance abuse. The impact of these factors may vary with age group, gender and type of care (e.g.: managed cared – individuals who are appointed by the court of law to enlist a rehabilitation program - as opposed to self-appointed care).

Social Support

Studies on the impact of social support in the treatment of substance abuse present mixed results. That impact may vary with factors such as gender and age. For instance, Richter, Brown & Mott (1991) conducted a longitudinal study to understand how social support affected the outcome following adolescent chemical dependency treatment. They concluded that social support was in fact important and that self-esteem was also a key post-treatment factor. Other studies have examined how general social support during adolescence provide a significant amelioration of all seven young-adult problem areas: health problems, psychosomatic symptoms, emotional distress, interpersonal relationships, family prob-

lems, loneliness in romantic relationships, and self-derogation (Newcomb & Bentler, 1988). In a different study aimed at a higher age group, and specifically on tobacco, results were mixed regarding the dyadic efficacy in partnered smokers indicating that partners' mutual support does not necessarily translate in higher quit rates (Sterba, Rabius, Villars, Wiatrek & McAllister, 2010).

Behavioral Counseling

There seems to be more of an agreement on the impact of this factor than on social support. Access to behavioral counseling, which includes access to information and resources such as telephone counseling and self-help materials, has a positive impact in overcoming addiction to alcohol, nicotine and illegal drugs (Whitlock, Polen, Green, Orleans & Klein, 2008).

Access to Information

While access to information can be part of behavioral counseling, it has a value on its own. Having access to information in the local hospitals r community centers positively impacts treatment of substance abuse (V. Rabius, personal communication, September 4, 2010).

Screening at Intake

Studies suggest that a large number of individuals who are admitted to treatment of substance abuse do not return to begin the program. The specific case of managed care has deserved studies in this area and they show that there seem to be differences associated with the type of dependency: individuals dependent on alcohol only have a higher probability of retuning to initiate treatment than those who are drug-dependent. Screening at intake has been employed to assess each individual context (work-place pressures as well as the patient's perception of the importance of treatment) and to that extent be a good indicator of prevision to starting treatment (Weisner, Mertens, Tam & Moore, 2001).

The screening at intake may also include the measurement of the addict's self-efficacy, a term coined by Albert Bandura (1997) to signify one's confidence in quitting the addictive behavior (in the context of this chapter that behavior is smoking, alcohol drinking and the intake of illegal drugs).

3. VW-ASSISTED HEALTH INTERVENTIONS FOR THE TREATMENT OF SUBSTANCE ABUSE

Factors Hindering the Generalized, Systematic Use of VWs in a Near Future in Health Interventions for the Treatment of Substance Abuse

Inclusiveness

Those of us who were early adopters of virtual worlds may feel compelled to see in them the ultimate *panacea*. However, users of virtual worlds are still a minority of the world population due to a number of factors not the least of which being how resource- demanding VWs are on the machines that run them. The number of VW users was estimated at .3% in 2008 and has been estimated as being 80% of active Internet users in 2011 (Gartner Inc, 2007). However, it is reasonable to believe that those who have the easiest and fastest access to VWs are not the gross of the priority target population in most national healthcare programs, and will not be so for several decades to come. This is a real hindrance when considering any health intervention program. As a case in point, MedicAid is a large program in the US to provide medical care to households that would otherwise have trouble accessing that aid (U.S. Department of Health & Human Services – Center for Medicare and MedicAid Services, 2009). Similar programs exist all over

the world, which help address health disparities in low income households. Unfortunately virtual worlds are resource intensive and to this date, worlds such as Second Life still impose certain hardware specifications that (still) translate to computer equipment at a cost that not anyone can afford (fast processors, up-to-date video cards). Furthermore, most worlds also require fast Internet connections and often, a monthly membership fee. All this means that the population that has access to the right equipment and the right Internet speed to interact with virtual worlds is not the same that is considered - in the US and in many other countries - as the priority population where to focus.

Learning Curve

Having enough skills in Second Life to navigate (walk, fl, communicate through voice, text and body gesture) follows a steep learning curve, which can be ruthless in the case of groups that have not been exposed to VWs. Furthermore, solving technological problems may get in the way of addressing the real, addiction, problems. Many scholars have noted this problem which is not particular to the study of addiction but that may permeate other areas (See, for example on a study about self-esteem among a Second Life in World group of women with disabilities, Nosek, Whelen, Hughes, Porcher, Davidson & Nosek, 2010).

Demographic Bias

The compounded effect of the two previous items-inclusiveness and learning curve – inexorably lead to a demographic bias, which is at odds with the ethical (and arguably utopian) principle that everyone should have the same access to health resources. I consider it as an independent factor hindering the wide adoption of VWs in the treatment of substance abuse as there may be many other factors (whose impact has not been sufficiently studied) such as age, average annual income and prior exposure to games, leading to a demographic bias in the use of VWs for the treatment of substance abuse.

Metrics

While VWs allow for the quantification of parameters that may be pertinent in VW-assisted health interventions, there are problems of human subject consent that can be more complex than in more traditional research settings. Furthermore, and though the interaction with the environment can be measured, some parameters may require costly and/or complex instruments of measurement that the health professional may not be equipped to tackle. An example is the systematic measurement of interpersonal distances among a support group, which is nothing but a simple parameter to measure in a world such as SL.

Researchers are concerned over the lack of access to good, manageable, quantitative and qualitative data, especially if that access is further complicated by the proprietary nature of the VW at hand.

Virtual Worlds with a Representation in Health Interventions

Virtual worlds that have been studied in relation to their potential in health issues include Second Life, Kaneva, There and IMVU (Norris, 2009). In addition, given the popularity of Second Life, studies conducted in this environment tackle a wide range of areas and methodologies. Good examples of this diversity of approaches are the celebration of The Worlds Aid's Day at Karuna's island on December first, and the pursuit of AA meetings at many SL sims. This is how a recovered alcoholic describes how anyone can seek help in the form of an AA support group in SL:

"To set up a 12 step meeting.

Figure out a weekly time that suits you.

Then IM Spike Willard to request a schedule weekly meeting.

That's it. Job done."

Of all VWs, Second Life is probably the best known. It claims 14 million registered accounts and many islands that have been occupied by colleges and universities, federal agencies and corporations. The average age of a Second Life resident is 35 and edges upward, showing the same demographics trend as Facebook and MySpace.

What virtual worlds have of unique is that they offer health professionals, practitioners and psychologists alike, an environment that allows the modeling of health behaviors in a way that can be highly immersive and reactive (because it reacts to actions in the environment).

Virtual Reality: Focus on Perceptual Tricking and Impact on Health Interventions

I will open this section by addressing not a virtual world per se but a technology that is (or may be) at the basis of virtual environments – Virtual Reality (VR). I say "may" because as Alan Craig and other experts in the field have stressed, there is no virtual reality in Second Life and similar VWs. The latter have evolved independently of the first, cumbersome, virtual reality simulators. Rather than acting on the perceptual system to trick it into experiencing an environment through immersion, they convey that immersive experience through mentally and emotionally engaging content.

Virtual reality has been used in behavioral change notably for the treatment of phobias from the first groundbreaking report demonstrating the efficacy of immersive computer-generated virtual reality (VR) and mixed reality for the treatment of arachnophobia (Carlin, Hoffman & Weghorst, 1997) to more recent studies on virtual reality exposure for the treatment of post-traumatic stress disorders experiences such as those following

9/11 (e.g.: Freedman, Hoffman, Garcia-Palacios, Weiss, Avitzour & Josman, 2010)

Virtual reality has been most used in health interventions aiming at the treatment of phobias. However, the fact that VR immersion is achieved through the compounded effect of computer graphics and peripheral devices allows a richness of input channels and consequently great potential to study combined stimuli in substance abuse (Rothbaum, Hodges, Ready, Graap, & Alarcon, 2001).

One particularly important area has been drug craving research (Bordnick et al, 2004). The analysis of drug triggers and stimuli is known as 'cue reactivity'. One caveat of traditional cue reactivity techniques is the lack of standardization. Techniques using VR cue reactivity extend previous research by offering a controlled setting for the analysis of reactions to drug cues.

In sum, virtual reality allows to explore cue exposure methods since exposure to stimuli VR is computer-controlled. Hence, health interventions using VR in the field of substance abuse have proved particularly helpful in craving research as assessments of reactivity to stimuli can be done in real time, as opposed to traditional settings.

Virtual reality interventions making use of virtual reality have proved effective in a number of RCTs for certain phobias. The limited type of psychosomatic problems that computers in general and virtual reality environments in particular have covered leads many sociologists to rule out large-scale use of computers for therapy and assessment in the near future (Emmelkamp, 2005)

Virtual reality has been used in the facilitation of emotional processing in the treatment of different disorders such as phobias (Rothbaum et al, 1995), complicated grief (Botella et al, 2008) and fear of flying (Rothbaum et al, 2000). In many cases there is some type of script or at least an activity that the patient should perform. To this extent, some of the applications using virtual reality in exposure therapy explore also computer games. This fusion of games and virtual reality has been used in the treatment of disorders such

as the fear of driving following a motor vehicle accident (Walshe et al, 2003)

4. PROOF-OF CONCEPT: 'BIOGRAPHIC SPACE', A STORYTELLING-BASED WATI (WEB-ASSISTED TOBACCO INTERVENTION) USING SECOND LIFE

I am proposing a model that I call 'biographic space', which embeds the successive stages that a smoker may go through during the attempt to quit smoking. I consider the type of intervention that this proof-of-concept as part of the WATIs since these can be defined as any web assisted health interventions for the treatment of tobacco and nicotine dependency.

The stages referred above, and embedded in the model include emotionally loaded aspects such as deciding to quit and post cessation withdrawal. The design of this space is informed by storytelling, a topic of my practice research, and explores the so called 'rich media' affordances of virtual environments as well as the possibility of integration (or mashing) different media in and with Second Life.

These 'biographic spaces' are spaces in Second Life (though there is no reason why they could not be implemented in other VWs), that can be explored by smokers anytime / anywhere internet access is available, and provide information to assist smokers wanting to quit. The information acquired that way is media-rich and addresses primarily the emotional component of the quitting process.

The space will enable the visitor to experience the successive stages of the quitting process by telling the life of a fictional character through the architectural space and the objects in that space. I am modeling these stages based on Prochaska and DiClemente's Stages of Change Model (1982). The stages are pre-contemplation, contemplation,

Figure 1.

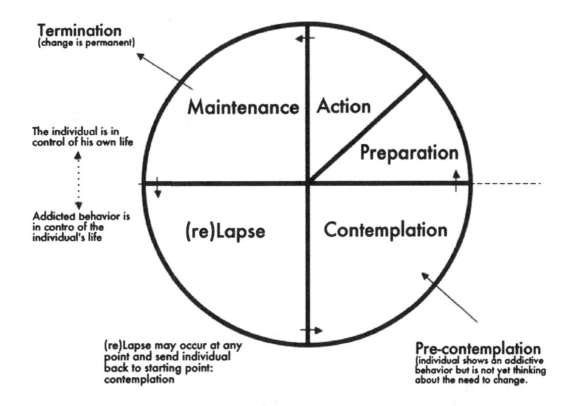

preparation, action and maintenance, and relapses may send the individual back to the contemplation stage (See Figure 1).

The visitor's state in the transtheoretical model is assessed through a survey that assigns her a stage. The house (intimate space) inhabited by the fictional character has a series of personal records and memories that reflect the stage identified for the user as a result of the answers to the survey. Under a narrative theory framework, this 'biographic space' is a diegetic one, insofar as situations and events are recounted, but has some mimetic aspects, to the extent that the space is 'experienced' in the first person, and thought this first person experience in channeled through an avatar.

The user can access the biographic space at any time and engage the life of the fictional character at the very user's own stage of behavioral change (including relapse) (See Figure 2). The scripted environment conveys the fictional character's life during his/her attempt to quit smoking through voice, written text, still images and movie clips – all of these media channels document the emotional stages experienced during a typical attempt to quit smoking.

For the concept of this storytelling model I strongly inspired by the first computer game blockbuster: Myst. In it, the technological restrictions at the time were partially responsible for a whimsical environment, where characters were not represented *per se*, but through objects evocative of their personalities and actions (Cyan, 1993).

The proof-of-concept explores two features of Second Life that I deem key to the support

Figure 2.

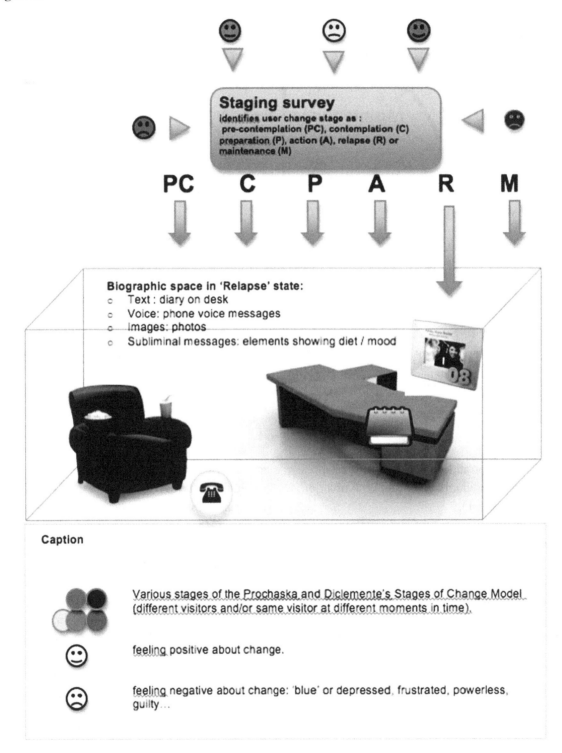

of addictive behavior change – the 'anywhere / anytime' support and media richness.

Users register to enter the space. The registration originates unique IDs so that users' interactions with objects, and number / duration of visits can be recorded using tools for metrics available in SL. The state of change according to the transtheoretical model, which was determined by the staging algorithm is recorded for each user and later part of a triangulation process.

CONCLUSION

In this chapter I have provided an overview of existing VWs assisted interventions for behavioral change associated with three types of addictive substances: tobacco, alcohol, and illegal drugs. The examples shown illustrate the potential that VWs have in the fighting addictions that are socially damaging, by offering an anonymous platform for meetings, especially important in the case of social stigma (that often accompanies addictions), and by offering it 24 h and arguably from any place (work or home). I have noted that the demographics targeted by most national Health programs tackling socially damaging addictions do not coincide with the demographics of use of virtual worlds, and this disparity increases with the sophistication of the platform in question. To this extent, and not unlike other areas (augmented reality for instance) there seem to be two polarized tendencies: towards the ease of use, and unobtrusive technology on one end and complex, hardware intense platforms, on the other. Geopositioning, by promoting the juxtaposition of real and virtual spaces, may promote simplicity (small, mobile) over complexity (large, cumbersome), but there will always be a place – notably in R&D whether led by universities or large corporations – for resource-demanding solutions that will not be within the layman's reach in any near future. Health practitioners should engage in this scenario in a very near future to ensure that their

voice is heard in discussion topics as important as credibility, accountability and metrics in VW supported health interventions for the treatment of substance abuse.

REFERENCES

Anonymous. (2008, November). *RE: Attending AA meetings in Second Life* [Web log post]. Retrieved from http://anon-recovery-archive.blogspot.com/

Bandura, A. (1971). *Social foundations of thought and action*. Englewood Cliffs, NJ.

Bartle, R. (2003). *Designing virtual worlds*. Berkeley, CA: New Riders.

Bem, D. J. (1972). Self-perception theory. In L. Berkowitz (Ed.), *Advances in Experimental Social Psychology, 6*, 1-62. New York, NY: Academic Press.

Boa-Ventura, A., & Saboga-Nunes, L. (2010). Biographic spaces: A personalized smoking cessation intervention in Second Life. In De Bra, P., Kobsa, A., & Chin, D. (Eds.), *User modeling, adaptation, and personalization. Lecture Notes in Computer Science, 6075*. Berlin, Germany: Springer. doi:10.1007/978-3-642-13470-8_43

Bock, B. C., Graham, A. L., Sciamanna, C. N., Krishnamoorthy, J., Whiteley, J., & Carmona-Barros, R. (2004). Smoking cessation treatment on the Internet: Content, quality, and usability. *Nicotine & Tobacco Research, 6*(2), 207–219. doi:10.1080/14622200410001676332

Bordnick, P., Graap, K., Copp, H., Brooks, J., Ferrer, M., & Logue, B. (2004). Utilizing virtual reality to standardize nicotine craving research: A pilot study. *Addictive Behaviors, 29*, 1889–1894. doi:10.1016/j.addbeh.2004.06.008

Botella, C., Osma, J., García Palacios, A., Guillén, V., & Baños, R. (2008). Treatment of complicated grief using virtual reality: A case report. *Death Studies, 32*(7), 674–692. doi:10.1080/07481180802231319

Brenner, V. (1998, January). *An initial report on the online assessment of Internet addiction: The first 30 days of the Internet usage survey.* Retrieved from http://www.ccsnet.com/prep/pap/pap8b/638b012p.txt

Carlin, A. S., Hoffman, H. G., & Weghorst, S. (1997). Virtual reality and tactile augmentation in the treatment of spider phobia: a case report. *Behaviour Research and Therapy, 35*(2), 153–158. doi:10.1016/S0005-7967(96)00085-X

Casetti, F. (1998). *Inside the gaze: The fiction film and its spectator* (pp. 8–9). Bloomington, IN: Indiana UP.

Cyan. (1993). *Myst.* Brøderbund.

Dean, E., Cook, S., Keating, M., & Murphy, J. (2009). Does this avatar make me look fat? Obesity and interviewing in Second Life. *Journal of Virtual Worlds Research, 2*(2). Retrieved August 12, 2010, from https://journals.tdl.org/jvwr/article/view/621/495

Dion, K., Berscheid, E., & Walster, E. (1972). What is beautiful is good. *Journal of Personality and Social Psychology, 24*(3), 285–290. doi:10.1037/h0033731

Emmelkamp, P. M. G. (2005). Psychotherapy & pychosomatics. *Technological Innovations in Clinical Assessment and Psychotherapy, 74*(6), 55–65.

Filbey, F. M., Schacht, J. P., Myers, U. S., Chavez, R. S., & Hutchison, K. E. (2009). Marijuana craving in the brain. *Proceedings of the National Academy of Sciences of the United States of America, 106*(31), 13016–13021. doi:10.1073/pnas.0903863106

Freedman, S., Hoffman, H., Garcia-Palacios, A., Weiss, P., Avitzour, S., & Josman, N. (2010). Prolonged exposure and virtual reality–enhanced imaginal exposure for PTSD following a terrorist bulldozer attack: A case study. *Cyberpsychology, Behavior, and Social Networking, 13*(1), 95–101. doi:10.1089/cyber.2009.0271

Gartner, Inc. (2007). *Gartner says 80 percent of active Internet users will have a second life in the virtual world by the end of 2011.* Gartner Symposium ITxpo, Emerging Trends, April 24, 2007.

Gary, J., & Remolino, L. (2000). *Coping with loss and grief through on-line support groups.* ERIC Clearinghouse on Counseling and Student Services. Retrieved September 10, 2010 from http://www.mental-health-matters.com /index.php?view=article& catid=175%3Agrief-and-loss&id=932%3Acoping-with-loss-and-grief-through-online-support-groups&format=pdf&option=com_content&Itemid=1906

Hansen, M. (2006). *Bodies in code: Interfaces with digital media.* New York, NY & London, UK: Routledge.

Haraway, D. (1991). A cyborg manifesto: Science, technology, and socialist-feminism in the late twentieth century. In D. Haraway (Ed.), *Simians, cyborgs, and women: The reinvention of nature,* (pp. 149-181). London, UK: Free Association Books. Retrieved from http://www.stanford.edu/dept/ HPS/Haraway/CyborgManifesto.html

Health, A. I. S. (2008). *Presence in virtual worlds could help health plans achieve real-world behavior change.* Retrieved from http://www.aishealth.com/ Bnow/hbd082808.html

Imholz, S. (2008). The therapeutic stage encounters the virtual world. *Thinking Skills and Creativity, 3*(1), 47–52. doi:10.1016/j.tsc.2008.02.001

Join Together. (2008). *First major study of marijuana addiction underway.* Retrieved from http://www.jointogether.org /news/headlines/inthenews/2008/ first-major-study-of.html

Kelley, A. E., & Berridge, K. C. (2002). The neuroscience of natural rewards: relevance to addictive drugs. *The Journal of Neuroscience, 22,* 3306–3311.

Koster, R. (2007). *What is a virtual world?* Retrieved September 8, 2007, from http://www.raphkoster.com/2007/ 06/15/whatis-a-virtual-world/

Lri Landay, L. (2009). Virtual KinoEye: Kinetic camera, machinima, and virtual subjectivity in Second Life. *Media Studies, 2*(1).

Lustria, M. L., Cortese, J., Noar, S. M., & Glueckauf, R. L. (2009). Computer tailored health interventions delivered over the Web: Review and analysis of key components. *Patient Education and Counseling, 74,* 156–173. doi:10.1016/j.pec.2008.08.023

Marsen, S. (2008). Becoming more than human: Technology and the post-human condition introduction. *Journal of Evolution & Technology, 19*(1), 1–5.

Matthews, S. (2008). Identity and Information Technology. In Jeroen van den Hoven, M., & Weckert, J. (Eds.), *Philosophy and Information Technology.* Cambridge University Press.

Meynell, L. (2009). Minding bodies. In Campbell, S., Meynell, L., & Sherwin, S. (Eds.), *Embodiment and agency.* Pennsylvania State University Press.

Myung, S. K., McDonnell, D. D., Kazinets, G., Seo, H. G., & Moskowitz, J. M. (2009). Effects of Web- and computer-based smoking cessation programs: Meta-analysis of randomized controlled trials. *Archives of Internal Medicine, 169*(10), 929–937. doi:10.1001/archinternmed.2009.109

Newcomb, M. D., & Bentler, P. M. (1988). Impact of adolescent drug use and social support on problems of young adults: A longitudinal study. *Journal of Abnormal Psychology, 97*(1), 64–75. doi:10.1037/0021-843X.97.1.64

Norris, J. R. (2009). The growth and direction of healthcare support groups in virtual worlds. *Journal of Virtual Worlds Research, 2*(2), 3–20.

Nosek, M., Whelen, S., Hughes, R., Porcher, E., Davidson, G., & Nosek, T. (2010). Self-esteem in Second Life: An in world group intervention for women with disabilities. In A. Boa-Ventura, O. Criner, E. Elam & M. Nosek (Chairs), SLACTIONS. Texas chapter, Houston, TX.

Prochaska, J. O., & DiClemente, C. C. (1983). Stages and processes of self-change of smoking: Toward an integrative model of change. *Journal of Consulting and Clinical Psychology, 51,* 390–395. doi:10.1037/0022-006X.51.3.390

Richter, S., Brown, S., & Mott, M. (1991). The impact of social support and self-esteem on adolescent substance abuse treatment outcome. *Journal of Substance Abuse, 3*(4), 371–385. doi:10.1016/S0899-3289(10)80019-7

Rizzo, A., Jarrell Pair, J., Graap, K., Manson, B., McNerney, P. J., & Wiederhold, B. … Spira, J. (2006). A virtual reality exposure therapy application for Iraq war military personnel with post traumatic stress disorder: From training to toy to treatment. In M. Roy (Ed.), *NATO Advanced Research Workshop on Novel Approaches to the Diagnosis and Treatment of Posttraumatic Stress Disorder,* (pp. 235-250). Washington DC: IOS Press.

Roberts, A. J., & Koob, G. F. (1997). The neurobiology of addiction: An overview. *Alcohol Health and Research World, 21*(2), 101–106.

Rothbaum, B., Hidges, L. F., Kooper, R., Opdyke, D., Williford, J. S., & North, M. (1995). Effectiveness of computer-generated (virtual reality) graded exposure in the treatment of acrophobia. *The American Journal of Psychiatry, 152*, 626–628.

Rothbaum, B., Hodges, L., Smith, S., Lee, J. H., & Price, L. (2000). A controlled study of virtual reality exposure therapy for the fear of flying. *Journal of Consulting and Clinical Psychology, 68*(6), 1020–1026. doi:10.1037/0022-006X.68.6.1020

Sterba, K., Rabius, V., Villars, P., Wiatrek, D., & McAlister, A. L. (2009, April). *Dyadic efficacy in partnered smokers motivated to quit.* Poster session presented at the 30th Meeting of the Society for Behavioral Medicine, Montreal, Canada.

Strecher Victor, J., Shiffman, S., & West, R. (2005). Randomized controlled trial of a Web based computer-tailored smoking cessation program as a supplement to nicotine patch therapy. *Addiction (Abingdon, England), 100*(5), 682–688. doi:10.1111/j.1360-0443.2005.01093.x

U.S. Department of Health & Human Services – Center for Medicare and MedicAid Services. (2009). *Medicaid program - General information.* Retrieved from http://www.cms.gov/Medicaid-GenInfo/

Volkow, N. D. (2007). *Addiction and the brain's pleasure pathway: Beyond willpower.* HBO. Retrieved from http://www.hbo.com/addiction/understanding_addiction/12_pleasure_pathway.html

Walshe, D. G., Lewis, E. J., Kim, S. I., O'Sullivan, K., & Wiederhold, B. K. (2003). Exploring the use of computer games and virtual reality in exposure therapy for fear of driving following a motor vehicle *accident. CyberPsychology & Behavior: The Impact of the Internet, Multimedia and Virtual Reality on Behavior and Society, 6*(3), 329–334.

Weisner, C., Mertens, J., Tam, T., & Moore, C. (2001). Factors affecting the initiation of substance abuse treatment in managed care. *Addiction (Abingdon, England), 96*(5), 705–716. doi:10.1046/j.1360-0443.2001.9657056.x

Whitlock, E. P., Polen, M. R., Green, C. A., Orleans, T., & Klein, J. (2004). Behavioral counseling interventions in primary care to reduce risky/harmful alcohol use by adults: A summary of the evidence for the U.S. Preventive Services Task Force. *Annals of Internal Medicine, 140*(7), 557–568.

Yee, N., & Bailenson, J. (2007). The Proteus effect: The effect of transformed self-representation on behavior. *Human Communication Research, 33*, 271–290. doi:10.1111/j.1468-2958.2007.00299.x

Section 6
Life Happens:
Religion, Morality, and Ethics

Chapter 19

Finding Liquid Salvation:
Using the Cardean Ethnographic Method to Document Second Life Residents and Religious Cloud Communities

Gregory Price Grieve
University of North Carolina at Greensboro, USA

Kevin Heston
Wake Forest University, USA

ABSTRACT

The Cardean Ethnographic Method was developed between 2007 and 2010 to study religious communities in the virtual world of Second Life. In our research, we faced a two-sided methodological problem. We had to theorize the virtual and its relation to the actual, while simultaneously creating practices for an effective ethnographic method. Our solution, named after the Roman goddess of the hinge, Cardea, theorizes the "virtual" as desubstantialized and nondualistic; "residents" as fluid, multiple, and distributed cyborg-bodies; and "cloud communities" as temporary, outsourced groups of emotionally bonded residents. These three qualities enable a classic form of ethnography based on participant observation, which is possible on Second Life because the platform enables immersion, a prolonged time in the field, as well as the bodily practices necessary for thick description. The Cardean method unveils online religion operating as "Liquid Salvation"—which is defined by consumerism, radical individualism, and pragmatic religious practice.

INTRODUCTION

On January 31, 2009, I logged onto the metaverse platform Second Life (SL) and teleported to a Christian dance club to talk with resident Deborah Devine.[1] Deborah had only been using SL for a

DOI: 10.4018/978-1-60960-854-5.ch019

few months, but she had considerable experience in other 3-D and 2-D multiuser environments, including World of Warcraft and email listserves. Over the past weeks, I had been keeping in touch with her and occasionally stopped by her virtual jewelry shop. After a few minutes of small talk, I asked Deborah about her Christian practice on SL. She explained to me that SL made spending

Figure 1. Cardean Virtual Research Team. Principal investigator Greg Grieve and five assistants: Sabrina Epps, Rebecca Davis, Kevin Heston, Michelle Lampley, and Jayme Mallindine. (Photo by Sabrina Epps)

time with the Christian community easier because "they are very visible, [and] there are scheduled activities like Sunday services, prayer meetings, and Bible studies." I asked her if the online community differed from that of her actual world. There was a pause: "Where in my RL [real life] could I go to a dance and meet people from around the globe and listen to a French man sing and play a mean guitar?"

Deborah is not alone in practicing religion in metaverse platforms. More and more people spend more and more of their lives online. As the Pew Internet and American Life Project notes, "cyberfaith" is the fastest growing form of religious practice (2000-2010). The Cardean method analyzes religious practices on 3-D metaverse platforms by documenting what Bronislaw Malinowski calls the "imponderabilia of actual life" (1961 [1922]). Imponderabilia are social phenomena of great importance that cannot possibly be recorded by interviews, recording devices, or quantitative methods, but must be interpreted in the full actuality of their cultural context.

Ethnography is the tried and tested approach for documenting the imponderabilia of life, virtual or otherwise. The main objective of this chapter is to sketch out the Cardean Ethnographic Method and the underlying theory and practice necessary to conduct research of religious groups on 3-D metaverse platforms such as SL. The Cardean Method was formulated by The Cardean Virtual Research Team (CVRT), which in its final form consisted of the principal investigator, one graduate, and four advanced undergraduates from the University of North Carolina, Greensboro, and which conducted research between September 2007 and September 2010 (Figure 1).

Our methodology was driven by three fundamental questions.[2] What is the relation between the virtual and the actual? How can one transfer and adapt traditional ethnographic methods, chiefly participant observation, to the cyberspace of 3-D metaverse platforms? And last, do the religious identities and communities found reflect their virtual environment, or are they representative of larger changes taking place in the late modern world?

Because the CVRT conducted some of the first ethnography in Second Life, we found ourselves facing a two-sided methodological problem. We had to theorize our main descriptive categories while simultaneously creating techniques for an effective ethnographic method. In practice, these two sides formed in a simultaneous and dialectic fashion with the theoretical emerging from the methodological and the methodological guided by the theoretical. Because we are limited here by print media, we proceed in a threefold linear fashion. First, we define the background concepts that position our topic. These include the "virtual," which we define as desubstantialized and nondualistic; "residents," those social entities that weave together avatars with their users and describe the bodily sensorium determined by 3-D metaverse platforms; and "cloud communities," online groups that are temporary, flexible, elastic, and inexpensive in the social capital required to join or to leave.

Second, as the main focus of the chapter, we illustrate the "Cardean Ethnographic Method," a team-based form of participant observation that is modeled on a hinge. As in the actual world, there are three qualities that make participant observation possible on virtual 3-D metaverse platforms: being present, prolonged time in the field, and thick description. Presence is the feeling that the landscape, buildings, and especially the inhabitants of a world are co-present with the user—they are *there*. A prolonged time in the field is required for a valid ethnography because it allows the researcher to become part of a group's everyday routine, to inhabit the insider's world, and to give the research the flexibility and fluidity it needs in order to follow alternative hypotheses that arise during the study. Thick description is a method for interpreting both a social practice and the context required for that practice to become meaningful to an outsider.

Third, we discuss some implications of our findings. On the broadest level, the Cardean method is necessary for the simple reason that tens of millions of people are entering and imagining new virtual worlds, yet we know little about their everyday life. More specifically, SL offers ideal models of "liquid salvation," which become observable because, as Christine Hine writes, "the Internet and similar networks provide a naturally occurring field site for studying what people do when they are online unconstrained by experimental design" (2000). What residents gain in SL is a re-enchantment that is impossible in the actual late modern world. Max Weber infamously claimed that we now live in an age of disenchantment—an epoch in which rationalization and intellectualization have destroyed traditional modes of wonder and mystery (1976 [1958]). We argue that online religions are both a cure and a symptom for our unpredictable, globalized consumer culture. We theorize these practices as "Liquid Salvation." Salvation can be understood as deliverance from suffering. Liquid Salvation—which is defined by consumerism, radical individualism, and pragmatic religious practice—defines an expression of, and a protest against, the suffering generated by what the sociologist Zygmunt Bauman calls "liquid modernity," the economic system that is historically linked to the second half of the twentieth century and is defined by the fluidity of financial capital, an intensification of the free market, globalization, and consumerism (2000).

BACKGROUND: THEORIZING THE VIRTUAL, RESIDENTS, AND CLOUD COMMUNITIES

Before we can sketch out the Cardean Method, it is necessary to describe the theory behind our practices. The first hurdle was to analyze the relation between the real and the virtual.[3] Theories of the virtual are based on a notion of the virtual as that which *seems* to be there as opposed to what is actually there (Rheingold, 1991). The virtual, then, in our current period usually denotes a distinction of "almost so." This understanding arose because the virtual is tethered to interactive computer systems. In other words, to more clearly see the virtual we need to disambiguate it from two currently intertwined concepts: "Internet" and "cyberspace." The "Internet" denotes the hardware and software that compose a global system of interconnected computer networks. "Cyberspace" denotes the mediated social space created by interconnected electronic communications. It differs from telecommunication, which has a sender and a receiver, because cyberspace occurs in a virtual social environment (Krueger, 1991). It differs from radio and television in that the communication is two-way, synchronous, and interactive. Linked to the Internet, cyberspaces enable interactive immersive environments that put a user in contact with other residents of digital worlds and offer new places and forms of socialization (Rheingold, 1993). Such worlds can be textual—as in newsgroups, chat rooms, and MUDs (Multi-User Dungeons)—or, as in SL, they can use computer graphics to render 3-D models.

Too often, virtual worlds are described as if they were something created whole cloth by these digital networks. Yet, being immersed in virtual worlds is nothing new. For instance, being immersed in a good novel, a film, or even a well-told story, can be understood as a form of the virtual. In fact, it can be argued that virtual worlds have followed human culture from its very beginning (Fornäs, 2002). As M. Serres and K. Sauer write in their book, *Atlas* (2006), "Imagination, memory, knowledge and religion are the vectors of virtualization that have enabled us to leave this 'there' long before the appearance of computerization and digital networks" (cited in Lévy, 1998). Nor are virtual spaces dependent upon cyberspace. For example, Margaret Wertheim argues that Giotto's Arena Chapel in Padua, Italy, transported viewers out of reality into an architecturally virtual space. She argues that Giotto's work "blur[s] the

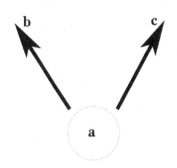

Figure 2. The Hinge. If virtual worlds are theorized as desubstantialized, then the experience (a) of the relationship between the virtual (b) and actual (c) is not one of real and unreal, but rather nondualistic. (Drawing by Greg Grieve)

boundary between the virtual space of the image and the physical space of the chapel" (Wertheim & Leonard, 1999).

If one disambiguates "virtual" from "cyberspace," then one finds that virtualities are neither "fake" nor immaterial, but are desubstantialized. That is, the virtual cannot be reduced to material or ideal, but it is a set of processes dependent upon the actual, and realized in it, but irreducible to a physical system. In such a case, the virtual, as Pierre Lévy argues, "has little affinity with the false, the illusory or imaginary. Nor does it mean the opposite of reality" (1995). For instance, the experience created by watching a film is dependent upon the physical celluloid, but its significance cannot be reduced to it. If one sees the virtual as desubstantialized, a second model appears. This can be theorized as the hinge, which models the virtual world and the actual as nondualistic (Figure 2).

Nondualism indicates that things appear distinct while not being separate, and affirms the understanding that while distinctions exist, dichotomies are illusory phenomena. The hinge places you in two worlds at once, and causes one to be transversal. That is, perception of the virtual pivots in two or more intersecting but parallel social positions. In fact, virtualization impedes us from thinking in schemes of binary dichotomies and in dialectic notions of synthesis (Nusselder, 2006). Instead, both are real because the virtual and the actual produce an effect (Lévy, 1998).

Residents: Fluid, Multiple, Distributed, and Sensorial Cyborg-Bodies

In SL, users assume an identity—such as Deborah Devine—by creating an online character, an "avatar." In computing, an avatar is the on-screen representation of the user(s), which can be a three-dimensional model such as in SL, a two-dimensional icon as used in many chat forums, or a textual description as used in MUDs. In SL, the default avatar shape is humanoid, but it can be customized through a graphical user interface that can modify gender, body shape, skin, hairstyle, and clothes. Moreover, one can purchase or create bodies and clothes, as well as attachments and animation and sonic (voice) overrides. Such customization results in the creation of male, female, and androgynous human avatars, as well as animals, robots, nekos, furries, and other fantasy creatures such as dragons.

A metaverse platform resident is a social entity that weaves together an avatar and its user within the broader social context of the cyberworld. In common usage, a resident is one who dwells in a particular place, and implies, as in *The Devil's Dictionary*, that one is "unable to leave" (Bierce & Steadman, 2003). Linden Research defines a "resident" as "a uniquely named avatar with the right to log into SL, trade Linden Dollars and visit the Community pages." In Second Life, residents are governed by terms of service (TOS), which specifically allow users to retain all intellectual property rights in the digital content they create or own in SL. In our research, we employ the word "user" to refer to the actual person "behind the keyboard," "avatar" to refer to the online image of a user's "virtual representative," and "resident" to indicate the cybersocial entity that is activated

Figure 3. A Resident (Drawing by Greg Grieve)

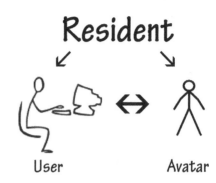

in SL by the presence of the avatar, operated by the user, and socialized by interaction with other residents, their avatars, and occasionally the users themselves (Figure 3).

It is important to remember that a "resident" is not always a one-to-one relationship between a real-life user and a virtual representation. As with most website user accounts, several avatars might belong to one user, and conversely one avatar might be operated by more than one user sequentially, or in some cases by more than one user at the same time, as in the situation of one avatar controlled by nine disabled persons (Au, 2008).

Theoretically, residents can be understood as cyborg, fluid selves, whose bodies are multiple and distributed across a number of "windows." As Valentine Daniel argues, selves are signs: "As a semiotic sign [they] are never actual: [they] are always virtual" (Daniel & Pugh, 1984). Donna Haraway writes that a "cyborg is a cybernetic organism, a hybrid of machine and organism, a creature of social reality as well as a creature of fiction" (2009: 149). Sherry Turkle uses the metaphor of computer screen windows to illustrate how residents cycle through cyberspace and the actual world (1984). For Turkle, "the self is no longer simply playing different roles in different settings at different times" (1996). Instead, "the life practice of windows is that of a decentered self that exists in many worlds, that plays many

Figure 4. Clint Using the "Triple Jewel HUD" to Perform a Gassho (Photo by Greg Grieve)

roles at the same time." As Turkle writes, "Now real life itself may be, as one of [her] subjects says, 'just one more window'" (1996).

What is important to remember here, is that these different windows are inhabited not just by minds, but also by bodies. As Anna Munster writes, "Information does not simply represent a body or corporeal experience; it renders the emergent properties and capacities of bodies" (2006). The current ideology surrounding metaverse platforms has been sustained by a rhetoric of dematerialization, which has driven even deeper the Cartesian wedge between mind and body. Katherine Hayles indicates that such dematerialization is exacerbated by "the postmodern ideology that the body's materiality is secondary to the logical or semiotic structures it encodes" (1999: 192). The normative assumption seems to be that when one logs into

cyberspaces, we leave our bodies behind. Here it is important to distinguish between what is meant by "body" and by "embodiment." Hayles argues that the body is a cultural norm, an idealized form, while "embodiment is a specific instantiation...enmeshed within the specifics of place, time, physiology, and culture" (196). In the same fashion that Lacan's "Real" undermines symbolic orders, Hayles's work suggests that embodiment "inherently destabilizes" semiotic systems (197; Lacan, 1966: 25; Lacan, 1978:49).

In SL, embodiment of self involves three minor factors and one major factor that are interdependent. The minor factors are appearance, actions, and communication. First, in SL embodiment is determined by how one appears to others. A user can change his or her avatar's shape, gender, race, species, as well as clothes, hair, and accessories.

Embodiment is also determined by actions. In SL, one can gesture and change posture. When it comes to religious practices, there are many religious gestures, such as "Worship the Lord!" and a Heads Up Device (HUD) called the Triple Jewel HUD that allows one to *gassho*—a position used for greeting, with the palms together and fingers pointing upwards in prayer position (Figure 4).

Last, a user can change modes of communication among different forms of text and voice. The major factor of virtual embodiment occurs when we are interpolated into a social network. Alterity is the very possibility and process of embodiment. While the body is never self-present, it is not fixed by nature—it is a cultural norm. Embodiment is created in relation to others, as one is perceived to be of a particular sex, race, or ethnic group in a particular social setting.

We are not arguing for a return to essentialized corporeal notions of the body. Instead, as Munster writes, "[l]ike all technologies associated with our sensorium, [new media require] us to undertake a labor of perception. Information bodies ["embodied information" in Hayles's terminology] no longer summon the immediate presence of corporeal existence, which can be affirmed through habitual codes and conventions" (180). What is important is the embodied sensorium. Walter Ong defines the sensorium as "the entire sensory apparatus as an operational complex...the organization of which is in part determined by culture, while at the same time it makes culture" (O'Leary, 1996; Ong, 1967). As shown in the work of Carpenter and McLuhan (1960), it is a natural extension to recognize that different media alter the normative perception of the world. That is, the "media is the message" because different mediascapes—from primarily oral, to manuscript, to print based, to analogue, and finally to digital—will create different "realities." Ideologically, the sensoriums are not neutral features; there are different winners and losers in each sensorium because of the production, circulation, and legitimization of knowledge,

especially as it pertains to an understanding of the transparent operation of the senses.

Cloud Communities: Temporary, Flexible, and Elastic Online Groups

Since at least April 1984, with the establishment of net.religion.jewish, computer-mediated religious groups—such as those to which Deborah Devine belongs—have existed in cyberspace. Howard Rheingold argues that such groups turn into communities "when people carry on public discussions long enough, with *sufficient human feeling,* to form webs of personal relationships" (1993). All communities are socially constructed, and even face-to-face groups, which use air to speak, in the end depend upon media for people to perceive themselves as members. There are many different types of communities on SL. Some communities re-enact specific historical or fictional spaces, such as medieval Japan, or John Norman's *Gor* novels. Some communities revolve around events such as airship races, philosophical debate, and role-play areas such as City of Lost Angels. This can also include religious groups and activities such as Bible study or silent meditation (Figures 5 and 6).

While the CVRT studied Muslim, Jewish, Pagan, Christian, Buddhist, Hindu, New Age, and agnostic groups, we base our theory on two SL religious communities: the Second Life Christians and their ALM CyberChurch (1,529 members) modeled by its devout but unordained founders after real-world Christian congregations, and the Upaya Sangha that is modeled on westernized Zen Buddhism. Participation in ALM CyberChurch includes Sunday services—with sermons, hymns, and collection plates—as well as everyday related discussions, fellowship meetings, and book groups, and for many the association extends to Christian-themed dance clubs. The Upaya Sangha is part of a Buddhist community on SL that consists of five groups—Buddha Center, Hikari Buddhist Group, Upaya Sangha, the Zen Center,

Figure 5. Zen Buddhist Silent Meditation at Zen Retreat (Photo by Greg Grieve).

Figure 6. Christian Altar Call Following a Sunday Sermon at ALM CyberChurch (Photo by Kevin Heston)

and the Zen Retreat. As of January 2010, these five groups had 2,756 members, five regions, and held approximately 75 events per week.

The term "community" defines a group that forms relationships over time by interacting on a regular basis around a shared set of experiences—this could be car enthusiasts or the members of a remote mountain village. A "cloud community" is an online group that is temporary, flexible, elastic, and is inexpensive in the social capital required to join or to leave (Figure 7).

We borrow the notion of the "cloud" from computing, where it signifies an architecture in which users access resources online from a host of different servers—Google Docs, Blist, and SlideRocket would be examples. Cloud computing users do not invest in infrastructure. Instead, they rent what they need when they need it.

Virtual cloud communities have become important because the passage into late modernity has dissolved traditional religious communities and institutions so that individuals have to actively explore and create novel, elastic, temporary, and flexible forms. Community experiences can be generated by place or interest, but what defines the concept of community is "communion" (Hodes,

Figure 7. Second Life's Zen Buddhist Community Cloud (Drawing by Greg Grieve)

1972). In fact, in the social sciences, since the late nineteenth century, the conception of community has been associated with the hope of living within more harmonious types of bonds, which are perceived to exist in more traditional societies and past ages (Hoggett, 1997; Tönnies & Harris, 2001). As Zygmunt Bauman writes, "'Community' stands for the kind of world which is not, regrettably, available to us—but which we would dearly wish to inhabit and which we hope to repossess" (2001). The longing for communion, even if it is just a myth, is what drives people's desire for online community. The temporary, flexible, elastic, and inexpensive nature of cloud communities makes this desire possible in what Baumann defines as "liquid modernity." As Bauman writes, "Liquid Life is a precarious life, lived under conditions of constant uncertainty.... A society in which the conditions under which its members act change faster than it takes the way of acting to consolidate into habits and routines" (Bauman, 2005: 1).

Cloud communities exist on SL, and are best analyzed by looking at "groups." Groups provide a way for residents to collaborate about shared interests, such as scripting, building, music, the arts, and games, to name just a few. For instance, one could join the group "East River Community" if one is interested in things nautical. Or one can join the "Seekers of the Black Caste of Gor," if one is interested in being an assassin. Members of SL groups are able to interact via group chat and also to send notices and to vote on proposals. Groups can also give members different administrative roles with different abilities, such as ejection, note card-sending, and invitation. Groups can be role-playing, such as the Toxian City—Main Group with 8,136 members. They can be educational, such as the Institute for SL Ethnography with 39 members. They can be for entertainment, such as the group Hot Sex with 544 members. On SL some of the longest lasting and most active of communities are religious, such as the Second Life Christians with 1,529 members, Islam Every Day with 213 members, or the Pagan site Anam Turas Pagan Learning Grove with 944 members.

THE CARDEAN ETHNOGRAPHIC METHOD: PARTICIPANT OBSERVATION BASED ON PRESENCE, PROLONGED TIME IN THE FIELD, AND THICK DESCRIPTION

Now that we have theorized the main descriptive categories, we can turn to the main focus of the chapter. Namely, illustrating the Cardean or hinge method for conducting ethnography in 3-D metaverse platforms such as SL. One worries, however, can ethnographers telecommute? Can one be immersed in other worlds while sitting in front of a computer screen? As Malinowski cautioned, to document the imponderabilia of life, researchers should not sit in their armchairs theorizing from a distance, but must spend time learning about, and from, groups of people in their natural surroundings (1961 [1922]). Yet, the myth of the ethnographic field as a discreet, bounded geographic locale is proving to be increasingly outdated and untenable as globalization blurs the boundary between "here" and "there" (Fox, 1991; Gupta & Ferguson, 1997; Kohn, 1995). In fact, a "field site" can no longer be seen merely as a physical location, but rather must be viewed as the intersection between people, practices, and shifting terrains, both physical and virtual.

Rather than a distant space, or a particular type of media, the ethnographic field is better defined through a set of methodological practices (Appadurai, 1986). What became clear during our research is that the need to theorize a new style of ethnographic research arises not only because SL differs from traditional actual world field sites, but also because SL's 3-D graphic interface differs from earlier text-based MUDs and the World Wide Web. The shift from a web-based to a 3-D platform changes the method needed to study a field. For instance, Christine Hine has developed a ten-point methodological framework for virtual ethnography (2000: 63-645). Yet her work focuses on listserves, websites, and chat rooms. None of these media have the wide range of new sensorial information that 3-D metaverse platforms, such as SL, offer.

Sometimes it is most efficient to put new wine in old bottles. During our research, we found what worked best was a classic ethnographic method consisting of practices of participant observation and thick description (Malinowski, 1961 [1922]; Geertz, 1973; see also Clifford & Marcus, 1986; Gupta & Ferguson, 1997). During our fieldwork, we meditated and prayed, explored temples and churches, prostrated before Buddha images, knelt before Christian altars, went to Dharma talks and Christian fellowship meetings, and argued in open discussions about the nature of Buddhism and Christianity. Our participant observation was recorded in shared field notes, snapshots, written documents, and material culture. What makes participant observation a scientific research method (as opposed to just "hanging out") is, in an oxymoronic fashion, that as one inhabits a

world, one also needs to stand back and observe by watching and listening, while taking both physical and mental notes. "Observation" means logging concrete documentation of social structures and examples of everyday life and utterances. While there is no standard set of methods for participant observation, the three key practices are presence in the field, emergent research design, and thick description.

Presence: Virtually Being There

Often virtual communities are not considered as valid fields because they lack the propinquity of face-to-face groups. Such skepticism is not limited to just experts. Many users see the Internet as merely a source of information. As a sixteen-year-old Christian, experienced with religious blogs and chats, said, "The Internet can never become to me what the church is" (Careaga, 2001). What seems to be missing online is presence, the feeling that the landscape, buildings, and especially the inhabitants are co-present with the user—that they are *there*. Three-dimensional metaplatforms counter this placelessness.

Imagine you already have a SL account. At home, at the office, or in a coffee shop, you get an electronic message reminding you that silent meditation is going to start. You log on to your SL viewer program much as you would a web browser, such as Safari or Firefox. Your avatar materializes in your home in SL. By looking at the map, you can tell that a number of people are already at the nearby meditation hall. It is a little too far to walk, and you cannot fly in this region, so you teleport over. You "rezz" (materialize) in front of a wooden building, through the glass door of which you can see a long wooden altar with incense, candles, flowers, and a large statue of Shakyamuni Buddha. This is the meditation hall. You push through the door and greet everyone with a *gassho*. You are welcomed with the emoticon for *gassho* and the word *namaste* by many of the sixteen practitioners, who run the gamut from those dressed in Zen monastic garb, to those who look as if they should be out clubbing—elves, one Gorean, and a small goat-like animal.

As the Buddhist example indicates, presence is enabled by "immersion" and "interactivity." In the context of metaverse platforms, immersion refers to the experience of being in the constructed world. The screen is not a surface in front of the user. Rather, the users lose themselves in the constructed world. Immersion creates an experience of locatedness "that organizes sensory information in such a way as to create a psychological state in which an individual perceives himself or herself as being present or having 'presence' in them" (Blascovich, 2002). Immersion occurs when the actual world is sufficiently muted, and the virtual world is sufficiently heightened, creating a feeling that one is no longer in the actual world. For instance, consider the feeling of being immersed in a good book and startled upon "return" to the actual world. What makes immersion more intense in virtual worlds is presence and interactivity. In 3-D cyberworlds, "presence" is enhanced by the greatly expanded sensorium and increased interactivity with not only the avatars of other residents, but also with the "virtual environment." Participation in SL usually involves physical, albeit virtual, activity on the part of the individual's avatar. Significantly, these activities are "publicly" observable and become part of the SL social fabric. Interests and associations are frequently signaled by tattoos, clothing, hairstyle, and body configuration.

What makes immersion in SL more intense than in other online media is the metaverse's three-dimensionally rich, highly interactive, and complex Internet platform. Such immersive navigation occurs when users move from seeking information to navigating through worlds. The goals of an immersed user are different from those of one seeking to extract information. Instead of text-based experience aimed at finding and connecting pieces of data, the goals of an immersed user include bodily sensory awareness. By using

mouse and keyboard instructions, one can explore SL, which includes 3-D builds, and environmental sounds. Avatars can communicate with other residents via voice and built-in public chat and instant messaging. Residents can buy and make clothes, objects, and buildings, as well as buy and rent property. One can conduct business using the in-world currency, run non-profit and educational groups, role-play, and socialize in any number of ways with others.

It is the "interactivity" with the platform that gives residents the feeling that they are more than "spectators," and turns the screen's pixels into what William Gibson, in his novel, *Neuromancer*, calls "consensual hallucinations" (1984). Also, it is interactivity that distinguishes the computer from the cinematic mode of engagement. As Allucquére Rosanne Stone argues, "Interaction is the physical concretization of a desire to escape the flatness and merge into the created system. It is the sense in which the 'spectator' is more than a participant, but becomes both participant in and creator of the simulation" (1991).

SL's immersive interactivity occurs through "virtual physicality," "hyper-interactivity," and the users' employment of imagination. Virtual physicality indicates that residents are able to walk, run, fly, swim, or teleport throughout immensely variable, virtual physical environments; and they are able to dance, cuddle, kiss, and hug one another. We refer to this as "hyper-interactivity" because it allows interaction with the dual "virtual-physicality" of SL—the ability to construct and interact with the environment as well as with the other avatars. This dual virtual-physicality enhances, relative to other platforms, what Yee and Bailenson describe as "the psychological experience of being able to move naturalistically in a different surrounding" (2009). The online experience becomes not only a "psychological experience of moving naturalistically," but also an experience of "being" naturalistically—both in body and in a different space. This sense of "being" is played out in a wide array of social interactions and relationships, including the religious, that many experienced residents report are equally significant to their real-world relationships.

That the form and activities of the avatars are on display for the residents creates a unique form of communication in which the importance of the image is greatly elevated over text-based Internet, and in which interactivity is greatly enhanced relative to both televangelism and text-based Internet religion. That an individual is "pulling the strings" to create the activities, and is responsible for the "physical" appearance of the avatar, creates a unique opportunity for a wide range of personal messages and private associations, including the "virtually" religious. Email groups and chat rooms utilize a limited array of simple images—emoticons—to convey meaning beyond text. Image-rich, interactive 3-D cyberspace opens up the possibility of expression by means of constructing "virtual" structures, forests, oceans, cities, universities, churches, synagogues, temples, and uniquely, the ability to use the richly expressive avatar "body language." Avatar facial expressions are possible in SL, but they are not regularly used. Other body language can be portrayed; for example, by using "gestures" that are readily available on the SL toolbar, it is possible to bow, curtsy, kneel, play an instrument, dance, or even toss a snowball. True, the body language is the product of computer code and therefore not spontaneous, but that does not prevent it from being communicative.

Metaverse platforms such as SL allow individuals to project themselves into, and to invite others into, their dramas and fantasies, enabling users to form communities and become comfortable with new ways of being. It is the incorporation of residents' imaginations that makes SL different from other 3-D interactive platforms that are engineered by game designers. The primary difference is in the fact that the users themselves "build" Second Life's content. The shift from the "traditional models of corporate-controlled production and distribution to more democratic,

non-hierarchical, [and] collaborative structures" (Schackman, 2009) affords an unprecedented level of interactivity. Such resident-created content is pushing computer-mediated communication from a modernist paradigm of calculation toward a postmodernist one of simulation, which links millions of users in new cyberspaces. Using "in-world" tools available to all residents, one can make objects with physical qualities and even give them scripted instructions, and thus create buildings, environments, and even the bodies that one inhabits. In SL, one can visit shopping malls, dance clubs, art and cultural sites, Hindu temples, Christian churches, synagogues, Pagan fire circles, and go on a virtual *hajj* and even visit a Buddhist hell (to name a few). These builds can be either "online religion," such as the Grove of the Greenman (Gai Rising Outerbanks 143, 181, 40) where cyberspace is the focus of practice, or they can be "religion online," such as the Saint Michael Shrine (Charleville 141, 246, 21) that is a copy of an actual church that exists in the actual world in Tarpon Springs, Florida (Helland, 2000; Karaflogka, 2002; Maxwell, 2002).

A Prolonged Time in the Field

Returning to SL, we find that the avatars are sitting on *zafu*s and *zabutons*. These meditation cushions are laid out in semi-circular lines so that when people sit on them they are facing the altar. There are two cushions facing away from the altar, and between them is a meditation gong (*kesu*), which is referred to as the "bell." Sitting on the right cushion facing away from the altar is the meditation leader or timekeeper who—and I quote from information given to me when I was trained for this job—"is the person who holds the meditative space for the sitting practice of others."

While the immersion and interactivity make possible a field site, for a valid ethnography one needs a prolonged time in the field because it allows the researcher to become part of the group's everyday routine, to inhabit the insider's world, and to give the research the flexibility and fluidity it needs to follow alternative hypotheses that arise during the study (O'Reilly, 2005). Moreover, prolonged time in the field is necessary because ethnographers have no clear idea what they will find, and thus need to have an open, fluid, and evolving research protocol. Unlike other social science methods whose aim is to test a hypothesis, ethnography by definition is inductive, fluid, and flexible, building upon the perspectives of the people studied. For instance, the Cardean research protocol evolved through four stages. Grieve, as the principal investigator, and Heston first logged onto SL in October 2007—before the platform had become known to the mainstream media, and really before any academic, let alone ethnographic papers had been written on the subject. We had been invited to view one of the first Asian religious sites, a Daoist temple run by resident Sufigari Xenith, and became curious about the possibilities of using the virtual world as an ethnographic site. Visitation of SL was sporadic at first but evolved into a minimum of three 2-hour sessions each week. Because our university's Institutional Review Board (IRB), a committee designated to monitor academic research involving human subjects, had not yet approved the study, no data was collected in this first stage of research, and we used the time to learn the language and culture of SL.

In the second stage of the research, Grieve and Heston became interested in how identities are formed in different SL religious groups, and we obtained an IRB in February 2008. Because of a vast already extant archive of primary and secondary sources, we concentrated on how gender identity is constituted by different SL religious groups. The research employed three different avatars—Brandy, Clint, and YT—who embodied female, male, and neuter genders. Using these three avatars on a random and rotating basis, we visited a number of different religious groups—Buddhist, Muslim, Christian, Jewish, and Pagan. Field notes were begun, and we compiled them

using the web-based application Google Documents (and later Dropbox). More time was spent in-world during this period, with a minimum of five 2-hour sessions each week for both researchers. Also during this period, more than 100 surveys were obtained, and Heston designed the "Aleph Technique," which reads the profiles of avatars to analyze the groups to which they belong (2008). Fairly quickly, the researchers discovered that it was difficult to "bond" with such quickly rotating avatars, and it was thus difficult to be immersed in SL. That is, it was difficult to advance to being a "resident." The term "bond" describes how users are psychologically attached to their avatars. When users are bonded and immersed, they become emotionally engaged with the community. Also, because the two researchers are both male in actual life, we decided that it would be prudent to involve women in the research team.

The third stage of research began in September 2008 with the addition of four advanced undergraduates—Epps, Davis, Lampley, and Mallindine. We also added the avatars Aleph, Da5id, Juanita, and Kaiya to the protocols. Researchers shared their field notes using Google Documents, and we also shared material culture and screenshots using the web-based program Dropbox. We were still interested in gender at this stage. Our original intention was for researchers to embody a particular avatar for six weeks, and then to exchange with another member of the team. Four weeks into the third stage, however, the direction of the study was again altered in two major ways: First, researchers were reluctant to abandon their avatars, so a final allocation was done and, for the most part, each person stuck with one avatar for the remainder of the study. Second, the study became both broader and more focused. It was broadened because the idea of studying only gender seemed limited, and so the study was enlarged to encompass religious selves, relationships, and communities. It became more focused because SL was growing and changing so quickly that the concept of studying all religion was abandoned, and we decided to concentrate on the Zen Buddhist cluster and the ALM CyberChurch. Participant observation continued with each researcher logging on for a minimum of two hours three times per week. In June 2009, we ceased participant observation, and engaged in one month of open interviews, in which the group spoke with forty-two participants.

The fourth stage, which is ongoing at the time of writing, began in September 2009 and will last until September 2010. After the student researchers graduated, Grieve worked alone. He concentrated on contemplative practices in Second Life's Buddhist cloud community. Grieve concentrated on documenting changes that were occurring in the Buddhist community—by leading meditation and reading groups, as well as attending new events such as dharma talks lead by actual-world Buddhist clergy. With the help of Heston, a final large survey is planned, in which we hope to gather around 200 responses. The completion of the survey will mark the end of three years of fieldwork.

Writing it Down: Thick Description in a Fluid World

As the time draws near, more people straggle in. Just before the start of the meditation period, the timekeeper types in public chat: "Please prepare for thirty minutes of silent meditation." The sitting period ends with one ring of the bell and a brief dedication, usually: "By this merit may all sentient beings attain complete awakening." The timekeeper then types the emoticon "_/!_" (for *gassho*). Most of the other people present also type this emoticon into their computers, which causes a cascade of _/!_s to flow down the screen. You then stand, *gassho* to the altar, and walk slowly out of the *zendo*. Once you have left, you say good-bye to your companions, teleport back to your house, and then log off.

The goal of ethnography is to create thick description. As Clifford Geertz defines the term, a "thick description" describes both a social practice and also the context in order for that practice to become meaningful to an outsider. Geertz uses the example of a wink. If someone winks, it could mean that they are expressing sexual desire, trying to communicate a secret, or they might "actually have been fake-winking, say, to mislead outsiders into imagining there was a conspiracy afoot" (Geertz, 1973). Without knowing the context, we reduce the wink to the thin description that the person is merely "rapidly contracting his right eyelid" (1973: 7). In a similar fashion, in the context of SL one could accurately describe the emoticon "_/!_" as a series of lines. Yet, such a "thin description" does not explain what this sign means to an insider. In Geertz's words, it neither "uncover[s] the conceptual structures that inform our subject's acts," nor allows us to "...construct a system of analysis" (1973: 27).

For example, a church service that concludes with avatars approaching the altar and kneeling in prayer suggests a different denominational bent than a service that concludes with avatars standing, arms reaching high as they sway to and fro. Or, consider an example that continues gender stereotypes from real life: A hands-folded, head-downcast posture of a conservatively dressed avatar will be interpreted as indicating a more demure personality than a hand-on-hip, head-held-high posture of a less conservatively dressed avatar, especially if the dynamics of a provocative walk are included in the latter. The intentionality should be recognized as a unique form of communication; the very fact that an avatar is assembled and operated entirely by personal intention provides rhetorical opportunities that SL residents use in their interpretation of others, their formation of community, their experience of religion, and to convey their own SL "personality." That these abilities are intrinsic to religious gatherings and activities in SL provides a significant increase, relative to previous media, in the personal and communal expression of religion in 3-D cyberspace.

Solutions and Recommendations

Near the end of a conversation with SL resident Deborah Devine, I told her about a National Broadcasting Company (NBC) segment, titled "Give Me that Online Religion: Virtual Religious Services are Gaining in Popularity," featuring Professor and Methodist Reverend Elaine Heath. I explained to Deborah how I was researching religious communities in SL, and how in the video segment Reverend Heath argues, "The Church cannot be the Church without flesh and blood interaction." Deborah Devine laughed back, "That RL [real-life] pastor is an idiot lol [laugh out loud]." Deborah paused and then added, "Really does the Holy Spirit have flesh and blood?" For Deborah, not only is interaction with fellow practitioners more readily available in SL, but the Holy Spirit is available as well. There was another pause, and then Deborah said, "This [Second] life is rich with experience, and I can do it sitting in my nightgown … sorry… now the dog needs me to take him out. BRB [be right back]." With this, Deborah took a break to attend to her dog in real life.

To document such "imponderabilia" that make up a virtual life, we described the Cardean Ethnographic Method—an ethnographic technique formulated to study religious practice on 3-D metaverse platforms. Methodologically, the Cardean Method demonstrates that one can transfer and adapt traditional ethnographic methods for the cyberspace of 3-D metaverse platforms. The Cardean Method's theoretical categories include the virtual as desubstantialized and nondualistic; residents as fluid cyborg-bodies; and cloud communities as temporary, flexible, outsourced groups. We have shown that these make participant observation possible on virtual 3-D metaverse platforms because they allow for the three classical elements: presence (immersion with interactivity), emergent research design, and thick description. On a theoretical level, our study causes one to rethink the relation between the virtual and the actual, especially as it relates to the materiality of the body. Realizing the material nature of virtual reality, however, indicates that the body is not dissolving into semiotic signs, but that the cyberbody is desubstantialized and nondual. Metaverse platforms hinge the cultural, abstract construct of the body with the imbricated experiences of an embodied sensorium. It is from here that we can recognize that the cultural construct of the body is abstract, it prejudices the mental, while embodiment is experiential, it prejudices the sensual. As Munster would have it, metaverse platforms "disclose a body's potential for becoming different, for transmutation" (180).

Last, the Cardean Method challenges definitions of what constitutes religion and expands our understanding of community in our highly mediated, late-capitalistic consumer culture. Our ethnography suggests that "virtual reality" is not an escape, but rather another "window" that people utilize. While we did not look over the native's shoulder, we did look through their windows and found that many people are practicing religion on SL because it is a form of "Liquid Salvation." That is, because the passage from "solid" to "liquid" modernity has dissolved traditional religious communities and institutions, users have had to actively explore and create novel, temporary, and flexible forms of salvation. For instance, when I asked Deborah how SL compared to other 3-D platforms, she said, "It is very different here in Second Life; I actually feel as though I'm supported here when I am tempted to do things I shouldn't do." Now that we have found Liquid Salvation, we need to use ethnography to analyze it. We need to focus on the details of how Second Life functions to re-enchant the lives of religious residents, and how such re-enchantment is tied to the expanded sensorium of Second Life and to the greatly increased opportunities for understanding the imponderabilia of a virtual life.

REFERENCES

Appadurai, A. (1986). Theory in anthroplogy: Center and periphery. *Comparative Studies in Society and History, 28*(2), 356–361. doi:10.1017/S0010417500013906

Au, W. J. (2008). *The making of Second Life: Notes from the new world.* New York, NY: Collins.

Bauman, Z. (2000). *Liquid modernity.* Cambridge, UK: Polity Press.

Bauman, Z. (2001). *Community: Seeking safety in an insecure world.* Cambridge, UK / Malden, MA: Polity Press/ Blackwell.

Bauman, Z. (2005). *Liquid life.* Cambridge, UK/ Malden, MA: Polity Press.

Bierce, A., & Steadman, R. (2003). *The devil's dictionary.* New York, NY: Bloomsbury, Holtzbrinck Publishers.

Blascovich, J. (2002). Social influence within immersive virtual environments. In Schroeder, R. (Ed.), *The social life of avatars: Presence and interaction in shared virtual environments* (pp. 127–145). London, UK: Springer-Verlag.

Campbell, J. E. (2004). *Getting it on online: Cyberspace, gay male sexuality, and embodied identity.* New York, NY: Harrington Park Press.

Careaga, A. (2001). *E-ministry: Connecting with the net generation* (p. 216). Grand Rapids, MI: Kregel Publications.

Carpenter, E. S., & McLuhan, M. (Eds.). (1960). *Explorations in communication: An anthology.* Boston, MA: Beacon Press.

Clifford, J., & Marcus, G. E. (Eds.). (1986). *Writing culture: The poetics and politics of ethnography.* Berkeley, CA: University of California Press.

Daniel, E. V. (1991). *Fluid signs: Being a person the Tamil way.* Berkeley, CA: University of California Press.

Daniel, E. V., & Pugh, J. F. (1984). *South Asian systems of healing.* Leiden, The Netherlands: E.J. Brill.

Fornas, J. (2002). *Digital borderlands: Cultural studies of identity and interactivity on the Internet.* (Digital formations, vol. 6). New York, NY: Peter Lang.

Fox, R. G. (1991). Introduction: Working in the present. In Fox, R. G. (Ed.), *Recapturing anthropology: Working in the present.* Santa Fe, NM: School of American Research Press, University of Washington Press.

Geertz, C. (1973). *Thick description: Toward an interpretative theory of culture. The interpretation of cultures* (pp. 3–30). New York, NY: Basic Books.

Geertz, C. (1983). *Local knowledge: Further essays in interpretive anthropology.* New York, NY: Basic Books.

Gibson, W. (1984). *Neuromancer.* New York, NY: Ace Books.

Gupta, A., & Ferguson, J. (1997). *Anthropological locations: Boundaries and grounds of a field science.* Berkeley, CA: University of California Press.

Haraway, D. J. (2009). *A cyborg manifesto: Science, technology, and socialist-feminism in the late twentieth century.*

Hayles, N. K. (1999). *How we became posthuman: Virtual bodies in cybernetics, literature, and informatics.* Chicago, IL: University of Chicago Press.

Helland, C. (2000). Online-religion/religion-online and virtual communitas. In J. K. Hadden & D. E. Cowan (Eds.), *Religion on the Internet: Research prospects and promises* (Religion and the social order, vol. 8). New York, NY: JAI.

Heston, K. S. (2008). The Aleph technique: Quantitative and ethnographic inquires into subjectification and religion in Second Life. In A. Mitra (Ed.), *National Communications Association Annual Convention 2008*. San Diego, CA.

Hine, C. (2000). *Virtual ethnography*. London, UK: SAGE.

Hodes, A. (1972). *Encounter with Martin Buber*. London, UK: Allen Lane.

Hoggett, P. (1997). *Contested communities: Experiences, struggles, policies*. Bristol, UK: Polity Press.

Ihde, D. (2002). *Bodies in technology*. Minneapolis, MN: University of Minnesota Press.

Karaflogka, A. (2002). Religious discourse and cyberspace. *Religion, 32*(4), 279–291. doi:10.1006/reli.2002.0405

Kohn, T. (1995). She came out of the field and into my home: Reflections, dreams and a search for consciousness in anthropological method. In Cohen, A. P., & Rapport, N. (Eds.), *Questions of consciousness* (pp. 41–59). London, UK: Routledge. doi:10.4324/9780203449486_chapter_2

Krueger, M. W. (1991). *Artificial reality II*. Reading, MA: Addison-Wesley Pub. Co.

Lacan, J. (1966). *Écrits*. Paris, France: Seuil.

Lévy, P. (1995). *Qu'est-ce que le virtuel?* Paris, France: La Découverte.

Lévy, P. (1998). *Becoming virtual: Reality in the digital age*. New York, NY: Plenum Trade.

Malinowski, B. (1961). *Argonauts of the Western Pacific*. New York, NY: E. P. Dutton & Co.

Maxwell, P. (2002). Virtual religion in context. *Religion, 32*(4), 343–354. doi:10.1006/reli.2002.0410

Merleau-Ponty, M. (1962). *Phenomenology of perception*. New York, NY: Humanities Press.

Munster, A. (2006). *Materializing new media: Embodiment in information aesthetics*. Hanover, NH: Dartmouth College Press, University Press of New England.

Nusselder, A. C. (2006). *Interface fantasy: A Lacanian cyborg ontology = Interface fantasie: een Lacaniaanse Cyborg Ontologie*. Amsterdam, The Netherlands: F&N Eigen Beheer.

O'Leary, S. D. (1996). Cyberspace as sacred space: Communicating religion on computer networks. *Journal of the American Academy of Religion. American Academy of Religion, 64*(4), 781–808.

O'Reilly, K. (2005). *Ethnographic methods*. London, UK: Routledge. Retrieved July 2, 2010, from http://www.pewinternet.org/

Ong, W. J. (1967). *The presence of the word: Some prolegomena for cultural and religious history. The Terry Lectures*. New Haven, CT: Yale University Press.

Pew Research Center's Internet & American Life Project. (2000-2010). *The Pew Internet & American Life Project is one of seven projects that make up the Pew Research Center, a nonpartisan, nonprofit "fact tank" that provides information on the issues, attitudes and trends shaping America and the world*. Retrieved July 2, 2010, from http://www.pewinternet.org/

Rheingold, H. (1991). *Virtual reality*. New York, NY: Summit Books.

Rheingold, H. (1993). *The virtual community: Homesteading on the electronic frontier*. Reading, MA: Addison-Wesley Pub. Co.

Schackman, D. (2009). Exploring the new frontiers of collaborative community. *New Media & Society, 11*(5), 875–885. doi:10.1177/1461444809106702

Serres, M., & Sauer, K. L. (2006). *Atlas*. Berlin, Germany: Verl. für das Künstlerbuch.

Stone, A. R. (1991). Will the real body please stand up? In Benedikt, M. (Ed.), *Cyberspace: First steps* (pp. 81–118). Cambridge, MA: MIT Press.

Taylor, C. (1989). *Sources of the self: The making of the modern identity*. Cambridge, MA: Harvard University Press.

Tönnies, F., & Harris, J. (2001). *Community and civil society*. Cambridge, UK/ New York, NY: Cambridge University Press.

Turkle, S. (1984). *The second self: Computers and the human spirit*. New York, NY: Simon and Schuster.

Turkle, S. (1996). Who am we? We are moving from modernist calculation toward postmodernist simulation, where the self is a multiple, distributed system. *Wired, 4*(1), 148.

Weber, M. (1976). *The Protestant ethic and the spirit of capitalism* (2nd ed.). London, UK: George Allen & Unwin.

Wertheim, M., & Leonard, A. (1999). The pearly gates of cyberspace: A history of space from Dante to the Internet. *The New York Times Book Review*, p. 12.

Yee, N., & Bailenson, J. N. (2009). The difference between being and seeing: The relative contribution of self-perception and priming to behavioral changes via digital self-representation. *Media Psychology, 12*(2), 195–209. doi:10.1080/15213260902849943

ENDNOTES

[1] As Charles Taylor has demonstrated in *Sources of the Self: The Making of the Modern Identity* (1989), the Modern first-person singular pronoun "I" is often problematic and slippery. As James Clifford has shown in *Writing Culture: The Poetics of Politics Ethnography* (1986), "I" is even more problematic for ethnographic writing. Our research team, in its final form, consisted of the principal investigator and five advanced undergraduates. We tried various methods, but eventually found it most effective to employ the first person, even if it indicates research conducted by different researchers. Accordingly, we treat the first-person singular not as representing an actual, bounded self, but as a social and discursive construct, which emerges from our data.

[2] These were sparked by the paper "Researching the Internet" given by Dr. Birgit Bräuchler (University of Munich) at the EASA Media Anthropology e-seminar in 2005. (http://www.media-anthropology.net/ braeuchler_internetresearch.pdf [accessed July 1, 2010])

[3] For the difference between "virtual-" and "actual-world" ethnography, see: Clifford, J. (1997). Spatial practices: Fieldwork, travel, and the disciplining of anthropology. In *Routes: Travel and translation in the late twentieth century* (pp. 52-91). Cambridge, MA: Harvard University Press; Escobar, Arturo. (2000). Welcome to Cyberia: Notes on the anthropology of cyberculture. In D. Bell & B. M. Kennedy (Eds.), *The Cybercultures reader* (pp. 56-76). London: Routledge. For examples of good textual based MUDs, see http://www.topmudsites.com/.

Chapter 20
Second Life, Second Morality?

Katleen Gabriels
Vrije Universiteit Brussel, Belgium

Joke Bauwens
Vrije Universiteit Brussel, Belgium

Karl Verstrynge
Vrije Universiteit Brussel, Belgium

ABSTRACT

This study is an examination of in-world morality of frequent residents of Second Life. Given the lack of systematic research on morality in non-gaming virtual worlds, the authors conducted an explorative small-scale, in-depth qualitative study with regular Second Life-residents. Drawing on cyber-anthropology, cyber-sociology, and game studies, they explore to what extent ideas and pictures of in-world moral behaviour differ from moral categories and definitions used in real life situations. Research findings show, firstly, that communication and sanction mechanisms (e.g. gossip), known from real life, are important means to create social control and group cohesion in Second Life. Secondly, the technologically mediated context intensifies and provides new tools for social control (e.g. alternative avatar). Thirdly, residents also make use of "out-world" systems to restrict or punish immoral behaviour (e.g. blogs, discussion forums, Web search engines). In general, findings indicate that morality in Second Life is not completely different from morality shown in real life. On the other hand, they also point at distinctiveness in a mediated environment because of specific technological tools.

INTRODUCTION

Although today millions of people are spending a considerable amount of time in three-dimensional non-gaming virtual worlds, little systematic research has been done regarding the question of morality and its distinctive nature in these

particular worlds. This lack is in sharp contrast to the numerous media debates on *Second Life*. Much ink has flowed in popular media discourses about the alleged absence of morality in this social virtual world. In those 'panic waves' the freedom that users have to experiment without restraints is often linked with the upsurge of immoral or amoral behaviour (e.g. Kuipers, 2006). Likewise game studies have shown much more

DOI: 10.4018/978-1-60960-854-5.ch020

interest in moral issues (e.g. sex, violence, aggression, cheating) in digital games like *World of Warcraft* or first person shooter games as *Call of Duty: Modern Warfare* or *America's Army* (see amongst many others Consalvo, 2005; Anderson, 2004; Anderson, & Bushman, 2002; Anderson, Gentile, & Buckley, 2007; Anderson, Sakaoto, Gentile, et al., 2008; Bushman, & Anderson, 2002; Ferguson, 2009; Mathiak, & Weber, 2006; Weber, Ritterfeld, & Mathiak, 2006; Longman, O'Connor, & Obst, 2009).

Taking these observations as our setting, we aim to provide a more evidence-based understanding of how people make sense of virtual morality. Our research focuses on the popular and widely known social virtual world *Second Life* (SL). SL was created in 2003 by Linden Lab and is defined as *"an immersive, user-created online world"* (Au, 2008, p. x). Linden Lab does not impose a game-oriented goal on its residents; they are free to choose how to spend their time in-world. Exactly this freedom to act and to experiment in a world that is believed to be a second, different or so-called *"otherworld"* (Dibbell, 1993) is the starting point of our investigation. We explore how people who often engage in SL think about morally un/acceptable values and behaviour in SL and how they relate morality in SL to morality in 'real life': as analogue and correlated or discontinuous and disconnected. Social life has produced different systems to restrict and punish immoral behaviour in 'real life'. One can ask oneself if these systems also stand in virtual worlds. Or to phrase the question more radically: does it *really* matter that immoral behaviour is limited or punished in virtual worlds, as these worlds are only 'virtual' and thus not rooted in actuality?

The specific focus in this chapter is on the dynamics and mechanisms of social control: how they are rooted in offline social conventions people bring along when they dwell in SL, but also how they are shaped and activated through the technological design and tools of SL. In what follows, we start with the theoretical background of our

study. We elaborate on a description of morality, on the idea of virtual space as a moral space and we discuss the distinctiveness of SL in relation to the virtual environments of gaming. Next, we present our methodology and research findings. We conducted a small-scale, in-depth qualitative study in order to examine the in-world morality of frequent residents. We interviewed devoted SL-residents and discussed their moral experiences in SL, in order to gain an understanding of the moral nature of social interactions in SL. In particular, the in-world prevention, exclusion, and punishment of immoral behaviour are discussed here.

MORALITY, ETHICS, AND SOCIALITY

Although morality and ethics are often interpreted and treated as synonyms, clear distinctions can be drawn between both concepts. In a stricter sense, ethics deal with the systematic and critical reflection on morals and morality, and in doing so they also refer to a specific field of philosophical study. Morals and morality, on the other hand, refer respectively to the habits and norms that are given within a specific cultural context, and to the individual reflection of those norms into personal codes of conduct. Morality comes about whenever a subject is conscious of his or her conduct, i.e. when personal behaviour is reflected in an awareness that is not determined by a supra-personal (external) normative source (e.g. law). Moral persons reflect on and evaluate their behaviour, principles, judgments, norms, and values on an individual, personal level (for further discussion, see a.o. Ross, 1967; Atkinson, 1969; Frankena, 1973; Williams, 1976; Mackie, 1990; Blackburn, 2001). Since every human being develops a kind of morality, it becomes an object of scientific research, i.e. in the academic discipline of ethics or moral philosophy.

In his 1989 book *Sources of the Self: The Making of the Modern Identity*, Charles Taylor offers an interesting outline of the modern self and modern morality. Taylor distinguishes three axes of modern moral thinking: first, our sense of respect for and obligations to others; second, our understandings of what makes a full life; and third, the notion of dignity, i.e. *"the characteristics by which we think of ourselves as commanding (or failing to command) the respect of those around us"* (Taylor, 1989, p. 15). Here as well, it is stressed that morality goes further than mere respect for others and obligations to them, as there is a notion of self-reflection and self-awareness. Taylor further focuses on the essential bond between identity and moral orientation, and places this within the framework of 'moral space'.

To know who you are is to be oriented in moral space, a space in which questions arise about what is good or bad, what is worth doing and what not, what has meaning and importance for you and what is trivial and secondary (Taylor, 1989, p. 28).

Morality is primarily concerned with our relation with the other and is therefore intrinsically linked to sociality: to be able to live and work together in harmony, public space and communities have created a consistent set of rules and norms. Likewise, different methods have also been developed to reduce the possibilities of cheating and to maximize the chances of successful cooperation (e.g. Stevens, & Hauser, 2004). Among other things, we analyze signals of others to predict if he or she is trustable (Hart, 1988; Bayliss, & Tipper, 2006); we have developed different methods for cheater detection (Mealy, Daood, & Krage, 1996; Yamagishi, et al., 2003; Chiappe, & Brown, 2004); we ascribe high importance to someone's reputation in order to know if we can trust her (Brown, & Moore, 2002); gossip creates social control and group cohesion (De Backer, 2005); and we have created different forms of punishment (Fehr, & Gächter, 2000).

Virtual Space as Moral Space

Both from a theoretical and empirical point of view, many cyber-anthropologists, -sociologists and -commentators assert that virtual worlds are socially constructed worlds (a.o. Castronova, 2007; Boellstorff, 2008). In spite of their computer-generated, artificial, and synthetic constitution, virtual worlds are *"places of human culture"* (Boellstorff, 2008, p. 17). Consequently, they become morally qualified spaces where people can look upon themselves as related to and responsible for online peers. In everyday offline life, the moral relationship between the self and the other is often conceived in terms of inter-related twin concepts, all expressing a spatially configured relationship between the self and the other: presence and absence, apparentness and invisibleness, proximity and distance, distinctiveness and anonymity, neighbours and strangers (Bauman, 1993; Silverstone, 2007).

As Taylor argues *"the very way we walk, move, gesture, speak is shaped from the earliest moments by our awareness that we appear before others, that we stand in public space, and that this space is potentially one of respect or contempt, of pride or shame"* (1989, p. 15). Clearly, in virtual encounters, we also appear before others in spatial respect, but in three-dimensional, graphic, artificial, and synthetic spaces, notions of 'walking', 'moving', 'gesturing', 'speaking' have taken on a different meaning. We often appear anonymously via 'user names', we talk via chat text, and we are able to construct a different identity (or presentation of it) in terms of sex, race, age, and nationality. As a consequence, technological innovations have created a new kind of communicative space that raises specific questions with regard to the meaning of moral claims and duties in virtual respect.

As we appear before technologically mediated others in cyberspace, one can ask oneself how we have to deal there with otherness and responsibility. For instance, the so-called 'cyber-other' is principally conceived as a technologically mediated other whose commands or moral claims are at least dubious or less compelling since proximal relations are missing (Virilio, 1996). Also, one always has the possibility of switching the mediated communication off (cf. Silverstone, 2003; Baym, 2007).

Social Virtual Worlds

The fact that present-day three-dimensional social virtual worlds have their origin in both virtual reality and video games can explain why so many people confuse virtual worlds with digital games and simulations (Boellstorff, 2008, p. 42). Apart from their massively multiplayer nature, games, virtual worlds, and simulations have in common that they are three-dimensional environments inhabited by avatars. Moreover, they can all be defined as highly interactive virtual environments (HIVEs) (Aldrich, 2009, p. 1). However, the absence of strictly controlled scenarios that have been designed to develop specific competencies and the lack of a predetermined goal (for instance, moving to the next level) differentiates social virtual words from virtual games (Aldrich, 2009, p. 1). Because of the dissimilar configuration of games on the one hand and virtual worlds on the other, the results of game studies cannot be automatically and completely extrapolated to virtual worlds. Nevertheless, there are overlaps between digital games and virtual worlds, for instance with regard to investment of time, emotions, and energy, social motivations, and close relationships (e.g. Yee, 2006).

With regard to morality, scientific research shows that specific mechanisms, for instance moral conventions, are also present in online communities. Baym (2007) states that one consistent finding on online groups is that they are normatively regulated. Other characteristics are empathetic communication and social hierarchies. The presence of offline moral conventions within online virtual surroundings is not remarkable, because users tend to identify with their avatar.

Because avatars are the digital representations of actual identities, they are not just fantasy or fictional objects: *"They [avatars] are the embodied conception of the participant's self through which she communicates with others in the community"* (Wolfendale, 2007, p. 114). Therefore, meaning must be ascribed to avatar attachment, as avatars are the means to appear before others in a community that aims at connectivity and interactivity. As a result of avatar identification, different forms of actual morality also emerge in the virtual world. Wolfendale states that avatar attachment must become as morally legitimate as real life attachment, for instance to material possessions or to other people (Wolfendale, 2007, p. 115). *"Avatar attachment is expressive of identity and self-conception and should therefore be accorded the moral significance we give to real-life attachment that play a similar role"* (Wolfendale, 2007, p. 111). Identification with the avatar is also related to the significance users assign to the reputation of their avatar (cf. infra).

Second Life

One of the most widely known and popular virtual worlds is called *Second Life*. Philip Rosedale, who also founded *Second Life*'s development company 'Linden Lab', created this virtual world. *Second Life* was launched on June 23, 2003, and is freely accessible via the Internet for any person above the age of eighteen. Residents, i.e. users of SL, interact with each other through avatars.

SL is defined as *"an immersive, user-created online world"* (Au, 2008, p. x) and can also be defined as an online Multi User Virtual Environment (MUVE). SL is user-created, which means that Linden Lab confines itself to the production of software and infrastructure, and allows residents to design the virtual world by building virtual objects and make real profit by selling them. Linden Lab does not impose a goal on its residents, who are free to choose how they want to spend their time in-world and how they attribute sense and meaning to their in-world activities.

Because it can be looked upon as a collaborative and cooperative microcosm filled with avatars that interact with each other in various ways, SL is an interesting platform to study morality and sociality. SL is particularly relevant to study social interactions, since it consists of numerous "sims" (abbreviation of "simulators", i.e. digital land in SL) on which people, among other things, socially bond, play role-playing games and go dancing. The infrastructure of SL offers several possibilities to make friends: there is a friend list, friendship can be offered, one can become a member of various groups on the basis of shared interests, avatars can be teleported and friends can be located online via the system. Linden Lab offers numerous ways to communicate via chat, varying from voice chat, instant messaging to group chat. This way, Linden Lab stimulates social interaction and networking and, consequently, SL can be described as a *social* virtual world.

Community building and sociality are essential in social virtual worlds like SL. Boellstorff (2008, pp. 232-233) mentions three encoded categories of social relations in SL: "friend", "partner", and "group". During his fieldwork in SL, Boellstorff found out that socializing with other residents, developing friendships and investing *"time and energy in finding, making, and maintaining friends"* was the *"most common activity"* (Boellstorff, 2008, p. 157, 181). Friendships, relationships, and several forms of fruitful cooperation are undoubtedly positive effects that are generated by SL, but there are also negative effects, mostly defined by the common term 'griefing', i.e. *"behavior in a virtual world intended to disrupt the experience of others"* (Boellstorff, 2008, p. 252). Frequent examples of griefing are, amongst others, sexual assault, harassment, crudity, offensiveness, stalking, stealing, fraud, and cheating.

RESEARCH DESIGN: PROBLEM, QUESTIONS, AND METHODOLOGY

The catchphrase "Free Yourself" in Linden Lab's video advertisement for *Second Life* points at the freedom that residents have, for instance, to construct a different online identity1. The liberty to experiment and to create a new self has incited a heated public debate, as many fear that everything seems to be allowed and possible within the anonymous and unrestricted settings of SL. In particular in connection with moral identity, the idea of avatars experimenting with moral values and behaviour, in beneficial and harmful respect, has been occupying the mind of many authors (Meadows, 2008; Castronova, 2005). We take this public concern and envisioned change as our starting point. Considering SL as a 'moral space', what are the mechanisms that regulate social control in-world?

Drawing on Taylor's ideas about morality in terms of ideas, pictures, and sense-making processes (cf. supra), interpretative research provides a valid methodological approach. In line with key assumptions and concepts within qualitative-interpretative methodology (a.o. Denzin, & Lincoln, 2000a; Schwandt, 2000), we attempt to understand what is morally un/acceptable in SL in terms of the meanings residents bring to it. One of the central aims is to acquire an inside understanding, i.e. an insight in actors' definitions of situations. This entails *Verstehen* or getting inside the mind of the actors to understand what motives, beliefs, desires, feelings, and thoughts guide their actions (Schwandt, 2000, p. 192). Equally, we aim to describe and unravel *"routine and problematic moments and meanings"* (Denzin, & Lincoln, 2000b, p. 3) SL-residents encounter. Because our research aims to grasp the meanings that constitute human and more particularly moral actions, we have asked SL-residents to explain to us their virtual experiences in their own words.

To this end, we conducted two focus group interviews and four individual interviews. Starting

Table 1. Overview respondents (N=14)

	Gender	Year of Birth	Education	Marital status / children	Self-reported primary motivation	Main activity in-world
R1	F	1984	College	Single / 0	Curiosity	Creation, work
R2	M	1946	High school	Married / 3	Curiosity	Social
R3	M	1979	College	Relationship / 0	Work	Work
R4	F	1943	High school	Widow / 2	Curiosity	Social
R5	M	1947	College	Married / 2	Leisure	Social, SL-real estate
R6	M	1965	College	Married / 0	Curiosity	Social, creation
R7	F	1953	University	Married / 2	Curiosity	Social
R8	M	1985	College	Single / 0	Leisure	Social
R9	M	1985	High school	Single / 0	Curiosity	Social, creation
R10	F	1972	High school	Divorced / 5	Social contacts	Social
R11	F	1959	University	Married / 2	Curiosity	Social, creation
R12	M	1966	College	Married / 1	Curiosity	Social
R13	M	1974	College	Cohabitation / 2	Work	Work
R14	M	1944	High school	Married / 2	Leisure / Because his wife is also active in SL	Social, creation

Explanation of the terms:

Creation: the primary motivation to reside in SL is to build virtual SL-objects or to create SL-art (e.g. photography).

Leisure: SL is a form of relaxation and enjoyment, without any obligations.

Social: the primary motivation consists of meeting friends, looking for a relationship or extending one's social network.

Work: the primary motivation is professional; these residents are in SL because of their job and are being paid to be in-world.

from the idea that interview contexts are always affected through the interaction and relation between the interviewer and the respondents (Fontana, & Frey, 2005), all interviews were conducted by the same researcher in order to control the effects of social dynamics as much as possible. The interviews were semi-structured: the interviewer started from an interview guide with a set of pre-determined topics, but equally left scope for discussion (in the focus groups) and excursions (in the individual interviews). Except for two electronic interviews through Voice Over IP, all interviews were face-to-face. However, given the availability of audio and visual cues and the synchronous course of communication, the VoIP interview comes close to face-to-face interaction.

We used purposive sampling strategy to select the respondents. Considering the importance of language in interpretive research, all respondents in our study were Dutch-speaking (13 Belgian and 1 Dutch participant). Another characteristic important to our study was familiarity with SL. All respondents first logged in between January 2005 and June 2007 and were actively engaged in SL since three to five years. The time that they are in-world varies from 4 hours per week (minimum) to 12 hours per day (maximum).

Apart from these characteristics, we aimed for a heterogeneous sample in order to explore the diversity and multiplicity of moral practices in SL. Dimensions of variety in the sample were socio-demographics (gender, age, education, SES), and the kind of investments, expectations, and gratifications people show in their SL-visits and -stays (see table 1 for overview).

In the analysis of the interview-transcripts, we used a distinct set of so-called sensitizing concepts (Blumer, 1954) as interpretive devices that draw attention to the key features of the overall research problem (Patton, 2002). For the sake of our argument, focus was on how social and technological factors determine the definition of morally un/acceptable values and behaviour and how SL-residents make sense of the difference and similarity between online and offline, second life and so-called first life experiences. Throughout the coding process, i.e. the process of labelling segmented parts of the interview texts, we took a double analytic approach to the interview data. On the one hand, we assumed that the respondents' statements refer to a reality that is experienced as a given, external reality (e.g. the existence of specific groups in SL). On the other hand, we assumed that in the way people describe their experiences, they equally construct the world they are part of (e.g. the categorizations they make of other groups in SL) (cf. Alasuutari, 1995; Silverman, 2000).

EXPLORATION OF THE FINDINGS

In agreement with other studies (Markham, 1998; Turkle, 1995; Boellstorff, 2008), the respondents in our study consider their involvement in a virtual world as part of significant life experiences. To them, 'virtual' most certainly does not equal 'not real'. As regular and mature users who have been in-world since a number of years, they all acknowledge the avatars as representations of human beings and identities and not as soulless objects. Equally, SL is a *social* virtual world to them and for that reason they ascribe high significance to the group and community they belong to. Apart from the solitary moments actively sought out to create or build objects, the experiences they talk about are together with others. Furthermore, our respondents consider SL not as a noncommittal game, but as a 'real' social world, which entails a 'serious' investment, whether in personal, emotional, psychological or professional terms. In this context, we noticed that our respondents talked about 'growing up' in SL. This process was described in terms of growing avatar attachment,

increasing recognition of the commitments, rules, and conventions in SL and, especially, stronger settling in social groups. When one becomes more embedded in a close group, SL gets serious. Increasing socialization (with the norms, skills, and customs) and identification (with their avatar) typify the process of 'growing up' in SL.

For a comprehensible reflection on our findings, we have inductively demarcated our results in three different fields. First, we discuss the correlation between motivations and main activities on the one hand and perceptions of morally un/acceptable behaviour on the other. Second, we elaborate on the moral consequences of anonymity, traceability, and sociality as experienced by SL-residents. Third, we consider the types of social sanctions the SL-residents we talked to discern and display when dealing with practices they morally disapprove of.

The Influence of Motives on Morality

The analysis of the interviews showed that motives for participating in SL and main activities displayed in-world regulate personal views on what residents believe is un/acceptable behaviour. Respondents who are in SL because of professional reasons (in table 1 labelled under 'work' and 'creation') are aware that they are being supervised and, this way, they make no distinction between SL-behaviour and real life behaviour. Throughout the interviews these respondents showed themselves as less emotionally involved, as their ties in SL are mostly work-related and their activities focus on professional gratification to explore the innovative use of SL and to develop software. These respondents accept telling untruths about age or gender in SL easier than in real life. For instance, R6 and R13 think lying about gender is not bad, as long as they have a good conversation and relation with this person.

However, they do have a problem with illegal issues, such as underage residents, infringement of intellectual property (e.g. the stealing of virtual objects that have been created by others), or having sex with a child or animal avatar. Also, telling untruths about profession-related skills and experiences is deemed bad. For example, R1 planned to work together with someone she met in SL and who had always been emphasizing in SL how skilful she was. When, after meeting her in real life, it became clear that she had been lying, R1 took offence at the deception. Clearly, this kind of moral indignation is distinguished from the more emotionally invested moral reactions they witness in-world. By using labels like 'drama' to describe the moral outrage of others, it becomes clear that they distance themselves from 'the fuss' others can make in-world. They realize that one always has to be aware of cheaters and not to take everything for truth or reality.

This professional-detached position contrasts sharply with the approach taken by respondents who are in-world for social reasons, which leads to higher emotional investment. Respondents who are looking for love or friendship, have more problems with lies about age and gender, especially when they are looking for a partner. Equally they believe that violations of Linden Lab's terms and conditions are impermissible. In general, they hold the conviction that playing with someone's feelings must be punished. In their stories they suggest that these basic principles influence their in-world behaviour. They also believe that it is permitted to make use of a wide range of technological tools offered and enabled in SL. For instance, they do not denounce spying on someone, whether by creating an 'alt' (i.e. an alternative avatar), asking someone else to do it, saving chatlogs, or making screenshots of disclosing behaviour.

What all respondents have in common is the importance they ascribe to 'SL-seniority': the longer someone is online, the more trustable he or she is. They are suspicious when someone pretends to be a 'noob', i.e. a new SL-resident, but turns out to be very experienced with the specific tools of SL (e.g. walking around, teleport, scripts, textures). All respondents indicate that when you

have built a close relationship with someone and have invested time, emotions, and energy in this person, lies are not accepted. There is also a general belief that cheaters will eventually fail, for instance by betraying themselves or by showing discontinuity in their behaviour. Many respondents also have the tendency to verify the truthfulness of a person on the web, through search engines like *Google* or on social networking sites like *Facebook*.

Anonymity, Traceability, and Sociality

The sense of anonymity and, related to that, the sense of traceability have an effect on how in-world morality is conceived of. Respondents (R1, R3, R9) who have linked their SL-profile to information that makes the real life connection explicit and traceability easier (e.g. name, website), show themselves more conscious about how they present and represent themselves in SL. They express a stricter sensitivity to self-regulation, as R1 explained:

From the moment that you realize that everything that your avatar does can be traced back to your real person, you do very few things that you would not do in real life (R1).

Conversely, when you do not reveal real life information and leave no traces of personal identity data, it seems easier to disappear and to start again (with an alt, i.e. an alternative avatar) because you have no commitments. Still, the respondents in our research all shared the idea that the tendency to remain anonymous and untraceable was only tempting when making its entry in SL. The ease of openly expressing emotions, flirting, telling lies, hence, the appeal of disengaged and uncommitted social interactions clashes at a certain point in time with the socialisation process residents go through. More particularly, respondents who do not share links to real life information experience stricter self-regulation when they become embedded in a network. As they have been in-world for an extensive period, they have invested resources like time, energy, emotions, and money and they do not want to put these at stake. During the years, our respondents have collected a group of friends and connections in-world and many of them have also met in real life. Being embedded in a close network leads to social control (group cohesion, group regulation) and regulates behaviour. They are less inclined to behave badly as this might lead to a loss of friends or being kicked out of the group (cf. infra). An interesting example is R2, who has created a female alt and thus has swapped gender in-world. He cannot get out of this lie, because if he will reveal the truth, he will lose his friends in-world:

It started as a game and it ended as friendship. If I tell it, I will lose their friendship. I can't get out of it (R2).

Therefore, the respondents in our study, who have been in-world for an extensive period, simply represent their actual identity in order to avoid situations as described by R2. Other academic research shows that people, who often engage in virtual environments, including digital games, prefer being themselves *"rather than experiment with new identities and personalities"* (Yee, 2006, p. 15). Moreover, our respondents explained that they often share personal information in intense conversations and that they are connected to out-world (i.e. not in SL) social networks, both offline (e.g. meetings in real life) and online (connections via *Skype, MSN, Facebook,* different blogs and forums). For all these reasons, managing and controlling lies, biased truths or fictionalized data about oneself is far from easy.

Obviously, residents who work or create in-world are also embedded in a network, albeit a professional or business set of social contacts. To them, it is essential to have and to maintain a good reputation, as a bad name might result in a

loss of clients or contacts. When they are accused falsely, they defend themselves, either in-world or on blogs and forums. Especially blogs are important means to restore one's reputation in the group. For instance, R1 has been falsely accused of lying about her gender and of copyright issues. As a defense, she wrote an extensive piece on her blog. Respondents also talk about others to learn more about their reputation and to find out if they are trustable to cooperate with.

Social Sanctions

Finally, the respondents in our study talked about the different mechanisms they know and apply when confronted with morally unacceptable practices. First of all, it is important to note that the residents, and not Linden Lab, seem to regulate these forms of sanctioning. As an everyday, familiar and concrete example of 'unacceptable behaviour', we discussed with our respondents cheating in the most general sense. In line with other studies on online communities (e.g. teenagers and social networking sites, instant messaging boards), the mechanisms virtual communities use for sanctioning objectionable behaviour are preeminently communicative (Reid, 1999; Baym, 2010).

First, there is sanction through inflated communication. This means that the deceived person will inform others, often close friends, about what has happened. Although the respondents state that they only do this when the damage is worth mentioning, they equally suggest that it is more accepted in SL to make commotion about less grave harm. Clearly, this form of punishment is closely linked to reputation, i.e. punishing the cheater by gossip to ruin his or her reputation. Respondents point out that this happens on a regular basis and is conventional in SL.

Second, punishing unacceptable behaviour also takes place through non-communication. This means that all contact will be broken in a quiet way, for instance, by ignoring the harm-doer or by muting him or her, which is technologically possible in SL. This way, chances are high that the harm-doer will eventually become an outcast and disappear.

Finally, the respondents in our study agree on the principle that victims of serious harm will exclude the harm-doer from his or her community and banish him of her from the communicative sphere, i.e. punishment by excommunication. The cheater will be pilloried, not only in-world but also on blogs and forums.

Although these three mechanisms recall practices in tribal societies as has been dealt with within anthropology, evolutionary psychology and moral sciences, the communication and information technological tools of SL enable an intensification and stronger coordination of social sanctioning. Compared to real life, it becomes easier for the deceived persons to start an active, almost organized campaign against the cheater. It is striking how much technological tools affect social behaviour, and more specifically forms of punishment. If there are proofs, for instance incriminating (disclosing) screenshots or chat-logs, they are distributed by the deceived ones. It is important to point at the significance of the blogosphere here: the reputation of the harm-doer is actively damaged on different blogs, not only to give a clear signal to the cheater, but also to warn others for him or her. There are also forms of group punishment to make clear that the harm-doer is no longer allowed in the group, for instance by collectively removing him or her out of the friend list or by banning him or her from sims.

DISCUSSION AND CONCLUSION

Regarding social control and the in-world preven-tion and punishment of immoral behaviour, our findings show that SL can be looked upon as a microcosm of actual social life. This is in line with other substantial empirical evidence demonstrat-ing that people behave in a similar way in virtual environments as in actual world situations (e.g. Yee, et al., 2007). We also pointed at the fact that our respondents are conscious of the person behind the avatar, which is intrinsically linked to the idea of virtual space as moral space. They not only feel related to other residents within their group, they show respect for residents with whom they have established a social relationship (personal or professional), and they are aware of moral and social duties. This way, SL is not an isolated world in which *"no such things as morals exist"* (Meadows, 2008, p. 78) nor a separated world for which users have a 'second' morality. Similar to actual life, activities in virtual worlds include various types of social interaction like hanging out with friends, collaborating in groups, establishing intimate relationships, and starting love affairs. As a consequence, several aspects of human sociality occur in SL, because residents take real life social conventions and conduct with them.

However, as social virtual worlds like SL are technologically designed and constructed, the question how moral practices are contingent on, activated by or disabled through technology needs also to be taken into consideration. We already pointed at the complexity of cheating, as the different views on what respondents consider as unacceptable behaviour depend on their personal perception of SL and their in-world activities. Nevertheless, if someone has done serious harm in SL, it feels unjust and, analogous to real life, the behaviour must be punished to restore the harmony. It is remarkable to see how residents make use of technological tools to start a well-structured campaign against a harm-doer (cf. supra, excommunication). Organizing a similar campaign in real life would be more complex, simply because the tools are lacking (friend list, screenshots, chatlogs). Also, causing commotion and drama because of a harm-doer seems more accepted in SL than in actual life.

The public debate on morality in social virtual worlds is heavily framed in 'moral panic'-terms. Many express their worries about these worlds without constraints where people are believed to have the freedom to cross moral boundaries. Interestingly, our data put these panics into perspective, as we see that different kinds of social mechanisms restrict unrestrained immoral behaviour. Being traceable, being embedded in a network, group cohesion, social control, amongst others, lead to both self- and group-regulation. Also, our respondents are 'normal' people as opposed to deviant and pathological. This contrasts with the stereotypical portrayal of a frequent user of virtual worlds in various popular media: ugly, isolated, alienated, escapist, and failed in his or her first life. Obviously, we must point out that we have been dealing with residents who were willing to participate and to open up about experiences that have been heavily stigmatized in various discourses. This study, albeit explorative, local, and small-scale, has aimed to contribute to a better understanding of lived experiences and meanings. In the future, the cultural and social diversity of SL-residents, SL-groups, and SL-sims will need to be taken more into account in order to reveal similarities and differences. Also, the question of how to study continuity and discontinuity between so-called first life and second life morality keeps bringing with it methodological challenges.

REFERENCES

Alasuutari, P. (1995). *Researching culture: Qualitative method and cultural studies*. London, UK: Sage.

Aldrich, C. (2009). Virtual worlds, simulations, and games for education: A unifying view. *Innovate, 5*. Retrieved May 26, 2010, from http://www.innovateonline.info/ index.php?view=article&id=727

Anderson, C. A. (2004). An update on the effects of violent video games. *Journal of Adolescence, 27*, 122–133. doi:10.1016/j.adolescence.2003.10.009

Anderson, C. A., & Bushman, B. J. (2002). The effects of media violence on society. *Science, 295*, 2377–2379. doi:10.1126/science.1070765

Anderson, C. A., Gentile, D. A., & Buckley, K. E. (2007). *Violent video game effects on children and adolescents*. New York, NY: Oxford University Press. doi:10.1093/acprof:oso/9780195309836.001.0001

Anderson, C. A., Sakaoto, A., & Gentile, D. A. (2008). Longitudinal effects of violent video games on aggression in Japan and the United States. *Pediatrics, 122*, 1067–1072. doi:10.1542/peds.2008-1425

Atkinson, R. F. (1969). *Conduct: An introduction to moral philosophy*. London, UK: MacMillan.

Au, W. J. (2008). *The making of Second Life. Notes from the new world*. New York, NY: HarperCollins Publishers.

Bauman, Z. (1993). *Postmodern ethics*. Oxford, UK & Cambridge, MA: Blackwell.

Bayliss, A. P., & Tipper, S. P. (2006). Predictive gaze cues and personality judgments: Should eye trust you? *Psychological Science, 17*, 514–520. doi:10.1111/j.1467-9280.2006.01737.x

Baym, N. K. (2007). Interpersonal life online. In Lievrouw, L. A., & Livingston, S. (Eds.), *Handbook of new media: Social shaping and consequences of ICTs* (pp. 62–76). London, UK: Sage.

Baym, N. K. (2010). *Personal connections in the digital age*. Cambridge, UK: Polity Press.

Blackburn, S. (2001). *Being good: A short introduction to ethics*. Oxford, UK: Oxford University Press.

Blumer, H. (1954). What is wrong with social theory? *American Sociological Review, 19*, 3–10. doi:10.2307/2088165

Boellstorff, T. (2008). *Coming of age in Second Life. An anthropologist explores the virtually human*. Princeton, NJ & Oxford, UK: Princeton University Press.

Brown, W. M., & Moore, C. (2002). Smile asymmetries and reputation as reliable indicators of likelihood to cooperate: An evolutionary approach. *Advances in Psychology Research, 11*, 59–78.

Bushman, B. J., & Anderson, C. A. (2002). Violent video games and hostile expectations: A test of the general aggression model. *Personality and Social Psychology Bulletin, 28*, 1679–1686. doi:10.1177/014616702237649

Castronova, E. (2005). *Synthetic worlds – The business and culture of online games*. Chicago, IL & London, UK: The University of Chicago Press.

Castronova, E. (2007). *Exodus to the virtual world: How online fun is changing reality*. New York, NY: Palgrave MacMillan.

Chiappe, D., & Brown, A. (2004). Cheaters are looked at longer and remembered better than cooperators in social exchange situations. *Evolutionary Psychology, 2*, 108–120.

Consalvo, M. (2005). Rule sets, cheating, and magic circles: Studying games and ethics. *International Review of Information Ethics, 3*, 7–12.

De Backer, C. (2005). Cheater detection reputation: Gossip as a punishment strategy and the problems of second-order free riders. In C. De Backer (2005). *Like Belgian chocolate for the universal mind. Interpersonal and media gossip from an evolutionary perspective*, (pp. 401-425). Ghent, Belgium: Ghent University.

Denzin, N. K., & Lincoln, Y. S. (Eds.). (2000a). *Handbook of qualitative research* (2nd ed.). Thousand Oaks, CA: Sage Publications.

Denzin, N. K., & Lincoln, Y. S. (2000b). Introduction: The discipline and practice of qualitative research. In Denzin, N. K., & Lincoln, Y. S. (Eds.), *Handbook of qualitative research* (2nd ed., pp. 1–28). Thousand Oaks, CA: Sage Publications.

Dibbell, J. (1993). *A rape in cyberspace*. Retrieved September 2, 2008, from http://www.juliandibbell.com /texts/bungle.html

Fehr, E., & Gächter, S. (2000). Cooperation and punishment in public goods experiments. *The American Economic Review, 90*, 980–994. doi:10.1257/aer.90.4.980

Ferguson, C. J. (2009). Violent video games: Dogma, fear and pseudo-science. *Sceptical Inquirer, 33*, 38–54.

Fontana, A., & Frey, J. H. (2005). The interview. From neutral stance to political interview. In Denzin, N. K., & Lincoln, Y. S. (Eds.), *Handbook of qualitative research* (2nd ed., pp. 695–728). Thousand Oaks, CA: Sage Publications.

Frankena, W. K. (1973). *Ethics* (2nd ed.). Englewood Cliffs, NJ: Prentice Hall.

Hart, K. (1988). Kinship, contract and trust: The economic organization of migrants in an African city slum. In Gambetta, D. (Ed.), *Trust: Making and breaking of cooperative relations*. Oxford, UK: Blackwell.

Kuipers, G. (2006). The social construction of digital danger: Debating, defusing and inflating the moral dangers of online humor and pornography in the Netherlands and the United States. *New Media & Society, 8*, 379–400. doi:10.1177/1461444806061949

Longman, H., O'Connor, E., & Obst, P. (2009). The effect of social support derived from World of Warcraft on negative psychological symptoms. *Cyberpsychology & Behavior, 12*, 563–566. doi:10.1089/cpb.2009.0001

Mackie, J. L. (1990). *Ethics: Inventing right and wrong*. London, UK: Penguin Books.

Markham, A. N. (1998). *Life online: Researching real experience in virtual space*. Walnut Creek, CA: AltaMira Press.

Markham, A. N. (2005). The methods, politics, and ethics of representation of online ethnography. In Denzin, N. K., & Lincoln, Y. S. (Eds.), *Handbook of qualitative research* (2nd ed., pp. 793–820). Thousand Oaks, CA: Sage Publications.

Mathiak, K., & Weber, R. (2006). Towards brain correlates of natural behavior: fMRI during violent video games. *Human Brain Mapping, 27,* 948–956. doi:10.1002/hbm.20234

Meadows, M. S. (2008). *I, avatar: The culture and consequences of having a Second Life*. Berkeley, CA: New Riders.

Mealy, L., Daood, C., & Krage, M. (1996). Enhanced memory for faces of cheaters. *Ethology and Sociobiology, 17,* 119–128. doi:10.1016/0162-3095(95)00131-X

Patton, M. Q. (2002). *Qualitative research & evaluation methods* (3rd ed.). Thousand Oaks, CA: Sage Publications.

Reid, E. (1999). Hierarchy and power: Social control in cyberspace. In Marc, A., & Smith, P. K. (Eds.), *Communities in cyberspace* (pp. 107–133). London, UK: Routledge.

Ross, W. D. (1967). *The right and the good*. Oxford, UK: Clarendon Press.

Schwandt, T. A. (2000). Three epistemological stances for qualitative inquiry: Interpretivism, hermeneutics, and social constructionism. In Denzin, N. K., & Lincoln, Y. S. (Eds.), *Handbook of qualitative research* (2nd ed., pp. 189–213). Thousand Oaks, CA: Sage Publications.

Silverman, D. (2000). Analyzing talk and text. In Denzin, N. K., & Lincoln, Y. S. (Eds.), *Handbook of qualitative research* (2nd ed., pp. 189–213). Thousand Oaks, CA: Sage Publications.

Silverstone, R. (2003). Proper distance: Towards an ethics for cyberspace. In Liestøl, G., Morrison, A., & Terje, R. (Eds.), *Digital media revisited: Theoretical and conceptual innovations in digital domains* (pp. 469–491). Cambridge, MA: MIT Press.

Silverstone, R. (2007). *Media & morality: On the rise of the Mediapolis*. Cambridge, MA: Polity Press.

Stevens, J. R., & Hauser, M. D. (2004). Why be nice? Psychological constraints on the evolution of cooperation. *Trends in Cognitive Sciences, 8,* 60–65. doi:10.1016/j.tics.2003.12.003

Taylor, C. (1989). *Sources of the self: The making of modern identity*. Cambridge, MA: Harvard University Press.

Turkle, S. (1995). *Life on the screen: Identity in the age of the Internet*. New York, NY: Touchstone.

Virilio, P. (1996). *Cybermonde, la politique du pire: Entretien avec Philippe Petit*. Paris, NY: Editions Textuel.

Weber, R., Ritterfeld, U., & Mathiak, K. (2006). Does playing violent video games induce aggression? Empirical evidence of a functional magnetic resonance imaging study. *Media Psychology, 8,* 39–60. doi:10.1207/S1532785XMEP0801_4

Williams, B. (1976). *Morality: An introduction to ethics*. Cambridge, UK: Cambridge University Press.

Wolfendale, J. (2007). My avatar, my self: Virtual harm and attachment. *Ethics and Information Technology, 9,* 111–119. doi:10.1007/s10676-006-9125-z

Yamagishi, T., Tanida, S., Mashima, R., Shimoma, E., & Kanazawa, S. (2003). You can judge a book by its cover: Evidence that cheaters may look different from cooperators. *Evolution and Human Behavior, 24*, 290–301. doi:10.1016/S1090-5138(03)00035-7

Yee, N. (2006). The psychology of MMORPGs: Emotional investment, motivations, relationship formation, and problematic usage. In Schroeder, R., & Axelsson, A. (Eds.), *Avatars at work and play: Collaboration and interaction in shared virtual environments* (pp. 187–207). London, UK: Springer-Verlag.

Yee, N., & Bailenson, J. N. (2007). The Proteus effect: The effect of transformed self-representation on behavior. *Human Communication Research, 33*, 271–290. doi:10.1111/j.1468-2958.2007.00299.x

Yee, N., Bailenson, J. N., Urbanek, M., Chang, F., & Merget, D. (2007). The unbearable likeness of being digital: The persistence of nonverbal social norms in online virtual environments. *Cyberpsychology & Behavior, 10*, 115–121. doi:10.1089/cpb.2006.9984

ADDITIONAL READING

Chesney, T., Coyne, I., Logan, B., & Madden, N. (2009). Griefing in virtual worlds: causes, casualties and coping strategies. *Information Systems Journal, 19*, 525–548. doi:10.1111/j.1365-2575.2009.00330.x

Craft, A. J. (2007). Sin in Cyber-Eden: Understanding the Metaphysics and Morals of Virtual Worlds. *Ethics and Information Technology, 9*, 205–217. doi:10.1007/s10676-007-9144-4

Hamelink, C. J. (2000). *The Ethics of Cyberspace.* London: Sage Publications.

Jackson, L. A., Zhao, Y., Qiu, W., Kolenic, A., Fitzgerald, H. E., Harold, R., & Von Eye, A. (2008). Cultural Differences in Morality in the Real and Virtual Worlds: A Comparison of Chinese and U.S. Youth. *Cyberpsychology & Behavior, 11*, 279–286. doi:10.1089/cpb.2007.0098

Jackson, L. A., Zhao, Y., Witt, E. A., Fitzgerald, H. E., & Von Eye, A. (2009). Gender, Race and Morality in the Virtual World and Its Relationship to Morality in the Real World. *Sex Roles, 60*, 859–869. doi:10.1007/s11199-009-9589-5

Schroeder, R. (Ed.). (2002). *The Social Life of Avatars: Presence and Interaction in Shared Virtual Environments*. London: Springer-Verlag.

Schroeder, R. (2007). An overview of ethical and social issues in shared virtual environments. *Futures, 39*, 704–717. doi:10.1016/j.futures.2006.11.009

Schroeder, R., & Axelsson, A. (Eds.). (2006). *Avatars at Work and Play: Collaboration and Interaction in Shared Virtual Environments*. London: Springer-Verlag.

Segovia, K., Bailenson, J. N., & Monin, B. (2010). Morality in Virtual Reality: The Moral and Immoral Self and Other. *Proceedings of the 60th Annual ICA Conference*, Singapore.

KEY TERMS AND DEFINITIONS

Alt: An alternative avatar. Many residents of *Second Life* have one or more alts.

Morality: Morals and morality refer respectively to the habits and norms that are given within a specific cultural context, and to the individual reflection of those norms into personal codes of conduct. We speak of morality when a subject is conscious of his or her conduct, i.e. when personal behaviour is reflected in an awareness that is not determined by a supra-personal normative source.

Noob or Newbie: A new resident of *Second Life*.

Prim(itive): Primitives are the fundamental building blocks in *Second Life*; they are essential to be able to build virtual objects.

Second Life: User-created and immersive social virtual world, founded by Linden Lab. *Second Life* is freely accessible via the Internet for any person above the age of eighteen.

Sim(ulator): A sim is a district of virtual land in *Second Life*. *Second Life*'s grid consists of numerous sims, which are all contained on actual world's servers.

Texture: An image that is essential for the creation of virtual objects in *Second Life*. Textures are used to cover the faces of a primitive (see *Second Life Wikia*: http://secondlife.wikia.com/wiki/Texture).

Virtual Worlds: Interactive, three-dimensional, computer-generated simulated places, enabled by online technologies and inhabited by persons. Contrary to digital games, virtual worlds lack a predetermined goal and controlled scenarios that have been designed to develop specific competencies.

ENDNOTE

[1] Linden Lab's video advertisement of *Second Life*. Retrieved April 19, 2010, from http://www.youtube.com/watch?v=z3gHCupXSMs

Chapter 21
Virtual World Professionals and the Interloper Effect in 3D Virtual Worlds

Victoria McArthur
York University, Canada

ABSTRACT

In this chapter we discuss virtual world professionals: real world employees deployed in virtual worlds for the purpose of representing a company or organization there. We investigate the notions of belonging and community in 3D virtual worlds, and identify the ways in which "belonging" and "not belonging" are constructed and perceived, especially in relation to so-called employee avatars. We explore the dimension of social stigma in virtual worlds and discuss the utility of the separate categories of outsiders and interlopers for inhabitant characterization. Our motivation for doing so is to determine the degree to which corporate presence can be mediated through the specific mechanism of employee avatar appearance. In considering the possibility that some employee avatars may be perceived as interlopers, we propose three methods for investigating the effect of their presence in virtual worlds, called the "interloper effect."

INTRODUCTION

Social virtual worlds such as *Second Life* are not only a place in which users can socialize with one another; companies have also turned to these environments in order to explore new ways to connect with one another, recruit new hires, and offer virtual world services (Brandon, 2007). Because of the complex nature of these environ-ments, social virtual worlds have been the subject of a number of high-level discussions surrounding online identity and online communities.

In addition to being a social virtual world, *Second Life* differs from other virtual worlds in that its users can conduct monetary business with one another directly through the use of Linden dollars (L$), *Second Life*'s own virtual currency. Currently, one can purchase 261 Linden dollars for one US dollar.[1] This differs from the economic systems present in other popular game-based worlds, such

DOI: 10.4018/978-1-60960-854-5.ch021

as *World of Warcraft* (http://www.worldofwarcraft.com), in that the direct conversion between real world currency and virtual currency is generally not a feature of these environments.[2] This ability to conduct monetary exchange, in combination with the ability to create virtual objects within *Second Life*, has led real world companies such as IBM and Sun Microsystems to invest in developing content for, and having a presence in, this virtual world (Brandon, 2007).

This chapter focuses on the virtual world professionals being deployed within *Second Life* *by* companies and the appearance of their avatars. Virtual world professionals are considered to be persons who are deployed within a virtual world, such as *Second Life*, for the purpose of representing their company or organization within the virtual world. We may also further distinguish these persons from other members of the virtual world community by describing the avatar they create and maintain for this purpose as an "employee avatar." In this distinction, we acknowledge the fact that these virtual world professionals may maintain more than one avatar in the same virtual environment; one or more for personal use and one for professional use.

Current literature on avatars and avatar appearance focuses primarily on the psychological aspects of the relationship between the human pilot and the avatar (e.g., Dibbell, 2001), or the mechanics of avatar creation interfaces (Pace, Houssian, & McArthur, 2009). In considering how and why users customize their avatars a number of key motivating factors have been identified in the literature, such as the desire to create an idealized version of oneself (Ducheneaut, Wen, Yee, & Wadley, 2009), and fitting in (Neustaedter & Fedorovskaya, 2008). However, little attention has been given to the appearance and behaviour of avatars created for professional interactions in virtual worlds. This chapter seeks to explore the mechanics of avatar creation for virtual world professionals and employee avatar appearance. Specifically, how are virtual world profession-

als customizing their avatars and how are these avatars perceived by other members of the virtual community?

Interestingly enough, *Second Life* is not the first multi-user virtual environment to be used by professionals. A paper by Churchill and Bly (1999) identified the use of text-based MUDs in the workplace. In their paper, the authors presented the results of a series of in-depth interviews with 8 professionals using MUDs for work-related interactions. The results revealed that use of the MUD filled a valuable communication niche for these distributed, off-site employees. The authors described these text-based virtual rooms as giving users a sense of "space" in which they can feel "co-present." On using the MUD to interact with co-workers, interviewees expressed mixed feelings. While some enjoyed using the space for collaboration, others disliked the metaphor and preferred the use of email. One respondent commented that she, "has multiple characters (or 'avatars') and uses [the MUD] for social and work purposes."

RELATED WORK

For many users, the avatar is not only a means to achieving agency within the virtual space; it is the vessel which is an integral component of their online identity (Meadows, 2008). The ability to customize our bodies in virtual worlds allows us to fine tune how we represent ourselves in this space. The creation and modification of an avatar in a particular virtual world is always mediated by the tools provided in that world; a factor that is known to its inhabitants and that actually plays a role in the formation of social perceptions. These are often known as character creation interfaces, or avatar editors.

While a great deal of research has examined avatars and identity, comparatively little work has been done to examine the mechanics of avatar customization. Due to space constraints, this chapter only discusses a handful of articles pertaining to avatar customization in social virtual worlds.

Avatar Customization

Papers by Ducheneaut et. al (2009)and Neustaedter and Fedorovskaya (2008) have identified some of the motivating factors that guide users in customizing their avatars a particular way.

In Body and Mind, Ducheneaut et. al (2009) note a lack of data explaining how and why users customize their avatars, as well as the user ease and satisfaction with existing avatar creation tools. They report on a study investigating these issues through a questionnaire administered to more than one hundred users of three virtual worlds: Maple Story, World of Warcraft, and *Second Life*.

In their attempt to characterize the motivations for the avatar modification trends they observed, they identified three conceptual factors that they hypothesized were contributing factors: idealized self, standing out, and following a trend. The first conceptual factor is self-explanatory: users may choose to create an avatar that may bear some resemblance to their real-life appearance, but with idealized or desired features. The second factor applied to users whose choice in avatar reflects a desire to have an unconventional look, where unconventional is described as being an avatar that stand out as much as possible or whose appearance is drastically different from that of the user's appearance IRL (in real life). The third describes avatars that have been modified to resemble a celebrity or reflect a popular trend in either the real world or the virtual world.

Comparatively, Neustaedter and Fedorovskaya (2008) identify four conceptual factors which they hypothesize are at play in avatar appearance trends: *realistics*, *ideals*, *fantasies*, and *roleplayers*. According to the authors, the first describes users who consider their virtual world life to be an extension of their real world life and therefore choose to create an avatar that most closely resembles themselves. The second is more in line

with the idealized self described by Ducheneaut et. al (2009). *Fantasies* are described as being users who desire an entirely different life in the virtual world. Lastly, *roleplayers* are described as being users who, like fantasies, enter the virtual world to experience life as someone else, but differ from this category in that they do not maintain identity continuity over time. The authors note that avatar appearance editors may or may not meet users' needs depending on which of the four aforementioned factors represent their virtual lives.

A particularly interesting component of Neustaedter and Fedorovskaya's paper is the discussion surrounding the social stigma of default avatars in *Second Life*. As was mentioned previously, upon joining *Second Life*, new users are prompted to choose an avatar from one of several default configurations before entering the virtual world. Once in-world, many users learn to customize the appearance of their avatar through use of the appearance editor, as well as potentially buying, acquiring, or making new clothes, hair, animations, for their avatar to wear or use. An illustration of the differences between the appearance of a default avatar and one that has undergone much modification is shown in Figure 1.

Once members of the community become familiar with the malleability of *Second Life* avatars, they are easily able to identify default avatars. The authors note that so-called veteran users identify users with default avatars as being "newbies." The effect of this social stigma is twofold: veterans view newbies as lacking in ability and assume that any social interaction with a default avatar will be related to technical issues surrounding the virtual environment. The second effect is that newbies feel the need to modify the appearance of their avatar as quickly as possible so that their avatar signifies "belonging" to the community.

From this it is very clear that the social signals triggered by avatar appearance have weight. Additionally, it is clear that there are ways to signal belonging and similarity between interactants in

Figure 1. Avatar with default cybergoth attributes (left) compared to specialized personal attributes (right)

order to have successful social interactions in virtual worlds. Other related work has investigated the link between credibility and avatar appearance, specifically with regard to anthropomorphic and non-anthropomorphic avatars. In the context of this chapter, we refer to an anthropomorphic avatar as being a non-human avatar with human traits, such as a "furry" (see Figure 2).[3]

Non-Anthropomorphic Avatars and Credibility

Even though avatar bodies in *Second Life* begin as human bodies, users can easily create or purchase avatar shapes of other anthropomorphic and non-anthropomorphic bodies. This has lead researchers to explore how credibility is linked to avatar appearance in virtual worlds and online environments (McGloin, et. al 2009; Nowak & Rauh, 2005, 2008) and how the presence of non-

anthropomorphic avatars effect social interaction (Morie & Verhuldonck, 2008).

In exploring the link between credibility and avatar choice in instant messaging, Nowak and Rauh (2005, 2008) conducted a series of studies. In the first step, 255 participants filled out a survey where they rated a set of 30 static avatars on their credibility, androgyny, and anthropomorphism. The second step was a between subjects experiment with 230 participants who interact with partners represented by one of 8 avatars (high and low androgyny, and anthropomorphism by high and low credibility).

Results of this study revealed that avatar characteristics are used in the person perception process. Participant perceptions of avatar androgyny influenced their perceptions of anthropomorphism, which influenced attributions of both avatar and partner credibility. Ultimately they found that chat partners who used more an-

Figure 2. Non-humanoid avatars in Second Life – anthropomorphic avatars or "furries" (left) and the flying spaghetti monster (right)[4]

drogynous avatars were perceived as being less credible than less androgynous partners. In addition to this, they also found that those participants with more instant messenger experience saw their partners as more credible regardless of the avatar that represented them.

McGloin et. al (2009) conducted a similar survey using the dimensions of credibility proposed by McCroskey and Yong (1981) in order to investigate how avatar appearance influences the processing of messages associated with avatars. Specifically, they investigated the relationship between credibility of text and credibility of avatar choice. Participants in this study were presented with what appeared to be a screenshot of a web page designed to look like a popular electronics retail site complete with customer reviews. Variants on the stimulus included pairings of high or low credibility avatars with high or low credibility text. For example, a low credibility avatar, such as a dinosaur, might be paired with a highly informative and well-written product review. The results of this study revealed that avatar credibility was predicted by perceptions of avatar anthropomorphism and realism. Additionally, review credibility seemed to be more dependent on avatar credibility than the credibility of the actual text. An even more

interesting result of this study was the positive link between avatar homophily and source trust.

While McGloin's results might imply that there is a certain comfort in the use of humanoid avatars, it is important to consider the environment for which the hypothesis was tested. While deviance from "real world" ideals had a negative impact on review credibility in an online store, this might not be the case in every computer-mediated environment. Consider the differences between the social climate of an online website hosting reviews of commercial products and a social virtual world such as *Second Life*. In many social virtual worlds, the social climate is "co-constructed" between its users.[5] We refer to this as the co-constructed nature of virtual worlds.

The Co-Constructed Nature of Virtual Worlds

The hypotheses presented in this chapter are largely based on the co-constructed nature of virtual worlds. Virtual worlds, whether text-based or three-dimensional, have presented us with a new space in which to communicate with others and build new communities. In the early text-based MUDs, users utilized text to create their physical surroundings. Users would describe the "rooms" they occupied in great detail, and these descriptions were generally agreed upon, and co-authored with the other inhabitants (Turkle, 1997).

The co-constructed nature of virtual worlds is not limited to atmosphere and décor; social contracts also emerged within these digital spheres. While a text-based virtual life may seem insignificant compared to our physical lives, the literature illustrates how deeply connected we are to our other selves. In his article "A Rape in Cyberspace", Dibbell (2001) describes a "cyberrape" that occurred in a MUD called LambdaMOO. A user piloting an avatar by the name of Mr. Bungle utilized a "voodoo doll" program that allowed him to essentially describe actions and falsely attribute them to other player characters. Mr. Bungle decided to use this program to make it appear as though other player characters were performing a variety of sexually explicit acts to themselves, to other player characters, and to Mr. Bungle. The human pilots, although safe in real life, were subjected to reading this text and having it appear as though it had originated from their own keyboards. Still, the incidents involving Mr. Bungle and the "voodoo doll" program left users feeling violated and raised awareness of user embedded values associated with avatar use.

The experience of constructing and sharing a virtual space of this nature also involves the co-construction of social contracts and their evolution. The difference between the social contracts in these spheres is perhaps best illustrated by Rheingold as he recounts his experiences in joining an online community called the WELL:

It became clear to me during the first months of that history that I was participating in the self-design of a new kind of culture. I watched the community's social contracts stretch and change as the people who discovered and started building the WELL in its first year or two were joined by so many others. Norms were established, challenged, *changed, re-established, rechallenged, in a kind of speeded-up social evolution (Rheingold, 1999).*

The fact that *Second Life*'s areas are divided up into individual islands makes it ideal for the compartmentalization of communities, their aesthetics, and social contracts. One such example is best illustrated in Meadows' I, Avatar, which describes the different social contracts and resultant interaction between Furries and Gor in *Second Life* (Meadows, 2008).

Virtual World Professionals and Avatar Appearance Codes

Professional appearance in real-world situations is important in business relations. For this reason it is not uncommon for corporations to employ dress codes, which can extend beyond attire to deal with hair colour and body piercing. These are the properties of appearance that are most easily manipulated in the real world. The degree to which one can manipulate the appearance of one's avatar in *Second Life* is almost infinite by comparison. The avatar editor in *Second Life* allows users to control every aspect of their avatar's appearance with great precision. For this reason, it is easy to consider how the notion of the dress code could easily become an "appearance code" when applied to virtual worlds (McArthur, 2008).

With regard to avatar appearance codes, how detailed are these policies and do they match the ideals of the virtual world? If a company wishes to court members of the virtual community, how will their employees be received? If the appearance code is simply a direct mapping of "real life" ideals of professionalism onto virtual world professionals, an appearance code could elicit a negative effect. Preliminary work conducted in 2009 investigating employee avatar appearance and avatar appearance codes suggests that a small number of real world companies do employ such policies (McArthur & Baljko, 2009). Some participants in that study stated that their company expected that representative avatars be human with professional or business-casual attire. Other participants stated that the policy only required that avatars be clothed and that representatives use common sense when making decisions regarding how their avatar looks and behaves within the virtual world. Interestingly, in our data we discovered that none of the policies neglected to address the issue of non-human avatars.

If avatar appearance can signal "belonging" within *Second Life*, what effects might an overly corporate appearance code have on employee avatars? One proposed effect of such a policy is the "interloper effect" (McArthur & Baljko, 2009). This term is borrowed from evolutionary biology (Smurda & Haselton, 2002), and in the context of this work it is used to describe the differences among attributions of professionalism and belonging in virtual worlds.

THE INTERLOPER EFFECT

In the case of employee-identified avatars, an overly corporate avatar may have a negative effect on a virtual world professional's social interactions. This can occur if the appearance code is simply a direct mapping of "real life" ideals of professionalism onto virtual world professionals, where the members of the community who are not there in a corporate capacity may have intentionally left these ideals out. We therefore hypothesize that an appearance code could have a negative effect on how virtual world professionals are received by members of the community.

The pragmatics of avatar modification has several facets. First, the particular selections made with respect to hair, clothing, and skin each have their own social signals. But in addition, there is a shared understanding among the members of the on-line world as to what these choices entailed --- the technical difficulty or ease or the "monetary" expense of a particular choice. The choices that a user makes have a social signal

that extends beyond mere appearance. What is at work here is not only a user's ability to use an avatar appearance editor in a particular way, but also the shared knowledge about the capabilities of the appearance editor. Since the capabilities off the appearance editor are known within the community, how one customizes their avatar can signal their intentions within the community.

In the case of employee avatars, the actual appearance of the particular avatar, combined with the shared knowledge about how appearance editing works, can signal to the community that an appearance code has been imposed. For example, clothing with logos are not part of the default repertoire of appearance attributes, so those encountering an avatar who is sporting such an article of clothing will deduce that the encountered user must have made some deliberate additional appearance modifications, either by purchasing the item in-world, or by creating the item themselves.

An online survey administered in late 2008 investigated employee avatar appearance for 37 virtual world professionals (McArthur, 2010). Of those 37, only 5 indicated that the appearance of their avatar was governed by an avatar appearance code. When asked if the policy addresses non-human avatars, all participants indicated yes, with three indicating that non-human avatars are allowed by the policy.

Since we expected the specifics of each policy to vary, thee participants were presented with additional open-ended questions that were designed to gather the details of these policies. When asked to describe the appearance code, some participants stated that their company expected that representative avatars be human with professional or business-casual attire. Other participants stated that the policy only required that avatars be clothed and that representatives use common sense when making decisions regarding how their avatar looks and behaves within the virtual world.

Next, participants were asked how much this policy has evolved over the course of its use. All participants indicated that the policy has remained substantively unchanged since its inception. Three of these participants did note that the policy had been implemented after the company or organization had moved into *Second Life*.

Lastly, we asked participants whether or not they felt as though their company's policy is suitable for virtual world professionals deployed within *Second Life*. Responses to this question varied greatly. Two participants indicated agreement with the statement. Two participants suggested that the appearance codes were not very suitable for 3D virtual worlds, but understood that the policies had been implemented so as to avoid offending clientele. The remaining participant expressed a lack of personal interest in the existence of the policy.

So while the sample size was small, it is clear that there may be mixed feelings among virtual world professionals regarding the appropriateness of policies governing employee avatar appearance. It is interesting to note that, while the five policies discussed varied, none of the policies neglected to address the issue of non-human avatars. Clearly those creating the policies have some understanding of the malleability of avatars in *Second Life* if their policies include such guidelines, but what is the basis for allowing or not allowing furries?

Neustaedter and Fedorovskaya (2008) documented the degree to which social stigma was associated with an inhabitant's use of the default appearance characteristics in *Second Life*. If an inhabitant's failure to modify their avatar's default appearance had the deleterious effect of marking him or her as and outsider in relation to the community, what other types of avatar configurations may have a detrimental effect on social interaction? In the case of avatar appearance codes, could corporate governance have a detrimental effect on in-world relations, and if so, how would we classify this effect? We turn to evolutionary biology and the idea of interlopers in order to formulate a hypothesis and methodological approach in exploring this.

Interlopers in Social Virtual Worlds

Within the field of evolutionary biology, a particular phenomenon has been identified with respect to interlopers. The phenomenon concerns the differences among attributions of sexual interest among different perceivers: if the perceiver is a person who is in a committed relationship with the purported target of the sexual interest, then the degree of sexual interest is perceived as much greater than if the perceiver is outside of the relationship. In commonplace terms, the perception of the threat is heightened for the party which is actually facing the threat, as opposed to a bystander.

In order to illustrate how the idea of interlopers can be adapted to describe employee avatars in virtual worlds, the parallels are outlined as follows: In evolutionary biology, the "interloper effect" refers to (1) the heightened awareness of (2) sexual advances by (3) couples in committed relationships. The interloper is therefore perceived as (4) threatening the ideals of the committed relationship. Adapted to virtual worlds, the "interloper effect" refers to the (1) heightened awareness of (2) social presence by (3) members of a virtual community. The interloper is perceived as (4) threatening the ideals of the virtual community.

What makes the interloper effect so interesting is that the actions of the one who has been labelled "interloper" in evolutionary biology may actually be completely benign in nature. One such false positive is outlined in an article by Haselton and Nettle (2006) in which they describe how social interaction between one's mate and an attractive other can result in the other being labelled as interloper – even if their actions are not sexually or romantically charged. This is what really gives the term mobility in the context of virtual world professionals; the interloper effect is not dependent on the actual intentions of the virtual world professionals, just the perception of them via the members of the community.

The interloper effect in virtual worlds, thus, would be a phenomenon concerning a difference between the perceptions of the world's inhabitants and the perceptions of those observing the world from outside (McArthur & Baljko, 2009). This is an important hypothesis for study because the individuals who are charged with the creation of "appearance code" corporate governance (e.g., those with HR affiliations) could very well be the "outside observers" to the virtual worlds. If so, then there very well could be a misalignment between the goals of the "appearance code" and its actual effect once deployed. While the appearance code may have been created in order to ensure professionalism in-world, the policy could potentially be perceived as threatening the community's ideals. This is especially apparent when we consider the cultural compartmentalization of specific islands in *Second Life*, and how non-compliance within those areas can be considered offensive.

When one considers the etymology of the "interloper" – the term may seem unnecessarily harsh. In the English language, the word interloper refers to persons or things who are not only considered to be outsiders; their presence is not only unwanted – it is also considered by some definitions to be disruptive. Most likely, virtual world professionals are not entering this sphere in order to infiltrate and interfere in the affairs of *Second Life* citizens, but how is their presence perceived by others? Since our interactions are mediated by our avatars in this space, we must first look to employee avatars in order to explore this idea of the interloper.

PROPOSED METHODS FOR INVESTIGATING THE INTERLOPER EFFECT

In order to determine whether or not an interloper effect is elicited, two methods based on established methodologies are proposed within this section.

Method 1: Ethnographic Study

Looking to some of the more prominent theories of online ethnographic studies proposed by Correll (1995), Hine (2000), and Kozinets (1998, 2002, 2006), a pilot study was designed to collect data on virtual world professionals and the appearance of their avatars. In our pilot study, we visited several corporate sites in *Second Life* and collected data in the form of interviews, observations, and screen shots. To extend this methodology to a study of the interloper effect, researchers would also collect the same data about the interactions between employee avatars and members of the virtual world community. The data collected would include observations about the interactions between employee-identified avatars and personal avatars, as well as follow-up survey data. A follow-up survey might include a list of questions intended to determine how the pilot of the personal avatar felt about their interaction with the employee-identified avatar.

Unfortunately, while the data we collected in our pilot study was very informative, a we encountered a few technical limitations, some of which are specific to *Second Life*. Firstly, when leaving an island in *Second Life*, it is not uncommon for users to teleport to another location, rather than walking or flying away. Additionally, users may also excuse themselves from the social interaction in order to log out of *Second Life*. While it would not be impossible to follow up with users who have teleported or logged out, the likeliness that such a participant declines an offer to follow up with the researcher presents a major issue. In addition to this, the popularity of *Second Life* for use by real world companies appears to be on the decline (possibly due to the more recent economic crisis). With this in mind, acquiring enough data with the aforementioned follow-up issues presents a problem with regard to quantitative analysis.

Method 2: Survey

One possible alternative to the in-world ethnographic study is one that is based purely on online surveys. Researchers who have opted to collect data from virtual world users via surveys have had a great deal of success in securing large numbers of respondents (e.g., Ducheneaut, et al., 2009). In exploring the interloper effect, questions used in this survey could be based on surveys designed by Nowak & Rauh (2005) and McGloin et. al (2009), which investigated the influence avatar choice has on users' perceptions of credibility. In these studies, users were presented with visual stimulus representing different avatar configurations and then asked a series of Likert scale questions to determine users' perceptions of anthropomorphism and credibility. The questions are based on categories of credibility proposed by McCroskey & Yong (1981).

While we aren't investigating credibility specifically, many of the dimensions of credibility are relevant to the interloper effect. For example, elements from the sociability dimension (e.g., "friendly" and "trustworthy") as well as the competence dimension (e.g., "informed" and "intelligent") are some of the key components we wish to investigate. Users' perceptions of employee avatars with regard to these dimensions can help us understand how different configurations of employee avatars are perceived by members of the virtual community.

A similar survey could be administered to members of the virtual world community in order to determine if employee-identified avatars do elicit an interloper effect. A series of images representing various configurations of employee-identified avatars, would be presented to participants. Multiple offerings of each of the variants would be produced in order to include male and female avatars, as well as varying degrees of corporate branding and alternative dress. The survey would be designed to be within-subjects, where all participants would be exposed to the same stimulus, but the order in which each participant was presented with each of the images would be randomized. This counterbalancing measure would be implemented to offset any exposure or ordering effect.

Figure 3 illustrates how the dimensions of credibility (McCroskey & Yong 1981) might be applied to this survey. Participants would be exposed to each image, one at a time, and asked to rate the avatar based on the dimensions presented.

The image in the above figure only represents one of the many configurations for employee avatars that would be tested. The images shown in Figure 4 are representative of some of the other configurations that should be tested. While the attire, skin, and hair of each of the avatars are strikingly different, their pose and body language is identical. All of the avatars in the table have identified themselves as representatives of a company through the use of group tags. In *Second Life,* the group tag is a textual affiliation marker that floats above the avatar's name. Based on our observations in the aforementioned pilot study, we have dressed these avatars in three different styles of clothing: casual attire, business or business casual attire, and branded attire. In the context of this chapter, casual attire can include, but is not limited to costumes, period clothing, gothic or alternative attire. The term "casual" was chosen to provide a category for all observed attire that did not fall under what we considered to fall outside of the commonly accepted categories of business attire.

The appearances of *variants B,* and *C* are closely aligned with "offline" configurations of professional dress whereas *variant A* takes into account the social climate of *Second Life. Variant B* pushes the boundaries with regard to business-appropriate attire in real-life, but her attire does not carry the same social stigma in *Second Life.* Understanding the differences between the two spheres is critical when creating policies like avatar appearance codes.

Figure 3. Sample survey page for the Survey Method

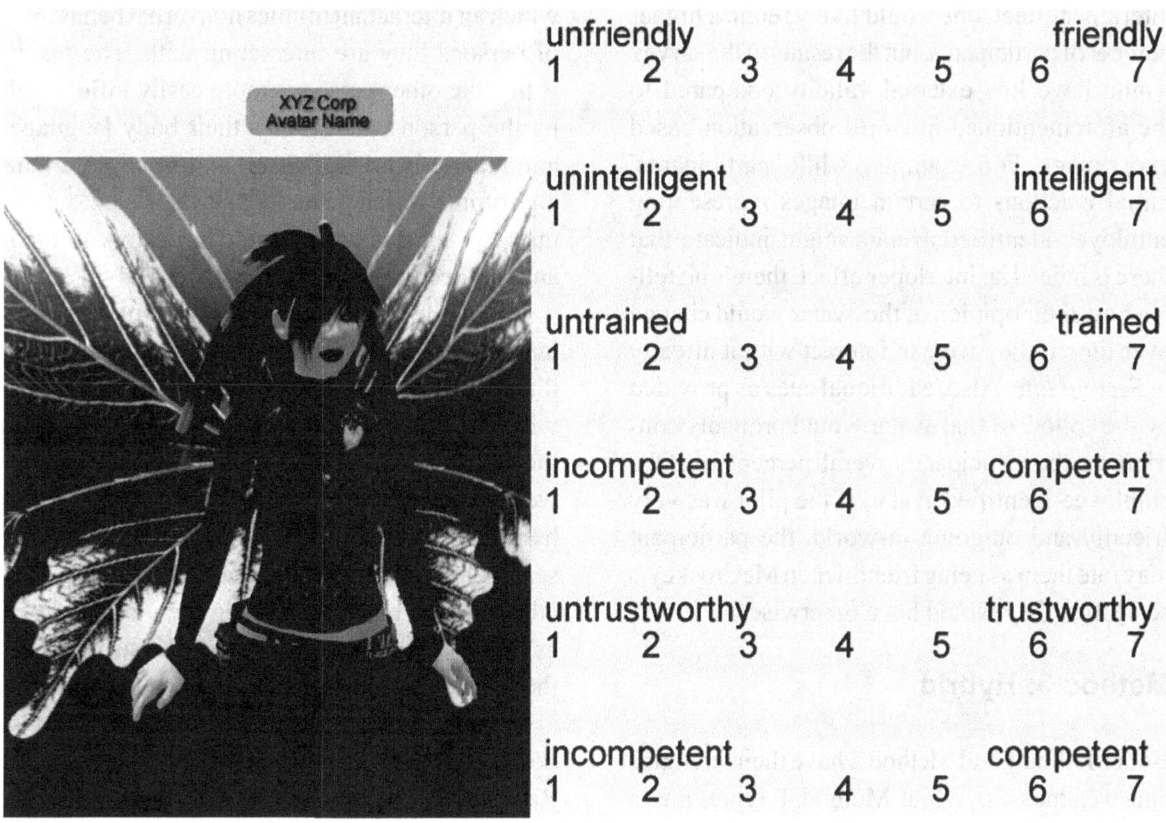

Figure 4. Three possible configurations for employee-identified avatars in Second Life[6]

By creating an online survey to investigate the interloper effect, one would likely retain a higher number of participants, but the results of the survey would have low external validity compared to the aforementioned in-world observation-based experiment. For example, while participants' initial reactions to certain images representing employee-identified avatars might indicate that there is indeed an interloper effect, there's no telling how their opinion of the avatar would change over time if they were to interact with it directly in *Second Life*. Also, additional cues as provided by the "pilot" of that avatar would probably contribute to the participant's overall perception of the employee-identified avatar. If the pilot was very friendly and outgoing in-world, the participant may rate them as being friendlier on McCroskey's scale than they would have otherwise.

Method 3: Hybrid

Both Method 1 and Method 2 have their strengths and weaknesses. While Method 1 represents a more sound ethnographic study with high external validity, the aforementioned limitations are problematic. Method 2 is a much more controlled experiment as all participants would be exposed to the same stimulus. The higher internal validity of Method 2, combined with the ability to secure more participants does make Method 2 seem ideal.

However, the limitations of Method 2 alone cannot be ignored. For example, the scripts a user chooses to adopt to control their avatar's body language may impact how they are received in-world; and why not? Bailenson and Beall (2006) identified how Transformed Social Interaction can affect our persuasiveness when interacting with others in virtual environments.

TSI can be broken down into two categories: transforming avatar appearance and transformations of avatar behaviour. In transformations of avatar behaviour, the authors note how the chameleon effect can be easily transferred over into the virtual world. The chameleon effect is described as a component of social interaction in which an interactant mimics nonverbal behaviour of persons they are interacting with. The result is that the other person is more easily influenced by the person who mimics their body language and mannerisms. Bailenson and Beall note that algorithms which generate an avatar's body language in a virtual world could be easily captured and applied to other avatars.

So, while a static image of an employee avatar might elicit a response that either proves or disproves the interloper effect, a brief encounter with that same avatar in-world might generate the opposite effect. Thus, with the strengths and weaknesses of both methods in mind, a third, hybrid method is proposed. In this method, researchers would take advantage of both the rich ethnographic data available in the virtual world as well as the internal validity of the survey, like the one utilized by Nowak and Rauh (2008).

In order to investigate the affects of anthropomorphism in instant messaging, Nowak and Rauh conducted a study in two phases: survey and experiment. The survey phase was very similar to the methodology described in Method 2: participants were exposed to 30 images in a static context and asked to rate them on various dimensions of credibility. In the second phase, the researchers conducted a between subjects experiment in which participants chatted in pairs using instant messaging software. Participants were represented by one of the avatars used in the first phase of the experiment and were asked to rate the avatar that represented their chat partner as well as their chat partner's credibility.

While the external validity of an in-house chat program might be lower than a study that involved more realistic variability, the fact that this study was conducted in the medium it studied is key. Similarly, a hybrid method that includes the survey discussed in Method 2 and an experiment involving a controlled condition in a virtual world (like Nowak and Rauh's instant messaging program) would likely result in more conclusive data. This could involve the construction of an in-house virtual environment, using something like Open Wonderland, a Java open source toolkit for creating collaborative 3D virtual worlds.

CONCLUSION

In 2007, John Brandon wrote an article for PC Advisor ranking the top 8 real world businesses to enter *Second Life* and set up shop. In this article, Brandon describes how each company has extended its operations into the virtual world. Visitors to Pontiac's site could test drive virtual models of real Pontiac vehicles. Members of Best Buy's Geek Squad, a technical support team, clocked-in to *Second Life* and offered their services to customers visiting the virtual location. At the time of the article, IBM had over 12 islands (virtual properties) in *Second Life* and used them for training, meetings, and recruitment. IBM even offered design solutions for other companies interested in having a presence in *Second Life*.

A lot has changed since Brandon's article. In early 2010, IBM has a strong presence in *Second Life*, occupying over 35 islands in-world. Sun still has three islands as of January 2010, but two of them are private and the third is empty. One explanation for this might be that Sun employees have moved into MPK20, Sun's virtual office building (Lynch, 2008). While their reasons for all but abandoning *Second Life* are not clear, they do state that MPK20 gives their non-collocated employees a feeling of shared space and is meant to allow for the types of spontaneous interactions and collaborative moments that happen in shared physical spaces, where a co-worker stops by your office to see what you're doing. Interestingly, this idea is very similar to the idea of shared space as discussed in Churchill and Bly's paper (1999). Dell and Cisco still have a handful of islands, but there were no employee avatars present. The other businesses described as "the top 8" in Brandon's

article are no longer present. Their islands aren't just unpopulated, they no longer exist.

While only a couple of the top 8 still maintain their presence in *Second Life,* companies continue to look to virtual worlds for online meetings, events, training, and marketing. The *Second Life* home page now has a section devoted to offering such services online (Linden Research, 2010). This section of the website lists many of the companies, academic institutions, and government organizations utilizing *Second Life* for work. Organizations such as Children's Memorial Hospital Chicago and Northrop Grumman have even provided case studies outlining their use of *Second Life* in augmenting their practices.

The information presented in this chapter can assist researchers with the ongoing study of avatar interactions in 3D virtual worlds. This information should also be beneficial to organizations that have developed, or are considering developing policies for employee avatar appearance. Familiarity with the social climate of the virtual world in question, as well as an understanding of the social signals associated with avatar appearance, is necessary if these policies are to facilitate interactions in the virtual world. These policies cannot be forged by simply grafting the ideals of the offline world directly onto the virtual world.

ACKNOWLEDGMENT

I would like to thank Dr. Melanie Baljko, Dr. Edward Jones-Imhotep, and Dr. Jennifer Jenson for their feedback regarding this project. This work has been made possible by the generous support of the Elia family and the Elia Scholars Program.

REFERENCES

Bailenson, J. N., & Beall, A. C. (2006). Transformed social interaction: Exploring the digital plasticity of avatars. In Schroeder, R., & Axelsson, A. S. (Eds.), *Avatars at work and play: Collaboration and interaction in shared virtual environments* (pp. 1–16). Dordrecht, The Netherlands & London, UK: Springer.

Brandon, J. (2007, May 21). The top 8 Second Life virtual businesses. *PC Advisor*. Retrieved from http://www.pcadvisor.co.uk/ news/index. cfm? newsid=9279

Churchill, E. F., & Bly, S. (1999). *Virtual environments at work: Ongoing use of MUDs in the workplace*. Paper presented at the International Joint Conference on Work Activities Coordination and Collaboration.

Correll, S. (1995). The ethnography of an electronic bar: The Lesbian Café. *Journal of Contemporary Ethnography*, *23*(3), 270–298. doi:10.1177/089124195024003002

Dibbell, J. (2001). A rape in cyberspace: Or how an evil clown, a Haitian trickster spirit, two wizards, and a cast of dozens turned a database into a society. In Trend, D. (Ed.), *Reading digital culture* (p. 374). Malden, MA: Blackwell.

Ducheneaut, N., Wen, M.-H., Yee, N., & Wadley, G. (2009). *Body and mind: A study of avatar personalization in three virtual worlds*. Paper presented at the 27th International Conference on Human Factors in Computing Systems.

Haselton, M. G., & Nettle, D. (2006). The paranoid optimist: An integrative evolutionary model of cognitive biases. *Personality and Social Psychology Review*, *10*(1), 47–66. doi:10.1207/s15327957pspr1001_3

Hine, C. (2000). *Virtual ethnography*. London, UK: Sage.

Kozinets, R. V. (1998). On netography: Initial reflections on consumer research investigations of cyberculture. *Advances in Consumer Research. Association for Consumer Research (U. S.)*, *25*, 366–371.

Kozinets, R. V. (2002). The field behind the screen: Using netography for marketing research in online communities. *JMR, Journal of Marketing Research*, *39*, 61–72. doi:10.1509/jmkr.39.1.61.18935

Kozinets, R. V. (2006). Click to connect: Netography and tribal advertising. *Journal of Advertising Research*, *46*, 279–288. doi:10.2501/S0021849906060338

Linden Research. (2010). *Second Life official site*. Retrieved October 1, 2010, from http://www.secondlife.com

Lynch, C. G. (2008). Inside Sun's virtual world for internal collaboration. Retrieved July 8, 2010, from www.cio.com/article/171655/Inside_Sun_s_Virtual_World_for_Internal_Collaboration

McArthur, V. (2008). *Real ethics in a virtual world*. Paper presented at the CHI '08 Extended Abstracts on Human Factors in Computing Systems.

McArthur, V. (2010). *Virtual world professionals and avatar appearance codes*. Paper presented at the ACM FuturePlay 2010.

McArthur, V., & Baljko, M. (2009). *Outsiders, interlopers, and employee-identified avatars*. Paper presented at the The 12th Annual International Workshop on Presence.

McCroskey, J., & Yong, T. (1981). Ethos and credibility: The construct and its measurement after three decades. *Central States Speech Journal*, *32*, 24–34.

McGloin, R. P., Nowak, K. L., Stifano, S. C., & Flynn, G. (2009). *The effect of avatar categorization on perceptions*. Paper presented at the 12th Annual International Workshop on Presence.

Meadows, M. (2008). *I, avatar*. New Riders Press.

Morie, J., & Verhuldonck, G. (2008). *Body/persona/action! Emerging non-anthropomorphic communication and interaction in virtual worlds*. Paper presented at the ACE 2008.

Neustaedter, C., & Fedorovskaya, E. (2008). *Establishing and maintaining relationships in a social virtual world*. (Eastman Kodak Company Technical Report 344195F).

Nowak, K. L., & Rauh, C. (2005). The influence of the avatar on online perceptions of anthropomorphism, androgyny, credibility, homophily, and attraction. *Journal of Computer-Mediated Communication*, *11*(1). doi:10.1111/j.1083-6101.2006.tb00308.x

Nowak, K. L., & Rauh, C. (2008). Choose your buddy icon carefully: The influence of avatar androgyny, anthropomorphism and credibility in online interactions. *Computers in Human Behavior*, *24*(4), 1473–1493. doi:10.1016/j.chb.2007.05.005

Pace, T., Houssian, A., & McArthur, V. (2009). Are socially exclusive values embedded in avatar creation interfaces of MMORPGs? *Journal of Information Communication and Ethics in Society*, *7*(2/3), 192–210. doi:10.1108/14779960910955909

Rheingold, H. (1999). Introduction to the virtual community. In Vitanza, V. J. (Ed.), *CyberReader* (pp. 63–94). Boston, MA: Allyn and Bacon.

Smurda, J., & Haselton, M. G. (2002). *Effects of relationship status and sexual strategy on perceptions of rivals' sexual intent: Preliminary evidence for the interloper effect*. Paper presented at the Human Behaviour and Evolution Society Conference.

Turkle, S. (1997). *Life on the screen: Identity in the age of the Internet*. New York, NY: Touchstone.

ADDITIONAL READING

Chartrand, T. L., & Bargh, J. (1999). The chameleon effect: The perception-behaviour link and social interaction. *Journal of Personality and Social Psychology*, *76*(6), 893–910. doi:10.1037/0022-3514.76.6.893

Clatterbuck, G. (1979). Attributional confidence and uncertainty in initial interaction. *Human Communication Research*, *5*(2), 147–157. doi:10.1111/j.1468-2958.1979.tb00630.x

Goffman, E. (1959). *The presentation of self in everyday life*. Garden City, NY: Doubleday.

Kafai, Y. B., Fields, D. A., & Cook, M. (2007). *Your second selves: avatar designs and identity play in a teen virtual world*. Paper presented at the DIGRA 2007.

McArthur, V. (2008). *Real ethics in a virtual world*. Paper presented at the CHI '08 extended abstracts on Human factors in computing systems.

Nakamura, L. (2002). *Cybertypes: race, ethnicity, and identity on the Internet*. New York: Routledge.

Rehak, B. (2003). Playing at being: psychoanalysis and the avatar. In Wolf, M. J. P., & Perron, B. (Eds.), *The video game theory reader* (pp. 103–127). New York, London: Routledge.

Weber, S., & Mitchell, C. (1995). *'That's funny, you don't look like a teacher': Interrogating images and identity in popular culture*. London: Falmer Press. doi:10.4324/9780203453568

Yee, N. (2007). *The Proteus effect: Behavioral modification via transformations of digital self-representation*. Stanford University.

KEY TERMS AND DEFINITIONS

Appearance Code: like a "dress code" for employee avatars, an avatar appearance code is a corporate policy that governs various aspects of employee avatar appearance. (McArthur, 2008, 2009).

Anthropomorphic Avatar: A non-human avatar with human traits, such as a "furry" (note: the term used to describe these avatars in the Presence community is non-anthropomorphic, but I believe this to be an incorrect as to be "anthropomorphic" is not to be "human" – thus, a non-anthropomorphic avatar would be an avatar with no humanoid traits or characteristics).

Avatar: An interactive, social representation of a user (Meadows, 2008).

Employee Avatar: An interactive, social representation of a virtual world professional. (McArthur, 2008, 2009).

Employee-Identified Avatar: An employee avatar whose corporate presence is expressed partially by their avatar's appearance (e.g.: corporate attire) (McArthur, 2009).

Social Virtual World: Online virtual worlds that differ from game-based virtual worlds like *World of Warcraft* in that there are no inherent "game mechanics" like lives, levels, and quests. The primary function of these virtual worlds is to facilitate social interaction.

Virtual World Professional: An employee or representative who conducts work-related duties in a virtual world. While the use of "professional" in this context might seem to exclude those whose work is not deemed so (e.g.: blue-collar workers) the term is meant to be inclusive of any and all employees who represent a company or academic institution in virtual worlds (McArthur, 2009).

ENDNOTES

[1] Exchange rate retrieved from the Linden Dollar Exchange website on October 15, 2010.

[2] While the conversion of real world currencies and virtual world currencies are not a feature of *World of Warcraft*, countless sites have emerged over the years offering such trades.

[3] *note:* the term used to describe these avatars in the Presence community is non-anthropomorphic, but we believe this to be have been possibly misapplied as to be "anthropomorphic" is not to be "human" – thus, a non-anthropomorphic avatar would be an avatar with no humanoid traits or characteristics. We believe this further distinction also acknowledges the drastic degree of anthropomorphism between furries and avatars such as the flying spaghetti monster.

[4] Images from http://2nddeath.wordpress.com/2007/06/28/anti-furry-discrimination/ and http://nwn.blogs.com/nwn/2007/12/new-world-new-3.html respectively.

[5] Arguably the social climate is also co-constructed by the virtual world's developers to an extent, as they do decide many of the allowable mechanics that become part of the underlying code. Still, there have been countless examples in which users have subverted these mechanics to allow or approximate desired mechanics, such as using chat in *World of Warcraft* as a means of having sex in-game.

[6] We consider that not all employee avatars may be visibly corporate in the virtual world. As such, a further distinction between employee avatar and employee-identified avatar is made, where an employee-identified avatar's corporate affiliation is immediately apparent by manner of dress and/or the use of the group tag in *Second Life*.

Chapter 22

One Self to Rule Them All:
A Critical Discourse Analysis of French–Speaking Players' Identity Construction in World of Warcraft

Omar V. Rosas
University of Twente, The Netherlands & University of Namur, Belgium

Grégory Dhen
Catholic University of Louvain, Belgium

ABSTRACT

This chapter provides a critical discourse analysis of French-speaking players' personal and collective identity construction in World of Warcraft. Based on sixteen semi-structured interviews conducted online, we have analyzed how players introduce their avatars, the extent to which avatars correspond to or differ from players' real selves, and how players perceive and construct collective identity within their guilds. The study revealed that most players make use of avatar introduction as a rhetorical pretext to fabricate narratives of personal experiences related to their game practice. In addition, players' discourses made it evident that avatars constituted either transparent (extensions) or translucent (enhancements) representations of their real selves. Finally, collective identity within guilds was mostly perceived and experienced through shared values that transcend the technical format of the game including sense of belonging, trust, respect, putting things into perspective, and modesty.

INTRODUCTION

It has become almost a cliché to say that Massively Multiplayer Online Role-Playing Games (MMORPGs) are laboratories in which individuals experiment with their identities. Like most clichés, it happens to be true. Since Sherry Turkle's

(1995) seminal work on identity construction in Multi User Dungeons (MUDs), there has been a huge amount of research exploring and documenting a wide range of motivations, behaviors, and consequences associated to players' identity construction and presentation in online games. To be sure, different theoretical and methodological approaches have been implemented, which testifies for the increasing interest of scholars from

DOI: 10.4018/978-1-60960-854-5.ch022

different quarters in understanding how personal and social identity is created, assumed, and negotiated in online games. But all share the common assumption that in-game identity construction involves complex articulations of players' personal and social backgrounds with affordances of embodiment and communication provided by specific online game technologies.

Constructing one's self-story through avatars or characters in World of Warcraft (henceforth WoW) typically involves adopting the plot and mythology provided by game designers but also adapting the play and narrative culture within which one grows up to WoW's gameplay affordances, although this may not be recognized as such by most players. Through this double process of adoption and adaptation, players juggle multiple roles, try on different hats, different lives, forging relevant selves that can either be relatively permanent or dissolved into new combinations when new game challenges arise. In a persistent fantasy world that demands flexibility in self-presentation and role-playing, identity construction may be conceived as an adaptive process governed by a confederacy of multiple self-conceptions. It is within this flexible and at the same time intricate context that we want to examine how French-speaking players construct their personal and collective identities via their digital counterparts or avatars.

Our aim in this chapter is to put forward a view identity construction in WoW as a socially embedded, situated personal narrative susceptible of being analyzed via players' discourses. We will argue that examining players' identity discourse provides insight into how they concretize perceptions of the ludic structure of the game, reconstruct their biographies as players, impute group identities, and align personal and collective identities. By drawing on Van Dijk's (2001) approach to Critical Discourse Analysis, we will examine sixteen online semi-structured interviews of WoW players to understand how players' self-presentation is narratively managed when introducing their avatars, what are parts of them that live in their avatars, and how they perceiv and/or construct collective identiety within guilds.

The structure of the chapter is as follows. We will start by briefly summarizing recent research focused on identity issues in WoW. After this brief summary, we will introduce the theoretical and methodological background for Critical Discourse Analysis in WoW and present the study results. Finally, we will provide some directions for future research and highlight some conclusions drawn from the present research.

BACKGROUND

Recent research on identity construction and presentation in WoW has showed that the ways in which players digitally (re)present themselves via avatars or characters reveal core assumptions about their actual and idealized self-conceptions. In order to understand the effects of these assumptions on players' avatar construction and game-based socialization, some researchers have examined how players create and negotiate their personal and social identity online by focusing on the role played by physical and personality traits (Ducheneaut, Yee, Nickell, & Moore, 2006; Bessière, Seay & Kiesler, 2007) as well as cultural and organizational models (Bainbridge, 2010a).

Research done by Ducheneaut, Yee, Nickell, & Moore (2006) examined avatar personalization in three online worlds: Mapple Story, Second Life, and WoW by focusing on two issues (1) evaluating current avatar creation and customization systems, and (2) examining the link between avatar system's features, the eventual avatars created by users, and users' physical and psychological characteristics. As far as identity-related issues in WoW are concerned, the study revealed that most players own multiple characters, which testifies for players need for a flexible appearance. Most WoW players granted relative importance to character features such as hair style, facial characteristics, and hair color but not to character skin color. Furthermore, female players were most likely to create avatars that are idealized versions of themselves than male players, and the latter tend to favor avatars that stand out more than female players. Analysis of reproduction of personality traits showed that, on average, participants rated their virtual character as being more conscientious, extraverted, and less neurotic than they themselves were. The authors conclude that while users do experiment with different body features to somewhat enhance their appearance, they do not tend to change their personality "in-avatar" too much (for a complementary analysis of player/avatar identity and personality based on self-discrepancy theory see Bessière, Seay & Kiesler, 2007).

Williams, Ducheneaut, Xiong, Yee, Nickell (2006) analyzed the social life of guilds in terms of the meanings, social capital, and networks formed by players inside WoW. Although they did not explicitly address identity issues, their analysis of guild typologies and practices (i.e., social, player versus player, raid, and role-playing) is useful to understand the extent to which guilds function as virtual counterparts of real-life identification spaces. The organic structure of guilds as collectives that share basic goals and play preferences allows players to simultaneously draw on and contribute to the in-game social capital accumulated by the guild-oriented networked action of their members. It may be thus expected that the supporting space so obtained functions as a relatively stable ground for developing trust among fellows, reducing game-related uncertainty, and promoting individual internalization of features that constitute the identity of guilds.

From a theoretical perspective, Tronstad (2008) examined the relationship between character appearance and character capacities in WoW and how this relationship affects the possibility of identifying with the character during play. According to the author, appearance does not reduce to physical appearance; rather, it should be understood as encompassing everything that is included in players' perception of the character. Based on the idea of character capacities, the author highlights two ways of identifying with one's character in WoW: empathic identity and sameness identity. Sameness identity concerns a player's entering the state where he or she has an experience of being the character (acting through the character's capacities). Empathic identity implies experiencing what the character experiences without the feeling of being identical to it (the player directly "experiences" the character's capacities as if they were her own). In role-playing settings a third kind of identity emerges. By drawing on Ricoeur's concept of narrative identity, the author argues that role-playing allows for players to narratively identify with their characters' in-game capacities and actions. This kind of identity along with the internalization of the controls, game mechanics, and knowledge about the game world provide a rewarding experience of flow by which players can accomplish almost utter identification with their characters.

Based on ethnographic and linguistic research, Hagström (2008) analyzed the relationships between avatar naming and player identity and showed that avatars' names reflect players' individual preferences and cultural models associated to linguistic background, literature, religion, art, sports, video games, popular media, etc. Furthermore, the author argues that within the social dynamics of WoW, the name is virtually both the character being played and the player who communicates with others via chat. Names are thus identity markers for avatars and players that bridge two game-related representational realms: being a character and a players.

Brignall (2008) conducted participant observation and informal interviews to study tribalistic behaviors in hard-core WoW players. Tribes frequently form because of the desires of members to be among others with shared identities. Seventy-four percent of his informants reported preferring socializing in WoW to offline socializing and the reasons for such behavior included feelings of strong friendship, group unity, role-playing with personal identity, hanging out with people who share similar likes, social anonymity, and the ability to ignore disliked people. The common reason reported to leave a guild was a desire to associate with players who had shared identities and playing styles. Based on previous MMORPG experience, some hard-core players in this study did not join guilds because they did not want the responsibilities or problems that came with guild membership. The author concludes that the structural environment of WoW fostered some of the negative aspects of tribalism such as quick judgments, stereotyping, and prejudicial behavior among players.

Salazar's (2009) research on Identity Liminal Event (ILE) is one of the rare studies that explicitly theorize social identity in WoW. By combining speech act theory with intergroup processes analysis, he defines IEL as "either an elicited or natural "happening" in a frame of time of a group's life" (p. 11). The author claims that such a happening is an ingroup speech event which triggers in players spontaneous co-construction of social identity boundaries, exclusion/inclusion codes, and narrative and spatial codes. This process of identity co-construction is meant to develop over time which implies that issues in social identity within WoW should be theoretically and methodologically approached to from a diachronic perspective.

Huh & Williams (2010) tested gender swapping in *EverQuestII*, focusing on swappers' real identity, their motivations, and what behaviors they enact within the game world. Although the study was not specifically conducted on WoW players, their results present useful perspectives to understand gender swapping in WoW. Contrary to their initial expectation, the authors found that females were not more likely to swap their gender online than males. However, homosexual users were more likely to change their online gender than straight users. Male players argued that they play a female avatar because it is a pleasing visual object, not a source of identification. As Huh &

Williams (2010) argue, "Whether people change their gender online or not, they still keep their offline gender roles in mind. In a sense, the virtual game world is more an extension of the real one than a separate place" (p. 171).

Finally, Bainbridge (2010b) combines his own experience as a WoW player with reflections coming from fantasy literature describing physical and mental attributes of different creatures. He argues that races in WoW are as subject to in-game stereotyping and prejudice as people are in real life. Players' perception of races and classes are certainly molded by the diegetic structure of the game but also by players' beliefs and feelings formed through their interaction with characters having different racial origins. In terms of identity construction and presentation, the problematic issue arises when an avatar's qualities are attributed to the player behind the character. In as much the same way as in real life, intergroup processes in WoW reflect complex dynamics of attribution, stereotyping, prejudice, and social evaluation which may have non-negligible impact on players' perception and construction of in-game social identity.

All these studies, together with research done on different online games (see Taylor, 2002, 2006) make it evident that players negotiate in somewhat complex ways aspects of their inner selves when engaging in individual and collective play inside WoW. Their results have largely improved our understanding of the different motivations, preferences, and culture-based models that impinge upon players' online ludic experiences. Researchers have used different language-based techniques to examine identity construction including questionnaires, online surveys, standardized scales, field notes, interviews, etc., which show the significance of getting linguistic access to players' identity-related cognitive and social processes and mechanisms implied in their online gaming. Consistent with this idea of finding a way to players' in-game identity experiences through language, we want to analyze WoW players' perception of their real and digitally reproduced selves via their self-crafted stories in order to understand how their personal and collective selves are discursively structured, how their linguistic choices denote particular stances towards themselves and their avatars, and how what they deem relevant to tell conveys assumptions about their real and possible selves.

FRAMING CRITICAL DISCOURSE ANALYSIS OF IDENTITY IN WORLD OF WARCRAFT

Theoretical Framework

Multidisciplinary research on discourse and identity has showed that the ways in which individuals narratively conceive of and communicate their self- and other-conceptions in different social contexts testify for a non-essentialist view of identity: personal and collective identity are not fixed, monolithic entities; rather they constitute unfinished projects which can be narratively reconstructed and deconstructed depending on particular features of interaction contexts as well as on individuals' preferences, goals, values, and communicative intentions (De Fina, Schiffrin, & Bamberg, 2006; Gergen, 1994; Widdicombe & Wooffitt, 1995). This non-essentialist, multifaceted view of the self does not imply, though, that no degree of stability can be granted to identity in narrative. Indeed, the self-concept can be conceived as having both narrative components that are relatively consistent over time (e.g., personality traits, past memories, values) and those that are more malleable and contextually based (Nurius, 1991). On the basis of such relatively stable components, self-relevant aspects can be added or subtracted as individuals "update" their working self-concept through sources such as social comparisons, personal performance, intersubjective feedback, adoption of new roles, etc.

Yet besides being constructions and descriptions in language, self-identity and collective identity are also products of agents whose actions are embedded in social practices. As Barker & Galasiński (2001) have argued, "Identities as descriptions in language are achieved in the everyday flow of language and stabilized as categories through their embedding in the pragmatic narratives of our day-to-day social conduct" (p. 44). These pragmatic narratives are useful to understand how people's interactional, rhetoric, and stylistic choices index their belonging to those categories. As De Fina (2006) has pointed out, "studies of narrative have shown that what defines people as members of a group is not only the content of their stories, but the way in which they use socially established resources to tell them" (p. 352).

One useful way to analyze these imbrications between narrative, identity, and social practices is provided by van Dijk's (2001) approach to Critical Discourse Analysis (henceforth CDA). Van Dijk (2001) conceives of CDA not as a fixed methodology but as a multidisciplinary orientation to investigate a wide range of social and political phenomena on the basis three interrelated axes: discourse, cognition, and society. Discourse concerns people's engagement in communicative actions by using several semiotic formats such as verbal and non-verbal language, written text, images, typographical layouts, etc. Cognition is to be understood as encompassing people's beliefs, goals, social representations, memory structures, affective appraisals, and mental models involved in discourse and interaction. Finally, society is to be understood as an umbrella term including intersubjective spaces provided by both microstructures (groups, communities, circles) and macrostructures (society, culture) which somewhat determine individual and collective patterns of discourse and interaction. In order to implement CDA as a useful heuristic to analyze identity construction and presentation in WoW some further specifications of the three aforementioned axes are in order.

The discourse axis implies that self-identity is formed by the ability to sustain a narrative of the self that develops a consistent feeling of biographical continuity over time. CDA may be expected to show more explicitly the differences and the functions of the perspectives involved in the understanding, description, and presentation of identity. It may, for instance, show how players actually go about representing and communicating their identities by disclosing themselves in a functional, descriptive (facts) or evaluative (mental state, episodic memory) way. Moreover, insofar as identities are often expressed in personal stories or accounts which are in line with their goals or interests, players can build up, use, and communicate identities strategically, depending on what they consider relevant to convey in a given interaction context. The notion of relevance (Sperber & Wilson, 1986) is helpful here to understand the pragmatic background against which players convey their identity narratives. According to Sperber & Wilson (1986), the principle of relevance states that every act of ostensive communication conveys a presumption of its own optimal relevance. In other words, when a speaker communicates a message in a given interaction context, he or she is at the same time making manifest to the audience a cluster of context-relevant assumptions. Such assumptions can be implicitly or explicitly communicated depending on whether the speaker uses implicatures (speech acts implying or suggesting one thing by saying something else) or explicatures (speech acts which explicitly communicate assumptions). In this sense, a player can, for instance, convey either explicit assumptions about his self-concept as a good player by saying "I am a good player" or implicit assumptions by stating "I have leveled my character up to 80 in record time". Furthermore, the principle of relevance also makes evident the speaker's positioning when communicating with the audience: relevance is helpful to disclose what

kind of information is selected and what narrative stance is adopted by a player when assembling and displaying who he or she is in interaction with others.

The cognition axis implies that identities are discursive-performative descriptions of personal and social models with which people cognitively and affectively identify. They can be best described as constructed through discursive practices which enact self- and other-conceptions by re-articulating memory structures, shared beliefs, and social representations. Cognition implies what van Dijk (1990) has elsewhere defined as "situation models", that is, "cognitive representations of personal experiences and interpretations, including personal knowledge and opinions … [that] are located in episodic memory" (p. 166). Memory structures play a key role in feeding up self-related narratives by providing both semantic or factual information such as name, date and place of birth, etc. (semantic memory) and episodic or biography-related information such as personal experiences, situated affective appraisals, etc. (autobiographic memory). Cognition is an important part of most online gaming. Besides being the basis for players to understand WoW's gameplay affordances, it also allows researcher to keep track of players' in-game categorizations, perception of gender stereotypes and/or prejudice, and memories concerning their gamer careers.

Finally, society is meant to include the whole range of social affordances provided by intersubjective settings and interactions. Players engage in discourse practices as past or current members of several guilds. This implies that identity narratives are produced and negotiated in specific contexts which allow for building relevant and situated meanings impregnated by specific kinds of normativity (norms, conventions) and world-views (values). Self-relevant conceptions and meanings can thus be constructed, negotiated, and legitimated in microstructures such as guilds and as well as in macrostructures composed of multiple guilds on a given server.

Method

In order to examine how French-speaking players discursively construct and convey their personal and collective identities in WoW, we adopted an online ethnographic approach (Hine, 2000) composed of participant observation, semi-structured interviews, and critical discourse analysis. During a few months of participant observation, one of us (Dhen) developed a main character named Oxxia (PvP/PvE) and two "alts" named Jeanolapin (PvP) and Pèrsifleur (RP) through which we gained first-hand insight into the technical, ludic, and social structure of the game. In order to earn participants' trust and thus provide them with a space for dialogue and personal disclosure, we decided to make Oxxia's identity as a researcher explicit during the call for informants posted on the trade chat channel integrated in the game communication interface. Criteria for selecting potential participants included their availability and willingness to participate in an approximately 60 minute online interview as well as their past and/or current active participation as guild members. 50 participants responded to the query and 36 were dropped because they did not meet selection criteria or were unavailable after half the interview was conducted. The final sample is composed of 16 players including 8 adolescents (1 female, 7 males, ages 14-17, M = 13,1) and 8 adults (3 females, 5 males, ages 20-36, M = 27,8). Participants were thus primarily male (12 men, 4 women). Interviews were conducted in French on three severs, namely Krasus (PvP), Cho'Gall (PvP/PvE), and Kirin Tor (RP) via two channels: whisper chat and group chat. Most of the interviews took place in relatively isolated places around Stormwind City that players considered quite enough to answer the interviewer-avatar questions. We decided to gather data from interviews in a written form. This decision was basically motivated by our aim to preserve the in situ textual structure of players' narratives. Even though we were aware of the communication

possibilities provided by TeamSpeak or other third-party software, we did not use them because VoIP channels require sharing a server address and password which is guild-specific and thus not available to outside players. Text was copy/pasted through the official Elephant chat log, translated into English, and organized in separate rtf files. All participants agreed on the recording of their answers and were asked whether they wanted us to keep their avatars' and guild's name preserved. Three of them requested the researcher to keep their guild's name and character names anonymous (See Table 1).

Semi-structured interviews were articulated around the following questions:

1. *Who is your avatar?* This question was explicitly aimed at allowing players the opportunity to introduce their avatars in whatever way they like. We wanted to check for identification patterns and discursive strategies players deem relevant to present their avatars (and themselves) to the online interviewer. This question also allowed us to keep track of overlapping narrative layers between avatars' history and players' game experiences.

2. *What is the part of you that lives in your avatar?* The aim of this question was to check whether avatars are narratively constructed as simple extensions of players' real selves, as game-based actualizations of their possible, idealized selves, or still as an amalgam of both. We wanted to identify the elements in players' self-narratives that point to implicit or explicit relevant assumptions about themselves as agents and their digital representations as proxies. Furthermore, this question was aimed at allowing players to invoke physical attributes, mental models, and personality traits as relevant source of information.

   2.1 *For you, what is the difference between playing solo and playing with the*

Table 1. Sample of the sixteen participants for this study. Asterisk (*) indicates pseudonyms that have been changed to keep players' avatar and guild names anonym

Player Name	Gender	Age	Kind of Avatar	Avatar Gender	Guild at the time of interview	Time played in WoW
Aernei	M	16	Night Elf Druid	M	Les Fondateurs d'Azeroth	2 years
Aldrak	M	27	Undead Warlock	M	OccO	4 years
Azeona	F	17	Draenei Shaman	F	Ømission*	2 years
Bluefaya	M	14	Draenei Shaman	M	I WoW You	5 months
Chasar	M	14	Night Elf Hunter	M	Gnostage*	2 years
Cystite	F	36	Night Elf Hunter	F	Le Cri du Hibou	4 years
Dõumdõum	M	30	Draenei Shaman	M	--	--
Eructite	M	29	Human Paladin	M	--	5 years
Lexiusxx Jenkinks	M	14	Human Warrior	M	NøRaj Baby Øn Est Weak	4 years
Malonever	M	33	Human Paladin	M	Níenna Ancalimon	1 ½ year
Sagitari	M	16	Dwarf Hunter	M	--	3 years
Shangrilâ	F	27	Night Elf Druid	F	Hazardous Formula	1 ½ year
Smiri	M	20	Dwarf Hunter	M	Troïka	5 years
Paos*	F	21	Gnome Warlock	M	DeathstarsX	--
Solanya	M	17	Draenei Death Knight	F	Níenna Ancalimon	--
Tamor	M	14	Night Elf Rogue	M	Le rêve d'émeraude	6 month

members of you guild? This question was aimed at extending question 2 by identifying players' motivations and behaviors related to both individual and collective in-game play. We expected narrative indicators of motivation, behavior, roles, commitments, and responsibilities to shed light on how players perceive personal and social values, attitudes, and regulatory structures which can in the end be internalized as components of their self-conception.

3. *Do you think you share a collective identity with your guild mates?* This question was intended as a first probe into players' perception of guilds as social settings fostering collective identity. We expected different empirical referents of guilds (name, tabard, charter, etiquette, private website or forum, etc.) and social values (etiquette, mutual respect, solidarity, reciprocity) to play a key role in collective identity construction.

3.1 *Could you specify that which you share with the other members of your guild?* This question was intended to extend question 3 by deepening potential monosyllabic answers to the collective identity question or insufficient understanding of the term "collective identity". We wanted to explore players' sharing of play-related beliefs, attitudes towards winning/failure, in-group customized lexicons, ideal of guilds, etc. The question also allows for examining the extent to which in-game and real-life mental models overlap with each other and how guild support for competence and relatedness fosters in-game social integration and collective identification.

Study Results

We have articulated participants' answers around three main themes according to the topics addressed in the interviews: (1) introducing one's avatar, (2) from real selves to (digitally) possible selves, and (3) guilds and collective identity.

Introducing One's Avatar

Within the context of our online interviews, we assumed that introducing one's avatar is at the same time a rhetorical way of introducing oneself. An avatar indicates that there is a real person—the avatar owner/player—present and actively engaged with the high-fantasy world, a person who has stories worth telling. In order to sort out the different modes of avatar introduction used by players, we have drawn on Van Leeuwen's (2008) categories for representing social actors. Avatars can be *nominated*, that is, (re)presented through their unique identity (i.e., name given by the player) or *categorized* in terms of identities and functions they share with others. This categorization can in turn be realized via functionalization or identification. *Functionalization* occurs when avatars are referred to in terms of what they do, that is, their occupation or role (professions). *Identification* takes place when avatars are defined, not in terms of what they do, but in terms of what they, more or less permanently, are. Here identification can be instantiated through (1) *classification* of avatars in terms of the major categories provided by game designers (faction, gender, race, class) and groups of players (guild's name) or (2) (re)presentation in terms of the *relational identification* they have with players by means of possessivation and affective attachment ("my shaman", "my creation", "my pet", "my babies").

These linguistic patterns of avatar introduction are to be considered here not as rigid categories but as a heuristic to understand the different ways players talk about their own avatars. As we will see from the interviews, the boundaries between these types of presentation are often blurred, which implies that nomination and categorization are frequently amalgamated at different levels in players' discursive (re)presentation of their avatars. Since players' choice of words is constrained by the interviewing context, and since words take on special significance in particular contexts, paying attention to the grammar of avatar introduction, in particular indexicality or the connection of utterances and pronouns to extra-linguistic reality, helped us track what players consider relevant to introduce their avatars to the interviewer as well as the relevant implicit or explicit assumptions about themselves they convey via their digitally represented counterparts.

Some players categorized their avatars by strictly alluding to their functions: "A level 80 night elf hunter" (Chasar), "A level 80 dwarf hunter" (Smiri). For these players, avatar introduction consisted in condensing their characters' level, class, and race into a single phrase. They felt no spontaneous need to fabricate a story about their avatars' name and/or imagined origins, which is consistent with the pragmatic and disengaged attitude towards WoW conveyed throughout their interviews. Yet for other players, avatar introduction contained mixtures of categorization and nomination. Some of them used combinations of name and function with additional information about their game practice or affective attachment to their avatars:[1]

Aldrak, warlock specialized in destruction but also in grief when needed…an old rogue who has been knocking about on this server for 4 years now and who nobody knows^^.[2]

Bluefaya, Draenei shaman, which I love:-)…Wow is a kind of game you fall in love with (very?) quickly…and you get too attached to your character.[3]

Dõumdõum, shaman heal…already three weeks played with it.[4]

Eructite, level 80 Human Paladin...but I've got 9 level 80 characters and a bunch of others in pexing or as bags.[5]

Avatar introduction in these cases provided us with a first glimpse into players' perception of themselves as gamers. Besides nominating and categorizing their digital representations in a somewhat standard way inside the game, players spontaneously told the interviewer about time invested in playing in WoW, how they feel about their characters, and how many characters they have created within the game. These additional indications also reveal the extent to which avatar introduction functions as a pretext to present aspects of the self and game practice players consider worth telling.

Other combinations of nomination and categorization in avatar introduction were framed within first- and third-person narratives articulated around diegetic elements provided by the game's plot and personal experiences and feelings stemmed from players' offline and online practices:

Cystite, young female night elf so named by her parents because it was her destiny to hurt. She comes from a noble family; she is usually serious and classy...she does not like vulgarity and has a mission to accomplish here, she likes hunting and above all her pet.[6]

Solanya, half-draenei (human father) death knight, I'd say between twenty and thirty years old, no brother or sister, parents dead long time ago.[7]

Aernei, level 80 druid who belongs to the guild The Founders of Azeroth. They all are my friends and I do my best to support them^^... Aernei (I) has lots of friends in order not to feel alone... My relationship with my avatar has certainly changed but it's true that I was already happy to find an avatar that typifies me ('cause this is my first online game so I was surprised), indeed the

more you get it stuffed and leveled up over time, the more you get attached to it...it's like building a house by yourself, you don't want to sell it, you want to live in...anyway, that's my opinion.[8]

My name is Malonever. I'm a paladin and have power to bring the dead back to life. I was born in the Gold Shire...when I was a child people called me noob and unstuffy. This made me seek revenge but also recognition from other players.[9]

In terms of avatar/player indexical identification and presentation, players' use of pronouns is revealing. Avatars are not only nominated but also personified via first- (I, me) and third-person pronouns (he, she) embedded in more or less creative and biographic narratives. For some players, patterns of avatar introduction show the ways in which an avatar' history is narratively intertwined with the player's relevant game experience. As stated above, this intertwining of avatars' and players' narratives furnishes some key elements to understand the extent to which telling an avatar's (hi)story from a first- or third-person perspective becomes a rhetorical pretext to talk about something else considered as relevant by the player, namely his or her evolution of play performance, his or her affective experiences within the game, or the needs he or she wants to be fulfilled. For instance, Malonever's narrative shows the way he mixes diegetic elements of WoW with items of his own autobiographic memory as a newbie thereby making evident that the hierarchical structure of the game imposes constraints on first-time players who are easily represented and categorized as poorly skilled. Malonever's words not only imply the usual stages any first-time player has to go through to improve his or her game practice, but also the fact that in-game prejudice against "newbies" via their avatars can bring about negative affective appraisals of other players (feelings of revenge) and the need for social recognition (Bainbridge, 2010a).

Unlike Malonever's utter indexical identification with his avatar, Aernei's avatar introduction started with a third-person pronoun but then he decided to put the pronoun "I" into brackets. This identity explicature is introduced before disclosing personal information about loneliness which probably conveys a mental model in which that kind of feelings is usually ascribed to non-digital, human beings. Furthermore, Aernei's narrative is marked by the importance of the guild for his game experience. Besides providing the guild's name as a distinctive sign of belongingness, introducing his avatar is the pretext to convey his need for and commitment to friendship within WoW. In addition, Aernei's use of the house building metaphor to describe avatar creation testifies for his personal view of an avatar as a player-made, time-consuming product which once finished provides affective gratifications to his/her owner. Further in his interview, Aernei explained that creating his social network inside WoW was like "building a second house".

Finally, other players consciously chose their avatars' names on the basis of, for instance, gender, in-game class coherence or past personal experiences:

I find that the letters or rather the sounds "o" and "a" harmonize nicely. Moreover, femininity is externalized by putting a final letter "a", and "z" is a very little used letter, which I love ^^... a strong identity while remaining feminine (Azeona).[10]

If you look in a dictionary of Latin, Sagitari relates to archery etc... So it fits nice into the class I have chosen (Sagitari).[11]

Muliang has a history; it is the Buddhist name that I got from a Zen Master in Korea. Shangrilä is an imaginary place in Tibet. Both names refer to my past, but also to a personal penchant. Muliang and Shangrilâ are two healing characters associated to "Buddhist" things, something that I mean on

purpose. That's it. Shangrila, an imaginary place, very much like this character (Shangrilâ).[12]

Azeona's choice of name is consistent with cultural models of gender-name coherence typical of some Romance languages like Italian, Portuguese, and Spanish in which female names usually contain a distinctive ending in "a". But her choice not only denotes her linguistic knowledge and preferences; it also reflects her will to remain feminine in a world where players can experiment with gender at will. Sagitari looked for semantic coherence between his avatar's class (dwarf hunter) and name and found it in Latin etymology. His choice reflects the satisfaction obtained by a name that faithfully denotes the technical capacities linked to his avatar's class. Shangrilâs' narrative about her avatars' names combined two sources related to a Buddhist worldview: her personal experience in Korea and her penchant for fictional novels (indeed, Shangri-La is a fictional place described by James Hilton in his 1933 novel *Lost Horizon*). Her avatars represent relevant aspects of her life that vivify and integrate her play experience and make it more or less meaningful within the game. In much the same way as Hagström's (2008) research on avatar naming in WoW, these players drawn on different cultural sources of inspiration to give their avatars a distinctive and self-related meaningful name.

As can be seen from their interviews, players introduced their avatars either by simply categorizing them as in-game facts or by telling a story in which initial diegetic elements of the game's plot are gradually and rhetorically mixed with players' real-life game practices. These narratives of avatar introduction involved different ways of telling and doing identity in which temporality is either implicitly or explicitly alluded to. Finally, the sense of identity that is perceived from, or projected through, players' language behavior when introducing their avatars can be seen as the consequence of moment-by-moment factor-driven decisions about what in-game and out-game self-related assumptions they deem relevant to communicate to the interviewer.

From Real Selves to (Digitally) Possible Selves

Nurius (1991) has argued that identity has been often approached to in the literature from two somewhat paradoxical conceptualizations of the self-concept. On the one hand, the self-concept can be understood in terms of its stable and unifying features (biographical self) and, on the other hand, it can be framed in terms of its situated and mutable features. According to the author, one way to somewhat resolve this tension is to put forward a working conception of the self understood in terms of actuality and potentiality, that is, as a constantly shifting configuration of self-conceptions between real and possible selves. Possible selves are thus conceptualized as working conceptions of the self concerning past-based and future-oriented beliefs and feelings about what people would like to be or are afraid of becoming (Markus & Nurius, 1986).

Within the context of online games, self-related actuality and potentiality have been examined in terms of the physical and personality traits as well as the behavioral patterns players "transfer" to their in-game digital representations. In this sense, endowing one's avatar with slightly modified or radically changed physical features can be understood as a way for players to cope with some of their bodily features they consider self-discrepant or socially undesirable. At the same time, the anonymity dimension encapsulated in the in-game required pseudonymity, may allow players to adopt behavioral patterns they do not normally display in real settings. Aspects of one's personality can thus be subject to more or less controlled experimentation within a context in which the risk of deception but also the benefits from pretence are high.

Different patterns and levels of self-experimentation transpired in our informants' discourses.

Some players reported that most of their real selves came out through their avatars' look and ways of speaking and acting:

I'm not so different when I play WoW, it's more like another facet of my personality...our characters are quite oddly like us, we do not make use of the virtual environment to be different (Cystite).[13]

For me the avatar is a tool that allows me to have fun and meet goals in the game, I do not behave differently from real life when I use it to play with other people (Sagitari).[14]

For these players, avatars constitute extensions or "transparent representations" of what they are and how they behave in real life. They did not feel any need to be someone else online, to adopt different behavioral patterns. Other players made moderate claims about player/avatar physical and personality resemblance. For them, their avatars' look and behavior reflected choices based on aesthetic values, personal ideals, social persuasion, or representing the two sides of the same coin:

Back to my avatar's physical appearance... let's say...for me it has some importance but not too much...as a druid I can change shapes so I rarely see his real physical appearance...and his white hair doesn't mean he is old, it just makes me think of snow^^...When I started playing, I wanted a male character who looks classy and experienced but young...that's why he has a young face and white hair...I chose that class because it concerns nature and animals and balance...quite spiritual... and at the same time it gave me the impression of being a justice and natural rights protector...but I'm not a green activist...(Aernei).[15]

My character is my creation and he evolves through me. He loves adventures like me but we do not have the same physical traits... I first wanted an orc, but my friends were playing in the alliance so they told me to choose a human... I do not like humans' heads so I have it stuffed to mask his head...My character has traits and clothes that I never dare wear in real life (Lexiusxx).[16]

There is a certain part of me in my paladin... The light protector, it fits nice with the vision I have of myself... By contrast, my warlock is quite the opposite of my personal mental image: ugly, little and nasty (Eructite).[17]

For Aernei and Lexiusxx (both of them are real-life fourteen-year-old males) the physical appearance of their avatars have different connotations. Aernei's choice of a classy, experienced, and young male character conveys the Western ideal of an "interesting" male who is young enough to correspond to his own age-related view yet mature enough to be more eye-catching. In addition, by explicitly stating that his avatar is young despite its white hair, he wanted to make sure the interviewer does not spontaneously associate white hair to old age. For Aernei, vindicating his real age through his avatar's look ("he" is not old), even though it can change shapes, was an indexical way to affirm his identity as a male teenager. His choice of avatar class reflects coherence between his role as a druid and his own nature-friendly and spiritual values. Positive feelings associated to seeing himself as a justice and nature rights protector represent the extent to which a digital version of his idealized self fosters his self-esteem, even though his real self has nothing to do with ecological activism. On the other hand, Lexiusxx's story conveys different but equally interesting points. Although his avatar represents things he loves doing and clothes he never dare wear in real life, his choice of a human avatar was determined by social influence which reflects what social psychologists have called "subjective norm", that is, judgments about and decisions made on the basis of what others who are important to the person think he or she should do (Fishbein, 1980). Yet the costs of "pleasing others" can bring about self-related conflicting values: playing an avatar he did not originally want to play and masking its physical

appearance because of aesthetic reasons. Eructite's answer somewhat exemplifies the Dr. Jekill/Mr. Hyde popular culture view of split personality and identity. He conveys the idea that avatars allow for digitally embodying opposite facets of one's personality worth experimenting with in an environment where the disclosure of one's bad and nasty selves may find an ideal place. This idea is nicely represented by Bluefaya: "I am who I want when I play, I can be normal, or piss off, or play the lover, I don't give it a damn because there is not much risk (Bluefaya).[18]

Masks and facades were among the reasons invoked by some players to account for their real/virtual self relationship:

[Oxxia]: What is the part of you that lives in your avatar?

[Azeona]: I remain myself. My avatar is a façade. And when I play, I use programs like Mumble, Teamspeak, so it is the "real" me who speaks... my character is a facade, not a hiding place. A facade because it is necessary in this game, it certainly expresses my tastes (hairstyle, etc.) but not my personality.[19]

[Oxxia]: is your avatar a kind of loophole for you?

[Paos]: uhm...talking about me through an avatar, something fake, a character...that's weird...my character = rather a mask, a bit like what I want to be or would like to be and at the same time hiding me because I do not normally talk about myself through it.[20]

Players' allusion to masks and facades is worth noting here. A mask is usually understood as something that conceals, partially or totally, one's face. It implies that no matter the perspective adopted there will always be some features of the actor's face that remain inaccessible to the audience. In this sense, Paos' metaphorical view of her avatar reflects a dramaturgical construction of virtual identity similar to that advanced by Goffman (1959) in which the self enacts multiple performances in order to negotiate context-related identities. Unlike masks, façades are a matter of available perspective (what can be seen from a specific point of view) and do not necessarily mean conscious hiding. Azeona's conception of her avatar as a façade can be understood as discarding any possible synecdochic sense of identity: an avatar does not stand for the whole player's self. This is consistent with her view that tastes and personality are two different things. Although, this point is largely arguable on psychological grounds, what is relevant in her answer is that her avatar's physical attributes do not denote her entire personality. Interestingly, Azeona's answer implies distinguishing between two ways of being in the game: as a character and as the real player behind it. Awareness of these two perspectives that tend to blend due to the feelings of presence fostered by the game's immersive interface, represents a somewhat instrumental view of avatars as digital artifacts, that is, avatars are simply ludic-oriented prostheses that allow players to engage with the game.

Most players showed gender consistency between them and their avatars. Only two of our informants played avatars of the opposite sex and their reasons for doing so include:

This character is a female because I created the story that way but I'm a man^^ (Solanya).[21]

I'll often build female characters because I'm a girl ^^...I'd like to create human or dranei characters because they have an aesthetic side I like much...I put some of my traits into my first two characters and then I got fun playing "fashion designer" with the others (Paos).[22]

For Solanya (a real life 17-year-old male player), the reason for playing a female avatar highlights his freedom to imagine and create gender possibilities he does not necessarily identify with. Paos' choice of female avatars is consistent with her real life gender and her aesthetic values. Although during the interview she was playing a male gnome warlock, her answers mostly concerned her past and current female avatars. For another player, technical changes introduced by game designers had a significant impact on his view or role-playing, gender, and avatar distinctiveness:

[Oxxia] do you give your characters special features?...

[Dõumdõum]: Arf... RP disappeared the day Blizzard decided to add a letter to its server "N Rp", normality quickly took over it so that giving your avatar a particular phrasing or a gender makes no longer any sense: (

...

[Oxxia]: do you use your avatar to change some of your features: gender, age, etc.. ?

[Dõumdõum]: Yuck, no, by the way I do not understand a male's need for playing a female avatar (have not met the opposite case).[23]

For Dõumdõum, role-playing in normal realms is no longer an exciting experience. What the player alludes to by "normality" implies the idea of technically standardizing players' control over their gameplay thereby altering the feeling of immersion they can derive from their play experiences. If everyone's gameplay gets standardized, endowing one's avatar with distinctive features such as way of speaking and gender makes no sense. Furthermore, gender swapping is something he is not comfortable with. His pejorative expression "Yuck" when speaking about males' reasons for playing female avatars probably conveys social stereotyping concerning maleness as something not to play with (even digitally).

Finally, other players deliberately concealed aspects of real selves via their avatars. Their reasons to do so include socially undesirable consequences inside the game but also personal coherence with ways of behaving in real life:

Sometimes I don't say I'm a girl lol because men in WoW get quickly aroused and overzealous once they know it (Paos).[24]

Usually, they [guild members] only accept adults when carrying out a raid, so I pretend to be older than my age (Tamor).[25]

[Malonever]: Given that I'm not a fervent fan of heroic fantasy I chose a black character, which as far as I know is something rarely alluded to in this universe...

[Oxxia]: you're not black in real life, are you?...

[Malonever]: no, but if you want more details, I've always loved hiding my face and skin color... my character is a bit like me because I play him ...he's rather obstinate.[26]

These strategic decisions imply carefully choosing what aspects of the self can be disclosed in a given context and being coherent with the strategically adopted role. As Paos argues, "sometimes" it is better for her not to say she is a woman, which implies that judging the woman-friendly dimension (or the absence of male "sexual pressure") of the play environment is crucial to communicate her real gender. In the case of Tamor, pretending to be older than his age—adopting an in-game second-order layer of make believe—is the way to enjoy going out for raids with his guild mates. Malonever's choice of a black avatar conveys his will to explore a fantasy universe mostly composed of Nordic-like human characters from a somewhat marginal perspective which echoes research done on racial inequality and ethnocultural stereotypes within WoW (Na-

kamura, 2008, Higgin, 2009). For these players, concealing or enhancing some aspects of their selves is possible because of the communication affordances of WoW. Yet unlike the abovementioned players for whom avatars are extensions or transparent representations of themselves, these players' avatars stand as translucent representations or their real selves, filtering and diffracting their physical and social identities.

Guilds and Collective Identity

Collective identity can be understood as the perceived sense of "we-ness" and joint agency anchored in real or imagined shared experiences and features of a social group (Snow, 2001). Consistent with this conception, our interviews showed that for some players collective identity is imagined, supposed, or hoped to exist rather than experienced directly. When explicitly asked if they share a collective identity with their guild mates those players answered, for instance: "I hope so otherwise there would be no reason for the guild to exist!!! (Aldrak)"[27] or "I wouldn't go so far as to say that" (Solanya).[28] Even though they were aware of their sharing distinctive symbols and play aspirations with members of their respective guilds, it seems that the very term "collective identity" makes little or no sense to them. By contrast, when asked to specify what they share with guild mates, they provided relevant components of collective identity such as sharing positive and negative feelings depending on whether they succeed or fail during raids, a friendly and trustful atmosphere, an ideal of serious and engaged playing, good writing (no SMS language), etc. So, even though the formal concept seems to make little sense to those players, collective identity was nevertheless *talked* into existence when asked to reflect on what they actually share with other guild members.

These answers are at odds with those of more "skeptical" players for whom membership in a guild does not constitute collective identity "even if people must think the same way to have affinities" (Bluefaya)[29]. Three of them provided personal reasons to justify why they think there is no collective identity within their guilds:

I'm not looking for virtual friendship here. I just use the system, of course, less than other people do, but I do use it (Dõumdõum).[30]

I don't attach myself to others because this is just a game (Chasar).[31]

If I leave the guild, some people will be disappointed but I don't think they would hate me like the slave who leaves her master... For me, the guild is not a family, it's just a hostel...A guild is just having fun killing bosses with people one likes (Azeona).[32]

Their synecdochic answers—each time collective identity is denoted by a potential single component: friendship, attachment, fraternal bonds—clearly reflect that they conceive of and engage with the game's ludic affordances in a rather instrumental way: as an entertaining system designed to provide fun. Overall, skeptical players often argued that belonging to a guild is a necessary and convenient condition to attain some goals and have fun playing the game but it does not create bonds strong enough to be perceived as establishing collective identity. In other words, for these players membership in a guild—the objective condition of belonging to the guild—does not imply assimilating their selves or attaching themselves to any supposed in-group identity prototype.

Other players did consider that they share a common identity with their guild mates. We have identified two kinds of referents in their answers around which collective identity appears to be articulated: (1) empirical referents including guilds' names, tabards, verbal styles, and charters, and (2) more abstract referents encompassing a variety of shared values like trust, mutual respect,

solidarity, game performance, putting things into perspective, etc.

For some players, the guild's name and tabard were distinctive empirical referents of their group identity. Moreover, since those referents are easily recognizable by members of other guilds, players are held accountable for any words and deeds performed when acting on behalf of the guild: "when we speak we've got the guild's name beneath our characters' so we do our best to look after the guild's profile" (Aernei)[33], "you 'personify' the guild: we have a tabard, the first sign of belonging, and also the guild's name under ours" (Shangrilâ)[34]. For still other players, the tabard represented the guild's shared sense of self-derision: "the guild's tabard is nice and also the ambiance...but the tabard is really great:p pink with a red heart on it... that's too much funny" (Smiri)[35]. Verbal styles were also alluded to as a specific referent of collective identity: "Think for example of Azura^^...they all share the same passion, they're always together. Their 'distinctive sign' is that they imitate troll language (Eructite).[36] Yet overall, verbal style was not a significant indicator of collective identity. Besides adopting the game-based lexicon for pragmatic reasons, the majority of our informants reported having no secret codes or guild-specific verbal styles. Finally, the basic function of guild charters can be seen as providing normative criteria for judging players' behavior. Yet in most interviews, guild charters were just considered as rules of etiquette for collective play but not as strong bases for building collective identity. Although all players were aware of the normative implications of guild charters, a number of them do not respect charters all the time or find ad hoc ways to get it round. On closer inspection, collective identity in most of the interviews seems to be derived from and reinforced by shared contents other than charter-based norms.

Players' apparent non-compliance with guild charters does not necessarily mean that guilds are utterly anarchic groups. Unlike most empirical referents, shared values were alluded to as playing a kcy role in structuring players' perception of a common identity within guilds. Values transpired in most of the non-skeptical players' interviews as the basic elements for the expression of collective identity insofar as they embody the playing ideals that prototypically define their past and current guilds. We have identified ten values players highlighted in their interviews and articulated them around three dimensions: (1) self-related values, (2) guild-related values and (3) play-related values (See Figure 1).

This scheme reflects three dimensions of motivational goals and valuing attitudes underlying collective identity in our informants' guilds. The fact that we analytically differentiate them does not mean that they belong to unrelated and merely juxtaposed spheres of desired states and outcomes. On the contrary, throughout our informants' interviews there seems to be a certain consistency among self-related, guild-related, and play-related values. The self-related dimension encompasses shared motivational goals that set the stage for personal achievement inside guilds. The point here is that players value the opportunities afforded by their guilds to satisfy their need for in-game performance and self-image improvement. Being able to accomplish challenging tasks, to use one's best assets in the game, and to feel that one is accepted as member of a guild are all end-states pursued by most of our players. Yet individual improvement is just one of the factors worth being valued. These self-related values also resonate with collective expectations and explicit demands for social accomplishment as a group on the basis of guild-related values embodying socially shared sentiments and desired group attributes. Being able to help others, to respect them, to trust them and to be modest imply a dynamics of intersubjective commitment to a particular way of being which characterizes the specificity of a guild in the eyes of players. Finally, the play-related dimension lays the ground for putting into practice self-related and guild-

related values as players look for the same kind of game-based experiences and assume self-reflecting attitudes towards their individual and collective behavior and accomplishments.

As suggested above, self-related values mostly concern players' in-game self-enhancement, that is, fostering or extending their capabilities as guild members. These values include the sense of belonging (being accepted and needed by the guild), self-fulfillment (fostering the best use of one's talents inside the game), and the sense of accomplishment (being able to succeed at what players, individually and collectively, want to do). Among our informants, Aernei illustrates the sense of belonging by building an analogy between his attachment to his guild and a particular version of patriotism:

It's a bit like patriotism but not so strong, we shouldn't exaggerate...patriotism is just that you've this nationality and you're permanently in this country so you want to protect it, and although you meet some bastards there, you know it's your country...whereas given that there are 70 of us in the guild if someone pisses us off we can get rid of him (Aernei)[37]

This analogy is, of course, limited but it nevertheless highlights some elements worth noting. On Aernei's view, belonging to a guild is like belonging to a country, having a nationality, and claiming the right to inhabit its land. The idea behind his discourse of "country" and "nationality" is that of a space/time situated condition in which everyone is granted a shared identity that is meant to be protected. But unlike discourse about countries and nationalities which, in principle, allows equal and permanent belonging conditions even to "bastards", Aernei's view is particular in that belonging to a guild is not a perpetually granted condition. If someone does not "adapt" to this shared value he or she can be ruthlessly excluded. Individual failures to adapt to a guild' way of functioning can thus trigger the guild's

Figure 1. Dimensions of values addressed by players

adoption of policies of member exclusion. For Aernei, belonging to a guild is something contingent, something players have to earn constantly by adapting themselves to and fostering the guild's expectations dynamics.

For another player, the sense of belonging is something that comes along with entering a guild:

When you enter a guild you conclude a tacit agreement…this passage gives you a feeling of belonging inside the pixelated jungle…you can count on the other guild members…for some, the guild provides security (Shangrilâ)[38]

By alluding to a "tacit agreement", Shangrilâ conveys the implicature that collective values exert normative force on players' behavior. On her view, tacitly adopting the guild's values implies complying with the guild's ethos as a condition for players not only to be granted a membership but especially to develop their "sense" of belonging, their trust in other members, and their feeling of being secured inside the pixelated jungle. This capacity to adopt guild's values also implies being able to balance personal goals and collective expectations, and to share the web of collective meanings and aspirations characteristic of a given guild.

Self-fulfillment was indirectly alluded to by one player when talking about what he shares with other guild members:

To show respect to other players: to optimize one's character in order not to slow other players down and to share information to help them improve their own characters (Eructite)[39]

On the one hand, this link between respect and self-fulfillment testifies for the relationship between self-related and guild-related values implied in collective identity discourse. On the other hand, the idea behind Eructite's view of respect is that of providing guild mates with opportunities and assistance to enhance their levels of performance and develop their talents inside the game. The fostering of self-fulfillment via respect entails here that respecting someone is not just a passive state of not harming her but an active (to show, to express) engagement to recognize her potential as a player as well as a fellow who shares and engages with a particular way of playing. It follows from Eructite's view that players' self-fulfillment is contingent both upon improving one's character technical capacities and upon players' readiness to share improvement-related information with each other.

As far as self-accomplishment is concerned, two players alluded to it as a shared aim within their guilds:

I'm looking for perfection…we all share the same aim: perfecting our characters' armor, gaining power, and being recognized (Lexiusxx)[40]

[We all share] a common aim: "we want to move forward, to progress" while respecting the fact that we can't oblige people to be present five times per week from 8:00pm till 12:00pm (Aldrak)[41]

For these players, perfection, power, recognition and progress are the ways to make self-accomplishment real. Lexiusxx' passage from "I" to "We" in which both pronouns come together to denote a shared goal of perfection is relevant for him to justify that there is consistency between what he is looking for within the game and the valuing framework provided by his guild. The "we" comes here to the fore as an intersubjective valuing support for him to be able to succeed at what he wants to do. Although Aldrak's view is to some extent similar to that of Lexiusxx's, his claim is more moderate in that real-life conditions can put constraints on what they want to achieve collectively. The idea behind this claim is that game-related self-accomplishment cannot be pursued to the detriment of other values holding for people's real lives.

In addition to self-related values, players also have addressed guild-related values which imply self-transcendence in the sense of valuing concern for other members' welfare and readiness to provide them with assistance and advice. Among these values are trust (being reliable and able to rely on other members when needed), solidarity (caring about other players, distributing loots among players who need them the most), respect (giving and receiving recognition inside the guild), and modesty (not showing off or being arrogant when accomplishing big raids and risky events).

Trust appeared implicitly in one of our interviews as a value which affects the guild's way of functioning:

An individual's bad behavior may cause problems to the guild…those behaviors generally include: stealing, lying, letting guild members down (Shangrilâ)[42]

The verbal labels used by Shangrilâ to refer to "bad behaviors" convey the idea of betrayal, of failing to live up to implicit or explicit commitments. The very fact that such behaviors are labeled as "bad" reflects the normative force granted to trust and trustworthy actions by the player. Even in highly competitive environments like WoW, in which selfish motives can impregnate some players' words and deeds, trust plays the role of social glue that binds players together when pursuing common goals.

Modesty was referred to as a value associated to being classy and showing "high level performance" patterns of behavior:

I feel that killing bosses without showing off is classy; so far, I find that the best guilds, at least in the Alliance faction, do not show off! (Azeona)[43]

Although it might seem odd for a young player to postulate modesty as a value, for Azeona modesty is a way to gain social recognition inside WoW. Modesty conveys the background idea of playing in a mature way and reacting soberly to big collective achievements. This also implies adopting a specific outlook on the game: the more you are modest when attaining some goal, the more you are recognized as being classy, elegant. For some of our young players modesty plays an instrumental role in allowing them to reach an ideal end-state: being socially recognized and admired.

Solidarity was addressed by one player as forming the core of any true guild:

I'd say this is my first true guild, a guild where people help each other, and if you need something there's someone who has it...that sort of things (Bluefaya)[44]

Bluefaya's qualification of a "true", genuine guild as one in which people help each other conveys his mental model of solidarity as altruistic action. Although this player may be largely unaware of the selfish motivations that can guide some "altruistic" behaviors, his view about solidarity highlights the value of intra-guild cooperation and fulfillment of others' needs inside the game.

Respect was evoked by one player as an essential yet not already found value within guilds:

I try to go my way without hurting others and I'm intolerant against those players who only care about leveling up to the detriment of other people... by and large I dream of a RP guild in which people value fair playing and show respect

for others in any situation. I've never seen this before in wow (Eructite)[45]

Eructite's disappointment about his past experiences in guilds denotes the idea that instrumental behaviors aimed at just leveling up characters by whatever means are incompatible, in his view, with respect for other people as a core value. His claim about respect here is consistent with his indirect way of speaking about self-fulfillment (see above) insofar as both values imply a sense of "social responsibility" to other players' technical and relational improvement within the guild. He is not objecting to leveling one's character up since this is part and parcel of the game. To his mind, what is unacceptable is that players consider game performance (level up) as a primary value without taking into account that "players" also are "people" that can be hurt.

Finally, play-related values encompass instrumental desired outcome such as reputation (building in-guild and out-guild individual and collective prestige) and end-states like fun and enjoyment (sharing the same hedonistic attitude towards the game) or putting things into perspective (being able to realize that WoW is just a place where social gaming can take place).

Insofar as WoW is a competitive game, reputation holds for individual and collective achievement. One of our informants referred to guild's reputation in terms of appreciation and popularity:

Yeah, [reputation] it's very important because the more people see you as strong the more your popularity ranking rises (Lexiusxx)[46]

Reputation is one of the values typically addressed by our youngest informants. Although for some of them reputation constitutes an end-state worth pursuing in itself, others take it from a more instrumental perspective and see it as a subsidiary outcome of playing "mature style". For Lexiusxx, reputation is a primary value in that it provides him with intra- and inter-guild appreciation. Throughout his interview, he was concerned with a specific idea of popularity as based on having his character stuffed, accomplishing difficult challenges, being wealthy, and posting short videos (also known as *machinimas*) of his guild killing big bosses. On his view, popularity and, by extension, reputation reflects his self-perception as someone appreciated for being a strong player and belonging to a strong, high level guild.

Fun and enjoyment concerned the hedonic dimension of the game, a dimension which, in the eyes of some players, most hard gamers tend easily to forget:

We only share playing time but in a good atmosphere (Cystite)[47]

The big difference is between "us" and the people who take it too much seriously...it's amazing to see lots of haters in the battlefields, they don't really enjoy it which in the end is the game's aim (Smiri)[48]

Unlike other guilds, which I won't mention here, that tear themselves apart, the most important things for us is to play and have fun (Tamor)[49]

Fun and enjoyment appear here as evaluative criteria for distinguishing between identity patterns referred to "us" and "others" who have troubles in realizing that, as a game, WoW represents a practice from which players can draw fun. These different perspectives on the ludic/hedonic dimension of WoW are also what motivate some players to quit their past guilds and to enter other ones that fit with their fun-related expectations.

Putting things into perspective was referred to by players as characterizing their game practice:

The capacity to put things into perspective, if we can't kill a boss it's not the end of the world, and if we succeed at it it's not a reason to showing off (Eructite)[50]

Eructite's claim underlies the capacity to see oneself as a player, to take some distance from the game without losing one's attachment to both the guild and the way of playing. Furthermore, it also stands for a balanced perspective on the way guilds manage to draw fun, success, and failure from collective actions. In a nutshell, putting things into perspective refers to a healthy, self-reflective attitude towards the self that permeates all the three valuing dimensions and ensures the persistence of the guild and the play over time.

As we can see, in most players' interviews values appear not just as optional extras about individual and collective behavior but also as standards for the self and the guild. They function as an "identity capital" from which players draw normative, symbolic, and emotional patterns of sharing which justify both their sense of joint agency and their motivations to be part of and work for the guild. It should be noted, though, that the values forming the core of a guild stem from the interplay between players' personal histories (desires, memories, and expectations) and the intersubjective affordances of the game. This is consistent with Pearce and Artemesia's (2009) claim that players arrive on the scene "with a certain set of values and a predisposition to socially emergent behaviors" (p. 73). Yet this does not imply that players' preexisting value systems and behavioral predispositions are so rigid that neither adaptation to nor adoption of in-game emergent values can take place inside the platform. In fact, the process of building collective identity appears to be marked by players' constant negotiation and monitoring of their value-based view of themselves, the guild, and the way of playing as can be seen from their belonging to past and current guilds. Such a negotiation is in line with Rettberg's (2008) claim that "the process of advancing in WoW is to some extent modeled on the process of getting an education" (p. 25). Players not only have to be "educated" in terms of learning how to master the technical and tactic intricacies of the game but also, and to some extent more critically, they are educated in what Klapp (1971, quoted in Klastrup, 2008 p. 163), speaking of social typing, called "collective values" and "socially necessary sentiments". These values and sentiments are triggered by the game's character narrative, which defines roles, types, attitudes, and levels of responsibility, but they still have to be felt and lived as characterizing both the guild's aims and the collective way of playing. Such feeling and living of values resonates with Gee's (2003) view of "projective identity" according to which players project their own values and desires onto virtual characters, see the latter as their "projects" in the making, and engage with relevant others who share or at least are able to negotiate on those values and desires. Values appear thus as significant components of collective identity as they encapsulate not only players' expectations about the game but also a reflective stance both towards themselves and towards others with whom they engage in collective playing. They define the specificity of a guild as they guide the selection of the means and ends of specific actions, and serve as criteria by which objects, actions or events are evaluated. Finally, unlike norms which are explicitly formulated in guild charters, values are carried latently through the social process of playing together and provide the sense of collective identity players experience, imagine, or dream of within guilds.

FUTURE RESEARCH DIRECTIONS

The present study reveals that critical discourse analysis is a helpful heuristic to understand language behavior patterns of identity construction inside WoW. It has showed, for instance, that players' narratives about their avatars convey relevant cognitive and social representations of their possible or imagined selves as well as self-related aspects of their game practices. Moreover, collective identity inside guilds was showed to be discursively enacted via evocation of shared

values among guild mates. Yet given its synchronic nature, this study constitutes a "snapshot" of how French-speaking WoW players construct and negotiate their personal and collective identities within the game. Since identity narratives are complex processes constructed and deconstructed over time, deeper insight into identity construction inside WoW can be gained by implementing critical discourse analysis longitudinal research aimed at examining, for instance, identity discourse at different times in players' and guilds' game careers. Furthermore, a more detailed view of players' discursive construction of identity could be attained by gathering face-to-face data and thus keeping track of how players verbally negotiate aspects of their in-game and real-life practices. Since players can also extend their game-based interactions to include meetings in real life, it would be useful to examine their patterns of interaction in out-game settings and the impact of real life events on the process of collective identity construction.

Finally, adopting a mixed methods approach based on discourse analysis and quantitative data mining can help researchers not only generalize their results to wider parts of the gamer population but also examine cross-cultural patterns of identity construction in WoW. Since narratives are widespread practices of constructing objects, roles, and collectivities grounded in cognitive models available in most if not all cultures (Barker & Galasiński, 2001, Sperber, 1996), analyzing and comparing intercultural patterns of in-game identity construction and presentation can shed light on the potential transcultural impact of WoW as a globalizing social practice.

CONCLUSION

In this chapter we have provided a critical discourse analysis of French-speaking WoW players' personal and social identity. We have showed that personal identity inside WoW is mostly (re) constructed as a narrative in which players merge their in-game perceptions via their avatars with their relevant real-life experiences as players. Avatar introduction has been showed to constitute a rhetorical mode of putting forward self-related assumptions and aspects of one' identity. These rhetorical modes have also revealed that for some players avatars function as extensions or transparent representations of themselves. For others, the representational flexibility of avatars inside WoW allows them to enhance and/or conceal some aspects of their real selves they deem self-discrepant or contextually undesirable. Finally, collective identity within guilds was perceived and constructed by players through some empirical referents such as guild's name, tabard, and verbal style but the majority of our informants reported shared values as denoting shared identity inside guilds. Consistent with major trends in the literature on online games, French-speaking WoW players' identity experiments are less a matter of becoming someone else online than negotiating and virtually representing self-discrepant aspects of their real lives.

REFERENCES

Bainbridge, W. S. (2010a). *Online multiplayer games*. San Rafael, CA: Morgan & Claypool.

Bainbridge, W. S. (2010b). *The Warcraft civilization: Social science in a virtual world*. Cambridge, MA: MIT Press.

Barker, C., & Galasińki, D. (2001). *Cultural studies and discourse analysis*. London, UK: Sage.

Bessière, K., Seay, F., & Kiesler, S. (2007). The ideal elf: Identity exploration in World of Warcraft. *Cyberpsychology & Behavior, 10*(4), 530–535. doi:10.1089/cpb.2007.9994

Brignall, T. (2008). Guild life in the World of Warcraft: Online game tribalism. In Adams, T., & Smith, S. (Eds.), *Electronic tribes: The virtual world of geeks, gamers, shamans, and scammers* (pp. 110–123). Austin, TX: University of Texas Press.

De Fina, A. (2006). Group identity, narrative and self-presentation. In De Fina, A., Schiffrin, D., & Bamberg, M. (Eds.), *Discourse and identity* (pp. 351–375). New York, NY: Cambridge University Press. doi:10.1017/CBO9780511584459.018

Ducheneaut, M., Yee, N., Nickell, E., & Moore, R. (2006). Alone together? Exploring the social dynamics of massively multiplayer online games. In *Proceedings of the SIGCHI Conference on Human Factors in computing systems* (pp. 407-416). Montreal, Canada.

Fishbein, M. (1980). Theory of reasoned action: Some applications and implications. In H. Howe & M. Page (Eds.), *Nebraska Symposium on Motivation* (pp. 65-116). Lincoln, NE: University of Nebraska Press.

Gergen, K. (1994). *Realities and relationships*. Cambridge, MA: Harvard University Press.

Goffman, E. (1959). *The presentation of self in everyday life*. Garden City, NY: Doubleday.

Hagström, C. (2008). Playing with names: Gaming and naming in world of warcraft. In Corneliussen, H., & Rettberg, J. (Eds.), *Digital culture, play and identity: A World of Warcraft® reader* (pp. 265–285). Cambridge, MA: MIT Press.

Higgin, T. (2009). Blackless fantasy: The disappearance of race in massively multiplayer online role-playing games. *Games and Culture, 4*(1), 3–26. doi:10.1177/1555412008325477

Hine, C. (2000). *Virtual ethnography*. London, UK: Sage.

Huh, S., & Williams, D. (2010). Dude looks like a lady: Gender swapping in an online game. In Bainbridge, W. S. (Ed.), *Online worlds: Convergence of the real and the virtual* (pp. 161–174). London, UK: Springer. doi:10.1007/978-1-84882-825-4_13

Keller, D. (2007). Gaming, identity, and literacy. In Selfe, C. L., & Gawisher, G. E. (Eds.), *Gaming lives in the twenty-first century* (pp. 71–87). New York, NY: Palgrave.

Klapp, O. (1971). Heroes, villains, and fools as agents of social control. In Almog, O. (Ed.), *Social types: Process, structure and ethos* (pp. 12–18). San Diego, CA: Aegis Publishing Company.

Klastrup, L. (2008). What makes World of Warcraft a world? A note on death and dying. In Corneliussen, H. G., & Rettberg, J. W. (Eds.), *Digital culture, play, and identity: A WoW reader* (pp. 143–166). Cambridge, MA: MIT Press.

Markus, H., & Nurius, P. (1986). Possible selves. *The American Psychologist*, *41*(9), 954–969. doi:10.1037/0003-066X.41.9.954

Nakamura, L. (2008). *Digitizing race: Visual cultures of the internet*. Minneapolis, MN: University of Minnesota Press.

Nurius, P. (1991). Possible selves and social support: Social cognitive resources for coping and striving. In Howard, J., & Callero, P. (Eds.), *The self-society dynamic: Cognition, emotion, and action* (pp. 239–258). Cambridge, MA: Cambridge University Press. doi:10.1017/CBO9780511527722.013

Pearce, C., & Artemesia. (2009). *Communities of play. Emergent cultures in multiplayer games and virtual worlds*. Cambridge, MA: MIT Press.

Rettberg, S. (2008). Corporate ideology in World of Warcraft. In Corneliussen, H. G., & Rettberg, J. W. (Eds.), *Digital culture, play, and identity: A WoW reader* (pp. 19–38). Cambridge, MA: MIT Press.

Salazar, J. (2009). Analyzing social identity (re)production: Identity liminal events in mmorpgs. *Journal of Virtual Worlds Research*, *1*(3), 3–22.

Snow, D. (2001). Collective identity and expressive forms. In Smelser, N. J., & Baltes, P. B. (Eds.), *International encyclopedia of the social and behavioral sciences* (pp. 2212–2219). London, UK: Elsevier Science.

Sperber, D. (1996). *Explaining culture: A naturalistic approach*. London, UK: Blackwell Publishing.

Sperber, D., & Wilson, D. (1986). *Relevance: Communication and cognition*. Oxford, UK: Basil Blackwell.

Taylor, T. L. (2002). Living digitally: Embodiment in virtual worlds. In Schroeder, R. (Ed.), *The social life of avatars: Presence and interaction in shared virtual environments* (pp. 40–62). London, UK: Springer.

Taylor, T. L. (2006). *Play between worlds: Exploring online game culture*. Cambridge, MA: MIT Press.

Tronstad, R. (2008). Character identification in World of Warcraft: The relationship between capacity and appearance. In Corneliussen, H., & Rettberg, J. (Eds.), *Digital culture, play and identity: A World of Warcraft® reader* (pp. 249–263). Cambridge, MA: MIT Press.

Van Dijk, T. (1990). Social cognition and discourse. In Giles, H., & Robinson, W. P. (Eds.), *Handbook of language and social psychology* (pp. 163–183). Chichester, UK: John Wiley & Sons.

Van Dijk, T. (2001). Multidisciplinary CDA: A plea for diversity. In Wodak, R., & Meyer, M. (Eds.), *Methods in critical discourse analysis* (pp. 95–120). London, UK: Sage.

Van Leeuwen, T. (2008). *Discourse and practice: New tools for critical discourse analysis*. New York, NY: Oxford University Press.

Widdicombe, S., & Wooffitt, R. (1995). *The language of youth subcultures*. London, UK: Harvester Wheatsheaf.

Williams, D., Ducheneaut, N., Xiong, L., Yee, N., & Nickell, N. (2006). From tree houses to barracks: The social life of guilds in World of Warcraft. *Games and Culture*, *1*(4), 338–361. doi:10.1177/1555412006292616

ADDITIONAL READING

Aarseth, E. (2004). Genre trouble: Narrativism and the art of simulation. In Wardrip-Fruin, N., & Harrigan, P. (Eds.), *First person* (pp. 45–54). Cambrigde, MA: MIT Press.

Adams, T. L., & Smith, S. A. (2008). *Electronic tribes. The virtual worlds of geeks, gamers, shamans, and scammers*. Austin: The University of Texas Press.

Crawford, G. (2009). Forget the magic circle (or towards a sociology of video games). Keynote presentation at the *Under the Mask* conference, University of Bedfordshire. Retrieved June 25 2010, from http://underthemask.wdfiles.com / local--files/key-note /Garry%20Crawford.doc

Egenfeldt-Nielsen, S., Smith, J. H., & Tosca, S. P. (2008). *Understanding video games: The essential introduction*. New York: Routledge.

Fischer, F., & Mandl, H. (2005). Knowledge convergence in computer-supported collaborative learning: The role of external representation tools. *Journal of the Learning Sciences*, *14*(3), 405–441. doi:10.1207/s15327809jls1403_3

Ford, M. J. (2005). The game, the pieces, and the players: generative resources from two instructional portrayals of experimentation. *Journal of the Learning Sciences*, *14*(4), 449–487. doi:10.1207/s15327809jls1404_1

Fornäs, J., Klein, K., Ladendorf, M., Sundén, J., & Sveningsson, M. (Eds.). (2002). *Digital borderlands: Cultural studies of identity and interactivity on the Internet*. New York: Peter Lang Publishing.

Gackenbach, J. (2006). Video game play and lucid dreams: Implications for the development of consciousness. *Dreaming*, *16*(2), 96–110. doi:10.1037/1053-0797.16.2.96

Gaggioli, A., & Breining, R. (2003). Perception and cognition in immersive virtual reality. In Riva, G., & Davide, F. (Eds.), *Identity community and technology in the Internet age* (pp. 71–86). Amsterdam: IOS Press.

Gamberini, L., & Bussolon, S. (2001). Human navigation in electronic environments. *Cyberpsychology & Behavior*, *4*(1), 57–65. doi:10.1089/10949310151088398

Gee, J. P. (2005). Video Games, Mind, and Learning. *The International Digital Media Arts Association Journal*, *1*(3), 37–43.

Giddings, S. (2007). Dionysiac machines. Videogames and the triumph of the simulacra. *Convergence: The International Journal of Research into New Media Technologies*, *13*(4), 417–431. doi:10.1177/1354856507082204

Giddings, S. (2009). Events and collusions: A glossary for the microethnography of video game play. *Games and Culture*, *4*(2), 144–157. doi:10.1177/1555412008325485

Golub, A. (2010). Being in the world (of warcraft): Raiding, realism, and knowledge production in a massively multiplayer online game. *Anthropological Quarterly, 83*(1), 17–46. doi:10.1353/anq.0.0110

Grimes, S. M. (2006). Online multiplayer games: A virtual space for intellectual property debates? *New Media & Society, 8*(6), 969–990. doi:10.1177/1461444806069651

Guardiola, E., & Natkin, S. (2005). Game theory and video game, a new approach of game theory to analyze and conceive game systems. In *Proceedings of the CGAMES'05 International Conference on Computer Games,* (pp. 166-170). Wolverhampton, UK: University of Wolverhampton. Available at http://cedric.cnam.fr/ PUBLIS/RC859.pdf

Harrigan, P., & Wardrip-Fruin, N. (Eds.). (2009). *Third person: Authoring and exploring vast narratives*. Cambridge, MA: MIT Press.

Humphrey, S. (2008). Ruling the virtual world: Governance in massively multiplayer online games. *European Journal of Cultural Studies, 11*(2), 149–171. doi:10.1177/1367549407088329

Hutchinson, R. (2007). Performing the Self: Subverting the Binary in Combat Games. *Games and Culture, 2*(4), 283–299. doi:10.1177/1555412007307953

Jansz, J., & Martens, L. (2005). Gaming at a LAN event: The social context of playing video games. *New Media & Society, 7*(3), 333–355. doi:10.1177/1461444805052280

Nasir, N. S. (2005). Individual Cognitive Structuring and the Sociocultural Context: Strategy Shifts in the Game of Dominoes. *Journal of the Learning Sciences, 14*(1), 5–34. doi:10.1207/s15327809jls1401_2

Poster, M., & Savat, D. (2009). *Deleuze and new technology*. Edinburgh: Edinburgh University Press.

Rummel, N., & Spada, H. (2005). Learning to collaborate: an instructional approach to promoting collaborative problem solving in computer-mediated settings. *Journal of the Learning Sciences, 14*(2), 201–241. doi:10.1207/s15327809jls1402_2

Salen, K., & Zimmerman, E. (2004). *Rule of play: Game design fundamentals*. Cambridge, MA: MIT Press.

Salen, K., & Zimmerman, E. (2005). *The game design reader: A rules of play anthology*. Cambridge, MA: MIT Press.

Simona, I. (2007). Ethnography of online role-playing games: the role of virtual and real contest in the construction of the field. *Forum Qualitative Sozialforschung/Forum: Qualitative Social Research, 8*(3), art. 36. Retrieved June 25 2010, from http://nbn-resolving.de/ urn:nbn:de:0114-fqs0703367

Taylor, T. L. (2006). Does WoW change everything? How a PvP server, multinational player base, and surveillance mod scene caused me pause. *Games and Culture, 1*(4), 318–337. doi:10.1177/1555412006292615

Turkle, S. (1995). *Life on the screen: Identity in the age of the internet*. London: Weidenfeld & Nicolson.

Walker, J. (2007). A network of quests in World of Warcraft. In Harrigan, P., & Wardrip-Fruin, N. (Eds.), *Second person: Role-playing and story in games and playable media* (pp. 307–311). Cambridge, MA: MIT Press.

KEY TERMS AND DEFINITIONS

Avatar: A digitally reproduced representation of a player in an online game environment also alluded to in-game as a "character".

Critical Discourse Analysis: A multidisciplinary orientation to investigate social and political phenomena by examining social actors' verbal and written discourses in order to unveil the impact of personal and social representations on their way of speaking and writing.

Collective Identity: The perceived or imagined sense of belonging to and identifying with a group.

Narrative: A verbal or written story-like piece accounting for individual or collective domain-specific experiences.

Relevance: The set of self- and context-related implicit or explicit assumptions a speaker conveys when communicating with others.

Values: Enduring beliefs and feelings associated to end-states worth pursuing and fostering.

ENDNOTES

[1]   All typing errors, grammatical mistakes, idioms, shortened forms, and slang in the original French quotations are reproduced verbatim.

[2]   «Aldrak, démoniste spécialisé en destruction et accessoirement affliction quand le besoin se fait sentir… Un vieux roublard qui traine sa bosse sur ce serveur depuish 4 ansh maintenant et que personnesh ne connait ^^ »

[3]   « BlueFaya Draneai Chaman Que j'affectionne:) … Wow est un jeu qu'on affectionne TRES (trop?) vite Et on s'attache assez rapidement a son perso »

[4]   « Dõumdõum, chaman heal…temps joué environs 3 semaines… »

[5]   « Eructite, paladin vindicte level 80, j'en ai 9 80 et une floppée en pexing ou qui servent juste de sacs »

[6]   «Cystite, jeune elfe de la nuit nommée ainsi par ses parents car elle était destinée à faire mal elle vient d'une famille noble, elle est en général classe et sérieuse elle aime la chasse par-dessus tout et son familier…elle n'aime pas la vulgarité et a une mission à remplir ici »

[7]   « Solanya, chevalier de la mort, demi-draeneï (père humain), Entre vingt et trente ans je dirais, Ni frère ni sœur, Parents morts il y a longtemps. »

[8]   «…un druide du nom de Aernei nivo 80 ki appartien à la guilde Les Fondateurs d'Azeroth ce sont tous mes amis et je les soutiens du mieu que je peux ^^…Aernei(moi) a bcp d'amis afin de ne pas se sentir seul… mon rapport à mon avatar a effectivement évolué mais il est vrai que au début j'étais déja vraiment content d'avoir un avatar qui me représentait (pk c'était mon 1er jeu online alors forcément j'étais un peu étonné), en fait le fait de le faire évoluer et stuffé fais kil est difficile de s'en séparé…En fait, plus tu le up plus tu met du tps sur ton avatar alors forcément à force tu as plus envie de le lacher c'est un peu comme une maison que l'on a construit de ces propres mains on a pas envie forcément de la vendre on préfère y vivre en tout cas c'est mon opinion »

[9]   « Je m appelle malonever. jsuis paladin et j'ai le pouvoir de ressusciter les morts je suis né dans le conté de l'or petit je me faisais insulté de noob et de unstuff ce qui a fini par me faire développer un sentiment de revanche et un besoin de reconnaissance auprès des autres joueurs

[10] « je trouve que la lettre, ou pluror les sons o et a s'accordent joliment, de plus la féminité s'exteriorise beaucoup par une derniere lettre en a et le z est une lettre assez peu utilisée, que j'aime beaucoup ^^…une identité forte en restant feminine »

[11] « si on regarde dans un dico de latin sagitari ce rapporte à la chasse à l'arc etc… donc ça allait bien à la classe que j'avais choisi »

[12] « Muliang est un nom qui a une histoire ; c'est le nom bouddhiste que j'ai reçu d'un maître zen en Corée ; shangrila est un lieu

imaginaire au Tibet. les deux noms font référence à la fois à mon passé, mais aussi à une appétence perso muliang et shangrila sont deux personnages heals associés donc à des choses "bouddhistes" ce qui n'est pas innocent de ma part voilou shangrila, lieu imaginaire tout comme ce personnage »

13 « je ne suis pas différente, c'est plus comme une autre facette de sa personnalité… nos persos nous ressemblent étrangement, nous ne profitons pas du virtuel pr être different »

14 « pour moi l'avatar n'est qu'un outil qui me permet de m'amuser et de remplir des objectifs dans le jeu je ne me comporte pas differemment avec les autres joueurs quand j'utilise cet avatar que dans la réalité »

15 « revenons à mon avatar alors mon phisik pour moi disons kil a une importance mais pas torp nn plus…étant droood je peux changer de forme il est rare ke je vois le réel phisik de mon perso..c'est pas pk il a les cheveux blancs kil est vieu mon perso sa me fait penser à la neige^^… qand jai commencé je voulais un mec ki a la classe et ki ait l'air d'un vétéran mais jeune d'où le visage jeune et les cheveux blancs… ma classe je sais pourkoi je l'ai choisi pk elle faisait rapport à la nature et aux animaux. Sa parlait d'équilibre….Sa faisait très spirituel et en mm tps sa me donnait l'impression d'être un fervent défenseur de la justice et des droits naturels… mais sa serait plus mes espérance dans mon cas pk je suis pas nn plus un écolo... »

16 « mon persoo c ma création et c moi qui l'évolue… a la base je voulé un orc mes mes pote étai a l'aliance alors on ma it pren un humain moi jaime pas trop leur tete alr je m'équipe a fond pour camouflé sa tete »

17 « Il y a une certaine part de moi dans mon paladin … Le défenseur de la lumière ca correspond assez a la vision que j'ai de moi… Par contre mon démoniste est tout le contraire

de mon image personnelle mentale: moche petit et méchant »

18 « Je suis qui je veut quand je joue, Je peut donc rester normal, ou faire chier, ou faire mon loveur, on s'en fout puisqu'il y a pas bcp de risques »

19 « [Oxxia]: Quel part de toi mets-tu dans ton avatar ? [Azeona]: je reste moi même. Mon avatar n'est qu'une facade, lorsque je joue, forcément, je vais sur des programmes comme mumble, Teamspeak, et c'est alors forcément la part "réelle" de moi qui s'exprime… Le personnage est une facade, pas une cachette. Une facade parce que dans ce jeu il en faut une, elle exprime forcément mes gouts (coiffire etc) mais pas ma personnalité »

20 « [Oxxia]: c'est un échappatoire pour toi ? [Paos]: surtout de parler de chose de moi, personnelle, a travers un avatar, un faux, un perso c'est vrai que c'est bizarre mon perso = un masque plutôt genre comme ce que j'aimerais être ou ce que j'aimerais paraître et me cacher en même temps parce que normalement je ne parle pas de moi avec »

21 « ce perso-là est féminin parce que j'ai créé l'histoire comme ça mais je suis un homme ^^ »

22 « le plus souvent je vais faire des personnages filles parce que je suis une fille ^^ j'aime bien me faire un perso humain ou dranei y'a un coté esthétique que je préfère chez eux… sur mes deux premiers personnages j'ai mis certains de mes traits et ensuite je me suis plutôt amusé a "jouer a la styliste" sur les autres on va dire »

23 « [Oxxia]: et les dotes-tu de traits de carcactères propres ? [Dõumdõum]: Arf...le RP à disparu le jour ou blizard à décidé de rajouter une lettre à ses serveur "N Rp",du coup la normalité à pris le dessus et donner un phrasé ou un genre à son perso n'a plus eu aucun sens:(… [Oxxia]: est ce que tu profites de ton avatar pour modifier certains

de tes traits ? genre, âge, etc. ? [Dõumdõum]: Beurk, non, je ne comprend d'ailleurs pas le fait de jouer un sexe feminin par un masculin (encore peu croisé l'inverse) »

24 « il m'arrive de pas dire que je suis une fille lol parce que les mecs dans wow sont beaucoup trop au taquet, et ils vont un peu de zelle une fois qu'ils le savent »

25 « en raid ils n'acceptent que des adultes donc je me fais passer plus vieux que mon age »

26 « [Malonever]: n'étant pas fervent fan de l'univers heroic fantaisy j ai pris express un personnage a peau noir ce qui a mon sens est rarement évoqué dans cet univers [Oxxia]: et tu n'es pas noir dans ta vie actuelle [Malonever]: non, si tu veux encore des precision jai tjrs aimer cacher mon visage et ma couleur de peau.. forcement mon perso me ressemble un peu vu ke c moi kil le joue… il est donc plutot tétu »

27 « J'espère sinon la guilde n'aurait pas raison d'être !!!! »

28 « … je ne pense pas que j'irais jusque là »

29 « Meme si il faut que les gens pensent pareil pour avoir des affinitées »

30 « Non je ne noue pas d'amitié virtuel, j'utilise le systeme, un peu moin que certains mais quand meme un peu »

31 « nn je ne m'attache pas ce n'est qu'un jeu »

32 « Si je quitte la guilde, certains pourront peut etre pincés, mais jamais on ne m'en voudra comme a un esclave qui quitte son maitre… La guilde c'est pas une famille selon moi, c'est un foyer d'accueil… Une guilde, c'est avoir le plaisir de tromber des boss avec des gens qu'on apprécie ».

33 « kand on parle on a juste en dessous de notre nom "Les Fondateurs d'Azeroth" alors forcément on essaie kand mm de soigner l'image de la guilde ».

34 « tu "représentes" la guilde: on a un "tabard" premier signe d'appartenance

on a aussi le nom de la guilde en dessous de son nom ».

35 « le tabard est sympa, puis l'ambiance aussi mais le tabard il est monstrueux:p Rose avec un coeur rouge dessus c'était marrant quoi ».

36 « Prends l'exemple d'Azura ^^ ils sont dans le même délire, ils s'entendent bien. Leur "signe distinctif" c'est par exemple d'immiter le language troll ».

37 « un peu comme du patriotisme mais bcp moin poussé fo pas abused non plus pk le patriotisme c juste ke tu es de cette nationalité tu es constament dans ce pays alors tu as forcément envie de le protégé et mm si tu rencontre des salop t usais ke c ton pays alors ka la guilde si une personne te fais chier, vu kon est 70, cdéja une personne de trop »

38 « quand on rentre dans une guilde, on formule un accord tacite ce passage te donne un sentiment d'appartenance dans la jungle pixellisée… tu peux compter sur les membres de ta guilde »

39 « le respect des autres joueurs (que ce soit en terme d'optimisation personnelle pour ne pas les ralentir mais aussi de partage d'informations pour qu'ils s'optimisent) »

40 « je veu vraiment la perfection. On partage le meme but la perfection du personnage armur, arme pouvoir etre reconnu »

41 « une idée de "on veut avancer" tout en respectant le fait qu'on ne peut pas obliger une personnes à être présente 5 soirs semaines de 20h à 00h00 »

42 « un comportement qui est malsain chez une personne peut poser pb à toute une guilde… ces comportements sont en général les suivants: voler (ninja), mentir, laisser tomber des gens de sa guilde »

43 « J'en sais rien, je trouve juste que c'est classe de tomber du boss sans se vanter. Je trouve qu'en ce moment toutes les bonnes

guildes, alliance du moins, ne se vantent pas ! »

44 « C'est ma premiere vraie guilde je dirais. Une guilde ou il y a beaucoup d'entraide, ou on a besoin de quelque cghose, quelqu'un l'a… ce genre de chose »

45 « J'essaie de suivre la voie du moindre mal et je suis intolérant quand je croise des joueurs qui ne sont là que pour évoluer même si ca doit être au détriment des autres. »

46 « oui très important car le fet ke beaucoup de personne te reconaissent forte augmente ta cote de popularité »

47 « on ne partage que du jeu, mais dans la bonne ambiance »

48 « la grosse différence c'est surtout entre "nous" et les gens qui prennet ça trop au sérieux par exemple quand on voit le nombre de rageux dans les champs de batailles c'est hallucinant ils s'amusent plus vraiment alors qu'au final c'est le but »

49 « le plus imortant pour nous c'est le jeu et l'amusement pas commes d'autres guildes que je ne citerais pas qui se déchirent de l'intérieru »

50 « la faculté de relativiser (si un boss ne tombe pas c'est pas la fin du monde…) »

Compilation of References

Aarseth, E. (1997). *Cybertext: Perspectives on ergodic literature*. Baltimore, MD: The John Hopkins University Press.

Aarseth, E. (2009). A hollow world. World of Warcraft as spatial practice. In Corneliussen, H. G., & Rettberg, J. W. (Eds.), *Digital culture, play, and identity. A World of Warcraft reader*. Cambridge: MIT Press.

Aas, B. G., Meyerbröker, K., & Emmelkamp, P. M. G. (2010). Who am I - and if so, where? A study on personality in virtual realities. *Journal of Virtual Worlds Research, 2,* 5.

Abbate, J. (1999). *Inventing the Internet*. Cambridge, MA: MIT Press.

Abramoviç, M. (1993). Art is about energy. *Art and Design, 8*(7-8), 32–37.

Abramoviç, M., von Daniken, H. P., & Ruf, B. (1996). A conversation with Marina Abramoviç. In Landert, M. (Ed.), *Marina Abramoviç: Double edge* (pp. 11–47). Warth, Austria: Museum of Fine Art of the Canton of Thurgau, Kartause Ittengen.

Abramoviç, M. (2010). *The pigs of today are the hams of tomorrow*. Plymouth Arts Centre. Retrieved October 17, 2010, from http://www.plymouthartscentre.org/Press/marinaAbramoviç.html

Abramoviç, M., & Abramoviç, V. *(1998). Time-space-energy or talking about asystemic thinking. In M. Abramoviç et al. (Eds.),* Marina Abramoviç: Artist body-Performances 1969-1998 *(pp. 400-17). Milano, Italia: Edizioni Charta.*

Alasuutari, P. (1995). *Researching culture: Qualitative method and cultural studies*. London, UK: Sage.

Albrechtslund, A. M. (2010). Gamers telling stories: Understanding narrative practices in an online community. *Convergence: The International Journal of Research into New Media Technologies, 16,* 112–124. doi:10.1177/1354856509348773

Aldrich, C. (2009). Virtual worlds, simulations, and games for education: A unifying view. *Innovate, 5*. Retrieved May 26, 2010, from http://www.innovateonline.info/ index.php?view=article&id=727

Alexander, C., Ishikawa, S., & Silverstein, M. (1977). *A pattern language: Towns, buildings, construction*. Oxford, UK: Oxford UP.

Aliaga, D. G., Rosen, P. A., & Bekins, D. R. (2007). Style grammars for interactive visualization of architecture. *IEEE Transactions on Visualization and Computer Graphics, 13*(4), 786–797. doi:10.1109/TVCG.2007.1024

American Cancer Society. (2010). *Relay for Life® in Second Life®*. Retrieved 3rd July 2010, from http://www.relayforlife.org/ relay/secondlife

American Psychological Association. (1986). *Guidelines for computer-based tests and interpretations*. Washington, DC: American Psychological Association.

American Psychological Association Committee on Professional Standards & Committee on Psychological Tests and Assessment. Division 40. (1987). Task force report in computer-assisted neuropsychological evaluation. *Clinical Neuropsychologist, 2,* 161–184.

Amyfreelunch. (2008). *New episode: Interview with Scott Kildall*. Retrieved November 14, 2010, from http://amyfreelunch.wordpress.com/2008/12/18/new-episode-interview-with-scott-kildall/

Anastasi, A., & Urbina, S. (1997). *Psychological testing* (7th ed.). New York, NY: McMillian.

Ancient Rome. (2010). *Ancient Rome*. Retrieved on June 13, 2010, from http://earth.google.com/rome/

Anders, P. (1998). *Envisioning cyberspace: Designing 3D electronic spaces*. New York, NY: McGraw-Hill Professional.

Anderson, C. A. (2004). An update on the effects of violent video games. *Journal of Adolescence, 27*, 122–133. doi:10.1016/j.adolescence.2003.10.009

Anderson, C. A., & Bushman, B. J. (2002). The effects of media violence on society. *Science, 295*, 2377–2379. doi:10.1126/science.1070765

Anderson, C. A., Gentile, D. A., & Buckley, K. E. (2007). *Violent video game effects on children and adolescents*. New York, NY: Oxford University Press. doi:10.1093/acprof:oso/9780195309836.001.0001

Anderson, C. A., Sakaoto, A., & Gentile, D. A. (2008). Longitudinal effects of violent video games on aggression in Japan and the United States. *Pediatrics, 122*, 1067–1072. doi:10.1542/peds.2008-1425

Anderson, T. (2003). Modes of interaction in distance education: Recent developments and research questions. In Moore, M. G., & Anderson, W. G. (Eds.), *Handbook of distance education* (pp. 129–144). Mahwah, NJ: Lawrence Erlbaum.

Angeli, C., & Valanides, N. (2009, January). Epistemological and methodological issues for the conceptualization, development, and assessment of ICT–TPCK: Advances in technological pedagogical content knowledge (TPCK). *Computers & Education, 52*(1), 154–168. doi:10.1016/j.compedu.2008.07.006

Anonymous. (2008, November). *RE: Attending AA meetings in Second Life* [Web log post]. Retrieved from http://anon-recovery-archive.blogspot.com/

Antonietti, A., & Cantoia, M. (2000). To see a painting versus to walk in a painting: An experiment on sense-making through virtual reality. *Computers & Education, 34*, 213–223. doi:10.1016/S0360-1315(99)00046-9

Antonietti, A., & Mellone, R. (2003). The difference between playing games with and without the computer: A preliminary view. *The Journal of Psychology, 137*(2), 133–144. doi:10.1080/00223980309600604

Appadurai, A. (1986). Theory in anthroplogy: Center and periphery. *Comparative Studies in Society and History, 28*(2), 356–361. doi:10.1017/S0010417500013906

Appel, J. (2006). Second Life develops education following: Virtual worlds being used by some educators and youth groups for teaching, socialization. *eSchoolNews: Tecnology News for Today's K-20 Educator.* Retrieved April 11, 2010, from http://www.eschoolnews.com/news/topnews/index.cfm?i=42030&CFID=3971087&CFTOKEN=31042212

Arnold, P., Farrell, M. J., Pettifer, S., & West, A. J. (2002). Performance of a skilled motor task in virtual and real. *Ergonomics, 45*(5), 348–361. doi:10.1080/00140130110120510

Asakawa, T., & Gilbert, N. (2003). Synthesizing experiences: Lessons to be learned from Internet-mediated simulation games. *Simulation & Gaming, 34*(1), 10–22. doi:10.1177/1046878102250455

Astur, R. S., Tropp, J., Sava, S., Constable, R. T., & Markus, E. J. (2004). Sex differences and correlations in a virtual Morris water task, a virtual radial arm maze, and mental rotation. *Behavioural Brain Research, 151*, 103–115. doi:10.1016/j.bbr.2003.08.024

Atkinson, R. F. (1969). *Conduct: An introduction to moral philosophy*. London, UK: MacMillan.

Au, W. J. (2008). *The making of Second Life*. New York, NY: Harper Collins Publishers.

Au, W. J. (2008). *The making of Second Life: Notes from the new world*. New York, NY: Collins.

Au, W. J. (2008). *The making of Second Life. Notes from the new world*. New York, NY: HarperCollins Publishers.

Bachelard, G. (1994). *The poetics of space*. Boston, MA: Beacon Press.

Back, M., Childs, T., Dunnigan, A., Foote, J., Gattepally, S., Liew, B., et al. (2010). *The virtual factory: Exploring 3D worlds as industrial collaboration and control environments.* Paper presented at the Virtual Reality Conference (VR).

Badger, C. (2008, December). *Recipe for success with enterprise virtual worlds.* Fortrera. Retrieved from http://www.forterrainc.com/ images/ stories/ pdf/ recipe_for_success_10509.pdf

Bailenson, J. N., Patel, K., Nielsen, A., Bajscy, R., Jung, S.-H., & Kurillo, G. (2008). The effect of interactivity on learning physical actions in virtual reality. *Media Psychology, 11*(3), 354–376. doi:10.1080/15213260802285214

Bailenson, J. N., & Beall, A. C. (2006). Transformed social interaction: Exploring the digital plasticity of avatars. In Schroeder, R., & Axelsson, A. S. (Eds.), *Avatars at work and play: Collaboration and interaction in shared virtual environments* (pp. 1–16). Dordrecht, The Netherlands & London, UK: Springer.

Bain, C., & Newton, C. (2003). Art games: Pre-service art educators construct learning experiences for the elementary art classroom. *Art Education, 56*(5), 33–40.

Bainbridge, W. S. (2007). The scientific research potential of virtual worlds. *Science, 317*(5837), 472–476. doi:10.1126/science.1146930

Bainbridge, W. S. (2007). The scientific research potential of virtual worlds. *Science, 317*, 472–476. doi:10.1126/science.1146930

Bainbridge, W. S. (2010a). *Online multiplayer games.* San Rafael, CA: Morgan & Claypool.

Bainbridge, W. S. (2010b). *The Warcraft civilization: Social science in a virtual world.* Cambridge, MA: MIT Press.

Bainbridge, W. S. (2008). The rights of an avatar. *The Journal of Personal Cyberconsciousness, 3*(4). Retrieved November 4, 2010, from http://www.terasemjournals.org/pc0302/wb3.html

Baker, C. (2003). Internal networks revisited: Telepathy meets technology. In *Digital Arts Conference 2003 Proceedings.* Retrieved September 23, 2009, http://hypertext.rmit.edu.au/dac/papers/Baker.pdf

Baldwin, M., & Hanel, P. (2003). *Innovation and knowledge creation in an open economy.* Cambridge, UK: Cambridge University Press. doi:10.1017/CBO9780511510847

Bambini, D., Washburn, J., & Perkins, R. (2009). Outcomes of clinical simulation for novice nursing students: Communication, confidence, clinical judgment. *Nursing Education Perspectives, 30*(2), 79–82.

Bandura, A. (1971). *Social foundations of thought and action.* Englewood Cliffs, NJ.

Barker, C., & Galasiński, D. (2001). *Cultural studies and discourse analysis.* London, UK: Sage.

Barlow, J. P. (1996). *A declaration of the independence of cyberspace.*

Barnes, S. (2007). Virtual worlds as a medium for advertising. *ACM SIGMIS Database, 38*(4), 55. doi:10.1145/1314234.1314244

Bartle, R. A. (2003). *Designing virtual worlds.* Berkeley, CA: Peachpit Press.

Bartle, R. A. (1990). *Interactive multi-user computer games.* MUSE Ltd. British Telecom.

Bartle, R. (2003). *Designing virtual worlds.* Berkeley, CA: New Riders.

Bateson, G. (1972). *Steps to an ecology of mind.* New York, NY: Ballantine Books.

Batson, T. (2008, June 8). It IS about technology: Integrating higher ed into knowledge culture. *Campus Technology.* Retrieved from http://campustechnology.com/ articles/ 2008/ 08/ it-is-about-technology -integrating-higher-ed -into-knowledge-culture.aspx

Batson, T. (2009, March 18). Is simulation as good as real life? *Campus Technology.* Retrieved from http://campustechnology.com/ Articles/ 2009/ 03/ 18/ Is-Simulation-as-Good- as-Real-Life.aspx? Page=1

Bauman, Z. (2000). *Liquid modernity.* Cambridge, UK: Polity Press.

Bauman, Z. (2001). *Community: Seeking safety in an insecure world.* Cambridge, UK / Malden, MA: Polity Press/ Blackwell.

Bauman, Z. (2005). *Liquid life*. Cambridge, UK/ Malden, MA: Polity Press.

Bauman, Z. (1993). *Postmodern ethics*. Oxford, UK & Cambridge, MA: Blackwell.

Baumer, A., & Magerko, B. (2009). Narrative development in improvisational theatre. In I. A. Iurgel, N. Zagalo, & P. Petta (Eds.) *Lecture Notes in Computer Science: International Conference on Interactive Digital Storytelling* (pp. 140-151) Berlin, Germany: Springer-Verlag.

Bausinger, H. (1984). Media, technology and daily life. *Media Culture & Society*, *6*, 343–351. doi:10.1177/016344378400600403

Bayliss, A. P., & Tipper, S. P. (2006). Predictive gaze cues and personality judgments: Should eye trust you? *Psychological Science*, *17*, 514–520. doi:10.1111/j.1467-9280.2006.01737.x

Baym, N. K. (2010). *Personal connections in the digital age*. Cambridge, UK: Polity Press.

Baym, N. K. (2007). Interpersonal life online. In Lievrouw, L. A., & Livingston, S. (Eds.), *Handbook of new media: Social shaping and consequences of ICTs* (pp. 62–76). London, UK: Sage.

Bechtel, W., & Abrahamsen, A. (1990). *Connectionism and the mind*. Cambridge, MA: Blackwell.

Beck, L., Wolter, M., Mungard, N. F., Vohn, R., Staedtgen, M., Kuhlen, T., & Sturm, W. (2010). Evaluation of spatial processing in virtual reality using functional magnetic resonance imaging (FMRI). *Cyberpsychology, Behavior, and Social Networwing*, *13*, 211–215. doi:10.1089/cyber.2008.0343

Begg, M., D. Dewhurst, and H. MacLeod. (2005). Game informed learning: Applying computer game processes to higher education. Innovate 1 (6).

Begg, M., Ellaway, R., Dewhurst, D., & Macleod, H. (2007). Transforming professional healthcare narratives into structured game-informed-learning activities. *Innovate* 3 (6). Retrieved on July, 13, 2009, from http://www.innovateonline.info/ index.php?view=article &id=419

Bell, M. W. (2008). Toward a definition of "virtual worlds.". *Journal of Virtual Worlds Research*, *1*(1). Retrieved from http://jvwresearch.org/ index.php ?_cms=1248915995.

Bell, M. W., & Robbins-Bell, S. (2008). Towards an expanded definition of "virtual worlds." In Villares, F. (Ed.), *New digital media: Audiovisual, games and music* (pp. 125–134). Rio de Janeiro, Brazil: E-Papers.

Bellotti, F., Berta, R., Gloria, A. D., Panizza, G., & Primavera, L. (2009). *Designing cultural heritage contents for serious virtual worlds*. Paper presented at the Proceedings of the 2009 15th International Conference on Virtual Systems and Multimedia.

Bem, D. J. (1972). Self-perception theory. In L. Berkowitz (Ed.), *Advances in Experimental Social Psychology, 6*, 1-62. New York, NY: Academic Press.

Benedikt, M. (1991). *Cyberspace: First steps*. Cambridge, MA: MIT Press.

Benford, S., Greenhalgh, C., Rodden, T., & Pycock, J. (2001). Collaborative virtual environments. *Communications of the ACM*, *44*(7), 79–85. doi:10.1145/379300.379322

Benoit, B., Kulpa, R., Ménardais, S., Fradet, L., Multon, F., & Delamarche, P. (2003). Real handball goalkeeper vs. virtual handball thrower. *Presence (Cambridge, Mass.)*, *12*(4), 411–422. doi:10.1162/105474603322391631

Benton, A. L. (1985). Some problems associated with neuropsychological assessment. *Bulletin of Clinical Neurosciences*, *50*, 11–15.

Berge, Z. L. (2008, May-June). Multi-user virtual environments for education and training? A critical review of Second Life. *Educational Technology*, *48*(3), 27–31. Retrieved from http://it.coe.uga.edu/ itforum/ ETSecLife.pdf.

Berger, A. A. (2009). *Video games: A popular culture phenomenon* (3rd ed., pp. 73–83). Piscataway, NJ: Transaction Publishers.

Bessa, M., Coelho, A. F. V. C. C., Moura, J. P., Ferreira, F. N., Cruz, J. B., & Sousa, A. A. d. (2005). *Modelação expedita de ambientes virtuais urbanos para utilização em dispositivos móveis*. Paper presented at the 13º Encontro Português de Computação Gráfica.

Bessière, K., Seay, F., & Kiesler, S. (2007). The ideal elf: Identity exploration in World of Warcraft. *Cyberpsychology & Behavior*, *10*(4), 530–535. doi:10.1089/cpb.2007.9994

Bierce, A., & Steadman, R. (2003). *The devil's dictionary*. New York, NY: Bloomsbury, Holtzbrinck Publishers.

Billig, M. (2009). Das surfende Klassenzimmer. An deutschen Hochschulen finden immer mehr Seminare in virtuellen Welten statt. *Berliner Zeitung*. Retrieved February 2, 2009, from www.berlinonline.de/berliner-zeitung/archiv/.bin/dump.fcgi/2009/0211/wissenschaft/0006/index.html

Bird, S. E. (2003). *The audience in everyday life: Living in a media world*. New York, NY: Routledge.

Blackburn, S. (2001). *Being good: A short introduction to ethics*. Oxford, UK: Oxford University Press.

Blackman, L. (2010). Embodying affect: Voice-hearing, telepathy, suggestion and modelling the non-conscious. *Body & Society, 16*, 163-190. Retrieved April 17, 2010, from http://bod.sagepub.com/cgi/content/abstract/16/1/163

Blascovich, J. (2002). Social influence within immersive virtual environments. In Schroeder, R. (Ed.), *The social life of avatars: Presence and interaction in shared virtual environments* (pp. 127–145). London, UK: Springer-Verlag.

Blumer, H. (1954). What is wrong with social theory? *American Sociological Review, 19*, 3–10. doi:10.2307/2088165

Boa-Ventura, A., & Saboga-Nunes, L. (2010). Biographic spaces: A personalized smoking cessation intervention in Second Life. In De Bra, P., Kobsa, A., & Chin, D. (Eds.), *User modeling, adaptation, and personalization. Lecture Notes in Computer Science, 6075*. Berlin, Germany: Springer. doi:10.1007/978-3-642-13470-8_43

Bock, B. C., Graham, A. L., Sciamanna, C. N., Krishnamoorthy, J., Whiteley, J., & Carmona-Barros, R. (2004). Smoking cessation treatment on the Internet: Content, quality, and usability. *Nicotine & Tobacco Research, 6*(2), 207–219. doi:10.1080/14622200410001676332

Boellstorff, T. (2008). *Coming of age in Second Life: An anthropologist explores the virtually human*. Princeton, NJ: Princeton UP.

Boellstorff, T. (2010). *Coming of age in Second Life: An anthropologist explores the virtually human*. Princeton, NJ: Princeton University Press.

Boellstorff, T. (2008). *Coming of age in Second Life: An anthropologist explores the virtually human*. Princeton, NJ: Princeton University Press.

Boellstorff, T. (2008). *Coming of age in Second Life: An anthropologist explores the virtually human*. Princeton, NJ: Princeton University Press.

Boellstorff, T. (2008). *Coming of age in Second Life*. Princeton, NJ: Princeton University Press.

Boellstorff, T. (2008). *Coming of age in Second Life. An anthropologist explores the virtually human*. Princeton, NJ & Oxford, UK: Princeton University Press.

Boellstorff, T. (2010). A typology of ethnographic scales for virtual worlds. In Bainbridge, W. S. (Ed.), *Online worlds: Convergence of the real and the virtual*. London, UK: Springer-Verlag. doi:10.1007/978-1-84882-825-4_10

Boelstorff, T. (2008). *Coming of age in Second Life - An anthropologist explores the virtual human*. Princeton, NJ & Oxford, UK: Princeton University Press.

Bolter, J. D., & Grusin, D. (2000). *Remediation – Understanding new media*. Cambridge, MA: MIT Press.

Bolter, J., & Grusin, R. (1999). *Remediation: Understanding new media*. Cambridge, MA: The MIT Press.

Bolter, J. D., & Grusin, R. (1999). *Remediation: Understanding new media*. Cambridge, MA & London, UK: MIT Press.

Bondía, J. L. (2002). Notas sobre a experiência e o saber de experiência. *Revista Brasileira de Educação, 19*, 20–28. doi:10.1590/S1413-24782002000100003

Bonsu, S. K., & Darmody, A. (2008). Co-creating Second Life. *Journal of Macromarketing, 28*(4), 355–368. doi:10.1177/0276146708325396

Bonsu, S., & Darmody, A. (2008). Co-creating Second Life: Market – consumer cooperation in contemporary economy. *Journal of Macromarketing, 28*(4), 355. doi:10.1177/0276146708325396

Bordnick, P., Graap, K., Copp, H., Brooks, J., Ferrer, M., & Logue, B. (2004). Utilizing virtual reality to standardize nicotine craving research: A pilot study. *Addictive Behaviors, 29*, 1889–1894. doi:10.1016/j.addbeh.2004.06.008

Bostrom, G., Fiocco, M., Puig, D., Rossini, A., Goncalves, J. G. M., & Sequeira, V. (2004). *Acquisition, modelling and rendering of very large urban environments.* Paper presented at the 3D Data Processing, Visualization, and Transmission (3DPVT), 2nd International Symposium.

Botella, C., Osma, J., García Palacios, A., Guillén, V., & Baños, R. (2008). Treatment of complicated grief using virtual reality: A case report. *Death Studies, 32*(7), 674–692. doi:10.1080/07481180802231319

Boulos, M. N., & Wheeler, S. (2007). The emerging Web 2.0 social software: An enabling suite of sociable technologies in health and healthcare education. *Health Information and Libraries Journal, 24,* 2–23. doi:10.1111/j.1471-1842.2007.00701.x

Boulos, M. N. K., & Toth-Cohen, S. (2009). The University of Plymouth sexual health SIM experience in Second Life®: Evaluation and reflections after 1 year. *Health Information and Libraries Journal, 26*(4), 279–288. doi:10.1111/j.1471-1842.2008.00831.x

Boulos, M. N. K. (2010). *Social Web (Web 2.0) and the 3D Web (Virtual worlds and Second Life®)* Retrieved from http://www.healthcybermap.org/ sl.htm

Boulous, M. N., Hetherington, L., & Wheeler, S. (2007). Second Life: An overview of the potential of 3-D virtual worlds in medical and health education. *Health Information and Libraries Journal, 24,* 233–245. doi:10.1111/j.1471-1842.2007.00733.x

Bouras, C., Tegos, C., Triglianos, V., & Tsiatsos, T. (2007). *X3D multi-user virtual environment Platform for collaborative spatial design.* Paper presented at the 27th International Conference on Distributed Computing Systems Workshops.

Bouvier, P. (2005). *Le lien social.* Paris, France: Gallimard.

Bramwell, C. (2009). The second life of Pye. *Artlink, 29*(3), 68–70.

Brandon, J. (2007, May 21). The top 8 Second Life virtual businesses. *PC Advisor.* Retrieved from http://www.pcadvisor.co.uk/ news/index.cfm? newsid=9279

Brea, J. L. (2007). Collective telepathy 2.0 (the interconnected multitudes theory). In J. M. Prada (Ed.), *Inclusiva-net: New art dynamics in Web 2 mode* (pp. 36-50). Madrid, Espana: Área de las Artes. Retrieved October 22, 2010, from http://www.medialab-prado.es/mmedia/1098

Brennan, D. M., Mawson, S., & Brownsell, S. (2009). Telerehabilitation: Enabling the remote delivery of healthcare, rehabilitation, and self management. *Studies in Health Technology and Informatics, 145,* 231–248.

Brenner, V. (1998, January). *An initial report on the online assessment of Internet addiction: The first 30 days of the Internet usage survey.* Retrieved from http://www.ccsnet.com/prep/ pap/pap8b/638b012p.txt

Brignall, T. (2008). Guild life in the World of Warcraft: Online game tribalism. In Adams, T., & Smith, S. (Eds.), *Electronic tribes: The virtual world of geeks, gamers, shamans, and scammers* (pp. 110–123). Austin, TX: University of Texas Press.

Brown, W. M., & Moore, C. (2002). Smile asymmetries and reputation as reliable indicators of likelihood to cooperate: An evolutionary approach. *Advances in Psychology Research, 11,* 59–78.

Bruce, V., & Green, P. (1990). *Visual perception: Physiology, psychology and ecology.* Hove, UK: Lawrence Erlbaum Associates.

Bruno, P. (1992). Le jeu de simulation dans. In B. Gilles (dir.), *Le jouet: valeurs et paradoxes d'un petit objet secret,* (p. 69). Paris, France: Autrement, collection Mutations

Burnham, B. R., & Walden, B. (1997). *Interactions in distance education: A report from the other side.* Paper presented at the 1997 Adult Education Research Conference, Stillwater, Oklahoma.

Burns, R. (2010). Preface. In Kapp, K. M., & O'Driscoll, T. (Eds.), *Learning in 3D: Adding a new dimension to enterprise learning and collaboration* (pp. xi–xiv). San Francisco, CA: Pfiffer.

Bushman, B. J., & Anderson, C. A. (2002). Violent video games and hostile expectations: A test of the general aggression model. *Personality and Social Psychology Bulletin, 28,* 1679–1686. doi:10.1177/014616702237649

Caillois, R. (1958). *Les jeux et les hommes.* Paris, France: Folio Gallimard.

Calongne, C. M. (2008, September/October). Educational frontiers: Learning in a virtual world. *EDUCAUSE Review, 43*(5). Retrieved from http://www.educause.edu/ EDUCAUSE% 2BReview/ EDUCAUSEReviewMagazineVolume43/ EducationalFrontiersLearningin/ 163163.

Campbell, J. E. (2004). *Getting it on online: Cyberspace, gay male sexuality, and embodied identity.* New York, NY: Harrington Park Press.

Cannon-Bowers, J. (2009). Synthetic learning environments: On developing a science of simulation, games, and virtual worlds for training. In Kozlowski, S. W. J. (Ed.), *Learning, training and development in organizations.* New York, NY: Routledge Academic.

Careaga, A. (2001). *E-ministry: Connecting with the net generation* (p. 216). Grand Rapids, MI: Kregel Publications.

Carlin, A. S., Hoffman, H. G., & Weghorst, S. (1997). Virtual reality and tactile augmentation in the treatment of spider phobia: a case report. *Behaviour Research and Therapy, 35*(2), 153–158. doi:10.1016/S0005-7967(96)00085-X

Carlsson, A. (2001). A paradigm shift in brain research. *Science, 294,* 1021–1024. doi:10.1126/science.1066969

Carney, O., McIntosh, J., & Worth, A. (1996). The use of the nominal group technique in research with community nurses. *Journal of Advanced Nursing, 23,* 1024–1029. doi:10.1046/j.1365-2648.1996.09623.x

Carpenter, E. S., & McLuhan, M. (Eds.). (1960). *Explorations in communication: An anthology.* Boston, MA: Beacon Press.

Carroll, J. (1994, August). Guerrillas in the Myst: From garage start-up to the first CD-ROM super-stars. *Wired,* 70-73.

Carroll, J. (September, 1997). (D)riven. *Wired Digital.* Retrieved June 15, 2009, from http://wwww.wired.com/ wired/ 5.09/ riven.html

Carrozzino, M., Tecchia, F., Bacinelli, S., Cappelletti, C., & Bergamasco, M. (2005). *Lowering the development time of multimodal interactive application: The real-life experience of the XVR project.* Paper presented at the ACM SIGCHI International Conference on Advances in Computer Entertainment Technology, ACE 2005.

Carrozzino, M., Tecchia, F., & Bergamasco, M. (2009). *Urban procedural modeling for real-time rendering.* Paper presented at the 3rd ISPRS International Workshop 3D-ARCH 2009: 3D Virtual Reconstruction and Visualization of Complex Architectures.

Casetti, F. (1998). *Inside the gaze: The fiction film and its spectator* (pp. 8–9). Bloomington, IN: Indiana UP.

Casey, E. S. (1997). *The fate of place: A philosophical history.* Berkeley, CA: University of California Press.

Castells, M. (1999). *A sociedade em rede.* São Paulo, Brazil: Paz e Terra.

Castells, M. (2003). *A Galáxia da Internet: Reflexões Sobre a Internet, os Negócios e a Sociedade.* Rio de Janeiro: Zahar.

Castronova, E. (2004). *Synthetic worlds: The business and culture of online games.* Chicago, IL: University of Chicago Press.

Castronova, E., Williams, D., Shen, C., & Ratan, R., Xiong, Li., Huang, Y., & Keegan, B. (2009). As real as real? Macroeconomic behavior in a large-scale virtual world. *New Media & Society, 11,* 685–707. doi:10.1177/1461444809105346

Castronova, E. (2005). *Synthetic worlds – The business and culture of online games.* Chicago, IL & London, UK: The University of Chicago Press.

Castronova, E. (2007). *Exodus to the virtual world: How online fun is changing reality.* New York, NY: Palgrave MacMillan.

Cavazza, F. (2007). *Virtual universes landscape.* Retrieved December 1, 2009, from http://www.fredcavazza. net/2007/10/04/virtual-universes-landscape/

Cernich, A., Brennana, D., Barker, L., & Bleiberg, J. (2007). Sources of error in computerized neuropsychological assessment. *Archives of Clinical Neuropsychology, 22,* 39–48. doi:10.1016/j.acn.2006.10.004

CGV. (2010). *Computer graphics and knowledge visualization.* Retrieved on May 31, 2010, from http://www. cgv.tugraz.at/CGV/Research/Projects

Chaffee, S. H., & Metzger, M. J. (2001). The end of mass communication? *Mass Communication & Society, 4*(4), 365–379. doi:10.1207/S15327825MCS0404_3

Chandra, V., Eröcal, D. P., Padoan, C., & Carlos, P. B. (2009). *Innovation and growth: Chasing a moving frontier*. World Bank & OECD Report. Retrieved from http://browse.oecdbookshop.org/oecd/pdfs/browseit/0309071E.PDF

Charbonneau, N., Boulerice, D., Booth, D. W., & Tidafi, T. (2006). *Understanding gothic rose windows with computer-aided technologies*. Paper presented at the 24th eCAADe Conference.

Chase, S. C. (2008). *Virtual worlds as collaborative environments for design and manufacturing: From idea to product*. Paper presented at the International Workshop on Virtual Manufacturing, Turin, Italy.

Chaytor, N., & Schmitter-Edgecombe, M. (2003). The ecological validity of neuropsychological tests: A review of the literature on everyday cognitive skills. *Neuropsychology Review, 13*, 181–197. doi:10.1023/B:NERV.0000009483.91468.fb

Chen, G., Esch, G., Wonka, P., Müller, P., & Zhang, E. (2008). Interactive procedural street modeling. *ACM Transactions on Graphics, 27*(3), 1–10. doi:10.1145/1360612.1360702

Chen, Y. S., & Raney, A. A. (2009). *Mood management and highly interactive video games: An experimental examination of Wii playing on mood change and enjoyment*. Paper presented at the International Communication Association Conference May 2009, Chicago.

Cherny, L. (1999). *Conversation and community: Chat in a virtual world*. Stanford, CA: CSLI Publications.

Chesbrough, H. W. (2006). *Open innovation. The new imperative for creating and profiting from technology*. Boston, MA: Harvard Business School Press.

Chiappe, D., & Brown, A. (2004). Cheaters are looked at longer and remembered better than cooperators in social exchange situations. *Evolutionary Psychology, 2*, 108–120.

Ching-Song, W., Yan, C., & Jiann-Gwo, D. (2009). *A 3D virtual world teaching and learning platform for computer science courses in Second Life*. Paper presented at the Computational Intelligence and Software Engineering.

Chodos, D., Stroulia, E., Boechler, P., King, S., Kuras, P., Carbonaro, M., & de Jong, E. (2010). *Healthcare education with virtual-world simulations*. Cape Town, South Africa: ACM.

Churchill, E. F., & Bly, S. (1999). *Virtual environments at work: Ongoing use of MUDs in the workplace*. Paper presented at the International Joint Conference on Work Activities Coordination and Collaboration.

Clancy, T. R., Effken, J. A., & Pesut, D. (2008). Applications of complex systems theory in nursing education, research, and practice. *Nursing Outlook, 56*(5), 248–256. doi:10.1016/j.outlook.2008.06.010

Clark, R. E. (1983). Reconsidering research on learning from media. *Review of Educational Research, 43*(4), 445–459.

Clark, M. A. (2009, August/September). Genome Island: A virtual science environment in Second Life. *Innovate, 5*(6). Retrieved from http://www.innovateonline.info/index.php? view=article& id=562

Clifford, J., & Marcus, G. E. (Eds.). (1986). *Writing culture: The poetics and politics of ethnography*. Berkeley, CA: University of California Press.

Club Penguin. (2010). *Club Penguin*. Retrieved on June 14, 2010, from http://www.clubpenguin.com/

Coelho, A., Bessa, M., Sousa, A. A. d., & Ferreira, F. N. (2007). Expeditious modelling of virtual urban environments with geospatial L-systems. *Computer Graphics Forum, 26*(4), 769–782.

Cohen, D. (2009). *Objet petit a(vatar): Psychoanalysis, posthumanism and the question of the self in Second Life*. Unpublished PhD thesis, University of Western Ontario, London Ontario Canada.

Collins, M., & Berge, Z. L. (1994, September/October). *Guiding design principles for interactive teleconferencing*. Paper presented at the Pathways to Change: New Directions for Distance Education and Training Conference, University of Maine at Augusta. Retrieved from http://www.emoderators.com/ papers/ augusta.html

Collins, M., & Berge, Z. L. (2000, November/December). Technological minimalism in distance education. *The Technology Source*. Retrieved from http://technology-source.org/ article/ technological_minimalism_ in_distance_education/

Consalvo, M. (2005). Rule sets, cheating, and magic circles: Studying games and ethics. *International Review of Information Ethics, 3*, 7–12.

Consalvo, M. (2003). *It's a queer world after all: Studying The Sims and sexuality*. Retrieved from http://www.glaad.org/ publications

Cooper, J. B., & Taqueti, V. R. (2004). A brief history of the development of mannequin simulators for clinical education and training. *Quality & Safety in Health Care, 13*(supplement 1), i11–i18. doi:10.1136/qshc.2004.009886

Correll, S. (1995). The ethnography of an electronic bar: The Lesbian Café. *Journal of Contemporary Ethnography, 23*(3), 270–298. doi:10.1177/089124195024003002

Csikszentmihalyi, M. (1996). *Flow and the psychology of discovery and invention*. New York, NY: Harpercollins.

Cyan. (1993). *Myst*. Brøderbund.

D'Ambrosio, U. (July, 2002). *Que matemática deve ser aprendida nas escolas hoje?* Teleconferência no Programa PEC – Formação Universitária, patrocinado pela Secretaria de Educação do Estado de São Paulo. Retrieved from http://vello.sites.uol.com.br/ aprendida.htm

Dalrymple Henderson, L. (1998). *Duchamp in context-Science and technology in the large glass and related works*. Princeton, NY: Princeton University Press.

Danforth, D. R. (2008). Development of an interactive virtual 3-D model of the human testis using the Second Life platform. *Biology of Reproduction, 78*(129), 319.

Danic, I. (2006). La culture des 12-15 ans: Les lascars pour modèle. In Sirota (dir.), *Eléments pour une sociologie de l'enfance*. Rennes, France: Presses universitaires de Rennes, collection Le sens social.

Daniel, B., Schwier, R. A., & Mccalla, G. (2003). Social capital in virtual learning communities and distributed communities of practice. *Canadian Journal of Learning and Technology, 29*(3).

Daniel, E. V. (1991). *Fluid signs: Being a person the Tamil way*. Berkeley, CA: University of California Press.

Daniel, E. V., & Pugh, J. F. (1984). *South Asian systems of healing*. Leiden, The Netherlands: E.J. Brill.

Darken, R. P., & Sibert, J. L. (1993). *A toolset for navigation in virtual environments*. New York, NY: ACM Press.

Darsøe, L., & Austin, R. (2009). Innovation processes and closure. *Journal of Management & Organization, 14*(5).

Davidson, D. (2008). *Stories in between: Narratives and mediums @ play*. ETC Press.

Davidson, D. (1999). *The journey of narrative: The story of Myst across two mediums*. National Communication Association Convention, Chicago, IL. Retrieved from http://waxebb.com/ writings/ journey.html

Davis, J., Sundbo, J., Gallina, A., & Serin, G. (Eds.). (2005). *Contemporary management of innovation*. London, UK: PalgraveMacmillan.

Davis, F. (1979). *A comunicação Não-verbal*. São Paulo, Brazil: Summus.

Dawley, L. (2009). Social network knowledge construction: Emerging virtual world pedagogy. *Horizon, 17*(2), 109–121. doi:10.1108/10748120910965494

De Backer, C. (2005). Cheater detection reputation: Gossip as a punishment strategy and the problems of second-order free riders. In C. De Backer (2005). *Like Belgian chocolate for the universal mind. Interpersonal and media gossip from an evolutionary perspective*, (pp. 401-425). Ghent, Belgium: Ghent University.

De Bono, E. (1968). *New think: The use of lateral thinking in the generation of new ideas*. New York, NY: Basic Books.

De Bono, E. (1970). *Lateral thinking: Creativity step by step*. New York, NY: Harper & Row.

De Bono, E. (n.d.). *Edward de Bono's authorised website*. Retrieved May 12, 2010, from http://www.edwdebono.com/ index.html

De Fina, A. (2006). Group identity, narrative and self-presentation. In De Fina, A., Schiffrin, D., & Bamberg, M. (Eds.), *Discourse and identity* (pp. 351–375). New York, NY: Cambridge University Press. doi:10.1017/CBO9780511584459.018

De Freitas, S., & Oliver, M. (2006). How can exploratory learning with games and simulations within the curriculum be most effectively evaluated? *Computers & Education*, *46*(Special Issue), 249–264. doi:10.1016/j.compedu.2005.11.007

Dean, E., Cook, S., Keating, M., & Murphy, J. (2009). Does this avatar make me look fat? Obesity and interviewing in Second Life. *Journal of Virtual Worlds Research*, *2*(2), 3–11.

Dean, E., Cook, S., Keating, M., & Murphy, J. (2009). Does this avatar make me look fat? Obesity and interviewing in Second Life. *Journal of Virtual Worlds Research*, *2*(2). Retrieved August 12, 2010, from https://journals.tdl.org/jvwr /article/view/621/495

Decelles, P. (2010). *OpenSim evolution simulation I* [Web page]. Retrieved July 1, 2010, from http://slbiology.blogspot.com/ 2010/02/opensim- evolution-simulation-i.html

Defense Advanced Research Projects Agency. (2010). *DARPA-BAA-10-62 healing heroes (HH) broad agency announcement (BAA) for information processing techniques office (IPTO)*. Retrieved July 1, 2010, from http://www.darpa.mil/ipto/ solicit/baa/BAA-1062_PIP.pdf

Delbecq, A. L., Van de Ven, A. H., & Gustafson, D. H. (1975). *Group techniques for programme planning: A guide to nominal group and Delphi process*. Glenview, IL: Scott Foresman and Company.

Denzin, N. K., & Lincoln, Y. S. (Eds.). (2000a). *Handbook of qualitative research* (2nd ed.). Thousand Oaks, CA: Sage Publications.

Denzin, N. K., & Lincoln, Y. S. (2000b). Introduction: The discipline and practice of qualitative research. In Denzin, N. K., & Lincoln, Y. S. (Eds.), *Handbook of qualitative research* (2nd ed., pp. 1–28). Thousand Oaks, CA: Sage Publications.

Dervin, B., & Foreman-Wernet, L. (Eds.). (2003). *Sense-Making Methodology reader: Selected writings of Brenda Dervin*. Cresskill, NJ: Hampton Press.

Dervin, B., & Song, M. (2005). *Reaching for phenomenological depths in uses and gratifications research: A quantitative empirical investigation.* Paper presented at the annual meeting of the International Communication Association, New York City, May. Retrieved from http://communication.sbs.ohio-state.edu/ sense-making/ art/ artabsdervinsong05 icaUG.html

Deutsche Post World Net. (2007). *In Second Life bestellen, in First Life ausprobieren. TESTBOX der Deutschen Post liefert aktuelle Markenprodukte frei Haus*. Retrieved November 10, 2009, from www.testbox.de/secondlife

Di Franco, G. (2001). *EDS: Esplorare, descrivere e sintetizzare i dati. Guida pratica all'analisi dei dati nella ricerca sociale*. Milano, Italia: Franco Angeli.

Dibbell, J. (1999). *My tiny life. Crime and passion in a virtual world*. London, UK: Fourth Estate Ltd.

Dibbell, J. (2001). A rape in cyberspace: Or how an evil clown, a Haitian trickster spirit, two wizards, and a cast of dozens turned a database into a society. In Trend, D. (Ed.), *Reading digital culture* (p. 374). Malden, MA: Blackwell.

Dibbell, J. (1993). *A rape in cyberspace*. Retrieved September 2, 2008, from http://www.juliandibbell.com /texts/bungle.html

Dickey, M. D. (2005). Three-dimensional virtual worlds and distance learning: Two case studies of Active Worlds as a medium for distance education. *British Journal of Educational Technology*, *36*(3), 439–451. doi:10.1111/j.1467-8535.2005.00477.x

Dion, K., Berscheid, E., & Walster, E. (1972). What is beautiful is good. *Journal of Personality and Social Psychology*, *24*(3), 285–290. doi:10.1037/h0033731

DiPaola, S., & Collins, D. (2002). A 3D virtual environment for social telepresence. *Proceedings of the Western Computer Graphics Symposium*.

Dodge, M., & Kitchin, R. (2001). *Mapping cyberspace*. New York, NY/ London, UK: Routledge.

Dodrill, C. B. (1997). Myths of neuropsychology. *The Clinical Neuropsychologist, 11,* 1–17. doi:10.1080/13854049708407025

Döllner, J., & Buchholz, H. (2005). *Continuous level-of-detail modeling of buildings in 3D city models.* Paper presented at the 13th Annual ACM International Workshop on Geographic Information Systems.

Dotsch, R., & Wigboldus, D. H. J. (2008). Virtual prejudice. *Journal of Experimental Social Psychology, 44,* 1194–1198. doi:10.1016/j.jesp.2008.03.003

Dovey, J., & Lister, M. (2009). Straw men or cyborgs? *Interactions: Studies in Communication and Culture, 1*(1), 129–145. doi:10.1386/iscc.1.1.129_1

Dreher, C., Reiners, T., Dreher, N., & Dreher, H. (2009). *3D virtual worlds as collaborative communities enriching human endeavours: Innovative applications in e-learning.* Paper presented at the Digital Ecosystems and Technologies.

Drinkall, J. A. (2006). *Telepathy in contemporary, conceptual and performance art.* Unpublished thesis, University of New South Wales, Sydney. Retrieved from http://unsworks.unsw.edu.au/vital/access/manager/Repository/unsworks:1561

Drinkall, J. A. (2007). *Social and political aesthetics of telepathy in Fluxus art and beyond.* Unpublished paper presented at Flux Conference, School of Art History, Cinema, Classics and Archeology, University of Melbourne.

Drinkall, J. A. (2009). Traumaculture and telepathetic cyber fiction. In I. A. Iurgel, N. Zagalo, & P. Petta (Eds.), *Lecture Notes in Computer Science: International Conference on Interactive Digital Storytelling* (pp. 163-173). Berlin, Germany: Springer-Verlag.

Drinkall, J. A. (2010). *Politics of telepathic collaborations: The 60s, the 80s and now.* Unpublished paper presented in Collaborations in Modern and Postmodern Visual Art Conference, Social and Aesthetics Research Unit, Monash University.

DSolve. (2010). *3DSolve.* Retrieved on January 5, 2010, from http://www.3dsolve.com/ov3d.html

Dubar, C. (1992). *Socialisations et identités professionnelles.* Paris, France: Armand Colin.

Dubey, G. (2001). *Le lien social à l'ère du virtuel.* Paris, France: PUF.

Ducheneaut, M., Yee, N., Nickell, E., & Moore, R. (2006). Alone together? Exploring the social dynamics of massively multiplayer online games. In *Proceedings of the SIGCHI Conference on Human Factors in computing systems* (pp. 407-416). Montreal, Canada.

Ducheneaut, N., Wen, M.-H., Yee, N., & Wadley, G. (2009). *Body and mind: A study of avatar personalization in three virtual worlds.* Paper presented at the 27th International Conference on Human Factors in Computing Systems.

Ducheneaut, N., Yee, N., Nickell, E., & Moore, R. J. (2006). *"Alone together?": Exploring the social dynamics of massively multiplayer online games.* Paper presented at the SIGCHI conference on Human Factors in computing systems.

Dudeney, H. E. (2008). *Os Enigmas de Canterbury. Espanha: RBA editora.* Desafios Matemáticos.

Durkheim, E. (1984). *The division of labour in society.* New-York, NY: Macmillan.

Eastwick, P. W., & Gardner, W. L. (2009). Is it a game? Evidence for social influence in the virtual world. *Social Influence, 4,* 18–32. doi:10.1080/15534510802254087

Eco, U. (2004). *Il nome della rosa.* Milano, Italia: Bompiani.

Edmunds, L., & Dundes, A. (1981). The sphinx in the Oedipus legend. In Edmunds, L. (Ed.), *Oedipus, a folklore casebook.* Madison, WI: The University of Wisconsin Press.

Eguchi, A., & Thompson, C. (2010). *Smart objects in a virtual world.* Presented at the Acxiom Laboratory for Applied Research, Conway Arkansas, April 9, 2010.

Elkind, J. S., Rubin, E., Rosenthal, S., Skoff, B., & Prather, P. (2001). A simulated reality scenario compared with the computerized Wisconsin card sorting test: An analysis of preliminary results. *Cyberpsychology & Behavior, 4,* 489–496. doi:10.1089/109493101750527042

Emmelkamp, P. M. G. (2005). Psychotherapy & pychosomatics. *Technological Innovations in Clinical Assessment and Psychotherapy, 74*(6), 55–65.

EnBW Energie Baden-Württemberg. (2009a). *Second-Life-Bildmotive zum Herunterladen*. Retrieved December 01, 2009, from http://www.enbw.com/content/de/impulse/enbw_webwelt/second_life/ download-bilder/index.jsp

EnBW Energie Baden-Württemberg. (2009b). *Verquizt noch mal – das erste Second-Life-Quiz zum Thema 'Energie'*. Retrieved January 10, 2009, from www.enbw.com/content/de/impulse/ enbw_webwelt/second_life/energyquiz

Engelbart, D. C. (1988). A conceptual framework for the augmentation of man's intellect. In Greif, I. (Ed.), *Computer-supported cooperative work: A book of readings* (pp. 35–65). Morgan Kaufmann Publishers Inc.

Erlanger, D., Kaushik, T., Cantu, R., Barth, J. T., Broshek, D. K., Freeman, J. R., & Webbe, F. M. (2003). Symptom-based assessment of the severity of a concussion. *Journal of Neurosurgery*, *98*, 477–484. doi:10.3171/jns.2003.98.3.0477

Erlanger, D. M., Kaushik, T., Broshek, D., Freeman, J., Feldman, D., & Festa, J. (2002). Development and validation of a Web-based screening tool for monitoring cognitive status. *The Journal of Head Trauma Rehabilitation*, *17*, 458–476. doi:10.1097/00001199-200210000-00007

Erler, H., Rieger, M., & Füller, J. (2009). Ideenmanagement und Innovation mit Social Networks – Die Swarovski i-flash Community. In Zerfaß, A., & Möslein, K. M. (Eds.), *Kommunikation als Erfolgsfaktor im Innovationsmanagement* (pp. 391–401). Wiesbaden: Gabler. doi:10.1007/978-3-8349-8242-1_24

Fang, Z.-C., & Cai, H. (2009). *Designing social commerce experience in 3D virtual world*. Paper presented at the 2009 IEEE Conference on Commerce and Enterprise Computing.

Farley, K., Nitsche, M., Bolter, J., & MacIntyre, B. (2009). Augmenting creative realities: The Second Life performance project. *Leonardo*, *42*(1), 96–97. doi:10.1162/leon.2009.42.1.96

Fauvell, J., & Gray, J. (1992). *The history of mathematics - A reader*. London, UK: The Macmillan Press ltd.

Fehr, E., & Gächter, S. (2000). Cooperation and punishment in public goods experiments. *The American Economic Review*, *90*, 980–994. doi:10.1257/aer.90.4.980

Feldon, D. F., & Kafai, Y. B. (2008). Mixed methods for mixed reality: Understanding users' avatar activities in virtual worlds. *Educational Technology Research and Development*, *56*, 575–593. doi:10.1007/s11423-007-9081-2

Ferguson, C. J. (2009). Violent video games: Dogma, fear and pseudo-science. *Sceptical Inquirer*, *33*, 38–54.

Ferreira, E., & Falcão, T. (2009). *Through the looking glass: Weavings between the magic circle and immersive processes in video games*. Digital Games Research Association 2009 Conference: Breaking New Ground: Innovation in Games, Play, Practice and Theory. London, UK.

Fetscherin, M., & Lattemann, C. (2008). User acceptance of virtual worlds. *Journal of Electronic Commerce Research*, *9*(3), 231–242.

Fields, D. A., & Kafai, Y. B. (2008). A connective ethnography of peer knowledge sharing and diffusion in a tween virtual world. *International Journal of Computer-Supported Collaborative Learning*, *4*(1), 47–68. doi:10.1007/s11412-008-9057-1

Filbey, F. M., Schacht, J. P., Myers, U. S., Chavez, R. S., & Hutchison, K. E. (2009). Marijuana craving in the brain. *Proceedings of the National Academy of Sciences of the United States of America*, *106*(31), 13016–13021. doi:10.1073/pnas.0903863106

Fink, E. (1966). *Le Jeu comme symbole du monde (1969)*. Paris, France: Minuit.

Fink, S. (2009). Strategische Kommunikation für Technologie und Innovation – Konzeption und Umsetzung. In Zerfaß, A., & Möslein, K. M. (Eds.), *Kommunikation als Erfolgsfaktor im Innovationsmanagement* (pp. 209–225). Wiesbaden: Gabler. doi:10.1007/978-3-8349-8242-1_11

Finkelstein, A. B. A. (1999). Nanotechnology and cyberspace: Two roads to the same city. In *Proceedings for the Ninth General Assembly of the World Future Society*. Montreal, Canada: MacGill University.

Fishbein, M. (1980). Theory of reasoned action: Some applications and implications. In H. Howe & M. Page (Eds.), *Nebraska Symposium on Motivation* (pp. 65-116). Lincoln, NE: University of Nebraska Press.

Fittkau & Maaß. (2007). *Ergebnisse der 24. W3B-Umfrage*. Retrieved August 1, 2008, from http://www.w3b.org/ergebnisse/w3b24/

Flanagan, M. (2003). Une maison de poupée virtuelle capitaliste? The Sims: domesticité, consommation et féminité. In M. Roustan (Ed.), *La pratique du jeu vidéo: Réalité ou virtualité?* Paris, France: L'Harmattan.

Flannery, K., & Walles, R. (2003). How does schema theory apply to real versus virtual memories? *Cyberpsychology & Behavior, 6*(2), 151–159. doi:10.1089/109493103321640347

Fleming, S. M. (2007). *The future of the brain.* In PhD 2, Neuroscience, Wellcome Trust Centre for Neuroimaging. Retrieved November 4, 2010, from www.ucl.ac.uk/.../ RfP_EssayComp_LIFE_Fleming_The_Brain_1_.pdf

Fluharty, L., Hayes, A. S., Milgrom, L., Malarney, K., Smith, D., Reklau, M. A., et al. (2011). A multisite, multiacademic track evaluation of end-of-life simulation for nursing education. *Clinical Simulation in Nursing.* In press. Retrieved May 2, 2011 from http://www.nursingsimulation.org/article/S1876-1399(10)00164-7/abstract

Fontana, A., & Frey, J. H. (2005). The interview. From neutral stance to political interview. In Denzin, N. K., & Lincoln, Y. S. (Eds.), *Handbook of qualitative research* (2nd ed., pp. 695–728). Thousand Oaks, CA: Sage Publications.

Fornas, J. (2002). *Digital borderlands: Cultural studies of identity and interactivity on the Internet.* (Digital formations, vol. 6). New York, NY: Peter Lang.

Forty, A. (2000). *Words and buildings: A vocabulary of modern architecture.* London, UK: Thames & Hudson.

Fournier, A., Fussell, D., & Carpenter, L. (1982). Computer rendering of stochastic models. *Communications of the ACM, 25*(6), 371–384. doi:10.1145/358523.358553

Fox, J., & Bailenson, J. N. (2009). Virtual virgins and vamps: The effects of exposure to female characters' sexualized appearance and gaze in an immersive virtual environment. *Sex Roles, 61*(3-4), 147–157. doi:10.1007/s11199-009-9599-3

Fox, R. G. (1991). Introduction: Working in the present. In Fox, R. G. (Ed.), *Recapturing anthropology: Working in the present.* Santa Fe, NM: School of American Research Press, University of Washington Press.

Franganito, S. T. (2007). *xox Voyager's (Skawennati Tricia Fragnito's) curatorial statement.* In Vancouver's Second Live 2007. Retrieved October 17, 2010, from http://secondlive2007.blogspot.com/

Frankena, W. K. (1973). *Ethics* (2nd ed.). Englewood Cliffs, NJ: Prentice Hall.

Franz, R., & Wolkinger, T. (2003). *Customer integration with virtual communities.* Paper presented at the 36th Hawaii International Conference on System Sciences.

Franzen, M. D., & Wilhelm, K. L. (1996). Conceptual foundations of ecological validity in neuropsychological assessment. In Sbordone, R. J., & Long, C. J. (Eds.), *Ecological validity of neuropsychological testing* (pp. 91–112). Boca Raton, FL: St Lucie Press.

Frasca, G. (2001). The Sims: Grandmothers are cooler than trolls. *The International Journal of Computer Game Research, 1*(1).

Frasca, G. (1999). *Ludology meets narratology: Similitude and differences between (video) games and narrative.* Retrieved January 12, 2010, from http://www.ludology.org/ articles/ ludology.htm

Freedman, S., Hoffman, H., Garcia-Palacios, A., Weiss, P., Avitzour, S., & Josman, N. (2010). Prolonged exposure and virtual reality–enhanced imaginal exposure for PTSD following a terrorist bulldozer attack: A case study. *Cyberpsychology, Behavior, and Social Networking, 13*(1), 95–101. doi:10.1089/cyber.2009.0271

Freire, P. (1982). *Pedagogia do oprimido* (11th ed.). Rio de Janeiro, Brazil: Paz e Terra.

Freud, S. (1999). *Triebe und Triebschicksale* (pp. 209–232). Frankfurt am Main, Germany: Fischer.

Friedman, D., Karniel, Y., & Dinur, A. L. (2009). Comparing group discussion in virtual and physical environments. *Presence (Cambridge, Mass.), 18*(4), 286–293. doi:10.1162/pres.18.4.286

Friedman, D., Steed, A., & Slater, M. (2007a). *Research bots in Second Life.* Retrieved October 10th 2010 from: http://portal.idc.ac.il/en/schools/Communications/ research/Virtuality/Pages/SLbots.aspx

Friedman, D., Steed, A., & Slater, M. (2007b). Spatial social behavior in Second Life. *Lecture Notes in Computer Science, 4722*, (p. 252).

Fritz, A. (2007). *Send us your art's birthday presence! Traces of art's birthday networks at the western front 1989-2007*. In Western Front Research Library. Retrieved November 4, 2010 from http://front.bc.ca/research/texts/3

Fuchs, A. (2006). *Outils numériques pour le relevé architectural et la restitution archéologique*. Nancy, France: Université Henri Poincaré.

Fuglsang, L., & Sundbo, J. (2002). *Innovation as strategic reflexivity*. London, UK: Routledge.

Füller, J., & Matzler, K. (2007). Virtual product experience and customer participation – A chance for customer-centred, really new products. *Technovation, 27*(6-7), 378–387. doi:10.1016/j.technovation.2006.09.005

Gaba, D. M. (2004). The future vision of simulation in health care. *Quality & Safety in Health Care, 13*(suppl 1), i2. doi:10.1136/qshc.2004.009878

Gadamer, H. G. (1999). *Verdade e método: Traços fundamentais de uma hermenêutica filosófica*. Petrópolis. Vozes, 3. ed.

Gaggioli, A., Keshner, E. A., Weiss, P. L., & Riva, G. (Eds.), *Advanced technologies in rehabilitation - Empowering cognitive, physical, social and communicative skills through virtual reality, robots, wearable systems and brain-computer interfaces*. Amsterdam, The Netherlands: IOS Press.

Galloway, A. (2006). *Gaming: Essays on algorithmic culture*. Minneapolis, MN: University of Minnesota Press.

Gartner, Inc. (2007). *Gartner says 80 percent of active Internet users will have a second life in the virtual world by the end of 2011*. Gartner Symposium ITxpo, Emerging Trends, April 24, 2007.

Gary, J., & Remolino, L. (2000). *Coping with loss and grief through on-line support groups*. ERIC Clearinghouse on Counseling and Student Services. Retrieved September 10, 2010 from http://www.mental-health-matters.com/index.php?view=article& catid=175%3Agrief-and-loss&id=932%3Acoping-with-loss-and-grief-through-online-support- groups&format=pdf&option=com_content&Itemid=1906

Gauntlet, D. (2009). Media studies 2.0: A response. *Interactions: Studies in Communication and Culture, 1*(1), 147–157. doi:10.1386/iscc.1.1.147_1

Gee, J. P. (2003). *What video games have to teach us about learning and literacy*. New York, NY: Palgrave MacMillan.

Geertz, C. (1973). *Thick description: Toward an interpretative theory of culture. The interpretation of cultures* (pp. 3–30). New York, NY: Basic Books.

Geertz, C. (1983). *Local knowledge: Further essays in interpretive anthropology*. New York, NY: Basic Books.

Gergen, K. (1994). *Realities and relationships*. Cambridge, MA: Harvard University Press.

Gibson, W. (1984). *Neuromancer*. New York, NY: Ace Books.

Giddings, S. (2009). Events and collusions: A glossary for the microethnography of video game play. *Games and Culture, 4*(2), 144–157. doi:10.1177/1555412008325485

Gierke, C., & Müller, R. (2008). *Unternehmen in Second Life: Wie Sie virtuelle Welten für Ihr reales Geschäft nutzen können*. Offenbach: GABAL Verlag GmbH.

Gillath, O., McCall, C., Shaver, P. R., & Blascovich, J. (2008). What can virtual reality teach us about prosocial tendencies in real and virtual environments? *Media Psychology, 11*(2), 259–282. doi:10.1080/15213260801906489

Gitelman, L., & Pingree, G. B. (2003). *New media, 1740-1915*. Cambridge, MA: The MIT Press.

Gladwell, M. (2010, October 4). Small change: Why the revolution will not be tweeted. *The New Yorker*. Retrieved November 4, 2010, from http://www.newyorker.com/reporting/2010/10/04/101004fa_fact_gladwell

Gloor; P. (2006). *Swarm creativity. Competitive advantage through collaborative innovation network*. Oxford, UK: Oxford University Press.

Goffman, E. (1959). *The presentation of self in everyday life*. Garden City, NY: Doubleday.

Goffman, E. (1974). *Frame analysis*. New York, NY: Harper & Row.

Goffman, E. (1959). *The presentation of self in everyday life* (pp. 106–140). Anchor Books.

Goffman, E. (1959). *The presentation of self in everyday life*. Garden City, NY: Doubleday.

Goldstein, F. C., & Levin, H. S. (1987). Disorders of reasoning and problem-solving ability. In Meier, M., Benton, A., & Diller, L. (Eds.), *Neuropsychological rehabilitation*. London, UK: Taylor & Francis Group.

Golub, A. (2010). Being in the World (of Warcraft): Raiding, realism, and knowledge production in a massively multiplayer online game. *Anthropological Quarterly*, *83*(1), 17–45. doi:10.1353/anq.0.0110

Goodrich-Hunsaker, N. J., & Hopkins, R. O. (2010). Spatial memory deficits in a virtual radial arm maze in amnesic participants with hippocampal damage. *Behavioral Neuroscience*, *124*, 405–413. doi:10.1037/a0019193

Gordon, C. J., & Buckley, T. (2009). The effect of high-fidelity simulation training on medical-surgical graduate nurses' perceived ability to respond to patient clinical emergencies. *Journal of Continuing Education in Nursing*, *40*(11), 491–498. doi:10.3928/00220124-20091023-06

Gordon, R., Bjorklund, N. K., Smith, R. J., & Blyden, E. R. (2009b). Halting HIV/AIDS with avatars and havatars: A virtual world approach to modelling epidemics. *BMC Public Health*, *9*(Suppl 1), 1–6.

Gorini, A., Gaggioli, A., Vigna, C., & Riva, G. (2008). A Second Life for e-health: Prospects for the use of 3-D virtual worlds in clinical psychology. *Journal of Medical Internet Research*, *10*, e21. doi:10.2196/jmir.1029

Gorini, A., Gaggioli, A., Vigna, C., & Riva, G. (2008). A second life for e-health: Prospects for the use of 3-D virtual worlds in clinical psychology. *Journal of Medical Internet Research*, *10*(3), e21. doi:10.2196/jmir.1029

Göritz, A. S., & Moser, K. (2006). Web-based mood induction. *Cognition and Emotion*, *20*, 887–896.

Gosling, S. D., Vazire, S., Srivastava, S., & John, O. P. (2004). Should we trust Web-based studies? A comparative analysis of six preconceptions about Internet questionnaires. *The American Psychologist*, *59*, 93–104. doi:10.1037/0003-066X.59.2.93

Green, C. (2000). Doppleganger and the third force: The artistic collaborations of Gilbert & George and Abramoviç/Ulay. *Art Journal*, *59*(2), 36–45. doi:10.2307/778099

Green, C. (2001). *The third hand: Collaboration in art from conceptualism to postmodernism. Minneapolis, MN & London, UK*: University of Minnesota Press.

Green, C. (2004). Group soul. Who own the artist fusion? *Third Text*, *18*(6), 595–608. doi:10.1080/0952882042000285005

Greenfield, P. M. (1984). *Mind and media: The effects of television, video games, and computers*. Cambridge, MA: Harvard University Press.

Greenfield, P. (1994). Les jeux video comme instrument de socialisation cognitive. *Reseaux*, 67.

Greuter, S., Parker, J., Stewart, N., & Leach, G. (2003). *Real-time procedural generation of 'pseudo infinite' cities*. Paper presented at the 1st International Conference on Computer Graphics and Interactive Techniques in Australasia and Southeast Asia.

Griebel, T. (2006). Self portrayal in a simulated life: Projecting personality and values in The Sims 2. *Games Studies, 6*. Retrieved from http://www.gamestudies.org

Guala, A. (2000). *Metodi della ricerca sociale*. Roma, Italia: Carocci.

Guenzel, S. (2008). The space-image. Interactivity and spatiality of computer games. In S. Guenzel, M. Liebe & D. Mersch (Eds.), *Conference Proceedings of the Philosophy of Computer Games 2008* (pp. 170-188). Potsdam, Germany: Potsdam University Press.

Guidi, G., Micoli, L., Russo, M., Frischer, B., Simone, M. D., Spinetti, A., et al. (2005). *3D digitization of a large model of imperial Rome*. Paper presented at the Proceedings of the Fifth International Conference on 3-D Digital Imaging and Modeling.

Guimarães, M. J. L. Jr. (2005). Doing anthropology in cyberspace: Fieldwork boundaries and social environments. In Hine, C. (Ed.), *Virtual methods: Issues in social research on the Internet* (pp. 141–156). Oxford, UK: Berg.

Gumbrecht, H. U. (2004). *Production of presence: What meaning cannot convey*. Stanford University Press.

Gunkel, D. J., & Gunkel, A. H. (1997). Virtual geographies. The new worlds of cyberspace. *Critical Studies in Mass Communication, 14*, 123–137. doi:10.1080/15295039709367003

Gupta, A., & Ferguson, J. (1997). *Anthropological locations: Boundaries and grounds of a field science.* Berkeley, CA: University of California Press.

Habbo Hotel. (2010). *Habbo Hotel.* Retrieved on June 14, 2010, from http://www.habbo.com/

Hagström, C. (2008). Playing with names: Gaming and naming in world of warcraft. In Corneliussen, H., & Rettberg, J. (Eds.), *Digital culture, play and identity: A World of Warcraft® reader* (pp. 265–285). Cambridge, MA: MIT Press.

Hall, R. S. (1983). The nominal group technique for planning and problem solving. *The Journal of Biocommunication, 10*, 24–27.

Hall, E. T. (1973). *The silent language.* New York, NY: Anchor.

Hall, E. (1968). A system for the notation of proxemic behavior. *American Anthropologist, 65*(5), 1003-1026. Retrieved May 23, 2008, from http://www.jstor.org/stable/668580

Hansen, M. (2006). *Bodies in code: Interfaces with digital media.* New York, NY & London, UK: Routledge.

Haraway, D. (1991). A cyborg manifesto: Science, technology, and socialist-feminism in the late twentieth century. In D. Haraway (Ed.), *Simians, cyborgs, and women: The reinvention of nature,* (pp. 149-181). London, UK: Free Association Books. Retrieved from http://www.stanford.edu/dept/ HPS/Haraway/CyborgManifesto.html

Haraway, D. J. (2009). *A cyborg manifesto: Science, technology, and socialist-feminism in the late twentieth century.*

Harder, B. N. (2010). Use of simulation in teaching and learning in health sciences: A systematic review. *The Journal of Nursing Education, 49*(1), 23. doi:10.3928/01484834-20090828-08

Hare, R. M. (1984). Supervenience. *Aristotelian Society, 58*, 1–16.

Harrison, D. (2009, February 02). Real-life teaching in a virtual world. *Campus Technology.* Retrieved from http://campustechnology.com/ Articles/ 2009/ 02/ 18/ Real-Life-Teaching-in-a- Virtual-World.aspx

Harry, D., Offenhuber, D., & Donath, J. (2008). Function follows form: The social role of virtual architecture. In Doesinger, S. (Ed.), *Space between people: How the virtual changes physical architecture* (pp. 64–70). Munich, Germany: Presetl.

Hart, K. (1988). Kinship, contract and trust: The economic organization of migrants in an African city slum. In Gambetta, D. (Ed.), *Trust: Making and breaking of cooperative relations.* Oxford, UK: Blackwell.

Haselton, M. G., & Nettle, D. (2006). The paranoid optimist: An integrative evolutionary model of cognitive biases. *Personality and Social Psychology Review, 10*(1), 47–66. doi:10.1207/s15327957pspr1001_3

Hatch, M. J., & Yanow, D. (2008). Methodology by metaphor: Ways of seeing in painting and research. *Organization Studies, 29*(1). doi:10.1177/0170840607086635

Hayles, N. K. (1999). *How we became posthuman: Virtual bodies in cybernetics, literature, and informatics.* Chicago, IL: University of Chicago Press.

Hayot, E., & Wesp, E. (2009). Towards a critical aesthetic of virtual-world geographies. *Game Studies, 9*(1).

Hayward, P. (1993). Situating cyberspace. The popularisation of virtual reality. In Hayward, P., & Wollen, T. (Eds.), *Future visions. New technologies of the screen* (pp. 180–204). London, UK: British Film Institute.

Health Level Seven International. (2010). *Health Level Seven International* [Web page]. Retrieved on 1st July 2010, from http://www.hl7.org

Health, A. I. S. (2008). *Presence in virtual worlds could help health plans achieve real-world behavior change.* Retrieved from http://www.aishealth.com/ Bnow/ hbd082808.html

Hébert, L. (2006). The functions of language. In L. Hébert (Dir.), *Signo: Theoretical semiotics on the Web.* Retrieved May 23, 2008, from http://www.signosemio.com/jakobson/a_fonctions.asp

Heidegger, M. (2006). *Sein und Zeit.* Tübingen: Niemeyer.

Heidegger, M. (1927, 2006). *Sein und Zeit.* Tübingen: Niemeyer.

Heidegger, M. (1971). Building dwelling thinking. In *Poetry, Language, Thought* (pp. 141-160). New York, NY: Harper Colophon.

Heinrichs, W. L. R., Youngblood, P., Harter, P. M., & Dev, P. (2008). Simulation for team training and assessment: case studies of online training with virtual worlds. *World Journal of Surgery, 32*(2), 161–170. doi:10.1007/s00268-007-9354-2

Helfrich, M. (2009). Community Generated Innovation – Vernetzung von Verbrauchern und Kreativen auf der Ideen-Community Tchibo ideas. In Zerfaß, A., & Möslein, K. M. (Eds.), *Kommunikation als Erfolgsfaktor im Innovationsmanagement* (pp. 367–378). Wiesbaden: Gabler. doi:10.1007/978-3-8349-8242-1_22

Helland, C. (2000). Online-religion/religion-online and virtual communitas. In J. K. Hadden & D. E. Cowan (Eds.), *Religion on the Internet: Research prospects and promises* (Religion and the social order, vol. 8). New York, NY: JAI.

Helmer, J. (2007). *Second Life and virtual worlds.* Learning Light Limited. Retrieved July 13, 2009, from http://www.epic.co.uk/content/ news/nov_07/Second_Life_and_Virtual_Worlds_JH.pdf

Hemp, P. (2006). Avatar-based marketing. *Harvard Business Review, 84*(6), 48–56.

Henri, F. (1992). Computer conferencing and content analysis. In A. Kaye (Ed.), *Collaborative learning through computer conferencing* (pp. 117-135). NATO ASI Series, 90, The Najaden Papers. Heidelberg, Germany: Springer-Verlag.

Henry, D. (1992). *Spatial perception in virtual environments: Evaluating an architectural application. Unpublished MScie.* University of Washington.

Hermes, J. (2009). Audience studies 2.0: On the theory, politics and method of qualitative audience research. *Interactions: Studies in Communication and Culture, 1*(1), 111–127. doi:10.1386/iscc.1.1.111_1

Heston, K. S. (2008). The Aleph technique: Quantitative and ethnographic inquires into subjectification and religion in Second Life. In A. Mitra (Ed.), *National Communications Association Annual Convention 2008.* San Diego, CA.

Higgin, T. (2009). Blackless fantasy: The disappearance of race in massively multiplayer online role-playing games. *Games and Culture, 4*(1), 3–26. doi:10.1177/1555412008325477

Hildebrand, J. (2008). *Anhaltende Flucht aus der virtuellen Scheinwelt.* Retrieved March 02, 2009, from www.welt.de/wams_print/article1655456/Anhaltende_Flucht_aus_der_virtuellen_Scheinwelt.html

Hillman, D. C. A., Willis, D. J., & Gunawardena, C. N. (1994). Learner- interface interaction in distance education: An extension of contemporary models and strategies for practitioners. *American Journal of Distance Education, 8*(2), 30–42. doi:10.1080/08923649409526853

Hindmarsh, J., Heath, C., & Fraser, M. (2006). (Im)materiality, virtual reality and interaction: Grounding the "virtual" in studies of technology in action. *The Sociological Review, 54*(4), 795–817. doi:10.1111/j.1467-954X.2006.00672.x

Hine, C. (2000). *Virtual ethnography.* Los Angeles, CA: Sage.

Hine, C. (2000). *Virtual ethnography.* London, UK: SAGE.

Hine, C. (2000). *Virtual ethnography.* London, UK: Sage.

Hine, C. (2000). *Virtual ethnography.* London, UK: Sage.

Hodes, A. (1972). *Encounter with Martin Buber.* London, UK: Allen Lane.

Hoelig, S., & Hasebrink, U. (2008). *What do people do when they use the internet? Communication modes as an integrated concept for the analysis of media use in converging media environments.* Paper presented at the 2nd European Communication Conference, ECREA, Barcelona, Spain, November 26-29.

Hoewner, J., Jansen, M., & Jantke, K. (2008). *Von der Spinnovation zur Sinnovation.* Düsseldorf.

Hofer, M. (2007). *Der geplatzte Traum vom zweiten Leben.* Retrieved March 2, 2009, from http://www.sueddeutsche.de/computer/939/320809/text/

Hoggett, P. (1997). *Contested communities: Experiences, struggles, policies.* Bristol, UK: Polity Press.

Hohmann, B., Krispel, U., Havemann, S., & Fellner, D. (2009). *CityFit: High-quality urban reconstructions by fitting shape grammars to images and derived textured point clouds.* Paper presented at the 3rd ISPRS International Workshop 3D-ARCH 2009: 3D Virtual Reconstruction and Visualization of Complex Architectures.

Holloway, D. (2009). Interview – DeeAnna Nagel and Kate Anthony. Online Therapy Institute. *The Metaverse Journal.* Retrieved July 1st 2010, from http://www.metaversejournal.com/2009/03/30/interview-deeanna-nagel-and-kate-anthony-online-therapy-institute/.

Holloway, D. (2010). ME/CFS Support in Second Life. *Metaverse Health.* Retrieved July 1st 2010, from http://www.metaversehealth.com/2010/03/me-cfs-support-in-second-life/

Holub, R. C. (1984). *Reception theory: A critical introduction.* New York, NY: Methuen.

Hornecker, E. (2004). Analogies from didactics and moderation/ facilitation methods: Designing spaces for interaction and experience. *Digital Creativity*, *15*(4), 239–244. doi:10.1080/1462626048520185

Huck-Sandhu, S. (2009). Innovationskommunikation in den Arenen der Medien – Campaining, Framing, Storytelling. In Zerfaß, A., & Möslein, K. M. (Eds.), *Kommunikation als Erfolgsfaktor im Innovationsmanagement* (pp. 195–208). Wiesbaden: Gabler. doi:10.1007/978-3-8349-8242-1_10

Hughes, I. (2009). We have all the pieces - Unity3d, OpenSim, Evolver, Smartfox. *Life At The Feeding Edge.* Retrieved July 4th 2010 from http://www.feedingedge.co.uk/blog/2009/12/15/we-have-all-the-pieces-unity3d-opensim-evolver-smartfox/

Huh, S., & Williams, D. (2010). Dude looks like a lady: Gender swapping in an online game. In Bainbridge, W. S. (Ed.), *Online worlds: Convergence of the real and the virtual* (pp. 161–174). London, UK: Springer. doi:10.1007/978-1-84882-825-4_13

Huizinga, J. (1939). *Homo Ludens. Vom Ursprung der Kultur im Spiel* (*Vol. 19*). Reinbek: Rowohlt.

Huizinga, J. (1950). *Homo ludens. A study of the play-element in culture.* Boston, MA: The Beacon Press.

Huizinga, J. (1955). *Homo Ludens, a study of the play element in culture* (p. 46). Boston, MA: Beacon Press.

Huizinga, J. (1990). *Homo Ludens: O jogo como elemento da cultura.* São Paulo, Brazil: Perspectiva.

Ichbiah, D. (1998). *La saga des jeux video.* Paris, France: Pocket.

Ihde, D. (2002). *Bodies in technology.* Minneapolis, MN: University of Minnesota Press.

Imholz, S. (2008). The therapeutic stage encounters the virtual world. *Thinking Skills and Creativity*, *3*(1), 47–52. doi:10.1016/j.tsc.2008.02.001

Imperial College London. (2010). *Medical media and design laboratory (MMDL).* Retrieved 15th June 2010, from http://www1.imperial.ac.uk/ medicine/research/researchthemes /healthtechnologies/ simulation/mmdl/

IMVU. (2010). *IMVU.* Retrieved on June 14, 2010, from http://www.imvu.com/

Ingold, T. (1994). General introduction. In Ingold, T. (Ed.), *Companion encyclopedia of anthropology* (pp. xiii–xxii). London, UK: Routledge.

Ingram, R., Benford, S., & Bowers, J. (1996). *Building virtual cities: Applying urban planning principles to the design of virtual environments.* Paper presented at the ACM Symposium on Virtual Reality Software and Technology (VRST'96)

Institute of Medicine (IoM), Division of Health Sciences Policy. (1985). *Assessing medical technologies.* Washington, DC: National Academies Press; Methods of Technology Assessment.

Jackson, L. A., Zhao, Y., Witt, E. A., Fitzgerald, H. E., & von Eye, A. (2009). Gender, race and morality in the virtual world and its relationship to morality in the real world. *Sex Roles*, *60*(11-12), 859–869. doi:10.1007/s11199-009-9589-5

Jacob, B. (2008). *Deutsche post world net, department market communication, project leader Second Life*. Written Interview, April 2, 2008.

Jacob, S. (2004). *The pop vernacular*. Retrieved 6 October, 2010, from http://www.strangeharvest.com/mt/archive/read_mes/the_pop_vernacular.php

Jana, R. (2006). *Starwood Hotels explore Second Life first*. Retrieved March 2, 2009, from www.businessweek.com/innovate/content/aug2006/id20060823_925270.htm

Javeau, C. (1990). *L'enquête par questionnaire: Manuel à l'usage du praticien*. Bruxelles, Belgium: Editions d'organisation.

Jeffries, P. R. (2005). A framework for designing, implementing, and evaluating simulations used as teaching strategies in nursing. *Nursing Education Perspectives, 26*(2), 96–103.

Jenkins, H. (1998). Complete freedom of movement: Video games as gendered play spaces. In Cassell, J., & Jenkins, H. (Eds.), *From Barbie to Mortal Kombat: Gender and computer games*. Cambridge, MA: MIT Press.

Jensen, S. S. (2009). Avatars and their use of avatars: An empirical study of avatar-based sense-makings and communication practices in the virtual worlds of EverQuest and Second Life. *MedieKultur, 47*, 29–44.

Jensen, H. S. (2008). *Research on innovation. Perspectives and views on processes of innovation*. Laboranova report.

Jensen, S. S. (2010). *Transformative interrelations of actors and their companion avatars: Sources of social innovation? Case studies of actors playing the game of EverQuest and inhabiting the social world of Second Life*. Paper presented at the 3rd ECREA Pre-Conference "Avatars and Humans: Representing Users in Digital Games", Hamburg, Germany, October 12th.

Jin, S.-A. A. (2009). Modality effects in Second Life: The mediating role of social presence and the moderating role of product involvement. *Cyberpsychology & Behavior, 12*(6), 717–721. doi:10.1089/cpb.2008.0273

Join Together. (2008). *First major study of marijuana addiction underway*. Retrieved from http://www.jointogether.org /news/headlines/inthenews/2008/ first-major-study-of.html

Joint Information Systems Committee. (2007). *Game-based learning. E-learning innovation programme*. Briefing papers. Retrieved on July 13, 2009, from http://www.jisc.ac.uk/publications /publications/pub_ game-basedlearningBP.aspx

Josephs, I. E. (2000). A psychological analysis of a psychological phenomenon: The dialogical construction of meaning. *Social Sciences Information. Information Sur les Sciences Sociales, 39*, 115–129. doi:10.1177/053901800039001007

Juul, J. (2005). *Half-real. Video games between real rules and fictional worlds*. Cambridge, MA: MIT Press.

Kancherla, A., Rolland, J., Wright, D., & Burdea, G. (1995). A novel virtual reality tool for teaching dynamic 3D anatomy. In *Proceedings of Computer Vision, Virtual Reality, and Robotics in Medicine '95* (CVRMed '95).

Kant, I. (1983). Crítica da Razão Pura. In *Os Pensadores*. São Paulo, Brazil: Abril Cultural.

Kanuka, H., & Anderson, T. (1999). Using constructivism in technology-mediated learning: Constructing order out of the chaos in the literature. *Radical Pedagogy, 1*(2).

Kapp, K. M., & O'Driscoll, T. (2010). *Learning in 3D: Adding a new dimension to enterprise learning and collaboration*. San Francisco, CA: Pfiffer.

Karaflogka, A. (2002). Religious discourse and cyberspace. *Religion, 32*(4), 279–291. doi:10.1006/reli.2002.0405

Katz, V. J. (2007). *The mathematics of Egypt, Mesopotamia, China, India, and Islam: A sourcebook*. Princeton, NJ: Princeton University Press.

Kearsley, G. (1994-2003). *Lateral thinking: DeBono*. Retrieved January 18, 2004, from http://tip.psychology.org/debono.html

Keller, D. (2007). Gaming, identity, and literacy. In Selfe, C. L., & Gawisher, G. E. (Eds.), *Gaming lives in the twenty-first century* (pp. 71–87). New York, NY: Palgrave.

Kelley, A. E., & Berridge, K. C. (2002). The neuroscience of natural rewards: relevance to addictive drugs. *The Journal of Neuroscience, 22*, 3306–3311.

Kelton, A. J. (2008, September/October). Virtual worlds? Outlook good. *EDUCAUSE Review*, *43*(5). Retrieved from http://www.educause.edu/ EDUCAUSE+Review/ EDUCAUSEReviewMagazineVolume43/ VirtualWorldsOutlookGood/ 163161.

Kildall, S. (2010). *Scott Kildall*. Retrieved November 4, 2010, from http://www.kildall.com/

Kim, J. Y., Allen, J. P., & Lee, E. (2008). Alternate reality gaming. *Communications of the ACM*, *51*(2), 36–42. doi:10.1145/1314215.1340912

Kinross, J. M., Lee, H., Patel, V., Chan, M., Das, A., & Miles, K. … Darzi, A (2009). *Virtual worlds are a novel interdisciplinary platform for medical device training*. In Society of American Gastrointestinal and Endoscopic Surgeons Annual Meeting. Phoenix, Arizona, USA.

Kirriemuir, J. (2009, June). *Early summer 2009 Virtual World Watch snapshot of virtual world activity in UK HE and FE*. Virtual World Watch. Retrieved from http://virtualworldwatch.net/ wordpress/ wp-content/ uploads/ 2009/ 06/ snapshot-six.pdf

Kivisto, P., & Pittman, D. (2007). *Goffman's dramaturgical sociology: Personal sales and service in a commodified world. In Kivisto, P. (Ed.), Illuminating social life: Classical and contemporary theory revisited*. London, UK: Pine Forge Press.

Klapp, O. (1971). Heroes, villains, and fools as agents of social control. In Almog, O. (Ed.), *Social types: Process, structure and ethos* (pp. 12–18). San Diego, CA: Aegis Publishing Company.

Klastrup, L. (2008). What makes World of Warcraft a world? A note on death and dying. In Corneliussen, H. G., & Rettberg, J. W. (Eds.), *Digital culture, play, and identity: A WoW reader* (pp. 143–166). Cambridge, MA: MIT Press.

Klastrup, L. (2003). *Towards a poetics of virtual worlds: Multi-user textuality and the emergence of story*. Unpublished PhD thesis, IT University of Copenhagen, Denmark.

Klastrup, L. (2003). *Towards a poetics of virtual worlds*. Doctoral Thesis presented to the IT University of Copenhagen.

Klevjer, R. (2006). *What is the avatar? Fiction and embodiment in avatar-based single player computer games*. Unpublished PhD thesis, University of Bergen, Norway.

Klevjer, R. (2006). *What is the avatar? Fiction and embodiment in avatar-based single player computer games*. Doctoral dissertation, University of Bergen in Norway.

Klinger, E., & Weiss, P. L. (2009). Shifting towards remote located virtual environments for rehabilitation. *Proceedings of the Chais Conference on Instructional Technologies Research*. Haifa, Israel.

Knapp, M. (1992). *Interpersonal communication and human relationships*. Boston, MA: Allyn & Bacon.

Knight, R. G., & Titov, N. (2009). Use of virtual reality tasks to assess prospective memory: Applicability and evidence. *Brain Impairment*, *10*, 3–13. doi:10.1375/ brim.10.1.3

Kohler, T., Matzler, K., & Füller, J. (2009). Avatar-based innovation: Using virtual worlds for real-world innovation. *Technovation*, *29*(6-7), 395–407. doi:10.1016/j. technovation.2008.11.004

Kohler, T. (2008). *Avatar-based innovation. Facilitating compelling co-creation experiences*. Unpublished dissertation, Innsbruck Universität.

Kohn, T. (1995). She came out of the field and into my home: Reflections, dreams and a search for consciousness in anthropological method. In Cohen, A. P., & Rapport, N. (Eds.), *Questions of consciousness* (pp. 41–59). London, UK: Routledge. doi:10.4324/9780203449486_chapter_2

KoinUp blog, the immersive worlds guide. (2009). *SaveMe Oh*. Retrieved October 22, 2010, from http://blog.koinup. com/2009/12/saveme-oh.html

Koster, R. (2004). A virtual world by any other name? *Terra Nova* blog. Retrieved from http://terranova.blogs. com/ terra_nova/ 2004/ 06/ a_virtual_world.html

Koster, R. (2007). *What is a virtual world?* Retrieved September 8, 2007, from http://www.raphkoster.com/2007/ 06/15/whatis-a-virtual-world/

Kozinets, R. V., Hemetsberger, A., & Schau, H. J. (2008). The wisdom of consumer crowds: Collective innovation in the age of networked marketing. *Journal of Macromarketing*, *28*(4), 339–354. doi:10.1177/0276146708325382

Kozinets, R. V. (1998). On netography: Initial reflections on consumer research investigations of cyberculture. *Advances in Consumer Research. Association for Consumer Research (U. S.), 25*, 366–371.

Kozinets, R. V. (2002). The field behind the screen: Using netography for marketing research in online communities. *JMR, Journal of Marketing Research, 39*, 61–72. doi:10.1509/jmkr.39.1.61.18935

Kozinets, R. V. (2006). Click to connect: Netography and tribal advertising. *Journal of Advertising Research, 46*, 279–288. doi:10.2501/S0021849906060338

Krauss, R. (1972). Léger, Le Corbusier, and purism. *Artforum, 10*(8), 50–53.

Krauss, R. (1976). Video: The aesthetics of narcissism. In Battcock, G. (Ed.), *New artists video: A critical anthology* (pp. 43–64). New York, NY: E. P. Dutton. republished 1978

Krohn, W., & van den Daele, W. (1998). Science as an agent of change: Finalization and experimental implementation. *Social Science Informatics, 37*(1), 191–122. doi:10.1177/053901898037001009

Krueger, M. W. (1991). *Artificial reality II*. Reading, MA: Addison-Wesley Pub. Co.

Krzywinska, T. (2009). World creation and lore: World of Warcraft as rich text. In Corneliussen, H. G., & Rettberg, J. W. (Eds.), *Digital culture, play, and identity. A World of Warcraft reader*. Cambridge, MA: MIT Press.

Kuhn, T. S. (1996). *The structure of scientific revolutions* (3rd ed.). Chicago, IL: University of Chicago Press.

Kuipers, G. (2006). The social construction of digital danger: Debating, defusing and inflating the moral dangers of online humor and pornography in the Netherlands and the United States. *New Media & Society, 8*, 379–400. doi:10.1177/1461444806061949

Kuutti, K. (1996). Activity theory as a potential framework for human computer interaction research. In Nardi, B. A. (Ed.), *Content and consciousness: activity theory and human-computer interaction* (pp. 17–44). Cambridge, MA: MIT Press.

KZero. (2010). *KZero chart*. Retrieved on June 14, 2010, from http://www.kzero.co.uk/universe.php

Lacan, J. (1996). *O seminário, livro 01: Os escritos técnicos de Freud*. Rio de Janeiro, Brazil: Jorge Zahar Editor.

Lacan, J. (1966). *Écrits*. Paris, France: Seuil.

Lagarto, M. J. (2009). *História da matemática medieval* (History of Medieval Mathematics). Retrieved on March 10, 2009, from http://www.malhatlantica.pt/ mathis/ Problemas/ macas/ macas.htm

Lanier, J. (2009). Future tense. Confusions of the hive mind. *Communications of the ACM, 52*(9), 112–113. doi:10.1145/1562164.1562192

Latour, B. (2005). *Reassembling the social. An introduction to actor-network-theory* (1st ed.). Oxford, UK & New York, NY: Oxford University Press.

Latour, B., & Woolgar, S. (1979/86). *Laboratory life*. Princeton, NJ/ Chichester, West Sussex, UK: Princeton University Press.

Laurel, B. (1993). *Computers as theatre*. Londres, UK: Addison Wesley.

Law, A. S., Logie, R. H., & Pearson, D. G. (2006). The impact of secondary tasks on multitasking in a virtual environment. *Acta Psychologica, 122*, 27–44. doi:10.1016/j.actpsy.2005.09.002

Le Corbusier. (2000). *Modulor 2: Let the user speak*. Basel, Switzerland: Birkhäuser.

Le Corbusier. (2008). *Toward an architecture*. London, UK: Frances Lincoln Limited.

Leathers, D. (1997). *Successful nonverbal communication: Principles and applications*. Boston, MA: Allyn & Bacon.

Lebel, J. (1968). On the necessity of violation. In Stiles, K., & Selz, P. (Eds.), *Theories and documents of contemporary art* (pp. 718–722). *Berkeley/Los Angeles, CA & London, UK*: University of California Press. republished 1996

Lemert, C., & Branaman, A. (Eds.). (1997). *The Goffman reader. Massachussets*. Blackwell Publishers.

Lemos, A. (2002). *Cibercultura. Tecnologia e Vida Social na Cultura Contemporânea*. Porto Alegre: Sulina.

Lenggenhager, B., Tadi, T., Metzinger, T., & Blanke, O. (2007). Video ergo sum: Manipulating bodily self-consciousness. *Science, 317*(5841), 1096–1099. doi:10.1126/science.1143439

Leong, J. J., Kinross, J., Taylor, D., & Purkayastha, S. (2008). Surgeons have held conferences in Second Life. *British Medical Journal, 337*(2), 683. doi:10.1136/bmj.a683

Lévy, P. (1995). *Qu'est-ce que le virtuel?* Paris, France: La Découverte.

Lévy, P. (1998). *Becoming virtual: Reality in the digital age.* New York, NY: Plenum Trade.

Levy, P. (1997). *Collective intelligence. Mankind's emerging world in cyberspace* (Bononno, R., Trans.). Cambridge, MA: Perseus Books.

Lévy, P. (1999). *Cibercultura.* Rio de Janeiro: Editora 34.

Lezak, M. D., Howieson, D. B., Loring, D. W., Hannay, H. J., & Fischer, J. S. (2004). *Neuropsychological assessment* (4th ed.). New York, NY: Oxford University Press.

Lichtenberg, P. A., Johnson, A. S., Erlanger, D. M., Kaushik, T., Maddens, M. E., & Imam, K. (2006). Enhancing cognitive screening in geriatric care: Use of an Internet-based system. *International Journal of Healthcare Information Systems and Informatics, 1*, 47–57. doi:10.4018/jhisi.2006070103

Lichtenberg-Ettinger, B. (2005). *The art-and-healing-oeuvre: Metramorphic relinquishment of the soul-spirit to the spirit of the cosmos. In de Zegher & H. Teicher (Eds.),* 3 x abstraction: New methods of drawing by Hilma af Klint, Emma Kunz and Agnes Martin. *New York, NY & New Haven, CT: The Drawing Center, and Yale University Press.*

Lichty, P. (2000). The cybernetics of performance and new media art. *Leonardo, 33*(5), 351–354. doi:10.1162/002409400552810

Lichty, P. (2009a). The translation of art in virtual worlds. *Leonardo Electronic Almanac, 16*, 4–5.

Lichty, P. (2008). Why art in virtual worlds? E-happenings, relational milieu & second sculpture. *CIAC, 31.* Retrieved November 1, 2010, from http://www.ciac.ca/magazine/archives/no_31/dossier.htm

Lichty, P. (2009b). Wikipedia as art? In *Rhizome at the new museum.* Retrieved November 4, 2010, from http://rhizome.org/discuss/view/41713

Lichty, P. (2009c). *I know Gaz Babeli.* Retrieved November 1, 2010, from http://gazirababeli.com/TEXTS.php?t=iknowgazbabeli

Lichty, P. (2009d). Lightening rod: Second front, reemergence of the happening and the integration of history. *CIAC, 33.* Retrieved October 29, 2010, from http://www.ciac.ca/magazine/perspective.htm

Lichty, P. *(2010).* Patrick Lichty: Theorist – artist – curator. Asking question through art and media. *Retrieved November 4, 2010, from* http://www.voyd.com/

Lievrouw, L. A., & Livingstone, S. (2002). The social shaping and consequences of ICTs. In L. A. Lievrouw & S. Livingstone (Eds.). *Handbook of new media* (1-16). Thousand Oaks, CA: Sage Publications.

Lifton, J. H. H. H. H., Laibowitz, M., Harry, D., Gong, N. W., Mittal, M., & Paradiso, J. A. (2009, July-September). Metaphor and manifestation - Cross-reality with ubiquitous sensor/actuator networks. *IEEE Pervasive Computing. Mobile and Ubiquitous Systems, 8*(3), 24–33.

Lifton, J. H. (2007). *Dual reality: An emerging medium.* PhD thesis, Massachusetts Institute of Technology. Retrieved from http://www.media.mit.edu/ resenv/ pubs/ theses/ lifton_phd.pdf

Lifton, J. H., & Paradiso, J. A. (2009, July 27-29). Dual reality: Merging the real and virtual. *Proceedings of the First International ICST Conference on Facets of Virtual Environments* (FaVE), Berlin, Germany. Retrieved from http://web.media.mit.edu/ ~lifton/ publications/ lifton_2009_07_fave.pdf

Lin, H. F., & Lee, G. G. (2006). Determinants of success for online communities: An empirical study. *Behaviour & Information Technology, 25*(6), 479–488. doi:10.1080/01449290500330422

Linden Lab. (2010a). *Economic statistics (Raw data files), logged_in_users.xls.* Retrieved February 6, 2010, from http://secondlife.com/statistics/economy-data.php

Linden Lab. (2010b). *Linden Lab Offiziell: Zusatz-Benutzerkonto FAQ*. Retrieved May 1, 2010, from http://wiki.secondlife.com/wiki/Zusatz-Benutzerkonto_FAQ_%28KB%29

Linden Research. (2008). *Second Life pricing list*. Retrieved December 8, 2008, from http://static-secondlife-com.s3.amazonaws.com/corporate/Second_Life_Pricing_List_20081208.pdf

Linden Research. (2010). *LindeX™ market data*. Retrieved May 5, 2010, from http://secondlife.com/statistics/economy-market.php

Linden Research. (2010). *Second Life official site*. Retrieved October 1, 2010, from http://www.secondlife.com

Lineage. (2010). *Lineage*. Retrieved on May 1, 2010, from http://www.lineage.com

Lipp, M., Wonka, P., & Wimmer, M. (2008). *Interactive visual editing of grammars for procedural architecture*. Paper presented at the ACM SIGGRAPH.

Lipsey, R. (1988). Frantisek Kupka: The realm of rhythms and signs. In Lipsey, R. (Ed.), *An art of our own: The spiritual in twentieth century art* (pp. 98–106). Boston, MA: Shambhala.

Lista EaD-L. (n.d.). *Distance education mailing list* (in Portuguese). Retrieved from http://www.ggte.unicamp.br/ gecon/ sites/ GGTE/ index_html?foco=HTML/ 753

Ljungström, M. (2005). *The use of architectural patterns in MMORPGs*. Paper presented at the Aesthetics of Play Conference, Bergen.

Lo, S. (2008). The impact of online game characters outward attractiveness and social status on interpersonal attraction. *Computers in Human Behavior*, 24(5), 1947–1958. doi:10.1016/j.chb.2007.08.001

Lofgren, E. T., & Fefferman, N. H. (2007). The untapped potential of virtual game worlds to shed light on real world epidemics. *The Lancet Infectious Diseases*, 7(9), 625–629. doi:10.1016/S1473-3099(07)70212-8

Long, C. J. (1996). Neuropsychological tests: A look at our past and the impact that ecological issues may have on our future. In Sbordone, R. J., & Long, C. J. (Eds.), *Ecological validity of neuropsychological testing* (pp. 1–14). Delray Beach, FL: GR Press/St. Lucie Press.

Longman, H., O'Connor, E., & Obst, P. (2009). The effect of social support derived from World of Warcraft on negative psychological symptoms. *Cyberpsychology & Behavior*, 12, 563–566. doi:10.1089/cpb.2009.0001

Lorentz, P. (2011). La construction des représentations sexuées à travers la pratique ludique: L'exemple des Sims. In Le Breton & Schmoll (Ed.), *Jeux et enjeux*. Strasbourg, France: Revue des Sciences sociales.

Lri Landay, L. (2009). Virtual KinoEye: Kinetic camera, machinima, and virtual subjectivity in Second Life. *Media Studies, 2*(1).

Luca, L. D., Véron, P., & Florenzano, M. (2007). A generic formalism for the semantic modeling and representation of architectural elements. *The Visual Computer, 23*(3), 181–205. doi:10.1007/s00371-006-0092-5

Lundvall, B.-A. (1985). *Product innovation and user-producer interaction*. Aalborg, Denmark: Aalborg University Press.

Luria, A. R. (1973). *The working brain: An introduction to neuropsychology*. New York, NY: Basic Books.

Lustria, M. L., Cortese, J., Noar, S. M., & Glueckauf, R. L. (2009). Computer tailored health interventions delivered over the Web: Review and analysis of key components. *Patient Education and Counseling, 74*, 156–173. doi:10.1016/j.pec.2008.08.023

Lynch, C. G. (2008). Inside Sun's virtual world for internal collaboration. Retrieved July 8, 2010, from www.cio.com/article/171655/ Inside_Sun_s_Virtual_World_for_Internal_ Collaboration

MacCallum-Stewart, E., & Parsler, J. (2009). Role-play vs. gameplay: The difficulties of playing a role in World of Warcraft. In Corneliussen, H. G., & Rettberg, J. W. (Eds.), *Digital culture, play, and identity. A World of Warcraft reader*. Cambridge, MA: MIT Press.

MacCallum-Stewart, E., & Parsler, J. (2007). *Illusory agency in vampire: The masquerade – Bloodlines*. Retrieved from http://bit.ly/ 9PJPjX

MacDonald, G. L., & Boyce, J. S. (2008). Nanotechnology: Considering the complex ethical, legal, and societal issues with the parameters of human performance. *NanoEthics, 2*, 265–275. doi:10.1007/s11569-008-0047-6

Machado, A. (2007). *O Sujeito na Tela. Modos de Enunciação no Cinema e no Ciberespaço*. São Paulo, Brazil: Paulus.

Mackie, J. L. (1990). *Ethics: Inventing right and wrong*. London, UK: Penguin Books.

Malaby, T. M. (2009). *Making virtual worlds: Linden Lab and Second Life*. New York, NY: Cornell University Press.

Malinowski, B. (1961). *Argonauts of the Western Pacific*. New York, NY: E. P. Dutton & Co.

Malpas, J. (2009). On the non-autonomy of the virtual. *Convergence: The International Journal of Research into New Media Technologies, 15*, 135–139. doi:10.1177/1354856508101579

Mandelbrot, B. B. (1982). *The fractal geometry of nature*. W. H. Freeman.

Mania, K., & Chalmers, A. (2001). The effects of levels of immersion on memory and presence in virtual environments: A reality centered approach. *Cyberpsychology & Behavior, 4*(2), 247–264. doi:10.1089/109493101300117938

Manovich, L. (2001). *The language of new media*. Cambridge, MA: The MIT Press.

Manovich, L. (2003). New media from Borges to HTML. In Wardrip-Fruim, N., & Montfort, N. (Eds.), *The new media reader* (pp. 13–25). Cambridge, MA: The MIT Press.

Markham, A. N. (1998). *Life online: Researching real experience in virtual space*. Walnut Creek, CA: AltaMira.

Markham, A. N. (1998). *Life online: Researching real experience in virtual space*. Walnut Creek, CA: AltaMira Press.

Markham, A. N. (2005). The methods, politics, and ethics of representation of online ethnography. In Denzin, N. K., & Lincoln, Y. S. (Eds.), *Handbook of qualitative research* (2nd ed., pp. 793–820). Thousand Oaks, CA: Sage Publications.

Markus, H., & Nurius, P. (1986). Possible selves. *The American Psychologist, 41*(9), 954–969. doi:10.1037/0003-066X.41.9.954

Marsen, S. (2008). Becoming more than human: Technology and the post-human condition introduction. *Journal of Evolution & Technology, 19*(1), 1–5.

Marshall, W. W., & Haley, R. W. (2000). Use of a secure Internet website for collaborative medical research. *Journal of the American Medical Association, 284*, 1843–1849. doi:10.1001/jama.284.14.1843

Martin, J. (2005). *The algorithmic beauty of buildings: Methods for procedural building generation*. Unpublished Honors Thesis, Trinity University.

Martinez Fabre, M. P., & Sentamans, T. (2007). The lapses of an avatar: Sleight of hand and artistic praxis in Second Life. In J. M. Prada (Ed.), *Inclusiva-net: New art dynamics in Web 2 mode* (pp. 51-76). Retrieved October 29, 2010, from http://www.medialab-prado.es/mmedia/1099

Marvin, C. (1988). *When old technologies were new: Thinking about electronic communication in the late nineteenth century*. New York, NY: Oxford University Press.

Mast, C., Huck, S., & Zerfaß, A. (2006). *Innovationskommunikation in dynamischen Märkten. Empirische Ergebnisse und Fallstudien*. Berlin, Münster: LIT.

Mast, C., & Zerfaß, A. (2005). *Neue Ideen erfolgreich durchsetzen. Das Handbuch der Innovationskommunikation. Frankfurt a. M*. FAZ Frankfurter Allgemeine Buch.

Mast, C., Huck, S., & Zerfaß, A. (2005). Innovation communication outline of the concept and empirical findings from Germany innovation. *Innovation Journalism, 2*(7). Retrieved May 20, 2009, http://www.innovationjournalism.org/archive/INJO-2-7.pdf

Mathiak, K., & Weber, R. (2006). Towards brain correlates of natural behavior: fMRI during violent video games. *Human Brain Mapping, 27*, 948–956. doi:10.1002/hbm.20234

Mattar, J. (2008, February 20). Second Life is not a learning environment... but why not? *De Mattar* (blog). Retrieved from http://blog.joaomattar.com/2008/02/20/second-life-is-not-a-learning-environment-but-why-not/

Mattar, J. (2009, October 21). Professional development models for educators. *De Mattar* (blog). Retrieved from http://blog.joaomattar.com/2009/10/21/professional-development-models-for-educators/

Matthews, S. (2008). Identity and Information Technology. In Jeroen van den Hoven, M., & Weckert, J. (Eds.), *Philosophy and Information Technology*. Cambridge University Press.

Matusitz, J. (2005). Deception in the virtual world: A semiotic analysis of identity. *Journal of New Media and Society*, *3*(1). Retrieved from http://www.ibiblio.org/nmediac/winter2004/matusitz.html.

Maxwell, P. (2002). Virtual religion in context. *Religion*, *32*(4), 343–354. doi:10.1006/reli.2002.0410

Mayer, P. (1996). Representation and action in the reception of Myst: A social semiotic approach to computer media. *Nordicon Review of Nordic Popular Culture*, *1*, 237–254.

McArthur, V. (2008). *Real ethics in a virtual world*. Paper presented at the CHI '08 Extended Abstracts on Human Factors in Computing Systems.

McArthur, V. (2010). *Virtual world professionals and avatar appearance codes*. Paper presented at the ACM FuturePlay 2010.

McArthur, V., & Baljko, M. (2009). *Outsiders, interlopers, and employee-identified avatars*. Paper presented at the The 12th Annual International Workshop on Presence.

McCroskey, J., & Yong, T. (1981). Ethos and credibility: The construct and its measurement after three decades. *Central States Speech Journal*, *32*, 24–34.

McGeorge, P., Phillips, L., Crawford, J. R., Garden, S. E., Della Sala, S., & Milne, A. B. (2001). Using virtual environments in the assessment of executive dysfunction. *Presence (Cambridge, Mass.)*, *10*, 375–383. doi:10.1162/1054746011470235

McGloin, R. P., Nowak, K. L., Stifano, S. C., & Flynn, G. (2009). *The effect of avatar categorization on perceptions*. Paper presented at the 12th Annual International Workshop on Presence.

McGonigal, J. (2008). Why I love bees: A case study in collective intelligence gaming. In Salen, K. (Ed.), *The ecology of games: Connecting youth, games, and learning* (pp. 199–208). Cambridge, MA: The MIT Press.

McGonigal, J. (2003). *This is not a game: Immersive aesthetics and collective play*. Paper presented at the 5th International Digital Arts and Culture Conference.

McLuhan, M. (1964). *Understanding media: The extensions of man*. Cambridge, MA: The MIT Press.

Mead, G. H. (1934). *Mind, self, and society* (Morris, C. W., Ed.). Chicago, IL: University of Chicago Press.

Meadows, M. S. (2008). *I, avatar: The culture and consequences of having a Second Life*. Berkeley, CA: New Riders.

Meadows, M. (2008). *I, avatar*. New Riders Press.

Mealy, L., Daood, C., & Krage, M. (1996). Enhanced memory for faces of cheaters. *Ethology and Sociobiology*, *17*, 119–128. doi:10.1016/0162-3095(95)00131-X

Mediaedge:CIA. (2005). *Playing with brands*. Retrieved February 18, 2008, from http://www.mecglobal.com/output/Page1463.asp

Medienboard Berlin-Brandenburg. (2008). *Games – Informationen zum Medienstandort Berlin-Brandenburg*. Retrieved August 18, 2008, from http://www.deutsche-gamestage.de/WebObjects/ Medienboard.woa/media/9064

Meier, S. (2004). *Jeux vidéo et médias du XXIème siècle. Quels modèles pour les nouveaux loisirs numériques?* (p. 6). Paris, France: Vuibert.

Merali, Y., & McKelvey, B. (2006). Using complexity science to effect a paradigm shift in Information Systems for the 21st century. *Journal of Information Technology*, *21*, 211–215. doi:10.1057/palgrave.jit.2000082

Merians, A. S., Jack, D., Boian, R., Tremaine, M., Burdea, G. C., & Adamovich, S. V. (2002). Virtual reality-augmented rehabilitation for patients following stroke. *Physical Therapy*, *82*(9), 898–915.

Merleau-Ponty, M. (2006). *Fenomenologia da percepção*. São Paulo, Brazil: Livraria Martins Fontes Editora.

Merleau-Ponty, M. (1962). *Phenomenology of perception*. New York, NY: Humanities Press.

Metzinger, T. (2003). *Being no one: The self-model theory of subjectivity*. Cambridge, MA: MIT Press.

Meyer, R. E. (1996). Neuropsychopharmacology: Are we ready for a paradigm shift? *Neuropsychopharmacology*, *14*, 169–179. doi:10.1016/0893-133X(95)00074-N

Meyerbröker, K., & Emmelkamp, P. M. G. (2010). Virtual reality exposure therapy in anxiety disorders: A systematic review of process- and outcome studies. *Depression and Anxiety, 27*(10). doi:10.1002/da.20734

Meynell, L. (2009). Minding bodies. In Campbell, S., Meynell, L., & Sherwin, S. (Eds.), *Embodiment and agency*. Pennsylvania State University Press.

Michaels, S. (2009, September 10). Courtney Love to sue over Kurt Cobain Guitar Hero appearance. *The Guardian*. Retrieved 13 July 2010, from http://www.guardian.co.uk/ music/ 2009/ sep/ 10/ courtney-love-kurt-cobain

Miles, D. (1999). The CD-ROM novel Myst and McLuhan's fourth law of media: Myst and its retrievals. In Mayer, P. (Ed.), *Computer media and communication: A reader* (pp. 307–319). Oxford, UK: Oxford University Press.

Miller, G. A. (2003). The cognitive revolution: A historical perspective. *Trends in Cognitive Sciences, 7,* 141–144. doi:10.1016/S1364-6613(03)00029-9

Milon, A. (2006). *La réalité virtuelle avec ou sans le corps?* Paris, France: Autrement, collection Le corps plus que jamais.

Mischel, W. (1999). *Introduction to personality* (6th ed.). Fort Worth, TX: Harcourt Brace.

Mishra, P., & Koehler, M. J. (2006). Technological pedagogical content knowledge: A new framework for teacher knowledge. *Teachers College Record, 108*(6), 1017–1054. doi:10.1111/j.1467-9620.2006.00684.x

Mitchell, W. J. (1995). *City of bits*. Boston, MA: MIT Press.

Mohr, J., Sengupta, S., & Slater, S. (2009). *Marketing of high-technology products and innovations* (3rd ed.). Upper Saddle River, NJ: Prentice Hall.

Molka-Danielson, J., & Deutschmann, M. (2009). *Learning and teaching in the virtual world of Second Life*. Trondheim, Norway: Tapir Academic Press.

Montola, M., Stenros, J., & Waern, A. (Eds.). (2009). *Pervasive games: Theory and design. Experiences on the boundary between life and play*. Amsterdam, The Netherlands: Morgan Kaufmann.

Moore, K., Wiederhold, B. K., Wiederhold, M. D., & Riva, G. (2002). Panic and agoraphobia in a virtual world. *Cyberpsychology & Behavior, 5*(3), 197–202. doi:10.1089/109493102760147178

Moore, R. J., Gathman, E. C. H., & Ducheneaut, N. (2009). From 3D space to third place: The social life of small virtual spaces. *Human Organization, 68*(2), 230–240.

Moore, M. G. (1989). Three types of interaction. *American Journal of Distance Education, 3*(2), 1–6. doi:10.1080/08923648909526659

Moores, S. (1993). *Interpreting audiences: The ethnography of media consumption*. Thousand Oaks, CA: Sage Publications.

Moravec, H. (1988). *Mind children: The future of robot and human intelligence*. Cambridge, MA & London, UK: Harvard University Press.

Moretti, G. (2009). *Mundos digitais virtuais em 3D e aprendizagem organizacional: uma relação possível e produtiva*. In IV Congreso de la CiberSociedad 2009: Crisis Analógica, Futuro Digital. Disponível em: http://www.cibersociedad.net/ congres2009/es/coms/ mundos-digitais-virtuais-em-3d-e-aprendizagem-organizacional-uma-relasao-possivel-e-produtiva/644/

Moretti, G. (2010). *La simulazione come strumento di produzione di conoscenza: Comunitã di apprendimento e di pratica nei mondi virtuali*. PhD thesis in Communication Sciences and Complex Organizations, LUMSA University, Rome, Italy, National Library of Rome.

Morie, J. F., Antonisse, J., Bouchard, S., & Chance, E. (2009). Virtual worlds as a healing modality for returning soldiers and veterans. *Studies in Health Technology and Informatics, 144,* 273–276.

Morie, J., & Verhuldonck, G. (2008). *Body/persona/action! Emerging non-anthropomorphic communication and interaction in virtual worlds*. Paper presented at the ACE 2008.

Müller, P., Wonka, P., Haegler, S., Ulmer, A., & Gool, L. V. (2006). Procedural modeling of buildings. *ACM Transactions on Graphics, 25*(3), 614–623. doi:10.1145/1141911.1141931

Müller, P., Zeng, G., Wonka, P., & Gool, L. V. (2007). Image-based procedural modeling of facades. *ACM Transactions on Graphics, 26*(3). doi:10.1145/1276377.1276484

Müller, P., Vereenooghe, T., Ulmer, A., & Gool, L. V. (2005). *Automatic reconstruction of Roman housing architecture*. Paper presented at the International Workshop on Recording, Modeling and Visualization of Cultural Heritage.

Müller, P., Vereenooghe, T., Vergauwen, M., Gool, L. V., & Waelkens, M. (2004). *Photo-realistic and detailed 3D modeling: The Antonine Nymphaeum at Sagalassos (Turkey)*. Paper presented at the Computer Applications and Quantitative Methods in Archaeology (CAA2004): Beyond the artifact - Digital interpretation of the past.

Müller, P., Vereenooghe, T., Wonka, P., Paap, I., & Gool, L. V. (2006). *Procedural 3D reconstruction of Puuc buildings in Xkipche*. Paper presented at the Symposium on Virtual Reality, Archaeology and Cultural Heritage (VAST).

Mullet, K. (2003). *The essence of effective rich Internet applications*. Macromedia White Paper.

Munster, A. (2006). *Materializing new media: Embodiment in information aesthetics*. Hanover, NH: Dartmouth College Press, University Press of New England.

Murray, J. (1997). *Hamlet on the holodeck: the future of narrative in cyberspace*. Cambridge, MA: MIT Press.

Murray, J. (1997). *Hamlet no Holodeck. O Futuro da Narrativa no Ciberespaço*. São Paulo, Brazil: UNESP.

Murray, J. (2003). *Hamlet no holodeck: O futuro da narrativa no ciberespaço*. São Paulo, Brazil: UNESP.

Musgrave, F. K., Kolb, C. E., & Mace, R. S. (1989). *The synthesis and rendering of eroded fractal terrains*. Paper presented at the 16th Annual Conference on Computer Graphics and Interactive Techniques.

Myung, S. K., McDonnell, D. D., Kazinets, G., Seo, H. G., & Moskowitz, J. M. (2009). Effects of Web- and computer-based smoking cessation programs: Meta-analysis of randomized controlled trials. *Archives of Internal Medicine, 169*(10), 929–937. doi:10.1001/archinternmed.2009.109

Nadeau, S. E. (2002). A paradigm shift in neurorehabilitation. *The Lancet Neurology, 1*, 126–130. doi:10.1016/S1474-4422(02)00044-3

Nakamura, L. (2008). *Digitizing race: Visual cultures of the internet*. Minneapolis, MN: University of Minnesota Press.

Natho, N., & Pfeiffer, O. (2010). *A knowledge management system for educational scenarios in 3D virtual worlds*. Paper presented at the Second International Conference on Mobile, Hybrid, and On-Line Learning.

Natkin, S. (2004). *Jeux vidéo et médias du XXIème siècle: Quels modèles pour les nouveaux loisirs numériques?* Paris, France: Vuibert.

Ndalianis, A. (2005). *Neo-Baroque aesthetics and contemporary entertainment*. Cambridge, MA: MIT Press.

Neustaedter, C., & Fedorovokya, E. (2008). *Presenting identity in a virtual world through avatar appearances*. In Kodak Research Labs and Graphics Interface Conference, (pp. 183-190). 25-27 May, Kelowna, British Columbia, Canada.

Neustaedter, C., & Fedorovskaya, E. (2008). *Establishing and maintaining relationships in a social virtual world*. (Eastman Kodak Company Technical Report 344195F).

Newcomb, M. D., & Bentler, P. M. (1988). Impact of adolescent drug use and social support on problems of young adults: A longitudinal study. *Journal of Abnormal Psychology, 97*(1), 64–75. doi:10.1037/0021-843X.97.1.64

Nielsen, K., Nielsen, H., & Jensen, H. S. (2008). *Skruen uden ende. Den vestlige teknologis historie* (3rd ed.). Odense, Denmark: Erhvervsskolernes Forlag.

Nielsen, H. S. (2010). The computer game as a somatic experience. *Eludamos, 4*(1), 25–40.

Nitsche, M. (2008). *Video game spaces: Image, play, and structure in 3D worlds*. Cambridge, MA: The MIT Press.

Nitsche, M. (2009). *Video game spaces. Image, play, and structure in 3D worlds*. Cambridge, MA: MIT Press.

Nonaka, I., & Konno, N. (1999). *The concept of "Ba": Building a foundation for knowledge creation*. USA: Butterworth – Heinemann.

Nonaka, I., & Takeuchi, H. (1998). *The knowledge creating company*. Milano, Italy: Guerini e Associati.

Norberg-Schulz, C. (2000b). *Principles of modern architecture*. London, UK: Andreas Papadakis Publisher.

Norberg-Schulz, C. (2000a). *Architecture: Presence, language and place*. Milano, Italia: Skira.

Nordfors, D. (2004). The role of journalism in innovation systems. *Innovation Journalism, 1*(7). Retrieved August 18, 2008, from www.innovationjournalism.org/archive/INJO-1-7.pdf

Nordfors, D. (2006). PR and the innovation communication system. *Innovation Journalism, 3*(5), Retrieved August 18, 2008, from www.innovationjournalism.org/archive/INJO-3-5.pdf

Norris, J. R. (2009). The growth and direction of healthcare support groups in virtual worlds. *Journal of Virtual Worlds Research, 2*(2), 3–20.

Nosek, M., Whelen, S., Hughes, R., Porcher, E., Davidson, G., & Nosek, T. (2010). Self-esteem in Second Life: An in world group intervention for women with disabilities. In A. Boa-Ventura, O. Criner, E. Elam & M. Nosek (Chairs), SLACTIONS. Texas chapter, Houston, TX.

Nowak, K. L., & Rauh, C. (2005). The influence of the avatar on online perceptions of anthropomorphism, androgyny, credibility, homophily, and attraction. *Journal of Computer-Mediated Communication, 11*(1). doi:10.1111/j.1083-6101.2006.tb00308.x

Nowak, K. L., & Rauh, C. (2008). Choose your buddy icon carefully: The influence of avatar androgyny, anthropomorphism and credibility in online interactions. *Computers in Human Behavior, 24*(4), 1473–1493. doi:10.1016/j.chb.2007.05.005

Nurius, P. (1991). Possible selves and social support: Social cognitive resources for coping and striving. In Howard, J., & Callero, P. (Eds.), *The self-society dynamic: Cognition, emotion, and action* (pp. 239–258). Cambridge, MA: Cambridge University Press. doi:10.1017/CBO9780511527722.013

Nussbaum, P. D., Goreczny, A., & Haddad, L. (1995). Cognitive correlates of functional capacity in elderly depressed versus patients with probable Alzheimer's disease. *Neuropsychological Rehabilitation, 5*, 333–340. doi:10.1080/09602019508401476

Nusselder, A. C. (2006). *Interface fantasy: A Lacanian cyborg ontology = Interface fantasie: een Lacaniaanse Cyborg Ontologie*. Amsterdam, The Netherlands: F&N Eigen Beheer.

O'Leary, S. D. (1996). Cyberspace as sacred space: Communicating religion on computer networks. *Journal of the American Academy of Religion. American Academy of Religion, 64*(4), 781–808.

O'Reilly, K. (2005). *Ethnographic methods*. London, UK: Routledge. Retrieved July 2, 2010, from http://www.pewinternet.org/

O'Guinn, T., Allen, C., & Semenik, R. (2008). *Advertising and integrated brand promotion*. Cincinnati, OH: South Western College Pub.

Oliver, P. (2003). *Dwellings: The vernacular house worldwide*. London, UK: Phaidon.

Oliver, M., & Carr, D. (2009). Learning in virtual worlds: Using communities of practice to explain how people learn from play. *British Journal of Educational Technology, 40*(3), 444–457. doi:10.1111/j.1467-8535.2009.00948.x

Ondrejka, C. (2007). Collapsing heography: Second Life, innovation, and the future of national power. *Innovations, 2*(3), 27–54. doi:10.1162/itgg.2007.2.3.27

Ondrejka, C. (2007). Collapsing geography (Second Life, innovation, and the future of national power). *Innovations: Technology, Governance, Globalization, 2*(3), 27–54. doi:10.1162/itgg.2007.2.3.27

Ong, W. J. (1967). *The presence of the word: Some prolegomena for cultural and religious history. The Terry Lectures*. New Haven, CT: Yale University Press.

OpenStreetMap. (2010). *OpenStreetMap*. Retrieved on May 31, 2010, from http://www.openstreetmap.org/

Ostrander, M. (2008). Talking, looking, flying, searching: Information seeking behaviour in Second Life. *Library Hi Tech, 26*(4), 512–524. doi:10.1108/07378830810920860

Pace, T., Houssian, A., & McArthur, V. (2009). Are socially exclusive values embedded in avatar creation interfaces of MMORPGs? *Journal of Information. Communication and Ethics in Society*, *7*(2/3), 192–210. doi:10.1108/14779960910955909

Padilla-Walker, L. (2006). Adolescents, developmental needs of, and media. In J. Jensen Arnett (Ed.), *Encyclopedia of children, adolescents, and the media*. SAGE Publications. Retrieved from http://www.sage-ereference.com/ childmedia/ Article_n419.html

Paech, V. (2007). *Secondfront: Performance art in Second Life*. Artshub. Retrieved October 26, 2010, from http://www.artshub.com.au/au/newsPrint.asp?sid=159056

Pallasmaa, J. (2005a). Identity, intimacy, and domicile: Notes on the phenomenology of home. In MacKeith, P. (Ed.), *Encounters: Architectural essays* (pp. 112–126). Helsinki, Finland: Rakennustieto Oy.

Pallasmaa, J. (2005b). The place of man: Time, memory, and place in architectural experience. In MacKeith, P. (Ed.), *Encounters: Architectural essays* (pp. 72–85). Helsinki, Finland: Rakennustieto Oy.

Palloff, R. M., & Pratt, K. (1999). *Building learning communities in cyberspace - Effective strategies for the online classroom*. São Francisco, CA: Jossey-Bass Publishers.

Parish, Y. I. H., & Müller, P. (2001). *Procedural modeling of cities*. Paper presented at the 28th Annual Conference on Computer Graphics and Interactive Techniques.

Park, S. M. (2005). *Tall building form generation by parametric design process*. Chicago, IL, USA: Illinois Institute of Technology.

Parlett, D. (1999). *The Oxford history of board games*. Oxford, UK: Oxford University Press.

Parsons, T. D., Bowerly, T., Buckwalter, J. G., & Rizzo, A. A. (2007). A controlled clinical comparison of attention performance in children with ADHD in a virtual reality classroom compared to standard neuropsychological methods. *Child Neuropsychology*, *13*, 363–381. doi:10.1080/13825580600943473

Parsons, T. D., Cosand, L., Courtney, C., Iyer, A., & Rizzo, A. A. (2009b). Neurocognitive workload assessment using the virtual reality cognitive performance assessment test. *Lecture Notes in Artificial Intelligence*, *5639*, 243–252.

Parsons, T. D., Larson, P., Kratz, K., Thiebaux, M., Bluestein, B., & Buckwalter, J. G. (2004b). Sex differences in mental rotation and spatial rotation in a virtual environment. *Neuropsychologia*, *42*, 555–562. doi:10.1016/j.neuropsychologia.2003.08.014

Parsons, T. D., & Rizzo, A. A. (2008a). Affective outcomes of virtual reality exposure therapy for anxiety and specific phobias: A meta-analysis. *Journal of Behavior Therapy and Experimental Psychiatry*, *39*, 250–261. doi:10.1016/j.jbtep.2007.07.007

Parsons, T. D., & Rizzo, A. A. (2008b). Neuropsychological assessment of attentional processing using virtual reality. *Annual Review of Cybertherapy and Telemedicine*, *6*, 23–28.

Parsons, T. D., & Rizzo, A. A. (2008c). Initial validation of a virtual environment for assessment of memory functioning: Virtual reality cognitive performance assessment test. *Cyberpsychology & Behavior*, *11*, 17–25. doi:10.1089/cpb.2007.9934

Parsons, T. D., Rizzo, A. A., & Buckwalter, J. G. (2004a). Backpropagation and regression: Comparative utility for neuropsychologists. *Journal of Clinical and Experimental Neuropsychology*, *26*, 95–104. doi:10.1076/jcen.26.1.95.23932

Parsons, T. D., Rizzo, A. A., Rogers, S. A., & York, P. (2009a). Virtual reality in pediatric rehabilitation: A review. *Developmental Neurorehabilitation*, *12*, 224–238. doi:10.1080/17518420902991719

Parsons, T. D., Rizzo, A. A., van der Zaag, C., McGee, J. S., & Buckwalter, J. G. (2005). Gender and cognitive performance: A test of the common cause hypothesis. *Aging, Neuropsychology, & Cognition*, *12*, 78–88.

Patton, M. Q. (2002). *Qualitative research & evaluation methods* (3rd ed.). Thousand Oaks, CA: Sage Publications.

Paul, R., Lawrence, J., Williams, L., Richard, C., Cooper, N., & Gordon, E. (2006). Preliminary validity of "integneuro": A new computerized battery of neurocognitive tests. *The International Journal of Neuroscience*, *115*, 1549–1567. doi:10.1080/00207450590957890

Pearce, C. (2006). *Toward a game theory of game. First Person: New Media as Story*. Performance, and Game.

Pearce, C., & Artemesia. (2009). *Communities of play. Emergent cultures in multiplayer games and virtual worlds*. Cambridge, MA: MIT Press.

Pecchioli, L., Carrozzino, M., & Mohamed, F. (2008). *ISEE: Accessing relevant information by navigating 3D interactive virtual environments*. Paper presented at the 14th International Conference on Virtual Systems and Multimedia, IEEE VSMM.

Pena, J., Hancock, J. T., & Merola, N. A. (2009). The priming effects of avatars in virtual settings. *Communication Research, 36*(6), 838–856. doi:10.1177/0093650209346802

Pera, H. (n.d.). *Humming Pera biography*. Last.fm. Retrieved October 18, 2009, http://www.last.fm/music/Humming+Pera/+wiki/diff?&a=1&b=2

Percheron, A. (1980). Se faire entendre. In Mendras, H. (Ed.), *La sagesse et le désordre*. Paris, France: Gallimard.

Perlin, K. (1985). An image synthesizer. *SIGGRAPH Computer Graphics, 19*(3), 287–296. doi:10.1145/325165.325247

Persky, S., & Blascovich, J. (2007). Immersive virtual environments versus traditional platforms: Effects of violent and nonviolent video game play. *Media Psychology, 10*(1), 135–156.

Peters, O. (2004). *A educação a distância em transição: tendências e desafios* (p. 62). Trad. Leila Ferreira de Souza Mendes. São Leopoldo, RS: Ed. Unisinos.

Petry, L. C. (2003). *Topofilosofia: O pensamento tridimensional na hipermídia*. Tese de Doutorado, São Paulo: PUC-SP.

Pew Research Center's Internet & American Life Project. (2000-2010). *The Pew Internet & American Life Project is one of seven projects that make up the Pew Research Center, a nonpartisan, nonprofit "fact tank" that provides information on the issues, attitudes and trends shaping America and the world*. Retrieved July 2, 2010, from http://www.pewinternet.org/

Phillips, R. A. (2000). *Facilitating online discussion for interactive multimedia project management*. Heriot-Watt University and Robert Gordon University. Retrieved 20 June, 2008, from http://otis.scotcit.ac.uk/eworkshop.htm

Piaget, J. (1973). *Estudos sociológicos*. Rio de Janeiro, Brazil: Companhia Editora Forense.

Piaget, J. (1970). *A Gênese das Estruturas Lógicas Elementares. Trad. Álvaro Cabral*. Rio de Janeiro: Zahar.

Piaget, J. (1977). *A tomada de consciência*. São Paulo, Brazil: Melhoramentos/Editora da Universidade de São Paulo.

Pijnappel, J., & Abramoviç, A. (1990). Biography by Johan Pijnappel, interview Amsterdam. In Wijers, L., & Pijnappel, J. (Eds.), *Art meets science and spirituality* (pp. 54–63). London, UK: Academy Editions.

Pike, K. (1967). *Language in relation to a unified theory of the structure of human behavior*. The Hague, The Netherlands: Mouton.

Popper, K. (1980). Three worlds (lecture given April 7, 1978). In Ashby, E., Popper, K., & Hare, R. M. (Eds.), *Tanner lectures on human values* (pp. 143–167). Salt Lake City, UT: University of Utah Press.

Portnoy, D., Smoak, N., & Marsh, K. (2010). Perceiving interpersonally-mediated risk in virtual environments. *Virtual Reality (Waltham Cross), 14*(1), 67–76. doi:10.1007/s10055-009-0120-7

Porush, D. (1998). Telepathy: Alphabetic consciousness and the age of cyborg illiteracy. In Broadhurst Dixon, J., & Cassidy, E. J. (Eds.), *Virtual futures: Cyberotics, technology and posthuman pragmatism, cyberculture singularities* (pp. 45–64). London, UK & New York, NY: Routledge.

Potter, W. J., & Tomasello, T. K. (2003). Building upon the experimental design in media violence research: The importance of including receiver interpretations. *The Journal of Communication, 53*(2), 315–329. doi:10.1111/j.1460-2466.2003.tb02593.x

Powers, M. B., & Emmelkamp, P. M. (2008). Virtual reality exposure therapy for anxiety disorders: A meta-analysis. *Journal of Anxiety Disorders, 22*, 561–569. doi:10.1016/j.janxdis.2007.04.006

Prensky, M. (2006). *Don't bother me mom – I'm learning*. St Paul, MN: Paragon House.

Prensky, M. (2007). *Digital game-based learning: Practical ideas for the application of digital game-based learning*. St. Paul, MN: Paragon House.

Prensky, M. (2005). *Adopt and adapt. 21st-century schools need 21st-century technology*. Edutopia. Retrieved on July 13, 2009, from http://www.digitaldivide.net/ articles/ view.php?ArticleID=786

Prensky, M. (2009). H. sapiens digital: From digital immigrants and digital natives to digital wisdom. *Innovate, 5*(3), 1. Retrieved on August 11, 2010, from http://www.uh.cu/ static/ documents/TD/H.%20Sapiens %20Digital.pdf

Prentice, S. (2007). *The five laws of virtual worlds*. Stamford, CT: Gartner Research, Gartner Inc. Publication ID: G00148019.

Pribram, K. H. (1971). *Languages of the brain*. Englewood Cliffs, NJ: Prentice-Hall.

Priebatsch, S. (2010). *The game layer on top of the world*. Paper presented at the TED Boston. from http://www. ted.com/ talks/ seth_priebatsch_the _game_layer_on_ top_of_the_world.html

Procedural Inc. (2009). *Procedural Inc*. Retrieved on June 24, 2009, from http://www.procedural.com/

Prochaska, J. O., & DiClemente, C. C. (1983). Stages and processes of self-change of smoking: Toward an integrative model of change. *Journal of Consulting and Clinical Psychology, 51*, 390–395. doi:10.1037/0022-006X.51.3.390

Prusinkiewicz, P., Lindenmayer, A., & Hanan, J. (1988). Development models of herbaceous plants for computer imagery purposes. *ACM SIGGRAPH Computer Graphics, 22*(4), 141–150. doi:10.1145/378456.378503

Pugnetti, L., Mendozzi, L., Attree, E. A., Barbieri, E., Brooks, B. M., & Cazzullo, C. L. (1998). Probing memory and executive functions with virtual reality: Past and present studies. *Cyberpsychology & Behavior, 1*, 151–162. doi:10.1089/cpb.1998.1.151

Quaranta, D. (2007). *Remediations: Art in Second Life*. Retrieved November 6, 2010, from http://www.hz-journal. org/n11/quaranta.html

Quaranta, D. (2007, August 31). *Displaced familiarity: Interview with Scott Kildall*. In Spawn of the Surreal. Retrieved November 6, 2010, from http://spawnofthesurreal.blogspot.com/

Quaranta, D. (2008). *For God's sake!* The Spawn of the Surreal. Retrieved November 6, 2010, from http:// spawnofthesurreal.blogspot.com/

Quelle InnovationsPartner. (2007a). *Experten-Chat im Quelle ErfinderLand*. Retrieved March 1, 2009, from http://www.quelle-innovationsinitiative.de/aktu-ell_detail.php?id=18&count=6&image=18/ image18. jpg&nav1=aktuell

Quelle InnovationsPartner. (2007b). *Quelle InnovationsInitiative öffnet ErfinderLand in Second Life*. Retrieved March 1, 2009, from http://www.quelle-innovationsinitia-tive.de/aktuell_detail.php? id=15&count=6&image=15/ image15.jpg&nav1=aktuell

Quinn, C. N. (2005). *Engaging learning: Designing e-learning simulation games*. San Francisco, CA: Pfeiffer.

Rabin, L., Barr, W., & Burton, L. (2005). Assessment practices of clinical neuropsychologists in the United States and Canada: A survey of INS, NAN, and APA Division 40 members. *Archives of Clinical Neuropsychology, 20*, 33–65. doi:10.1016/j.acn.2004.02.005

Rabin, L. A., Burton, L. A., & Barr, W. B. (2007). Utilization rates of ecologically oriented instruments among clinical neuropsychologists. *The Clinical Neuropsychologist, 5*, 727–743. doi:10.1080/13854040600888776

Raichle, M. E. (2009). A paradigm shift in functional brain imaging. *The Journal of Neuroscience, 29*, 12729–12734. doi:10.1523/JNEUROSCI.4366-09.2009

Randall, T., Terwiesch, C., & Ulrich, K. T. (2005). Principles of user design of customized products. *California Management Review, 47*(4), 68–85.

Redfield, M. (1992). Book review Nicholas Royle- Telepathy and literature: The fictions of telepathy. *Surfaces, 2*, 27. Retrieved November, 6, 2010, from http://www. pum.umontreal.ca/revues/surfaces/vol2/redfield.html

Reeves, W. T. (1983). Particle systems - A technique for modeling a class of fuzzy objects. *ACM Transactions on Graphics, 2*(2), 91–108. doi:10.1145/357318.357320

Reid, E. (1999). Hierarchy and power: Social control in cyberspace. In Marc, A., & Smith, P. K. (Eds.), *Communities in cyberspace* (pp. 107–133). London, UK: Routledge.

Reinhard, C. D. (2010b). Interviews within experimental frameworks: How to make sense of sense-making in virtual worlds. *Journal of Virtual Worlds Research, 3*(1). Retrieved from http://jvwresearch.org.

Reinhard, C. D. (2008). *Gendered media engagings as user agency mediations with sociocultural and media structures: A Sense-Making Methodology study of the situationality if gender divergences and convergences.* Doctoral dissertation, Ohio State University.

Reinhard, C. D. (2010a). *Our definitions and metaphors: Discussion of how researchers and designers as users make sense of virtual world technologies.* Paper presented at Virtual Worlds Research Group International Research Workshop, June 7-9, Copenhagen.

Reinhard, C. D., & Dervin, B. (2010). *Situations of media engagings: Comparing the new and the old through sense-making.* Paper presented at the Association of Internet Researchers Conference 11.0, October 21-23, Gothenburg, Sweden.

Rettberg, S. (2008). Corporate ideology in World of Warcraft. In Corneliussen, H. G., & Rettberg, J. W. (Eds.), *Digital culture, play, and identity: A WoW reader* (pp. 19–38). Cambridge, MA: MIT Press.

Reynolds, C. W. (1987). *Flocks, herds and schools: A distributed behavioral model.* Paper presented at the 14th Annual Conference on Computer Graphics and Interactive Techniques.

Rheingold, H. (1993). *The virtual community: Homesteading on the electronic frontier.* Reading, MA: Addison-Wesley.

Rheingold, H. (1991). *Virtual reality.* London, UK: Secker & Warburg.

Rheingold, H. (1991). *Virtual reality.* New York, NY: Summit Books.

Rheingold, H. (1993). *The virtual community: Homesteading on the electronic frontier.* Reading, MA: Addison-Wesley Pub. Co.

Rheingold, H. (1999). Introduction to the virtual community. In Vitanza, V. J. (Ed.), *CyberReader* (pp. 63–94). Boston, MA: Allyn and Bacon.

Rheingold, H. (2000). *Tools for thought. The history and future of mind-expanding technology* (new edition (first edition 1985) ed.). Cambridge, MA: The MIT Press.

Rheingold. H. (2004). The virtual community: Homesteading at the electronic frontier. Retrieved from http://www.rheingold.com/vc/book

Rice, C. (2007). *The emergence of the interior: Architecture, modernity, domesticity.* London, UK: Routledge.

Rice, J. W. (2007). New media resistance: Barriers to implementation of computer video games in the classroom. *Journal of Educational Multimedia and Hypermedia, 16*(3), 249–261.

Richards, L., & Moore, J. M. (2009). *Fare ricerca qualitativa.* Milano, Italy: FrancoAngeli.

Richardson, W. (2006). *Blogs, wikis, podcasts, and other powerful web tools for classrooms.* Thousand Oaks, CA: Corwin Press.

Richter, S., Brown, S., & Mott, M. (1991). The impact of social support and self-esteem on adolescent substance abuse treatment outcome. *Journal of Substance Abuse, 3*(4), 371–385. doi:10.1016/S0899-3289(10)80019-7

Riva, G., Waterworth, J. A., & Waterworth, E. L. (2004). The layers of presence: A bio-cultural approach to understanding presence in natural and mediated environments. *Cyberpsychology & Behavior, 7*(4), 402–416. doi:10.1089/cpb.2004.7.402

Rizzo, A. A., Schultheis, M. T., Kerns, K., & Mateer, C. (2004). Analysis of assets for virtual reality applications in neuropsychology. *Neuropsychological Rehabilitation, 14*, 207–239. doi:10.1080/09602010343000183

Rizzo, A. A., Pair, J., Graap, K., Treskunov, A., & Parsons, T. D. (2006). User-centered design driven development of a VR therapy application for Iraq war combat-related post traumatic stress disorder. *Proceedings of the 2006 International Conference on Disability, Virtual Reality and Associated Technology,* (pp. 113-122).

Rizzo, A., Jarrell Pair, J., Graap, K., Manson, B., Mc-Nerney, P. J., & Wiederhold, B. ... Spira, J. (2006). A virtual reality exposure therapy application for Iraq war military personnel with post traumatic stress disorder: From training to toy to treatment. In M. Roy (Ed.), *NATO Advanced Research Workshop on Novel Approaches to the Diagnosis and Treatment of Posttraumatic Stress Disorder*, (pp. 235-250). Washington DC: IOS Press.

Robbins-Bell, S. (2008). *Using a faceted classification scheme to predict the future of virtual worlds.* Presented at the Association of Internet Research Conference, 9.0, Copenhagen, Denmark.

Roberts, A. J., & Koob, G. F. (1997). The neurobiology of addiction: An overview. *Alcohol Health and Research World, 21*(2), 101–106.

Rodrigues, N., Dionísio, M., Gonçalves, A., Magalhães, L., Moura, J. P., & Chalmers, A. (2008b). Rule-based generation of houses. *Computer Graphics & Geometry, 10*(2), 49–65.

Rodrigues, N., Dionísio, M., Gonçalves, A., Magalhães, L., Moura, J. P., & Chalmers, A. (2008a). *Incorporating legal rules on procedural house generation.* Paper presented at the Spring Conference on Computer Graphics.

Rodrigues, N., Magalhães, L., Moura, J. P., & Chalmers, A. (2007). *Geração automática de estruturas Romanas.* Paper presented at the CAA Portugal.

Rodrigues, N., Magalhães, L., Moura, J. P., & Chalmers, A. (2008). *Automatic reconstruction of virtual heritage sites.* Paper presented at the Symposium on Virtual Reality, Archaeology and Cultural Heritage (VAST 08).

Rodrigues, N., Magalhães, L., Moura, J. P., Chalmers, A., Santos, F., & Morgado, L. (2009, 24-25 September). *ArchHouseGenerator - A framework for house generation.* Paper presented at the Slactions 2009 International Conference: Life, imagination, and work using metaverse platforms, Babbage Amphiteatre, NMC Conference Center, Second Life.

Rome Reborn. (2010). *Rome Reborn.* Retrieved on June 13, 2010, from http://www.romereborn.virginia.edu/

Roschek, J. (2009). Web 2.0 als Innovationsplattform – Wie multimediale Kollaboration bei Cisco interne und externe Innovationspotenziale mobilisiert. In Zerfaß, A., & Möslein, K. M. (Eds.), *Kommunikation als Erfolgsfaktor im Innovationsmanagement* (pp. 379–389). Wiesbaden: Gabler. doi:10.1007/978-3-8349-8242-1_23

Rose, F. D., Brooks, B. M., & Rizzo, A. A. (2005). Virtual reality in brain damage rehabilitation [Review]. *Cyberpsychology & Behavior, 8,* 241–262. doi:10.1089/cpb.2005.8.241

Ross, W. D. (1967). *The right and the good.* Oxford, UK: Clarendon Press.

Rothbaum, B., Hidges, L. F., Kooper, R., Opdyke, D., Williford, J. S., & North, M. (1995). Effectiveness of computer-generated (virtual reality) graded exposure in the treatment of acrophobia. *The American Journal of Psychiatry, 152,* 626–628.

Rothbaum, B., Hodges, L., Smith, S., Lee, J. H., & Price, L. (2000). A controlled study of virtual reality exposure therapy for the fear of flying. *Journal of Consulting and Clinical Psychology, 68*(6), 1020–1026. doi:10.1037/0022-006X.68.6.1020

Rourke, L., Anderson, T., Garrison, D. R., & Archer, W. (2001). Assessing social presence in asynchronous text based computer conferencing. *Journal of Distance Education, 14*(2). Retrieved June 6, 2006, from http://cade.athabascau.ca/vol14.2/rourke_et_al.html

Ruff, R. M. (2003). A friendly critique of neuropsychology: Facing the challenges of our future. *Archives of Clinical Neuropsychology, 18,* 847–864. doi:10.1016/j.acn.2003.07.002

Ruhrberg, K., Schneckenberger, M., Fricke, C., Honnef, K., & Ingo, W. F. (2000). *Art of the 20th century.* London, UK/ Madrid, Spain/ New York, NY/ Paris, France/ Tokyo, Japan: Taschen.

RunEscape. (2008). *RunEscape.* Retrieved on May 1, 2008, from http://www.runescape.com

Ryan, M. L. (2001). *Narrative as virtual reality. Immersion and interactivity in literature and electronic media.* Baltimore, MD: The John Hopkins University Press.

Salazar, J. (2009). Analyzing social identity (re)production: Identity liminal events in mmorpgs. *Journal of Virtual Worlds Research, 1*(3), 3–22.

Salen, K., & Zimmerman, E. (Eds.). (2006). *The game design reader. A rules of play anthology.* Cambridge, MA/London, UK: The MIT Press.

Sanchez-Vives, M. V., & Slater, M. (2005). From presence to consciousness through virtual reality. *Nature Reviews. Neuroscience, 6*, 332–339. doi:10.1038/nrn1651

Sant, T. (2009). Performance in Second Life: Some possibilities for learning and teaching. In Molka-Danielsen, J., & Deutschmann, M. (Eds.), *Learning and teaching in the virtual world of Second Life* (pp. 145–166). Norway: Tapir Academic Press.

Saponaro, A. (2007). *Assignment 3: Second Life as didactic environment.* Retrieved online from http://www.ielmers.com/ saponaro/ portfolio/ ITDE8012/ Assignment_3 _SecondLifeInEducation.pdf

Saposnik, G., Teasell, R., Mamdani, M., Hall, J., McIlroy, W., & Cheung, D. (2010). Effectiveness of virtual reality using Wii gaming technology in stroke rehabilitation: A pilot randomized clinical trial and proof of principle. *Stroke, 41*(7), 1477–1484. doi:10.1161/STROKEAHA.110.584979

Sauvé, L., Renaud, L., Kaufman, D., & Marquis, J. S. (2007). Distinguishing between games and simulations: A systematic review. *Educational Technology & Society, 10*(3), 247-256. Retrieved on July 13, 2009, from http://www.ifets.info/journals /10_3/17.pdf

Saveme Oh. (2010). *Death of an avatar.* Retrieved October 19, 2010, from http://savemeoh.yolasite.com/death-of-an-avatar.php

Saveria Melissa Oh. (2010). *High heels but no soul.* Retrieved October 18, 2010, from http://www.vimeo.com/15462380

Schackman, D. (2009). Exploring the new frontiers of collaborative community. *New Media & Society, 11*(5), 875–885. doi:10.1177/1461444809106702

Schatz, P., & Browndyke, J. (2002). Applications of computer-based neuropsychological assessment. *The Journal of Head Trauma Rehabilitation, 17*, 395–410. doi:10.1097/00001199-200210000-00003

Schechner, R. (1988). Drama, script, theater and performance. In Schechner, R. (Ed.), *Performance theory.* New York, NY: Routledge.

Schell, J. (2010). *When games invade real life.* Paper presented at the DICE 2010.

Schindler, K. (2010, May 28). Life after death: An interview with Eva and Franco Mattes. *Art 21.* Retrieved October 27, 2010, from http://blog.art21.org/2010/05/28/life-after-death-an-interview-with-eva-and-franco-mattes/

Schläffer, C. (2009). Interne Innovations-Communities mit Bewegtbild-Formaten – Generierung von Innovationsideen bei der Deutschen Telekom und T-Mobile. In Zerfaß, A., & Möslein, K. M. (Eds.), *Kommunikation als Erfolgsfaktor im Innovationsmanagement* (pp. 403–413). Wiesbaden: Gabler.

Schlemmer, E. (1998). *A representação do espaço cibernético pela criança, na utilização de um ambiente virtual. Programa de Pós Graduação em Psicologia, Universidade Federal do Rio Grande do Sul. Dissertação.* Porto Alegre: Mestrado em Psicologia do Desenvolvimento.

Schlemmer, E. (2009). *Telepresença.* Curitiba: IESDE Brasil S.A.

Schlemmer, E., Trein, D., & Oliveira, C. (2009). Metaverse: Telepresence in 3D avatar-driven digital-virtual worlds. *TIC Revista D'Innovación Educativa, 2*, 26–32.

Schlemmer, E. (2005). Metodologias para Educação a Distância no Contexto da Formação de Comunidades Virtuais de Aprendizagem. In Barbosa, R. M. (Ed.), *Ambientes Virtuais de Aprendizagem* (pp. 29–49). Porto Alegre.

Schlemmer, E, (2008). ECODI – A criação de espaços de convivência digital virtual no contexto dos processos de ensino e aprendizagem em Metaverso. IHU Ideias, São Leopoldo, ano 6. n. 103 (caderno).

Schlemmer, E. (2002). AVA: Um ambiente de convivência interacionista sistêmico para comunidades virtuais na cultura da aprendizagem. Porto Alegre: URFGS. *Tese (Doutorado em Informática na Educação) Programa de Pós Graduação em Informática na Educação, Universidade Federal do Rio Grande do Sul.*

Schlemmer, E. (2005). Ambiente virtual de aprendizagem (AVA): Uma proposta para a sociedade em rede na cultura da aprendizagem. *In: Carla Beatris Valentini; Eliana Maria do Sacramento Soares. (Org.). Aprendizagem em Ambientes Virtuais: compartilhando idéias e construindo cenários*, (pp. 135-160). Caxias do Sul.

Schlemmer, E., Trein, D., & Oliveira, C. J. (2009).The metaverse: Telepresence in 3D avatar-driven digital-virtual worlds. *Revista d'Innovació Educativa, 2*, 26-32. Retrieved from http://gpedunisinos.files.wordpress.com/2009/ 03/ 02.pdf

Schmoll, P. (2000). Les mondes virtuels, entre imagerie et imaginaire. *Sociétés, 70*(4), 33–46.

Schnapp, J. T., & Shanks, M. (2009). Artereality (Rethinking craft in knowledge economy). In Maddoff, S. H. (Ed.), *Art school (Propositions for the 21st century)* (pp. 141–157). Cambridge, MA: MIT Press.

Schroeder, R. (2008). Virtual worlds research: Past, present & future. *Journal of Virtual Worlds Research, 1*(1).

Schubert, T., Friedmann, F., & Regenbrecht, H. (2001). The experience of presence: Factor analytic insights. *Presence (Cambridge, Mass.), 10*, 266–281. doi:10.1162/105474601300343603

Schubert, T., Friedmann, F., & Regenbrecht, H. (1999). Embodied presence in virtual environments. In Paton, R., & Neilson, I. (Eds.), *Visual representations and interpretations* (pp. 268–278). London, UK: Springer-Verlag.

Schultze, M. (2008). *EnBW, Director CRM und New Media*. Telephone Interview, April 25, 2008.

Schwandt, T. A. (2000). Three epistemological stances for qualitative inquiry: Interpretivism, hermeneutics, and social constructionism. In Denzin, N. K., & Lincoln, Y. S. (Eds.), *Handbook of qualitative research* (2nd ed., pp. 189–213). Thousand Oaks, CA: Sage Publications.

Scotti, E., & Sica, R. (2007). *Community management. Processi informali, social networking e tecnologie Web 2.0 per la gestione della conoscenza nelle organizzazioni*. Roma: Apogeo.

Second Front. (2010). *The pioneering performance art group in Second Life*. Retrieved November 4, 2010, from http://www.secondfront.org

Second Life. (2010). *Second Life destination guide*. Retrieved November 4, 2010, from http://secondlife.com/destinations

Second Opinion. (2006). *Infinite vision media. Expressing brands in 3D*. Retrieved March 2, 2009, from http://secondlife.com/newsletter/2006_12/html/developer.html

SecondLife. (2009). *Second Life*. Retrieved on July 29, 2009, from http://secondlife.com/

Seidel, I., & Berger, H. (2007). *Integrating electronic institutions with 3D virtual worlds*. Paper presented at the 2007 IEEE/WIC/ACM International Conference on Intelligent Agent Technology.

Seipp, B. (2008). *Den neuen Hotelmarken in die Betten geguckt*. Retrieved March 1, 2009, from www.welt.de/reise/article2573514/Den-neuen-Hotelmarken-in-die-Betten-geguckt.html

Serres, M., & Sauer, K. L. (2006).*Atlas*. Berlin, Germany: Verl. für das Künstlerbuch.

Shaffer, D. W. (2007).*How computer games help children learn*. Palgrave Macmillan.

Shin, D. (2009). The evaluation of user experience of the virtual world in relation to extrinsic and intrinsic motivation. *International Journal of Human-Computer Interaction, 25*(6), 530–553. doi:10.1080/10447310902963951

Siddiqi, S., Mama, S., & Lee, R. E. (in press). Developing an obesity prevention intervention in networked virtual environments: The international health challenge in Second Life. *Journal of Virtual Worlds Research*.

Sihvonen, T. (2009). *Players unleashed! Modding The Sims and the culture of gaming*. Doctoral dissertation, University of Turku, Finland.

Silva, F., Rodrigues, D., & Gonçalves, A. (2004). *House of the skeletons - A virtual way*. Paper presented at the XXXII CAA - Computer Applications and Quantitative Methods to Archaeology Conference.

Silverman, D. (2000). Analyzing talk and text. In Denzin, N. K., & Lincoln, Y. S. (Eds.), *Handbook of qualitative research* (2nd ed., pp. 189–213). Thousand Oaks, CA: Sage Publications.

Silverstein, S. M., Berten, S., & Olson, P. (2007). Development and validation of a World Wide Web-based neurocognitive assessment battery: WebNeuro. *Behavior Research Methods*, *39*, 940–949. doi:10.3758/BF03192989

Silverstone, R. (2007). *Media & morality: On the rise of the Mediapolis*. Cambridge, MA: Polity Press.

Silverstone, R. (2003). Proper distance: Towards an ethics for cyberspace. In Liestøl, G., Morrison, A., & Terje, R. (Eds.), *Digital media revisited: Theoretical and conceptual innovations in digital domains* (pp. 469–491). Cambridge, MA: MIT Press.

Simon, H. (1977). *Models of discovery*. Dortrecht, Holland: Reidel.

Sims, R. (2006). Beyond instructional design: Making learning design a reality. *Journal of Learning Design*, *1*(2), 1–7. Retrieved from http://www.jld.qut.edu.au/ publications/ vol1no2/ documents/ beyond% 20instructional% 20design.pdf.

Sivunen, A., & Siitonen, M. (2010). *Comparing experiences on leadership in virtual teams and online multiplayer gaming clans*. Paper presented at the International Communication Association Conference, June 2010, Singapore.

Slater, M., Perez-Marcos, D., Ehrsson, H. H., & Sanchez-Vives, M. (2008). Towards a digital body: The virtual arm illusion. *Frontiers in Human Neuroscience*, *2*, 6. doi:10.3389/neuro.09.006.2008

Sloterdijk, P. (2008). Excerpts from Spheres III: Foams. *Harvard Design Magazine*, *29*, 38–52.

Smith, M., & Berge, Z. L. (2009, June). Social learning theory in Second Life. *MERLOT Journal of Online Learning and Teaching*, *5*(2), 439-445. Retrieved from http:// jolt.merlot.org/ vol5no2/ berge_0609.pdf

Smurda, J., & Haselton, M. G. (2002). *Effects of relationship status and sexual strategy on perceptions of rivals' sexual intent: Preliminary evidence for the interloper effect*. Paper presented at the Human Behaviour and Evolution Society Conference.

Smyth, J. M. (2007). Beyond self-selection in video game play: An experimental examination of the consequences of massively multiplayer online role-playing game play. *Cyberpsychology & Behavior*, *10*(5), 717–721. doi:10.1089/cpb.2007.9963

Snelson, C. (2008). Web-based video in education: Possibilities and pitfalls. *Proceedings of the Technology, Colleges & Community Worldwide Online Conference*, (pp. 214-221). Retrieved from http://etec.hawaii.edu/ proceedings/ 2008/ Snelson2008.pdf

Snow, C. E., & Hoefnagel-Höhle, M. (1978). The critical period for language acquisition: Evidence from second language learning. *Child Development*, *49*(4), 1114–1128. doi:10.2307/1128751

Snow, D. (2001). Collective identity and expressive forms. In Smelser, N. J., & Baltes, P. B. (Eds.), *International encyclopedia of the social and behavioral sciences* (pp. 2212–2219). London, UK: Elsevier Science.

Snowdon, D., Churchill, E. F., & Munro, A. J. (2001). Collaborative virtual environments: Digital spaces and places for CSCW: An introduction. In Churchill, E. F., Snowdon, D. N., & Munro, A. J. (Eds.), *Collaborative virtual environments: Digital places and spaces for interaction* (pp. 3–17). London, UK: Springer-Verlag.

Sony Ericsson. (2007). *Sony Ericsson builds at Second Life*. Retrieved March 13, 2007, from http://www.sonyericsson-secondlife.com/downloads/Pressemitteilung_Second%20Life_CeBIT_ English.pdf, press release

Sperber, D. (1996). *Explaining culture: A naturalistic approach*. London, UK: Blackwell Publishing.

Sperber, D., & Wilson, D. (1986). *Relevance: Communication and cognition*. Oxford, UK: Basil Blackwell.

Squire, K. (2002). Cultural framing of computer/video games. *The International Journal of Computer Game Research*, *2*(1). Retrieved on July 13, 2009, from http:// www.gamestudies.org/ 0102/squire/

Stein, E. (2003). *Nas proximidades da antropologia: Ensaios e conferências filosóficas*. Ijuí. Editora UNIJUÍ.

Steinkuhler, C., & Williams, D. (2006). Where everybody knows your (screen) name: Online games as third places. *Journal of Computer-Mediated Communication*, *11*(4), 885–909. doi:10.1111/j.1083-6101.2006.00300.x

Sterba, K., Rabius, V., Villars, P., Wiatrek, D., & McAlister, A. L. (2009, April). *Dyadic efficacy in partnered smokers motivated to quit*. Poster session presented at the 30th Meeting of the Society for Behavioral Medicine, Montreal, Canada.

Sternberg, R. J. (1997). Intelligence and lifelong learning: What's new and how can we use it? *The American Psychologist, 52*, 1134–1139. doi:10.1037/0003-066X.52.10.1134

Stevens, J. R., & Hauser, M. D. (2004). Why be nice? Psychological constraints on the evolution of cooperation. *Trends in Cognitive Sciences, 8*, 60–65. doi:10.1016/j.tics.2003.12.003

Stiles, K. (2003). Anomaly, sky, sex, and Psi in Fluxus. In Hendricks, G. (Ed.), *Critical mass: Happenings, Fluxus, performance, intermedia and Rutgers University 1958-1972* (pp. 60–88). Nebraska and New Jersey: Rutgers University Press.

Stone, A. R. (1998). *The war of desire and technology at the close of the mechanical age*. Cambridge, MA: MIT Press.

Stone, A. R. (1991). Will the real body please stand up? In Benedikt, M. (Ed.), *Cyberspace: First steps* (pp. 81–118). Cambridge, MA: MIT Press.

Strecher Victor, J., Shiffman, S., & West, R. (2005). Randomized controlled trial of a Web based computer-tailored smoking cessation program as a supplement to nicotine patch therapy. *Addiction (Abingdon, England), 100*(5), 682–688. doi:10.1111/j.1360-0443.2005.01093.x

Stroulia, E., Chodos, D., Boers, N. M., Huang, J., Gburzynski, P., & Nikolaidis, I. (2009). Software engineering for health education and care delivery systems: The smart condo project. *Proceedings of the 2009 ICSE Workshop on Software Engineering in Health Care*, (pp. 20-28).

Sturm, L. P., Windsor, J. A., Cosman, P. H., Cregan, P., Hewett, P. J., & Maddern, G. J. (2008). A systematic review of skills transfer after surgical simulation training. *Annals of Surgery, 248*(2), 166–179. doi:10.1097/SLA.0b013e318176bf24

Suh, K. S., & Chang, S. (2006). User interfaces and consumer perceptions of online stores: The role of telepresence. *Behaviour & Information Technology, 25*(2), 99–113. doi:10.1080/01449290500330398

Sundbo, J. (2001). *The strategic management of innovation: A sociological and economic theory*. Cheltenham, UK: Edward Elgar.

Sundbo, J. (2001). *The theory of innovation: Entrepreneurs, technology and strategy*. Cheltenham, UK: Edward Elgar.

Sundstedt, V., Chalmers, A., & Martinez, P. (2004). *High fidelity reconstruction of the ancient Egyptian temple of Kalabsha*. Paper presented at the 3rd International Conference on Computer Graphics, Virtual Reality, Visualisation and Interaction in Africa.

Süss, D. (2006). Socialization and media. In J. Jensen Arnett (Ed.), *Encyclopedia of children, adolescents, and the media*. SAGE Publications. Retrieved from http://www.sage-ereference.com/ childmedia/ Article_n419.html

Svanaes, D., & Verplank, W. (2000). In search of metaphors for tangible user interfaces. Designing augmented reality environments. In *Proceedings of DARE 2000 on Designing Augmented Reality Environment* (pp. 121-129). New York, NY: ACM.

Szuchewycz, B. (1995). Power in language: Verbal communication and social influence. *Canadian Journal of Communication, 20*(2). Retrieved May 29, 2008, from http://www.cjc-online.ca/index.php/journal/article/view/874/780

Tajfel, H., & Turner, J. C. (1986). The social identity theory of intergroup behavior. In Worchel, S., & Austin, W. (Eds.), *Psychology of intergroup relations* (pp. 7–24). Chicago, IL: Nelson-Hall.

Tarde de, G. (2003). *Les lois de l'imitation, étude sociologique*. Book Surge Publishing.

Tavinor, G. (2005). Video games, fiction, and emotion. In Y. Pisan (Ed.), *The Second Australasian Conference on Interactive Entertainment* (pp. 201-206). Sidney, Australia: University of Technology, Sydney.

Taylor, T. L. (2006). *Play between worlds: Exploring online game culture*. Cambridge, MA: The MIT Press.

Taylor, T. L. (2006). *Play between worlds. Exploring online game culture*. Cambridge, MA & London, UK: MIT Press.

Taylor, C. (1989). *Sources of the self: The making of the modern identity*. Cambridge, MA: Harvard University Press.

Taylor, C. (1989). *Sources of the self: The making of modern identity*. Cambridge, MA: Harvard University Press.

Taylor, T. L. (2006). *Play between worlds: Exploring online game culture*. Cambridge, MA: MIT Press.

Taylor, T. L. (2002). Living digitally: Embodiment in virtual worlds. In Schroeder, R. (Ed.), *The social life of avatars: Presence and interaction in shared virtual environments* (pp. 40–62). London, UK: Springer.

Tedeschi, B. (2007, June 11). Awaiting real sales from virtual shoppers, e-commerce report. *The New York Times*. Retrieved February 28, 2009, from www.nytimes.com/2007/06/11/business/ 11ecom.html

Thatcher, M. (2005, March 15). The back page (vol. 16). Q&A with Chris Dede. *Tech&Learning*. Retrieved from http://www.techlearning.com/ article/ 3704

Thomas, W., & Stammermann, L. (2007). Der Markt für In-Game Advertising. In W. Thomas & L. Stammermann (Eds.), *In-Game Advertising – Werbung in Computerspielen* (pp. 11-25). Wiesbaden: Gabler.

Thompson, C. W., & Hagstrom, F. (2008). Modeling healthcare logistics in a virtual world. *IEEE Internet Computing, 12*(5), 100–104. doi:10.1109/MIC.2008.106

Tisseron, S. (dir.). (2006). *L'enfant au risque du virtuel*. Paris, France: Dunod.

Toffler, A. (1980). *The third wave (Vol. 1)*. New York, NY: Morrow.

Tonéis, C. N., & Petry, L. C. (2008). Experiências matemáticas no contexto de jogos eletrônicos. *Ciências & Cognição, 13*(3), 300-317. Retrieved from http://www.cienciasecognicao.org/ pdf/ v13_3/ m318317.pdf

Tönnies, F., & Harris, J. (2001). *Community and civil society*. Cambridge, UK/ New York, NY: Cambridge University Press.

Toomey, M. (2000). The power of language. In M. Toomey (Ed.), *Liberation psychology: The choice of intimacy not conquest*. Retrieved May 29, 2008 from http://www.mtoomey.com/book_language.html

Toro-Troconis, M. and Mellström, U. (2010), Game-based learning in Second Life®. Do gender and age make a difference?, *Journal of Gaming and Virtual Worlds* 2:1, pp. 53-76, doi: 10.1386/jgvw.2.1.53_1

Toro-Troconis, M., Mellström, U., Partridge, M., Meeran, K., Barrett, M., & Higham, J. (2008). Designing game-based learning activities for virtual patients in Second Life. *Journal of CyberTherapy and Rehabilitation* 1(3):227–239. Retrieved on July 13, 2009, from http://www1.imperial.ac.uk/ resources/62DCE340-6816-4254-B4C0-03A16B54EF0A/

Toumi, I. (2002). *Networks of innovation*. Oxford, UK: University Press.

Trein, D. (2010). *Educação online em metaverso: a mediação pedagógica por meio da telepresença via avatar em MDV3D*. Master Thesis, Universidade do Vale do Rio dos Sinos - Unisinos, São Leopoldo-RS, Brasil.

Trommsdorff, V., & Steinhoff, F. (2007). *Innovationsmarketing*. München: Vahlen.

Trompenaars, F. (1995). *The seven cultures of capitalism*. Piatkus Books.

Tronstad, R. (2008). Character identification in World of Warcraft: The relationship between capacity and appearance. In Corneliussen, H., & Rettberg, J. (Eds.), *Digital culture, play and identity: A World of Warcraft® reader* (pp. 249–263). Cambridge, MA: MIT Press.

Turkle, S. (1995). *Life on the screen: Identity in the age of the Internet*. New York, NY: Simon & Schuster.

Turkle, S. (1984). *The second self: Computers and the human spirit*. New York, NY: Simon and Schuster.

Turkle, S. (1996). Who am we? We are moving from modernist calculation toward postmodernist simulation, where the self is a multiple, distributed system. *Wired, 4*(1), 148.

Turkle, S. (1995). *Life on the screen: Identity in the age of the Internet*. New York, NY: Touchstone.

Turkle, S. (1997). *Life on the screen: Identity in the age of the Internet*. New York, NY: Touchstone.

Turkle, S. (1999). Fronteiras do real e do virtual. Entrevista concedida a Federico Casalegno. In *Revista FAMECOS, 11*, dezembro.

Turner, J. O. (2006). *Onto Distro's official Yahoo time capsule speech*. Retrieved November 4, 2010, from http://video.google.com/videoplay?doc id=7699712386719429816# Turner, J. O. (2010a). *In memory of Wirxli FlimFlam (2006-2010)*. May 2007. Retrieved October 17, 2010, from http://wirxliflimflam.blogspot.com/2007_05_01_archive.html

Turner, J. O. (2010b). *Jeremy Owen Turner's classic blogs*. Retrieved October 29, 2010, from http://classicblogs.blogspot.com/

Turner, J. O. (2010c). *Last exit – Ars virtua*. Retrieved November 1, 2010, from http://www.youtube.com/watch?v=q6DmzPrmH3A

Turner, J. O. (2010d). *Qyxxql Merlin's LiveJournal*. Retrieved October 17, 2010, from http://qyxxql-merlin.livejournal.com/

U.S. Department of Health & Human Services – Center for Medicare and MedicAid Services. (2009). *Medicaid program - General information*. Retrieved from http://www.cms.gov/MedicaidGenInfo/

Unity3D. (2010). *UNITY: Game development tool*. Retrieved on June 14, 2010, from http://unity3d.com/

Van Dijk, T. (1990). Social cognition and discourse. In Giles, H., & Robinson, W. P. (Eds.), *Handbook of language and social psychology* (pp. 163–183). Chichester, UK: John Wiley & Sons.

Van Dijk, T. (2001). Multidisciplinary CDA: A plea for diversity. In Wodak, R., & Meyer, M. (Eds.), *Methods in critical discourse analysis* (pp. 95–120). London, UK: Sage.

Van Kleef, G. A., De Dreu, C. K. W., & Manstead, A. S. R. (2004). The interpersonal effects of anger and happiness in negotiations. *Journal of Personality and Social Psychology, 86*, 57–76. doi:10.1037/0022-3514.86.1.57

Van Leeuwen, T. (2008). *Discourse and practice: New tools for critical discourse analysis*. New York, NY: Oxford University Press.

Veen, W., & Vrakking, B. (2006). *Homo zappiens. Growing up in a digital age*. London, UK: Network Continuum Education.

Venturi, R. (2002). *Complexity and contradiction in architecture*. New York, NY: The Museum of Modern Art.

Virilio, P. (1996). *Cybermonde, la politique du pire: Entretien avec Philippe Petit*. Paris, NY: Editions Textuel.

Virtual Fluxus. (2010). *Virtual Fluxus*. Retrieved October 28, 2010, from http://www.mefeedia.com/watch/33503241

Volkow, N. D. (2007). *Addiction and the brain's pleasure pathway: Beyond willpower*. HBO. Retrieved from http://www.hbo.com/addiction/ understanding_addiction/12_pleasure_pathway.html

Voulgari, I., & Komis, V. (2010). "Elven Elder LVL59 LFP/RB. Please PM me": Immersion, collaborative tasks and problem-solving in massively multiplayer online games. *Learning, Media and Technology, 35*(2), 171–202. doi:10.1080/17439884.2010.494429

Wadley, G. (2008). Talking and building: Two studies of collaboration in Second Life. *Workshop on virtual worlds, collaboration, and workplace productivity, at CSCW, San Diego*.

Wadley, G., Gibbs, M. R., & Ducheneaut, N. (2009). *You can be too rich: Mediated communication in a virtual world*. Paper presented at OZCHI 2009, November 23-27, 2009, Melbourne, Australia.

Wagner, C. (2008). Learning experience with virtual worlds. *Journal of Information Systems Education, 19*(3), 4.

Walker, V., & Rockinson-Szapkiw, A. (2009). Educational opportunities for clinical counseling simulations in Second Life. *Innovate, 5*(5). Retrieved from http://www.innovateonline.info/ index.php? view=article& id=711

Wallace, P., & Maryott, J. (2009). The impact of avatar self-representation on collaboration in virtual worlds. *Innovate, 5*(5). Retrieved from http://www.innovateonline.info/ index.php? view=article& id=689

Walshe, D. G., Lewis, E. J., Kim, S. I., O'Sullivan, K., & Wiederhold, B. K. (2003). Exploring the use of computer games and virtual reality in exposure therapy for fear of driving following a motor vehicle *accident. CyberPsychology & Behavior: The Impact of the Internet. Multimedia and Virtual Reality on Behavior and Society, 6*(3), 329–334.

Walton, K. (1993). *Mimesis as make-believe.* London, UK: Harvard University Press.

Wang, F. Y. (2007). Toward a paradigm shift in social computing: The ACP approach. *IEEE Intelligent Systems, 22,* 65–67. doi:10.1109/MIS.2007.4338496

Wankel, C., & Kingsley, J. (2009). *Higher education in virtual worlds: Teaching and learning in Second Life.* Bingley, UK: Emerald Group Publishing Limited.

Wankel, C., & Kingsley, J. (2009). *Higher education in virtual worlds: Teaching and learning in Second Life.* United Kingdom: Emerald Group Publishing Limited.

Warner, M. (2006). *Phantasmagoria: Spirit vision, metaphors and media into the twenty-first century.* Oxford, UK: Oxford University Press.

Waters, J. K. (2009, January 1). A Second Life for educators. *THE Journal.* Retrieved from http://thejournal.com/ Articles/ 2009/ 01/ 01/ A-Second-Life-For-Educators. aspx? Page=1

Waterworth, J. A., Waterworth, E. L., Mantovani, F., & Riva, G. (2010). On feeling (the) present. *Journal of Consciousness Studies, 17*(1–2).

Watson, B., Müller, P., Wonka, P., Sexton, C., Veryovka, O., & Fuller, A. (2008). Procedural urban modeling in practice. *IEEE Computer Graphics and Applications, 28*(3), 18–26. doi:10.1109/MCG.2008.58

Watson, J. B. (1912). Psychology as the behaviorist views it. *Psychological Review, 20,* 158–177. doi:10.1037/ h0074428

Weber, M. (1976). *The Protestant ethic and the spirit of capitalism* (2nd ed.). London, UK: George Allen & Unwin.

Weber, R., Ritterfeld, U., & Mathiak, K. (2006). Does playing violent video games induce aggression? Empirical evidence of a functional magnetic resonance imaging study. *Media Psychology, 8,* 39–60. doi:10.1207/ S1532785XMEP0801_4

Weisner, C., Mertens, J., Tam, T., & Moore, C. (2001). Factors affecting the initiation of substance abuse treatment in managed care. *Addiction (Abingdon, England), 96*(5), 705–716. doi:10.1046/j.1360-0443.2001.9657056.x

Weissberg, J.-L. (2000). *Présences à distance. Déplacement virtuel et réseaux numériques: Pourquoi nous ne croyons plus la télévision?* Paris, France: L'Harmattan, collection Communication et civilisation.

Weitz, S. (1979). *Nonverbal communication: Readings with commentary.* New York, NY: Oxford University Press.

Wenger, E. (2006). *Comunità di pratica. Apprendimento, significato, identità.* Milano, Italy: Raffaello Cortina.

Wenger, E., Mcdermott, R., & Snyder, W. (2007). *Coltivare comunità di pratica.* Milano, Italy: Guerini e Associati.

Wenger, E. (2010). *Communities of practice: A brief introduction.* Retrieved from http://www.ewenger.com/ theory/index.htm

Wertheim, M., & Leonard, A. (1999). The pearly gates of cyberspace: A history of space from Dante to the Internet. *The New York Times Book Review,* p. 12.

Westall, R., Perkey, M. N., & Chute, D. L. (1989). Millisecond timing on Apple's Macintosh revisited. *Behavior Research Methods, Instruments, & Computers, 21,* 540–547. doi:10.3758/BF03202886

Weusijana, B. V., Svihla, D. G., & Bransford, J. (2009). MUVEs and experiential learning: Some examples. *Innovate, 5*(5). Retrieved from http://www.innovateonline. info/ index.php? view=article& id=702

Whelan, D. L. (2005). Let the games begin! *School Library Journal, 51*(4), 40–43.

Whitlock, E. P., Polen, M. R., Green, C. A., Orleans, T., & Klein, J. (2004). Behavioral counseling interventions in primary care to reduce risky/harmful alcohol use by adults: A summary of the evidence for the U.S. Preventive Services Task Force. *Annals of Internal Medicine, 140*(7), 557–568.

Widdicombe, S., & Wooffitt, R. (1995). *The language of youth subcultures.* London, UK: Harvester Wheatsheaf.

Wilkens, A. (2006). *IBM weitet Aktivitäten auf „Second Life" aus.* heise.de. Retrieved January 3, 2009, from http://www.heise.de/newsticker/IBM-weitet-Aktivitaeten-auf-Second-Life-aus--/meldung/82490

Williams, D. (in press). The mapping principle, and a research framework for virtual worlds. *Communication Theory.*

Williams, B. (1976). *Morality: An introduction to ethics.* Cambridge, UK: Cambridge University Press.

Williams, D., Ducheneaut, N., Xiong, L., Yee, N., & Nickell, N. (2006). From tree houses to barracks: The social life of guilds in World of Warcraft. *Games and Culture, 1*(4), 338–361. doi:10.1177/1555412006292616

Willmott, J., Wright, L. I., Arnold, D. B., & Day, A. M. (2001). *Rendering of large and complex urban environments for real time heritage reconstructions.* Paper presented at the conference on Virtual reality, archaeology, and cultural heritage.

Wilson, B. A. (1993). Ecological validity of neuropsychological assessment: Do neuropsychological indexes predict performance in everyday activities? *Applied & Preventive Psychology, 2,* 209–215. doi:10.1016/S0962-1849(05)80091-5

Winter, M. (2010). *Second Life education in New Zealand: Evaluation research final report.* New Zealand: CORE Education. Retrieved 5th July 2010, from http://slenz.files.wordpress.com /2010/03/slenz-final-report-2_-080310cca.pdf

Wolfendale, J. (2007). My avatar, my self: Virtual harm and attachment. *Ethics and Information Technology, 9,* 111–119. doi:10.1007/s10676-006-9125-z

Wonka, P., Wimmer, M., Sillion, F., & Ribarsky, W. (2003). Instant architecture. *ACM Transactions on Graphics, 22*(3), 669–677. doi:10.1145/882262.882324

Wonka, P., Wimmer, M., Zhou, K., Maierhofer, S., Hesina, G., & Reshetov, A. (2006). *Guided visibility sampling.* Paper presented at the ACM SIGGRAPH.

Woo, E. (2008). Computerized neuropsychological assessments. *CNS Spectrums, 13,* 14–17.

Wood, D. P., Wiederhold, B. K., & Spira, J. (2010). Lessons learned from 350 virtual reality sessions with warriors diagnosed with combat-related posttraumatic stress disorder. *Cyberpsychology, Behavior, and Social Networking, 13*(1), 3–11. doi:10.1089/cyber.2009.0396

Woodcock, B. (2008). *MMOG chart.* Retrieved on April 21, 2008, from http://www.mmogchart.com/Chart8.html

World of Warcraft. (2010). *World of Warcraft.* Retrieved on May 1, 2010, from http://www.worldofwarcraft.com

Yamagishi, T., Tanida, S., Mashima, R., Shimoma, E., & Kanazawa, S. (2003). You can judge a book by its cover: Evidence that cheaters may look different from cooperators. *Evolution and Human Behavior, 24,* 290–301. doi:10.1016/S1090-5138(03)00035-7

Yee, N., & Bailenson, J. (2007). The Proteus effect: The effect of transformed self representation on behavior. *Human Communication Research, 33,* 271–290. doi:10.1111/j.1468-2958.2007.00299.x

Yee, N., Bailenson, J. N., Urbanek, M., Chang, F., & Merget, D. (2007). The unbearable likeness of being digital: The persistence of nonverbal social norms in online virtual environments. *Cyberpsychology & Behavior, 10,* 115–121. doi:10.1089/cpb.2006.9984

Yee, N., Ellis, J., & Ducheneaut, N. (2009). The tyranny of embodiment. *Artifact, 2,* 1–6.

Yee, N., Bailenson, J. N., Urbanek, M., Chang, F., & Merget, D. (2007). The unbearable likeness of being digital: The persistence of nonverbal social norms in online virtual environments. *The Journal of CyberPsychology and Behavior, 10,* 115–121. doi:10.1089/cpb.2006.9984

Yee, N., & Bailenson, J. (2007). The Proteus effect: The effect of transformed self-representation on behavior. *Human Communication Research, 33,* 271–290. doi:10.1111/j.1468-2958.2007.00299.x

Yee, N., & Bailenson, J. N. (2009). The difference between being and seeing: The relative contribution of self-perception and priming to behavioral changes via digital self-representation. *Media Psychology, 12*(2), 195–209. doi:10.1080/15213260902849943

Yee, N., & Bailenson, J. N. (2007). The Proteus effect: The effect of transformed self-representation on behavior. *Human Communication Research, 33*, 271–290. doi:10.1111/j.1468-2958.2007.00299.x

Yee, N., Bailenson, J. N., Urbanek, M., Chang, F., & Merget, D. (2007). The unbearable likeness of being digital: The persistence of nonverbal social norms in online virtual environments. *Cyberpsychology & Behavior, 10*, 115–121. doi:10.1089/cpb.2006.9984

Yee, N. (2006). The psychology of MMORPGs: Emotional investment, motivations, relationship formation, and problematic usage. In Schroeder, R., & Axelsson, A. (Eds.), *Avatars at work and play: Collaboration and interaction in shared virtual environments* (pp. 187–207). London, UK: Springer-Verlag.

Yee, N. (2007). *The Proteus Effect: Behavioral modification via transformations of digital self-representation.* Unpublished PhD thesis, Stanford University, USA.

Yee, N. (2007). *The Proteus effect. Behavioral modification via transformations of the digital-self representation.* Unpublished Doctoral Thesis presented to the Department of Communication and the Committee of Graduate Studies of Stanford University.

Yerkes, R. M. (1917). Behaviorism and genetic psychology. *Journal of Philosophy, Psychology, and Scientific Methods, 14*, 154–160. doi:10.2307/2940700

Yoakum, C. S., & Yerkes, R. M. (1920). *Army mental tests.* New York, NY: Holt. doi:10.1037/11054-000

Younes, M., Hill, J., Quinless, J., Kilduff, M., Peng, B., & Cook, S. (2007). Internet-based cognitive testing in multiple sclerosis. *Multiple Sclerosis, 13*, 1011–1019. doi:10.1177/1352458507077626

Young, J. R. (2010, February 14). After frustrations in Second Life, colleges look to new virtual worlds. *The Chronicle of Higher Education.* Retrieved from http://chronicle.com/ article/ After-Frustrations-in-Second/ 64137/

Zackariasson, P., & Wilson, T. L. (2010). Paradigm shifts in the video game industry. *Competitiveness Review, 20*, 139–151.

Zerfaß, A. (2005a). Innovation readiness. A framework for enhancing corporations and regions by innovation communication. *Innovation Journalism, 2*(8), 1–27.

Zerfaß, A., & Möslein, K. (2009). *Kommunikation als Erfolgsfaktor im Innovationsmanagement: Strategien im Zeitalter der Open Innovation.* Wiesbaden: Gabler. doi:10.1007/978-3-8349-8242-1

Zerfaß, A., Swaran, S., & Huck, S. (2004). Kommunikation von Innovationen. Neue Ideen und Produkte erfolgreich positionieren. *Kommunikationsmanager, 1*(2), 56–58.

Zerfaß, A., Sandhu, S., & Huck, S. (2004). Innovationskommunikation. Strategisches Handlungsfeld für Corporate Communications. In Bentele, G., Piwinger, M., & Schönborg, G. (Eds.), *Kommunikationsmanagement.* Loseblattwerk.

Zerfaß, A., & Huck, S. (2007). Innovationskommunikation: Neue Produkte, Technologien und Ideen erfolgreich positionieren. In Piwinger, M., & Zerfaß, A. (Eds.), *Handbuch Unternehmenskommunikation* (pp. 847–858). Wiesbaden: Gabler.

Zerfaß, A. (2009). Kommunikation als konstitutives Element im Innovationsmanagement – Soziologische und kommunikationswissenschaftliche Grundlagen der Open Innovation. In Zerfaß, A., & Möslein, K. M. (Eds.), *Kommunikation als Erfolgsfaktor im Innovationsmanagement. Strategien im Zeitalter der Open Innovation* (pp. 23–56). Wiesbaden: Gabler. doi:10.1007/978-3-8349-8242-1

Zerfaß, A. (2005b). Innovationsmanagement und Innovationskommunikation. Erfolgsfaktor für Unternehmen und Region. In C. Mast & A. Zerfaß (Eds.), *Neue Ideen erfolgreich durchsetzen. Das Handbuch der Innovationskommunikation* (pp. 16-42). Frankfurt a. M.: Frankfurter Allgemeine Buch.

About the Contributors

Nelson Zagalo is Assistant Professor at the University of Minho (UM). He got his PhD in Communication Technology from the University of Aveiro about new interaction paradigms in virtual environments. He is member of the board of directors of the Master of Technology and Digital Art at UM and of the Center for Communication and Society Studies. He co-chairs the research group EngageLab at Computer Graphics Center and chairs the Portuguese Society of Videogame Sciences. He has more than forty peer-reviewed publications in the fields of film, videogames, interactive storytelling, and emotion and has chaired the Digital Games 2008 – National Research Conference; the SLACTIONS 2009 International Conference: Life, imagination, and work using metaverse platforms; and the ICIDS2009 - 2nd International Conference on Interactive Digital Storytelling. Nelson is the author of the book "Interactive Emotions, from Film to Videogames" (2009).

Leonel Morgado is an Assistant Professor at the University of Trás-os-Montes e Alto Douro, in Portugal, where he lectures on programming and the use of virtual worlds. His main research interest is the use of virtual worlds as tools for learning and business. Before pursuing an academic career, he was terminologist for a MS Office 97 localization team, a manager of Web-development and software-deployment teams, a business technical manager, and a programmer.

Ana Boa-Ventura is a researcher at the University of Texas at Austin. She has managed several international projects aiming at the design and promotion of virtual professional collaboration. Boa-Ventura has worked with digital storytelling (DST) in various contexts of practice research in the metaverse. Her research on virtual communities for tobacco cessation intersects with storytelling to the extent that stories are at the basis of community and trust building. Boa-Ventura designed two interactive platforms for the Portuguese Ministry of Health: for the promotion of breast-feeding and of tobacco cessation. In Portugal, she co-founded Media Shots, a Portuguese organization that works with corporations in the design and implementation of innovative programs in the area of corporate social responsibility (CSR). These include strategic and community–oriented digital storytelling, as well as other social media driven solutions to leverage social intervention by ONGs and corporations in a time of recession.

* * *

Benjamin Gregor Aas was born in 1980, in Bamberg, a rural part of southern Germany as the second of three brothers. In 1999 he received 'Abitur' at the Dientzenhofer-Gymnasium Bamberg. After a year of fulfilling social service at a school for disabled children, he entered the Otto-Friedrich Universität Bamberg, to study German language and geography. After receiving 'Vordiplom' in both subjects, he visited the Universiteit I Bergen, Norway, where his interest in psychology grew, which eventually resulted in moving to Amsterdam, The Netherlands, in 2004, where he is currently about to finish a double Master's of science in psychology (clinical and research Master). His widespread interests and production range from new research paradigms as virtual worlds and complex systems theory, to literature, basketball, and art.

Joke Bauwens is professor of Media Sociology at the Department of Media and Communication Studies, Free University of Brussels (VUB). Her research activities, situated in the research groups CEMESO (Centre for Studies on Media and Culture) and IBBT-SMIT, involve young people's media use, and morality and media use. In Belgium she coordinated a research on teenagers' ICT usage and the entailed risks and opportunities (Cyberteens, Cyberrisks, Cybertools, published in 2009). She is also Belgian team member of the EU Kids Online research network.

Alan Chalmers is a Professor of Visualisation at the International Digital Laboratory, WMG, University of Warwick, UK. He has an MSc with distinction from Rhodes University, 1985 and a PhD from University of Bristol, 1991. He has published over 200 papers in journals and international conferences on high-fidelity graphics, multi-sensory perception, High Dynamic Range (HDR) imaging, virtual archaeology, and parallel rendering. He is Honorary President of Afrigraph and a former Vice President of ACM SIGGRAPH. He is the Founder and a Director of the spin-off company, goHDR Ltd., which aims to be the leader in the software that enables HDR technology. Chalmers' research goal is "Real Virtuality," obtaining physically-based, multi-sensory, high-fidelity virtual environments at interactive rates through a combination of parallel processing and human perception techniques.

Grégory Dhen is a Ph.D. student in the department of Political and Social Sciences at the Catholic University of Louvain, Belgium. He's currently conducting fieldwork in *World of Warcraft* where he focuses on players' building of social relationships. His doctoral dissertation proposes an analysis of the guilds' governance logics and examines the ways guild members negotiate their offline and online identities as well as their personal and collective play practices. His interdisciplinary work draws on both French and English approaches to game studies and virtual worlds. He is also member of the OMNSH association (Observatoire des Mondes Numériques en Sciences Humaines).

Jacquelene Drinkall researches telepathy in contemporary art and digital media. She is an artist working in video, performance, installation, photography, sculpture, and painting - exhibiting in Australia and internationally. Jacquelene holds a PhD in Art History and Theory, Master's of Research in Visual Art, and a BA in Visual Art (Painting). She recently collaborated with Jeremy Owen Turner and others in a Second Life avatar performance. She has lectured at Australian National University; COFA University of New South; Design Lab, Faculty of Architecture at University of Sydney; and James Cook University. Jacquelene has received many awards and grants: Curriculum Refresh grant, NAVA grant, two COFA Student Art Prizes, Artspace residency, Cite International Paris residency, Australian Postgraduate Award, Marten Bequest, Telecom Travelling Scholarship, Janet Johnston Award, two AGNSW awards, University Medal, and 7 time finalist (5 time exhibitor) for the Helen Lempriere Travelling Art Scholarship.

Thiago Falcao is a PhD Student at the Contemporary Communication and Culture Postgraduate Program of the Federal University of Bahia, where he is member of both the Research Group on Society, Digital Technology, and Interaction (GITS) and the Research Group on Cybercities (GPC). He currently develops a research concerning aspects of social theory and narrative-cognitive processes involved in online gaming; he is also editor of the peer-reviewed journal Realidade Sintética, the first Portuguese-language based resource to fully dedicate itself to issues regarding research on the video game culture.

Katleen Gabriels is a doctoral student at the Vrije Universiteit Brussel (VUB, Belgium). She is working on a PhD on morality and ethics in social virtual worlds. Katleen is part of the Department of Communication Sciences and the Department of Philosophy. She is also a member of IBBT-SMIT (Interdisciplinary Institute for Broadband Technology - Studies on Media, Information and Telecommunication) and the Centre for Ethics. She holds Master's degrees in Germanic Languages (KULeuven) and Moral Philosophy (Ghent University).

Gregory Price Grieve researches and teaches in the intersection of South Asian religions, New Media, and postmodern and pluralistic approaches to the study of religion. Grieve is associate professor of Religious Studies and the Director of MERGE: A Network for Interdisciplinary and Collaborative Scholarship at the University of North Carolina at Greensboro. He is the author of numerous articles, the monograph Retheorizing Religion in Nepal and the co-editor of the edited volume Historicizing Tradition in the Study of Religion. Grieve has been a research fellow at the Asia Research Institute, the National University of Singapore, and the Center for Religion and Media at New York University. He is currently working on a book titled, Waking Up Online: Buddhism, Second Life and the Reenchantment of Late Modernity, which analyzes Second Life's Zen Buddhist cluster to comprehend the early effort of practitioners to reshape religious practices on the virtual frontier.

Kevin S. Heston researches the rhetoric of religious movements in late modernity and the impact on subjectivity of the multiple identities that confront the individual in contemporary society. He is a graduate student in the Department of Communication at Wake Forest University. He served as Director of the Cardia Virtual Research Team and presented on religion and subjectivity in Second Life at the National Communication Association annual conventions in 2008 and 2010. His most recent research involves the Creation Museum of Petersburg, Kentucky as a rhetorical movement. He presented on his research at the Biennial Wake Forest Argumentation Conference in 2009. Most recently he presented his paper The Creation Museum as Rhetorical Savior, and presented on three panels at the NCA annual convention in 2010. He is currently working on a book titled, Fragmented Reality or Cosmopolitan Vitality: Contemporary Media, the Shifting Sensorium, and the Formation of the "Real Self."

David Holloway is a Registered Nurse who has been involved with virtual worlds since 1993, when he was one of 25 worldwide selected to test the use of a MOO (Multi-User Dungeon Object Orientated) environment as an adjunct to online music collaboration. He has been writing on virtual worlds since 2006 for his own sites, The Metaverse Journal and Metaverse Health, in addition to a range of Australian mainstream publications. David has recently commenced his PhD studies on the use of virtual environments in clinical simulation for nurses. He currently holds a Master of Nursing and a Master of Business Administration.

Sisse Siggaard Jensen is a Professor of Digital Communication at the Department of Communication, Business and Information Technologies, Roskilde University, Denmark. Her current research interests are questions about how actors make sense of their chosen virtual world(s), avatars, and relationships, research that aim to study the co-construction of self and world-makings. Virtual ethnography and qualitative in situ video analysis are some of her preferred methods of studying the micro-moments of actors' sense-making and engagement. Currently, she is head of a large research project about sense-making and user-driven innovation in virtual worlds (2008-2012) supported by the Danish Strategic Research Council. She has a long record of practice and research in fields of networked learning and communication. Sisse Siggaard Jensen is one of the initiators of a newly started Experience Lab aimed to carry out experimental research on virtual world-makings and mixed and augmented realities.

Bjarke Liboriussen holds a PhD in Media Studies from the University of Southern Denmark, earned for work on the application of landscape aesthetics and architectural theory to the study of virtual worlds. His current research interests include game studies, media production studies, and the philosophy of technology.

Pascaline Lorentz is currently working as an Associate Professor in Sociology for the University of Paris – La Sorbonne at the French College in Saint-Petersburg in Russia. Completing her PhD in Social Sciences at the University of Strasbourg and the Research lab "Cultures and Societies in Europe" (CNRS FRE 3229), her sociological research investigates the impacts of knowledge the gamer can gain from his relationship with his avatars in the video game, The Sims®. She has conducted fieldwork on gaming with teenagers in France, Russia and United Arabic Emirates. Then, she will lead addtional research about embodiment and its consequences in Australia at the Centre for New Media Research and Education at the Faculty of Humanities and Social Sciences at Bond University in Brisbane.

Luís Magalhães is an Assistant Professor at the University of Trás-os-Montes e Alto Douro, in Portugal. He has an MSc and a PhD in Computer Science. His research interests include the use of computer vision techniques for the production of 3D models from video sequences, augmented reality, computer graphics, and more recently, on the use of these techniques to develop cultural heritage applications. He has also some studies on the use of visual perception in computer graphics.

Bettina Maisch holds a degree in electronic business as well as a degree in social and business communication from the University of the Arts in Berlin, Germany. She gained several years of work experience in the international advertising network of Ogilvy and in the marketing department of the German research and development network of Fraunhofer Society before commencing her PhD candidature at the Institute for Media and Communications Management at the University of St. Gallen, Switzerland. Her current research focuses on the potential of Web 2.0 applications such as wikis, weblogs, and social networks for the communication of innovations. In her dissertation, Bettina investigates the influencing factors of Facebook on the market introduction of electric cars. She was able carry out the data collection during her time as a visiting researcher at the Center for Design Research at Stanford University, United States.

João Mattar has a Bachelor Degree in Language and Literature (Universidade de São Paulo – USP) and Philosophy (Pontifícia Universidade Católica de São Paulo – PUC-SP), Extension (University of California Berkeley and Boise State University), Graduate Degree in Business and Administration (Fundação Getúlio Vargas – FGV-SP), Doctorate Degree in Literature (Universidade de São Paulo – USP), and was a Post-Doctorate Researcher and Visiting Scholar (Stanford University). He has been Professor and Researcher in Higher Education Institutions in Brazil since 1994, intensively working with Distance Education, authoring multimedia didactic material and tutoring, and specialized in Web 2.0 tools and Second Life. He is also author of several books, such as: *Second Life e Web 2.0 na educação: o potencial pedagógico das novas tecnologias*; *ABC da EaD: a educação a distância hoje*; *Games em Educação: como os nativos digitais aprendem.*

Victoria McArthur is a Ph.D. candidate in the Communication & Culture programme at York University, Canada. She received her honours BA in Music from Brock University in 2007 and her MA in Interdisciplinary Studies at York University in 2010. In 2003 she received a full scholarship to study at Nagoya Gakuin University in Japan, where she graduated with a certificate in Japanese area studies. Her primary research interests include human-computer interaction (HCI), self-representation and social interaction in virtual environments, and social inclusion. Her research is currently funded by the Elia Scholars Program.

Gaia Moretti earned a PhD in Communication Science and Complex Organizations from LUMSA University, Rome, Italy. She has published several papers and essays on digital communication and complex organizations. She is consultant in the field of Communication and Training, and Junior Networking Manager in the Italian company IANUS Srl. She is junior researcher of CRESEC, Research Center in Social Responsibility, Events and Communication, of LUMSA University, and also member of GP-edu UNISINOS/CNpQ, research group of UNISINOS, S. Leopoldo, RS, Brazil. She is professor of Web Marketing, Innovation, and Business Communication at ISCEM – Instituto Superior de Comunicação Empresarial, Lisboa, Portugal, where she collaborates also in the European planning of research projects.

João Paulo Moura is an Assistant Professor in Engineering Department at the University of Trás-os-Montes e Alto Douro and member at Knowledge Engineering and Decision Support Research Center, in Portugal. His main research interests include: computer graphics, Geographic Information Systems, and multimedia.

Michael Nitsche is interested in digital spaces and where and how they intersect with physical environments. Mainly using video games, mobile technology, and digital performances, he experiments with these borderline areas. He heads the Digital World and Image Group and is Associate Director of the Experimental Game Lab at Georgia Tech. In the course of his research he has worked with game developers such as SCEE, EA, Bluebyte, and Turner Broadcasting. His book Video Game Spaces was published at MIT Press early 2009 and he co-edited the first reader on Machinima (TBP, MIT Press). Michael's most current research is on locative social media. He works as Associate Professor in Digital Media at the School of Literature, Communication & Culture (LCC) at the Georgia Institute of Technology where he teaches in the Digital Media M.S. and Ph.D. program, as well as for the Computational Media undergraduate program.

Thomas D. Parsons, PhD is a Clinical and Experimental Neuropsychologist, Assistant Research Professor, and Research Scientist at the University of Southern California's Institute for Creative Technologies. He directs the NeuroSim (Neuroscience and Simulation) Laboratory, helping to facilitate human-computer interface research. His work with human-computer interfaces began with invasive brain-computer interfaces and the cognitive sequelae of deep brain stimulation. The long-range goal of Dr. Parsons's laboratory is to develop noninvasive brain-computer interfaces and psychophysiologically adaptive virtual worlds that may be used for neuropsychological assessment, stress inoculation, virtual reality exposure therapy, cognitive training, and rehabilitation. This goal is being pursued with a combination of theoretical and experimental approaches at several levels of investigation ranging from the biophysical level to the systems level. In addition to his patents (with eHarmony.com), he has over 100 publications in peer-reviewed journals and other fora.

Martyn Partridge is Professor of Respiratory Medicine at Imperial College London. His research interests are in evaluating the delivery of healthcare to those with respiratory illnesses. He has a particular interest in the subject of health literacy and in simplifying information materials and questionnaires (such as the Epworth score) to enhance widespread comprehension. Professor Partridge chairs the clinical years sub-committee of the Undergraduate Education Committee at Imperial College where he is also deputy Director of Education. Professor Partridge is past President of the British Thoracic Society (BTS), previous Chief Medical Adviser to Asthma UK, and he currently chairs the UK Department of Health Asthma Steering Group. He is also on the DH Respiratory Programme board. In October 2010 he took up the additional position of Senior Vice Dean to the new Imperial College Nanyang Medical School in Singapore, a position to which he will devote most of his time.

Luís Pedro is an Assistant Professor in Communication and Arts Department, University of Aveiro, Portugal. He is engaged in research activities in educational technology and communication sciences and technologies, namely in the multimedia communications Master's, and in the multimedia in education and in the information and communication in digital platforms Doctoral programs. His research interests are related with technology enhanced learning, PLEs, and MUVE in Education.

Luis Petry graduated in School of Arts in Old House - Novo Hamburgo - Degree course in psychology by UNISINOS – São Leopoldo – Philosophical Studies Training with Ernildo Stein in Hermeneutic Phenomenology - UFRGS - Porto Alegre - PhD in Communication and Semiotics – PUCSP – Brazil. He is a researcher and Professor at PUC-SP: Pontifical Catholic University of São Paulo, in the Graduate Program Technologies of Intelligence and Digital Design (TIDD), and Superior Technology Course in Digital Games. He is a researcher Leader NuPHG: The Center for Research in Hypermedia & Games (PUC-SP), where he participated in Biennale Art Cerveira (2008) with the conceptual game and meta-verse "AlletSator 4.5." His current research project focuses on the ontological foundations of games and metaverse and ontological implications in the design and production applied research and communication.

Sara Pita is a researcher at Projecto Matemática Ensino at University of Aveiro, Portugal. She is engaged in research activities, namely the creation of multimedia contents to apply in Portuguese schools. Her research interests are related with the use of MUVE and of games in Education, Web 2.0 tools, and Portuguese literature.

CarrieLynn D. Reinhard received her Ph.D. in Communication from Ohio State University studying how people engage with the media. For the past two years she has been a post-doctoral researcher at Roskilde University, Roskilde, Denmark, for the Virtual Worlds Research Project. Her research for the project has focused on how a variety of users make sense of virtual worlds as innovative media technologies. Her research focuses on the application of Dervin's Sense-Making Methodology to reception studies of newer media, such as the Internet, digital games, and virtual worlds, as well as the moment-by-moment sense-making and everyday recodings of traditional media, such as film and television.

Nicola Roberts graduated with a BSc (Hons) in Biological Sciences from Napier University and completed her PhD in Respiratory Medicine at Queen Mary and Westfield College. She was a lecturer in respiratory healthcare delivery at Imperial College until December 2010 where her research interests focused on health services research in particular, investigating delivery of care and medical education in Respiratory Medicine. In February 2010 she took up the post of research fellow at Glasgow University and is now expanding her expertise in health economics and epidemiology in respiratory and dental disease.

Nuno Rodrigues is an Assistant Professor at the School of Technology and Management of the Polytechnic Institute of Leiria. He is also a researcher at the Polytechnic Institute Computer Science and Communication Research Centre. His main research interests and development projects concern Computer Graphics, Virtual Reality, and Procedural Modelling.

Omar Rosas is a Postdoctoral researcher in the department of Political, Social, and Communication Science at the University of Namur, Belgium. He's currently conducting a research project on audiences' trust in both mainstream and citizen-based online news in French-speaking Belgium. He also works as associate researcher in the department of philosophy at the University of Twente and the 3TU Center for Ethics and Technology at the Delft University of Technology, the Netherlands. He is member of the international research project "Evaluating the Cultural Quality of New Media" which investigates the relationships between ICT and people's quality of life and well-being.

Filipe Santos is an Assistant Professor at the School of Education and Social Sciences of the Polytechnic Institute of Leiria. He is also a researcher at the Polytechnic Institute Centre for Research and Development in Education. His main research interests and development projects concern technologies for education and technologies for development. For these purposes, he works closely to some pedagogical movements, as the Portuguese Modern School Pedagogical Movement, and non-governmental organizations that promote development in Portuguese speaking African countries. Some of his recent projects concern building educational games in CD-ROMs for primary school children to promote sustainability and the study of social media in lifelong learning.

Eliane Schlemmer is a PhD in Computing in Education and Master in Psychology at Federal University of Rio Grande do Sul – UFRGS – Brasil. She is researcher for Postgraduate Programme in Education at University of Vale do Rio dos Sinos (UNISINOS); Coordinator of the Digital Education Research Group – GPe-dU UNISINOS/CNPq; Member of the Managing Committee in the Catholic Network of Higher Education Institutions — RICESU. She was conceiver and developer of the educational software and environment: Virtual Learning Environment (AVA-UNISINOS), Virtual Worlds (AWSINOS in Metaverse Active Worlds, Ilha UNISINOS and Ilha RICESU in Metaverse Second Life) Communicative Agent (MARIÁ), Space of Digital Virtual Living Together (ECODI - technological hybridism), and the Virtual Learning Environment for Mobile Learning COMTEXT (Skills in Context).

Sue Smith graduated with a BSc in pharmacology from the University of Liverpool, then studied part time for a PhD at Charing Cross Hospital Medical School where she investigated the effects of tobacco smoke on proteolytic activity on the lung surface. Having successfully completed her PhD, Dr. Smith became a full time researcher, but with a teaching role as a pharmacology tutor. A merger of Charing Cross with Imperial College London provided an exciting opportunity to become involved in curriculum development, and she contributed to a number of areas of a new six year MBBS/BSc programme, most notably Pharmacology and Therapeutics, which she co-led for the first few years of its existence and which continues essentially unchanged to the present day. Further opportunities to build her teaching portfolio followed. She was appointed Reader in Medical Education in 2007 and became Deputy Director of Education in the Faculty of Medicine at Imperial College London in 2009.

Katrin Tobies studied communication management, business science, sociology, and politics in Berlin and is now doing her PhD in communication science at the University of Leipzig. Additionally, she works as European Project Manager for the Berlin Senate Department for Economics and Technology since 2008 in the areas of cluster development, open innovation, digital media, and creative industries. Prior to this, she has worked some years as a researcher and public relations consultant to several organizations in industry, science and culture. Lastly, she was research assistant and lecturer at the Games & Interactive Media Competence Centre of the Berlin University of Applied Sciences. Katrin Tobies has contributed to several national and international studies, conferences, and advisory boards. Her current research interests comprise innovation communication, live communication, construction of space, innovation management, design & innovation, and open government.

Cristiano Tonéis has a degree in Mathematics from UNESP and a Master in Technology of Intelligence and Digital Design – PUCSP. He developed research on the application of puzzles in Myst – Riven – as potentials to build the cognitive structures, that we call logical-mathematical thinking. He also worked as researcher in NuPHG: The Research Center on Hypermedia and Games at the Pontifical Catholic University of São Paulo, contributing to the project Cabu Island with the transposition of the classical puzzles to metaverse puzzles. He is a Professor of Math Application in Games, Analytical Geometry and Logic in the Faculdades Metropolitanas Unidas de São Paulo – FMU – Brazil.

Maria Toro-Troconis is the E-learning Strategy and Development Manager at the Faculty of Medicine, Imperial College London. Her main role is to support the development and delivery of the Faculty's e-learning strategy. Maria has extensive experience working in e-learning, having developed several e-learning programmes for various UK Universities. Maria's background is in computer science and human factors. Her research interest is game-based learning and virtual worlds. Her key skills include instructional design, coordination across distributed teams, business analysis, and project management. She also has an in depth knowledge of international learning standards and their implementation across platforms. Maria chairs the E-learning Implementation Group (ELIG) at the Faculty of Medicine and represents the Faculty at the College E-learning Strategy Committee (eLSC).

Karl Verstrynge is Professor of Media Ethics and Applied Ethics at the Department of Philosophy and the Department of Media and Communication Studies, Free University of Brussels (VUB). His research activities, situated in the Centre for Ethics, involve media ethical themes (especially with regard to virtual media) and existential ethics. He is also the director of the Søren Kierkegaard translation project in the Netherlands and Flanders.

Index

W

X

Y

Z